Reflections

HBJ Reading Program
Margaret Early

Bernice E. Cullinan
Roger C. Farr
W. Dorsey Hammond
Nancy Santeusanio
Dorothy S. Strickland

LEVEL 14

Reflections

HBJ **HARCOURT BRACE JOVANOVICH, PUBLISHERS**
Orlando   San Diego   Chicago   Dallas

Copyright © 1987 by Harcourt Brace Jovanovich, Inc.

All rights reserved. No part of this publication may be reproduced or transmitted in any form or by any means, electronic or mechanical, including photocopy, recording, or any information storage and retrieval system, without permission in writing from the publisher.

Requests for permission to make copies of any part of the work should be mailed to: Permissions, Harcourt Brace Jovanovich, Publishers, Orlando, Florida 32887

Printed in the United States of America

ISBN 0-15-330514-2

Acknowledgments

For permission to reprint copyrighted material, grateful acknowledgment is made to the following sources:

Atheneum Publishers, Inc. and The Canadian Publishers, McClelland and Stewart Limited, Toronto: Adapted from *Frozen Fire: A Tale of Courage* by James Houston. Copyright © 1977 by James Houston. A Margaret K. McElderry book.

Tom Clark: "Clemente (1934–72)" from *Blue* by Tom Clark. Published by Black Sparrow Press, 1974.

Harold Courlander: "How Ologbon-Ori Sought Wisdom" from *Olode the Hunter and Other Tales from Nigeria* by Harold Courlander. Copyright © 1968 by Harold Courlander. Published by Harcourt Brace Jovanovich, Inc.

Coward, McCann & Geoghegan: Adapted from *Katherine Dunham* (Titled: "The African Roots of American Dance"), a biography by James Haskins, Copyright © 1982 by James Haskins.

Dodd, Mead & Company, Inc.: Adapted from "How Whirlwind Saved Her Cub" in *Buffalo Woman* by Dorothy M. Johnson. Copyright © 1977 by Dorothy M. Johnson. "The Case of the Little Green Men" (Retitled: "Jocelyn Bell's Puzzle") from *Test-Tube Mysteries* by Gail Kay Haines. Copyright © 1982 by Gail Kay Haines.

Doubleday & Company, Inc.: From *War Cry on a Prayer Feather* (Titled: "Ute Indian Poem") by Nancy Wood, Copyright © 1979 by Nancy Wood.

Farrar, Straus & Giroux, Inc.: From *Annie John* by Jamaica Kincaid. Copyright © 1983, 1984, 1985 by Jamaica Kincaid. Originally published in *The New Yorker*.

The Feminist Press: Illustration by Pamela Baldwin Ford from "Three Strong Women" by Claus Stamm on p. 43 in *Tatterhood and Other Tales*, edited by Ethel Johnston Phelps.

Ginn and Company: Adapted from "The Sampler" in *Young Americans* by Cornelia Meigs. Copyright © 1936 by Ginn and Company.

Executors of the Estate of Robert Graves: "What Did I Dream?" from *Collected Poems 1975* by Robert Graves. © 1975 by Robert Graves.

Harcourt Brace Jovanovich, Inc.: Abridged and adapted from pp. 225–226 in *HBJ Health*, Level Gold, Grade 8. Copyright © 1983 by Harcourt Brace Jovanovich, Inc. Abridged and adapted from pp. 350–352 in *Mathematics Today*, Grade 8. Copyright © 1985 by Harcourt Brace Jovanovich, Inc. Abridged from pp. 46–47 in *American History* by John A. Garraty, Aaron Singer, and Michael J. Gallagher. Copyright © 1982 by Harcourt Brace Jovanovich, Inc. Abridged and adapted from p. 376 in *America: Its People and Values*, Heritage Edition by Leonard C. Wood, Ralph H. Gabriel, and Edward L. Biller. Copyright © 1985 by Harcourt Brace Jovanovich, Inc. From p. 245 and from pp. 307–308 in *Matter: An Earth Science*, Curie Edition by Paul F. Brandwein, Warren E. Yasso, and Daniel J. Brovey. Copyright © 1980 by Harcourt Brace Jovanovich, Inc. Abridged and adapted from pp. 255–256 in *Language for Daily Use*, Voyager Edition, Level Gold, Grade 8. Copyright © 1986 by Harcourt Brace Jovanovich, Inc. From *I Remember Mama* by John van Druten. Copyright 1944, 1945 by John van Druten; renewed 1972, 1973 by Carter Lodge, Executor for the Estate of John van Druten. Pronunciation key from p. 33 and the short key from p. 35 in *HBJ School Dictionary*. Copyright © 1985 by Harcourt Brace Jovanovich, Inc.

Harper & Row, Publishers, Inc.: Abridged and adapted from pp. 32–52 in *The Talking Earth* by Jean Craighead George. Copyright © 1983 by Jean Craighead George. Abridged and adapted from Chapters 1, 2, and 3 and specified photographs in *SPORTS MEDICINE: Scientists At Work* by Melvin Berger. Copyright © 1982 by Melvin Berger. Both published by Thomas Y. Crowell.

Hill and Wang, a division of Farrar, Straus & Giroux, Inc.: "The Story-Teller" from *Collected and New Poems 1924–1963* by Mark Van Doren. Copyright © 1963 by Mark Van Doren.

Houghton Mifflin Company: From pp. 90–109 in "The Dragon of Pendor" in *A Wizard of Earthsea* by Ursula K. LeGuin. Copyright © 1968 by Ursula Le Guin. A Parnassus Press book.

Lothrop, Lee & Shepard Books, a division of William Morrow & Company, Inc.: Abridged from pp. 1–3, 99, 101–103, 108–117, and 205 of *In Kindling Flame: The Story of Hannah Senesh 1921–1944* (Titled: "Hannah Senesh") by Linda Atkinson. Copyright © 1985 by Linda Atkinson.

Macmillan Publishing Company: From pp. 115–133 in *The Golden Fleece and the Heroes Who Lived Before Achilles* by Padraic Colum. Copyright © 1921 by Macmillan Publishing Company; renewed 1949 by Padraic Colum.

Macmillan Publishing Company and William Heinemann Limited: "The Hairy Dog" from *Phillicock Hill* by Herbert Asquith. Published by Macmillan Publishing Company, 1926.

Harold Matson Company, Inc.: "Dark They Were, and Golden-Eyed" by Ray Bradbury. Copyright 1949 by Standard Magazines, Inc.; copyright renewed 1976 by Ray Bradbury. Originally published in *Thrilling Wonder Stories* under the title "The Naming of Names."

McGraw-Hill Book Company: From "The Treasures of King Tutankhamen" in *Wrapped for Eternity: The Story of the Egyptian Mummy* by Mildred Mastin Pace. Copyright © 1974 by Mildred Mastin Pace. Published by McGraw-Hill Book Company.

Toni Mendez Incorporated: From "The Adventure of the Musgrave Ritual" in *Sir Arthur Conan Doyle's THE ADVENTURES OF SHERLOCK HOLMES* by Catherine Edwards Sadler. Copyright © 1981 by Catherine Edwards Sadler. Published by Avon Books.

Lillian Morrison: "The Sprinters" from *Sprints and Distances* by Lillian Morrision. Copyright © 1965 by Lillian Morrison. Published by Thomas Y. Crowell Company.

William Morrow & Company, Inc.: Abridged and adapted from pp. 18–28 in *A Deaf Child Listened* by Anne E. Neimark. Copyright © 1983 by Anne E. Neimark.

Harold Ober Associates Incorporated: "Jigsaw Puzzle" from *Allsorts 3* by Russell Hoban. Copyright © 1970 by Russell Hoban. Published by Macmillan Publishing Company.

Murray Pollinger: From "A Crown of Wild Olive" in *Heather, Oak, and Olive: Three Stories* by Rosemary Sutcliff. Published by E. P. Dutton & Co., Inc., 1972.

G. P. Putnam's Sons: Abridged from *Roberto Clemente, Batting King* by Arnold Hano. Copyright © 1968, 1973 by Arnold Hano. Abridged from *Dear Greta Garbo* by Toby Talbot. Copyright © 1978 by Toby Talbot.

Random House, Inc.: Adapted from *We Shook the Family Tree* by Hildegarde Dolson. Copyright 1941, 1942, 1946 by Hildegarde Dolson.

St. Martin's Press and Harold Ober Associates, Incorporated: From pp. 417–426 in *All Creatures Great and Small* (Titled: "Going to the Dogs . . . and Cats") by James Herriot. Published by St. Martin's Press, 1972.

Charles Scribner's Sons: Adapted from *A Gathering of Days: A New England Girl's Journal, 1830–32* by Joan W. Blos. Copyright © 1979 by Joan W. Blos.

Shocken Books Inc. and Vallentine, Mitchell & Co. Ltd., London, England: From Hannah Senesh's diary and correspondence, and the written recollections of Catherine Senesh, Yoel Palgi, and Reuven Dafne in *Hannah Senesh: Her Life and Diary* (Titled: "Hannah Senesh") by Hannah Senesh, translated by Marta Cohn. Copyright © 1966 by Hakibbutz Hameuchad Publishing House Ltd; English edition copyright © 1971 by Nigel Marsh.

Silver Burdett Company: From p. 436 in *THE WORLD AND ITS PEOPLE: One Flag, One Land,* Annotated Teacher's Edition by Richard C. Brown and Herbert J. Bass. © 1985 by Silver Burdett Company. Published by Silver Burdett Company.

Rosemary A. Thurber, Attorney–in–Fact for Helen W. Thurber: From "Look Homeward, Jeannie" in *Thurber's Dogs: A Collection of the Master's Dogs, Written and Drawn, Real and Imaginary* by James Thurber. Copyright © 1955 by James Thurber; renewed 1983 by Helen W. Thurber and Rosemary A. Thurber. Published by Simon and Schuster.

Viking Penguin Inc.: Adapted from "The Far Forests" in *The Far Forests* by Joan Aiken. Copyright © 1977 by Joan Aiken. From "Three Strong Women" by Claus Stamm. Copyright © 1962 by Claus Stamm.

Photographs

The following abbreviations indicate the position of the photographs on the page: *t,* top; *b,* bottom; l, left; *r,* right; c, center.

Cover: Michael Stuckey/Comstock, Ind.

Page xvi–1, 148–149, 152–153, 296–297, 300–301, 444–445, 448–449, 612–613, Ken Karp/OPC; 25, Leonard Lee Rue III/Photo Researchers; 27, Lawrence Fried/The Image Bank; 30, Robin Scogell/Ickenham, Uxbridge, England; 33, Smithsonian Institution, Washington, D. C.; 53, Isy-Schwartz/The Image Bank; 54, Lee Boltin; 55, Shostal Associates; 56–60, Lee Boltin; 61, The Metropolitan Museum of Art, NY; 63, Lee Boltin; 67, Steve McCutcheon; 124, David Falconer/Time Magazine, Time Inc.; 175, NASA; 192–195, National Theatre of the Deaf, Chester, CT.; 180, The Bettmann Archive; 219, John Margolies/Esto; 249, Pat Lanza Field/ Bruce Coleman Inc.; 251, Nancie Battaglia/Duomo; 252, Brian Payne/Black Star Photos; 255–259, Massachusetts General Hospital News Office, Boston; 262–263, Gerry Cranham/Photo Researchers; 266, The Bettmann Archive; 369, Michael O'Connor/The Image Bank; 371, Peter Davey/Bruce Coleman Inc.; 388, James Houston; 389. National Film Board of Canada; 390, Watson/Atheneum Books; 466–469, Katherine Dunham Papers, Special Collection, Morris Library, Southern Illinois University at Carbondale; 495, Museum of the American Indian, NY; 516–520, Rick Browne; 529, The Granger Collection; 530, Focus on Sports; 532, Focus on Sports; 535, 538, Al Satterwhite/Camera 5; 542, Ken Regan/Camera 5; 542, 566, The Zionist Archives and Library, NY; 568, 573, George Senesh; 570, The Bettmann Archive; 575, YIVO, NY; 580, Culver Pictures

Illustrators

Esther Baron; 412/413; Chris Calle: 172/173; Floyd Cooper: 230, 235, 237, 243, 270, 273, 276, 279, 281, 286, 288, 291, 293, 354, 356, 359, 361, 363, 364, 374, 377, 380, 382, 384, 416; Debra Edgerton: 454, 457, 459, 462/463, 465; Paul Gourhan: 90, 92, 96, 103, 104; Ron Himler: 225, 226, 227, 546, 548, 551, 552/553, 556, 559, 561, 562; Rosenkrans Hoffman: 21, 582, 583, 584, 585, 586, 587, 588, 589, 590, 591, 592, 593, 594, 595, 596, 597, 598, 599, 600, 601, 602, 603, 604, 605, 606, 607, 608, 609, 610; Leonard Jenkins: 396, 397, 399, 402/403, 405, 408; Christa Kieffer: 496, 498, 501, 502, 505, 507; Paul Lackner: 8, 11, 13, 16; Tom Leonard: 199; Richard Loehle: 110, 112, 115, 117, 118, 158, 160, 165, 166/167, 168; Lyle Miller: 202, 204, 207, 212, 214, 322, 323, 326, 331; Ed Parker: 247, 248, 475; Jim Pearson: 180, 182, 183, 184, 187, 189, 190/191, 304, 307, 308, 310, 478, 480, 482/483, 484, 486, 489; Charles Robinson: 70; Sue Rother: 24, 334, 337, 338, 340, 343, 345; Margaret Sanfilippo: 419, 420/421, 423, 426, 428/429, 432, 436, 439; Arvis Stewart: 36, 38, 41, 43, 45, 46/47, 127, 128, 131, 133, 135, 139, 142, 144; Jas Szygiel: 72, 75, 78, 81, 84/85, 86; Joe Veno: 315

Design, Production: Kirchoff/Wohlberg, Inc.

Contents

Unit 1 Quests and Conquests 1

Fantasy... 2
  (Literature Study)

Dark They Were, and Golden-Eyed................. 4
  by Ray Bradbury (Science Fiction)

The Story-Teller.................................. 20
  by Mark van Doren (Poem)

Cause and Effect................................ 22
  (Comprehension Study with Textbook
  Application in Science)

Jocelyn Bell's Puzzle............................ 28
  by Gail Kay Haines (Informational Article)

Jason and the Golden Fleece.................... 36
  by Padraic Colum (Myth)

Book Parts..................................... 50
  (Study Skills)

The Treasures of King Tutankhamen.............. 54
  by Mildred Mastin Pace (Informational Article)

Comparisons and Contrasts...................... 66
  (Comprehension Study with Textbook
  Application in Social Studies)

Frozen Fire.................................... 72
  by James Houston (Realistic Fiction)

vii

The Talking Earth........................... 90
   by Jean Craighead George   (Realistic Fiction)

Descriptive Language 108
   (Vocabulary Study)

Going to the Dogs . . . and Cats....................110
   by James Herriot   (Autobiography)

Plot..122
   (Literature Study)

Author Profile: Ursula K. Le Guin..................124

Bonus: **The Dragon of Pendor**......................126
   by Ursula K. Le Guin   (Fantasy)

Thinking About "Quests and Conquests" 148

Read on Your Own................................150

Unit 2 Galaxies — 153

Realistic Fiction 154
   (Literature Study)

A White Heron 156
   by Sarah Orne Jewett   (Realistic Fiction)

Jigsaw Puzzle 172
   by Russell Hoban   (Poem)

Make Generalizations 174
   (Comprehension Study with Textbook
   Application in Social Studies)

A Deaf Child Listened 180
   by Anne E. Neimark   (Biography)

The National Theatre of the Deaf 192
   (Photo Essay)

Greek and Latin Roots 198
   (Vocabulary Study)

The Adventure of the Musgrave Ritual 200
   by Sir Arthur Conan Doyle   (Mystery)

Author's Purpose 218
   (Comprehension Study with Textbook
   Application in Language Arts)

How Ologbon-Ori Sought Wisdom 224
   retold by Harold Courlander   (Folktale)

Dear Greta Garbo 230
   by Toby Talbot   (Realistic Fiction)

ix

Libraries 246
    (Study Skills)

What Is Sports Medicine? 250
    by Melvin Berger (Informational Article)

The Sprinters 262
    by Lillian Morrison (Poem)

Characterization 264
    (Literature Study)

Author Profile: Rosemary Sutcliff 266

Bonus: A Crown of Wild Olive 268
    by Rosemary Sutcliff (Historical Fiction)

Thinking About "Galaxies" 296

Read on Your Own 298

Unit 3 Wit and Wisdom 301

Essays and Anecdotes 302
   (Literature Study)

Look Homeward, Jeannie 304
   by James Thurber   (Essay)

The Hairy Dog 314
   by Herbert Asquith   (Poem)

Main Idea 316
   (Comprehension Study with Textbook
   Application in Health)

Jimmy Valentine 322
   by O. Henry   (Realistic Fiction)

We Shook the Family Tree 334
   by Hildegarde Dolson   (Autobiography)

Tests 350
   (Study Skills)

Three Strong Women 354
   by Claus Stamm   (Tall Tale)

Predict Outcomes 368
   (Comprehension Study with Textbook
   Application in Mathematics)

Annie John 374
   by Jamaica Kincaid   (Realistic Fiction)

James Houston: Tales of the Far North 388
   by Bernice E. Cullinan   (Biography)

xi

Analogies 394
    (Vocabulary Study)

The Far Forests 396
    by Joan Aiken   (Fantasy)

What Did I Dream? 412
    by Robert Graves   (Poem)

Point of View 414
    (Literature Study)

Author Profile: Kathryn Forbes 416

Bonus: Scenes from I Remember Mama 418
    by John van Druten   (Play)

Thinking About "Wit and Wisdom" 444

Read on Your Own 446

Unit 4 Legacies 449

Nonfiction 450
    (Literature Study)

The African Roots of American Dance
from **Katherine Dunham** 452
    by James Haskins   (Biography)

Katherine Dunham 466
    (Photo Essay)

Fact and Opinion 472
    (Comprehension Study with Textbook
    Application in Science)

How Whirlwind Saved Her Cub 478
    by Dorothy M. Johnson   (Historical Fiction)

Ute Indian Poem 494
    by Nancy Wood   (Poem)

A Gathering of Days 496
    by Joan W. Blos   (Historical Fiction)

Job Applications 512
    (Study Skills)

Margaret Sanfilippo: A Discriminating Artist 516
    by Neil Ryder Hoos   (Biography)

Paraphrase Information 524
    (Comprehension Study with Textbook
    Application in Social Studies)

Roberto Clemente, Batting King 530
    by Arnold Hano   (Biography)

Clemente (1934–72) 542
    by Tom Clark   (Poem)

Context Clues 544
    (Vocabulary Study)

The Sampler 546
    by Cornelia Meigs   (Historical Fiction)

Hannah Senesh 566
    by Linda Atkinson   (Biography)

Description 578
    (Literature Study)

Author Profile: Rudyard Kipling 580

Bonus: Mowgli's Brothers 582
    by Rudyard Kipling   (Fantasy)

Thinking About "Legacies" 612

Read on Your Own 614

Glossary 616

Pronunciation Guide 637

Index of Titles and Authors 639

Reflections

Unit 1
Quests and Conquests

An adventure is an exciting experience. Sometimes it is a dangerous undertaking. *Life* is an adventure! It is a quest for understanding and fulfillment. We are constantly changing, growing, and seeking new experiences. Sometimes our quests lie in the outside world. At other times our conquests are over our own weaknesses.

We don't always have to seek adventures ourselves. We can learn by reading about the quests and conquests of others. Stories often sharpen our observations of the world. They give insights into the way people behave. Some of the stories you will read in this unit are about events that happened to real people. Others are adventures involving fantastic creatures and imaginary worlds.

As you read, perhaps you will be able to identify with the characters on their various quests. Think about their actions. Think about their battles to overcome doubts and fears. Think about the challenges they face. Imagine yourself involved in their adventures!

Literature Study

Fantasy

Fantasy can take you to imaginary worlds where impossible events take place. In the world of fantasy, you find very unusual characters. You might even find characters that are "out of this world." Animals talk! Inanimate objects think and have feelings! In fantasy, characters can do things that are truly incredible. They can move backward or forward in time and can accomplish superhuman feats. A fantasy author makes you believe in an imaginary world by mixing the real with the fantastic. Part of the fun of reading a fantasy is seeing what the author has done to make the plot and the characters believable. By presenting a world where fantastic events are possible, a fantasy author sometimes presents truths about problems that concern people around the world.

Here are some characteristics of fantasy:

- imaginary worlds made believable
- characters who have supernatural qualities
- themes that deal with the struggle between good and evil

Now read the following story:

>   Gothar the warrior trembled as he stood before the dragon-king. "I have come to strike a bargain," the young man said, "a bargain for the safety of Reah Valley."
>   The dragon-king looked down at Gothar. Yellow smoke curled above the dragon's head. Fire danced along his forked tongue. He lifted himself up, looming above the young warrior, and roared, "Who is it that dares to come before the dragon-king with a bargain? What can you bargain? Where is your strength?" The dragon-king burst into laughter. "Surely, you are joking!"

What clues tell you this story is a fantasy? There are clues that one of the characters is a dragon and that the dragon does things people would do — talk. This story is a fantasy because there is a mix of the real and the fantastic — an imaginary creature doing things associated with humans.

Science fiction is like fantasy in many ways. It also mixes the real with the fantastic. It has unusual characters and plots. It allows characters to do many of the highly imaginative things that are characteristic of fantasy. Most science fiction, however, deals with scientific possibilities and the changes these advancements may bring about. Unlike fantasy, science fiction suggests theories about life in the future. Science fiction deals with worlds that are possible.

Here are some characteristics of science fiction:

- alternate views of the future
- information based on fact and theories
- consideration of the impact of science and technology on life

Read the following story:

> Rob lay on his back in the tall metallic grass. It still was a delight to look up into a *green* sky. The planet Zoron was not his world, but it had become his second home. Much had happened since the Granites had come down to Earth to rescue their relatives — the living rocks of the mountains. Only a few people were allowed to go back to Zoron with the Granites, and Rob was one of them.

Think about the fantasy details in this story — metallic grass, a green sky, the imaginary planet Zoron, and the Granites. Think about the realistic details — a boy resting in the grass looking up at the sky. Like fantasy, this science fiction story mixes the real with the fantastic. But two other details are mentioned — space travel and beings on another planet. *These* details, which deal seriously with possibilities for the future, make this story science fiction.

Remember, in fantasy and science fiction, the characters, the setting, and the plot may be unbelievable. You can meet strange creatures, explore unusual settings, or read about them in incredible plots.

In this science fiction adventure, a family from the planet Earth move to Mars. How will they adjust to their new life?

This story, like most science fiction stories, combines realism and fantasy. As you read, look for examples of realism and examples of fantasy.

Dark They Were, and Golden-Eyed

by Ray Bradbury

The rocket metal cooled in the meadow winds. Its lid gave a bulging *pop*. From its clock interior stepped a man, a woman, and three children. The other passengers whispered away across the Martian meadow, leaving the man alone among his family.

The man felt his hair flutter and the tissues of his body draw tight as if he was standing at the center of a vacuum. His wife, before him, seemed almost to whirl away in smoke. The children, small seeds, might at any instant be sown to all the Martian climes.

The children looked up at him, as people look to the sun to tell what time of their life it is. His face was cold.

"What's wrong?" asked his wife.

"Let's get back on the rocket."

"Go back to Earth?"

"Yes! Listen!"

The wind blew as if to flake away their identities. At any moment the Martian air might draw his soul from him, as marrow comes from a white bone. He felt submerged in a chemical that could dissolve his intellect and burn away his past.

They looked at Martian hills that time had worn with a crushing pressure of years. They saw the old cities, lost in their meadows, lying like children's delicate bones among the blowing lakes of grass.

"Chin up, Harry," said his wife. "It's too late. We've come over sixty million miles."

The children with their yellow hair hollered at the deep dome of Martian sky. There was no answer but the racing hiss of wind through the stiff grass.

He picked up the luggage in his cold hands. "Here we go," he said — a man standing on the edge of a sea, ready to wade in and be drowned.

They walked into town.

Their name was Bittering, Harry and his wife Cora; Dan, Laura, and David. They built a small white cottage and ate good breakfasts there, but the fear was never gone. It lay with Mr. Bittering and Mrs. Bittering, a third unbidden partner at every midnight talk, at every dawn awakening.

"I feel like a salt crystal," he said, "in a mountain stream, being washed away. We don't belong here. We're Earth people. This is Mars. It was meant for Martians. For heaven's sake, Cora, let's buy tickets for home."

But she only shook her head. "One day the atom bomb will fix Earth. Then we'll be safe here."

"Safe and insane!"

Tick-tock, seven o'clock sang the voice-clock; *time to get up.* And they did.

Something made him check everything each morning — warm hearth, potted blood-geraniums — precisely as if he expected something to be amiss. The morning paper was warm from the 6 A.M. Earth rocket. He broke its seal and tilted it at his breakfast place. He forced himself to be convivial.

"Colonial days all over again," he declared. "Why, in ten years there'll be a million Earthmen on Mars. Big cities, everything! They said we'd fail. Said the Martians would resent our invasion. But did we find any Martians? Not a living soul! Oh, we found their cities, but no one in them. Right?"

A river of wind submerged the house. When the windows ceased rattling, Mr. Bittering swallowed and looked at the children.

"I don't know," said David. "Maybe there're Martians around we don't see. Sometimes nights I think I hear 'em. I hear the wind. The sand hits my window. I get scared. And I see those towns way up in the mountains where the Martians lived a long time ago. And I think I see things moving around those towns, Papa. And I wonder if those Martians *mind* us living here. I wonder if they won't do something to us for coming here."

"Nonsense!" Mr. Bittering looked out the windows.

"We're clean, decent people." He looked at his children. "All dead cities have some kind of ghosts in them. Memories, I mean." He stared at the hills. "You see a staircase and you wonder what Martians looked like climbing it. You see Martian paintings and you wonder what the painter was like. You make a little ghost in your mind, a memory. It's quite natural. Imagination." He stopped. "You haven't been prowling up in those ruins, have you?"

"No, Papa." David looked at his shoes.

"See that you stay away from them. Pass the jam."

"Just the same," said little David, "I bet something happens."

Something happened that afternoon.

Laura stumbled through the settlement, crying. She dashed blindly onto the porch.

"Mother, Father—the war, Earth!" she sobbed. "A radio flash just came. Atom bombs hit New York! All the space rockets blown up. No more rockets to Mars, ever!"

"Oh, Harry!" The mother held onto her husband and daughter.

"Are you sure, Laura?" asked the father quietly.

Laura wept. "We're stranded on Mars, forever and ever!"

For a long time there was only the sound of the wind in the late afternoon.

Alone, thought Bittering. Only a thousand of us here. No way back. No way. No way. Sweat poured from his face and his hands and his body; he was drenched in the hotness of his fear. He wanted to strike Laura, cry, "No, you're lying! The rockets will come back." Instead, he stroked Laura's head against him and said, "The rockets will get through someday."

"Father, what will we do?"

"Go about our business, of course. Raise crops and children. Wait. Keep things going until the war ends and the rockets come again."

The boys stepped onto the porch.

"Children," he said, sitting there, looking beyond them, "I've something to tell you."

"We know," they said.

In the following days, Bittering wandered often through the garden to stand alone in his fear. As long as the rockets had spun a silver web across space, he had been able to accept Mars. For he had always told himself: Tomorrow, if I want, I can buy a ticket and go back to Earth.

But now: The web gone, the rockets lying in jigsaw heaps of molten girder and unsnaked wire. Earth people left to the strangeness of Mars, the cinnamon dusts and wine airs, to be baked like gingerbread shapes in Martian summers, put into harvested storage by Martian winters. What would happen to him, the others? This was the moment Mars had waited for. Now it would eat them.

He got down on his knees in the flower bed, a spade in his nervous hands. Work, he thought, and forget.

He glanced up from the garden to the Martian mountains. He thought of the proud old Martian names that had once been on those peaks. Earthmen, dropping from the sky, had gazed upon hills, rivers, Martian seas left nameless in spite of names. Once Martians had built cities, named cities; climbed mountains, named mountains; sailed seas, named seas. Mountains melted, seas drained, cities tumbled. In spite of this, the Earthmen had felt a silent guilt at putting new names to these ancient hills and valleys.

Nevertheless, man lives by symbol and label. The names were given.

Mr. Bittering felt very alone in his garden under the Martian sun, planting Earth flowers in a wild soil.

Think. Keep thinking. Different things. Keep your mind free of Earth, the atom war, the lost rockets.

He perspired. He glanced about. No one watching. He removed his tie. Pretty bold, he thought. First your coat off, now your tie. He hung it neatly on a peach tree he had imported as a sapling from Massachusetts.

He returned to his philosophy of names and mountains. The Earthmen had changed names. Now there were Hormel Valleys, Roosevelt Seas, Ford Hills, Vanderbilt Plateaus, Rockefeller Rivers, on Mars. It wasn't right. The American settlers had shown wisdom, using old Indian prairie names: Wisconsin, Minnesota, Idaho, Utah, Milwaukee, Waukegan, Osseo. The old names, the old meanings.

Staring at the mountains wildly, he thought: Are you up there? All the dead ones, you Martians? Well, here we are, alone, cut off! Come down, move us out! We're helpless!

The wind blew a shower of peach blossoms.

He put out his sun-browned hand, gave a small cry. He touched the blossoms, picked them up. He turned them, he touched them again and again. Then he shouted for his wife.

"Cora!"

She appeared at the window. He ran to her.

"Cora, these blossoms!"

She handled them.

"Do you see? They're different. They've changed! They're not peach blossoms anymore!"

"Look all right to me," she said.

"They're not. They're *wrong!* I can't tell how. An extra petal, a leaf, something, the color, the smell!"

The children ran out in time to see their father hurrying about the garden, pulling up radishes, onions, and carrots from their beds.

"Cora, come look!"

They handled the onions, the radishes, the carrots among them.

"Do they look like carrots?"

"Yes . . . no." She hesitated. "I don't know."

"They're changed."

"Perhaps."

"You know they have! Onions but not onions, carrots but not carrots. Taste: the same but different. Smell: not like it used to be." He felt his heart pounding, and he was afraid. He dug his fingers into the earth. "Cora, what's happening? What is it? We've got to get away from this." He ran across the garden. Each tree felt his touch. "The roses. The roses. They're turning green!"

And they stood looking at the green roses.

And two days later Dan came

running. "Come see the cow. I was milking her and I saw it. Come on!"

They stood in the shed and looked at their one cow.

It was growing a third horn.

And the lawn in front of their house very quietly and slowly was coloring itself like spring violets. Seed from Earth but growing up a soft purple.

"We must get away," said Bittering. "We'll eat this stuff and then we'll change — who knows to what? I can't let it happen. There is only one thing to do. Burn this food!"

"It's not poisoned."

"But it is. Subtly, very subtly. A little bit. A very little bit. We mustn't touch it."

He looked with dismay at their house. "Even the house. The wind's done something to it. The air's burned it. The fog at night. The boards, all warped out of shape. It's not an Earthman's house anymore."

"Oh, your imagination!"

He put on his coat and tie. "I'm going into town. We've got to do something now. I'll be back."

"Wait, Harry!" his wife cried.

But he was gone.

In town, on the shadowy step of the grocery store, the men sat with their hands on their knees, conversing with great leisure and ease.

Mr. Bittering wanted to fire a pistol in the air.

What are you doing, you fools! he thought. Sitting here! You've heard the news — we're stranded on this planet. Well, move! Aren't you frightened? Aren't you afraid? What are you going to do?

"Hello, Harry," said everyone.

"Look," he said to them. "You did hear the news, the other day?"

They nodded and laughed. "Sure. Sure, Harry."

"What are you going to do?"

"Do, Harry, do? What can we do?"

"Build a rocket, that's what!"

"A rocket, Harry? To go back to all that trouble? Oh, Harry!"

"But you *must* want to go back. Have you noticed the peach blossoms, the onions, the grass?"

"Why, yes, Harry, seems we did," said one of the men.

"Doesn't it scare you?"

"Can't recall that it did much, Harry."

"Idiots!"

"Now, Harry."

Bittering wanted to cry. "You've got to work with me. If we stay here, we'll all change. This air. Don't you smell it? Something in the air. A Martian virus, maybe; some seed, or a pollen. Listen to me!"

They stared at him.

"Sam," he said to one of them.

"Yes, Harry?"

"Will you help me build a rocket?"

"Harry, I got a whole load of metal and some blueprints. You want to work in my metal shop on a rocket, you're welcome. I'll sell you that metal for five hundred dollars. You should be able to construct a right pretty rocket, if you work alone, in about thirty years."

Everyone laughed.

"Don't laugh."

Sam looked at him with quiet good humor.

"Sam," Bittering said. "Your eyes —"

"What about them, Harry?"

"Didn't they used to be gray?"

"Well now, I don't remember."

"They were, weren't they?"

"Why do you ask, Harry?"

"Because now they're kind of yellow-colored."

"Is that so, Harry?" Sam said.

"And you're taller and thinner —"

"You might be right, Harry."

"Sam, you shouldn't have yellow eyes."

"Harry, what color eyes have *you* got?" Sam said.

"My eyes? They're blue, of course."

"Here you are, Harry." Sam handed him a pocket mirror.

"Take a look at yourself."

Mr. Bittering hesitated, and then raised the mirror to his face.

There were little, very dim flecks of new gold captured in the blue of his eyes.

"Now look what you've done," said Sam a moment later. "You've broken my mirror."

9

Harry Bittering moved into the metal shop and began to build the rocket. Men stood in the open door and talked and joked without raising their voices. Once in a while they gave him a hand on lifting something. But mostly they just idled and watched him with their yellowing eyes.

"It's suppertime, Harry," they said.

His wife appeared with his supper in a wicker basket.

"I won't touch it," he said. "I'll eat only food from our Deepfreeze. Food that came from Earth. Nothing from our garden."

His wife stood watching him. "You can't build a rocket."

"I worked in a shop once, when I was twenty. I know metal. Once I get it started, the others will help," he said, not looking at her, laying out the blueprints.

"Harry, Harry," she said, helplessly.

"We've got to get away, Cora. We've got to!"

The nights were full of wind that blew down the empty moonlit sea meadows past the little white chess cities lying for their twelve-thousandth year in the shallows. In the Earthmen's settlement, the Bittering house shook with a feeling of change.

Lying abed, Mr. Bittering felt his bones shifted, shaped, melted like gold. His wife, lying beside him, was dark from many sunny afternoons. Dark she was, and golden-eyed, burnt almost black by the sun, sleeping, and the children metallic in their beds, and the wind roaring forlorn and changing through the old peach trees, the violet grass, shaking green rose petals.

The fear would not be stopped. It had his throat and heart. It dripped in a wetness of the arm and the temple and the trembling palm.

A green star rose in the east.

A strange word emerged from Mr. Bittering's lips.

"*Iorrt. Iorrt.*" He repeated it.

It was a Martian word.

He knew no Martian.

In the middle of the night he arose and dialed a call through to Simpson, the archaeologist.

"Simpson, what does the word *Iorrt* mean?"

"Why, that's the old Martian word for our planet Earth. Why?"

"No special reason."

The telephone slipped from his hand.

"Hello, hello, hello, hello," it kept saying while he sat gazing out at the green star. "Bittering? Harry, are you there?"

The days were full of metal sound. He laid the frame of the rocket with the reluctant help of three indifferent men. He grew very tired in an hour or so and had to sit down.

"The altitude," laughed a man.

"Are you eating, Harry?" asked another.

"I'm eating," he said, angrily.

10

"From your Deepfreeze?"
"Yes!"
"You're getting thinner, Harry. And taller."
"I'm not!"
"Liar!"

His wife took him aside a few days later. "Harry, I've used up all the food in the Deepfreeze. There's nothing left. I'll have to make sandwiches using food grown on Mars."

He sat down heavily.

"You must eat," she said. "You're weak."

"Yes," he said.

He took a sandwich, opened it, looked at it, and began to nibble at it.

"And take the rest of the day off," she said. "It's hot. The children want to swim in the canals and hike. Please come along."

"I can't waste time. This is a crisis!"

"Just for an hour," she urged. "A swim'll do you good."

He rose, sweating. "All right, all right. Leave me alone. I'll come."

"Good for you, Harry."

The sun was hot, the day quiet. There was only an immense staring burn upon the land. They moved along the canal, the father, the mother, the racing children in their swim suits. They stopped and ate meat sand-

wiches. He saw their skin baking brown. And he saw the yellow eyes of his wife and his children, their eyes that were never yellow before. A few tremblings shook him, but were carried off in waves of pleasant heat as he lay in the sun. He was too tired to be afraid.

"Cora, how long have your eyes been yellow?"

She was bewildered. "Always, I guess."

"They didn't change from brown in the last three months?"

She bit her lips. "No, why do you ask?"

"Never mind."

They sat there.

"The children's eyes," he said. "They're yellow, too."

"Sometimes growing children's eyes change color."

"Maybe *we're* children, too. At least to Mars. That's a thought." He laughed. "Think I'll swim."

They leaped into the canal water, and he let himself sink down and down to the bottom like a golden statue and lie there in green silence. All was water-quiet and deep, all was peace. He felt the steady current drift him easily.

If I lie here long enough, he thought, the water will work and eat away my flesh until the bones show like coral. Just my skeleton left. And then the water can build on that skeleton — green things, deep water things, red things, yellow things. Change. Change. Slow, deep, silent change. And isn't that what it is up *there*?

He saw the sky submerged above him, the sun made Martian by atmosphere and time and space.

Up there, a big river, he thought, a Martian river, all of us lying deep in it, in our pebble houses, in our sunken boulder houses, like crayfish hidden, and the water washing away our old bodies and lengthening the bones and—

He let himself drift up through the soft light.

Dan sat on the edge of the canal, regarding his father seriously.

"*Utha,*" he said.

"What?" asked his father.

The boy smiled. "You know. *Utha*'s the Martian word for 'father.'"

"Where did you learn it?"

"I don't know. Around. *Utha!*"

"What do you want?"

The boy hesitated. "I — I want to change my name."

"Change it?"

"Yes."

His mother swam over. "What's wrong with Dan for a name?"

Dan fidgeted. "The other day you called Dan, Dan, Dan. I didn't even hear. I said to myself, That's not my name. I've a new name I want to use."

Mr. Bittering held to the side of the canal, his body cold and his heart pounding slowly. "What is this new name?"

"Linnl. Isn't that a good name?

Can I use it? Can't I, please?"

Mr. Bittering put his hand to his head. He thought of the silly rocket, himself working alone, himself alone even among his family, so alone.

He heard his wife say, "Why not?"

He heard himself say, "Yes, you can use it."

"Yaaa!" screamed the boy. "I'm Linnl, Linnl!"

Racing down the meadowlands, he danced and shouted.

Mr. Bittering looked at his wife. "Why did we do that?"

"I don't know," she said. "It just seemed like a good idea."

They walked into the hills. They strolled on old mosaic paths, beside still-pumping fountains. The paths were covered with a thin film of cold water all summer long. You kept your bare feet cool all the day, splashing as in a creek, wading.

They came to a small deserted Martian villa with a good view of the valley. It was on top of a hill. Blue marble halls, large murals, a swimming pool. It was refreshing in this hot summertime. The Martians hadn't believed in large cities.

"How nice," said Mrs. Bittering, "if we could move up here to this villa for the summer."

"Come on," he said. "We're going back to town. There's work to be done on the rocket."

But as he worked that night, the thought of the cool blue marble villa entered his mind. As the hours passed, the rocket seemed less important.

In the flow of days and weeks, the rocket receded and dwindled. The old fever was gone. It frightened him to think he had let it slip this way. But somehow the heat, the air, the working conditions —

He heard the men murmuring on the porch of his metal shop.

"Everyone's going. You heard?"

"All going. That's right."

Bittering came out. "Going where?" He saw a couple of trucks, loaded with children and furniture, drive down the dusty street.

"Up to the villas," said the men.

"Yeah, Harry. I'm going. So is Sam. Aren't you, Sam?"

"That's right, Harry. What about you?"

"I've got work to do here."

"Work! You can finish that rocket in the autumn, when it's cooler."

He took a breath. "I got the frame all set up."

"In the autumn is better." Their voices were lazy in the heat.

"Got to work," he said.

"Autumn," they reasoned. And they sounded so sensible, so right.

"Autumn would be best," he thought. "Plenty of time, then."

No! cried part of himself, deep down, put away, locked tight, suffocating. No! No!

"In the autumn," he said.

"Come on, Harry," they all said.

"Yes," he said, feeling his flesh melt in the hot liquid air. "Yes, in the autumn, I'll begin work again then."

"I got a villa near the Tirra Canal," said someone.

"You mean the Roosevelt Canal?"

"Tirra. The old Martian name."

"But on the map—"

"Forget the map. It's Tirra now. Now I found a place in the Pillan mountains—"

"You mean the Rockefeller range," said Bittering.

"I mean the Pillan mountains," said Sam.

"Yes," said Bittering, buried in the hot, swarming air. "The Pillan mountains."

Everyone worked at loading the truck in the hot afternoon of the next day.

Laura, Dan, and David carried packages. Or, as they preferred to be known, Ttil, Linnl, and Werr carried packages.

The furniture was abandoned in the little white cottage.

"It looked just fine in Boston," said the mother. "And here in the cottage. But up at the villa? No. We'll get it when we come back in the autumn."

Bittering himself was quiet.

"I've some ideas on furniture for the villa," he said after a time. "Big, lazy furniture."

"What about your encyclopedia? You're taking it along, surely?"

Mr. Bittering glanced away. "I'll come and get it next week."

They turned to their daughter. "What about your New York dresses?"

The bewildered girl stared. "Why, I don't want them anymore."

They shut off the gas, the water, they locked the doors and walked away. Father peered into the truck.

"Gosh, we're not taking much," he said. "Considering all we brought to Mars, that is only a handful!"

He started the truck.

Looking at the small white cottage for a long moment, he was filled with a desire to rush to it, touch it, say good-bye to it, for he felt as if he were going away on a long journey, leaving something to which he could never quite return, never understand again.

Just then Sam and his family drove by in another truck.

"Hi, Bittering! Here we go!"

The truck swung down the ancient highway out of town.

There were sixty others traveling the same direction. The town filled with a silent, heavy dust from their passage. The canal waters lay blue in the sun, and a quiet wind moved in the strange trees.

"Good-bye!" said Mr. Bittering.

"Good-bye, good-bye town," said the family, waving to it.

They did not look back again.

Summer burned the canals dry. Summer moved like flame upon the meadows. In the empty Earth settlement, the painted houses flaked and peeled. Rubber tires upon which children had swung in backyards hung suspended like stopped clock pendulums in the blazing air.

At the metal shop, the rocket frame began to rust.

In the quiet autumn Mr. Bittering stood, very dark now, very golden-eyed, upon the slope above his villa, looking at the valley.

"It's time to go back," said Cora.

"Yes, but we're not going," he said quietly. "There's nothing there anymore."

"Your books," she said. "Your fine clothes."

"Your *lles* and your fine *ior uele rre*," she said.

"The town's empty. No one's going back," he said. "There's no reason."

The daughter wove tapestries and the sons played songs on ancient flutes and pipes, their laughter echoing in the marble villa.

Mr. Bittering gazed at the Earth settlement far away in the low valley. "Such odd, such ridiculous houses the Earth people built."

"They didn't know any better," his wife mused. "Such ugly people. I'm glad they've gone."

They both looked at each other, startled by all they had just finished saying. They laughed.

"Where did they go?" he wondered. He glanced at his wife.

She was golden and slender as his daughter. She looked at him, and he seemed almost as young as their eldest son.

"I don't know," she said.

"We'll go back to town maybe next year, or the year after, or the year after that," he said, calmly. "Now—I'm

warm. How about taking a swim?"

They turned their backs to the valley. Arm in arm they walked silently down a path of clear-running spring water.

Five years later a rocket fell out of the sky. It lay steaming in the valley. Men leaped out of it, shouting.

"We won the war on Earth! We're here to rescue you! Hey!"

But the American-built town of cottages, peach trees, and theaters was silent. They found a flimsy rocket frame rusting in an empty shop.

The rocket men searched the hills. The captain established headquarters in an abandoned bar. His lieutenant came back to report.

"The town's empty, but we found native life in the hills, sir. Dark people. Yellow eyes. Martians. Very friendly. We talked a bit, not much. They learn English fast. I'm sure our relations will be most friendly with them, sir."

"Dark, eh?" mused the captain. "How many?"

"Six, eight hundred, I'd say, living in those marble ruins in the hills, sir. Tall, healthy. Beautiful women."

"Did they tell you what became of the men and women who built this Earth-settlement, Lieutenant?"

"They hadn't the foggiest notion of what happened to this town or its people."

"Strange. You think those Martians killed them?"

"They look surprisingly peaceful. Chances are plague did this town in, sir."

"Perhaps. I suppose this is one of those mysteries we'll never solve. One of those mysteries you read about."

The captain looked at the room, the dusty windows, the blue mountains rising beyond, the canals moving in the light, and he heard the soft wind in the air. He shivered. Then, recovering, he tapped a large fresh map he had thumbtacked to the top of an empty table.

"Lots to be done, Lieutenant." His voice droned on and quietly on as the sun sank behind the blue hills. "New settlements. Mining sites, minerals to be looked for. Bacteriological specimens taken. The work, all the work. And the old records were lost. We'll have a job of remapping to do, renaming the mountains and rivers and such. Calls for a little imagination."

"What do you think of naming those mountains the Lincoln Mountains, this canal the Washington Canal, those hills — we can name those hills for you, Lieutenant. Diplomacy. And you, for a favor, might name a town for me. Polishing the apple. And why not make this the Einstein Valley, and further . . . are you *listening*, Lieutenant?"

The lieutenant snapped his gaze from the blue color and the quiet mist of the hills far beyond the town.

"What? Oh, *yes*, sir!"

Discuss the Selection

1. How did the Bitterings finally adjust to their new life?
2. What changes did Mr. Bittering notice, first in the settlement on Mars, then in his family?
3. What do you think about Mr. Bittering's concerns about his changing environment? What else could he have done?
4. What do you think will happen to the group of new Earthmen who arrive on Mars?
5. At what point in the story did you realize what was happening to the Bitterings? Give examples from the story.

Apply the Skills

Science fiction combines fantasy and realism. It may include characters with supernatural qualities, imaginary worlds made real, and incredible plots. It may also include things that could actually happen in a future time, based on current scientific knowledge.

1. Give three examples of realism from this story.
2. Give three examples of fantasy from this story.

Think and Write

Prewrite

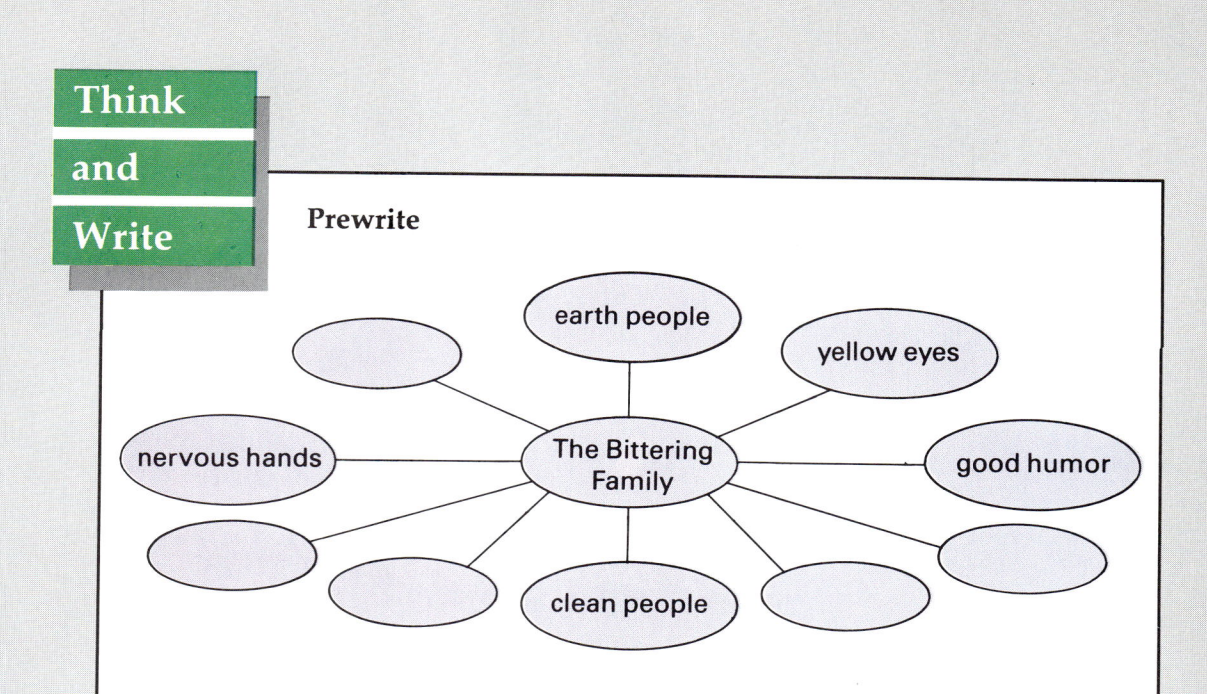

Ideaburst diagram: "The Bittering Family" in the center, connected to: earth people, yellow eyes, good humor, nervous hands, clean people, and three empty ovals.

Descriptions of people are called character sketches. They describe physical characteristics and personality traits.

The diagram shown above is an ideaburst. Copy the ideaburst above on a sheet of paper. Include Ray Bradbury's descriptions of the Bittering family that are already on the diagram. Then extend the diagram with your own descriptions of the Bitterings.

Compose

Using the information in the ideaburst and the story, write a paragraph describing the Bittering family. Include two physical characteristics and two personality traits.

Revise

Read the paragraph that you wrote. Notice the way you used the descriptions from the diagram. Check your character sketch with the reader in mind. Did you make the Bitterings seem real to someone who might not have read the story? If not, revise it. Most good writers are rarely satisfied with their first draft.

The Story-Teller
by Mark Van Doren

He talked, and as he talked
Wallpaper came alive;
Suddenly ghosts walked,
And four doors were five;

Calendars ran backward,
And maps had mouths;
Ships went tackward,
In a great drowse;

Trains climbed trees,
And soon dripped down
Like honey of bees
On the cold brick town.

He had wakened a worm
In the world's brain,
And nothing stood firm
Until day again.

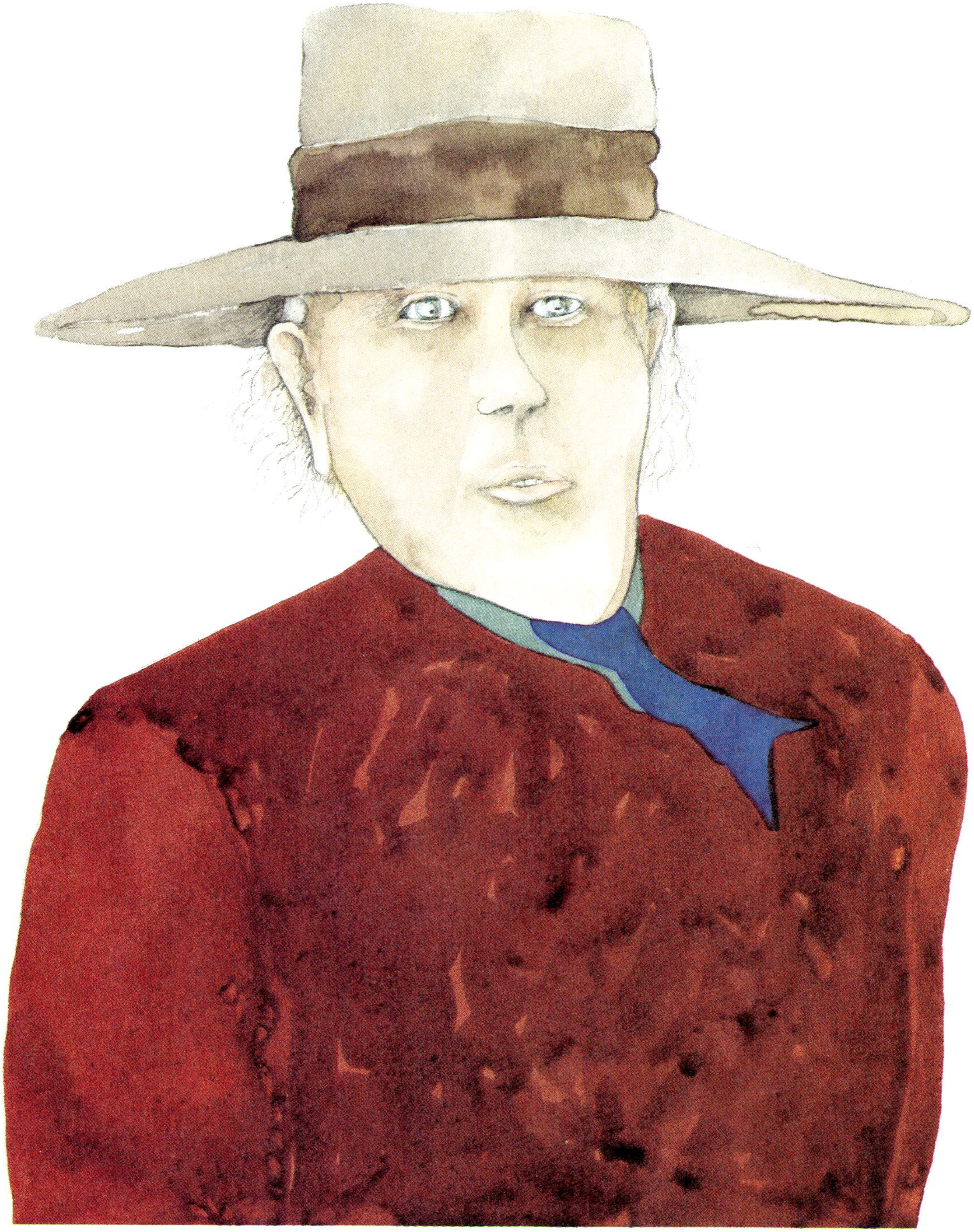

Comprehension Study

Cause and Effect

If someone knocked over a table loaded with food, the food would fall off. This is an example of a **cause-and-effect relationship**. One action — the knocking over of a table — results in another action — the falling of the food. The first action is the cause; the second is the effect.

To fully understand cause and effect, you must be able to tell how events are related. Two questions will help you do this: *What happened?* and *Why did this happen?* The "what" is the **effect**; the "why" is the **cause**. Ask these questions about the sentence that follows and you will be able to find the cause and the effect.

> The number of movie and radio fans has decreased because television has become very popular.

What happened in the first part of the sentence? *The number of movie and radio fans has decreased.* This is the effect. Why did this happen? *Television has become very popular.* This is the cause. The word *because* signaled the cause in this sentence.

Signal Words

Words and phrases such as *because, therefore, since, consequently, so,* and *as a result* often signal cause-and-effect relationships. It is helpful to know these words, but they are not always there to help you. Read the following sentences:

> John forgot to put the ice cream in the freezer before he left. He had quite a mess to clean up when he returned home four hours later.

What is the effect? *John had quite a mess to clean up.* What is the cause? *John forgot to put the ice cream in the freezer.* Although no word signaled the cause, it is easy to figure out what happened — the ice cream melted.

One Effect, Several Causes

When you read a story, you often have to think about a number of causes in order to understand a single effect. Read the following story about the legendary King Arthur. The story gives several causes for Arthur's becoming king. What causes are mentioned?

> As a result of several things, Arthur became king of Britain. Although he did not know it, his father had been king of Britain at one time; therefore, Arthur was destined to be king, too. The magician Merlin trained young Arthur so he could assume his royal responsibilities. Through his magic, Merlin caused a sword to be embedded in a large stone. Merlin did it in such a way that only a future king could remove it. People all over Britain knew of this test. Years later, when Arthur was able to pull out the sword, the people knew he was the true king. They acknowledged his right to the throne.

The single effect discussed in this story is how Arthur came to be king. According to the story, what causes led to his becoming king?

- Arthur's father had been king of Britain.
- The magician Merlin trained young Arthur so he could assume the responsibilities of a king.
- Through his magic, Merlin caused a sword to be embedded in a large stone as a test to identify any future king.
- Arthur was able to pull the sword out of the stone, thus proving that he was the true king.
- Finally, the people of Britain acknowledged Arthur's right to the throne.

Some of these causes brought about effects that in turn caused other effects. This kind of cause-and-effect relationship is referred to both as a **causal chain** and as a **chain reaction**.

One Cause, Several Effects

One event can lead to other events. For example, suppose an enormous tidal wave hit an island. The tidal wave might be the cause of several effects:

> flooding   crop damage   food shortages

Some of these effects could produce a causal chain or chain reaction. Flooding—an effect of the tidal wave—could cause crop damage. Crop damage could in turn cause food shortages.

Read the following paragraph. What is the cause? What are the effects?

> Last year Maria won a million dollars in a contest. As a result, she was able to pay her bills and buy a new house. She quit her job and became a writer. She has already written a best-selling book about her life since she won the money. Last week she appeared as a guest on a TV show to talk about her book.

This paragraph discusses the effects of Maria's winning a million dollars. According to the paragraph, what are the effects?

- Maria was able to pay her bills and buy a new house.
- She quit her job and became a writer.
- She has written a best-selling book.
- She appeared as a guest on a television show and talked about her book.

Maria's winning of the million dollars produced all the effects listed. Each effect in turn became part of a causal chain or chain reaction.

Now read the following paragraph about forest fires and answer the questions that follow:

> Forest fires bring about many changes in a forest. There are, of course, many unpleasant results. Trees are burned, animals are killed or driven from their homes, and the property of people living in or near the forest is destroyed. Sometimes these fires result in new life in a wilderness area. After a fire, much new growth begins in a forest. Many plants and low grasses that had been shaded by large trees grow quickly in the sunshine. Young trees begin to sprout. Insect and animal life increase as the smaller animals return. Life begins anew as the forest is reborn.

1. What are the positive effects of a forest fire?
2. What causes the new plant life to grow?
3. What are the unpleasant effects of a forest fire?

Textbook Application: Cause and Effect in Science

Information in textbooks is often organized to show cause-and-effect relationships. Causes are often signaled by words such as *because, since, consequently, so,* and *as a result.* Effects are often signaled by words such as *therefore* and *resulting in.* Read the following textbook selection. Use the sidenotes to help you recognize the cause-and-effect relationships.

> **What effects of the gas shortage are mentioned in this paragraph?**
>
> In 1973, many gas stations were closed because they had no gasoline to sell. Long lines of cars formed at stations that were open. And most of these limited the amount of gasoline you could buy. Many people gave up plans for long car trips. As a result of the gasoline shortage, resort areas had few visitors.
>
> **What were the causes of the gas shortage?**
>
> The gasoline shortage was the result of many factors. For one thing, oil—from which gasoline is produced—was not coming into the United States from the Middle East. Fifty years ago, we were a nation dependent on our coal resources. Over the years, oil and gas replaced coal as our chief source of energy. Without easy access to supplies of oil, a truly severe energy crisis could await us in the future. What effect did this energy crisis have?
>
> **What one important effect did the energy crisis have?**
>
> One important result of the crisis was our new awareness of the importance of an energy supply. People living in industrial nations learned that bright lights, warm homes, big cars, and long-distance vacations are luxuries. We became aware that industrial nations use energy too quickly. For example, in 1973, the United States, with 6 percent of the world's population, was using 35 percent of the world's energy supply.

And so, following the fuel crisis, many Americans bought smaller, more fuel-efficient cars. They also became more conservation-minded. But only two years later, large cars were popular again. People seemed willing to pay almost any price for gasoline. The fuel crisis seemed to be forgotten—at least for a time.

— *Matter: An Earth Science,*
Harcourt Brace Jovanovich

- What one event mentioned in the selection is both an effect and a cause? Give reasons for your answer.

In her quest to learn more about a new kind of astronomy, Jocelyn Bell discovers some strange signals coming from space. What age-old mystery does she solve through her study of the signals?

This selection explains why certain events take place. As you read, look for examples of cause-and-effect relationships.

Jocelyn Bell's Puzzle

by Gail Kay Haines

In a Nancy Drew mystery book, the young detective usually grapples with two separate puzzles which turn out to help solve each other. In 1967, a young researcher named Jocelyn Bell uncovered a real-life mystery that puzzled astronomers all over the world — until they added another unsolved mystery more than nine hundred years old.

Jocelyn Bell had always wanted to be an astronomer. As a little girl, she talked with scientists at the planetarium near her home in Northern Ireland. But one thing bothered her. She couldn't keep awake late at night. All her friends at the observatory had told her that staying up all night was an important part of the job.

Then Bell learned about a new kind of astronomy. It searched, not for light from far-off stars, but for another kind of radiation from outer space called microwaves. Microwaves are waves of energy a million times longer than light-waves. In fact, they are very much like short radio waves. The scientists who study them are called radio astronomers.

About the time Bell graduated from college, a new project in radio astronomy was getting under way at the Mullard Radio Astronomy Observatory in England. The study seemed made just for her: Almost all the work was done during the day. Bell joined the group as a graduate student researcher.

The huge radio telescope took two years to build. It was made up of 2,048 radio receivers, spread out over a space larger than four football fields. With it, there was no need to peer through a lens at the sky, because the waves the telescope picked up could not be seen. Instead, automatic instruments connected to the receivers translated data into three wavy lines traced onto graph paper.

Jocelyn Bell's job was to analyze those tracings. The huge radio telescope put out almost a hundred feet of data every day. She studied it all carefully, picking out sources of microwaves from different parts of the sky and charting their locations.

Local static from car ignitions and refrigerators made her job harder. Radio waves from outer space are so weak that a radio telescope must be extra-sensitive. That sensitivity causes it to record all kinds of human-made interference. But Bell soon learned to tell which squiggles on the paper were really from space and which came from the surrounding countryside.

Then one day in October, she found something strange as she was catching up on some old charts. A funny blip appeared, on an August chart, that didn't look like anything she had seen before. She couldn't figure out what it might be. Six more times on the charts from August to the end of September, Bell found this same mysterious blip.

Bell showed the strange tracings to Anthony Hewish, the director of her project. He was puzzled, too. They decided to give the blip a closer look.

The simplest way to study a section of graph made by a tracing pen is to run the instrument faster. That spreads out the lines and makes them easier to study. But the speed-up adjustment had to be done by hand, at just the right moment.

Bell went to the observatory right before the blip was due to appear. She switched the recorder to high speed. But nothing happened. The pen traced a normal pattern for that part of the sky.

Day after day, she watched the high-speed tracings move in a steady pattern. No blips, no mystery. Finally, Bell skipped a day to hear a special lecture. When she went out to pick up the graphs for that day, there was the mysterious blip. "It's back," she told Hewish.

The next day, Bell speeded up the recorder, and this time caught the elusive blip. In fact, it turned out to be a series of blips, evenly spaced about one and one-third seconds apart.

At first, she was disappointed and suspicious. Magnified by speed, the tracings began to look like the kind made by a human-made signal generator. She wondered if some of the lab people were playing a trick on her. Bell explained her suspicions to Dr. Hewish.

Scientists are always curious. Neither the young student nor the experienced astronomer could give up until they had solved the mystery, even if it only meant finding out who was playing the joke.

The next day, Dr. Hewish came to the observatory to see the puzzling blip. It was there, right on time, spaced out by the high-speed tracing: a series of mysterious marks, from a spot in the sky where no microwaves ought to be.

There the real mystery began. Someone might have tried to play a joke on a graduate student, but no one would try to trick Dr. Hewish. So the puzzling blips had to be real. But what were they?

Jocelyn Bell examining tracings on which the blip appeared.

The blips were pulsing much too often to be from a star. Stars are huge. They produce bursts of microwaves every few hours, but not every second.

Whatever was causing the blips had to be much smaller than a star. In fact, it seemed obvious that the blips had to be coming from somewhere on Earth, except for one more confusing detail Bell had noticed. The blips were operating on star time, not Earth time.

To astronomers, the "day" is not quite the twenty-four hours most people know. It is only twenty-three hours and fifty-six minutes. So things that happen on star time happen four minutes earlier each day. And that is exactly how the blip was behaving. Every day it pulsed four minutes sooner than it had the day before.

Then someone suggested that the signal might be coming from another civilization trying to contact Earth.

Astronomers are always skeptical of flying saucer stories, but this time they were not so sure. If there really were civilizations somewhere in outer space, they would live on planets. Maybe the mysterious signal from space was a message from living beings on another planet.

One evening, Bell went out to the lab to work. Just before closing time, she was surprised to find another blip on a chart from a different part of the sky. She began thumbing back through the graphs. Yes, the new blip had appeared several times before. She had discovered another key to the puzzle, a new blip, with pulses one and one-fourth seconds apart.

Soon after that, two more pulsing blips were discovered. By that time the group had almost given up on the idea that the signals were messages from a different civilization. It didn't seem very likely that intelligent beings in four different parts of the sky would be beaming the same kind of signal in Earth's direction. And even though the signals were weak, they were using up an incredible amount of energy. No civilization would be likely to waste so much energy when they didn't even know who they were contacting.

Finally, if the signals were coming from a planet, they should change slightly as the planet revolved around its own sun. They didn't. The scientists decided to name the blips "pulsars." The name matched the mysterious "quasars."

Now the mystery was back to the start: not from a star, not from Earth, not from civilizations on distant planets. Anthony Hewish began searching the library, looking for an answer. And there, he found another mystery.

This mystery was first recorded in 1054, in China. A royal astronomer named Yang Wei-t'e observed a "guest star" that appeared where no star had been seen before. It was so bright it could be seen in the daytime, but in just over a year, it disappeared completely.

Modern astronomers identified the "guest star" as a supernova, which is a huge star that blows up suddenly, spewing radiation as bright as a million suns.

Fred Zwicky, an astronomer in the 1930's, was interested in supernovas. He wanted to see one, but supernovas are rare. Zwicky couldn't find a single star where any supernova had been thought to be. It seemed that once their brilliance dimmed, they were gone forever.

Zwicky and his colleague, Walter Baade, thought that most of the material in the star must have been turned into energy by the gigantic explosion. But what happened to the matter left over? It was a mystery.

Zwicky and Baade thought of a solution to their mystery. They reasoned that the force of the star's explosion would squeeze the inner core of the star. Gravity would squeeze it even tighter until the atoms inside began to collapse. Since atoms are mostly empty space, the collapsed atoms in a star millions of miles across could be compressed by gravity into a dense ball no more than twenty miles across.

Zwicky named these strange, collapsed stars he had imagined "neutron stars," because the compressed atoms would have turned into neutrons.

Anthony Hewish had read about neutron stars in the library. But now they sounded like just what he was looking for. They were something much smaller than an ordinary star, moving with the stars, that might be giving off energy in the form of microwaves. Hewish felt very sure he had solved both mysteries. Pulsars and neutron stars must be the same thing.

But being sure is not scientific proof. Hewish and Bell announced the discovery of pulsar to the world in February, 1968. They used neutron stars as a possible explanation.

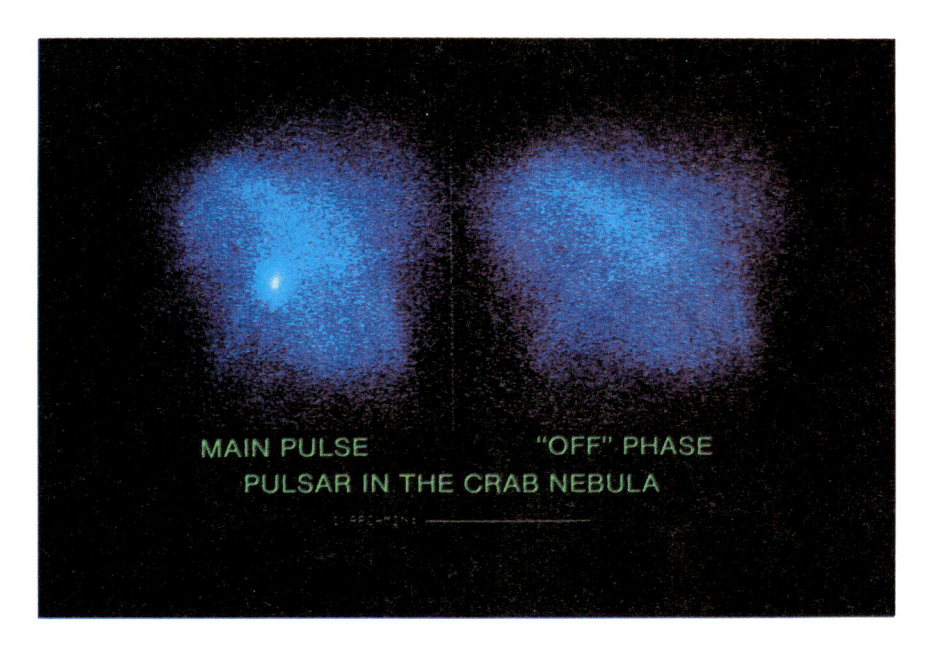

As the pulsar spins x-rays seem to flash on and off.

MAIN PULSE   "OFF" PHASE
PULSAR IN THE CRAB NEBULA

Immediately, radio astronomers everywhere began to look for pulsars. By late 1968, more than twenty had been discovered. Several of these were found where supernovas had been expected to be. One pulsar was in a part of the sky called the Crab Nebula—right where the famous "guest star" had been seen.

That was almost, but not quite, enough proof that pulsars are really neutron stars.

Astronomers in Arizona found the final proof. They set up a carefully planned experiment to try to see a pulsar. They used a telescope that could "collect" light until it had enough to show even very faint stars on a screen. They aimed for the pulsar in the Crab Nebula.

On January 15, 1969, conditions were perfect. When all the apparatus was turned on, a line of green dots began to climb across the screen. Astronomers were actually seeing light from Yang Wei-t'e's "guest star" for the first time in 914 years.

In 1974, Anthony Hewish and Sir Martin Ryle, who had developed the radio antenna used in the discovery of pulsars, were awarded the Nobel prize in physics.

More than 300 pulsars are now known. The solution to the puzzling blips did not locate any life on other planets, but it did produce a whole new field of research.

Discuss the Selection

1. What age-old mystery did Jocelyn Bell help to solve because of her discovery of strange signals coming from outer space?
2. Explain how two unsolved puzzles led to a new discovery.
3. What characteristics of Bell's personality do you think most helped her make and verify her discovery? Give reasons for your answers.
4. Why do you think the mystery of supernovas could not be solved until the twentieth century?
5. This selection traces the steps scientists took to verify a discovery. Locate the parts of the selection where the following steps are described: speculating about possible solutions, researching in the library, and setting up experiments.

Apply the Skills

In order to understand a single event, you may have to think about a number of related causes. Two questions will help you do this: *What happened?* and *Why did this happen?* The answer to the first question is the effect; and the answer to the second question is the cause. Give two examples of cause-and-effect relationships from this selection. Identify the causes and the effects.

Think and Write

Prewrite

Problem	Resolution
1. Jocelyn's sleepiness at night	1. Observatory with daytime research
2. Human-made interference	2. Interpreting squiggles
3.	3.

Good writing often holds the reader's interest by presenting problems to be resolved. "Jocelyn Bell's Puzzle" is about a scientist with various problems related to her work and personal life. The chart above identifies two of these problems and their resolutions.

Copy the chart on a sheet of paper. Then extend it by adding another conflict and resolution from the story.

Compose

Write a paragraph about one of the problems listed on the chart. Your topic sentence should state the problem. You might begin this way: *Jocelyn, an aspiring astronomer, couldn't keep awake at night when most astronomers conducted their research.*

After your topic sentence, add two detail sentences to support it. Refer to the story as you write.

Now write a second paragraph. Your topic sentence should state the solution to the problem discussed in your first paragraph. You might write: *At the observatory in England, most research was conducted during the day.*

Add two supporting detail sentences.

Revise

Read the paragraphs that you wrote. Check to make sure that each topic sentence is followed by two detail sentences. Revise your paragraphs so that the details clearly relate to their topic sentences.

In this Greek myth, Jason has set out on a quest to find the Golden Fleece. Who possesses the Fleece and where is it kept?

As you read the myth, look for characteristics of fantasy.

Jason and the Golden Fleece

by Padraic Colum

In Greek mythology, Jason was heir to the throne of Aeson, the king of Iolcus. When Jason's uncle, Pelias, seized the throne, Jason and his mother were forced to flee the country. Many years later, Jason returned to Iolcus to claim his father's throne. He was determined to win back the kingdom that had been taken from him. To get rid of Jason, Pelias persuaded him to go on an expedition to the distant land of Colchis. Pelias told Jason that his task was to bring back the Golden Fleece, the wool of a flying ram that had been sacrificed to the god Zeus.

After many dangerous adventures, Jason and his crew, known as Argonauts after their ship *Argo,* finally reached Colchis. As our story begins, at a meeting in the royal palace of Colchis, Jason has pleaded with Aeetes, the king of Colchis, to let him have the Golden Fleece.

Aeetes was not made friendly by Jason's words. His heart was divided as to whether he should summon his armed men and have them slain upon the spot, or whether he should put them into danger by the trial he would make of them. And then he spoke to Jason, saying:

"Strangers to Colchis, it may be true what my nephews have said. It may be that ye are truly of the seed of the immortals. And it may be that I shall give you the Golden Fleece to bear away after I have made trial of you."

As he spoke, Medea, brought there by his messenger so that she might observe the strangers, came into the chamber. She entered softly and she stood away from her father and the four who were speaking with him. Jason looked upon her, and although his mind was filled with the thought of bending King Aeetes to his will, he saw what manner of maiden she was, and what beauty and what strength was hers.

She had a dark face that was made very strange by her crown of golden hair. Her eyes, like her father's, were wide and full of light, and her lips were so full and red that they made her mouth like an opening rose. But her brows were always knit as if there was some secret anger within her.

"With brave men I have no quarrel," said Aeetes. "I will make a trial of your bravery, and if your bravery wins through the trial, be very sure that you will have the Golden Fleece to bring back in triumph to Iolcus.

"But the trial that I would make of you is hard for a great hero even. Know that on the plain of Ares yonder I have two fire-breathing bulls with feet of brass. These bulls were once conquered by me; I yoked them to a plow of adamant, and with them I plowed the field of Ares for four plow-gates. Then I sowed the furrows, not with the seed that Demeter gives, but with the teeth of a dragon. And from the dragon's teeth that I sowed in the field of Ares armed Earth-born Men sprang up. I slew them with my spear as they rose around me to slay me. If you can accomplish this that I accomplished in days gone by, I shall submit to you and give you the Golden Fleece. But if you cannot accomplish what I once accomplished you shall go from my city empty-handed, for it is not right that a brave man should yield aught to one who cannot show himself as brave."

So Aeetes said. Then Jason, utterly confounded, cast his eyes upon the ground. He raised them to speak to the king, and as he did he found the strange eyes of Medea upon him. With all the courage that was in him he spoke:

"I will dare the contest, monstrous as it is. I will face this doom. I have come far, and there is nothing else for me to do but to yoke your fire-breathing bulls to the plow of adamant, and plow the furrows in the field of Ares, and struggle with the Earth-born Men." As he said this he saw the eyes of Medea grow wide as with fear.

Then Aeetes said, "Go back to your ship and make ready for the trial." Jason, with Peleus and Telamon, left the chamber, and the king smiled grimly as he saw them go.

When darkness came upon the earth; when, at sea, sailors looked to the Bear and the stars of Orion; when, in the city, there was no longer the sound of barking dogs nor of men's voices; Medea went from the palace. She came to a path; she followed it until it brought her into the part of the grove that was all black with the shadow that oak trees made.

She called up Hecate, the Moon. She saw the moon rise above the treetops, and then the hissing and shrieking and howling died away. Holding up a goblet in her hand Medea poured out a libation of honey to Hecate.

She stood outside the temple of Hecate. She waited, but she had not long to wait, for, like the bright Star Sirius rising out of the ocean, soon she saw Jason coming toward her. She made a sign to him, and he came and stood beside her in the portals of the temple.

They would have stood face to face if Medea did not have her head bent. A blush had come upon her face, and Jason seeing it, and seeing how her head was bent, knew how grievous it was to her to meet and speak to a stranger in this way. He took her hand and he spoke to her reverently.

"Lady," he said, "I implore you by Hecate and by Zeus who helps all strangers to be kind to me and to the men who have come to your country with me. Without your help I cannot hope to prevail in the grievous trial that has been laid upon me. If you will help us, Medea, your name will be renowned throughout all Greece. And I have hopes that you will help us, for your face and form show you to be one who can be kind and gracious."

The blush of shame had gone from Medea's face and a softer blush came over her as Jason spoke. She looked upon him and she knew that she could hardly live if the breath of the brazen bulls withered his life or if the Earth-born Men slew him. She took the charm from out her girdle. Ungrudgingly she put it into Jason's hands. And as she gave him the charm that she had gained with such danger, the fear and trouble that was around her heart melted as the dew melts from around the rose when it is warmed by the first light of the morning.

Then they spoke standing close together in the portal of the temple. She told him how he should anoint his body all over with the charm; it would give him, she said, boundless and untiring strength, and make him so that the breath of the bulls could not wither him nor the horns of the bulls pierce him. She told him also to sprinkle his shield and his sword with the charm.

And then they spoke of the dragon's teeth and of the Earth-born Men who would spring from them. Medea told Jason that when they arose out of the earth, he was to cast a great stone amongst them. The Earth-born Men would struggle about the stone, and they would slay each other in the contest.

Her dark and delicate face was beautiful. Jason looked upon her, and it came into his mind that in Colchis there was something else of worth besides the Golden Fleece. And he thought that after he had won the Fleece there would be peace between the Argonauts and King Aeetes, and that he and Medea might sit together in the king's hall. But when he spoke of being joined in friendship with her father, Medea cried:

"Think not of treaties nor of covenants. In Greece such are regarded, but not here. Ah, do not think that the king, my father, will keep any peace with you! When you have won the Fleece you must hasten away. You must not tarry in Aea."

She said this and her cheeks were wet with tears to think that he should go so soon, that he would go so far, and that she would never look upon him again.

Then they parted; Medea went swiftly back to the palace, and Jason, turning to the river, went to where the *Argo* was moored.

The heroes embraced and questioned him: He told them of Medea's counsel and he showed them the charm she had given him. That savage man Arcas scoffed at Medea's charm.

Jason bathed in the river; then he anointed himself with the charm; he sprinkled his spear and shield and sword with it. He came to Arcas who sat upon his bench and he held the spear toward him.

Arcas took up his heavy sword and he hewed at the butt of the spear. The edge of the sword turned. The blade leaped back in his hand as if it had been struck against an anvil. And Jason, feeling within him a boundless and tireless strength, laughed aloud.

They took the ship out of the backwater and they brought her to a wharf in the city. At a place that was called "The Ram's Couch" they fastened the *Argo*. Then they marched to the field of Ares, where the king and the Colchian people were.

Jason, carrying his shield and spear, went before the king. From the king's hand he took the gleaming helmet that held the dragon's teeth. This he put into the hands of Theseus, who went with him. Then with the spear and shield in his hands, with his sword girt across his shoulders, and with his mantle stripped off, Jason looked across the field of Ares.

He set his feet firmly upon the ground and he held his shield before him. He awaited the onset of the bulls. They came clanging up with loud bellowing, breathing out fire. They lowered their heads, and with mighty, iron-tipped horns they came to gore and trample him.

Medea's charm had made him strong; Medea's charm had made his shield impregnable. The rush of the bulls did not overthrow him. His comrades shouted to see him standing firmly there, and in wonder the Colchians gazed upon him. All around him, as from a furnace, there came smoke and fire.

The bulls roared mightily. Grasping the horns of the bull that was upon his right hand, Jason dragged him until he had brought him beside the yoke of bronze. Striking the brazed knees of the bull suddenly with his foot, he forced him down. Then he smote the other bull as it rushed upon him, and it too he forced down upon its knees.

Castor and Polydeuces held the yoke to him. Jason bound it upon the necks of the bulls. He fastened the plow to the yoke. Then he took his shield and set it upon his back, and grasping the handles of the plow he started to make the furrow.

With his long spear he drove the bulls before him as with a goad. Terribly they raged, furiously they breathed out fire. Beside Jason, Theseus went holding the helmet that held the dragon's teeth. The hard ground was torn up by the plow of adamant, and the clods groaned as they were cast up. Jason flung the teeth between the open sods, often turning his head in fear that the deadly crop of the Earth-born Men was rising behind him.

By the time that a third of the day was finished the field of Ares had been plowed and sown. As yet the furrows were free of the Earth-born Men. Jason went down to the river and filled his helmet full of water and drank deeply. And his knees that were stiffened with the plowing, he bent until they were made supple again.

He saw the field rising into mounds. It seemed that there were graves all over the field of Ares. Then he saw spears and shields and helmets rising up out of the earth. Then armed warriors sprang up, a fierce battle cry upon their lips.

Jason remembered the counsel of Medea. He raised a boulder that four men could hardly raise and with arms hardened by the plowing he cast it. The Colchians shouted to see such a stone cast by the hands of one man. Right into the middle of the Earth-born Men the stone came. They leaped upon it like hounds, striking at one another as they came together. Shield crashed on shield, spear rang upon spear as they struck at each other. The Earth-born Men, as fast as they arose, went down before the weapons in the hands of their brethren.

Jason rushed upon them, his sword in his hand. He slew some that had risen out of the earth only as far as the shoulders; he slew others whose feet were still in the earth; he slew others who were ready to spring upon him. Soon all the Earth-born Men were slain, and the furrows ran with their dark blood as channels run with water in springtime.

The Argonauts shouted loudly for Jason's victory. King Aeetes rose from his seat that was beside the river and he went back to the city. The Colchians followed him. Day faded, and Jason's contest was ended.

But Aeetes would not suffer the strangers to depart peaceably with the Golden Fleece that Jason had won. In the assembly place, with his son beside him, and with the furious Colchians all around him, the king spoke.

He would have them attack the strangers and burn the *Argo*. There was a prophecy, he declared, that would have him be watchful of the treachery of his own offspring. He feared that his daughter, Medea, had aided the strangers. So the king spoke, and the Colchians, hating all strangers, shouted around him.

Word of what her father had said was brought to Medea. She knew that she would have to go to the Argonauts and bid them flee hastily from Aea. They would not go, she knew, without the Golden Fleece; then she, Medea, would have to show them how to gain the Fleece.

Then she could never again go back to her father's palace, she could never again sit in this chamber and talk to her handmaidens, and be with Chalciope, her sister. Forever afterward she would be dependent on the kindness of strangers. Medea wept when she thought of all this. And then she cut off a tress of her hair and she left it in her chamber as a farewell from one who was going afar. Into the chamber where Chalciope was she whispered farewell.

Swiftly she went along the ways that led to the river. She came to where fires were blazing and she knew that the Argonauts were there.

She called to them, and Phrontis, Chalciope's son, heard the cry and knew the voice. To Jason he spoke, and Jason quickly went to where Medea stood.

She clasped Jason's hand and she drew him with her. "The Golden Fleece," she said, "the time has come when you must pluck the Golden Fleece off the oak in the grove of Ares." When she said these words all Jason's being became taut like the string of a bow.

Along a path that went from the river Medea drew Jason. They entered a grove. Then Jason saw something that was like a cloud filled with the light of the rising sun. It hung from a great oak tree. In awe he stood and looked upon it, knowing that at last he looked upon THE GOLDEN FLEECE.

His hand let slip Medea's hand and he went to seize the Fleece. As he did he heard a dreadful hiss. And then he saw the guardian of the Golden Fleece. Coiled all around the tree, with outstretched neck and keen and sleepless eyes, was a deadly serpent. Its hiss ran all through the grove and the birds that were wakening up squawked in terror.

Like rings of smoke that rise one above the other, the coils of the serpent went around the tree — coils covered by hard and gleaming scales. It uncoiled, stretched itself, and lifted its head to strike. Then Medea dropped on her knees before it, and began to chant her Magic Song.

As she sang, the coils around the tree grew slack. Like a dark, noiseless wave the serpent sank down on the ground. But still its jaws were open, and those dreadful jaws threatened Jason. Medea, with a newly cut spray of juniper dipped in a mystic brew, touched its deadly eyes. And still she chanted her Magic Song. The serpent's jaws closed; its eyes became deadened; far through the grove its length was stretched out.

Then Jason took the Golden Fleece. As he raised his hands to it, its brightness was such as to make a flame on his face. Medea called to him. He strove to gather it all up in his arms; Medea was beside him, and they went swiftly on.

They came to the river and down to the place where the *Argo* was moored. The heroes who were aboard started up, astonished to see the Fleece that shone as with the lightning of Zeus. Over Medea Jason cast it, and he lifted her aboard the *Argo*.

"O friends," he cried, "the quest on which we dared the gulfs of the sea and the wrath of kings is accomplished, thanks to the help of this maiden. Now may we return to Greece; now have we the hope of looking upon our fathers and our friends once more. And in all honor will we bring this maiden with us, Medea, the daughter of King Aeetes."

Then he drew his sword and cut the hawsers of the ship, calling upon the heroes to drive the *Argo* on. There was a din and a strain and a splash of oars, and away from Aea the *Argo* dashed. Beside the mast Medea stood; the Golden Fleece had fallen at her feet, and her hand and face were covered by her silver veil.

Discuss the Selection

1. Who possessed the Golden Fleece and where was it kept?
2. How did Jason accomplish the three tasks set for him by the king?
3. What do you think about Jason's decision to ask Medea to help him? Did he take a chance? Give reasons for your answer.
4. Why did Medea go against her father and help Jason?
5. At first, Jason accepts the king's trial with little hope of success. Where in the story do you find evidence that Jason's attitude toward the outcome of the trial has changed?
6. Do you think Jason could have defeated the fire-breathing bulls and warriors without Medea's help? Give reasons for your answer.

Apply the Skills

A myth is one kind of fantasy because it has many of the same characteristics as fantasy. Give three examples of fantasy from this selection.

Think and Write

Prewrite

1. Jason first encounters King Aeetes.	2. Jason then sees the lovely Medea.	3. Aeetes sets a trial.
4.	5.	6.

When a storyteller narrates a series of events from the earliest to the most recent, he or she is using time order.

The chart above contains three boxes summarizing events from "Jason and the Golden Fleece." Each box is numbered sequentially (in the order in which the event occurred in the story).

Copy the chart on a sheet of paper. Then extend it by adding three subsequent events from the tale.

Compose

Referring to the boxes and the story, write a one-page account that synthesizes (brings together) these six events. Your first sentence might be *Aeetes was displeased with Jason's words.* Try to use time-order words such as *first, next,* and *later* to make the order in which each event occurred very clear.

Revise

Read the account that you wrote. Pay particular attention to your use of time-order words. Check to make sure that you presented each event in the order in which it took place in the story. Revise your first draft to make the sequence of events as clear as possible to anyone who might read your work.

Study Skills

Book Parts

Many books, especially nonfiction books, are divided into three parts: the front matter, the main part of the book, and the back matter. Having books organized in this manner makes it easier to find information quickly.

The Front Matter

The front matter includes the title and copyright pages, the table of contents, and usually a preface or introduction.

The **title page** contains the title of the book, the name of the author or editor, the publisher, and the city where the book is published.

The **copyright page** usually follows the title page. The copyright date tells when the book was published. This shows you whether the book is up-to-date and whether the information in the book is current. When seeking the most recent information on a subject, it is best to look for a book with a current copyright date. If you were doing research on the use of robots in industry, which of the following books would be more useful to you: a book with a 1964 copyright date or a book with a 1986 copyright date?

Another part of the front matter is the **Table of Contents**. It shows how the book is organized. Most books are organized either by units and chapters or simply by chapters. The Table of Contents lists each chapter in the order in which it appears in the book and gives the page number on which it begins. Look at the Table of Contents from *Animals as Hunters*. The book is organized into units and chapters. What chapters are found in the first unit?

Some books have a **Preface** or **Introduction**. It often is written by the author or editor of the book. It explains the importance of the topic and gives the reasons why the book was written. Sometimes this part of the book is written by someone other than the author or editor. It is then known as the **Foreword**.

CONTENTS

Introduction	9	III. **The Final Kill**	
		On Land	48
I. **In Search of Food**		In the Air	53
Learning to Track	11	In Waters	59
The Use of Camouflage	17	At Night	64
The Aid of Senses	22		
		Glossary	70
II. **Natural Weapons**		Bibliography	73
Teeth and Fangs	29	Index	75
Various Venoms	35		
Jaws, Claws, and Paws	41		

The Back Matter

There is a lot of helpful information found in the back matter of a book.

One part that might be included is an **Appendix**. It contains information that is not included in the main text. Maps, charts, lists, and diagrams are often found in the appendix.

The author may also choose to include a **Glossary** in the back matter. A glossary defines certain words that appear in the book. Like the dictionary, the entries in a glossary are arranged in alphabetical order. Some glossaries might include a pronunciation key. Is there a pronunciation key in the glossary of this book?

One of the most useful parts of a book is the **Index**. It is an alphabetical list of topics mentioned in the book. The numbers of the pages on which the topics appear are also listed. Look at the following sample index page:

Insects
  venom, 36

Jaguars, 42, 49
Jungles, 26

Kingfisher, 60

Leopards, 29, 42, 49
Lions, 42, 50
Lizards
  as hunters, 51
  venom, 37

Mammals
  as hunters, 50
  diet, 13

Nighthawks, 55
Nightingale, 54

Parasites, 24
Pirate birds, 55

Notice that the topic **Lizards** has been divided into smaller parts — as *hunters* and *venom*. These divisions are called subtopics. The subtopics are also arranged in alphabetical order. On which page would you find information about lizards as hunters?

Sometimes you may need to find more information about a topic. The author or editor may include a **bibliography**. The bibliography lists books and other reference sources used in the writing of the text as well as further reading material about the topic. Most bibliographies usually appear in the back matter, but sometimes bibliographies appear at the end of a chapter or unit in a book. Where does the bibliography appear in this book? Look at the following sample bibliography. In what order are the entries listed?

> Deegan, Paul. *Animals of East Africa*. Mankato, Minn.: Creative Education, Inc., 1971.
>
> Hartman, Jane E. *Animals That Live in Groups*. New York: Holiday House, Inc., 1978.
>
> Patent, Dorothy. *Hunters and the Hunted: Surviving in the Animal World*. New York: Holiday House, Inc., 1981.
>
> Ricciuti, Edward R. *Sounds of Animals at Night*. New York: Harper & Row Publications, Inc., 1977.
>
> Walter, Eugene J., Jr. *Why Animals Behave the Way They Do*. New York: Charles Scribner's Sons, 1981.

An important point to remember is that not all books have all the parts mentioned. However, familiarizing yourself with the different parts of a book will help in finding information from books easily and quickly.

- In which part of the book might you find each of the following items?

    a. A list of topics and subtopics that appear in the book
    b. The date when the book was published
    c. Maps, charts, and additional information
    d. A list of additional books and references on the topic

The quest of archaeologist Howard Carter ends with an important discovery. What is the discovery and why is it so important?

A chain of events almost prevents Carter from making his discovery. As you read, notice the causal chain that almost prevents him from doing so.

The Treasures of King Tutankhamen

by Mildred Mastin Pace

The young king's name was Tutankhamen. His queen was named Ankhesenamun. Little is known of them, but they married very young, perhaps when eleven or twelve years old.

His reign was short and his tomb was small and unpretentious. It was made up of three modest whitewashed rooms and a burial chamber so small there was barely space in it for his sarcophagus.

The richness and beauty of the objects found in this minor king's tomb give us a dazzling sample of the treasure, the fortune in jewels and gold, that was buried with the greater Pharaohs.

Had his tomb been emptied of its treasure by thieves, or had it remained hidden beneath its rubble, Tutankhamen's name would be almost unknown today.

But fortunately the treasure lay hidden. And thanks to the determination of an English archaeologist, Howard Carter, the tomb was discovered.

For years Carter had been excavating in a bleak and barren area known as the Valley of the Kings. Sun-scorched by the unbearable heat in summer, hot and arid the year through, the valley is a desolate place of rocks and cliffs and mounds of sand. Cut into the faces of the rocks and cliffs are many openings. These are entrances leading to tombs under the ground built in the day of the ancient Pharaohs. The valley got its name from the fact that so many kings were buried there.

For five years Carter excavated, searching for the tomb. He had no money of his own. But he had a benefactor: Lord Carnarvon, an Englishman of wealth who was interested in Egyptian archaeological finds.

At long last Lord Carnarvon, too, decided there was nothing more to find in the valley. He asked Carter to come to visit him at his home in England, Highclere Castle, and there told Carter he could no longer support him.

One night, while still in England, Carter was poring over maps of the valley and pinpointed a small triangular space they had not explored. It was a barren area covered with loose rocks, sand, and rubble. Small, unpromising, and situated at the base of the great tomb of Rameses VI, it was an unlikely spot for another Pharaoh's tomb. Diggers, quite reasonably, had passed it by.

But Carter pointed it out to Carnarvon and begged him to finance just one more season of digging. Carnarvon agreed.

Carter returned to Egypt and on November 1, 1922, he and his crew began clearing the wedge of land. Three days later they discovered a step cut in the rock beneath an ancient worker's hut they had uncovered. A little more clearing revealed this to be the first of sixteen steps leading down into more rock. At the foot of the stairs there was a door, blocked with piles of stone.

After the workers removed the stones, Carter was excited to see impressions of seals pressed into the door, indicating a royal burial. He now knew, at long last, that he had found a royal tomb.

Carter later said, "I needed all my self-control to keep from breaking down the doorway . . . then and there."

To open it at once he felt would not be fair to his benefactor, Lord Carnarvon, who was still in England. He went to the nearby city of Luxor and cabled Carnarvon:

> . . . MADE WONDERFUL DISCOVERY IN VALLEY.
> A MAGNIFICENT TOMB WITH SEALS INTACT.
> RE-COVERED SAME FOR YOUR ARRIVAL.
> CONGRATULATIONS.

So the workers blocked the door once more and filled in the stairway with rubble. Carter placed guards on watch and, half mad with impatience, awaited Carnarvon's arrival.

Lord Carnarvon reached Luxor on November 23. By the following day the rubble and stones were again cleared, and the two men, accompanied by a few aides, went down to examine the door. To their bitter disappointment they saw now that Carter was mistaken. The seals had been broken, and resealed. They removed the door and entered the narrow, empty corridor. At the end of the corridor was another door, the door to the tomb itself. To the men's despair they saw that this door, too, had been forced open and resealed.

Graverobbers had been there before them! Would they find just another empty tomb?

With trembling hands Carter made a small opening in the upper left-hand corner of the door. He held a lighted candle to the opening and peered in.

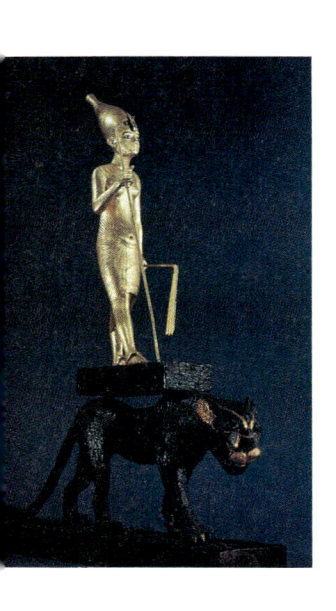

The candle sputtered. For a moment he saw nothing. Then, in Carter's own words,

"As my eyes grew accustomed to the light, details of the room within emerged slowly from the mist, strange animals, statues, and gold—everywhere the glint of gold. For the moment—an eternity it must have seemed to the others standing by—I was struck dumb with amazement. And when Lord Carnarvon, unable to stand the suspense any longer, inquired anxiously, 'Can you see anything?' It was all I could do to get out the words, 'Yes. Wonderful things.'"

Carter handed Lord Carnarvon the candle. When the door was removed, the men saw that all was in disorder. Thieves had been there—probably shortly after the king's burial.

Apparently they had been surprised and scared off by guards or priests before they did much harm. But they had left their greasy fingerprints where they had emptied valuable oils from alabaster vases. There was a footprint on the floor. In their haste to flee when discovered, they had left behind waterskins partly filled with oil. One thief had dropped a number of gold rings he had wrapped in a linen cloth. Two gold struts were broken from a golden chair. A small statue, probably of gold, was missing, ripped from its base.

But very little had been taken, very little damage done.

Carter, Carnarvon, and their aides had entered a virtually intact tomb of a Pharaoh—the only one that had ever been found.

This room, which Carter called the antechamber, was the largest of the four rooms they were to find in the tomb. Even so, it was small by comparison with chambers in other royal tombs—25 feet long and just 12 feet wide. The whitewashed walls were plain and unadorned.

But this room, and two smaller "storage rooms" they entered later, were crammed with treasures. The wealth that had been buried with this boy-king for more than three thousand years dazzled the eyes and boggled the mind. Objects of gold and silver, turquoise, carnelian, lapis lazuli, carved ivory and alabaster . . .

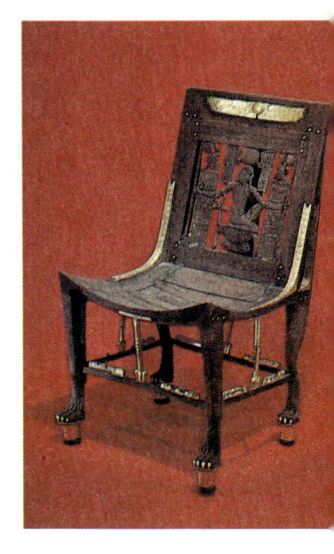

There was the young Pharaoh's gold and silver throne, set with semiprecious stone; there was a whole fleet of model boats — ready to fill the Pharaoh's every sailing wish — including one of alabaster, inlaid with gold and precious stone.

The gold-sheathed ceremonial chariots he had used on earth were there — dismantled because they were too large to be drawn through the narrow corridor into the small room.

To serve him in his second life, there were servants: more than a hundred statuettes of men and women, called ushabti. And with them were almost two thousand tools and implements they would use in their king's service.

In magnificently decorated chests were his royal robes, some covered with gold sequins, others decorated with pure gold rosettes; his sandals worked with gold.

These and hundreds of other things were in the tomb, ready for his use in the next world.

Among the many objects of beauty, a few cast some light on the shadowy figure of the young king, Tutankhamen. His marriage to the girl-queen is pictured as a happy one. Scenes from their daily life are exquisitely drawn on the side panels of a gold shrine or chest.

The tomb tells us that the young king was a great hunter. Hundreds of bows and arrows were placed there for his use. There are pictures showing him hunting large game and small animals, wild ducks and other fowl. But he was fond of animals, too; he had a pet lion.

We know he enjoyed a popular chesslike game called senet. A number of handsome sets of varying sizes, made of ebony and ivory and inlaid with gold, were found in the tomb, their pieces, or "men," intact, ready for a game.

He played the trumpet. Two were buried with him. One of solid silver was placed in the shrine that held his sarcophagus.

When Carter first entered the antechamber, piled high with treasures, his eyes were caught by two life-size statues of the king. Handsome in black and gold, holding scepters of gold, they stood at each side of a sealed door. Carter guessed at once that they guarded the royal sarcophagus. Behind that door he should find the mummy of the Pharaoh Tutankhamen.

59

If the sarcophagus had not been broken into, if the mummy remained intact, this would be the most important archaeological find in all Egypt and one of the most important in all the world. This would be the first royal mummy ever found in its original coffins, its wrappings undisturbed.

As anxious as Carter and Lord Carnarvon were to see the sarcophagus, almost three months passed between discovery of the tomb and opening of the door to the burial chamber.

First they had to empty the antechamber. Every object in the room had to be examined, cataloged, and photographed before it could be moved. Steps had to be taken, too, to preserve objects that might be harmed when exposed to outside air. For example, there were fragile objects that might disintegrate. Experts working with Carter hastened to preserve these in wax: the ostrich feathers of the king's fans, the wreaths of flowers still standing against the walls.

Finally, only the two black and gold statues of the king were left in place, guarding the door.

By now the discovery of the tomb had attracted worldwide attention. When he was finally ready to open the burial chamber, Carter had an invited audience seated on folding chairs in the emptied whitewashed room. The room was charged with excitement.

Carter make a small opening in the top of the sealed door. Using a flashlight, he peered in. There, within a yard of the doorway, he was astonished to see a solid wall of gold. It stretched as far as he could see and seemed to block the entrance to the chamber.

When the door was removed, Carter and Lord Carnarvon squeezed into the narrow passage between the "wall" of gold and the walls of the burial chamber. They found it was not a wall of gold. It was a large gilt shrine, apparently built around the sarcophagus for protection. It practically filled the burial chamber. Almost 11 feet wide, more than 16 feet long, and 9 feet high, it nearly touched the ceiling. The space between it and the four walls of the room was a little more than 2 feet. That left a very narrow space for the men to move around in.

There were two doors to the shrine, which Carter removed. Inside was another gold shrine. Now Carter's excitement was intense! The seals on the doors had never been tampered with. For the first time since the days of ancient Egypt, men would soon see the intact sepulcher of an Egyptian king, his mummy in its coffins just as it was on the day of his burial.

Removing the doors of the second shrine, Carter found a third one. And nested inside that, a fourth.

As the men carefully removed each shrine, they found rich and beautiful objects: elaborate lamps of milky alabaster, staffs of gold and silver, painted alabaster jars with lids of carved figures, small chests inlaid with gold. Over one shrine hung a sheer canopy sprinkled with bright gilded daisies.

The fourth, and last, golden shrine contained the magnificent red quartzite sarcophagus. At each corner, in high relief, was the figure of a goddess, her winged arms spread out protectingly.

When the sarcophagus was opened, Carter found three coffins, each shaped like a mummy. They nestled tightly, one within the other, so tightly that Carter could scarcely wedge his little finger between them.

Opening these coffins was to prove one of the toughest jobs in Carter's entire career. To make the job more difficult, the room in which he worked was always crowded with men watching him. This bothered Carter.

But he and all who watched were astonished by the beauty of the coffins. Each was a figure of the young king wearing the false beard and headdress of the pharaohs. His hands, folded across his chest, held the crook and flail, symbols of Egyptian royalty.

The first and second coffins were made of gilded wood. They were inlaid with bits of gold and brilliant red and blue stones: carnelian and lapis lazuli. The third coffin was of solid gold.

Carter and those with him gazed in awe. The rich beauty of the golden figure of the young Pharaoh was overwhelming.

The coffin was massive. More than 6 feet long, it contained 2,448 pounds of twenty-two-carat gold. But there was a delicacy in its elegance, the flowing lines of the goddesses etched in gold, the soft glow of stones set in graceful designs. Inside this coffin of gold was the mummy of the king.

Within the wrappings that enfolded him was found a whole treasury of ornaments: on his head the royal diadem of gold set with carnelian, lapis lazuli, and turquoise; collars and necklaces, golden girdles, amulets and pendants, pectorals—intricately wrought treasures of great beauty and exquisite workmanship. His splendid hands were heavy with jewel-studded gold rings. And gold nail stalls were fitted on his fingers and toes.

Most wondrous of all was the portraitlike mask that had been placed on the bandaged face. Wrought of gold inlaid with gems, it covered the king's head and shoulders and extended down to the middle of his body. It was almost an exact likeness of the young king: the wide-open eyes luminous, the shining golden face noble and serene.

Tragically, Lord Carnarvon did not live to see the coffins opened and the young king's mummy revealed. Less than five months after the tomb was discovered, he was bitten by an insect in the Valley of the Kings. Blood poisoning set in and he died in a hospital in Cairo.

Almost six years elapsed from the day the tomb was discovered by Carter until it was emptied and its treasures moved to the museum in Cairo.

No, not emptied. For the mummy of the young king was left in its simple whitewashed tomb, lying in the second coffin, resting in the handsome quartzite sarcophagus where it had been placed more than three thousand years before.

Discuss the Selection

1. What did Carter discover and why was it so important?
2. What things could be learned about the young king because of what was found?
3. If you had been Lord Carnarvon, would you have agreed to continue the excavation?
4. Why did Carter wait for Carnarvon's arrival before opening the tomb?
5. What special technique did the author use to describe the first look in the tomb? Find that part of the selection. Why do you think the author used this technique?

Apply the Skills

Remember that in order to understand cause and effect, it is helpful to ask these two questions: *What happened?* and *Why did this happen?* The answer to the first question is the effect; the answer to the second one is the cause. Howard Carter was almost prevented from looking for King Tutankhamen's tomb because of a chain of events that preceded the actual digging. What events almost prevented Carter from looking for King Tutankhamen's tomb?

Think and Write

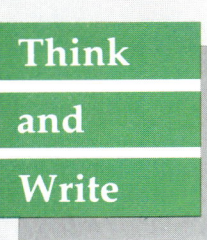

Prewrite

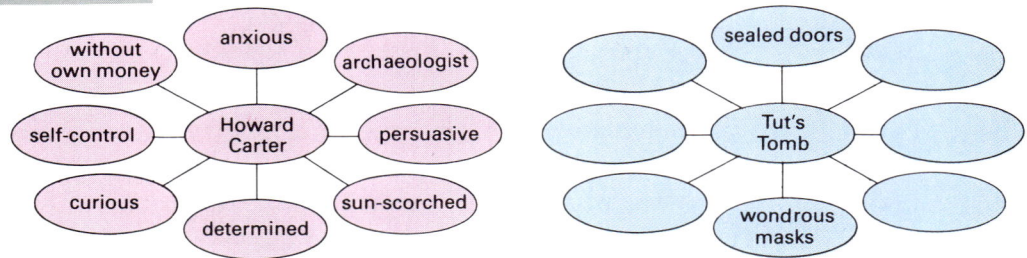

Ideaburst 1 — Howard Carter: anxious, archaeologist, persuasive, sun-scorched, determined, curious, self-control, without own money

Ideaburst 2 — Tut's Tomb: sealed doors, wondrous masks (other circles blank)

The diagrams shown above are what might be called ideabursts. The information in the center circle of each one represents its subject. Study the first ideaburst. Notice how the surrounding circles all relate to Carter.

On a sheet of paper, copy the partial ideaburst about King Tut's tomb. Complete the diagram with appropriate words from the story.

Compose

Using the information from the ideabursts and the story, write one paragraph about Howard Carter's quest and another about his discovery of the treasure. Your first paragraph might begin like this: *Sun-scorched, exhausted, and without funds, Carter refused to stop excavating.*

Your second paragraph might start with a sentence such as this one: *The rich beauty of the mummy's gold mask was a wondrous sight.*

Revise

Read the paragraphs that you wrote. As you read, check to be sure that your sentences are consistent with the ideabursts and with the selection "The Treasures of King Tutankhamen." Edit your writing to make every sentence a vivid and accurate summary of both Howard Carter's quest and the discovery of King Tutankhamen's tomb.

Comprehension Study

Comparisons and Contrasts

Do you sometimes have the experience of meeting someone who reminds you of another person? Maybe the way the person looks or acts calls to mind someone familiar. What you are actually doing is noticing the similarities between the two people. You are making a comparison. When you **compare** two or more things, people, or situations, you notice their similarities. When you **contrast** two or more things, people, or situations, you notice their differences.

Related Topics

An author may compare and contrast when presenting information. As you read the following paragraph, notice how the author compares and contrasts two related topics.

> Many people mistakenly think that the Arctic and the Antarctic are very similar to one another. After all, they point out, both are cold, snowy places. But unlike the Arctic, Antarctica is a continent. There is a vast amount of land beneath the thick ice shelf. The area known as the Arctic consists of the Arctic Ocean dotted by a few small islands.

The author notes the similarities and differences of the two polar regions. In what ways are these regions the same? "Both are cold, snowy places." The word *both* is a clue that a comparison is being made. How are the Arctic and Antarctic different? Antarctica is a continent; the Arctic is not. The words *but* and *unlike* signal this contrast.

Making the Unfamiliar Familiar

Sometimes an author introduces an idea or subject to the reader through comparison and contrast. To help the reader understand the new idea, the author may compare it to, or contrast it with, something the reader is likely to know. Read the paragraph that follows to find out what the author considers unfamiliar to the reader.

> Eskimos rely greatly on the kayak for transportation across frigid northern waters. A kayak is generally made of seal skins and resembles a canoe. Unlike the canoe, however, the kayak seats only one person.

The author compares the kayak to a canoe, thereby creating a mental image for the reader who is unfamiliar with the kayak. What are the stated differences between the kayak and the canoe? What word is a clue to the contrast being made?

Comparisons That Describe

An author might use comparison to emphasize a particular characteristic or create a vivid image. Read the sentence that follows:

> When it reached the small ice pan on which they stood, the huge polar bear heaved its bulk out of the water and shook itself like an immense dog.

What is being compared in the sentence? The movement of the polar bear is being compared to that of an immense dog. The author is creating an image for the reader.

Comparisons and Contrasts Through Graphic Aids

Authors can show comparisons and contrasts through the use of graphic aids, too. Graphs and charts are useful tools for comparing and contrasting. Look at the following sample graph:

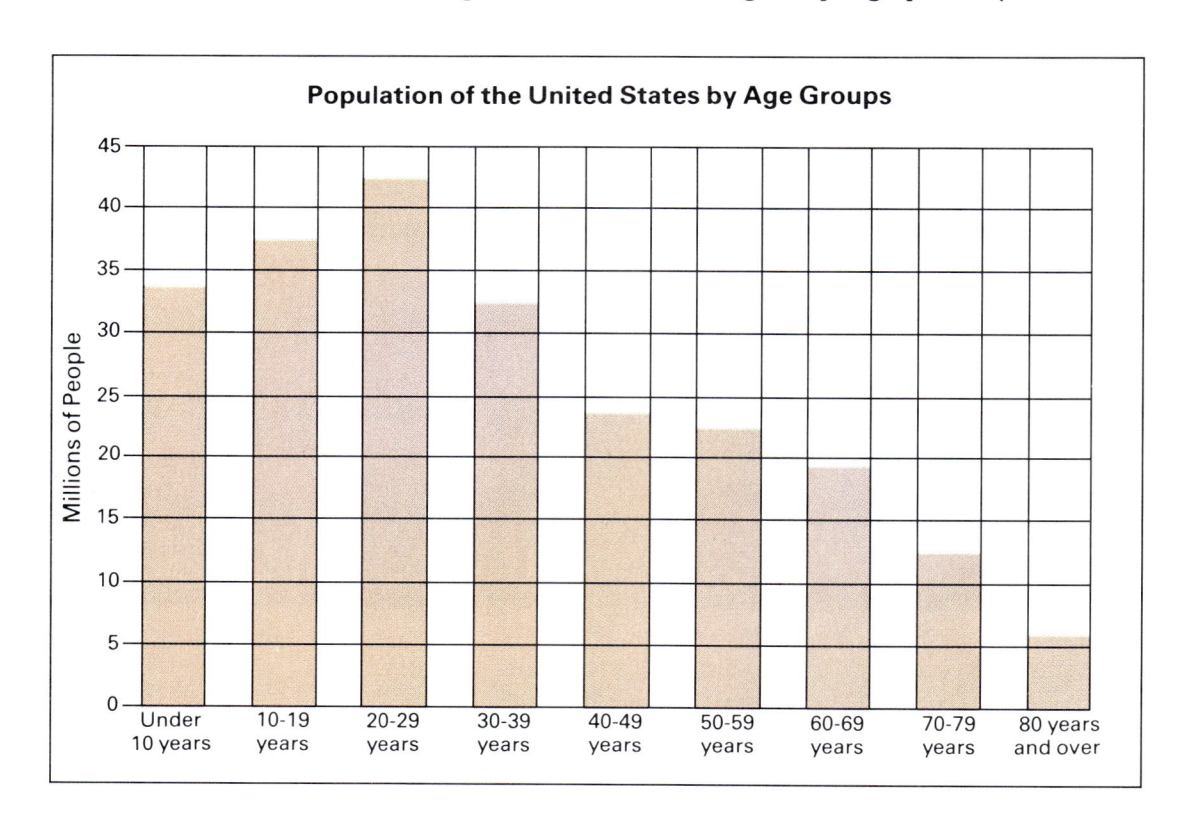

Population of the United States by Age Groups

Age Group	Millions of People
Under 10 years	33
10-19 years	37
20-29 years	42
30-39 years	32
40-49 years	23
50-59 years	22
60-69 years	19
70-79 years	12
80 years and over	5

What advantages does a graph have over written text? It presents a great deal of information in one illustration. A graph presents comparisons and contrasts visually and helps the reader to locate information easily.

1. What two things are being compared in each of these sentences?
   a. The full moon glowed like a mysterious spaceship sailing through the clouds spinning a path of silver across the mountains and the open water.
   b. My headlights had picked out the creeping drifts of snow; pretty pointed fingers feeling their way inch by inch across the strip of tarmac.
2. Read the paragraph and answer the questions that follow:

   Harriet Quimby and Matilde Moisant made aviation history when they became the first women licensed pilots. Their enthusiasm for flying led them to pilot many flights that had never been attempted before. Harriet Quimby flew across the English Channel, while Matilde set records of her own in Mexico City. The women shared a common interest in flying, but they were different in personality. Harriet took precautions. Her planes were carefully inspected. On the other hand, Matilde Moisant believed she could handle any danger. She was less careful. Ironically, Harriet died in an air accident. Matilde retired from flying at the request of her family.

- How were Harriet and Matilde alike? How were they different?

Textbook Application: Comparisons and Contrasts in Social Studies

Read the following textbook excerpt. Refer to the sidenotes to help you recognize the author's comparisons and contrasts.

> The Pilgrims decided to settle at a place they called **Plymouth**. The rock on which they are thought to have landed is now a national

monument. They came ashore with almost nothing, no "butter or oil, not a sole to mend a shoe." They were true pilgrims, these wanderers, uncertain of what lay over the next hill.

In some respects the Pilgrims were like the first immigrants from Asia, people who owned little more than what they had on their backs, isolated in an unknown land. They were totally dependent on one another, but this was their strength. They recognized their common purpose and the need for unity. They were ready to give up the familiar world for the uncertain wilderness.

> What comparison is being made in this paragraph?

Their early experiences were similar to those of the Jamestown settlers. Disease swept through the exhausted party. The survivors might well have starved to death if an Indian named Squanto had not befriended them. Squanto taught the Pilgrims how to grow corn. He showed them the best streams for fishing.

Things changed for the better in the spring. Unlike the first Virginians, the Pilgrims worked hard, planted their crops, and in the autumn gathered in a bountiful harvest. For this, in November, 1621, the settlers came together to give thanks. Thus was established the American tradition of **Thanksgiving Day**.

> What is being contrasted in this paragraph?

—*American History*,
Harcourt Brace Jovanovich

1. In what ways were the Pilgrims like the first immigrants from Asia?
2. How were the Pilgrims different from the first Virginians?

On a quest to find his father, Matthew and his friend Kayak struggle to stay alive in the frozen Arctic. What dangers do they encounter?

Matthew and Kayak sometimes react in different ways to dangerous situations. As you read, compare their reactions as they struggle to stay alive.

Frozen Fire

by James Houston

Thirteen-year-old Matthew Morgan arrives in the town of Frobisher, in the Canadian Arctic, with his father, Ross Morgan. Ross is a prospector and geologist who believes that his next expedition will yield a great discovery of some rare mineral. Ross has come to the Canadian Arctic in search of a rich copper deposit that he believes is near Frobisher. At the airport, Matthew meets Kayak, an Eskimo boy. The two quickly become friends.

Matthew's dad sets off in the *Waltzing Matilda*, a helicopter piloted by his friend Charlie, in search of the copper. When the helicopter does not return, Matthew and Kayak set out on their own in a snowmobile to find Mr. Morgan and Charlie.

During a day's ride from Frobisher, the snowmobile's gas cap is lost and the boys lose all their fuel. They are forced to continue on foot. As our selection begins, the boys are looking for a place to build a makeshift igloo in which to spend the night.

A cold sharp wind blew against their backs and seemed to drive them forward. Matthew was so hungry he felt light enough to take off and sail across the snow. They entered the mountains just before darkness came and hurried through a long valley.

"Just a little farther," Kayak called to him. "I want to build our igloo right up there."

When they reached the height of land, darkness had come.

Kayak ran to Matthew and gripped him by the arm and shook him. "We did it! We did it!" he whispered.

Matthew could not tell if Kayak was laughing or crying.

"See over there. Across the bay. See the glow of lights? That's Frobisher. That's where we came from!"

Far away on the horizon Matthew could see a faint yellow glow in the sky, as though some strange moon was about to rise.

"I wonder if my dad is over there?" said Matthew. "Let's keep on going!"

Matthew took a step forward, but his legs bent like spongy rubber that might let him down at any moment.

"No, no," said Kayak, "that glow must be thirty miles away." He drew the long snow knife from his pack. "We'll build an igloo here and sleep. We'll feel stronger in the morning."

They left at dawn and traveled down the long slope toward the frozen bay. When they finally reached the ice, Matthew felt light-headed.

Kayak squatted in the snow and, taking the broken half of the bow that he had saved, he lashed the snow knife to its grip.

"Why are you doing that?" asked Matthew.

"See that black fog rising way out there?" said Kayak. "The ice has changed. It's broken open. When we get out there, I'm going to have to feel beneath the snow for open water. I don't trust moving ice. You walk only in my footsteps," he added, as he carefully probed the ice before him. "Hurry," he said. "See that crack up ahead. It may be opening. It may be getting wider."

They ran toward the blue-green line that zigzagged like a frozen streak of lightning across their path. To the south, Matthew could see a great green shining lake where the seawater had flooded over the ice.

"Too wide for us to cross," exclaimed Kayak.

He hurried north along the edge of the crack. Matthew dreaded the look of the black water that stood gaping before them, sometimes eight feet, sometimes twelve feet wide.

"We'll never get across that crack," said Matthew, and he felt like falling down and weeping on the snow.

"Come on," said Kayak. "Hurry! We've got to keep on moving."

The crack stretched like a long ragged tear in a piece of white paper for as far as Matthew could see.

73

"There's a seal," whispered Kayak.

Matthew saw a head as round and black as a bowling ball floating in the icy water not thirty paces from them.

"If it was summer, we could swim across like seals," Matthew muttered.

"Swim?" said Kayak. "Even in summer that water is so cold it would kill both you and me in a few minutes. What did you learn in school in the south? I mean in Aree-zona and British Columbia and Mex-ico?"

"Reading, writing, geography, history, and archery and tennis. They were more fun."

"That's what I learned in school, too," said Kayak, "but no archery or tennis. Which one of those subjects is going to help you now, Mattoosie?"

"I don't know. I don't think any of them will help us."

"That's true, they won't," said Kayak. "Did they teach you about ice in school, Mattoosie?"

"No, not about ice."

"A *kaluna* once told me my grandfather was ignorant. You hear that? Ignorant! But everything we do right yesterday, today, tomorrow, comes from my grandfather. You'd be dead, I'd be dead already, without the knowledge of my grandfather.

"Today the subject is ice!" said Kayak. "Moving ice. And tides. Those two can kill you. So today we travel by my grandfather's school. He could only count to twenty — using his fingers and toes.

He died thinking the world was flat. He knew spirits moved the ice or stopped it from moving. He said on moonlit nights sometimes you can see the little people lying on their backs beside the tide cracks, scissoring their legs in the air and hear them screaming and laughing, teasing the poor humans. Would you say he was ignorant, Mattoosie?"

"No, he was not," said Matthew. "He understood the ice. Your grandfather never spent a day in school and yet today he is my teacher."

"Look here," Kayak pointed. "There is our only chance."

Matthew saw his friend run forward and kick hard at a four-foot chunk of ice that had cracked away from the main ice and then frozen fast again. Carefully Kayak knelt and cleared the snow away. Then seeing the weak fault where the ice pan had refrozen, he started chipping with the snow knife at the crack.

"Help me," he called to Matthew, who opened the largest blade of his Swiss Army knife.

Kneeling, they worked desperately. Small chips of ice flew up their sleeves, melted and ran along their arms in icy rivulets. Suddenly with a soft swoosh the small pan of ice let go and drifted. Kayak caught it with his knife and slowly drew it to him.

"I'll go first," he said, cautiously putting one foot on the ice pan.

Matthew saw it shudder and sink a little.

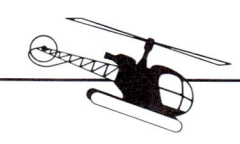

"It should hold me," Kayak said.

As though he trod on eggs, he carefully eased one knee and then the other onto the trembling pan of ice.

"Now push the ice," he said to Matthew. "Not so hard you'll tip me in, but hard enough to float me over to the other side."

Matthew lay on his stomach and with both hands he gave the ice a steady push. Kayak was on his hands and knees. A light breeze whipped across the ice and caught him like a sail, so the ice pan turned half around. Matthew closed his eyes and prayed.

"*Nakomik*, thanks a lot," he heard Kayak shout, and when Matthew opened his eyes, he saw Kayak scrambling onto the strong ice on the other side of the widening crack.

Kayak then began to chip two holes in the ice pan about four inches apart. He worked downwards in a V-shape until the two holes touched. Then he forced the piece of tent line through the ice and tied it tight.

"Get ready," he called to Matthew and, pushing the ice with his foot, sent it drifting back across the crack. "You're heavier than I am and that ice is very tippy even though it's thick," shouted Kayak. "You be mighty careful."

With the deadly cold black water all around him, Matthew felt like an elephant balancing on a cold round ball. Slowly, cautiously, Kayak drew Matthew toward him across the widening gap between the heavy shore ice of the bay and the great central body of ice, until Matthew, too, could crawl onto the strong ice.

If the two boys could have seen where they were going from an airplane, they would not have been in such a hurry to cross that deadly gap. The ice in the center of Frobisher Bay was broken into a dangerous jigsaw puzzle of slowly moving pans of ice, rising and falling as much as thirty feet on the huge tides pulled by the terrifying forces of the moon.

"I think we're going to be all right now," Kayak called to Matthew. "The wind should make it easier to get onto the shore ice across the bay near Frobisher."

He was wrong. Dead wrong. For the next six hours they hurried across the vast broken ice fields, driving the knife in before taking every step, testing. Kayak warned Matthew a dozen times to step only in the footprints that he, himself, had made.

In the late afternoon they watched with terror as the huge tide flooded the ice, creating deadly lakes just south of them. With each step Matthew imagined he could feel the broken ice beneath them moving south toward the Hudson Straits where they would be swept to certain death in the North Atlantic Ocean.

As darkness came again, Kayak squatted on the ice and placed his head in his hands. He was trembling, and Matthew could not tell whether it was from cold or hunger or fear.

"It's no use going any further," said Kayak. "I can feel it, we are being swept away. The tide is carrying us too far south. We will never reach the other side."

"What do you mean?" said Matthew, horrified.

"See that hill," said Kayak. "It was far to the south of us this morning, when we crossed the tide crack. Now it is so far to the north I can scarcely see it. We have moved fifteen miles south already. By morning we will have drifted thirty, almost forty miles away. We are lost, I tell you. Lost forever. Look. Look how the ice has split." Kayak showed him. "We were once on pans a mile square in size. Look how all of them have broken. You could not walk fifteen paces now without falling into the water. I am sorry, Mattoosie, we are truly finished."

A cruel blast of wind swept out of the north, driving chilling swirls of ice fog around them.

"We must build an igloo," said Matthew, unlashing Kayak's snow knife from the broken bow.

"It is difficult here," Kayak mumbled. "The snow is wet with salt water."

"Still we must try our best," said Matthew, and he paced out the small circle as he had seen Kayak do and began to cut the thin damp blocks. Big wet flakes of snow came driving on the wind.

"Come and help me," Matthew called to Kayak.

"Don't move," answered Kayak in a whisper. There was terror in his voice.

Cautiously Matthew turned and saw the white head and black beady eyes as it moved snakelike through the icy water. When it reached the small ice pan on which they stood, the huge polar bear heaved its bulk out of the water and shook itself like an immense dog. It looked yellow against the stark white snow.

Matthew saw the great bear swing its head back and forth, sniffing the air suspiciously. Its huge blue-black mouth hung open showing its terrible teeth. With a rumbling growl, the giant bear lowered its head and came shambling toward them.

The bear snaked forward cautiously until it reached the very edge of the ice where it had seen a seal. It reached out its paw and scratched against the ice.

The seal must have heard the sound beneath the water and, being curious, it once more raised its head above the surface. Seeing nothing but a yellowish heap of snow, it swam cautiously along the edge of the ice.

Suddenly, with lightning swiftness, the bear's right paw shot out and struck the seal's head a killing blow. The left paw lunged forward and hooked the seal inward with its great curved claws. Using its teeth, the bear easily hauled the hundred-pound seal up onto the ice pan.

Matthew watched it sniff the dead seal all over, then roll it on its back. Then the bear started to devour his prey.

"Stay still," Kayak hissed through his teeth, now chattering from cold and fear.

At last Matthew saw that the big bear was finished eating. With its belly rumbling, it padded once more to the edge of the ice and slipped silently into the freezing water. Kayak sat up carefully as the bear swam south. They saw it climb upon another pan and amble off, disappearing into the whirling snow.

Kayak rolled stiffly onto his hands and knees, then crouched like an animal, still watching the place where they had last seen the bear.

"I'm soaking wet." He trembled. "Get up," he called quietly to Matthew. "We're in trouble now, worse than we've ever been before."

The north wind seemed to press its freezing hand against Matthew's soaking clothes. It glazed them with a thin white sheath of ice as stiff as armor.

"Being wet will kill us sure," said Matthew, shivering like a dog. "What will we do?"

"I don't know. We'll have to think of

something," said Kayak, and he went forward and felt inside the seal.

In the half darkness Matthew saw him cut the big artery, then pull its heart out and set it on the ice.

"Quick, we got to build a shelter. Work hard and it will warm you up a little. Move your arms and legs," Kayak said, "so your clothing won't freeze stiff."

On one end of their pan, sheets of ice the size of tabletops lay scattered like playing cards, forced there by the pressures of the rising tides. Kayak stood three upright, leaning them against each other. Then together they hauled two more into place to form a rough circle.

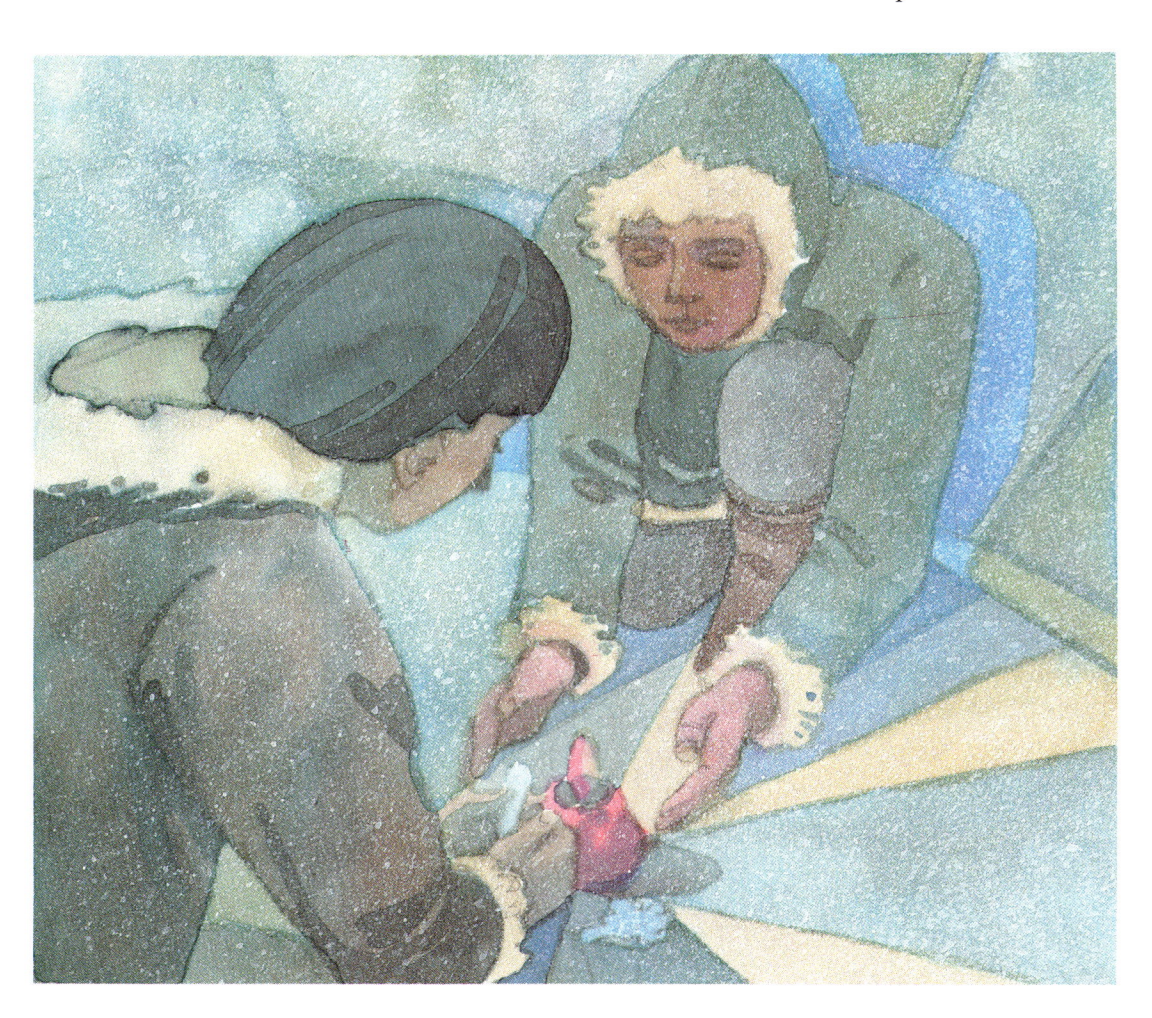

"Now gather snow," said Kayak, kicking it into wet piles with his soaking boots. "We'll chink up the holes and cracks between the ice to make it strong. If the house blows down with the wind tonight we could never build a new one in the dark."

When their crude shelter was finished, it looked like nothing but another miserable pile of ice.

Kayak hurried away and returned with the frozen heart and the torn remains of the seal. He dragged them inside the little ice cave.

"It's just as cold in here," said Matthew. "We've only built a grave for ourselves."

"Unless we make a fire."

Kayak took the last matches carefully from his pocket and felt them. "They are soaking wet," he groaned, "and their heads have come off. Useless," he said and flung them on the snow.

"Then we can't make a fire," cried Matthew through his chattering teeth. "We've got no lamp, no matches, and everything is soaking wet."

He saw Kayak take the snow knife and hack white chunks of seal fat from the inside of the carcass and set the frozen heart up in the snow like a small melon with its top cut open.

"Give me your little knife," he said and with it he trimmed a narrow piece off the back tail of his shirt in a place where it was still dry.

"I hope I didn't lose it," Kayak said, searching his pockets with his freezing hands. "I've found it. My little piece of flintstone." He handed it to Matthew.

"Hold it carefully. Don't drop it. It's worth more to us than gold."

Matthew had to help Kayak cut open the freezing front of his parka, so that he could reach into his inside breast pocket to get the little carving file and the wad of fine steel wool, the ones Matthew had seen him using at the school.

"They're soaking wet," said Kayak. "Feel in your hip pockets. They're still dry. Can you find any pieces of lint or string?"

"Only just this bit of string," said Matthew.

"Nearly nothing."

"It may be enough. Roll it into a loose ball," Kayak said. "Now, Mattoosie, you do everything exactly as I tell you. If you get your hands a little bit burned, don't mind it, understand me?"

Matthew wanted to laugh at him or cry. "How are you going to burn my hands? They're almost frozen."

He watched as Kayak struck the flint along the steel teeth of the little file. On the third try sparks flew into the wet steel wool and Matthew gasped in surprise, as he saw the fine steel wire spark and begin to flare red and burn. The fire fizzled out.

"Now," said Kayak. "If I can light it again, you put the dry string in the spark with your finger. Do it right! My hands are freezing."

He struck the file again a dozen times before the steel wool sputtered into running sparks. Matthew held the wad of string against the tiny flame.

"Hold it here. Don't let it go out."

Kayak took the shirttail wick that he had made, rubbed it with seal fat and held it in the tiny glow.

"Don't breathe on it just yet," he said, and waited.

Matthew felt a blister rising on his finger.

"Don't move it," Kayak ordered.

Slowly the seal fat sizzled, then a real flame burst into life. Kayak blew gently on it, then carefully stuffed one end of the wick into the well of glistening seal fat that he had stuffed into the open cavity of the frozen seal's heart. The white candle-like flame expanded, as the seal fat softened and soaked upward into the homemade wick. Working as painstakingly as a surgeon, Kayak spread the cloth wick with his knife until the flame widened. He let out his breath in satisfaction when he saw that there were at least three inches burning hotly. The ice shelter reflected the joyful light. Matthew held his hands out, spreading his stiffened fingers in the life-giving warmth.

"I would never have believed that," Matthew said quietly. "That you could make a lamp stove out of a frozen seal's heart and make wet steel wool burn. It smells good," he said, "like my mother's burning toast!"

"It's something," said Kayak, "I didn't learn in school."

With Matthew's knife he cut strips of rich red seal meat from the carcass where the bear had scarcely touched it. Together they warmed the strips over the little lamp and ate them. Matthew thought that he had never tasted anything so good.

"Now come on," Kayak demanded. "We go out of here and run around this little house as many times as you have fingers on your hands and I have toes."

When they came inside once more, Matthew felt warm all over as though the seal meat in his stomach was fuel on fire within him. His face and hands seemed to burn in the strong warmth and flickering light of Kayak's clever lamp.

Kayak unrolled the sleeping bags, which were only a little damp.

"Tonight we sleep resting on our knees and elbows," he said. "The snow's too wet to lie down."

Kayak pulled off his parka and beat it with the piece of broken bow until the sheath of ice fell away, then he put his parka on backwards.

"Why are you doing that?" asked Matthew.

"Because I'm going to pull up my hood and breathe into it. That way I catch all my body heat. You do the same. It's a trick I heard about from my mother's relatives. It might help to save our lives."

In the first light of the morning, Matthew heard the ice grinding and had

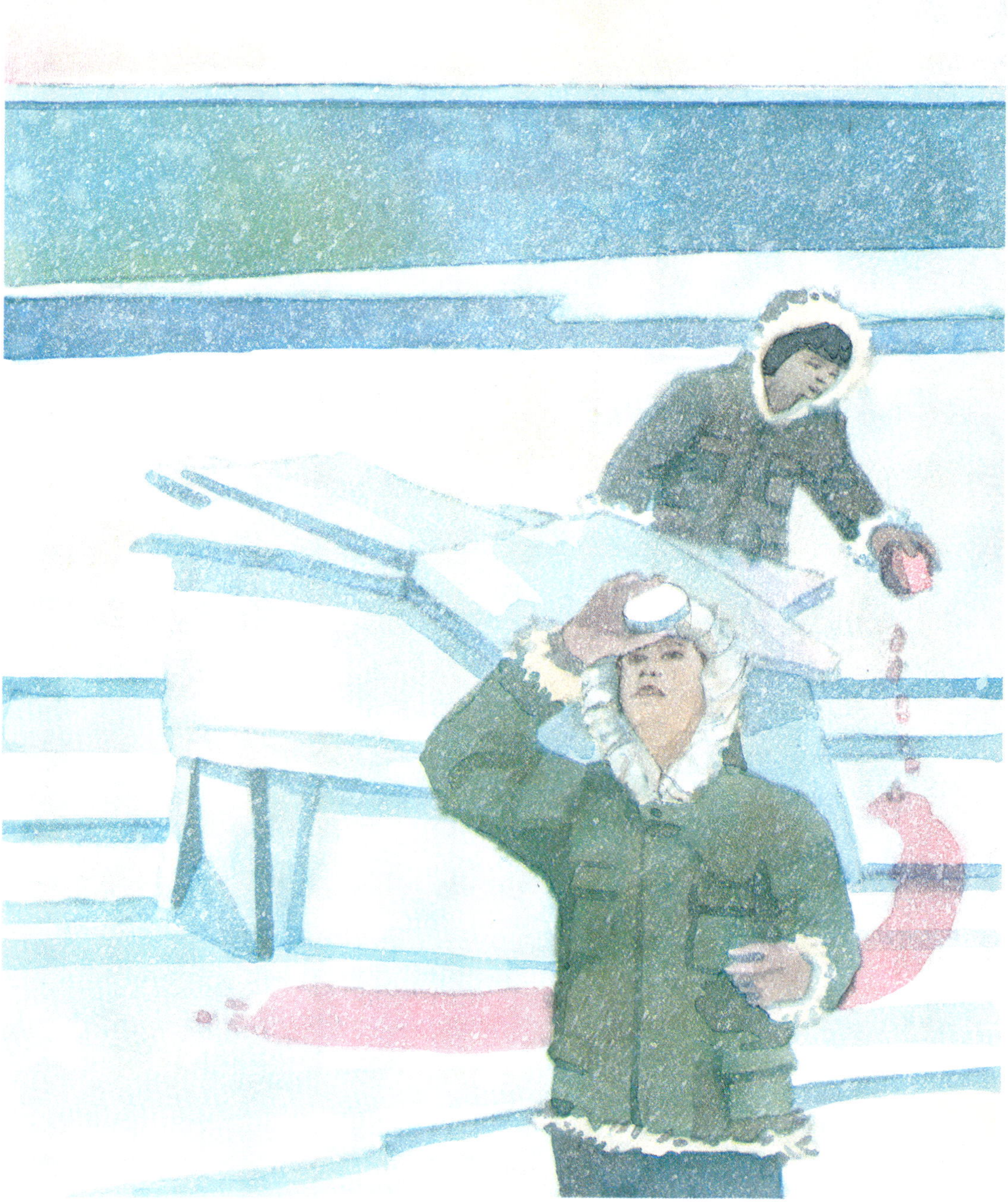

the uneasy sense that their whole house was slowly turning. Kayak pushed out the piece of ice that he had used to block the entrance.

"Look up there!" he yelled at Matthew.

Matthew, still crouching stiffly, looked up and in the sky saw a long thin white contrail.

"It's the big plane," said Kayak, "going into Frobisher Bay or maybe over to Greenland. No use waving your arms," he said in a discouraged voice. "It can never see you. It must be two miles high."

Matthew whirled around, dived back through the entrance, reached into his pack and leaped outside holding the snowmobile's mirror.

"Give me the knife, the knife!" he shouted.

With its point he scratched a small cross in the mercury behind the glass. Then, standing in the rays of the morning sun, he placed it against his eye and sighted the plane. Through the tiny opening he could see it moving through the cold blue sky like a slow silver bullet. He tipped the glass back and forth, back and forth, back and forth. He continued to watch the airplane through the hole until it was out of sight.

"What's that? Some kind of magic you are doing?" Kayak asked him.

"No," answered Matthew. "It was nothing, I guess. My dad told me that sometimes a pilot can see a mirror flashing from a very long way off. You know, it's that old Indian trick."

"Well, it didn't make them turn around," said Kayak. "They're all just sitting up there warm and dry and comfortable, drinking coffee in the sky."

"I guess you're right," said Matthew, and he dropped the mirror in the snow.

"The ice, it's breaking in half," screamed Kayak. "Quick!"

He grabbed Matthew by the arm and forced him to jump across the gap. As they watched, half of their shelter broke apart and slipped into the freezing water.

"The sleeping bags and pack are gone," cried Matthew, and he lunged toward the edge to grab the heart lamp and the seal remains. He felt the ice pan tipping, as he slithered forward.

A steady wind blew out of the north and the cold spring sun glared off the snow-covered ice. They pumped their feet and swung their arms about their bodies to keep their blood circulating. Matthew watched the tide go slack, then turn, as the ice moved north again, but the north wind was against them and all too soon they felt the pull of the outgoing tide carrying them toward destruction in the open sea.

The cold that comes with night swept in and with it ghostly vapors rising like steam between the cracks of broken ice. The full moon rose, staring at them like a dead man's face, and once more they heard the dreadful ringing as the tide rose and drove them south with awesome force. Matthew closed his eyes and saw the image of his father and thought what he would give to see him once again.

"I wish we had known each other for a longer time," Kayak said, "but I . . . I'm going to say good-bye to you now, Mattoosie."

"Oh, don't say that." Matthew spoke in a choked voice.

"Why not?" said Kayak. "What is going to be — will be."

He started to pull the last remains of the seal into the crude little house and then suddenly changed his mind and began to circle around the house, pressing down hard, leaving a dark red trail of seal blood in the snow.

"Now you're trying magic," Matthew cried. "What good will that do?"

Kayak didn't answer him. The only sound was the moaning of the ice in the gathering gloom. Together they crawled inside and huddled side by side, and ate some seal meat.

"Aren't you going to light the lamp?" said Matthew.

"Maybe later. What's the use? Oh, I'll try to light it, if you want me to."

They slept, crouching like animals in the lamp's faint glow, until the first light of morning filtered faintly through their ice shelter.

"What's that?" gasped Kayak. He cocked his head and listened.

"I don't hear anything," said Matthew. "Wait! Wait! Yes, I do. I do!"

They kicked away the thin ice door and scrambled out the narrow entrance.

"It's Matilda!" Kayak yelled. "It's the *Waltzing Matilda*. She's all patched up."

They could see Charlie in the gleaming blister, waving at them wildly. One door of the helicopter slid open and Charlie flipped out a short rope ladder with metal rungs. Kayak staggered across the ice pan and grabbed it.

"I'm too weak to climb," he screamed at Matthew.

"I'll help you," Matthew shouted, and with his last remaining strength he heaved Kayak onto the dangerously swaying ladder.

"Get in!" Charlie shouted over the roar of the engine.

Kayak grabbed Matthew by the hood of his parka and helped pull him up the ladder. Matthew slumped down behind them. There was very little room inside.

"You two all right? Feet not frozen? No bones broken?" Charlie shouted.

They shook their heads.

He reached across Matthew and slid the door closed, then gunned the engine. *Waltzing Matilda* whirled up above their little ice shelter. Kayak looked down for the last time at what had almost been their grave.

Charlie pointed down and said, "Whoever made that red circle around that ice shack of yours certainly saved your lives. I would never have found you without that red bull's-eye. Where did you get the paint?"

83

"It's not paint," said Matthew. "He thought of the idea." Matthew nodded toward Kayak. "He saved us."

"It worked like magic," Charlie shouted. "And where did you get the mirror? The one you flashed at the Nordair flight that was coming into Frobisher. If they hadn't seen that mirror shining, we'd never have found you. The aircraft and the rescue teams were looking for you inland. That mirror saved your lives!"

"He thought of that," said Kayak. "Mattoosie saved us with his Aree-zona Indian trick."

Kayak reached out and put his hand on his friend's shoulder. "Look, Mattoosie, there's Apex, there's my house."

The bright red helicopter whirled in toward the airport.

"There's our school," said Matthew.

Kayak turned and looked at him. "I never thought we'd have a chance to go to school again."

The helicopter landed in a whirling haze of snow crystals. Charlie turned off the engine and the big black blades stopped and hung silent in the harsh Arctic light of morning. Matthew could see a stream of people running out of the hangar toward them.

Charlie slid open the door and Kayak stepped out. He collapsed onto his knees from exhaustion but, taking hold of one of Matilda's big rubber helicopter floats, he lifted himself up and helped Matthew.

"Be careful," he said. "You probably feel as weak as I do."

A young policeman and a nurse and Kayak's family helped the two boys across the airstrip. When Kayak's cousin smiled at them and held open the door, Matthew felt like he was coming home. Inside the airport he was sure he would see his father. But when he looked around, the whole big room was hot and empty. He felt his knees buckle under him, and he slumped down onto the floor.

When Matthew awoke, he turned his head and stared out the window. It was night. Beyond the lights of the airstrip he could see a long way down Frobisher Bay. Where he and Kayak had been, there was now only a sea of blackness. The full moon glowed like a mysterious spaceship sailing through the clouds spinning a path of silver across the mountains and the open water.

He looked the other way and saw Kayak, who was sitting up in the neat white hospital bed, eating a bowl of chicken soup. He stared at Matthew. His face looked gaunt and thin. The nurse came in.

"Where's my father?" he asked, and his voice was trembling so that he could hardly speak.

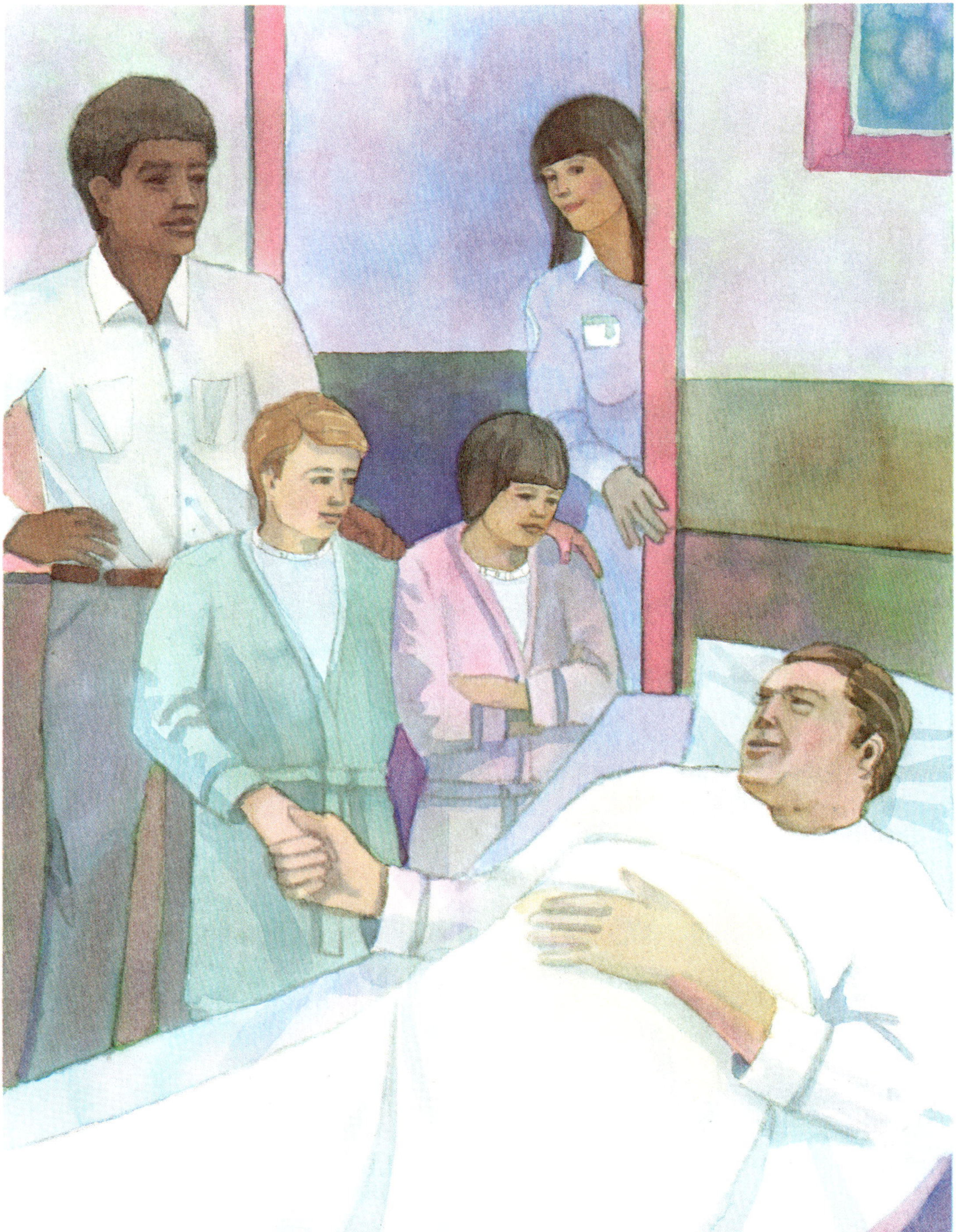

"Do you feel strong enough to stand?" the nurse asked quietly.

"Yes, I think . . . I can," said Matthew.

"Then put on your slippers and your robe," she said.

"Can I come with him?" asked Kayak.

The nurse hesitated.

"I can help him walk," said Kayak. "We often help each other. He's in my family. He's sort of . . . well, he really is my brother."

Kayak's father, Toogak, was sitting just outside their door. He got up when he saw them.

At the end of the hall the nurse opened a door cautiously, then said, "You can go in now. You can't stay long."

Matthew had to hold onto Kayak, when he first saw his father lying in the bed. He looked old and tired, as though his big strong body had given out on him. His eyes were sunken, and there were black frost patches on his cheeks and forehead.

"Oh, you're safe," his father said to Matthew and grabbed his hand along with Kayak's. "You two boys never should have come out looking for us, and yet . . ." His eyes had tears in them. "I'm so very proud you did."

"Your dad is a strong man," said the nurse. "He must have walked almost a hundred freezing miles to find his way back here. He saved Charlie's life as well as his own. His feet were not too badly frozen and those black frost marks on his face will go away."

"What matters most," said Matthew's father, "is that all of us are back here safe together." He paused, then shook his head. "I wanted to find copper so much I almost caused all of us to lose our lives.

"Like lots of my ideas, it didn't work. But I've still got a little bit of luck. Look, Matt," his father said, holding out a letter. "The government of the Northwest Territories has asked me to be the science teacher here. That means that as soon as the snow is gone, I can start my outdoor classes again, teaching geology in a tent right here on Baffin Island."

Matthew was quiet for a minute while he took in what his father was saying. That meant he could stay too — and be near Kayak. And he would study geology.

"That's wonderful Dad!" he finally said.

"You can teach me too!" said Kayak. "And I'll teach Mattoosie to speak Eskimo while I learn to hunt for *saviksak* — that means iron, material for making knives. You'll see I'm good at hunting." Kayak gave Matthew a knowing look and Matthew nodded slightly and grinned.

"It all sounds great to me." Charlie laughed. "The government says they will pay for thirty hours flying time while we take your students out and teach them mineral hunting from the air. We'll all be flying again together."

Discuss the Selection

1. What dangers did Matthew and Kayak encounter?
2. How were Matthew and Kayak able to survive?
3. How was the polar bear both a threat and a help?
4. Why do you think Kayak circled the igloo with the seal remains and left a trail of blood?
5. At what point in the story do you think Matthew and Kayak were in the *most* trouble? Find that part in the story.

Apply the Skills

You compare two or more things, people, or situations by noticing their similarities. You contrast two or more things, people, or situations by pointing out their differences. Compare and contrast Matthew's reaction to a dangerous situation with that of Kayak.

Think and Write

Prewrite

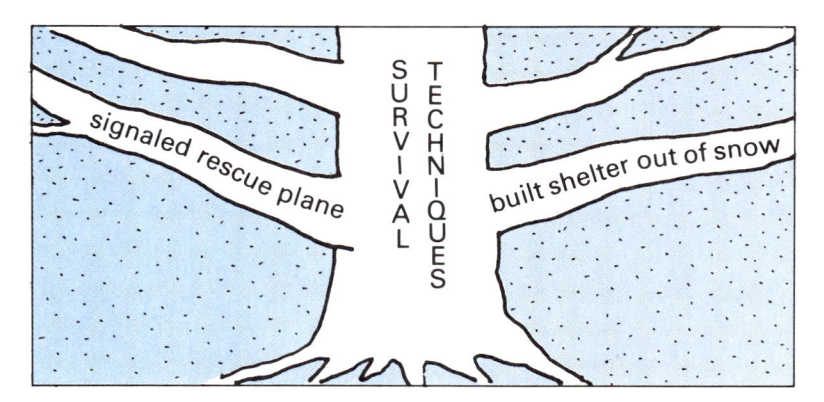

[tree diagram with trunk labeled SURVIVAL TECHNIQUES and branches labeled "signaled rescue plane" and "built shelter out of snow"]

Classifying information is the first step in organizing material for most writing tasks. Look at the tree diagram above. Notice the information on the trunk and the branches.

Copy the diagram on a sheet of paper. Now extend it by identifying two more survival techniques used by the boys. Your tree diagram should now have four branches connected to the trunk, or main topic.

Compose

Referring to "Frozen Fire" and to the diagram, write two paragraphs, focusing each on a different technique that helped to save Matthew and Kayak. One of your topic sentences might be *By using a snowmobile mirror, Matthew was able to signal a rescue plane.*

Follow each topic sentence with two detail sentences to make your paragraphs as informative and lively as they can be.

Revise

Read the paragraphs that you wrote. Check to be sure that your detail sentences do a good job of explaining how Matthew and Kayak were able to survive against all odds. Delete anything that cannot be classified as a survival technique in "Frozen Fire."

An American Indian girl's adventure in the wilderness helps her learn about her ancestors. Read to find out what the girl, Billie Wind, discovers about her ancestors.

Billie Wind has a negative attitude toward her ancestors' beliefs. Compare her negative attitude with her attitude at the end of the story.

The Talking Earth

by Jean Craighead George

Billie Wind, a thirteen-year-old Seminole Indian girl, has doubts about the legends of her ancestors. She has trouble believing that animal gods can talk. She has difficulty believing that there is a great serpent who lives in the Everglades and that there are little people who live underground. Charlie Wind, Billie Wind's uncle and the tribal medicine man, brings her a message that she must be punished for being a doubter. As a punishment, Billie Wind suggests that she go into the *pa-hay-okee,* the Everglades, to test the legends. The first day of her journey Billie Wind is almost killed by a raging fire that spreads through the swampy grassland, turning the area into an inferno. Billie Wind escapes by diving into a sinkhole — a sunken hole in the ground that connects with an underground passage. In a cave at the bottom of the sinkhole she begins to learn about and to believe in the people she loves.

Billie Wind awoke around noon but she did not get up. Instead she lay quietly on her back, staring at the limestone wall. Where was she? Why was she looking at a wall? With a shiver she remembered. She was entombed by the fire serpent. She felt her legs. "I'm alive." Then she added, "I think." She moved her fingers and toes. "Yes, I am." Turning cautiously to her side, she peered out of the cave. The roaring fire of last night could not be heard. She sat up. The sun fell in pale patches on the log and the pool. The air was smoky but sunlit.

Sliding from her bed, she walked out on the log and looked up. A few strands of smoke curled along the rim of the pit; an occasional flare marked the last gasp of a flame. The trees were black stalks, and the once-lacy green canopy was gone. Although hot coals glowed along the rim of the pit, the worst of the fire seemed to be over. She was cheered. As her shoulders relaxed she became aware of a gnawing hunger and took out her supply of corn bread. She ate all but a small bite, then squatted on her heels and studied the sinkhole and sky. Where the walls had been festooned with ferns and mosses yesterday, they were now bare. Without the plants as a cover, she could see that there were not just two ledges in the pit, but many. She studied them.

"Steps," she said. "I think they are steps. And steps are cut by persons." She crossed the log and measured them with her hand. "Yes, they are. Some person came and went on them." She pondered as to who it might have been. "Perhaps she was hiding from a fire . . . like me. No, fires did not burn the moist islands in those days. Perhaps she hid from the conquistadores. Or maybe she was the leader of the little underground people, and this was the stairway to her council house." She smiled at her joke. "I wish it was so — then I could go home and tell Charlie Wind there *are* little underground people who build strange cities and save curious little Seminole Indians."

She pushed the little people out of her head and considered the stairs again. They were pocked and black with fire burn and oxidation; old but maybe not ancient. The Calusa, Seminole ancestors, built ramps. White men and Seminoles built steps. And yet, the Everglades and the south Florida west coast were dotted with the ruins of ingenious constructions; canals that led to fish-holding ponds, elevated village sites.

She jumped down the steps to pack up her possessions and the ancient bowl that she discovered in the cave. She was eager to go home.

She pulled on her sneakers and leggings, checked her pocket

to make sure her penknife was there, shouldered her pouch, and ran across the log and up the steps. Near the top she was stopped by a blast of heat. She covered her face with her arm. The stones and soil were oven hot. She could not touch anything. Standing on her tiptoes, she peered over the rim of the pit. Flames leaped along fallen trees and red fires smoldered in the loam.

"I'm trapped," she said. "The earth is too hot to walk on." Biting her lips to keep them from trembling, she turned and walked slowly back to the cave.

"I can't wait very long," she said. "I've got one piece of venison left." She sat down on the bed. "I'm going to die here. It will take a long, long time for the earth to cool. I shall die in this pit." She dropped her head on her knees.

Presently a thought replaced her fear. She remembered that a tortoise had fallen into the water and that many, many snakes had slithered into the pit. All were good food. She unpacked her deerskin pouch, placed the pot on the ground and pondered.

In the light of the afternoon she saw that the bumps on the floor of the cave that she had thought to be rocks last night were piles of oysters, conches, and cochinas. The sea must have been a short distance away when the ancient person lived here. Charlie Wind told old legends about the sea once covering all the *pa-hay-okee*. Maybe he was right.

Taking out her machete, she dug into a shell pile and uncovered a conch, its top cut off and the spiral removed.

"A cup," she exclaimed. She put the cup aside and dug more carefully into the broken shells and dust. A few inches down she uncovered an oyster shell that had been chipped into a stirring spoon and near it, the heavy central column of an enormous fighting conch.

"A hammer." She brought it down sharply on the ground, and was surprised by how well it was balanced. She dug on, uncovering a wedge-shaped conch with a sharp edge. Two holes had been drilled in this instrument, which she recognized to be an adze.

After uncovering a few more cups and spoons, broken and unbroken, she noticed that the far wall was blackened.

"A cooking hearth," she said, wondering where the smoke vented. She glanced up and saw that the roof of the cave was riddled with holes typical of the Everglades limestone. The smoke, of course, went up through the porous rock.

A shrill whistle sounded. Billie Wind leaped to her feet and ran joyfully to the entrance of the cave.

"Hello, Charlie Wind!" She slowed as she neared the top. It couldn't be Charlie Wind. The earth was a red-hot inferno. Not even a medicine man could cross it. She peered at the smoldering forest floor.

No one was there.

Her hopes shattered, she sat down on a step and covered her face with her hands. She felt alone and frightened, even more so than that moment when she saw the fire coming toward her.

The whistle sounded again.

She lifted her hand with renewed interest. "It's coming from inside the wall of the pit."

Someone grunted and coughed in a sooty hole at her feet. She leaned over and peered into a shadowy cavern.

"Who's there?" The humanlike cough sounded again. Two bright eyes gleamed above a flat nose and upturned mouth. "I see a little person," she said, then added aloud: "Charlie Wind, forgive me." She thought again. This time more clearly. "Nonsense, there are no such things as underground men."

The mouth in the hole moved as if to speak and she saw that the lips were rimmed with silvery whiskers.

"A petang, a petang," she cried joyfully. "Little otter, what are you doing here?" Holding out her hand she waited for him to smell her odor of friendship and come to her.

"Come, little friend," she said. "Come here to me. I shall take care of you whom the Indians of the north call petang. We are the only living things in this charred world."

Petang's nostrils flared. He backed up.

"Did you escape the fire by crawling into a pit like me? If

so, we are fire spirits. We must console each other." Petang's eyes rolled from right to left and then up into Billie Wind's face. He seemed to sense something reassuring about her, for he poked his head out of the hole and whimpered. Then he grabbed the meat in her hands with his small teeth so vigorously that Billie Wind was forced to hold it with both hands.

Hesitatingly, moving forward, back, forward, the little otter finally came all the way out of the hole, and placing one large webbed foot on her hand, grunted wistfully. Then he sat up, propping himself erect like a little man with the support of his stout, tapering tail. Strong muscles rippled under his silver-brown fur. Billie Wind judged him to be about two months old, for she had once played with a young otter at the zoo on the Big Cypress Reservation.

Talking softly to this beautiful friend, she slipped one hand under him and drew him to her with the other. She held him against her body, stroking his head and body as do mother otters to encourage their little ones to eat. He sucked the meat. At the same time she peered into other holes searching for a mother or sister or brother. She saw nothing else alive, not even a snake, not even a mosquito. Then a frog piped from the bottom of the sinkhole.

"That makes three of us," she said. "You and me, Petang, and a frog."

Petang devoured most of the venison by simply sucking it down. When he was satisfied, he snuggled against her and instantly fell asleep. She was happy to see him relax, for it meant that he trusted her. Gingerly tiptoeing, so as not to awaken him, she carried the little otter to the cave and sat down. She wondered what to do next. She must hunt food, and yet she did not want to put him down for fear he would run away.

As she sat holding the beautiful wild thing, she scanned the water in the bottom of the pit until at last her eyes came to rest on the frog. His head was protruding above the surface of the water near the log.

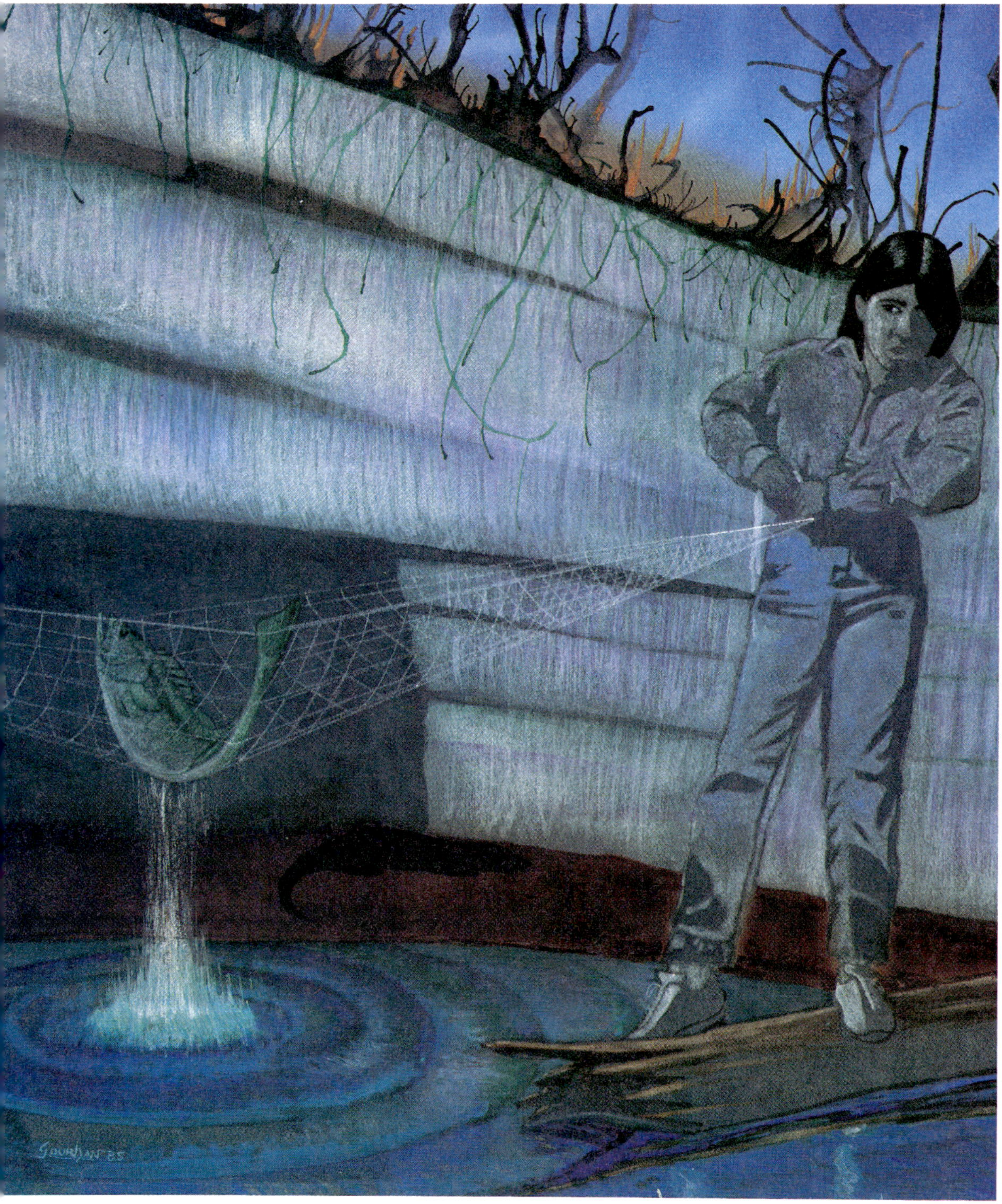

"How," she said to Petang, "how do I catch him? Even so small a bite will keep you and me alive for another day. And tomorrow it might rain and we can leave." She looked at the remains of the venison. "Half a meal for each of us. I'd better catch the frog."

A peal of thunder rumbled, and she looked up out of the pit. The sky was filled with rolling clouds; rain was indeed coming. She wouldn't have to catch the frog. The rumbling deluge would cool the soil, she hoped, and they could leave the pit today. She leaned back to wait for the thunderstorm to break, and then thought better of it. She had been fooled before. These were, after all, the years of drought, and drought perpetuated drought. She eased Petang to the floor beside her deerskin pouch and carefully pulled out the hammock. He did not awake, and she smiled, cut off three feet of the hammock with her penknife and knotted the ragged ends so they would not unravel. She spread the net on the floor. Along one side she strung the heaviest of the shells and three long cords cut from the hammock ties. At the end of each cord she tied more shells. When she was done she had a fishnet, which she carried out on the log.

"Where are you, frog?" she asked. The wind trumpeted as it blew over the rim of the pit. Sparks exploded somewhere above her; she did not heed them. Instead she concentrated on dropping the weighted end of the net across the deepest part of the pool. So that she could pull it up, she draped the cords over the log. The shells held them in place. Next she tied one corner of the unweighted side to a fig root on the wall, the other to a sapling on the other side of the pit. The net was set. Squatting, she poised herself to grab the cords and yank. The frog would have to come to the surface to breathe pretty soon, for he had been under a long time, and he was an air breather. With a swish, the sapling thrashed. Billie Wind grabbed the cords and pulled. Flopping in the net was a big large-mouthed bass.

"Petang," she shouted excitedly. "We will live. A fish, a fish." With a quick jab she thrust her fingers into the gills to make sure the bass did not escape, set the net again, and ran back to the cave.

"We can live a long time down here, Petang," she said. We have a bed, a fireplace, a cooking bowl — and food."

"Petang," she said to the still-sleeping otter. "How do you suppose a fish got down in this pit? He can not crawl on land or fly. Did a bird drop him? Did an egg wash in on a flood? Did the little underground men bring him here?"

She smiled. "Little underground men are very useful. They explain all nature's mysteries." Then a thought occurred to her and she glanced around the cave.

"Do you suppose this was a fish pond for the ancients? Perhaps they brought them here eons ago. Perhaps a fish keeper lived in this cave. The Calusa cultivated fish, you know."

Petang smelled the fish in his sleep and came awake. He bounced to Billie Wind's side.

"Here," she said, cutting off a large chunk of the tail. "You must learn to eat, not suckle." The otter tossed the food in the air, caught it, and dug in with his teeth. Billie Wind put the remainder of the catch in the bowl with water from the pool.

"Now, how do I make a fire?" She glanced up at the top of the pit. "All that fire and no fire," she said, "but perhaps . . ."

Climbing to the last step of the sinkhole, she searched the embers until she found a flaming stick within reach. Licking her fingers, she picked it up and backed down to the cave. To it she added chips from the log, whacked off with her machete. The chips caught fire.

When the coals were red she placed the ancient bowl carefully among them, hoping the old clay could still withstand fire. Then she squatted on her heels. The water bubbled, but did not boil. It must boil. She dropped a hot stone into the pot and the water rolled, then boiled; the fish simmered, and the smoke climbed through the porous holes in the limestone ceiling of the cave.

"Petang," she announced when the fish was tender. "Dinner is served." She need not have been concerned about this problem. The little otter had chewed and swallowed the uncooked tail of the bass and was sitting on his haunches, short front legs crossed on his chest, begging for more, cooked or uncooked.

Billie Wind held out a warm bite and watched him eat it with gusto and pleasure. The sapling thrashed.

She put down her bowl and ran. Petang was close at her heels. What a mother otter does, a little otter does. Her next movements baffled him, however. She knelt down, reached out and pulled up a net. Then she lifted a fish above her head and cheered. Petang turned and scratched a flea.

"Fish," Billie Wind said addressing the bass. "Charlie Wind says that the animals talk. Tell me how you got here?"

The fish twisted in her hand. Its cold open mouth gave no answer.

Several days passed and the hot fires still burned. Each day Billie Wind would go to the surface hoping to be free, see that she was not, and climb down to play with Petang. When he slept she dug into the floor, uncovering more and more treasures.

One morning she dug up the beak of a sawfish. It resembled a double-edged saw almost precisely, and she wondered if it was strong enough to cut wood.

She walked out on the log and drew the strange beak across one of the limb stubs. The ancient bone crumbled.

"No more of that," she said, putting it back where she had found it. "I am going to come back here someday. I will bring an archaeologist and Charlie Wind, and they will look at these things and tell me who the ancient person was and how the fish got into this hole on this island.

"Maybe the cave will give up a secret that will solve the mystery of where the Calusa came from."

That night she lay awake for a long time thinking of her ancestors and the daily lives they lived. They had fire and tools and fish and they made beautiful pots. The ghosts of the distant past seemed to snuggle closely around her, and she felt safe.

For two days no fish swam into the net.

"This is bad news, Petang," she said, the third morning.

"I think we've caught all the fish there are in this hole, and the earth is still too hot for us to leave."

Seeing Billie Wind, Petang ran up her back to her shoulders. There he looked down at the water. Although he had seen water before, this time he really saw it. He leaned over and sniffed, then reached out and tapped it with his paw. It rippled. He struck it. It splashed. He leaned closer, put his head in, sneezed and pulled back. With his eyes he asked Billie Wind what it was all about. She was about to demonstrate the essence of water by splashing him, when some inherited gene told him what to do. He dove in headfirst and swam without instruction. It was as if he had been swimming since he was born. Circling and snorting water, he barked, rolled on his back and took a back dive to the bottom. Up he came, chortling and whistling. Bubbles of water clung to his whiskers.

"Petang, you're marvelous." Billie Wind exclaimed. "You are a water spirit." She reached out her hand to him; he climbed to her shoulder, turned and dove again. Shooting forward, he rounded the pool, leaped up into the air like a geyser and came to her. He tugged on her fingers.

"I get it. I get it," she said. "You want me to swim too, and I guess I'll have to." She held her nose and jumped into the pool with a splash that sent water sparkling up the walls of the pit. Then she rolled onto her back and kicked. Petang swam around her like a spinning, turning porpoise.

On the other side of the pool Billie Wind let her feet down. She could not touch the bottom. The water was very deep. Petang sensed this, barked as if telling her to follow the leader, and dove deep. Billie Wind treaded water and peered down through the clear depths to see what he was up to. Surrounded with bubbles, he moved like a silver missile into an underwater cavern. She held her nose and went down.

The sun dimly illuminated the bottom, and she could see the bones of alligators and armadillos that had fallen into the pit and drowned. She recognized the skull of a black bear and a raccoon. Surfacing for a breath, she went down again. She swam toward the cavern where Petang had gone, then turned back. It was too dark, its course too frightening; for it wound off under the *pa-hay-okee,* a river beneath the river of grass. Petang shot out of the darkness. In his mouth was a fish.

The two popped to the surface simultaneously and swam side by side to the log. Billie Wind pulled herself into the warm air. Petang leaped after, holding tightly to his fish.

"Petang, you have told me how the fish got into the pit. When the glades dry up, the fish are not dead as we've always assumed; they are down in the underground pools and rivers waiting for the rains to return and fill the *pa-hay-okee* so they can come back to the saw grass.

"That seems so sensible, I don't know why no one has thought of it before. Little underground men, ha." She reached for Petang's fish but he ran down the log and up the steps.

"Okay, okay," she called. "You can have it. I don't want your old fish. I have something important to do."

She slipped into the water and swam back to the underwater cavern for one more look. Could it be, she wondered, that the ancients carved the tunnel from the sea to the pit to raise fish for the village? Was that why the steps were there? So the ancients could come down to the water and catch fish? She touched the walls and wished she knew more.

Clambering back onto the log, she looked for Petang. He was on the steps, swinging the fish from side to side.

"Come here," she said, stamping her foot. Petang dove into the pool. He surfaced, tossed the fish into the air and caught it before it escaped. Then he swam to the far side of the pit, crawled up on the ledge and stared across the water at her.

"If I didn't know better," she said, "I would say there is a naughty person inside that fur coat of yours." He sidled a few feet toward her, leaped into the water and came up on the log. She reached for him. Eyes shining, he ran into the cave, circled it twice, then dropped the fish and sat up on his haunches. He dangled his paws, his eyes black and lively.

"You are quite a playmate," she said, picking him up and hugging him. "It's very nice down here with you as a friend."

Billie Wind was cleaning the fish for dinner when Petang dove into the water, came out and shook all over her.

"Stop it!" she said. He shook again. She rocked back on her heels and stared at him. "Are you grinning, Petang? Do I see a smile on your face?"

"No," she answered. "Of course, I don't. Otters don't tease people." She touched his head. "I've been down here too long."

Around noon the next day a wind blew across the island, plucking sad tunes on the burned tree limbs. Billie Wind climbed to the top of the pit to see if a storm was coming. The sky was clear. She despaired. She would never get out of the pit. Then she noticed that the loam had burned down to the bedrock. The soil was gone. It would take hundreds, maybe thousands of years for the plants to grow, die, and build back the rich loam.

Nevertheless, when she crawled into her bed that night and snuggled down with Petang, she was pleased that the fire had reached the bedrock. It could not burn anymore. She would soon be able to go home.

Billie Wind and Petang lived on fish the otter caught in the underground river, and she watched the sky and waited. Every morning she climbed the steps to look across the forest floor, and with each trip she was cheered to see that one more fire had burned out. The ground became cooler and cooler. One morning as she came down the steps, she stopped and stared into the water. In the shallows near the cave entrance a bright green object shone.

"A plant," she said. "Petang, Petang, the sun is pulling life out of death."

Rolling up her pants, she waded onto the mud shelf and cut off the new shoot of a pickerel weed. The young leaves were pleasant to taste and Billie Wind ate them where she was, for she had not had green vegetables for many days.

"Where did a plant come from in this burned world?" she asked herself. Reaching into the mud, she felt hard, round balls, and brought them up.

"Seeds," she said. "Dropped by the birds who ate them?" She wondered how long they had lain there waiting for the sun: months, years, decades, perhaps. One question solved only presented another. This she did know: The seeds would never have sprouted had not the fire burned off the trees and let the sun into the pit.

"Nature plans ahead for her disasters," she said, reaching for another sproutling.

Before dusk that night, Petang tumbled and boxed with Billie Wind until both were exhausted. They sat on the log to rest and cool off. Billie Wind looked up. A flock of wood storks was winging southward.

"The fire must be out," she said to Petang. "The wood storks are crossing over the island again." Petang was asleep, his paws folded on his chest.

"Is that what you are saying?" she asked the birds. Hardly had she spoken when a white heron alighted on the black limb of the dead oak above. She stared at the bird for a long time, not daring to admit that it meant good luck; and yet she did think that and hoped that it was so.

As the sun came up the next morning, Billie Wind heard thunder, opened her eyes and once more listened hopefully. She longed to be home with her mother, Whispering Wind. She sat up and sniffed. The air smelled damp as it does before a rainstorm; but she had been disappointed too often to trust her nose. She lay back on her bed, noticing Petang's nose twitching in his sleep.

"Do you smell rain, too?" she asked. "Your nose is twitching, and it is a much smarter nose than mine."

A lightning flash illuminated the cave. Billie Wind slipped from her bed and walked to the entrance. Bolt after bolt shot across the ruined forest. Petang joined her, whimpering at her feet. She picked up and held him close.

"Why are you afraid? What do you know that I don't know? Tell me, please." An earsplitting thunder crack sent Petang leaping to the floor. He dove into her trouser leg. Billie Wind screamed and, reaching up, grabbed a ledge in the ceiling and dangled from it as she wildly kicked her foot, trying to dislodge the clawing, scrambling Petang. He fell to the floor. The ledge snapped, and Billie fell, too. She covered her head as pebbles, dust, and sand rained down upon her, but she did not move, for she was listening. Above the rifle shots of thunder and the crash of stones a hiss could be heard.

"Rain," she said. "Petang, the rain is falling. Listen." The hiss turned to a hum, then a rumble, and the clouds above released their water in torrents.

After an hour of heavy rain with no letup in sight, she began to fear that the pool would rise and fill the cave.

"No," she said, recalling the ant lions. "They live in dry places." Nevertheless she and Petang huddled in the bedroom as high off the floor as they could get, listening until the rain slowed to a light patter.

She could leave. How glad her family and Charlie Wind would be when she returned from the *pa-hay-okee*. Her eyes concentrated on the ledge in the ceiling that had broken under her weight. The corner of a square object stuck over the edge. She stepped out of bed, reached up, and took down a dry leather pouch folded three times. It cracked when she opened it. A snake's fang fell out.

"A medicine bundle," she said in awe. "Just like the one Charlie Wind explained about, Petang. Where are we? What is this place?" Her spine tingled; then a buffalo horn fell from the pouch.

"The buffalo are no longer here." She looked around slowly. "This is an old and important place." With care she replaced the fang and horn and put the medicine bundle back.

"I must not disturb anything more. I will come back with people who will know what this place is."

The rain stopped. Hoping she would not be disappointed again, but afraid she might be, Billie Wind nevertheless climbed to the surface to test the rocks. They were cool. The once-red coals on the forest floor were black. Above the ravished island the sun was shining brightly.

"Petang," she called to the little otter, who was climbing up on the log from a fishless fishing expedition. "We can go home. We can go home."

Discuss the Selection

1. What did Billie Wind discover about her ancestors?
2. How did Petang, the otter, help Billie Wind to confirm her beliefs about her ancestors?
3. How do you think the others of her tribe will react when Billie Wind tells them of the many things she discovered in the cave?
4. If Billie Wind had been able to leave the cave, she might not have made these discoveries. Why did she have to stay in the cave for so long after the fire?
5. What did you read that made you think that Billie had begun to better appreciate her ancestors? Identify the parts of the story where she made discoveries about her ancestors and their legends.

Apply the Skills

When we compare two or more things, we point out their similarities. When we contrast, we point out their differences. What was Billie Wind's attitude toward her ancestors' beliefs at the beginning of the story? Compare and contrast that attitude with her attitude at the end of the story. Give evidence from the story to support your answer.

Think and Write

Prewrite

> I. Billie's discoveries about her ancestors
>   A. Made tools and pots
>   B. Raised and caught fish
>
> II. Billie's inability to leave cave
>   A. Burning trees
>   B. Smoldering loam
>
> III. Billie's ancestors' beliefs
>   A.
>   B.

A good way to prepare for writing a report, or anything else, is to make an outline. Study the partial outline above. It is based on "The Talking Earth."

On a separate piece of paper, extend the outline by completing Part III. Refer to the story as needed.

Compose

Follow the outline to write three paragraphs that summarize "The Talking Earth." Use the headings next to the roman numerals to develop your topic sentences. Use the subheadings to develop your detail sentences. Refer to the story as often as necessary for help with writing an accurate, well-organized summary.

Revise

Read the paragraphs that you wrote. Check to see if you included enough information: Could someone understand what "The Talking Earth" is about simply by reading your summary of it? Revise your paragraphs for greater clarity and interest level. Words and sentences can be moved, combined, taken out, or added.

Vocabulary Study

Descriptive Language

The most famous author of fables is Aesop. In the Aesop fable that follows, two elements of weather compete against each other. Read "The Wind and The Sun."

The Wind and The Sun

Once upon a time when everything could talk, the Wind and the Sun had an argument as to which was the stronger. They decided to put the matter to a test; they would see which one could make a certain man, who was *walking* down the road, throw off his cape. The Wind tried first. He blew and blew and he blew. The traveler *trudged* along wrapping his cape tightly about him. The Wind finally gave up and told the Sun to try. As the Sun grew warmer, the traveler became more comfortable and *sauntered* onward. But the Sun shone brightly and the man became weary. Seating himself on a stone, he quickly removed his cape. You see, gentleness had accomplished what force could not.

Notice the words *walking*, *trudged*, and *sauntered*, printed in italic type. What do these words have in common? The words *trudged* and *sauntered* are synonyms for the word *walking*. The use of synonyms in writing can make a story more interesting. The synonyms, *trudged* and *sauntered*, help the reader visualize the action. What image is portrayed by the word *trudged*? By the word *sauntered*?

Good writers use a variety of words. Writers want to make their writing exciting and interesting. Using descriptive words will help the reader visualize the object or action.

Read the following sentence:

> The woman walked into the auditorium and spoke to the orchestra conductor.

Do you know anything about the way the woman was walking? Do you know how she was speaking? You could visualize her actions in many ways. The next sentence gives a more specific description of the woman's actions.

> The woman tiptoed into the auditorium and whispered to the orchestra conductor.

How did the new words change the idea of the sentence? The words *tiptoed* and *whispered* alter the meaning of the sentence. They show that the woman may not have wanted to disturb anyone.

Read the sentence that follows to see how the meaning is changed when words are substituted for *tiptoed* and *whispered*.

> The woman stormed into the auditorium and yelled to the orchestra conductor.

The words *stormed* and *yelled* show that the woman might not have been pleased with the orchestra conductor.

Read the paragraph that follows. Think of descriptive words that can be used as substitutes for the words printed in italic type. Rewrite the paragraph using the new words.

> The young man climbed out of the taxi and *walked* across the busy intersection toward the phone booth on the corner. He entered the phone booth and *shut* the door. He then proceeded to *look* in his briefcase for some loose change. From his coat pocket, he *took* out his note pad. The phone number was *written* on the first page. He picked up the receiver and dialed the number. *Looking* at the people passing by, he listened as the phone continued to ring. Why was no one answering? Was there something wrong? He began to wonder whether his friends had forgotten that he purposely rearranged his schedule so he could visit them.

In his writings, James Herriot shares his adventures as a veterinarian. Read to find out what satisfactions Herriot gets from his job.

James Herriot's case histories contain many colorful words. As you read, look for words or phrases that help to give vivid descriptions.

Going to the Dogs . . . and Cats

by James Herriot

It looked as though I was going to make it back to the road all right. And I was thankful for it because seven o'clock in the morning, with the wintry dawn only just beginning to lighten the eastern rim of the moor, was no time to be digging my car out of the snow.

This narrow, unfenced road skirted a high tableland and gave on to a few lonely farms at the end of even narrower tracks. It hadn't actually been snowing on my way out to this early call, but the wind had been rising steadily and whipping the top surface from the white blanket which had covered the ground for weeks. My headlights had picked out the creeping drifts; pretty, pointed fingers feeling their way inch by inch across the strip of tarmac.

Soon the drifts stopped being pretty and lay across the road like white bolsters; but my little car managed to cleave through them, veering crazily at times, wheels spinning, and now I could see the main road a few hundred yards ahead, reassuringly black in the pale light.

But just over there on the left, a field away, was Cote House. I was treating a bullock there — he had eaten some frozen turnips — and a visit was fixed for later today. I didn't fancy trailing back up there if I could avoid it, and there was a light in the kitchen window. The family was up, anyway. I turned and drove down into the yard.

The farmhouse door lay within a small porch and the wind had driven the snow inside, forming a smooth, two-foot heap against the timbers. As I leaned across to knock, the surface of the heap trembled a little, then began to heave. There was something in there, something quite big. It was eerie standing in the half light watching the snow parting to reveal a furry body. Some creature of the wild must have strayed in, searching for warmth — but it was bigger than a fox or anything else I could think of.

Just then the door opened and the light from the kitchen streamed out. Peter Trenholm beckoned me inside and his wife smiled at me from the bright interior. They were a cheerful young couple.

"What's that?" I gasped, pointing at the animal that was shaking the snow vigorously from its coat.

"That?" Peter grinned. "That's awd Tip."

"Tip? Your dog? But what's he doing under a pile of snow?"

"Just blew in on him, I reckon. That's where he sleeps, you know, just outside the back door."

I stared at the farmer. "You mean he sleeps there, out in the open, every night?"

"Aye, allus. Summer and winter. But don't look at me like that, Mr. Herriot, it's his own choice. The other dogs have a warm bed in the cow house but Tip won't entertain it. He's fifteen now and he's been sleeping out there since he were a pup. I remember when me father was alive he tried all ways to get t'awd feller to sleep inside but it was no good."

I looked at the old dog in amazement. I could see him more clearly now. He wasn't the typical sheep dog type, he was bigger boned, longer in the hair; and he projected a bursting vitality that didn't go with his fifteen years. It was difficult to believe that any animal living in these bleak uplands should choose to sleep outside — and thrive on it. I had to look closely to see any sign of his great age. There was the slightest stiffness in his gait as he moved around, perhaps a fleshless look about his head and face, and of course the tell-tale lens opacity in the depths of his eyes. But the general impression was of an unquenchable jauntiness.

He shook the last of the snow from his coat, pranced jerkily up to the farmer, and gave a couple of reedy barks. Peter Trenholm laughed. "You see he's ready to be off — he's a beggar for work is Tip." He led the way towards the buildings and I followed, stumbling over the frozen ruts, like iron under the snow, and bending my head against the knife-like wind. It was a relief to open the byre door and escape into the sweet bovine warmth.

There was a fair mixture in the long building. The dairy cows took up most of the length; then there were a few young heifers, some bullocks, and finally, in an empty stall deeply bedded with straw, the other farm dogs. The cats were there too, so it had to be warm. No animal is a better judge of comfort than a cat and they were just visible as furry balls in the straw. They had the best place, up against the wooden partition where the warmth came through from the big animals.

Tip strode confidently among his colleagues — a young dog and a female with three half-grown pups.

One of the bullocks was my patient and he was looking a bit better. I smiled to myself in satisfaction.

As I prepared to leave, Peter's brother came down the byre with a full bucket on the way to the cooler. As he passed the dogs' stall he tipped a few pints of the warm milk into their dishes and Tip strolled forward casually for his breakfast. While he was drinking, the young dog tried to push his way in, but a soundless snap from Tip's jaws missed his nose by a fraction and he retired to another dish. I noticed, however, that the old dog made no protest as the mother and her pups joined him. The cats, black and white, tortoise-shell, tabby gray, appeared, stretching, from the straw and advanced in a watchful ring. Their turn would come.

Mrs. Trenholm called me in for a cup of tea and when I came out it was full daylight. But the sky was a burdened gray and the sparse trees near the house strained their bare branches against the wind which drove in long, icy gusts over the white empty miles of moor. It was what the Yorkshiremen called a "thin wind" or sometimes a "lazywind" — the kind that couldn't be bothered to blow round you but went straight through instead. It made me feel that the best place on earth was by the side of that bright fire in the farmhouse kitchen.

Most people would have felt like that, but not old Tip. He was capering around as Peter loaded a flat cart with some hay bales for the young cattle in the outside barns; and as Peter shook the reins and set off over the fields, he leapt onto the back of the cart.

As I threw my tackle into the boot, I looked back at the old dog, legs braced against the uneven motion, tail waving, barking defiance at the cold world. I carried away the memory of Tip, who scorned the softer things and slept in what he considered the place of honor—at his master's door.

A little incident like this has always been able to brighten my day and, fortunately, I have the kind of job where things of this kind happen.

And there was that letter from the Bramleys—that really made me feel good. You don't find people like the Bramleys now; radio, television, and the motorcar have carried the outside world into the most isolated places so that the simple people you used to meet on the lonely farms are rapidly becoming like people anywhere else. There are still a few left, of course—old folk who cling to the ways of their fathers and, when I come across any of them, I like to make some excuse to sit down and talk with them and listen to the old Yorkshire words and expressions, which have almost disappeared.

But even in the thirties, when there were many places still untouched by the flood of progress, the Bramleys were in some ways unique. There were four of them; three brothers and an older sister, and their farm lay in a wide, shallow depression in the hills. You could just see the ancient tiles of Scar House through the top branches of the sheltering trees in Drewburn village and in the summer it was possible to drive down over the fields to the farm. I had done it a few times, the bottles in the trunk jingling and crashing. The other approach to the place was right on the other side, through Mr. Broom's stockyard and then along a track with ruts so deep that only a tractor could negotiate it.

There was, in fact, no road to the farm, but that didn't bother the Bramleys because the outside world held no great attraction for them. Miss Bramley made occasional trips to the town of Darrowby on market days for provisions and Herbert, the middle brother, had come into town in the spring of 1929 to have a tooth out, but apart from that, they stayed contentedly at home.

A call to Scar House always came as rather a jolt because it meant that at least two hours had been removed from the working day. In all but the driest weather it was safer to leave the car at Mr. Broom's and make the journey on foot. One February night at about eight o'clock, I was splashing my way along the track, feeling the mud sucking at my boots; it was to see a horse with colic and my pockets were stuffed with the things I might need. My eyes were half closed against the steady drizzle, but about half a mile ahead I could see the lights of the house winking among the trees.

After twenty minutes of slithering in and out of the unseen puddles and opening a series of broken, string-tied gates, I reached the farmyard and crossed over to the back door. I was about to knock when I stopped with my hand poised. I found I was looking through the kitchen window and in the interior, dimly lit by an oil lamp, the Bramleys were sitting in a row.

They weren't grouped round the fire but were jammed tightly on a long, high-backed wooden settle that stood against the far wall. The strange thing was the almost exact similarity of their attitudes; all four had their arms folded, chins resting on their chests, feet stretched out in front of them. The men had removed their heavy boots and were stocking-footed, but Miss Bramley wore an old pair of carpet slippers.

I stared, fascinated by the curious immobility of the group. They were not asleep, not talking or reading or listening to the radio — in fact, they didn't have one — they were just sitting.

I never had seen people just sitting before, and I stood there for some minutes to see if they would make a move or do anything at all, but nothing happened. It occurred to me that this was probably a typical evening; they worked hard all day, had their meal, then they just sat till bedtime.

A month or two later I discovered another unsuspected side of the Bramleys when they started having trouble with their cats. I knew they were fond of cats by the number and variety that swarmed over the place and perched confidently on my car hood on cold days with their unerring instinct for a warm place. But I was unprepared for the family's utter desolation when the cats started to die. Miss Bramley was on the doorstep at Skeldale House nearly every day carrying an egg basket with another pitiful patient — a cat or sometimes a few tiny kittens — huddling miserably inside.

Even today, with the full range of modern antibiotics, the treatment of feline enteritis is unrewarding. I did my best. I even took some of the cats and kept them at the surgery so that I could attend to them several times a day, but the mortality rate was high.

The Bramleys were stricken as they saw their cats diminishing. I was surprised at their grief because most farmers look on cats as pest killers and nothing more. But when Miss Bramley came in one morning with a fresh consignment of invalids, she was in a sorry state. She stared at me across the surgery table and her rough fingers clasped and unclasped on the handle of the egg basket.

"Is it going to go through 'em all?" She quavered.

"Well, it's very infectious and it looks as though most of your young cats will get it anyway."

For a moment Miss Bramley seemed to be struggling with herself, then her chin began to jerk and her whole face twitched uncontrollably. She didn't actually break down but her eyes brimmed and a couple of tears wandered among the network of wrinkles on her cheeks. I looked at her helplessly as she stood there, wisps of gray hair straggling untidily from under the incongruous black beret pulled over her ears.

"It's Topsy's kittens I'm worried about," she gasped out at length. "There's five of 'em and they're the best we've got."

I rubbed my chin. I had heard a lot about Topsy, one of a strain of incomparable ratters and mousers. Her last family was only about ten weeks old and it would be a crushing blow to the Bramleys if anything happened to them. But what could I do? There was, as yet, no protective vaccine against the disease — or, wait a minute, was there? I remembered that I'd heard a rumor that there was a drug company working on one.

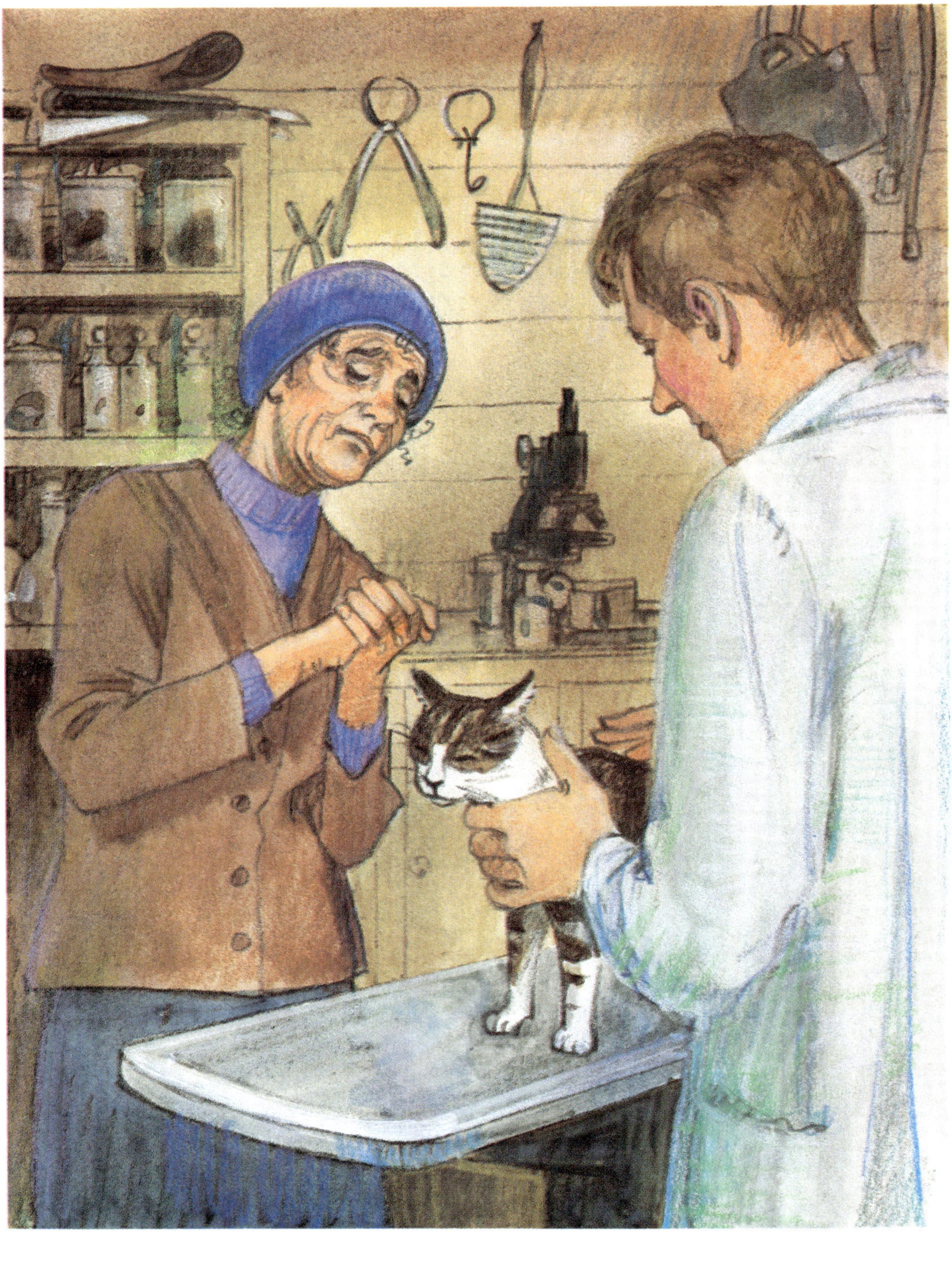

I pulled out a chair. "Just sit down a few minutes, Miss Bramley. I'm going to make a phone call." I was soon through to the laboratory and half expected a sarcastic reply. But they were kind and cooperative. They had had encouraging results with the new vaccine and would be glad to let me have five doses if I would inform them of the results.

I hurried back to Miss Bramley. "I've ordered something for your kittens. I can't guarantee anything but there's nothing else to do. Have them down here on Tuesday morning."

The vaccine arrived promptly and as I injected the tiny creatures Miss Bramley extolled the virtues of the Topsy line. "Look at the size of them ears! Did you ever see bigger 'uns on kittens?"

I had to admit that I hadn't. The ears were enormous, sail-like, and they made the ravishingly pretty little faces look even smaller.

Miss Bramley nodded and smiled with satisfaction. "Aye, you can allus tell. It's the sure sign of a good mouser."

The injection was repeated a week later. The kittens were still looking well.

"Well, that's it," I said. "We'll just have to wait now. But, remember, I want to know the outcome of this, so please don't forget to let me know."

I didn't hear from the Bramleys for several months and had almost forgotten about the little experiment when I came upon a grubby envelope which had apparently been pushed under the surgery door. It was the promised report and was, in its way, a model of conciseness. It communicated all the information I required without frills or verbiage.

It was in a careful, spidery scrawl and said simply: "Dere Sir, Them kittens is now big cats. Yrs trly, R. Bramley."

Discuss the Selection

1. What satisfaction do you think Herriot gets from his job?
2. What was remarkable about the Trenholms' dog, Tip?
3. Why did Herriot find the Bramleys' way of life so unusual?
4. In what ways do you think the dog Tip and the Bramleys were alike?
5. This story has two episodes, or complete stories. Find the episodes and tell what each episode is about. What idea is shared by the episodes?

Apply the Skills

Good writers use a variety of words to make their writing exciting and interesting. Descriptive words help a reader visualize an object or action. Give one example of descriptive language in this selection. Tell why the example is a good description.

Think and Write

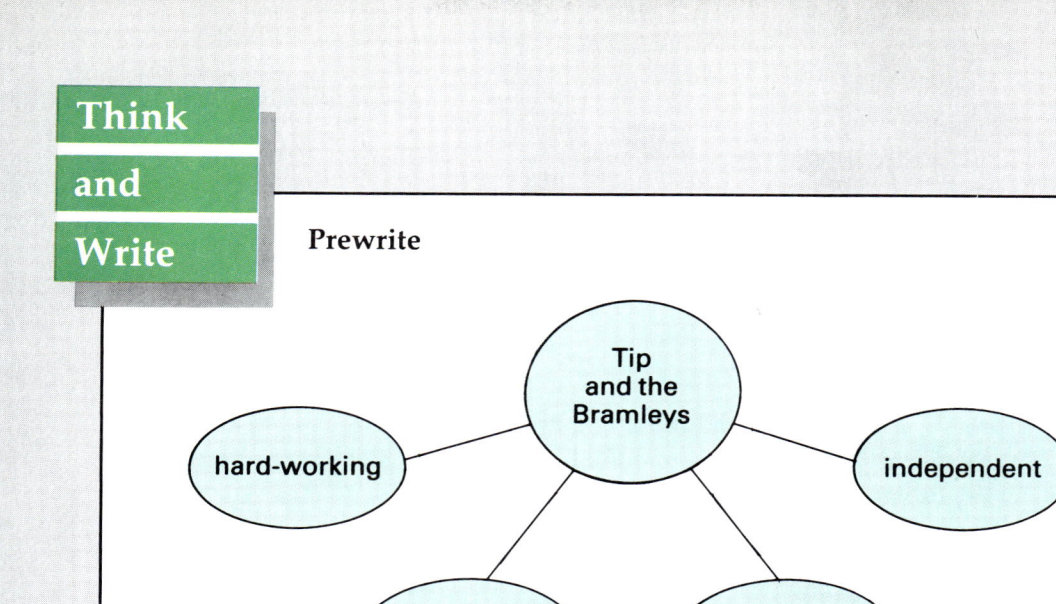

Prewrite

```
        Tip
    and the
    Bramleys
   /    |    \
hard-  gentle  independent
working
```

Study the ideaburst above. Notice that it compares similarities between Tip and the Bramleys.

Copy the diagram on a sheet of paper. Then extend it by adding another similarity between Tip and the Bramleys. Refer to the story as necessary.

Compose

Using the information in the diagram and from the story, write a comparison paragraph describing similarities between Tip and the Bramleys. You might start with this topic sentence: *Just as Tip scorned the "easy" life, the Bramleys were disinterested in modern ways.*

Follow your topic sentence with two detail sentences from the story. You might use some of James Herriot's colorful words, such as *knife-like wind*.

Revise

Read the paragraph that you wrote. Check to see if you pointed out the similarities between Tip and the Bramleys. Would someone who hasn't read the story understand how they are alike? If not, revise what you wrote to emphasize their similar characteristics.

Literature Study

Plot

Kim just finished reading a short story titled "Travelers in Time." Her best friend asked her what the story was about. This is what Kim told her:

"It's a story about a girl named Jane who builds a time machine in her basement. When her friends Ted and Pat doubt that it's really a time machine, Jane agrees to let them go with her on a test run. In what seems like only a minute or two, they find themselves looking through the window of the time machine at a lush jungle. They leave the time machine to explore the jungle. There they see giant lizards, which chase them and almost kill Pat. Jane throws a large rock at the lizards, and the three of them are able to reach the safety of the time machine for the short ride home."

Kim described what happened in the story. In other words, she gave the **plot**—the actions in a story. The plot shows how, when, and why things happen in a story.

The plot of a story is developed around the **conflict**, which is the struggle that takes place between two opposing forces. Without a conflict there simply would not be a story.

A conflict can take place between a character and a natural force, like a bear or a hurricane; between two characters; or between opposing views held by separate characters or groups of characters. Such conflicts are *external* conflicts. What is the conflict in "Travelers in Time"? It is a battle between three young people and a group of giant lizards.

Sometimes the conflict is *internal*. A character struggles with a problem in his or her own mind. The character with an internal conflict must make a difficult decision or overcome a fear. Here is an example: A child copes with the loss of a pet.

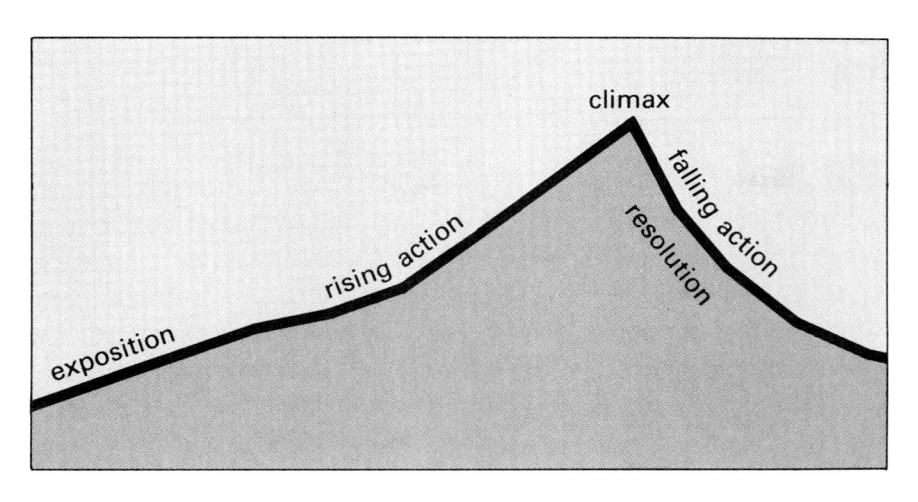

Stages of Plot Development

Most plots go through different stages. The first stage is **exposition**. During this stage, basic information is given about the story. These basics—the who, what, where, and when—are usually given in the first few paragraphs of the story. What basics would be given for "Travelers in Time"? Jane, Ted, and Pat—the main characters—would be introduced. The fact that Jane has built a time machine would be given. The fact that they are going to travel in the time machine would be given.

The second stage is called the **rising action**. The events that take place during this stage move the plot along and get you, the reader, more interested in the story. In "Travelers in Time," the rising action includes the trip itself, the exploration of the jungle, and the sighting of the giant lizards.

During the next stage, the story reaches the **climax**, or turning point. It is the high point in the story. It is often the most exciting part of the story. What is the climax in "Travelers in Time"? The climax takes place when Jane, Ted, and Pat are chased by the giant lizards.

The events following the climax make up the final stage, which is called the **falling action** or **resolution**. During the falling action or resolution, conflicts are resolved. In "Travelers in Time," the resolution takes place when Jane throws the rock at the lizards and the group reaches the time machine safely.

Understanding the different stages of a story's plot will help you appreciate the story.

Author Profile

Ursula K. Le Guin

"I have been writing since I was six, mostly fantasies and science fiction," states Ursula K. Le Guin, an American author of science fiction and fantasy. Her first completed short story, which she wrote at age nine, was a fantasy in which a man is persecuted by evil elves. By the time Le Guin was twenty-two, some of her poems and a short story had been published. She had also written five novels, but she could not get them published. She explains, "You must either fit a category or have a name to publish a book in America. As the only way I was ever going to achieve Namehood was *by* writing, I was reduced to fitting a category. Therefore my first efforts to write science fiction were motivated by a pretty distinct wish to get published: nothing higher or lower."

In 1966, her first science fiction books were published. Written for adults, they show an interest in anthropology and have a romantic, magical tone. "I was beginning to get the feel of the medium [of writing]," Le Guin says of her early work. "In the next books I kept pushing at my own limitations and at the limits of science fiction. That is what the practice of an art is; you keep looking for the outside edge. When you find it, you make a whole, solid, real, and beautiful thing; anything less is incomplete."

The books that followed were some of Le Guin's most successful works in fantasy. She was asked by her publisher to write a novel for young adults. The result was *A Wizard of Earthsea,* from which

"The Dragon of Pendor" is taken. Le Guin was recognized for her writing when this book won the *Boston Globe-Horn Book* Award for excellence. *A Wizard of Earthsea,* along with two other award-winning books, *The Tombs of Atuan* and *The Farthest Shore,* form the trilogy about the fantasy world of Earthsea. In this series, Le Guin combines mystical elements with the familiar.

As a writer of science fiction and fantasy, Le Guin is often asked where she gets her ideas and if she would ever want to write about the *real* world. She answers, "I do write about the real world, and I get all my weird ideas from it, too. It is just that reality is much stranger than many people want to admit. After all, the real world is not made up only of the actual. If it were, it would stop right now. It is also made up of the possible and the probable: They are part of it now and always have been."

Le Guin has such an enthusiasm for science fiction that she encourages others to write it, too. She has taught courses in the writing of science fiction and fantasy at universities. She has also held workshops in science-fiction writing. Le Guin says that she finds participating in the workshops exciting and invigorating.

Fantasy and science fiction appeal to Le Guin because they depend heavily on the use of imagination. She states, "Imagination is one of humanity's greatest tools. It can be badly used, just as an ax can. A writer can lie, or refuse to admit facts he [or she] doesn't like, just as a scientist can. But skillfully and honestly used, imagination is our best means of understanding reality, and the chief tool of both the scientist and the artist." Le Guin is a user of imagination. For that her readers are grateful.

Ged, a young wizard, begins a quest to resolve an inner conflict. What is Ged's inner conflict?

As you read, notice the stages of plot in the story.

The Dragon of Pendor

by Ursula K. Le Guin

Ged, a fifteen-year-old wizard, first shows his unusual powers when his home town is attacked by a warlike tribe. Ged hides the town in a mist that allows the people to surprise and destroy their enemies. In creating the mist, however, Ged exhausts himself and falls into a kind of coma. The master wizard, Ogion, hears of Ged's feat and comes to revive him. Ogion then makes Ged his apprentice.

With Ogion's blessing, Ged soon sails to Roke Knoll and enrolls in a school for wizards. There he accidentally unleashes a mysterious creature called the shadow, who haunts Ged wherever he goes. When Ged leaves school, he takes an assignment that he hopes will take his mind off the shadow.

He is to take a position as a resident wizard in a lonely corner of the Ninety Isles. Low Torning is an island bordering the West Reach, near the dragon-spoiled isle of Pendor. What challenges will the young wizard face in his new assignment?

West of Roke in a crowd between the two great lands of Hosk and Ensmer lie the Ninety Isles. The nearest to Roke is Serc, and the farthest is Seppish, which lies almost in the Pelnish Sea; and whether the sum of them is ninety is a question never settled, for if you count only isles with freshwater springs you might have seventy, while if you count every rock you might have a hundred and still not be done; and then the tide would change. Narrow run the channels between the islets, and there the mild tides of the Inmost Sea, chafed and baffled, run high and fall low, so that where at high tide there might be three islands in one place, at low there might be one. Yet for all that danger of the tide, every child who can walk can paddle, and has his own little rowboat; housewives row across the channel to take a cup of rushwash tea with the neighbor; peddlers call their wares in rhythm with the stroke of their oars. All roads there are salt water, blocked only by nets strung from house to house across the straits to catch the small fish called turbies, the oil of which is the wealth of the Ninety Isles. There are few bridges, and no great towns. Every islet is thick with farms and fishermen's houses, and these are gathered into townships, each of ten or twenty islets. One such town was Low Torning, the westernmost, looking not on the Inmost Sea but outward toward the empty ocean, that lonely corner of the Archipelago where only Pendor lies, the dragon-spoiled isle, and beyond it the waters of the West Reach, desolate.

A house was ready there for the township's new wizard. It stood on a hill among green fields of barley, sheltered from the west wind by a grove of pendick trees that now were red with flowers. From the door one looked out on other thatched roofs and groves and gardens, and other islands with their roofs and fields and hills, and amongst them all the many bright winding channels of the sea. It was a poor house, windowless, with earthen floor, yet a better house than the one Ged was born in. The Isle-Men of Low Torning, standing in awe of the wizard from Roke, asked pardon from its humbleness. "We have no stone to build with," said one. "We are none of us rich, though none starve," said another, and a third, "It will be dry at least, for I saw to the thatching myself, Sir." To Ged it was as good as any palace. He thanked the leaders of the township frankly, so that the eighteen of them went home, each in his own rowboat to his home isle, to tell the fishermen and housewives that the new wizard was a strange young grim fellow who spoke little, but he spoke fairly, and without pride.

There was little cause, perhaps, for pride in this first magistry of Ged's. Wizards trained on Roke went commonly to cities or castles, to serve high lords who held them in high honor. These fishermen of Low Torning, in the usual way of things, would have had among them no more than a witch or a plain sorcerer, to charm the fishing nets and sing over new boats and cure beasts and men of their ailments. But in late years the old Dragon of Pendor had spawned: nine dragons, it was said, now laired in the ruined towers of the Sealords of Pendor, dragging their scaled bellies up and down the marbled stairs and through the broken doorways there. Wanting food on that dead isle, they would be flying forth some year when they were grown and hunger came upon them. Already a flight of four had been seen over the southwest shores of Hosk, not alighting but spying out the sheepfolds, barns, and villages. The hunger of a dragon is slow to wake, but hard to sate. So the Isle-Men of Low Torning had sent to Roke begging for a wizard to protect their folk from what boded over the western horizon, and the Archmage had judged their request well-founded.

"There is no comfort in this place," the Archmage had said to Ged on the day he made him wizard, "no fame, no wealth, maybe no risk. Will you go?"

"I will go," Ged had replied, not from obedience only. Since the night on Roke Knoll, his desire had turned as much against fame and display as once it had been set on them. Always now he doubted his strength and dreaded the trial of his power. Yet also the talk of dragons drew him on with a great curiosity. In Gont there have been no dragons for many hundred years; and no dragon would ever fly within scent or sight or spell of Roke, so that there also they are a matter of tales and songs only, things sung of but not seen. Ged had learned all he could of dragons at the School, but it is one thing to read about dragons and another to meet them. The chance lay bright before him, and heartily he answered, "I will go."

The Archmage Gensher had nodded his head, but his look was somber. "Tell me," he said at last, "do you fear to leave Roke? Or are you eager to be gone?"

"Both, my lord."

Again Gensher nodded. "I do not know if I do right to send you from your safety here," he said very low. "I cannot see your way. It is all in darkness. And there is a power in the North, something that would destroy you, but what it is and where, whether in your past or in your forward way, I cannot tell: it is all shadowed. When the men of Low Torning came here, I thought at once of you, for it seemed a safe place and out of the way, where you might have time to gather your strength. But I do not know if any place is safe for you, or where your way goes. I do not want to send you out into the dark. . . ."

It seemed a bright enough place to Ged at first, the house under the flowering trees. There he lived, and watched the western sky often, and kept his wizard's ear tuned for the sound of scaly wings. But no dragon came. Ged fished from his jetty, and tended his garden-patch. He spent whole days pondering a page or a line or a word in the Lore-Books he had brought from Roke, sitting out in the summer air under the pendick trees, while the otak slept beside him or went hunting mice in the forests of grass and daisies. And he served the people of Low Torning as healall and weatherworker whenever they asked him. It did not enter his head that a wizard might be ashamed to perform such simple crafts for he had been a witch child among poorer folk than these. They, however, asked little of him, holding him in awe, partly because he was a wizard from the Isle of the Wise, and partly on account of his silence and his scarred face. There was that about him, young as he was, that made men uneasy with him.

Yet he found a friend, a boatmaker who dwelt on the next islet eastward. His name was Pechvarry. They had met first on his jetty, where Ged stopped to watch him stepping the mast of a little catboat. He had looked up at the wizard with a grin and said, "Here's a month's work nearly finished. I guess you might have done it in a minute with a word, eh, Sir?"

"I might," said Ged, "but it would likely sink the next minute, unless I kept the spells up. But if you like . . ." He stopped.

"Well, Sir?"

"Well, that is a lovely little craft. She needs nothing. But if you like, I could set a binding-spell on her, to help keep her sound; or a finding-spell, to help bring her home from the sea."

He spoke hesitantly, not wanting to offend the craftsman, but Pechvarry's face shone. "The little boat's for my son, Sir, and if you would lay such charms on her, it would be a mighty kindness and friendly act." And he climbed up onto the jetty to take Ged's hand then and there and thank him.

After that they came to work together often, Ged interweaving his spellcrafts with Pechvarry's handwork on the boats he built or repaired, and in return learning from Pechvarry how a boat was built, and also how a boat was handled without aid of magic, for this skill of plain sailing had been somewhat scanted on Roke. Often Ged and Pechvarry and his little son Ioeth went out into the channels and lagoons, sailing or rowing one boat or another, 'til Ged was a fair sailor, and friendship between him and Pechvarry was a settled thing.

Along in late autumn the boatmaker's son fell sick. The mother sent for the witchwoman of Teak Isle, who was a good hand at healing, and all seemed well for a day or two. Then in the middle of a stormy night came Pechvarry's hammering at Ged's door, begging him to come save the child. Ged ran down to the boat with him and they rowed in all haste through dark and rain to the boatmaker's house. There Ged saw the child on his pallet-bed, and the mother crouching silent beside him, and the witchwoman making a smoke of corly-root and singing a Nagian chant, which was the best healing she had. But she whispered to Ged, "Lord Wizard, I think this fever is the redfever, and the child will die of it tonight."

When Ged knelt and put his hand on the child, he thought the same, and he drew back a moment. In the latter months of his own long sickness the Master Herbal had taught him much of the healer's lore, and the first lesson and the last of all that lore was this: Heal the wound and cure the illness, but let the dying spirit go.

The mother saw his movement and the meaning of it, and cried out aloud in despair. Pechvarry stooped down by her saying, "The Lord Sparrowhawk will save him, wife. No need to cry! He's here now. He can do it."

Hearing the mother's wail, and seeing the trust Pechvarry had in him, Ged did not know how he could disappoint them. He mistrusted his own judgment, and thought perhaps the child might be saved, if the fever could be brought down.

He set to bathing the little boy with cold rainwater that they brought new-fallen from out of doors, and he began to say one of the spells of feverstay. The spell took no hold and suddenly he thought the child was dying in his arms.

Summoning his power all at once and with no thought for himself, he sent his spirit out after the child's spirit, to bring it back home. He called the child's name, "Ioeth?" Thinking some faint answer came in his inward hearing, he pursued, calling once more. Then he saw the little boy running fast and far ahead of him down a dark slope, the side of some vast hill. There was no sound. The stars above the hill were no stars his eyes had ever seen. Yet he knew the constellations by name: the Sheaf, the Door, the One Who Turns, the Tree. They were those stars that do not set, that are not paled by the coming of any day. He had followed the dying child too far.

Knowing this, he found himself alone on the dark hillside. It was hard to turn back, very hard.

He turned slowly. Slowly he set one foot forward to climb back up the hill, and then the other. Step by step he went, each step willed. And each step was harder than the last.

The stars did not move. No wind blew over the dry steep ground. In all the vast kingdom of the darkness only he moved, slowly, climbing. He came to the top of the hill, and saw the low wall of stones there. But across the wall, facing him, there was a shadow.

The shadow did not have the shape of man or beast. It was shapeless, scarcely to be seen, but it whispered at him, though there were no words in its whispering, and it reached out towards him. And it stood on the side of the living, and he on the side of the dead.

Either he must go down the hill into the desert lands and lightless cities of the dead, or he must step across the wall back into life, where the formless evil thing waited for him.

His spirit-staff was in his hand, and he raised it high. With that motion, strength came into him. As he made to leap the low wall of stones straight at the shadow, the staff burned suddenly white, a blinding light in that dim place. He leaped, felt himself fall, and saw no more.

Now what Pechvarry and his wife and the witch saw was this: the young wizard had stopped midway in his spell, and held the child a while motionless. Then he had laid little Ioeth gently down on the pallet, and had risen, and stood silent, staff in hand. All at once he raised the staff high and it blazed with white fire as if he held the lightning-bolt in his grip, and all the household things in the hut leaped out strange and vivid in that momentary fire. When their eyes were clear from the dazzlement they saw the young man lying huddled forward on the earthen floor, beside the pallet where the child lay dead.

To Pechvarry it seemed that the wizard also was dead. His wife wept, but he was utterly bewildered. But the witch had some hearsay knowledge concerning magery and the ways a true wizard may go, and she saw to it that Ged, cold and lifeless as he lay, was not treated as a dead man but as one sick or tranced. He was carried home, and an old woman was left to watch and see whether he slept to wake or slept forever.

The little otak was hiding in the rafters of the house, as it did when strangers entered. There it stayed while the rain beat down

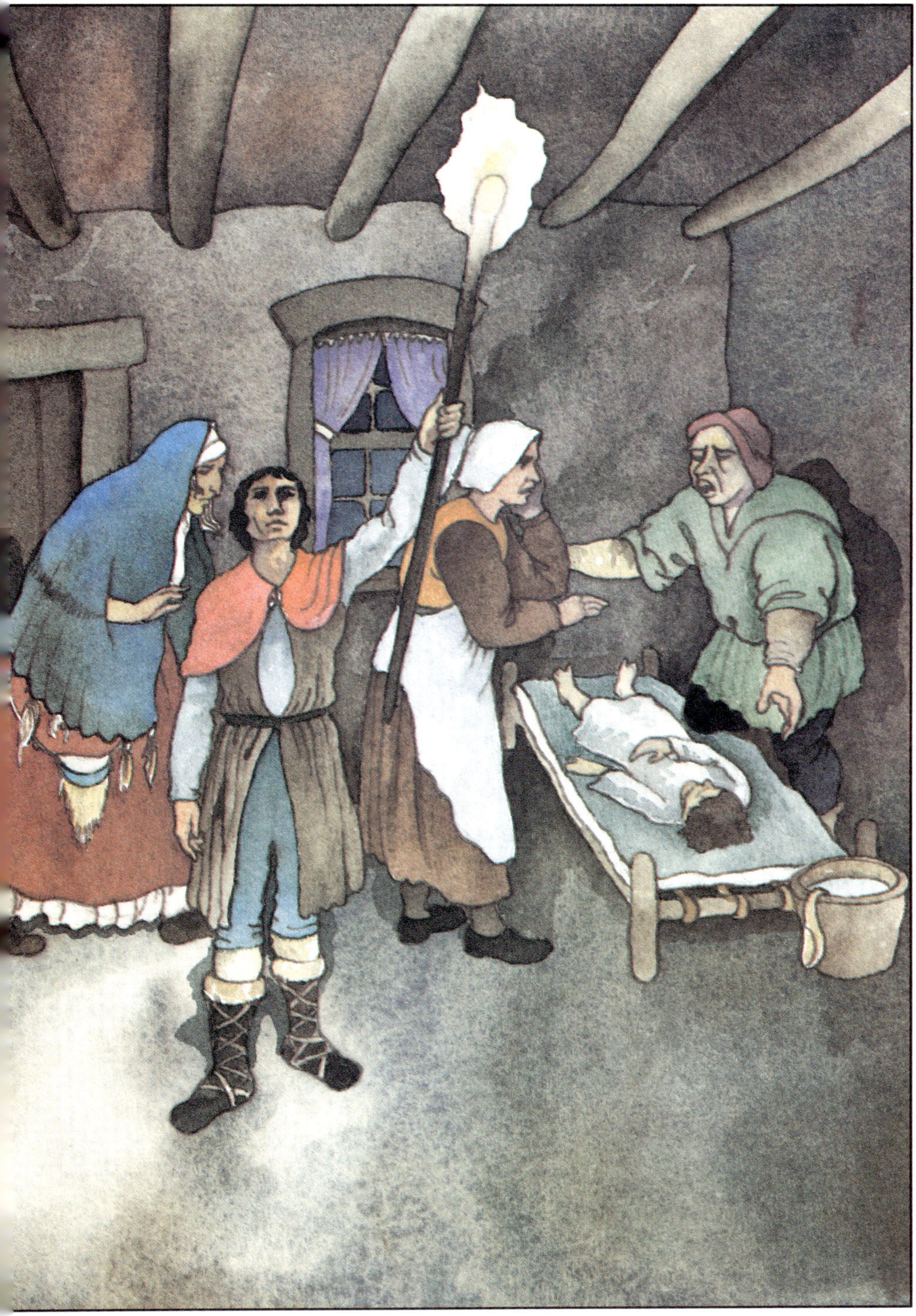

on the walls and fire sank down and the night wearing slowly along left the old woman nodding beside the hearthpit. Then the otak crept down and came to Ged where he lay stretched stiff and still upon the bed. It began to lick his hands and wrists, long and patiently, with its dry leaf-brown tongue. Crouching beside his head, it licked his temple, his scarred cheek, and softly his closed eyes. And very slowly under that soft touch Ged roused. He woke, not knowing where he had been or where he was or what was the faint gray light in the air about him, which was the light of dawn coming to the world. Then the otak curled up near his shoulder as usual, and went to sleep.

Later, when Ged thought back upon that night, he knew that had none touched him when he lay thus spirit-lost, had none called him back in some way, he might have been lost for good. It was only the dumb instinctive wisdom of the beast who licks his hurt companion to comfort him, and yet in that wisdom Ged saw something akin to his own power, something that went as deep as wizardry. From that time forth he believed that the wise man is one who never sets himself apart from other living things, whether they have speech or not, and in later years, he strove long to learn what can be learned, in silence, from the eyes of animals, the flight of birds, the great slow gestures of trees.

He had now made unscathed, for the first time, that crossing-over and return which only a wizard can make with open eyes, and which not the greatest mage can make without risk. But he had returned to a grief and a fear. The grief was for his friend Pechvarry, the fear was for himself. He knew now why the Archmage had feared to send him forth, and what had darkened and clouded even the mage's foreseeing of the future. For it was darkness itself that had awaited him, the unnamed thing, the being that did not belong in the world, the shadow he had loosed or made. In spirit, at the boundary wall between life and death, it had waited for him these long years. It had found him there at last. It would be on his track now, seeking to crawl near to him, to take his strength into itself, and suck up his life, and clothe itself in his flesh.

Soon after, he dreamed of the thing like a bear with no head or face. He thought it went fumbling about the walls of the house, searching for the door. Such a dream he had not dreamed since the healing of the wounds the thing had given him. When he woke he was weak and cold, and the scars on his face and shoulder drew and ached.

Now began a bad time. When he dreamed of the shadow or so much as thought of it, he felt always that same cold dread: sense and power drained out of him, leaving him stupid and astray. He raged at his cowardice, but that did no good. He sought for some protection, but there was none: the thing was not flesh, not alive, not spirit, unnamed, having no being but what he himself had given it—a terrible power outside the laws of the sunlit world. All he knew of it was that it was drawn to him and would try to work its will through him, being his creature. But in what form it could come, having no real form of its own yet, and how would it come, and when would it come, this he did not know.

He set up what barriers of sorcery he could about his house and about the isle where he lived. Such spell-walls must be ever renewed, and soon he saw that if he spent all his strength on these defenses, he would be of no use to the islanders. What could he do, between two enemies, if a dragon came from Pendor?

Again he dreamed, but this time in the dream the shadow was inside his house, beside the door, reaching out to him through the darkness and whispering words he did not understand. He woke in terror, and sent the werelight flaming through the air, lighting every corner of the little house till he saw no shadow anywhere. Then he put wood on the coal of his firepit, and sat in the firelight hearing the autumn wind fingering at the thatch roof and whining in the great bare trees above; and he pondered long. An old anger had awakened in his heart. He would not suffer this helpless waiting, this sitting trapped on a little island muttering useless spells of lock and ward. Yet he could not simply flee the trap: to do so would be to break his trust with the islanders and to leave them to the imminent dragon, undefended. There was but one way to take.

The next morning he went down among the fishermen in the principal moorage of Low Torning, and finding the Head Isle-Man there said to him, "I must leave this place. I am in danger, and I put you in danger. I must go. Therefore I ask your leave to go out and do away with the dragons on Pendor, so that my task for you will be finished and I may leave freely. Or if I fail, I should also fail when they come here, and that is better known now than later."

The Isle-Man started at him all dropjawed. "Lord Sparrowhawk," he said, "there are nine dragons out there!"

"Eight are still young, they say."

"But the old one—"

"I tell you, I must go from here. I ask you leave to rid you from the dragon-peril first, if I can do so."

"As you will, Sir," the Isle-Man said gloomily. All that listened there thought this a folly or crazy courage in their young wizard, and with sullen faces they saw him go, expecting no news of him again. Some hinted that he meant merely to sail back by Hosk to the Inmost Sea, leaving them in the lurch; others, among them Pechvarry, held that he had gone mad, and sought death.

For four generations of men all ships had set their course to keep far from the shores of Pendor Island. No mage had ever come to do combat with the dragon there, for the island was on no traveled sea road, and its lords had been pirates, slave-takers, war-makers hated by all that dwelt in the southwest parts of Earthsea. For this reason none had sought to revenge the Lord of Pendor, after the dragon came suddenly out of the west upon him and his men where they sat feasting in the tower, and smothered them with the flames of his mouth, and drove all the townsfolk screaming into the sea. Unavenged, Pendor had been left to the dragon, with all its bones, and towers, and jewels stolen from long-dead princes of the coasts of Paln and Hosk.

All this Ged knew well, and more, for ever since he came to Low Torning he had held in mind and pondered over all he had ever learned of dragons. As he guided his small boat westward—not rowing now nor using the seaman's skill Pechvarry had taught him, but sailing wizardly with the mageuum in his sail and a spell set on prow and keel to keep them true — he watched to see the dead isle rise on the rim of the sea. Speed he wanted, and therefore used the mago wind, for he feared what was behind him more than what was before him. But as the day passed, his impatience turned from fear to a kind of glad fierceness. At least he sought this danger of his own will; and the nearer he came to it the more sure he was that, for this time at least, for this hour perhaps before his death, he was free. The shadow dared not to follow him into a dragon's jaws. The waves ran white-tipped on the gray sea, and gray cloud streamed overhead on the north wind. He went west with the quick mago wind in his sail, and came in sight of the rocks of Pendor, the still streets of the town, and the gutted, falling towers.

At the entrance of the harbor, a shallow crescent bay, he let the windspell drop and stilled his little boat so it lay rocking on the waves. Then he summoned the dragon: "Usurper of Pendor, come defend your hoard!"

His voice fell short in the sound of the breakers beating on the ashen shores; but dragons have keen ears. Presently one flitted up from some roofless ruin of the town like a vast black bat, thin-winged and spiny-backed, and circling into the north wind came flying towards Ged. His heart swelled at the sight of the creature that was myth to his people, and he laughed and shouted, "Go tell the Old One to come, you wind-worm!"

For this was one of the young dragons, spawned there years ago by a she-dragon from the West Reach, who had set her clutch of great leathern eggs, as they say she-dragons will, in some sunny broken room of the tower and had flown away again, leaving the Old Dragon of Pendor to watch the young when they crawled like baneful lizards from the shell.

The young dragon made no answer. He was not large of his kind, maybe the length of a forty-oared ship, and was worm-thin for all the reach of his black membranous wings. He had not got his growth yet, nor his voice, nor any dragon-cunning. Straight at Ged in the small rocking boat he came, opening his long, toothed jaws as he slid down arrowy from the air: so that all Ged had to do was bind his wings and limbs stiff with one sharp spell and send him thus hurtling aside into the sea like a stone falling. And the gray sea closed over him.

Two dragons like the first rose up from the base of the highest towers. Even as the first one they came driving straight at Ged, and even so he caught both, hurled both down, and drowned them; and he had not yet lifted up his wizard's staff.

Now after a little time there came three against him from the island. One of these was much greater, and fire spewed curling from its jaws. Two came flying at him rattling their wings, but the big one came circling from behind, very swift, to burn him and his boat with its breath of fire. No binding spell would catch all three, because two came from north and one from south. In the instant that he saw this, Ged worked a spell of Changing, and between one breath and the next flew up from his boat in dragon-form.

Spreading broad wings and reaching talons out, he met the two head on, withering them with fire, and then turned to the third, who was larger than he and also armed with fire. On the wind over the gray waves they doubled, snapped, swooped, lunged, till smoke roiled about them red-lit by the glare of the fiery mouths. Ged flew suddenly upward and the other pursued, below him. In midflight the dragon Ged raised wings, stopped, and stooped as the hawk stoops, talons outstretched downward, striking and bearing the other down by neck and flank. The black wings flurried and black dragon-blood dropped in thick drops into the sea. The Pendor dragon tore free and flew low and lamely to the island, where it hid, crawling into some well or cavern in the ruined town.

At once Ged took his form and place again on the boat, for it was most perilous to keep that dragon-shape longer than need demanded. His hands were black with the scalding worm-blood, and he was scorched about the head with fire, but this was no matter now. He waited only till he had breath back and then called, "Six I have seen, five slain, nine are told of: come out, worms!"

No creature moved nor voice spoke for a long while on the island, but only the waves beat loudly on the shore. Then Ged was aware that the highest tower slowly changed its shape, bulging out on the side as if it grew an arm. He feared dragon-magic, for old dragons are very powerful and guileful in a sorcery like and unlike the sorcery of men: but a moment more and he saw this was no trick of the dragon but of his own eyes. What he had taken for a part of the tower was the shoulder of the Dragon of Pendor as he uncurled his bulk and lifted himself slowly up.

When he was all afoot his scaled head, spike-crowned and triple-tongued, rose higher than the broken tower's height, and his taloned forefeet rested on the rubble of the town below. His scales were gray-black, catching the daylight like broken stone. Lean as a hound he was, huge as a hill. Ged stared in awe. There

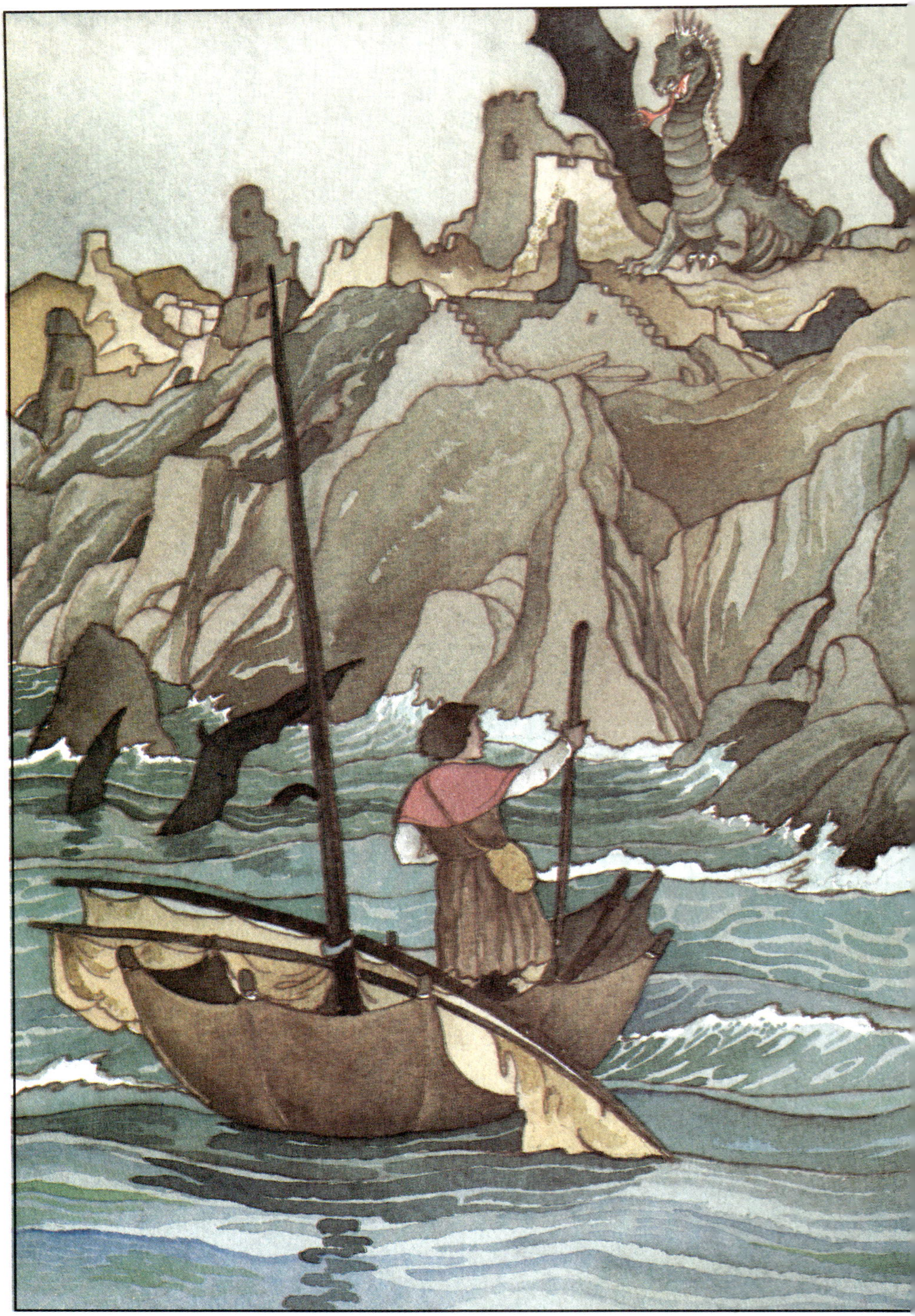

was no song or tale could prepare the mind for this sight. Almost he stared into the dragon's eyes. He glanced away from the oily green gaze that watched him, and held up before him his staff, that looked like a splinter, like a twig.

"Eight sons I had, little wizard," said the great dry voice of the dragon. "Five died, one dies: enough. You will not win my hoard by killing them."

"I do not want your hoard."

The yellow smoke hissed from the dragon's nostrils: that was his laughter. "Would you not like to come ashore and look at it, little wizard? It is worth looking at."

"No, dragon." The kinship of dragons is with wind and fire, and they do not fight willingly over the sea. That had been Ged's advantage so far and he kept it; but the strip of seawater between him and the great gray talons did not seem much of an advantage anymore.

It was hard not to look into the green, watching eyes. "You are a very young wizard," the dragon said. "I did not know men came so young into their power." He spoke, as did Ged, in the Old Speech, for that is the tongue of the dragons still. Although the use of the Old Speech binds a man to truth, this is not so with dragons. It is their own language, and they can lie in it, twisting the true words to false ends, catching the unwary hearer in a maze of mirrorwords each of which reflects the truth and none of which leads anywhere. So Ged had been warned often, and when the dragon spoke he listened with an untrustful ear, all his doubts ready. But the words seemed plain and clear: "Is it to ask my help that you have come here, little wizard?"

"No, dragon."

"Yet I could help you. You will need help soon, against that which hunts you in the dark."

Ged stood dumb.

"What is it that hunts you? Name it to me."

"If I could name it—" Ged stopped himself.

Yellow smoke curled above the dragon's long head, from the nostrils that were two round pits of fire.

"If you could name it you could master it, maybe, little wizard.

Maybe I could tell you its name, when I see it close by. And it will come close, if you wait about my isle. It will come whenever you come. If you do not want it to come close you must run, and run, and keep running from it. And yet it will follow you. Would you like to know its name?"

Ged stood silent again. How the dragon knew of the shadow he had loosed, he could not guess, nor how it might know the shadow's name. The Archmage had said that the shadow had no name. Yet dragons have their own wisdom; and they are an older race than man. Few men can guess what a dragon knows and how he knows it, and those few are the Dragonlords. To Ged, only one thing was sure: that though the dragon might well be speaking truth, though he might indeed be able to tell Ged the nature and name of the shadow-thing and so give him power over it—even so, even if he spoke the truth, he did so wholly for his own ends.

"It is very seldom," the young man said at last, "that dragons ask to do men favors."

"But it is very common," said the dragon, "for cats to play with mice before they kill them."

"But I did not come here to play, or to be played with. I came to strike a bargain with you."

Like a sword in sharpness but five times the length of any sword, the point of the dragon's tail arched up scorpion-wise over his mailed back, above the tower. Dryly he spoke: "I strike no bargains. I take. What have you to offer that I cannot take from you when I like?"

"Safety. Your safety. Swear that you will never fly eastward of Pendor, and I will swear to leave you unharmed."

A grating sound came from the dragon's throat like the noise of an avalanche far off, stones falling among mountains. Fire danced along his three-forked tongue. He raised himself up higher, looming over the ruins. "You offer me safety! You threaten me! With what?"

"With your name, Yevaud."

Ged's voice shook as he spoke the name, yet he spoke it clear and loud. At the sound of it, the old dragon held still, utterly still. A minute went by, and another; and then Ged, standing there in his rocking chip of a boat, smiled. He had staked his venture and his life on a guess drawn from old histories of dragon-lore learned on Roke, a guess that this Dragon of Pendor was the same that had spoiled the west of Osskil in the days of Elfarren and Morred, and had been driven from Osskil by a wizard, Elt, wise in names. The guess had held.

"We are matched, Yevaud. You have the strength: I have your name. Will you bargain?"

Still the dragon made no reply.

Many years had the dragon sprawled on the island where golden breastplates and emeralds lay scattered among dust and bricks and bones; he had watched his black lizard-brood play among crumbling houses and try their wings from the cliffs; he had slept long in the sun, unwaked by voice or sail. He had grown old. It was hard now to stir, to have this mage-lad, this frail enemy, at the sight of whose staff Yevaud, the old dragon, winced.

"You may choose nine stones from my hoard," he said at last, his voice hissing and whining in his long jaws. "The best: take your choice. Then go!"

"I do not want your stones, Yevaud."

"Where is man's greed gone? Men loved bright stones in the old days in the north. . . . I know what it is you want, wizard. I, too, can offer you safety, for I know what alone can save you. There is a horror follows you. I will tell you its name."

Ged's heart leaped in him, and he clutched his staff, standing as still as the dragon stood. He fought a moment with sudden, startling hope.

It was not his own life he bargained for. One mastery, and only one, could he hold over the dragon. He set hope aside and did what he must do.

"This is not what I ask for, Yevaud."

When he spoke the dragon's name it was as if he held the huge being on a fine, thin leash, tightening it on his throat. He could feel the ancient malice and experience of humans in the dragon's gaze that rested on him, he could see the steel talons each as long as a man's forearm, and the stone-hard hide, and the withering fire that lurked in the dragon's throat: and yet always the leash tightened, tightened.

He spoke again: "Yevaud: Swear by your name that you and your sons will never come to the Archipelago."

Flames broke suddenly bright and loud from the dragon's jaws, and he said, "I swear it by my name!"

Silence lay over the isle then, and Yevaud lowered his great head.

When he raised it again and looked, the wizard was gone, and the sail of the boat was a white fleck on the waves eastward, heading towards the flat bejeweled islands of the inner seas. Then in rage the old Dragon of Pendor rose up breaking the tower with the writhing of his body, and beating his wings that spanned the width of the whole ruined town. But his oath held him, and he did not fly, then or ever, to the Archipelago.

To find out more about Ged's struggle with the shadow, read A Wizard of Earthsea *by Ursula K. Le Guin.*

Discuss the Selection

1. What was Ged's inner conflict?
2. When did Ged first encounter the shadow?
3. Why did Ged decide to go after the dragons?
4. Why do you think the dragon agreed to make a bargain with Ged?
5. When he sends Ged to Roke Knoll, Gensher seems to think there is more danger for Ged than just dragons. Locate Gensher's statements that imply an unknown danger.

Apply the Skills

The plot tells what happens in a story. Most plots go through four stages of development: exposition, rising action, climax, and falling action or resolution. What are the four stages of plot development in "The Dragon of Pendor"?

147

Thinking About "Quests and Conquests"

In this unit, you have read about some characters who lived in ancient times and some who lived in modern times. You have read about fantastic people and imaginary creatures. All these stories share a common theme. Each involved a character's quest to reach a difficult goal.

Some characters were successful in their quest. Jason obtained the Golden Fleece. Ged defeated the dragon of Pendor. James Herriot was able to help both his human friends and his animal patients.

In the excerpt from *Frozen Fire*, you met Matthew and Kayak. In the excerpt from *The Talking Earth*, you met Billie Wind. These three youths shared a common goal—survival. Think about Matthew and Kayak's battle to survive in the bitter Arctic environment. Did you identify with Billie Wind as she fought fear in the aftermath of a forest fire?

Jocelyn Bell and Howard Carter had certain qualities that helped them reach their goals. Think about how they remained steadfast and determined to prove their beliefs. These qualities helped them contribute major discoveries to the world. Jocelyn Bell's discovery of strange signals coming from outer space led to a new understanding about the way stars decay. Howard Carter's discovery of King Tutankhamen's tomb helped archaeologists learn about ancient Egypt.

Even the Bitterings faced challenges in trying to make a home for themselves on Mars. Think about their quest.

The stories in this unit gave you insights into the way people behave. Perhaps you enjoyed some stories more than others. Authors write different kinds of stories from which you pick and choose. They use many ideas and writing styles to please you—the reader.

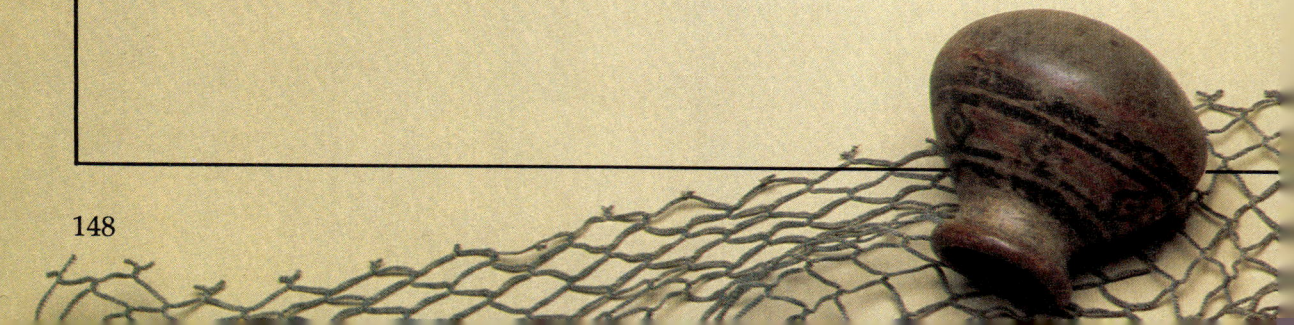

1. Think of the characters you met in "Quests and Conquests." Choose a character from two different selections and compare and contrast their quests. In what ways were they alike? How were they different? What do you think the characters learned from their experiences?

2. Many of the stories in "Quests and Conquests" contained fantasy. Think of other books or stories you have read or heard that contain fantasy. Choose one book or story and give an example of fantasy in it. If the book or story you choose is science fiction, point this out.

3. Matthew, Kayak, and Billie Wind all shared a common goal—survival. In what ways was Matthew and Kayak's battle to survive like that of Billie Wind? In what ways was it different?

4. The characters in "Quests and Conquests" had certain qualities that helped them reach their goals. What qualities do you think are important in reaching a goal?

5. Jocelyn Bell and Howard Carter were involved in quests that resulted in important scientific contributions to the world. Think about other people you have read about or have heard about who made important contributions to the world—scientific or otherwise. Choose one person and tell why you think his or her contribution is important.

6. "Going to the Dogs . . . and Cats" was appealing because James Herriot used colorful language to describe his friends and animal patients. Look through the other selections in "Quests and Conquests" and choose one that contains examples of descriptive language. Give an example of descriptive language in it. Tell why it is a good description.

7. Think about a quest that you might like to make. Tell about the quest. Why do you want to make the quest? What problems do you think you might encounter? How would you go about solving the problems?

Read on Your Own

Bright Stars, Red Giants and White Dwarfs by Melvin Berger. Putnam. The author describes the stages in the birth, life, and death of stars.

New Found Land by John Christopher. Dutton. Simon and his cousin Brad encounter a strange fireball and are transported back in time, where fascinating adventures await them.

King Tut's Game Board by Leona Ellerby. Lerner. Jason Sanders makes a startling discovery about his friend Nate in the Valley of the Kings, burial place of Egypt's pharaohs.

The Talking Earth by Jean Craighead George. Harper & Row. Billie Wind goes out alone into the Florida Everglades to find out about the legends of her Indian ancestors.

Breakthrough: Women in Science by Diane C. Gleasner. Walker. Included are short biographies of six women scientists whose efforts led to important scientific discoveries.

All Creatures Great and Small by James Herriot. Bantam. Under the pen name of James Herriot, a British veterinarian gives accounts of the people he meets and his animal patients.

Frozen Fire by James Houston. Atheneum. Matthew Morgan and his friend Kayak brave storms, starvation, and wild animals during their search for Matthew's father in the Canadian Arctic.

The Keeper of the Isis Light by Monica Hughes. Atheneum. Olwen lives on the planet Isis, where she encounters a group of settlers from Earth.

The Farthest Shore by Ursula K. Le Guin. Atheneum. Ged, the Archmage of Roke Knoll, sets out to meet unknown dangers, to confront his own past, and to test ancient prophecies.

The Tombs of Atuan by Ursula K. Le Guin. Atheneum. Ged, the young wizard of Roke Knoll, seeks a treasure hidden in a desolate cavern called the Place of Tombs.

A Wizard of Earthsea by Ursula K. Le Guin. Houghton Mifflin. Ged, a young apprentice wizard, is pursued by an unknown power called the shadow.

A Wrinkle in Time by Madeleine L'Engle. Farrar, Straus & Giroux. Meg, Charles Wallace, and Calvin O'Keefe search for Meg's father, a scientist who disappeared while working on a secret project.

Ancient Civilizations by Anne Millard. Warwick Press. The author describes major archaeological digs around the world.

Singularity by William Sleator. Dutton. The relationship between twins Harry and Barry changes when they discover a gateway to another universe, where time and space are distorted.

King Beetle-Tamer and Other Lighthearted Wonder Tales by Isabel Wyatt. Dawne-Leigh Publications. Included are lighthearted tales about fantastic creatures and incredible people.

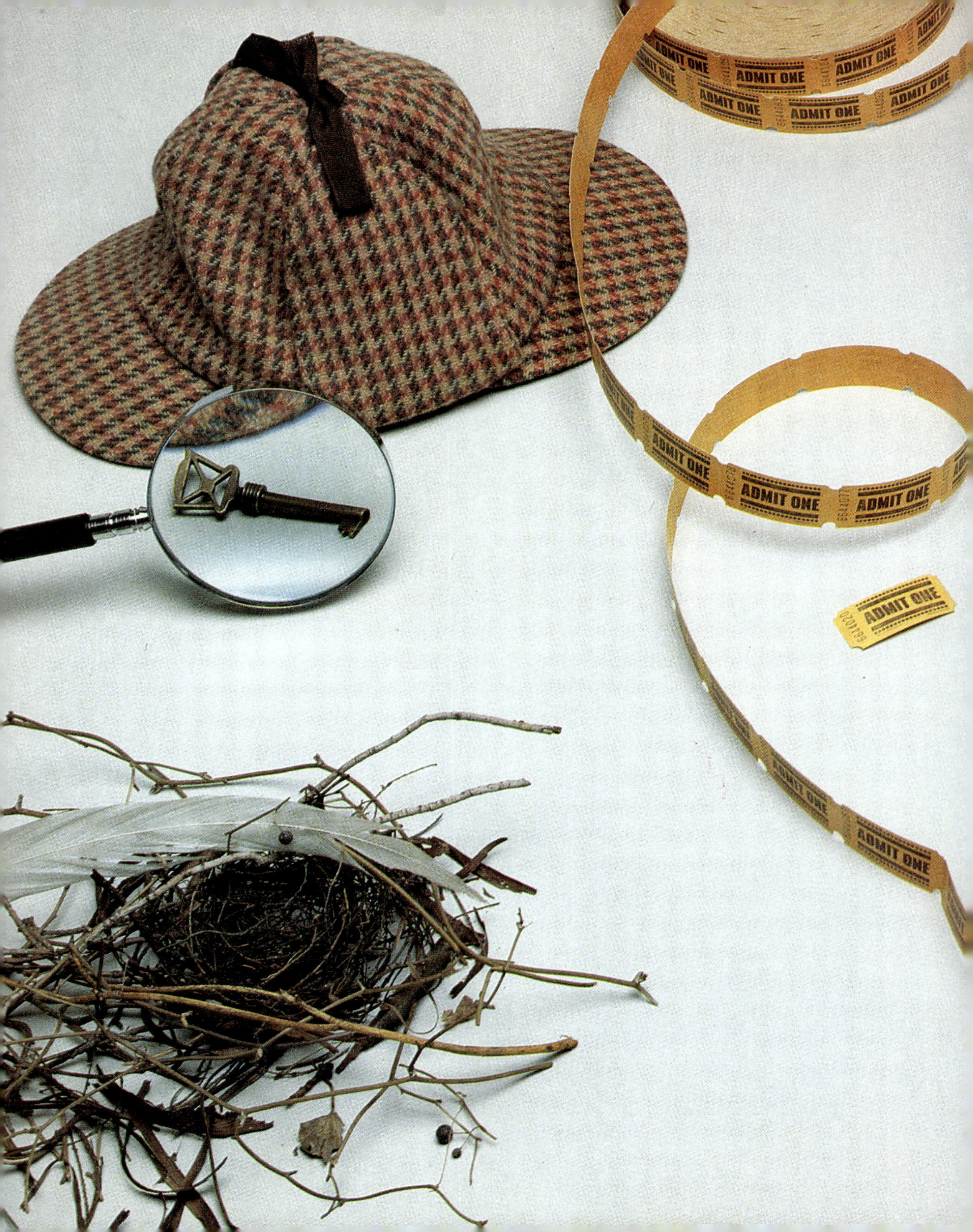
ADMIT ONE

Unit 2

Galaxies

You are now entering a new and exciting stage of your life. It is time for you to set new goals — to expand your horizons. You will be looking for answers to many questions: What do you believe in? What do you value in life? What kind of a person do you want to be?

As you explore the world around you, you will find new hobbies and interests. Some may be passing fancies, while others could be a source of enjoyment for many years. Among these new pursuits, you may discover talents and abilities you didn't know you had. You might even find an ability or interest that will lead to a long-lasting career.

Just as our planet is part of a galaxy or system of stars, so each of us is part of the galaxy of human experience. One way to explore this galaxy is by reading about people who have lived in other places and at other times. Stories you read can help you discover things about yourself. Would you make a choice in the same way a story character does? Would you solve the problem in a different way? Reading can help you discover new worlds of knowledge. You will become aware of subjects you want to learn more about. You will learn about people, places, and things that are shaping the world of the future — your future.

As you read the selections in this unit, think about what you have discovered. See what place each discovery has in your own personal galaxy.

Literature Study

Realistic Fiction

A story that seems real but has made-up characters and events is called **realistic fiction**. In this kind of story, you will meet characters who are like many people you know in real life. They live in houses, shop in stores, and ride in cars, buses, trains, and airplanes. The characters and events are made up by an author, are believable, and seem real; yet realistic fiction never really happened. It only seems, while you are reading it, as if it could happen because the setting and characters are realistic.

Here are some characteristics of realistic fiction:

- an illusion of reality, a believable "slice-of-life"
- characters who are like many people we know
- real-world settings
- themes that deal with basic truths of human nature
- language similar to natural spoken language

Setting in Realistic Fiction

Most realistic fiction is set in the present. It can, however, be set in the past. Sometimes realistic fiction set in the past gives facts about important real people or events from history. This kind of realistic fiction is called **historical fiction**. Historical fiction mixes historical facts with fictional details.

Realistic-fiction authors try to make their characters do things in a way that will be familiar to the reader. An author often begins a story by giving clues that tell readers when and where a story takes place. In this way, the reader will know what kind of a story to expect. Read this example of realistic fiction.

>   Jimmy and Marcia walked with their lunchboxes to the corner where the school bus stopped each morning. They couldn't talk about anything except the Clayton Junior High Track Meet that was going to be held at four

o'clock in the afternoon. This was to be the most important meet of the month, and they were both afraid of running in it. They kept wondering if they would get over their fear by the time the meet began. The more they tried to talk about something else, the more they thought of the track meet. Jimmy's left hand squeezed tightly around the handle of his lunchbox. Marcia just clenched her fist and whistled.

As you read the passage above, what clues did you notice that tell you this story is realistic fiction? For example, the characters and the events seem real. Jimmy and Marcia seem to be like many young people their age. They are acting in the same way many boys and girls would act before an important track meet at school.

Plot in Realistic Fiction

When you tell what happens in a story, you are talking about the plot. Plot is the sequence of events in a story. Short stories, novels, dramas, and narrative poems all have plots. Many times, especially in novels and plays, there will be more than one plot.

In realistic fiction, the plot is usually less complicated than in other kinds of fiction. This is because it is hard to present an illusion of realism within a very complicated plot. For example, readers can become suspicious of too many lucky occurrences during an unusual and difficult struggle. When the series of events seem too good to be true, the plot doesn't seem logical to the reader. For this reason, realistic fiction often presents an ordinary day in someone's life — a time and place in which nothing extraordinary happens, as in a lot of people's lives.

Presenting an ordinary day in one's life is called **slice-of-life fiction.** The author presents the reader with a mood, a sense of atmosphere, or a look into someone's life. A lot of unusual things don't have to happen in slice-of-life fiction. In fact, only realistic fiction can handle the slice-of-life approach to writing. Other kinds of fiction are more dependent on plot, especially on the element of conflict where a struggle of some kind takes place.

In realistic fiction, the characters, settings, and plots are generally quite believable. In this kind of fiction, you meet people who seem and act like many people you know. Much fiction is based on real personal experience even though it almost always involves invented characters, actions, settings, or details.

A stranger's visit helps a young girl expand her horizons and make an important decision. What important decision does the girl, Sylvia, make?

As you read, notice the characteristics of realistic fiction in this story and look for examples of each.

A White Heron

by Sarah Orne Jewett

The woods were already filled with shadows one June evening, just before eight o'clock, though a bright sunset still glimmered faintly among the trunks of the trees. A little girl was driving home her cow — a plodding, provoking creature in her behavior, but a valued companion for all that. They were going away from the western light, and striking deep into the dark woods, but their feet were familiar with the path, and it did not matter whether their eyes could see it or not.

There was hardly a night the summer through when the old cow could be found waiting at the pasture edge. On the contrary, it was her greatest pleasure to hide herself away among the high huckleberry bushes. Though she wore a loud bell, she had made the discovery that if she stood perfectly still it would not ring. So Sylvia had to hunt for her until she found her, and call "Co'! Co'!" with never an answering moo, until her childish patience was quite spent.

If the creature had not given good milk and plenty of it, the case would have seemed very different to her owners. Besides, Sylvia had all the time there was, and very little use to make of it. Sometimes in pleasant weather it was a consolation to look upon the cow's pranks as an intelligent attempt to play hide and seek. As Sylvia had no playmates, she lent herself to this amusement with a good deal of zest. Though this chase had been long, Sylvia had only laughed when she came upon the cow at the swampside. Then she urged the cow affectionately homeward with a twig of birch leaves. The old cow was not inclined to wander farther — she even turned in the right direction for once as they left the pasture, and stepped along the road at a good pace. She was quite ready to be milked now, and seldom stopped to graze. Sylvia wondered what her grandmother would say because they were so late. It was a great while since she had left home at half past five o'clock, but everybody knew the difficulty of making this errand a short one. Mrs. Tilley had chased the horned torment too many summer evenings herself to blame anyone else for lingering. She was only thankful as she waited that she had Sylvia, nowadays, to give such valuable assistance. The good woman suspected that Sylvia loitered occasionally on her own account. There never was such a child for straying out-of-doors since the world was made! Everybody said that it was a good change for a little maid who had tried to grow for eight years in a crowded manufacturing town. As for Sylvia herself, it seemed as if she never had been alive at all before she came to live at the farm.

"Afraid of folks," old Mrs. Tilley said to herself, with a smile, after she had made the unlikely choice of Sylvia from her daughter's houseful of children, and was returning to the farm. " 'Afraid of folks,' they said! I guess she won't be troubled with 'em up at the old place!" When they reached the door of the lonely house and stopped to unlock it, and the cat came to purr loudly, and rub against them, Sylvia whispered that this was a beautiful place to live in, and she never would wish to go home.

The companions followed the shady wood road, the cow taking slow steps, and the child very fast ones. The cow stopped long at the brook to drink, and Sylvia stood still and waited, letting her bare feet cool themselves in the water. The great twilight moths flew softly against her. She waded on through the brook as the cow moved away, and listened to the thrushes with a heart that beat fast with pleasure. There was a stirring in the great boughs overhead. They were full of little birds and beasts that seemed to be wide awake, and going about their world, or else saying good night to each other in sleepy twitters. Sylvia herself felt sleepy as she walked along. However, it was not much farther to the house, and the air was soft and sweet. She was not often in the woods as late as this. It made her feel as if she were a part of the gray shadows and the moving leaves. She was just thinking how long it seemed since she first came to the farm a year ago. She wondered if everything went on in the noisy town just the same as when she was there. The thought of the great red-faced boy who used to chase and frighten her made her hurry along the path to escape from the shadow of the trees.

Suddenly this little woods-girl was horror-stricken to hear a clear whistle not very far away. Not a bird's whistle, which would have a sort of friendliness, but a boy's whistle, determined, and somewhat aggressive. Sylvia left the cow to whatever sad fate might await her, and stepped discreetly aside into the bushes. But she was just too late. The enemy had discovered her, and called out in a very cheerful and persuasive tone, "Hello, little girl, how far is it to the road?" Trembling, Sylvia answered almost inaudibly, "A good ways."

She did not dare to look boldly at the tall young man, who carried a gun over his shoulder, but she came out of her hiding place and again followed the cow, while he walked alongside.

"I have been hunting for some birds," the stranger said kindly. "I have lost my way, and need a friend very much. Don't be afraid," he added gallantly. "Speak up and tell me what your name is. Do you think I can spend the night at your house, and go out hunting early in the morning?"

Sylvia was more alarmed than before. Would not her grandmother consider her much to blame? But who could have foreseen such an accident as this? It did not appear to be her fault. She hung her head as if the stem of it were broken, but managed to answer "Sylvy," with much effort when her companion again asked her name.

Mrs. Tilley was standing in the doorway when the trio came into view. The cow gave a loud moo by way of explanation.

"Yes, you'd better speak up for yourself, you old trial! Where'd she tuck herself away this time, Sylvy?" Sylvia kept an awed silence. She knew her grandmother must be mistaking the stranger for a farmer-lad of the region.

The young man stood his gun beside the door, and dropped a heavy game bag beside it. Then he bade Mrs. Tilley good evening, and repeated his wayfarer's story, and asked if he could have a night's lodging.

"Put me anywhere you like," he said. "I must be off early in the morning, before day. But I am very hungry indeed. You can give me some milk at any rate."

"Dear sakes, yes," responded the hostess, whose long-slumbering hospitality seemed to be easily awakened. "You might fare better if you went out on the main road a mile or so, but you're welcome to what we've got. I'll milk right off, and you make yourself at home. Now step round and set a plate for the gentleman, Sylvy!" Sylvia promptly stepped. She was glad to have something to do, and she was hungry herself.

It was a surprise to find so clean and comfortable a little dwelling in this New England wilderness. The young man listened eagerly to the old woman's quaint talk. He watched Sylvia's pale face and shining gray eyes with ever-growing enthusiasm, and insisted that this was the best supper he had eaten for a month. Then, afterward, the new friends sat down in the doorway together while the moon came up.

Soon it would be berry time, and Sylvia was a great help at picking. The cow was a good milker, though a plaguy thing to keep track of. The hostess gossiped frankly, adding presently that she had buried four children, so that Sylvia's mother and a son in California were all the children she had left. "Dan, my boy, was a great hand to go hunting," she explained sadly. "I never wanted for partridges or gray squer'ls while he was at home. He's been a great wanderer, I expect, and he's not one to write letters. There, I don't blame him, I'd have seen the world myself if it had been so I could.

"Sylvia takes after him," the grandmother continued affectionately, after a minute's pause. "There ain't a foot of ground she don't know her way over, and the wild creatures counts her one of themselves. Squer'ls she'll tame to come and feed right out of her hands, and all sorts of birds. Last winter she got the jaybirds here, and I believe she'd have scanted herself of her own meals to have plenty to throw out amongst 'em, if I hadn't kept watch. Anything but crows, I tell her, I'm willin' to help support. Dan, he went and tamed one of them that did seem to have reason same as folks. It was round here a good spell after he went away."

"So Sylvy knows all about birds, does she?" he exclaimed, as he looked round at the little girl who sat, very demure but increasingly sleepy, in the moonlight. "I am making a collection of birds myself. I have been at it ever since I was a boy." Mrs. Tilley smiled. "There are two or three very rare ones I have been hunting for these five years. I mean to get them on my own ground if they can be found."

"Do you cage them up?" asked Mrs. Tilley doubtfully, in response to this enthusiastic announcement.

"Oh, no, they're stuffed and preserved, dozens and dozens of them," said the ornithologist. "I have shot or snared every one myself. I caught a glimpse of a white heron three miles from here on Saturday, and I have followed it in this direction. They have never been found in this district at all. The white heron." He turned again to look at Sylvia with the hope of discovering that the rare bird was one of her acquaintances.

But Sylvia was watching a hoptoad in the narrow footpath.

"You would know the heron if you saw it," the stranger continued eagerly. "A strange tall white bird with soft feathers and long thin legs. And it would have a nest perhaps in the top of a high tree, made of sticks, something like a hawk's nest."

Sylvia's heart gave a wild beat. She knew that strange white bird, and had once stolen softly near where it stood in some bright green swamp grass, away over at the other side of the woods. There was an open place where the sunshine always seemed strangely yellow and hot, where tall, nodding rushes grew, and her grandmother had warned her that she might sink in the soft black mud underneath and never be heard of more. Not far beyond were the salt marshes. Beyond those was the sea, the sea which Sylvia wondered and dreamed about, but never had looked upon, though its great voice could often be heard above the noise of the woods on stormy nights.

"I can't think of anything I should like so much as to find that heron's nest," the handsome stranger was saying. "I would give ten dollars to anybody who could show it to me," he added desperately. "I mean to spend my whole vacation hunting for it if need be. Perhaps it was only migrating, or had been chased out of its own region by some bird of prey."

Mrs. Tilley gave amazed attention to all this. Sylvia still watched the toad, not understanding, as she might have done at some calmer time, that the creature wished to get to its hole under the doorstep, and was much hindered by the unusual spectators at that hour of the evening. No amount of thought, that night, could help Sylvia decide how many wished-for treasures the ten dollars, so lightly spoken of, would buy her.

The next day the young sportsman hovered about the woods, and Sylvia kept him company. She had lost her first fear of the friendly lad, who proved to be most kind and sympathetic. He told her many things about the birds and what they knew and where they lived and what they did with themselves. And he gave her a jackknife, which she thought as great a treasure as if she were a desert-islander. All day long he did not once make her troubled or afraid except when he brought down some unsuspecting singing creature from its bough. Sylvia would have liked him vastly better without his gun. She could not understand why he killed the very birds he seemed to like so much. But as the day waned, Sylvia still watched the young man with loving admiration. She had never seen anybody so charming and delightful. The two stopped to listen to a bird's song. They pressed forward again eagerly, parting the branches — speaking to each other rarely and in whispers; the young man going first and Sylvia following, fascinated, a few steps behind, with her gray eyes dark with excitement.

She grieved because the longed-for white heron was elusive, but she did not lead the guest, she only followed, and there was no such thing as speaking first. The sound of her own unquestioned voice would have terrified her. It was hard enough to answer yes or no when there was need of that. At last evening began to fall, and they drove the cow home together. Sylvia smiled with pleasure when they came to the place where she heard the whistle and was afraid only the night before.

Half a mile from home, at the farther edge of the woods, where the land was highest, a great pine tree stood, the last of its generation. Whether it was left for a boundary mark, or for what reason, no one could say. The wood choppers who had felled its mates were dead and gone long ago, and a whole forest of sturdy trees — pines and oaks and maples — had grown again. But the stately head of this old pine towered above them all and made a landmark for sea and shore miles and miles away. Sylvia knew it well. She had always believed that whoever climbed to the top of it could see the ocean. The little girl often laid her hand on the great rough trunk and looked up wistfully at those dark boughs that the wind always stirred, no matter how hot and still the air might be below. Now she thought of the tree with a new excitement. If one climbed it at break of day, could not one see all the world, and easily discover whence the white heron flew, and mark the place, and find the hidden nest?

What a spirit of adventure, what wild ambition! What fancied triumph and delight and glory for the later morning when she could make known the secret to her new friend! It was almost too real and too great for her to bear.

All night the door of the little house stood open. The whippoorwills came and sang upon the very step. The young sportsman and his old hostess were sound asleep, but Sylvia's great design kept her awake and watching. She forgot to think of sleep. The short summer night seemed as long as the winter darkness. At last when the whippoorwills ceased, and she was afraid the morning would after all come too soon, she stole out of the house and followed the pasture path through the woods. She hastened toward the open ground beyond, listening with a sense of comfort and companionship to the drowsy sound of a half-awakened bird whose perch she had jarred in passing.

There was the huge tree asleep yet in the paling moonlight. Small and hopeful Sylvia began with utmost bravery to climb to the top of it. First she must climb the white oak tree that grew alongside, where she was almost lost among the dark branches and the green leaves heavy and wet with dew. A bird fluttered off its nest, and a red squirrel ran to and fro and scolded pettishly at the harmless housebreaker. Sylvia felt her way easily. She had often climbed there. She knew that higher still one of the oak's upper branches rubbed against the pine trunk, just where its lower boughs were set close together. There, when she made the dangerous pass from one tree to the other, the great enterprise would really begin.

She crept out along the swaying oak limb at last, and took the daring step across into the old pine tree. The way was harder than she thought. She must reach far and hold fast. The sharp dry twigs caught and held her and scratched her like angry talons. The pitch that oozed from the bark made her thin little fingers clumsy and stiff as she went round and round the tree's great stem, higher and higher upward. The sparrows and robins in the woods below were beginning to wake and sing to the dawn, yet it seemed much lighter there aloft in the pine tree, and the child knew that she must hurry if her project were to be of any use.

   The tree seemed to lengthen itself out as she went up, and to reach farther and farther upward. It was like a great mainmast to the voyaging earth. It must truly have been amazed that morning through all its ponderous frame as it felt this determined spark of human spirit creeping and climbing from higher branch to branch.

Sylvia's face was like a pale star, as she stood trembling and tired but wholly triumphant, high in the treetop. Yes, there was the sea with the dawning sun making a golden dazzle over it, and toward that glorious east flew two hawks with slow-moving pinions. How low they looked in the air from the height when before one had only seen them far up, and dark against the blue sky. Their bright feathers were as soft as moths. They seemed only a little way from the tree, and Sylvia felt as if she too could go flying away among the clouds. Westward, the woodlands and farms reached miles and miles into the distance; here and there were church steeples, and white villages. Truly it was a vast and fascinating world.

The birds sang louder and louder. At last the sun came up bewilderingly bright. Sylvia could see the white sails of ships out at sea. The clouds that were purple and rose-colored and yellow at first began to fade away. Where was the white heron's nest in the sea of green branches? Was this wonderful sight and pageant of the world the only reward for having climbed to such a giddy height? Now look down again, Sylvia, where the green marsh is set among the shining birches and dark hemlocks. There where you saw the white heron once, you will see it again. Look, look! A white spot of it like a single floating feather comes up from the dead hemlock and grows larger, and rises, and comes close at last, and goes by the landmark pine with steady sweep of wing and outstretched slender neck and crested head. Wait! Wait! Do not move a foot or a finger, little girl. Do not send an arrow of light and consciousness from your two eager eyes, for the heron has perched on a pine bough not far beyond yours, and cries back to its mate on the nest, and plumes its feathers for the new day!

   The child gives a long sigh a minute later when a company of shouting catbirds comes also to the tree. Vexed by their fluttering and lawlessness the solemn heron goes away. She

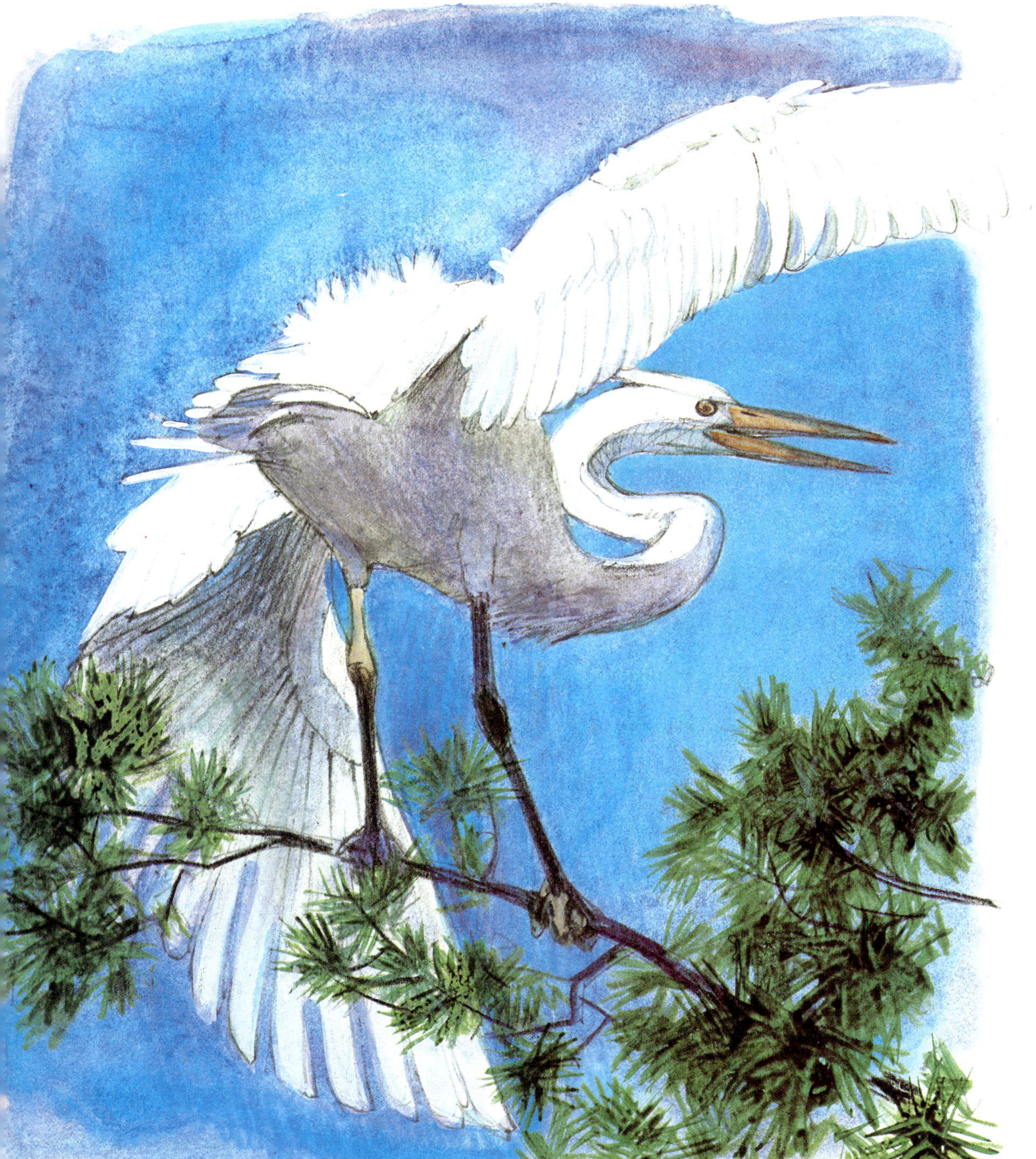

knows its secret now — the wild, light, slender bird that floats and wavers, and goes back like an arrow presently to its home in the green world beneath. Then Sylvia, well-satisfied, makes her perilous way down again, not daring to look far below the branch she stands on, ready to cry sometimes because her fingers ache and her lamed feet slip. She wonders over and over again what the stranger will say to her, and what he will think when she tells him how to find his way straight to the heron's nest.

"Sylvy, Sylvy!" called the busy old grandmother again and again, but nobody answered. The small bed was empty, and Sylvia had disappeared.

The guest waked from a dream, and remembering his day's pleasure, hurried to dress himself that it might sooner begin. He was sure from the way the shy little girl looked once or twice yesterday that she had at least seen the white heron, and now she must really be persuaded to tell. Here she comes now, paler than ever. Her worn old frock is torn and tattered, and smeared with pine pitch. The grandmother and the sportsman stand in the door together and question her. The splendid moment has come to speak of the dead hemlock tree by the green marsh.

But Sylvia does not speak after all, though the old grandmother fretfully rebukes her, and the young man's kind appealing eyes are looking straight into her own. He can make them rich with money. He has promised it, and they are poor now. He is so well worth making happy, and he waits to hear the story she can tell.

No, she must keep silent! What is it that suddenly forbids her and makes her mute? Has she been nine years growing, and now, when the great world for the first time puts out a hand to her, must she thrust it aside for a bird's sake? The murmur of the pine's green branches is in her ears. She remembers how the white heron came flying through the golden air and how they watched the sea and the morning together. Sylvia cannot speak. She cannot tell the heron's secret and give its life away.

Discuss the Selection

1. What important decision did Sylvia make?
2. How did Sylvia's feelings toward the ornithologist change during the story?
3. Find the paragraph that describes Sylvia's feelings toward the ornithologist when she first meets him. Then find the paragraph that describes Sylvia's change in feelings.
4. If it had not been for the stranger's interest in the white heron, do you think Sylvia would have climbed the tree to find the nest?
5. Why did Sylvia decide not to reveal where the white heron could be found?

Apply the Skills

In realistic fiction, the characters, settings, and plots are usually quite believable. What characteristics of realistic fiction did the author include in this story? Give an example of each.

Think and Write

Prewrite

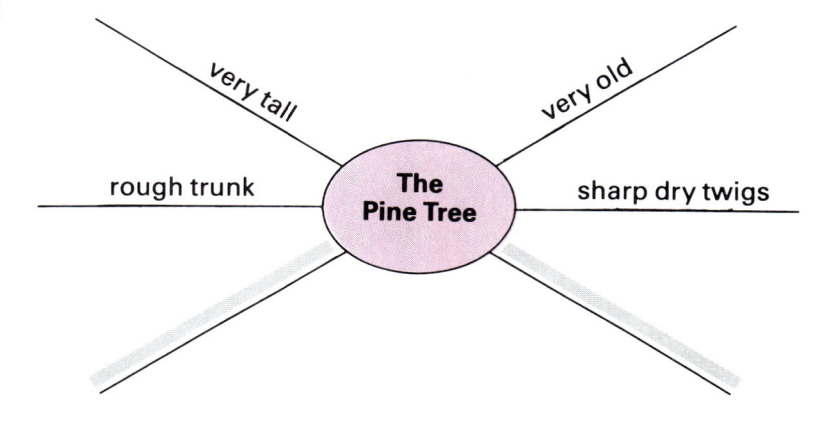

```
    very tall          very old
              ┌──────┐
              │ The  │
  rough trunk │ Pine │ sharp dry twigs
              │ Tree │
              └──────┘
```

Paragraphs that describe places and things are built around sensory experiences — the things one sees, hears, touches, tastes, and smells. Putting sensory experiences into words is part of the author's craft. Copy the diagram shown above, including the descriptions of the pine tree that are already on the diagram. Then add descriptive words used by author Sarah Orne Jewett in "A White Heron."

Compose

Using the information in the diagram and the story itself, write a paragraph describing the pine tree. Include as many sensory details as possible. You might start with this topic sentence: *To seafarers, the old pine tree was like a lighthouse; to small woodland creatures, it was a shelter.*

Revise

Read the descriptive paragraph that you just wrote. Did you include examples of sensory language? Will someone who has not read "A White Heron" be able to picture the pine tree? If not, revise your work.

Jigsaw Puzzle
by Russell Hoban

My beautiful picture of pirates and treasure
Is spoiled, and almost I don't want to start
To put it together; I've lost all the pleasure
I used to find in it: There's one missing part.

I know there's one missing — they lost it, the others,
The last time they played with my puzzle — and maybe
There's more than one missing: along with the brothers
And sisters who borrow my toys there's the baby.

There's a hole in the ship or the sea that it sails on,
And I said to my father, "Well, what shall I do?
It isn't the same now that some of it's gone."
He said, "Put it together; the world's like that too."

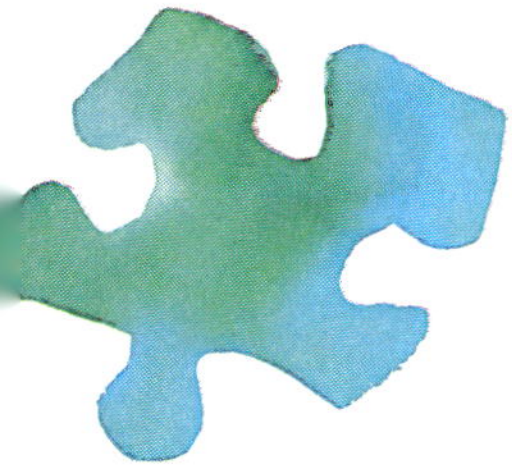

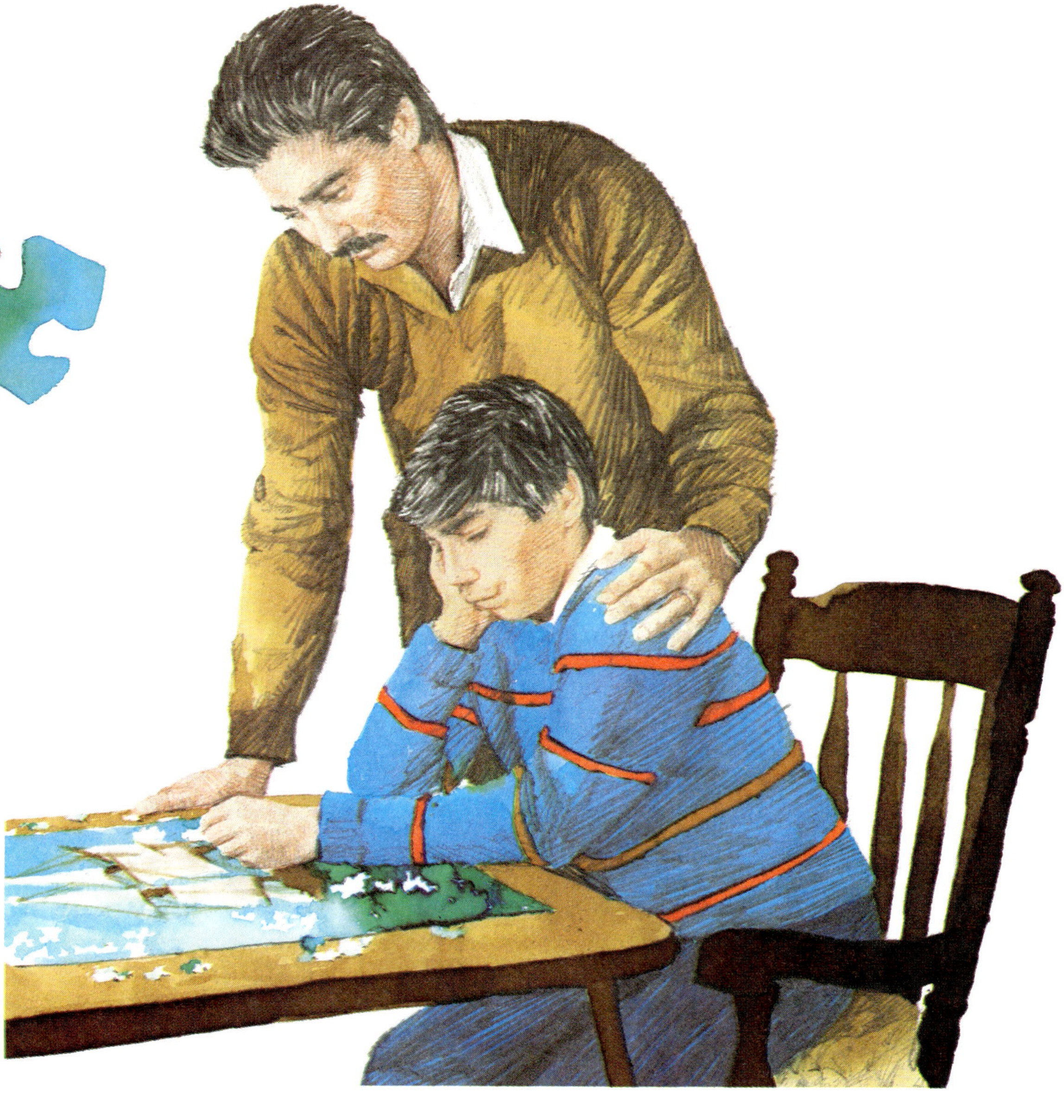

Comprehension Study

Make Generalizations

A **generalization** is a broad general statement that is supported by facts and that, in most cases, is true. Recognizing generalizations is an important reading skill.

You may have heard a statement similar to this one: *Exercise makes people feel better*. Although that statement is generally true, there are exceptions. For example, some people can't exercise because of their physical condition. Others just don't like to exercise. But since most people feel better if they exercise, the statement is a **valid** generalization. This means that the generalization is true most of the time. If you and your friends and relatives like to exercise, you probably judged the statement as a valid generalization. We all tend to generalize from our personal experiences.

Read the following paragraph and find the broad, general statement. Notice the facts that come before the generalization. Then, judge whether the generalization is valid.

> Some Greek legends describe mythological characters who tried to fly. Centuries later, during the Italian Renaissance, Leonardo da Vinci sketched a flying machine powered by the muscles of the human leg. Today, space flights are routine, and spacecraft have carried people to the moon. Sky diving, an increasingly popular sport, allows people to glide through the air in giant, motorless kites. For centuries, many people have dreamed of flying.

In the paragraph you have just read, the author's generalization is given in the last sentence: *For centuries, many people have dreamed of flying.*

What facts are given to support this generalization? The author mentions three periods of history — the era of the ancient Greeks, the Renaissance, and the present. For each period, an example of people's interest in flying is given. The author's generalization about people's desire to fly is based on the facts presented.

Reread the generalization about people dreaming of flying. Notice the use of the word *many*. Qualifying words such as *many, most, all, some, none, always, often, usually, generally, sometimes*, and *never* are often used to signal generalizations. When you come across one of these words in your reading, examine the sentence to see whether the author is making the type of broad statement known as a generalization.

Valid Generalizations and Faulty Generalizations

A generalization is considered valid if it gives enough facts, takes all the facts into account, and is true in most cases. In the paragraph on flying, notice that the generalization in the last sentence is supported by facts contained in the sentences before it. Whether the supporting facts come before or after the generalization, they are needed to make the statement valid.

A generalization has to be true in most cases, not in every case, in order to be valid. It is unlikely that everyone throughout history has wanted to fly. The author acknowledges this by saying that many people, not all people, dream of flying.

A generalization is not valid, it is **faulty,** if it is not true in most cases, or if it is not supported with enough facts. The following paragraph contains a faulty generalization. Find the generalization and decide what is wrong with it.

> Leonardo da Vinci had many talents other than painting. He was a town planner, mathematician, engineer, and inventor. He was also interested in many sciences, including geology and botany. Great artists are very versatile.

Notice that the author's generalization is given in the last sentence: *Great artists are very versatile*. This generalization is faulty because it is not backed up by enough facts. Leonardo da Vinci was versatile, but that does not mean that every great artist is talented in so many different areas. There are probably a great number of exceptions to the generalization. Remember, for a generalization to be valid, it must be true in most cases. If it is not true in most cases, it is faulty.

What you already know and have experienced can help you decide whether a generalization is valid. When you read about Leonardo da Vinci's many talents, you probably realized that most artists are not as versatile as he was. If you are not sure whether a generalization is valid, look for more facts in a reference book.

Generalizing and Drawing Conclusions from Graphic Aids

Authors often use tables, charts, and other graphic aids to present facts. Then, they draw conclusions based on facts they present. They may also go another step by drawing a generalization from the conclusions.

Study the following table and the generalization drawn from it.

Museum Attendance for One Week

	Air Museum	Art Museum	History Museum	Nature Museum	Science Museum
Mon.	85	closed	closed	110	170
Tues.	closed	150	140	100	closed
Wed.	118	130	124	91	180
Thurs.	98	160	132	100	144
Fri.	160	200	180	125	205
Sat.	220	415	250	230	390
Sun.	374	550	426	390	600

The five museums shown in the table offer different types of exhibits. Nevertheless, you can draw several conclusions about attendance patterns at these museums. Using the table for reference, you may conclude that attendance at all five museums is highest on Sunday, with the second highest attendance on Saturday. Attendance at the four museums that are closed one day a week increases on the day after the museum is closed, but decreases the next day. Notice that the conclusions are drawn from the specific facts shown in the table.

Based on the facts, this generalization, or broad statement can be made: *Generally, more people visit museums on weekends than in the middle of the week.*

This generalization is valid in light of the facts. Notice that the word *generally* is used to show that the generalization is not true all the time, just most of the time.

Textbook Application: Make Generalizations in Social Studies

In textbooks and other nonfiction works, good authors back up their generalizations with facts. They also use words such as *generally*, *usually*, and *many* to signal a generalization. The facts presented by the author, along with what you already know, can help you decide whether a generalization is valid. Remember, to be valid, a generalization must be true in most cases.

Read the following excerpt from a social studies textbook. Use the sidenotes to help you find the generalizations.

In the difficult years following the American Revolution, some schools had to close. The few that continued to operate were supported by churches or private individuals.

> In this paragraph, the generalization comes before the facts. Notice the qualifying word *often* in the third sentence.

These free schools had many problems. They were overcrowded and could not afford to pay well-trained teachers. As a result, the number of subjects taught in the free schools was often limited. Pupils studied reading, writing, and arithmetic, but little else.

> The last sentence in this paragraph is a generalization. Notice the qualifying word *usually*.

Since the schools depended mainly on charity for support, many parents considered it a disgrace to send their children to these schools. Some well-to-do parents hired tutors to teach their children. People with less money usually did not educate their children at all.

As time went by, however, many of the nation's leaders became troubled by the lack of equal opportunity in education. To correct this situation, they began to demand free public schools supported by taxes.

> Americans realized that in a nation where the people govern themselves, all citizens should be educated. Thomas Jefferson was an outstanding supporter of this belief. He tried to start a system of free public schools in Virginia that would educate even the poorest children.
>
> — *America: Its People and Values,*
> Harcourt Brace Jovanovich

The first sentence in this paragraph is a generalization. Probably not all Americans cared about education in this way.

From the facts presented in the excerpt you just read, which of the following generalizations do you consider valid?

1. In the time soon after the American Revolution, no one received a good education.
2. In the time soon after the American Revolution, education was far different from what it is today.

The facts support the second generalization. Learn to base generalizations on facts.

Paying close attention to the world around him led Thomas Gallaudet to a discovery that widened the horizon of his life. Read to find out about Thomas Gallaudet's discovery and how it affected his life.

As you read, try to make some generalizations based on the selection.

A Deaf Child Listened

by Anne E. Neimark

Thomas Gallaudet was an idealistic young man who wanted to do something to benefit humanity. Although he was physically weak because of poor health, his mind was strong from many years of studying hard.

Thomas Gallaudet kept a diary in which he wrote of how he "used to delight to dwell upon what *might* be, and to conjure up such scenes of prosperity for myself and friends and all mankind."

After graduating from Yale College at the age of nineteen, Thomas wrote stories for children, tutored at Yale, and became a traveling merchant and then a traveling minister. Through these jobs, he discovered his passion for educating people, sharing his vision of "what *might* be." This excerpt from his biography begins in 1814, when Thomas was twenty-six years old. He was feeling disappointed that his poor health kept him from doing something "worthy" with his life.

On a warm day in early summer, Thomas Gallaudet walked down Main Street in Hartford, Connecticut, pausing in the dimness of the Jeremy Addams Inn for a glass of water and circling past the millinery shop with its window full of whalebone bonnets on stands. On Prospect Street, he unbuttoned his waistcoat and removed his hat. Trees splayed their branches into arches of brown and green, and squirrels were darting across picket fences. At the front path to the family house, Thomas felt weary. The shade of the small wooden porch tempted him, and he sat down on the steps and balanced his hat on one knee.

A cardinal soared from the porch roof, a flash of brilliant red, and then the quiet of the afternoon was broken by a burst of laughter. Turning toward the left end of the house, Thomas saw a group of children in a boisterous game of tag. Some of his younger sisters and brothers were at the heels of a boy in checkered britches. The children waved at Thomas and raced on, whooping like buccaneers. Soon the boy in the checkered britches was caught and stood, blindfolded, in a circle of his former chasers. Tottering forward, he was to tag the next object of sport.

All at once, at the edge of the lawn, Thomas noticed a little girl who had not taken part in the play. She looked about eight or nine years of age and was neatly dressed in a pink pinafore. A blankness in her face arrested Thomas's interest. He saw the child stare at the commotion around her. She didn't appear ill. Why hadn't one of the children asked her to join the game?

He called out to his brother Teddy. As the nine-year-old hopped onto the steps, face aflame, he was questioned about the little girl in the ruffled pink dress. Oh! Teddy said, she was Alice from down the street. Dr. Cogswell's daughter. She was deaf. She couldn't hear anything or talk. She didn't know she was Alice.

Teddy sped away to the clamoring children, and Thomas walked slowly across the lawn toward Alice Cogswell. Under a tree, he bent down to pluck a tiny violet and offer it to the child. She sniffed at the flower warily but let Thomas take her hand, and together they walked to the porch and sat on the wooden steps. Rubbing the flower over her eyelids, Alice finally held it against her nose.

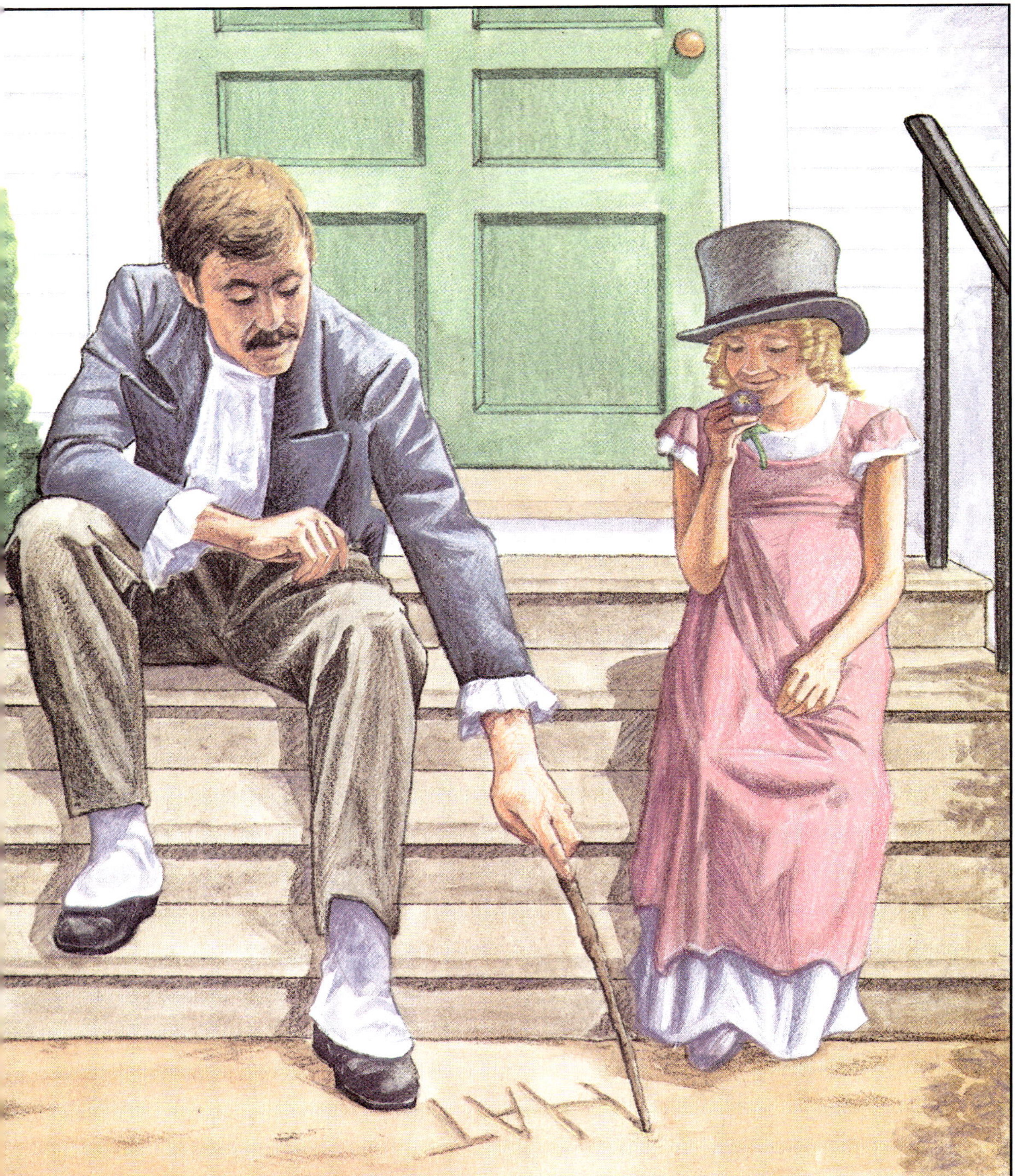
HAT

Deafness in the 1800's meant a life of hopelessness and uselessness. The winter before, while in Boston to preach, Thomas had rescued a deaf-mute boy from a grimy alley. Two dock workers had clapped their hands over the boy's ears and mocked him with guttural sounds.

Now, Thomas glanced at the child who sat so quietly at his side. Her blond hair fell in ringlets to her shoulders. She didn't seem afflicted — but then, why should she? Deafness was not a crippled leg or missing arm. It didn't show. Who would have presumed that Dr. Cogswell's young daughter lived without words in a silent prison?

"You don't even know that your name is Alice," he said.

Putting his hat on Alice Cogswell's head, he smiled at her. An idea was taking root in his mind. He reached to pick up a stray stick from beneath the steps and drew the letters *H A T* in the sandy dirt. With the word completed, he retrieved his top hat and positioned it directly above the printed letters. A beginning, he asked himself, or a wasted, presumptuous act?

Alice giggled, a thin, high sound, and touched the tiny petals of the violet. She waved the flower in the air and dropped it into a pocket of Thomas's waistcoat.

Once more he smiled at the child. Catching her eye, he pointed straight at the hat. Then he pointed to the stick-drawn word. Deliberately, he retraced the *H A T* with the stick. He pointed back to his hat.

This time Alice Cogswell tapped her shoes on the steps and wiggled her fingers. She must have thought, Thomas later wrote, that they both were playing a game. First he would do a trick, then so would she. How could teaching truly begin?

For more than an hour, Thomas patiently pulled Alice's attention to the indented letters and to his gray top hat. Her eyes showed no dawning of a connection between the design made by the stick and the object worn on the head. Teddy ran by with a neighborhood dog. He yelled that Alice didn't know things had names, that her father had tried teaching her.

By late afternoon, Thomas Gallaudet and Alice Cogswell were fast friends. Having younger sisters and brothers had given Thomas a feeling of ease among children. And his own childhood, where he, too, had stood apart, spurred an instant kinship with this child who could not hear.

He would never know the exact moment when comprehension was born in Alice Cogswell. If she wondered why he kept touching his hat and pointing and tracing fingers over the dirt — while she jumped and wiggled and tossed stones and tugged her hair — her wondering and her delight with Thomas must at last have let a door swing open just far enough for her to see the link between the *H A T* and the unnamed object that the smiling man put on his head. Alice suddenly grabbed the top hat to clamp it down, lopsided, over her curls. She pointed to the word made by Thomas, eagerly tapped his hat, and jumped off the steps in excitement. *H A T* and hat? The link had been made. She waited.

Leaping to the ground, Thomas swung the child into his arms. His weariness was gone. What an incredible day! How had this happened? He heard Alice's high-pitched giggle and he plunged after it, pointing a finger directly at the word in the dirt. *Correct!* Thomas wanted to shout.

Several houses away, a carriage rolled into a pebbled driveway, wheels clattering, horses snorting. Thomas recognized Dr. Mason Cogswell, and he turned Alice toward the sounds, watching her face light up at the sight of her father. A yank on Thomas's arm said that she wanted him to come with her, but then she stopped and looked quizzically at her new friend. She lunged for the stick and dragged Thomas onto the patch of dirt. Frantically, she pushed the stick into his hands and began thumping her fists on her own shoulders. *Me? Me? Me?* she seemed to be saying.

Again Thomas smiled. He saw Dr. Cogswell waving to him and to Alice, but he knelt down to smooth out a clear place in the sandy dirt. With the stick moving in his fingers like the most magical of wands, he started to write a large letter *A*, the very first letter of Alice Cogswell's name.

In Dr. Mason Cogswell's study, Thomas was surrounded by a profusion of books. One wall of shelves was filled with medical texts, another with historical volumes, two with encyclopedias and volumes on philosophy, religion, and science. Books were stacked like pillars on a desk and tables. After Thomas had been fed buttered biscuits by Mrs. Cogswell and Alice persuaded by her mother's kisses and gestures to lie down for a nap, Dr. Cogswell threw an arm around Thomas's shoulders and swept him into the study.

The doctor still seemed unable to believe what had occurred. He adored his daughter — that Thomas could see — and spoke of the scarlet fever that had robbed her of her hearing at age two. Any words Alice had known slowly ebbed from her consciousness. The sounds she made grew garbled, a torrent of grunts or a high wailing cry. By the time she was four, she was judged a deaf-mute — unable to hear or speak and thought incapable of understanding.

Dr. Cogswell had never accepted the judgment on his daughter. He didn't believe she was mentally impaired. He was certain that intelligence lived within the child, even if it lived under lock and key. In his medical texts, he researched early nineteenth-century theories on deafness, studying diagrams of ear dissections and of the three interior areas of the ear — the opening, or meatus; the middle ear; and the shell-shaped cochlea, or inner ear. Italian scientist Dominico Cotugno had discovered that the cochlea was an important center of hearing and was filled with fluid rather than air. Alice's scarlet fever had probably destroyed nerve fibers in the cochlea or in the main auditory nerve that transmitted sound impulses to the brain. No cure for deafness was known, and Dr. Cogswell turned to his history books to read whatever he could about the deaf.

Thomas listened to Dr. Cogswell speak of deafness and of nine-year-old Alice trapped in her soundless prison. Being deaf, Thomas learned, brought a greater penalty than being blind. Deaf-born children, receiving no words, couldn't learn to think in organized language. The panorama of the world passed before them without much reassurance. Ordinary sounds — rain thrumming, the pleasant drone of faraway voices — might tell the hearing that all was safe. But for the deaf, there was only the terror of a silence without end.

The Cogswells had hesitated to send Alice across the seas to one of the few European schools for the deaf. Her helplessness frightened them, and they had tried without success to educate her themselves. But now, Dr. Cogswell exclaimed, Alice wouldn't need to go away. She wouldn't have to live in ignorance. In one afternoon, young Mr. Gallaudet had wrought some kind of miracle. He would continue to help Alice, wouldn't he? He would become her teacher?

By supper, Thomas left the study of the Cogswell house with the questions posed by Dr. Cogswell and with two French volumes entitled *Theory of Signs,* written by a French priest, the Abbé Sicard. In his attic bedroom, Thomas leafed through printed drawings and Dr. Cogswell's English translations of a one-handed manual alphabet and of hand gestures, or signs, representing words, phrases, or sentences. The alphabet letter *A*, Thomas saw, was formed by simply folding down the fingers onto the top of the palm and laying the unfolded thumb against the side of the index finger. Each alphabet letter required particular positions of fingers and hand.

BABY

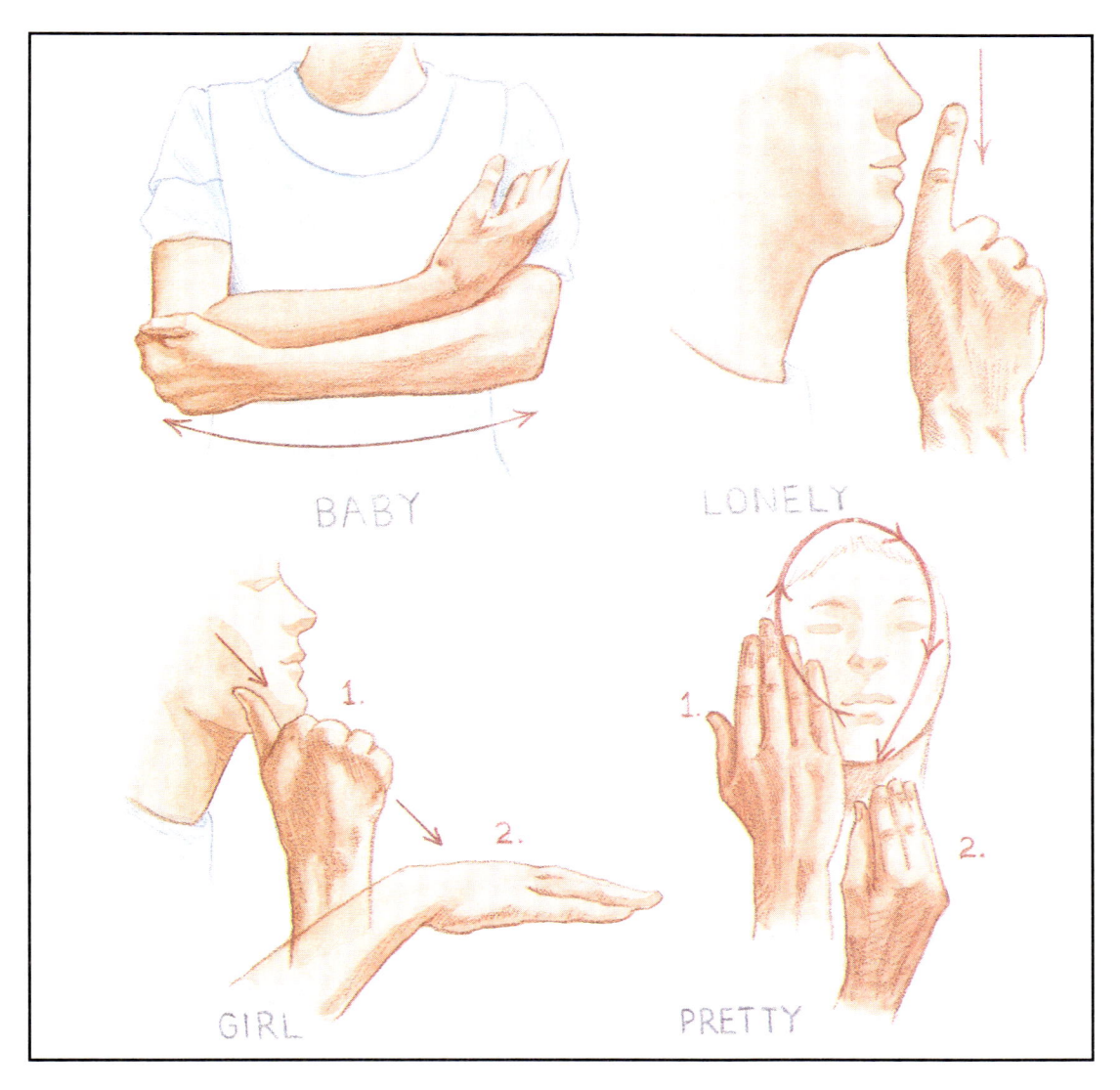

LONELY

GIRL

PRETTY

Some of the signs created an image, a pantomime, of the intended word. The sign for *baby* was made by placing and rocking the right hand in the crook of the left arm. Many signs, however, were less obvious. The word *lonely* was signed by drawing the right index finger down across the lips, the palm facing left. And since pointing could readily indicate *I*, *you*, *he*, *she*, or *us*, this language of gestures did not provide for pronouns or articles. It also changed some of the familiar word order of English; noun subjects were given emphasis over adjectives, as in *girl pretty* instead of *pretty girl*.

These are the signs for baby, lonely, *and* pretty girl *in American Sign Language.*

Deaf children, Dr. Cogswell had told Thomas, fortunate enough to be schooled were taught by one of two methods: an oral method, which trained people to watch or "read" lips and parrot some words; and the silent or natural method, based on the use of sign language instead of vocalized speech. The first method could only help the more skillful, while the second could enable anyone who knew the signs to communicate. Schools hotly defended one system or the other, with England and Scotland on the oral side, and France promoting the silent gestures.

The morning after talking to Dr. Cogswell, Thomas took Alice down Prospect Street. Exuberant, the child raced from object to object, skimming them with her fingertips and looking to Thomas for the words. He wrote large letters into a notebook, and having already memorized the Abbé Sicard's manual alphabet, he spelled each word for Alice with his fingers. Did she understand? Later — tomorrow — he would begin teaching her signs and the one-handed letters. Teach her. Teacher. Yes, that's what he would agree to do and be. Weekends would see him in the pulpits of churches in New England. On weekdays, he would return to teach Alice Cogswell a language spoken by hand and not by mouth.

Soon, Thomas's younger sisters and brothers were trooping behind teacher and student, practicing the signs and finger alphabet and applauding Alice for mastering words. Her occasional tears of frustration at making mistakes were wiped away by the other children. She learned almost twenty words a day, each word urging her further through the door and beyond the wall that had kept her apart. Passersby stopped to watch the slight, eldest son of Peter Gallaudet lead the small band that etched pictures in midair like mimes upon a stage. To indicate the word *boy*, fingers of hands grasped imaginary hat brims. To say *girl*, thumbs on closed hands traced pretend bonnet strings from cheek to chin.

In April of 1815, Thomas was asked to speak at an evening meeting of ten merchants and educators in Dr. Mason Cogswell's parlor. Alice had advanced so rapidly that her father wanted the young minister to describe his teaching.

A census of New England, said Dr. Cogswell, showed eighty-four deaf-mutes in Connecticut alone; thousands more from across the country were, if not totally deaf, hearing-impaired. The United States was to be the land of opportunity, yet no school for unfortunate children had been established. Might not Thomas inspire the men in the parlor to found such a school? If a little girl like Alice could be educated, how many other girls and boys, or deaf adults for that matter, were capable of being taught?

Thomas stood in the hazy kerosene warmth of the Cogswell parlor before a semicircle of chairs and a polite but skeptical audience. Hands rested on knees or in laps, hands that were accustomed to ordinary use. Thomas must have wondered how he would convince these men of Hartford that a deaf child's hands might create words by shape. He'd learned that the deaf did not have to be ignorant or mute. Alice's fingers could speak in a silent language of nouns, verbs, and adjectives that even, by means of a specific sign, put sentences in past, present, or future tense.

Through the evening, Thomas explained to his audience that a school for the deaf would be a just and humane undertaking. At nine o'clock, an interruption came from a sleepy Alice in flannel nightgown and cotton slippers. Carried into the parlor by her father, the child sat on a rug by the fireplace. Thomas stooped beside her and tapped her hands. Gently, his own fingers asked his student to tell the ten gentlemen of Hartford what she felt about learning words.

Shyly, she smiled. From the edge of the rug, Alice's right hand rose, opening like a flower on its stem, and she swayed toward the music of her fingers. The little finger of her right hand touched her chest to indicate herself, and then her index finger, hand palm up, made a clockwise circle. She tapped her forehead and crooked and uncrooked her fingers. Finally, after folding her fingers and curling her thumb beneath the first joint of her middle and index finger, Alice lifted her index finger and placed her hand in front of her forehead.

Thomas kissed the top of her head and turned to the men to translate Alice's signing. *I always want — understand*, she said.

A unanimous vote was taken that evening among the ten merchants and educators. The men agreed to try to collect enough money to send an emissary to Europe to study the available methods of teaching the deaf. If more funds were collected, the first school in America for deaf students might be opened in Hartford. The town, boasted one merchant, contained the first stone state house in the country. Why shouldn't it be the site of another noteworthy first?

Thomas shook hands with each of the men. As he was leaving the Cogswell parlor, however, he stopped suddenly to clap his hands together in two sharp bursts of sound. Startled, the men looked at him. Clapping again, Thomas remarked that such a hand motion was not only a means of expressing approval or commanding respect. Two claps of the hands, he said, was French — and now American — sign language for the word *school*.

"Clap with me," Thomas invited the men. And echoing behind him, slow and awkward at first but soon growing firm, came a long series of double hand claps in behalf of the deaf.

The National Theatre of the Deaf

The National Theatre of the Deaf, from Hartford, traveled to Los Angeles to perform at the 1984 Olympics.

An actor "signs" his lines.

The actors express themselves with pantomime and sign language.

193

In the play "Farewell, My Lovely," the troupe pays tribute to an American institution, the Ford Model T, the original economy car.

Since 1967, The National Theatre of the Deaf has entertained millions of people. It has been to Europe, Asia, and Australia many times. The group has performed on television and appeared at the 1984 Olympics. The company's ten deaf actors sign and pantomime their lines while the two hearing actors recite them. Its Little Theatre of the Deaf performs plays for young people.

The group's repertoire is diverse.

Broad gestures communicate to the audience.

In December the Little Theatre plays a classic, Dickens' "A Christmas Carol."

Discuss the Selection

1. What discovery did Thomas Gallaudet make? How did this discovery affect his life?
2. By the end of the story, Thomas Gallaudet began to realize that he would spend his life working on behalf of the deaf. What led to this decision?
3. How did you feel when Alice Cogswell was first able to express her feelings in sign language?
4. Locate the paragraph in which the sign Alice Cogswell used to tell the audience that she wanted to learn is described.
5. In what ways do you think the audience will help Thomas Gallaudet?

Apply the Skills

A generalization is a broad statement that is true in most cases. To make a valid generalization based on the information in a selection, first consider the information the author gives you. Do the facts relate to each other? Are there enough facts to make a generalization? What generalizations can you make based on the information given in "A Deaf Child Listened"? Cite evidence from the selection.

Think and Write

Prewrite

1. Thomas notices a lonely girl.	2. Thomas gives Alice a violet.	3. Thomas spells H-A-T and Alice understands.
4.	5.	6.

Each of the top three note cards shown above describes an event from "A Deaf Child Listened." The events are described in sequence, with the first card representing what happened first. Think about the story. Get or make three more note cards and on them describe additional events from the story.

Compose

Referring to the story and using the information on the note cards, write a summary of the main events. Describe each event in sequence. Try to use time-signaling words such as *first, next, later,* and *finally.*

Revise

Read the paragraph that you just wrote. Have you included the main events of the story in sequence? Have you used time-signaling words? If not, revise your work to accurately summarize the story.

Vocabulary Study

Greek and Latin Roots

Many English words are Greek and Latin in their origins. These Greek and Latin words can help you to unlock the meanings of many unfamiliar English words. Readers who are aware of the meanings of Greek and Latin roots will be able to increase their vocabularies easily.

Greek Roots

Knowing Greek roots can sometimes help you determine the meaning of an English word. Read the following sentence:

> Phil put his new record on the phonograph.

You know that a *phonograph* is a machine on which records are played. Let's take a closer look at the word *phonograph*. This word is made up of two Greek words. The word *phono* comes from the Greek root *phone*, which means "sound." The Greek root *graph* means "write." The word *phonograph* got its name because sounds are "written" on a record and then read by the phonograph. Suppose you don't know the meaning of *telephoto* in this sentence:

> Maria put a telephoto attachment on her camera to take a picture of the stampeding elephants.

The word *telephoto* is made up of two Greek words. The Greek root *tele* means "far." The word *photo* comes from the Greek word *photos*, which means "light." If you don't know the meaning of the word *telephoto*, can you guess? The word *telephoto* suggests something that is used to see things far away. You can begin to understand that a telephoto attachment was designed to help take pictures of things that are far away. Knowing Greek words can start you on the way to defining an English word.

Latin Roots

Knowing Latin roots can also help you determine the meaning of an English word. Very often a single Latin root can be the base for several different English words. Here are a few common Latin roots and their English meanings.

Latin Root	spec	vid, vis	script
English Meaning	look	see	write

Read the following sentence:

> A detective's most important work is a full inspection of all the clues that he or she can gather.

Let's take a closer look at the word *inspection*. This word contains the Latin root *spec*, which means "look." What does this clue suggest about the meaning of the word *inspection*? You can begin to understand that a detective's most important work is looking at clues carefully. Knowing a common Latin root has started you on the way to defining an English word.

The Latin roots *vid* and *vis* come from a word that means "see." What does this tell you about the words *videotape* and *visible*? The word *videotape* suggests something that is taped to be seen. The word *visible* suggests that something can be seen.

The Latin root *script* comes from a word that means "write." What is a script? Knowing the meaning of the Latin root *script* should help you decide. A script is something that is written down. What is a prescription? It is something "written" by a doctor. Again, knowing the meaning of the Latin root should help.

Greek and Latin roots can unlock the meanings of many English words and help build your reading vocabulary. Look for these useful roots as you read.

The famous detective, Sherlock Holmes, looks deep into his own background to solve a case. To what does he owe his success?

When you come to an unfamiliar word in the story, see if you can recognize its root. If you can, use the root to figure out the meaning of the word.

The Adventure of the Musgrave Ritual

by Sir Arthur Conan Doyle
Adapted by Catherine Edwards Sadler

Sherlock Holmes had one of the most organized and methodical of minds. But when it came to his personal habits, he was one of the most untidy men I have ever met! I myself am not the neatest of people, but with me there is a limit. Holmes kept his cigars in the coal-scuttle, his tobacco in the toe-end of a Persian slipper, and his unanswered letters attached by a jackknife to the very center of our wooden mantelpiece!

Our rooms were always full of chemicals, and souvenirs from past criminal cases were always turning up in the butter dish or some other odd place. But what truly bothered me were Holmes's papers. He hated to destroy documents, especially those connected to past cases. Yet he only managed to straighten them up once or twice a year. Month after month his papers would pile up so that eventually every corner of the room was stacked with them. And look out the person who tried to burn them or even store them away!

One winter's night we sat together by the fire. Holmes had just finished pasting clippings into his scrapbook. As usual, the room was scattered with paper, and I suggested that he spend the next two hours making the room a bit more tidy. He could not deny that it needed straightening up. Without enthusiasm, Holmes went off to his bedroom. He came back, pulling a large tin box behind him which he placed in the middle of the floor. He squatted down upon a stool in front of it and threw back the lid. I could see that it was a third full of bundles of paper, each bundle tied with red tape.

"My dear Watson," said Holmes mischievously, "if you knew what was in this box, you'd be asking me to pull papers out rather than put papers in."

"These must be the records of your early work," I said. "I have often wished that I had the notes of those cases."

"Yes, my boy. These were all done in my early days, before you had come along to write about me." He lifted bundle after bundle in a tender sort of way. "They are not all successes, Watson," said he. "But there are some rather interesting cases among them. Here's the record of the Tartleton murders, and the case of Vamberry, the wine merchant, and the adventure of the old Russian woman, and the curious affair of the aluminum crutch as well as a full account of Ricoletti and his wife. And here — ah, now! This is something really special!"

He dived down to the bottom of the chest and brought out a small wooden box with a sliding lid. From within he produced a crumpled piece of paper, an old-fashioned brass key, a peg of wood with a ball of string attached to it, and three rusty old discs of metal.

"Well, my boy, what do you make of this lot?" Sherlock Holmes asked.

"It is a curious collection," I answered.

"Very curious. And the case in which they were involved will strike you even more curious."

"These relics have a history then?"

"So much so that they are history."

"What do you mean by that?"

Sherlock Holmes picked them up one by one and laid them along the edge of the table. Then he reseated himself in his chair and looked them over. There was a gleam of satisfaction in his eyes.

"These are all I have left to remind me of 'The Adventure of the Musgrave Ritual.' "

I had heard him mention the case more than once, but he had never told me the details.

"I would be very interested in hearing about the case."

"And I get to leave this litter right here!" Holmes cried, smiling. "Your desire for tidiness is short-lived, Watson! I should be glad to tell you of the Musgrave Ritual and have you write about it. There are many points in it which are quite unique in the criminal records of this country. A collection of my stories about my small achievements as a detective would certainly be incomplete without an account of this unusual adventure.

"You see me now when my name has become known far and wide. People travel to see me when the police cannot solve their doubtful cases. Even when you first met me I had already established myself as a consulting detective. You can hardly realize how difficult it was to start off in this unusual business of mine.

"When I first came to London I had rooms in Montague Street just around the corner from the British Museum. I spent long hours at that museum studying everything I felt might help me in my work. Now and again fellow students would bring me a case to solve. The third of these cases was that of the Musgrave Ritual. It is to that one case that I owe my later success.

"Reginald Musgrave had studied at the same college as myself. We were slight acquaintances. He looked very aristocratic with his thin, high nose and large eyes. In fact, he was from one of the oldest families in the kingdom. His family had lived in Western Sussex in Hurlstone Manor, which is quite famous as an ancient estate. Once or twice we had a conversation at college and I can remember that he expressed a keen interest in my methods of observation and detection.

"For four years I had seen nothing of him. Then one morning he walked into my rooms in Montague Street. He had changed little. He was dressed like a man of fashion and seemed as distinguished as ever.

" 'How have things gone with you, Musgrave?' I asked after we had shaken hands.

" 'You probably heard of my poor father's death,' said he. 'He died about two years ago. Since then I have had the estate to manage and I am most busy. I understand, Holmes, that you are now using your amazing powers of observation professionally?'

" 'Yes,' said I, 'I have taken to living by my wits.'

"'I am delighted to hear it. Your advice would be most valuable to me now. There are some very strange happenings down at Hurlstone and the police have not been able to shed any light upon the matter. It is really a most extraordinary business.'"

"You can imagine, Watson, how eager I was to work on this case. I had been waiting for months for just such an opportunity. I was sure that I could succeed where others had failed."

"'Pray let me have the details,'" I cried.

"Reginald Musgrave sat down opposite me.

"'You know that I have to keep a large staff of servants at Hurlstone. It is a rambling old place and takes a good deal of looking after. Altogether there are eight maids, the cook, the butler, two footmen, and a boy. The garden and the stables have a separate staff, too.

"'Of all the servants the butler, Brunton, has been in our service the longest. He had planned to be a schoolmaster, but had not been able to find work. My father hired him as our butler. He was a man of great energy and intelligence and soon became invaluable in the household. He is a handsome man. He has been with us for twenty years but cannot be older than forty. With his looks and extraordinary talents — he can speak several languages and plays nearly every instrument — it is a bit surprising that he stayed on as a butler for so long. But I suppose he was comfortable and lacked the energy to make any change.

"'But Brunton has one fault: He is a ladies' man. All the women are mad for him. A few months ago we thought he was going to settle down. He became engaged to Rachel Howells, our second housemaid. But he has broken up with her and now courts Janet Tregellis, the daughter of the head gamekeeper. Rachel is a very good woman, but she has a very excitable temperament. After he threw her over, she became ill with fever. She went about the house like someone who had gone mad — or at least she did until yesterday. That was when the first drama occurred at Hurlstone.

"'I have said that the house is a rambling one. One night last week — on Thursday night to be more exact — I could not sleep. And so at about two in the morning I rose from my bed and lit a candle with the intention of reading a novel. The book I wanted to read, however, was in the billiard room. So I pulled on my dressing gown and started off to get it.

"'To get to the billiard room I had to go down a flight of stairs and cross a hallway that led to the library and gun room. I looked down this corridor and saw a light coming from the library. Naturally, my first thought was of burglars. The walls at Hurlstone are decorated with old weapons so I picked up a battle-ax. I left the candle behind me, tiptoed down the passage, and peeped in at the open door.

"'Brunton, the butler, was in the library, sitting in an easy chair. He had a slip of paper that looked like a map upon his knee. His forehead was sunk forward upon his hand in deep thought. I stood watching him in the darkness. I was numb with astonishment. A small candle on the edge of the table shed a weak light. Suddenly he rose from his chair and walked over to a bureau. He unlocked it, pulled open one of its drawers, and from this he took a piece of paper. He returned to his seat, flattened it out beside the candle, and began to study it carefully. I was enraged at his calm inspection of my family documents. I took a step forward. It was then that Brunton saw me standing in the doorway. He sprang to his feet, his face livid with fear. He quickly thrust the maplike paper into his pocket.

"'So!' said I, "this is how you repay us for the trust we have placed in you! You go through our private papers! You will leave my service tomorrow!"

"'He looked like a man who was utterly crushed. He slunk past me without a word. The candle was still on the table. By its light I could see the piece of paper he had taken from the bureau. To my surprise, it was nothing of importance at all. It was simply a copy of the Musgrave Ritual. It is a curious old ceremony which each Musgrave recites on coming of age. The tradition has been carried on for centuries but is of little interest to anyone except the family — and perhaps some archaeologist studying ancient family rituals.'

"'We had better come back to that paper later,' said I.

"'If you think it really necessary,' he answered. 'To continue: I relocked the bureau with the key Brunton had left. Then I turned to go. I was surprised to find Brunton had returned and was standing before me.

"'Mr. Musgrave, sir," he cried. His voice was hoarse with emotion. "I can't bear disgrace, sir. I've always been proud. Disgrace would kill me. If you cannot keep me after what has passed, then let me give you my resignation. I will leave in a month as if of my own free will. I could stand that, Mr. Musgrave, but I could not stand to be cast out in front of all the people I know so well."

"'You don't deserve much consideration, Brunton. Your conduct has been shocking. However you have been with the family a long time. I have no wish to bring public disgrace upon you. A month, however, is too long. Leave in one week, and tell people whatever you like."

"'Only a week, sir?" he cried in despair. "A fortnight, sir . . . two weeks . . . ."

"'A week," I repeated.

"'He crept away, his face sunk on his chest like a broken man.

"'For two days Brunton went about his duties as usual. I did not mention what had passed. I was curious to see how he was going to cover his disgrace. On the third morning, however, he did not appear after breakfast for his usual instructions. As I was leaving the dining room, I happened to meet Rachel Howells, the maid. She looked deathly pale.

"'You should be in bed," I said. "Come back to your duties when you are stronger."

"'She looked at me with a strange expression.

"'I am strong enough, Mr. Musgrave," said she.

"'We will see what the doctor says," I answered. "You must stop work now. When you go downstairs tell Brunton I wish to see him."

"'The butler is gone, sir," said she.

"'Gone! Gone where?"

"'He is gone. No one has seen him. He is not in his room. Oh, yes, he is gone — he is gone!" She fell back against the wall with shriek after shriek of laughter. I was horrified at her mad behavior. I rushed to the bell to summon help. The woman was taken to her room, still screaming and sobbing. Meanwhile I made inquiries after Brunton and found there was no doubt that he had disappeared. His bed had not been slept in, and he had not been seen since he retired to his room the night before. Yet it was difficult to see how he left the house. Both the windows and doors were found locked in the morning as usual. His clothes, his watch, even his money, were found in his room. However, the black suit he usually wore was missing. His slippers, too, were gone, but his boots were left behind. Where, then, could butler Brunton have gone in the night and what could have become of him?

" 'We searched the house from cellar to garret. There was no trace of him. It was incredible to me that he could have gone away and left all his property behind. Yet where could he be? I called in the local police, but they found nothing. Rain had fallen the night before, and so we examined the lawn and the paths all around the house. Again we found nothing. It was then that a second drama occurred.

" 'For two days Rachel Howells had been ill. We had hired a nurse to sit with her day and night. On the third night after Brunton's disappearance, Rachel was sleeping nicely. The nurse decided, therefore, to take a nap in the armchair. When she awoke in the early morning she found that the window was open and there was no sign of Rachel. I was awakened immediately. The two footmen and I started off in search of the missing woman. We started our search directly under her window. We could see her footsteps in the earth. We followed them easily across the lawn. But they vanished at the edge of the lake, close by the gravel driveway which leads out of the grounds. The lake is eight feet deep. You can imagine our feelings when we saw that the woman's trail ended at its edge.

" 'Of course, we had the lake dragged at once but we did not find a trace of the woman. What we did bring up was a linen bag, containing some rusty bits of metal and several dull-colored pieces of pebble or glass. This strange find was all that we could get from the lake. Despite all our efforts, we still know nothing of the fate of Rachel Howells or Richard Brunton. The country police are at their wits' end, and so, I have come to you.'

"I listened eagerly to this extraordinary tale. I tried in my mind to find a common thread which would pull these strange events together.

"The facts of the case were these: The butler was gone and the maid was gone. The maid had loved the butler, but had afterward reason to hate him.

206

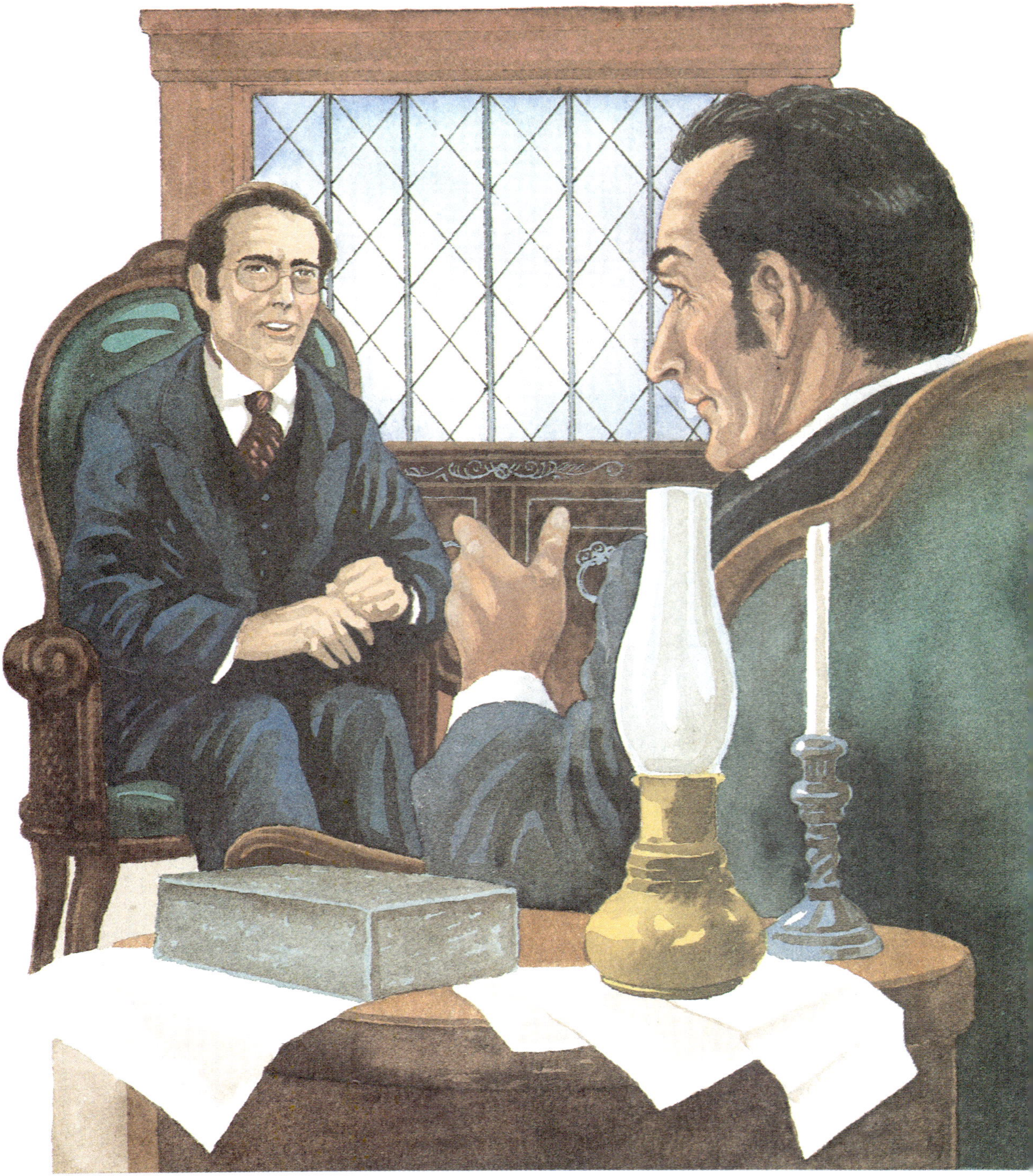

She had an excitable temperament. She had been terribly upset, almost insane, after his disappearance. She had flung a bag into the lake. That bag had contained some curious objects. All these facts were important. Yet none gave me a clue into the true heart of the matter. What was the starting point of this chain of events? There lay the end of this tangled thread.

" 'I must see that paper, Musgrave,' said I. 'The one Brunton took from the bureau.'

" 'This Ritual of ours is an absurd business,' he answered. 'But it is very ancient. I have a copy of the questions and answers here.'

"He handed me the very paper which I have here, Watson. This is the strange Ritual each Musgrave had to recite when he reached adulthood. I will read you the questions and answers:

" 'WHOSE WAS IT?'
" 'HIS WHO IS GONE.'
" 'WHO SHALL HAVE IT?'
" 'HE WHO WILL COME.'
" 'WHERE WAS THE SUN?'
" 'OVER THE OAK.'
" 'WHERE WAS THE SHADOW?'
" 'UNDER THE ELM.'
" 'HOW WAS IT STEPPED?'
" 'NORTH BY TEN AND BY TEN, EAST BY FIVE AND BY FIVE, SOUTH BY TWO AND BY TWO, WEST BY ONE AND BY ONE, AND SO UNDER.'
" 'WHAT SHALL WE GIVE FOR IT?'
" 'ALL THAT IS OURS.'
" 'WHY SHOULD WE GIVE IT?'
" 'FOR THE SAKE OF THE TRUST.'

" 'The original has no date. But the spelling is of the seventeenth century,' remarked Musgrave. 'I am afraid it can be of little help to you in solving this mystery.'

" 'What it does,' said I, 'is give us another mystery — one which is even more interesting than the first. It may be that the solution to one may prove to be the solution to the other. You will excuse me if I say that your butler appears to have been a very clever man. He seems to have understood the meaning of this Ritual more than ten generations of his masters.'

" 'I hardly follow you,' said Musgrave. 'The paper seems to me to be of no practical importance.'

" 'But to me it seems immensely practical. I fancy Brunton saw it the same way. He had probably seen this Ritual before the night you caught him.'

" 'It is very possible. We did not hide it.'

" 'I imagine that he simply wanted to refresh his memory that last time. You say he had some sort of map as well? And that he thrust it in his pocket on seeing you?'

" 'That is true. But what could Brunton have to do with this old family custom of ours? And what does this rigamarole mean?'

" 'I don't think we'll have much difficulty finding that out,' I said. 'With your permission, we will take the first train down to Sussex. We can go more deeply into the matter there.'

"That afternoon we went down to Hurlstone Manor. Perhaps you have seen pictures and read descriptions of that famous old building. It is built in the shape of an 'L.' The long arm is the more modern portion while the short arm is the ancient part of the building. The date 1607 is chiseled over the door in the center of the original wing. Experts say that the beams and stonework are even older than this. Its enormously thick walls and tiny windows forced the family to build a newer, more modern building. The old one is now used as a storehouse and a cellar. A splendid park with fine old trees surrounds the house. The lake lies close by the drive and is about two hundred yards from the building.

"I was convinced that there were not three separate mysteries here. There was but one. I felt that if I could only read the Musgrave Ritual correctly, I could solve its mystery — and find the missing butler and maid. I now turned all my energies to that task. I asked myself why the butler wanted to understand this old Ritual. The answer was plain: because he saw something in it — something which generations of country squires had not understood. He must have expected to gain something by figuring out its questions and answers. What, then, did the Ritual mean? And what did it have to do with the butler and the maid's strange disappearance?

"It seemed obvious to me that the measurements were directions to some particular spot on the property. We now had to find that spot. There were two clues or guides — one was the oak and the other was the elm. As to the oak, there could be no question at all. Right in front of the house there stood a great giant oak, one of the most magnificent trees I have ever seen.

" 'Was that tree there when your Ritual was first drawn up?' said I as we drove past.

" 'It was probably there a thousand years ago. It has a girth of 23 feet!'

" 'Have you any old elms?' I asked.

" 'There used to be a very old one over yonder. It was struck by lightning ten years ago. We cut down the stump.'

" 'Can you still see where it used to be?' I asked.

" 'Oh, yes.'

" 'There are no other elms?'

" 'No old ones, but plenty of beeches.'

" 'I should like to see where it grew,' I said.

"We got out of the carriage and he led me to where the elm had stood. It was nearly midway between the oak and the house. My investigation seemed to be progressing. 'I suppose it is impossible to find out how high the elm was?' I asked.

" 'I can tell you that at once. It was 64 feet,' answered Musgrave. 'When I was a lad my tutor made me measure the heights of things. I had to work out the height of every tree and building on the estate.'

"This was an unexpected piece of luck. My information was coming more quickly than I could have hoped for!

" 'Tell me,' I asked, 'did your butler ever ask you that question?'

"Reginald Musgrave looked at me in astonishment. 'Now that you call it to mind, Brunton did ask me about the height of the tree some months ago. He said he needed to know it to settle an argument with the grooms.'

"This was excellent news, Watson. It showed me that I was on the right road. The ritual had said: 'Where was the sun?' 'Over the oak.' I looked up at the sun. It was low in the heavens. I calculated that in less than one hour it would lie just above the topmost branches of the old oak. One instruction in the old Ritual would then be met. 'Where was the shadow?' it had asked. 'Under the elm.' I now had to find out where the end of the elm's shadow would fall when the sun was just above the oak."

"But that must have been difficult, Holmes. The elm was no longer there!"

"If Brunton could do it, then so could I. I went with Musgrave to his study and whittled myself a peg. I attached a very long string to it. I marked off each yard with a knot. Next I fetched Musgrave's 6-foot fishing rod. Musgrave and I went back to where the elm had stood. I looked up. The sun was just over the oak. I stuck the rod into the earth. Its shadow pointed toward the house and measured 9 feet in length. What had I learned by this? At this time of day a 6-foot rod casts a 9-foot shadow — the shadow was half-again the rod's length. Therefore, a 64-foot tree would cast a shadow 96 feet long at the same time of day. Likewise, the tree's shadow would point in the same direction as had the rod's. I placed my string at the base of the rod. This was my starting point. I then began to walk in the direction of its shadow. As I walked I measured the distance with my string. Ninety-six feet later I found myself almost at the wall of the manor. I thrust my peg into the spot. Then I saw a small hole in the ground only two inches away. You can imagine my delight, Watson. I knew that it had been made by Brunton. I was still on the right trail.

"The Ritual had next said to 'step north ten and by ten, east five and by five, south two and by two and west one and by one.' Ten steps north with each foot took me alongside the wall. Again I marked the spot. Then I carefully paced off five double steps to the east and two double steps to the south. They brought me to the old door. And 'west one and by one' seemed to mean that I was to go two paces beyond that door. I should now be standing where the secret of the Musgrave Ritual was hidden.

"The sun shone down on the old gray stones. They were firmly cemented and had not been moved in years. I tapped upon the floor, but it sounded the same all over. There was no sign of a crack or crevice. Never had I been so disappointed. Luckily, Musgrave had begun to understand what I was doing. He was now as excited as myself. He took out the Ritual to check its instructions.

" 'And under!' he cried. 'You have forgotten the "and so under." '

"I had thought 'and so under' meant that we were to dig. But now I saw that I was wrong. 'Is there a cellar under us?' I cried.

" 'Yes, and it is as old as the house. Down here, through this door!'

"We went down a winding stone staircase. My companion struck a match. A lantern stood nearby on a barrel. He lit it and the cellar brightened. There was no doubt that we had come to the right place . . . and that others had been there recently.

"The cellar had been used to store planks of wood. Someone had pulled the planks to one side. In the center of the floor was one particularly large flagstone. A rusted iron ring was attached to it and to this was tied a wool muffler.

" 'By Jove!' cried Musgrave, 'that's Brunton's muffler! I have seen it on him. I could swear it! What has he been doing here?'

"I suggested that we call the local police immediately. It was not long before two strong policemen arrived on the scene. I then tried to raise up the stone by pulling on the muffler. I could barely move it. One of the policemen came to my aid, and together we managed to slide the stone to one side. A black hole loomed beneath. We all peered into the pit. Musgrave knelt at its edge and pushed the lantern down into it.

"A small chamber about seven feet deep and four feet square lay open beneath us. To one side was a squat wooden box. Its hinge lid lay open and an old-fashioned key was in its lock. The box was covered in a thick layer of dust. Damp and worms had eaten through the wood and mold was growing within. Several discs of metal were scattered over the bottom of the box. They seemed to be old coins of some sort. The box contained nothing else.

"At that moment, however, we had little thought for that old chest. Our eyes were glued to what lay beside it. There, frozen in position, crouched the figure of a man. He was dressed in a suit of black and his arms were outstretched towards us. All the blood had drained from his face and it was now unrecognizable. But the height, the dress, and the hair convinced Musgrave that this was his missing butler.

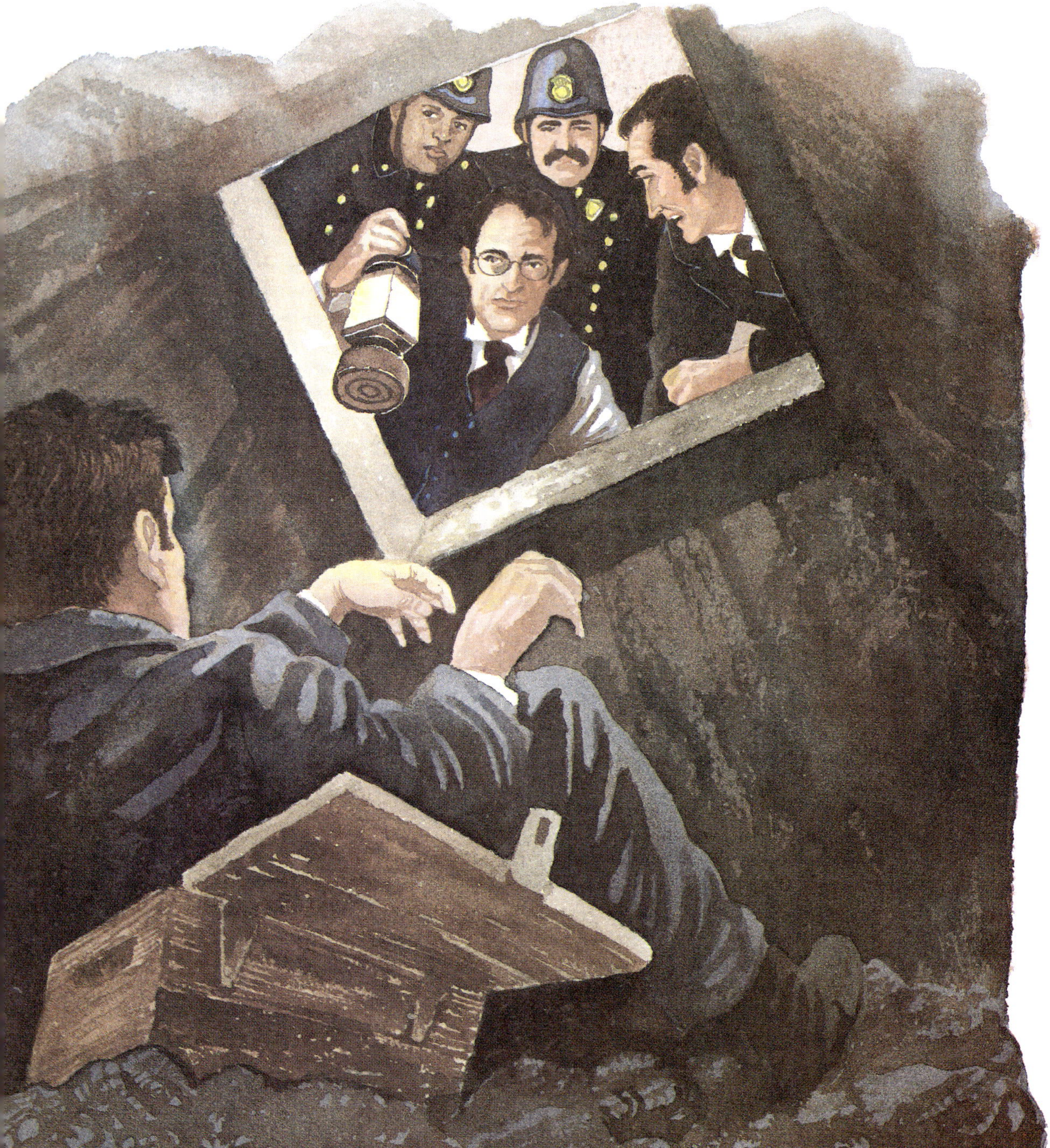

He had been dead for some days. There was no wound or bruise on his body to show how he had met his death. The police dragged the body from its tomb and carried it away.

"I must confess that I was disappointed with my investigation at this point. I had thought the discovery of the hiding-place would reveal both what was the Ritual's secret and what had happened to the butler and the maid. But now it seemed only to have raised further questions. What had been in the chest? Why had the Musgraves hidden it so securely and put the directions to its whereabouts into such a curious Ritual? And the butler . . . how had he met his fate? And the maid . . . what part had she played in this drama? I sat myself down upon a barrel and thought out the entire matter most carefully.

"You know my methods in such cases, Watson. I put myself in the butler's place. He had discovered the Ritual and had figured out that it contained a message to future Musgraves. The message was that they had been entrusted with some object of importance. It was to be found according to the directions in the Ritual. He knew that something of value was to be found at the trail's end. And so he worked out the instructions and came upon the huge stone in the floor. But it was too heavy for him to move alone. He needed someone's aid. But whose? The windows and the doors of the manor were barred every night. It would be risky to let someone in and out because there was too much chance of being discovered. No, far better to use someone who lived right in the house. Of course, he would think of Rachel Howells, the maid. She had loved him. He had thrown her over for someone else, but he probably thought he could win her back with flattery. And so it seemed that he had.

"Together the butler and the maid went down to the cellar. But it must have been difficult to raise that heavy stone. A large policeman and I had trouble enough doing it. They needed something to help them in their great task. But what would they use? I tried to think what I would have done. I walked over to the nearest pile of wood. It was not long before I found what I was looking for. One particular plank of wood had a large gash or groove at one end. They had managed to lift up the stone slightly, and then they had slipped this plank into the crack and used it as a lever to help them shift the stone to one side.

"Only one person could fit into the small hole. That person was Brunton. He had crawled down, while the maid had waited above. Brunton had unlocked the box and handed up the contents to Rachel. And then — what had happened? Perhaps the plank slipped and the stone snapped shut.

Brunton must have screamed and scratched at the stone in terror but Rachel could do nothing to save him. In my mind, I could see Rachel as she clutched at her treasure and rushed up the winding stairs while Brunton's cries rang in her ears.

"This then was the cause of her white face, her shaken nerves, her hysterical laughter. But what had been in the box . . . and what had she done with it? It had to have been the old metal and pebbles dragged from the lake. She had thrown them in the water to remove the last trace of the theft.

"For twenty minutes I sat motionless thinking the matter out. Musgrave still peered down into the hole, his face deathly pale.

" 'These must be the coins of King Charles I,' he said. 'He was the King of England when the Ritual was written.'

" 'And we may find something else of Charles I,' I cried suddenly. 'Let me see the contents of the bag you fished from the lake.'

"We went up to his study and he lay its contents before me. The metal was almost black and the stones were dark and dull. I rubbed one of them on my sleeve. It sparkled brilliantly. The metal work was in the shape of a double ring, but it had been bent and twisted out of its original shape.

" 'If my mind serves me, Charles I was executed. His son, Charles II, fled the country with many of the royal families. They probably had to leave their most precious possessions buried behind them. I am sure they intended to return for them in more peaceful times.'

" 'My ancestor, Sir Ralph Musgrave, was a knight during King Charles's day. He later left England with Charles II,' said my friend.

" 'Ah, indeed!' I answered. 'Well, I think I now have the last link in this mystery. It is sad that you had to make such a discovery through so tragic a drama. But you now possess a relic of truly great historic value.'

" 'What is it, then?' Musgrave gasped in astonishment.

" 'It is nothing less than the ancient crown of the Kings of England,' Sherlock Holmes answered.

" 'The crown!' Musgrave exclaimed.

" 'Precisely. Consider what the Ritual says. How does it run? "Whose was it?" "His who is gone." It had belonged to Charles I, but Charles I was now dead. Then, "Who shall have it?" "He who will come." That was Charles II. He had fled the country, but would later return as king. There can be no doubt that this battered and shapeless object once crowned royal heads.'

" 'And how did it get into the pond?' Musgrave asked.

" 'That is a question which will take some time to answer,' I said and began to explain my theory.

" 'And why didn't Charles II recover his crown when he returned to England?' asked Musgrave.

" 'Ah, that we may never know. It is likely that only one Musgrave knew where the crown was buried. He probably died while Charles II was abroad. By some oversight he must have left his Ritual without explaining its meaning. From that day to this it has been handed down from father to son . . . until it fell into the hands of a man who solved its mystery and lost his life for it.'

"And that's the story of the Musgrave Ritual, Watson. They now have the crown down at Hurlstone. I am sure they will show it to you if you mention my name. Nothing was ever heard of Rachel Howells. She probably carried herself — and the memory of that horrible accident — to some distant land."

With that, Sherlock Holmes shut his tin box and dragged it back into his bedroom. The bundles of paper scattered all about remained exactly as they were. As for me, I forgot all about the mess, and happily spent the rest of the evening writing down "The Adventure of the Musgrave Ritual."

Discuss the Selection

1. What case did Sherlock Holmes solve? To what did he owe his success?
2. What did the Musgrave Ritual turn out to be? To what discovery did it lead?
3. At what point in the story did you learn what the Musgrave Ritual was?
4. Why do you think the talented and educated Brunton remained a butler at Hurlstone Manor for so long?
5. How did Holmes solve the problem of measuring the shadow of an elm tree that had been cut down ten years earlier?

Apply the Skills

English owes much of its richness to words from other languages. Sometimes, word roots form the base for whole families of words. Principal sources for roots of English words have been Greek and Latin.

1. The Musgrave Ritual was an important document. The word *document* comes from the Latin root *doc*, meaning "teach." All but one of these words comes from the same root: *doctor, doctrine, dockyard, indoctrinate*. Can you guess which word does not belong?
2. Dr. Watson describes Holmes's mind as "methodical." *Methodical* comes from the Greek root *odo*, meaning "a way, a road, or a means." All but one of these words comes from the same root: *odometer, exodus, oddity, episodic*. Can you guess which word does not belong?

Think and Write

Prewrite

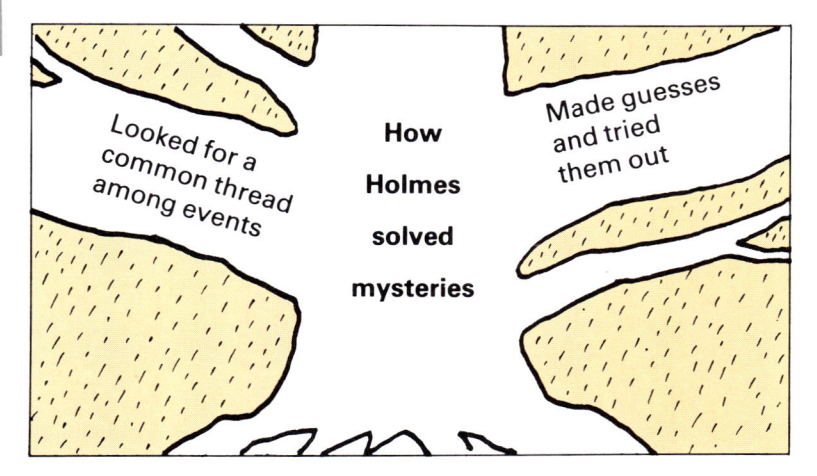

Diagram: "How Holmes solved mysteries" — branches labeled "Looked for a common thread among events" and "Made guesses and tried them out" (two branches empty).

Sherlock Holmes was an excellent classifier of information. Two of the branches on the diagram shown above give methods that Sherlock Holmes used to solve "The Adventure of the Musgrave Ritual." Copy the diagram, and complete it by identifying two more of Holmes's mystery-solving methods on the empty branches. Refer to the story as needed.

Compose

Using information from the story and the diagram, write two paragraphs, focusing each on a different investigative method used by Holmes. One of your topic sentences might be *Unlike those around him, Sherlock Holmes could find a common thread among diverse events.* Follow each topic sentence with at least two detail sentences.

Revise

Read your paragraphs. Do your topic sentences describe the Holmesian methods contained in the diagram? Do your detail sentences explain how Holmes put his methods into practice? If not, revise your work.

Comprehension Study

Author's Purpose

Recognizing the Author's Purpose

Authors have different points of view, and they have different reasons for writing, but they all share one goal. They want to communicate certain ideas or information to their readers.

One author might try to inform the reader by presenting facts. Another author might try to persuade the reader by presenting convincing arguments in support of an idea, product, or cause. Other authors write to judge, criticize, and analyze the work, ideas, or behavior of others. Some authors simply write to give their readers a good time — to entertain them. These are all examples of authors' purposes. It is an author's purpose that influences his or her message.

Suppose that all of these authors were writing about movies. The author who writes to present you with information might tell which movies are playing and where they are playing. The author who writes to persuade might try to convince you that a certain movie is the best one to see. Another kind of author, the movie critic, would state his or her opinion of the movie. Finally, the author who writes purely to entertain might tell you something about the personal lives of the stars in the movie.

Writing to Inform

The best way to present information is to give the facts without any personal opinions. This is called **objective writing**. Objective writers try very hard to avoid personal opinion when presenting facts. For example, a TV news reporter describes the big stories of the day without giving his or her own views of these events. Look at the following two paragraphs. Notice how personal thinking has been excluded from this piece of objective writing.

The first motion pictures were created by Louis Aimé Augustin Le Prince as early as 1885. In that year, in his New York office, he screened a film on a white wall on which faint outlines moved. A few years later he patented a film in Britain that showed a man walking in a garden.

On April 14, 1894, the first movie theater opened in New York. People paid twenty-five cents to see five films through special viewing devices. In France, the Lumière brothers presented the first public screening of a film in 1895. The earliest sound movie was commercially screened in 1923. The first all-talking movie was presented in 1928.

Writing to Persuade

To convince others to share a point of view, an author must appeal to the audience. Can you tell anything about the audience that the author of the following paragraph is trying to persuade?

There is no way that anyone in eighth grade can afford to miss the movie that I saw about a group of kids who take on the world — and win! At first, there are a lot of adults who don't understand what the kids want and why they want it so much. But at last the adults understand. Then they even help the kids to succeed. There isn't any fourteen-year-old who won't cheer the gang in this movie. When their bicycles go flying through the air, the whole movie house goes wild. This one is not to be missed by any eighth grader. It's the best movie ever made. Go see it today.

Writing to Express Criticism

Critical writing is different from pure persuasion because it relies more on facts to make its case. It is similar to debating. Critical writing tries to provoke thought rather than blind acceptance of the author's point of view. In fact, the author usually examines the details and analyzes them before identifying the writing purpose. See how the following example of critical writing supports the author's purpose.

> I have been thinking a lot about a number of recent movies for teenage audiences. The girls in these films are often treated differently from the boys. Usually, there will be some pretense that girls are as smart or as brave as boys. Yet all too often the story doesn't give girls a chance to show any such thing. In one movie, a boy becomes a starfighter and goes off to fight cosmic evil. Meanwhile, his girlfriend stays home, wringing her hands and waiting for him. In another movie, a boy must pull the world out of a disaster by using his knowledge of computers. His girlfriend just stands by and watches him with wide eyes. These movies are very unfair because they don't show girls as they really are. Girls can grow up to be astronauts and computer scientists if they want to, but this certainly isn't the message that most movies present. It's about time for a change.

Writing to Entertain

Writing that is meant to give people pleasure often makes its own rules. It can take the form of a short story, a fantasy, an interview, a personal essay, or almost anything else. The following paragraph is from an essay by an author who is trying to entertain the reader. How is this writing different from the examples given before?

> I get very emotional at movies. Most of the time I don't dare to show it. But at scary movies, I have no choice. I spill my soda over my shoes. I scatter my popcorn over the heads in front of me. I climb my chair trying to escape from the monster that seems to be coming straight at me. Maybe I have 3-D eyes, because I always take everything on the screen as being personally intended for me and me alone. I also clutch at my friends, leaving them with black-and-blue fingerprints on their arms that take days to fade. No wonder some of them refuse to go to suspense movies with me anymore. Or else they show up in armor or football padding. I prefer padding. Knocking on armor can cause a lot of noise in a movie theater. I got thrown out for that once.

Loaded Words and Slanted Writing

Almost any word that expresses a strong opinion can be called a **loaded word**. Such words trigger an instant reaction without facts to back them up. Here are some examples: It was a *brilliant* movie. It was a *rotten* movie. The adjectives *brilliant* and *rotten* might be used by different people about the same film without evidence to support these adjectives.

Slanted writing means using loaded words and other questionable persuasion techniques to push a point of view. The messages in most print advertisements are examples of slanted writing. An advertiser might claim, "Our soap cleans 10 percent better." The careful consumer and reader will want to know, "Better than what and based on what set of facts?" Of course, everyone knows that an advertiser's purpose is to sell products, so loaded words are expected in advertising messages.

Slanted writing used for purposes other than advertising, however, can do much harm. When used in political campaigns, for example, slanted writing is called **propaganda**. This kind of slanted writing is meant to mislead the targeted audience. The thoughtful and critical reader can rarely be fooled by slanted writing, loaded words, or propaganda techniques.

Textbook Application: Author's Purpose in Language Arts

You know that authors can have several different purposes for writing. As you read the following excerpt from a language arts textbook, refer to the sidenotes. They will help you to understand the author's purpose.

> What is the author criticizing in the first paragraph?

> What facts does the author present in paragraphs two, three, and four to support the claim that littering is a "terrible situation" at this beach resort?

> Why aren't the sentences about the need for medical care examples of slanted writing?

Whether you are a resident of our town or a visitor, you cannot help but notice the large amount of litter on our beaches. This is a terrible situation.

For one thing, food scraps attract more birds and insects than would normally be at the beaches. Many people complain about it, but few connect the problem with their own littering.

Broken bottles and rusty cans pose a danger, too. People playing on the beaches, especially children, are liable to stumble over these dangerous objects. In fact, the first-aid station at the main beach reported sending five people to the hospital for tetanus shots as a result of stumbling over broken bottles and rusty cans. Three others required stitches as a result of these accidents.

Finally, the trash makes our beaches less attractive to the resort crowd. Our summer economy depends on these people, so we want to surround them with beauty — not garbage.

> Littering is turning our town's biggest asset into a dump. We need to police our beaches and fine all litterers $100 or more — whatever it takes to make them find a trash can.
>
> — *Language for Daily Use,*
> Harcourt Brace Jovanovich

How does the last paragraph help to strengthen the author's criticism of littering?

1. A good author writes in a way that is meaningful to his or her audience. Who is the author of the textbook excerpt on littering trying to reach, and for what purpose?
2. Why is the excerpt on littering a better example of critical writing than of pure persuasion?

Being able to recognize an author's purpose will help in your understanding of a selection.

An African villager looks beyond the horizon of his village in search of wisdom. Does the man, Ologbon-Ori, find wisdom? Where does he find it?

As you read, ask yourself what the author's purpose is in writing this tale. Does he achieve that purpose?

How Ologbon-Ori Sought Wisdom

A Folktale from Nigeria

retold by Harold Courlander

In a certain village there was a man named Ologbon-Ori. He himself had never been far from his village, but he had heard many travelers speak of the wonders and wisdom to be found in the outside world. Ologbon-Ori yearned to see what the world beyond the bush country was like and to obtain some of the wisdom that was to be found there. And one day after the yams had been harvested, he decided to go on a journey with his small son to find some of it.

Ologbon-Ori had things prepared. He and his son bathed and put on their finest clothes. He fed his camel and watered him. Then he mounted the camel and seated his boy behind him. His friends stood at the trail as he departed, wishing him a safe journey. Ologbon-Ori and his son rode away.

In time they came to a town. There were many buildings. Many women were going and coming with produce on their heads. In the distance there was the hum of the marketplace. Ologbon-Ori rode to where the trading was going on. He was amazed at so much activity. "See," he said to his son, "around us is wisdom in great quantities. Let us see, let us learn."

Ologbon-Ori watched all the goings on with fascination. But soon he noticed that people were pointing at him and making comments. He listened. "What kind of man is this?" he heard someone say. "He makes his half-starved camel carry two persons." Someone else said: "Yes, he must come from the bush country. He has no feelings. See how exhausted his camel is."

When he had passed through the town, Ologbon-Ori said to his son: "You see, there are things to be learned in the world. I had not known it before, but a camel should not carry two people. So dismount, my son, and walk alongside."

The boy dismounted. He walked while his father rode. And in time they came to another town. As they passed through it, Ologbon-Ori marveled at the sights. But again he saw people pointing at him and making comments. He heard one man say: "See how the father rides while he makes the small child walk. Can such a man have a heart?" Another said: "Yes, it is so. Why should a strong man treat a boy this way?" A third man said: "He rides as though he were an Oba and the little one his slave."

Ologbon-Ori was troubled. He stopped, saying, "The knowledge of the world is hard to learn. How could we have gotten wisdom like this in our village?"

He dismounted and put his boy on the camel. The boy rode, and the father walked, and in this manner they came to the next town. It, also, was full of wonders. But once again Ologbon-Ori noticed that people were talking about him. "What is everything coming to," one man said, "when the young ride and the old must walk?" "Yes," another said, "is there no respect anymore for the aged? Since when does the child go in comfort while the father's feet are covered with dust?"

This time Ologbon-Ori was greatly perplexed. He thought about it deeply. At last he said: "There is much to learn in the outside world, things we never dreamed of in our village. How lucky we are to have made this journey. It is clear that neither of us may ride the camel, else shame comes on one or the other. Let us walk, therefore, the father and son side by side."

So walking together and leading the camel by his halter, they arrived in the fourth town, intrigued by the wonders around them. But as it was before, so it was again. People pointed, laughed, and made remarks. One said: "Look. A man, a boy, and camel, walking together like friends." Another said: "Whenever before has anyone seen such idiots? They are footsore and tired, yet they walk. Why don't they mount that camel and ride like any sensible people would do?"

This time when Ologbon-Ori stopped to consider the matter, he remained in thought a long while. At last he said: "I believe our journey has come to an end. We have learned a great thing — that the wisdom of one town is the stupidity of another. Whatever a man does to please someone will surely annoy others. Let us mount. Let us ride. Let us return whence we came." They mounted and rode back to their village in the bush country.

When they arrived, Ologbon-Ori's friends stood at the trail to greet him. They asked: "Where is it? Where is the wisdom of the world?"

Ologbon-Ori replied: "There is much wisdom to be found. I have returned with only a small portion of it. It is this:

'Seek wisdom, but do not throw away common sense.'"

Discuss the Selection

1. Did Ologbon-Ori find wisdom? Where did he find it?
2. In what different ways did Ologbon-Ori and his son use the camel?
3. Do you think Ologbon-Ori was wise to pay attention to the comments he heard? Explain.
4. Do you think that Ologbon-Ori's reply to his friends' question was a good one? Give reasons to support your answer.
5. At what point in the story did you realize that Ologbon-Ori would not be able to please everyone he and his son met?

Apply the Skills

Authors write for a number of purposes; they write to inform, to convince, and to entertain. Sometimes they write for all three purposes. What do you think the author's purpose was in writing this tale? Do you think he achieved his purpose? Explain your answer.

Think and Write

Prewrite

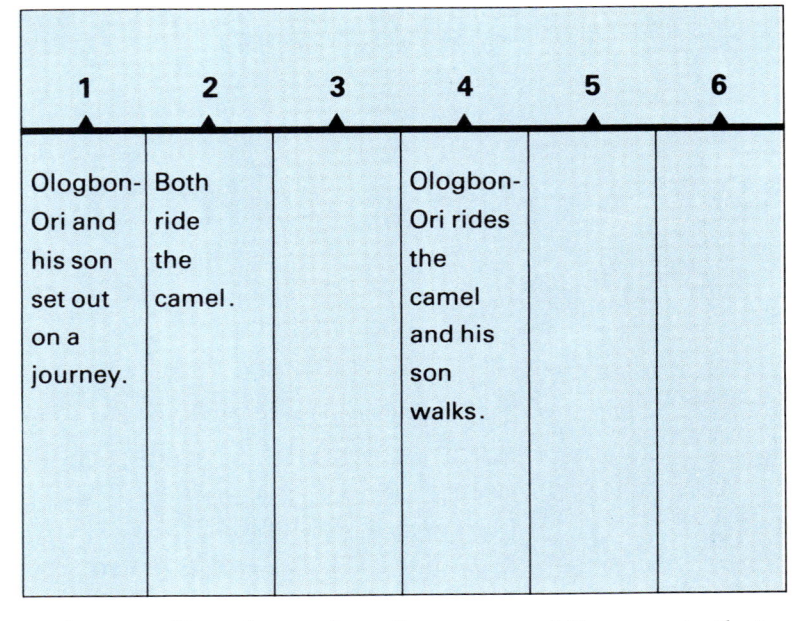

1	2	3	4	5	6
Ologbon-Ori and his son set out on a journey.	Both ride the camel.		Ologbon-Ori rides the camel and his son walks.		

The time line above describes some of the events that took place in "How Ologbon-Ori Sought Wisdom." When writing a summary of a story, you may find it helpful to make a time line to sequence the events that took place in the story. Copy the time line and fill in the missing events.

Compose

Write a short summary of the story "How Ologbon-Ori Sought Wisdom." Refer to the entries on the time line to make sure that you tell the events in sequence. Use time-order words such as *then*, *next*, and *finally*.

Revise

Read your summary. Did you include all the important events of the story? Are they in the correct order? Did you use some of the time-order words? If not, revise your work.

Facing the horizons of "growing up," Miranda seeks answers to questions about her life. How does Miranda's grandmother help her find an answer?

Miranda and her grandmother resemble each other. As you read, look for the similarities between the two of them.

Dear Greta Garbo

by Toby Talbot

Thirteen-year-old Miranda is spending the summer with her mother at their country house on Long Island. She will be returning home to New York City soon. Even though she is sad to see the summer end, she is looking forward to seeing her friends and moving into her sister's room while her sister is away at college. Then, without warning, her father calls from the city with the news that Grandpa is very sick. Miranda and her mother return immediately. By the time they arrive, he has died.

Miranda is very sad, remembering the fun she had with her grandfather and how much she loved him. Grandma moves into Miranda's sister's room in their apartment. As Miranda and her grandmother spend time together, they grow closer. The whole family feels empty because Grandpa is gone. In the months that follow, Miranda and her grandmother both try to look toward the future and struggle to live their own lives.

Miranda's mother waved the cake cutter in the air for emphasis and laid a slice of pumpkin pie in front of her mother. "Mother, you're only sixty-four years old. You look fifty-four. Youth is in the heart. It'll be just like home here. Dad would have wanted it this way, for you to live with us, not to be alone."

Miranda's father agreed. "We have plenty of room. You can come and go as you wish. Our house is your house."

"You're both good to me," said Grandma.

"You ought to start thinking about giving up your apartment. Life will be much simpler for you here. You won't have to worry about taking care of things, laundry, marketing, cleaning, paying rent. . . ."

Miranda began swaying on the front legs of her chair, wondering if her mother's life was very difficult. It must be hard for her to fit in everything. But what could she eliminate? Her work, her household tasks, her obligations to Grandma, to her family . . . to Miranda. Everyone counted on her, expected things of her. And she always came through.

Life isn't a picnic, they say. Was it always that complicated to be grown-up? Maybe it was better to be a child. Their next-door neighbor liked to tell Miranda that this was the best time of her life. Maybe she was right. Maybe thirteen years old was a good age to be.

"Miranda, please stop swinging on your chair," her mother put in, interrupting what she'd been saying.

"I wasn't swinging on my chair," Miranda grumbled, unaware that indeed she had been.

Her mother looked at her crookedly and went on. "As I was saying, there's no need for you to have the burden. . . . We *want* to have you here."

As Miranda continued listening uneasily, she crossed her legs and jiggled the right leg over the left knee. With each jiggle the leg banged the trestle under the table.

Her father turned to her. "Miranda, please stop kicking the table!" She uncrossed her legs and remained poised on the edge of her seat. Why were grown-ups so nervous, so irritable, about little things? Suddenly, she heard her grandmother speaking.

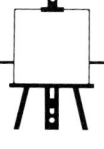

"I have my social security and your father's now, too. I can afford to keep my apartment. . . ."

"There are so many activities you could do," her mother went on. "At the Y they have an active Senior Citizen's Club with lectures and poetry readings. You can see old movies at the Museum of Modern Art. You and Dad were such movie fans. You can take French lessons at the Alliance Française, as you've always threatened to do, and pottery classes too. Working with clay would be wonderful for the arthritis in your fingers." Miranda's mother spoke with an optimistic tone, as if all possibilities lay ahead. "But the first thing to do is give up your apartment."

Miranda's grandmother rose and started to clear the table. "We'll see," she said.

"Leave all that, Mother. You don't have to clear. I'd like you to take it easy."

"It's all right, Hannah. I want to."

Miranda jumped from her chair, picked up the empty pie plate, and followed her grandmother into the kitchen. They both were silent and Miranda dawdled around the stove, rummaging around inside herself for some hidden thought that teased like a buzzing fly. In a moment she heard her mother call from the living room. "Miranda, have you finished your homework?" At this reminder, the secret thought burst forth. Why did her mother think she could organize Grandma's life the way she tried to organize Miranda's? As if they were both library books that could be tucked away safely in their proper shelf. Again, Miranda felt that tug to pull away, to run contrary to her mother's plans, battling with the other urge, to stay little Miranda.

"I finished my homework," Miranda called out crossly. "I don't have to be reminded. I'm not a baby."

Grandma looked at her but did not comment. She dried her hands on the kitchen towel and headed for the hall closet. Taking out her coat, she put it on.

"Where are you going?"

"Over to the store to pick up some honey." Grandma always drank hot milk and honey before going to bed. She'd done it since she was a child, she once told Miranda. It helped her fall asleep.

"Can I go with you?"

"Ask your mother."

As Miranda was going in to ask, her mother came out to the hall.

"Mama, you're not going out at this hour, are you?"

"It's only half past seven."

"It's not really safe to walk in the streets of New York at this hour."

"It's only half past seven and the streets are well lit. I've always gone for a walk after dinner."

Miranda knew that she had always gone out with Grandpa. "Mom, please let me go with Grandma. I'm all finished with my work."

"Well . . . I guess so, but come back soon so that you don't take your bath at all hours of the night."

At Pick 'N Pay, the twenty-four-hour store on Broadway, they bought a jar of honey, and then, the excuse for the walk accomplished, continued to stroll along. They paused at the Riviera movie house to study the photographs and the coming attractions. Today *Ninotchka* was playing, with Greta Garbo. A billboard displayed a large close-up of Garbo. She reminded Miranda of a statue of Venus on the ground floor of the Metropolitan Museum of Art. A broad forehead, slender nose, lofty cheekbones, large eyes. Garbo's hair, however, was chin length, while Venus's hair was long. Both Venus and Garbo seemed the essence of womanhood.

Miranda's grandmother gazed at the photos intently, as if they were an album recalling fragments of her own past.

"You know, Miranda, Greta Garbo was your grandfather's favorite actress. When I was younger, I used to be jealous of her. Can you imagine?" She smiled. "But Grandpa loved me to the end of his life. He loved me even more, I think, as we grew older. We understood each other better. He used to call me 'my gray-haired love.' "

It seemed funny to Miranda to think that old people could still talk about love romantically. She half-closed her eyes into slits and tried to imagine her grandmother as a young girl. Possibly she had looked like Miranda. People often remarked on the family resemblance. Maybe that was one of the reasons Miranda felt so close to her. Would she look and be like Grandma one day?

As they turned to leave, Miranda cast a parting glance at Garbo and then noticed that her grandmother was walking over to the box office. For a moment Miranda had the happy thought that her grandmother had impulsively decided to buy tickets.

"How many, please?" the cashier asked, chewing gum a mile a minute. She was wearing a frizzy blond wig.

"Uh . . . none, thank you," Grandma said, but continued to stand there. She was looking at a sign that read: WANTED. CASHIER. PART TIME. INQUIRE MANAGER INSIDE.

"Would you please step aside?" said the cashier. "You're blocking the line." The "line" consisted of one man waiting to buy a ticket.

Grandma stepped aside long enough for him to do so, and then asked, "Is the manager here?"

The cashier snapped her gum. "What's it in reference to?"

"The cashier position," Grandma said. Miranda looked at her in surprise. The cashier scrutinized her skeptically, a sneaky smile lurking round her lips as if to say, "You're too old." Miranda felt like tearing off her wig.

"He's on his lunch break," the cashier replied, pursing her lips. *How could anyone be eating lunch at eight o'clock at night?* Miranda wondered.

Grandma persisted. "When will he be back?"

"He won't be back," said the cashier, her nose twitching. "He has to go to the bank afterward." It was obviously a lie.

As they turned to leave, a man in a formal black suit, white shirt, and silver-striped tie came up to the box office.

He was dressed as if for a wedding. "How are we doing tonight?" he asked the cashier. Miranda saw her wink and signal to Grandma.

Her grandmother marched straight up to the man. "Are you the manager?"

He cleared his throat and tightened his tie. "Yes," he responded in a stuffy tone.

"I'm interested in the cashier vacancy," Grandma said with almost equal formality. Somehow she sounded more like a librarian than a cashier.

The manager expertly cased the elderly woman, dubiously eyeing her gray hair, her old-fashioned oxfords, the pearls around her neck. Miranda felt that he even noticed her knobby arthritic fingers. He cleared his throat again. "Well, I believe the position is filled, but you may leave your name and address if you wish."

He's just trying to get rid of her, Miranda thought. The cashier, with her smug look on her face, handed over pencil and paper, and Grandma wrote down her name, address, and phone number on a slip of paper that looked as if it would get thrown away as soon as their backs were turned.

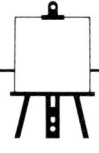

"Do you really want to work?" Miranda asked her grandmother on the way home.

"I hadn't considered it till this moment, but it's an idea. As they say, the days are long, but the years drag by. I'm so used to being with your grandfather. . . . Sometimes I'm afraid I've lost all my force. I've forgotten how it is to lead a life alone."

"But you're not alone, Grandma," said Miranda. "You have us . . . *me*."

Her grandmother squeezed her hand.

At home Miranda's mother had a steaming bath ready for Miranda. Somehow that annoyed Miranda. It was so babyish. At the same time she felt a twinge of guilt for resenting her mother's thoughtfulness.

"Mom, I wish I had hair like Greta Garbo's. Short, silky. Not this snarly old seaweed. It's always greasy these days."

"Miranda, what *are* you talking about? Your hair is beautiful, blond, and silky as corn tassels."

She thinks I look like Alice in Wonderland, thought Miranda, making a dash for the bathroom. *Next thing, she'll call it cute, and tie it with a pink satin ribbon.* . . . She slammed the door, locked it, and undressed. In front of the medicine-chest mirror, she sucked in her cheeks and held her hands over the bottom part of her hair. Despite these efforts, her round face and stubby nose looked more like W.C. Fields's than Greta Garbo's. Her head squatted on her shoulders like a turtle's. No neck. Miranda No-Neck. She plunged into the tub and submerged her head in the soapy water. A shampoo was the best medicine for anything.

"It's for you, Mother. Telephone."

Miranda awoke to the sound of her mother thumping on Grandma's door. Saturday morning, the one day Miranda could sleep late. No classes, no Sunday school. No peace. Miranda came to the breakfast table, sullen.

"What's come over you lately, Miranda?" her mother asked.

Miranda poured herself some cereal and stuck the box in

front of her face. Her grandmother walked in. She was all dressed, especially neat. Ready to go out.

"Good morning, everybody," she said.

"Who phoned you so early?" Miranda's mother asked. And before an answer was made, "And where are you going?" She sounded so nosy, thought Miranda, though she must admit, she herself was kind of curious.

"To work," Grandma answered.

"What?" Miranda's mother held the percolator in midair, as shocked as if Grandma had announced she was going to hold up a bank.

"Yes," Grandma nodded. "The manager of the Riviera called to offer me a job. I start in half an hour. They're having a kiddy show, and another cashier that they hired quit before she began."

"The Riviera? What are you talking about?" Miranda's mother demanded. Just then her father came into the kitchen.

"What's this I hear about the Riviera?" He went over and kissed Miranda on the head. "Miranda, are you going off to the sunny Riviera?" He laughed. Dad was the best audience for his own jokes.

"I wish I were," Miranda replied glumly.

"No, I am, Michael. I have a job as a cashier at the Riviera Theatre."

"I can't believe it, Mother. You must be fooling. You wouldn't work as a *cashier*, out on the sidewalk, exposed to full view! It's not right, it's...."

Miranda mentally finished her mother's sentence — *it's below you*.

Grandma smiled. "Oh, Hannah, don't be such a snob." Miranda bit her lips to hold back her approval.

"It's not that, Mother. But you haven't worked in years."

"Don't you think I can do it, Hannah?"

"It's not that, but you're too...." She broke off.

"Too old?" Grandma finished. *Glory, glory!* Miranda sang inside. Her grandmother sure knew how to say things straight out.

"No, that's *not* what I was going to say; you're too qualified."

"Qualified for what? Pottery classes, French lessons, senior citizens' socials?"

"You know that's not what I mean. You're a librarian, like I am."

"Hannah, how old are you?" Grandma asked.

"Thirty-nine."

"Well, I haven't been a librarian for thirty-nine years. I stopped being a librarian a month before you were born. I don't even remember the Dewey Decimal System."

Miranda smiled happily. Neither did she.

"There's no reason why I can't get you a volunteer job at our library. We always need help."

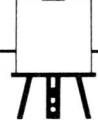

"I don't want a volunteer job, Hannah, and I don't need you to get me a job at your library," Grandma said quietly. "Look, we'll talk later. I have to leave or I'll be late."

"Without tea?" Miranda asked. Tea was Grandma's staff of life.

"Don't worry, Miranda. I'll have some later."

"I still don't think it's safe. You hear such stories these days. . . and read such terrible headlines." Miranda's mother looked anxious, as if she wanted to cling to her mother.

"Don't worry, Hannah dear," Grandma repeated. "I can take care of myself."

"When will you be back?" Miranda's mother stirred her spoon round in her cup.

"I don't know. Later. Good-by, everybody."

"I can't believe it," Miranda's mother said after the front door closed.

"What is so terrible about Grandma taking a job?" Miranda asked. "*You* work."

"Imagine her sitting in that cage all day. And my friends passing by and seeing her."

So that is it, thought Miranda. Her mother, in addition to everything, didn't want Grandma to be on public display. To take what *she* considered a lowly job. Miranda wondered if her mother feared that one day she might be reduced to being a cashier. What would happen if Miranda announced that she was going to be one? It was less boring than being a tollbooth taker or an elevator operator. In fact, come to think of it, it was *interesting* — watching the stream of people go by, observing the scene.

"It's certainly something *I'd* never do," her mother said.

Miranda gloated inwardly at her correct guess. "I don't see anything wrong with Grandma taking that job."

"Oh, Miranda, you don't understand! You're too young!"

Miranda *knew* she'd say that.

"I'm not too young to know that Grandma has a right to lead her own life," she shot back. And she felt like adding, "And me too!"

"What is this, Miranda, are you and your grandmother in cahoots?" her father put in. "Your mother is right. It isn't safe."

"Or . . . or proper," his wife concluded.

"Let's drop it now," said Miranda's father. "We'll discuss it when Grandma gets back."

Miranda stood up from the table. She knew they'd discuss it more when she was out of earshot. They thought she was too childish, too immature to take into their confidence. Sometimes she had the feeling they saved *really* important matters for private discussion. After all, what value did her opinion have?

Miranda stationed herself across the street from the Riviera to watch her grandmother in action. A line of noisy kids was crowding in front of the cashier's box while Grandma, inside the little booth, was taking money, giving change, tearing off tickets, answering the telephone. She seemed a trifle flustered as the kids bumped and jostled one another, but she was managing. Miranda felt proud of her, as if her grandmother had gone public.

Grandma now seemed doubly precious for those private moments they'd been sharing in the last month and a half. She was such a comfort to Miranda. You could tell her anything, even secrets. She was never a judge, though she had her own opinions and expressed them freely. She was one person who could come out and say what she felt. How Miranda admired that.

Miranda leaned against a lamppost and looked at her grandmother. *I knew she would do it*, she said to herself.

Miranda turned and gazed idly into a shop window. It was one of the oldest stores in the neighborhood. They rented tuxedos. Two mannequins, a bride and groom, stood in the window, smiling in eternal wedding bliss. A sign said: YOU GET MARRIED ONLY ONCE. WHY BUY A TUXEDO? RENT. Next door to the tuxedo rental was a beauty parlor. Three disembodied heads gaped at the sidewalk, one wearing a black wig, another a red wig, the third, a blond. Their reflections were caught in a rear window. A sign in the window read: WE SPECIALIZE IN LONG HAIR. *That means me*, thought Miranda, and she studied herself in a mirror. Her hair, despite last night's shampoo, was greasy and straggly.

In the mirror she caught herself making faces. She began fingering the allowance that had been given her that morning. She about-faced toward the Riviera. But this time it was not only Grandma and the Riviera she saw. Soaring above the building, like a radiant mirage, was Greta. Dear Greta Garbo! With ethereal free hair . . . A symbol of womanhood, of independence.

The decision no longer rested in Miranda's power. Her feet on their own floated into the beauty parlor. Fumes of lotions, hair spray, shampoo, creams, ammonia, other unidentifiable odors drifted forth. The place was humid and musky as a dense underbrush. A low hum of voices formed the background, like twittering birds when you enter a clearing in the woods. A voice in a pink uniform stepped forward.

"May I help you?"

Peering past the pink uniform into the parlor, Miranda viewed a row of seated women, heads bound in rollers, seemingly attached to the domed dryers overhead. Miranda pushed her hair behind her ears, swallowed, and said casually, "How much is a haircut, please?"

The magic words set gears in motion. Miranda was instantly turned over to another pink uniform, a young, brisk beautician with a cropped head.

"Step up, miss," she said, guiding Miranda into a high leather chair.

Miranda, facing the mirror, pulled her skirt over her knees the way she did at the dentist's, and stared at herself. Her sidewalk assurance had deserted her, and a froglike woebegone look made her eyes seem twice their natural size. A white length of gauze was wound round her neck; she felt like a mummy being prepared for funeral rites. Then a green plastic cape fell over her shoulders, leaving the head exposed as a target. Miranda closed her eyes a moment to resuscitate Garbo's image.

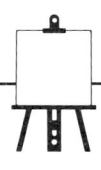

"How short would you like it?" the beautician asked.

Miranda inserted a length of front hair between her middle and index fingers. The young woman nodded and in a wink had made a wide decisive first snip. Her fingers moved quick as a sleight-of-hand magician's.

Miranda was in the chair only ten minutes. In those ten minutes her hair was halved. The beautician stood back and surveyed Miranda's head, scissors still snipping the air. She looked as if she could go on forever. Miranda was a hairdresser's dream.

"Would you like me to take off a smidge more?" she asked.

Miranda gazed at herself in the mirror. Her new self. Her hair was chin length, like Garbo's, and her neck rose straight as a column, where before it had jutted out squat as a turtle's. The straggly ends were gone; the bottom was straight as an arrow.

"Would you?" the beautician repeated. "A *little* more?"

Miranda glanced at the floor, at the peacock fan of hair, *her* hair, that encircled the chair, and then looked sideways at the beautician's cropped head.

"I think that will be enough," she said in the polite but firm tone of someone refusing second helpings.

She looked beautiful. Suddenly she had a neck, visible, exposed, a proper resting place for her head. Miranda practiced a little smile in the mirror. Without all that hair, her features seemed more expressive. She was more herself!

All her doubts and hesitations were gone. She couldn't believe how easy it was to cut, to remove, to change — once you made up your mind. She'd never had a haircut in her life. Can you imagine? Thirteen years old and still sporting the original mat she'd been born with — plus. It was primitive. Her mother had always regarded Miranda's hair as her best feature. But for Miranda, the long hair was a vestige of babyhood; Goldilocks, curly locks, to please Mama, the epitome of Shirley Temple rather than Greta Garbo.

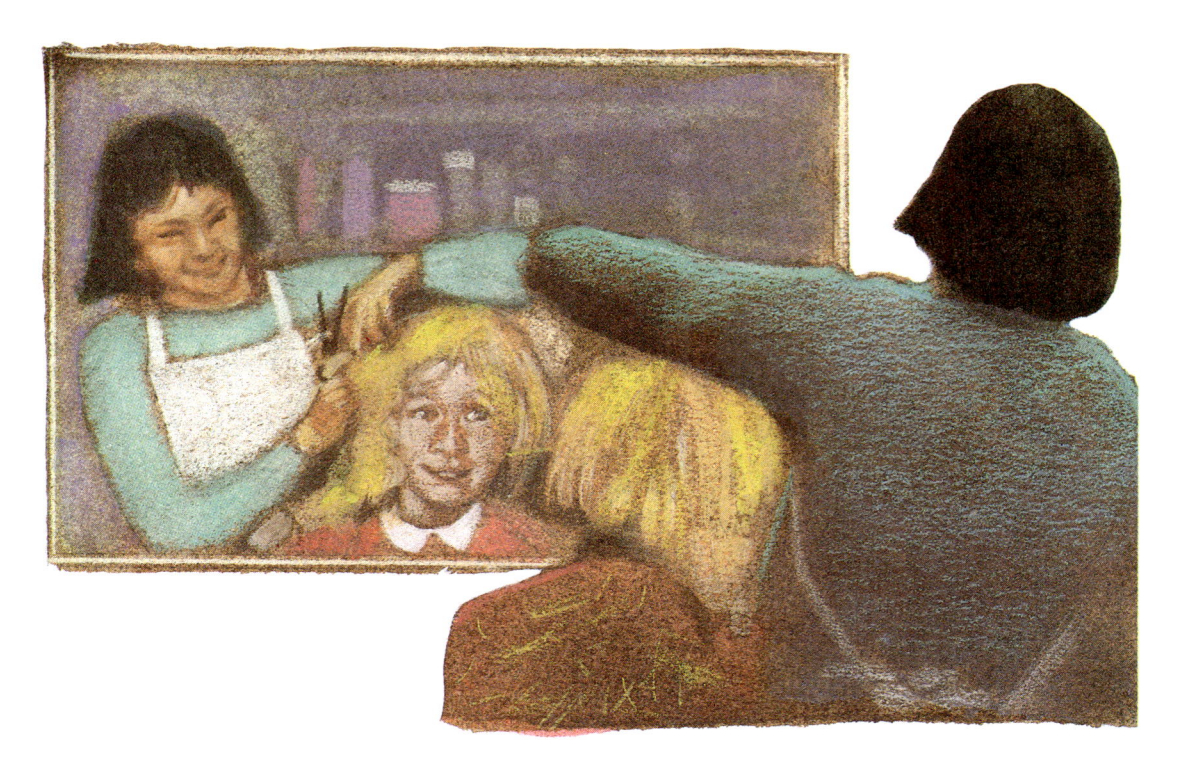

"Would you like to take it home with you?" the beautician asked, like a waiter offering a doggie bag.

"What for?" asked Miranda, glad to be rid of it.

"I don't know. Some people save their hair...." The young woman smiled lamely as she rang up the money in the cash register.

Miranda, the new Miranda, sister of Garbo, sailed into the street. She felt inches taller. She was a long-stemmed rose. A drum majorette high-stepping down Broadway, toes first, arms swinging, head bobbing with little airs and graces. Suddenly the day had wings. If it was that easy to change her hair, why not other things, too?

Head elevated like a swan's, she smiled at the mannequins in the tuxedo rental shop and then crossed Broadway. She nodded in a queenly manner to a man eating a roll, a woman feeding the pigeons, and to the pigeons themselves. Was everyone noticing how different she was?

The sky was a cloudless luminous blue, a banner for her new sense of freedom. As she strode home, the breeze from the river stroked her neck.

Discuss the Selection

1. How did Miranda's grandmother help her find her answer?
2. Why did Miranda's grandmother apply for the job as a ticket cashier?
3. Miranda admired her grandmother. Cite examples in the story that indicate what Miranda admired about her grandmother.
4. How could a change in Miranda's physical appearance change her outlook about her life?
5. How did you think Miranda's mother will react to Miranda's new haircut? What explanation do you think Miranda will give her mother?

Apply the Skills

When you compare two or more things, people, or situations, you notice their similarities. What similarities did you find between Miranda and her grandmother?

Think and Write

Prewrite

Event
Date
Time
Place
For whom
For information contact

Signs were an important part in changing the lives of Miranda and her grandmother in "Dear Greta Garbo." Signs and notices should be designed to attract attention. The use of color, print, or pictures are ways of doing this. The chart above lists the information one might use for a notice. Copy the chart and complete it with information about the tryouts for a school play.

Compose

Prepare a notice for the school bulletin board announcing tryouts for a school play. Use the information that you wrote in the chart. Remember to make your notice appealing and attention-getting.

Revise

Reread your notice. Did you include all the important details? Will your notice be understood by all? Will it attract attention? If not, revise your work.

Study Skills

Libraries

An up-to-date term for finding out something that you want to know is information retrieval. Of course, sometimes you aren't really retrieving the information. Rather, you're searching for facts that you never knew in the first place. Today, there are more ways than ever of finding out whatever it is that you need to know.

We live in an information age. Librarians are always thinking of new ways to store all this information so that it is available for research. The largest part of a library's collection is made up of books, newspapers, and magazines. Most libraries also store information on tape, film, and even on computers.

Libraries are generally divided into four sections — fiction, nonfiction, reference, and periodicals.

The fiction section holds novels and books of short stories. These books are arranged alphabetically by the author's last name. If the same author has written several books, they are arranged under his or her name and then alphabetized by title.

The nonfiction section holds books about science, engineering, music, art, religion, and history. It also holds books of poems and books of plays. Nonfiction books are arranged by subject. For example, books about music will be grouped together.

Biographies, a type of nonfiction, are sometimes put in another part of the library. They are arranged alphabetically by subject. If more than one author has written a biography about the same person, the books are then arranged alphabetically by the author's last name.

In the reference section, you will find encyclopedias, almanacs, dictionaries, and atlases. You will also find books such as biographical dictionaries and guidebooks.

In the periodical section, you will find the latest newspapers and magazines. Back issues of newspapers and magazines may be bound together in book form. Sometimes they are stored on film. Pages reduced photographically are put on microfilm. These pages may then be put together on a large sheet of film called a microfiche. The periodical section also holds pamphlets, which are arranged in folders by subject. This is called the vertical file of the periodical section.

The Readers' Guide to Periodical Literature

The *Readers' Guide to Periodical Literature* is a monthly listing of all the articles that appear in major magazines. The articles listed in the *Readers' Guide* are arranged in alphabetical order. The *Readers' Guide* is the most up-to-date listing of articles on different subjects.

The Dewey Decimal System

The **Dewey Decimal System** is a fast and easy way to find a nonfiction book. It groups all nonfiction books by subject. In all, there are ten groups. Here are the ten groups:

000—099	General works (encyclopedias, periodicals)
100—199	Philosophy (conduct, ethics, psychology)
200—299	Religion (Bible stories, myths, religious history)
300—399	Social sciences (economics, law, education)
400—499	Linguistics (dictionaries, grammars)
500—599	Pure science (mathematics, astronomy, physics)
600—699	Applied science (engineering, radio, aeronautics)
700—799	Arts and recreation (art, music, games)
800—899	Literature (poems, plays, essays — not fiction)
900—999	History (travel, geography, biography)

The Dewey Decimal number, called the call number, is printed on the spine of each nonfiction book. The books are arranged on the shelves in numerical order by call number.

Letters Used in Call Numbers

Besides numbers in a call number, you'll often see letters. Here are some of the letters:

- R = Reference (usually these books cannot be taken from the library)
- B = Biography (sometimes found in a separate section)
- J = Juvenile (usually found in a separate section)
- YA = Young adult (often found in the adult section)
- F = Fiction (arranged alphabetically by author and found in a separate section)

Whether you know exactly what you want or have only a general idea, the Dewey Decimal System can help you. If you want a certain book on music, for instance, you can check the card catalog under the title of the book. You can also check under the author's last name. The call number, which is found on the upper left-hand corner of the card, will tell you where the book can be found. On the other hand, if any music book will do, check the card catalog under *Music*. Then read the cards that describe books on music until you find one that seems most useful to you.

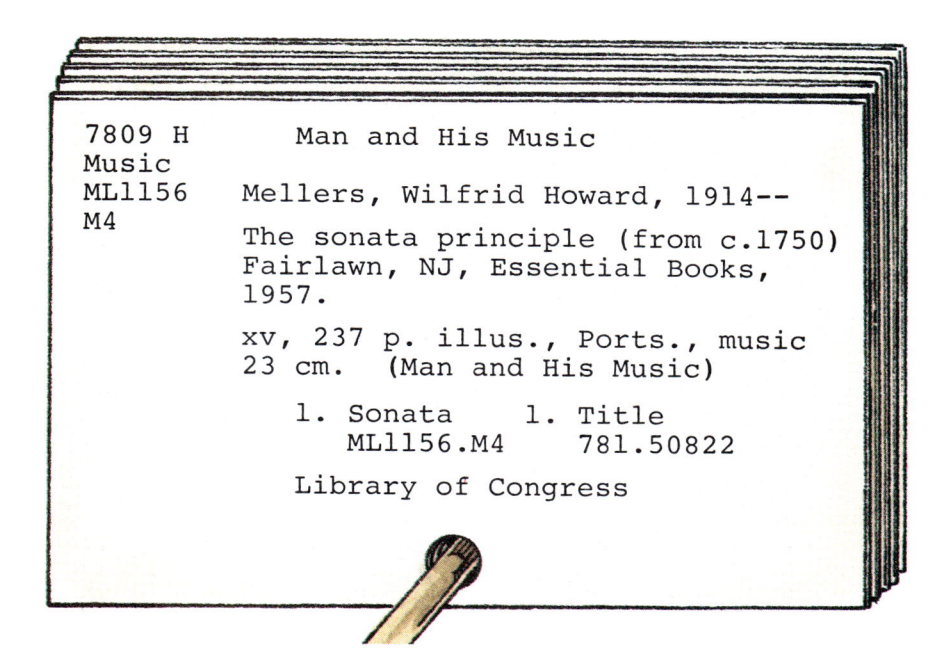

```
7809 H        Man and His Music
Music
ML1156        Mellers, Wilfrid Howard, 1914--
M4
              The sonata principle (from c.1750)
              Fairlawn, NJ, Essential Books,
              1957.

              xv, 237 p. illus., Ports., music
              23 cm.  (Man and His Music)

                 1. Sonata    1. Title
                    ML1156.M4    781.50822

              Library of Congress
```

Library Files and Records

Two helpful files in the library are the **picture file** and the **vertical file.** The picture file, as its name tells you, contains pictures of all kinds. The vertical file contains informational pamphlets published by various organizations. Both the picture file and the vertical file are arranged alphabetically by subject.

Many libraries are now setting up listening laboratories. Such laboratories contain headphones, cassette tapes, and other audio-visual aids. This equipment, of course, cannot be checked out of the library.

Special Services

Bookmobiles are bus-size vehicles stocked with hundreds of books. They go to hospitals and schools to provide library service to those who cannot get to the library.

Many popular books have been reprinted in large type for people who have trouble seeing regular print. These large-print books are unabridged and are found in a separate part of the library.

Talking books are recordings of stories and other kinds of reading material. These books were recorded while someone read them aloud. Talking books were originally recorded as a service for the blind. Now, these books are finding their way to classrooms everywhere.

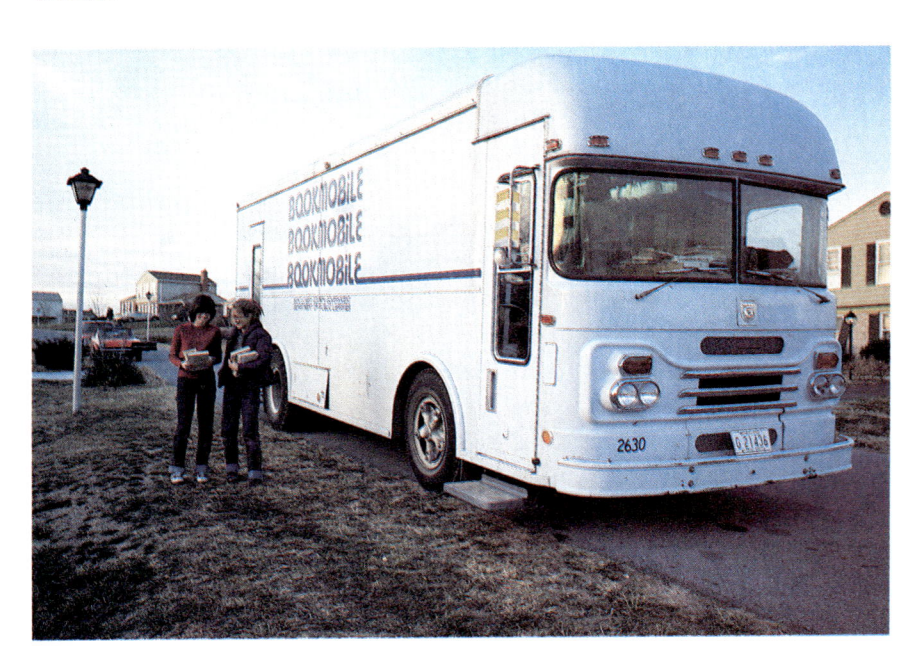

The growing awareness of physical fitness has led to the rapid expansion of a new medical field — sports medicine. What is sports medicine? Where did it get its start?

As you read, notice the author's use of details in describing various aspects of sports medicine.

What Is Sports Medicine?

by *Melvin Berger*

A famous football star is afraid his career is over because of a bad knee.

A player on a high school soccer team sprains his shoulder during a game.

A champion ice skater wants a training program that will get her into top shape for the day of her Olympic race.

A running-shoe manufacturer is trying to design the best possible shoe for joggers who run on hard pavement.

A first-grader breaks her arm in a fall while roller-skating.

A sixty-two-year-old man who has had heart surgery wants to know whether it is safe for him to play tennis.

These people are typical of the many persons who need treatment, help, or advice because they take part in sports. In the past, such people would go to their doctor or coach to get medical attention. Now, more and more of them are turning to experts in the new field of sports medicine.

Simply put, sports medicine is the science of preventing and treating sports injuries. But it is more than that. It also includes building physical fitness, improving athletic skills, developing good mental health, and doing basic research on people and sports and sports equipment.

Who Are the Sports Scientists?

A number of different kinds of scientists are at work in the field of sports medicine. At the head of most sports medicine teams is the orthopedic surgeon. He or she is a doctor who treats diseases or deformities of the body's structure. These doctors may suggest a few days of rest or give some special exercises. They may prescribe drugs, braces, or casts. Or, in some cases, they may decide to operate.

Working with the orthopedic surgeons are experts who study the human body. They study the effects of exercise on the body. These specialists do many jobs in sports medicine. They test the strength of the different muscles of the body. They measure the patient's lung capacity. They learn the proportion of fat to lean tissue in the patient's body. They develop special exercises for their patients.

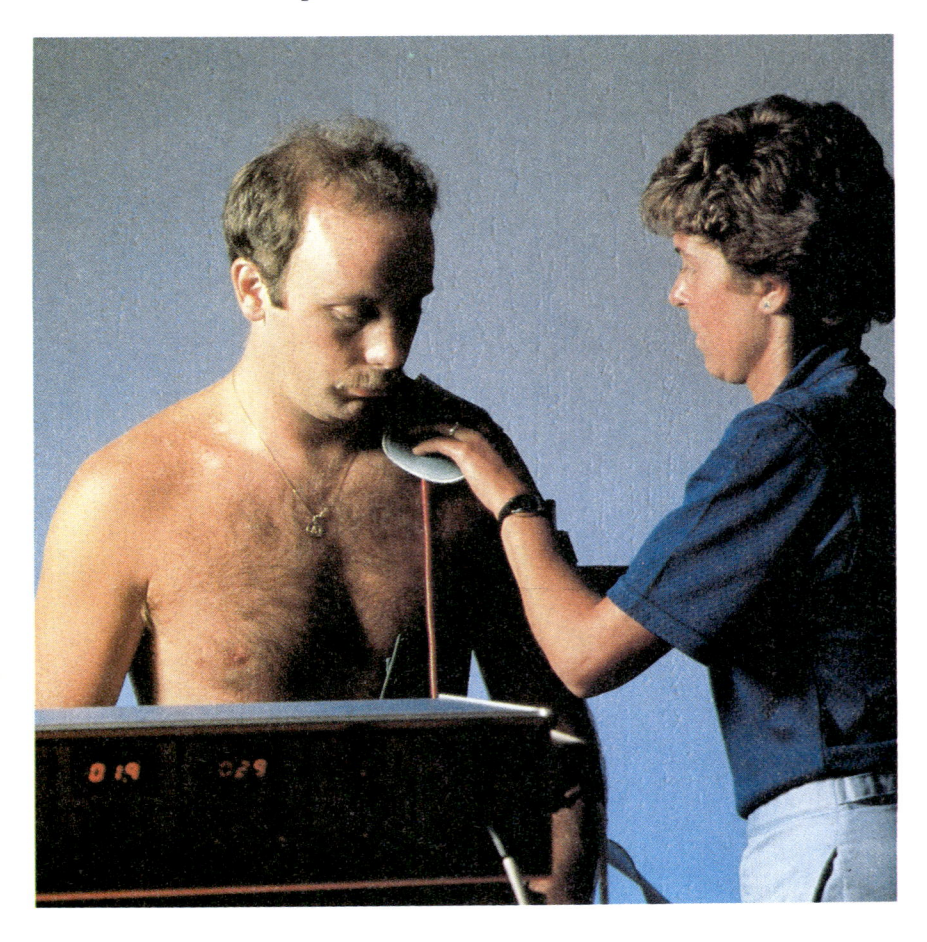

Athlete being treated with a Dyna-Wave, Dyna-Sound machine.

Physical condition is not the only factor in sports success. Mental condition is also important. The scientists who study the relationships between mind and body are psychologists. They help athletes overcome any mental blocks that may be keeping them from success in sports. By talking over their problems with them, the psychologists are often able to help athletes improve their performance, enjoy their sport more, and in general, become happier people.

Behind the scenes in sports medicine are many scientists who study the human body as a machine. These studies help athletes perform better.

Other medical specialists are sometimes called in to help the sports scientists. Among them are podiatrists, who study the feet, cardiologists, who study the heart, and dermatologists, who study the skin. Also, the sports scientist may consult with nutritionists, who help plan diets for athletes.

Sports scientists come from different backgrounds and do a

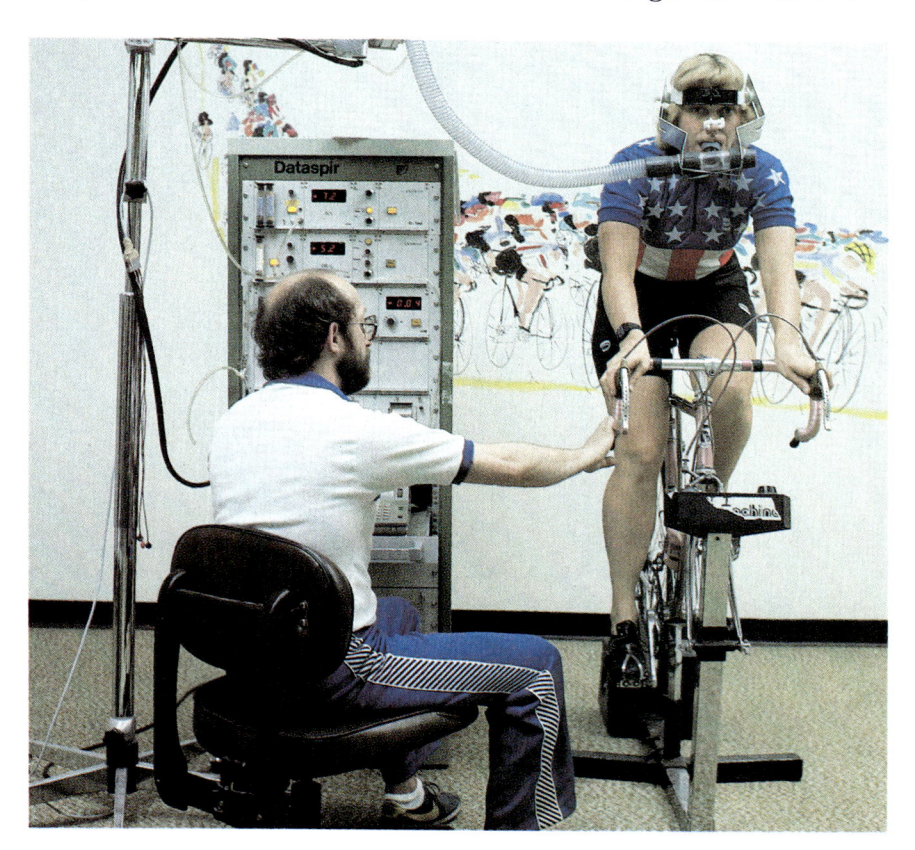

A researcher in biomechanics studies the leg movements of a cyclist.

great many different tasks. They hold many points of view. But in one way they are all the same. All care deeply about sports. In their hospitals and offices, they are working to bring the delights of safe, health-giving sports to everyone.

Where Did Sports Medicine Start?

The idea that athletes need special care goes all the way back to ancient Greece. In those days the sports medicine doctors were called *gymnasts,* a Greek word for the people who trained and treated athletes. Hippocrates, the father of modern medicine, was a gymnast for some of the early Olympic games held at Olympia in Greece.

Over the following years, though, sports medicine dropped in importance. Doctors were mostly concerned with the survival of their patients. And since sports was such a small part of daily life, they saw little need to develop this branch of medicine.

The situation stayed about the same until early in the twentieth century. By then, medical science had advanced to the point where doctors could look beyond just helping people live longer. Some began to think about improving the quality of life through physical fitness.

Three early sports scientists, Robert Osgood, P.D. Wilson, and Gus Thorndike, started the first fitness laboratory at Harvard University in 1919. It is considered the first sports medicine facility in the United States.

Sports medicine centers, concerned with injuries as well as fitness, began opening in the mid-1950's. Since then they have grown quickly. By 1980 about eighty-five sports medicine centers were in full bloom around the country. And new ones are opening all the time.

Why the Growth in Sports Medicine?

The rapid gain in sports science seems to have two basic explanations. First, many more people are active in sports. More free time and more and better sports equipment and facilities are making it easier for people of all ages to take part in sports.

It is estimated that in the United States about fifty-five million adults exercise daily. Some twenty-five million youngsters under the age of sixteen play at some sport after school.

All this sports activity is surely improving the health and well-being of the players. But it is also increasing the number of sports-related injuries. An estimated twenty million adults and ten million youngsters are treated for sports injuries every year.

Sports medicine has also grown because of advances in modern science. Only recently has it become possible to prevent and treat successfully the many different kinds of sports injuries. But often it takes someone who knows sports medicine to treat these patients. Most doctors are best at treating one part of the body, such as the heart or the eyes. What the hurt athlete needs are health experts who treat only those in sports and athletics.

Treating a Sports Injury

A sports injury can be frightening. An athlete may worry about losing the skills needed for his or her sport. At such a time, an expert in sports medicine is the best doctor to see. Susan, a twenty-year-old college student who plays tennis, went to such a doctor. Let's follow her case.

Not long ago Susan came to the office of Dr. Dinesh Patel, an orthopedic surgeon at Massachusetts General Hospital in Boston. She was frightened and in terrible pain. The day before, in the middle of a game, Susan's right knee had suddenly locked in place. Would she ever be able to play tennis again? How long would she have to stay away from school?

The Examination

First, Dr. Patel questioned Susan carefully about the injury. "How did you get hurt?" he asked. "Did you twist your leg? Did you bang your knee? Did you fall down on it? Has this happened before?"

Susan told the doctor how the accident had happened. She had twisted around quickly for a backhand shot. Suddenly she felt a sharp pain in her knee. That is when she fell. As she started to get up and tried to straighten her leg, the pain got worse. She found that she could not move the knee at all.

From Dr. Patel's experience as a sports medicine doctor, as well as an amateur tennis player, he believed that Susan had probably torn the cartilage in her knee. The cartilage in the

Dr. Patel, co-director of the Sports Medicine Clinic, examines the injury.

knee joint is made up of two half-moon-shaped wedges of tough, elastic tissue on either side of the knee. They serve as cushions or shock absorbers for the bones in the knee joint. They help to keep the joint stable. When the upper body twists without moving the foot, the cartilage can tear.

Torn cartilage in the knee is a very common sports injury. When it tears, cartilage does not heal. If the person is in pain, the only treatment is to remove the damaged cartilage by surgery.

Dr. Patel moved and bent Susan's knee in different directions. He carefully felt around the joint, looking for tenderness, swelling, or other symptoms of injury. Step by step, he judged the extent of the injury.

When he finished this part of the exam, Dr. Patel ordered X-rays of Susan's knee. After this, Dr. Patel called in Ara Sakayan, a registered physical therapist. Mr. Sakayan sat Susan at a machine that measured the strength, power, and endurance of her good leg. Dr. Patel then set himself the goal of making Susan's injured leg at least 90 percent as strong as the healthy one.

By now, Dr. Patel was quite sure that Susan had indeed torn the cartilage in her right knee. But he took the time to talk to her and to get to know her better. Using a plastic model of the knee joint, he told her exactly what had happened inside her knee. Then he told her what he would like to do to repair the damage. As a tennis player himself, he was able to make it very clear that he understood just how important the game was to her.

Dr. Patel planned surgery to remove the damaged tissue. Further, he planned to use a surgical method called *arthroscopy*. The basic tool of this new kind of surgery is the arthroscope. This is a long, narrow, hollow tube like a metal drinking straw. The surgeon inserts the arthroscope into the joint, and can see the condition of the bones, lining, cartilage, and ligaments inside. A number of different tools can then be used to perform the many tasks necessary in knee surgery.

In order for Susan to understand the operation, Dr. Patel took her to the audiovisual room in his office. There he showed her a videotape that explained every step of the procedure.

Dr. Patel and Susan chose a day for the surgery. It would not be necessary for her to spend even one night in the hospital. She would arrive early that morning, be operated on that same morning, and return home late that afternoon. Before surgery, Mr. Sakayan would show her special exercises so that she would not suffer any weakness in her legs.

The Operation

Susan could not help being a little frightened when she arrived at the hospital early on the day of the operation. But she had complete trust and confidence in Dr. Patel.

Susan was prepared for the surgery, and taken to the operating room. Here she was given a general anesthetic. She would feel absolutely no pain during the surgery.

Dr. Patel started by making a small, quarter-inch incision, or cut, on the side of her knee. He inserted the arthroscope through the incision. A light shining through the tube allowed Dr. Patel to see inside the joint.

Dr. Patel, though, preferred to use a miniature, hand-held TV camera that he attached to the outside end of the arthroscope. The greatly magnified picture appeared on a TV monitor in the operating room.

The closed-circuit TV offered several advantages. It showed features inside the knee that might be hard to see. It let Dr. Patel work without craning his neck. The nurses and other staff were able to help more because they could see all that was happening inside the knee. Since he did not have to peer through the arthroscope, Dr. Patel kept his head away from the incision, lessening the chance of infection. And finally, Dr. Patel was able to videotape the whole operation for later study.

While holding the arthroscope and attached TV camera in one hand, Dr. Patel used his other hand to insert a probe through a second incision. With this probe he checked the

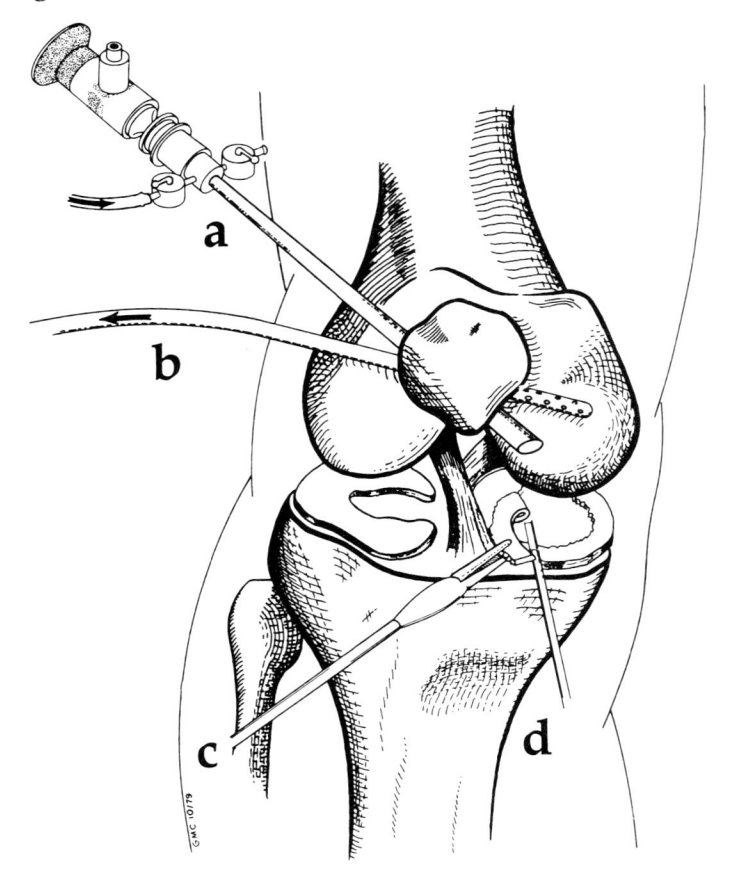

Four instruments used in the operation: an arthroscope (a), a tube to remove fluids (b), a "grabber" (c), and a knife (d).

257

Surgeon views an enlarged picture of the knee on a monitor.

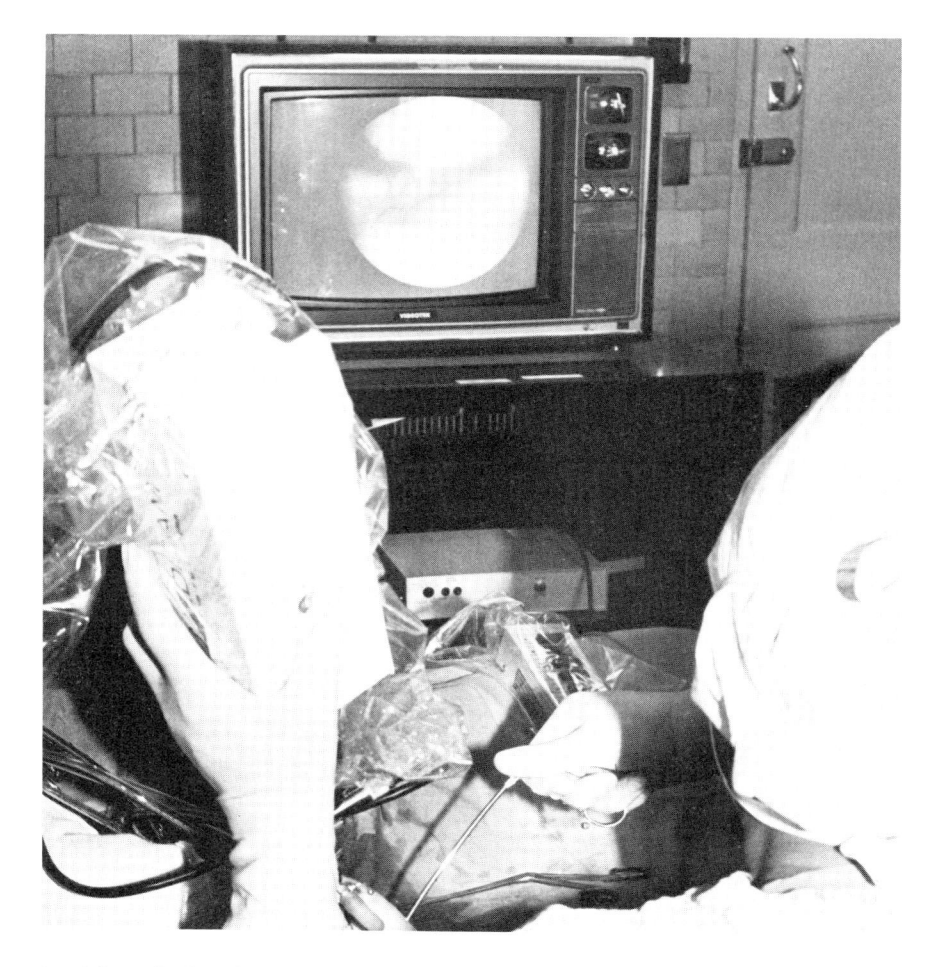

inside of the knee. He looked for any bits of loose material within the joint. As far as he could see, the only problem was the damaged cartilage.

Dr. Patel removed the probe. Then he inserted a miniature instrument with a small, sharp knife blade at the end. Guided by the image on the TV screen, he snipped off the torn section of cartilage.

The doctor next put a grabber, a kind of tiny plier, into the incision. He grasped the torn piece of cartilage and removed it from the knee. Next, he flushed the knee joint out with a salt-water solution to remove any loose particles and debris. Then, with a few stitches, he closed up the tiny cuts. The operation was over in less than a half hour.

Susan was wheeled from the operating room to a recovery

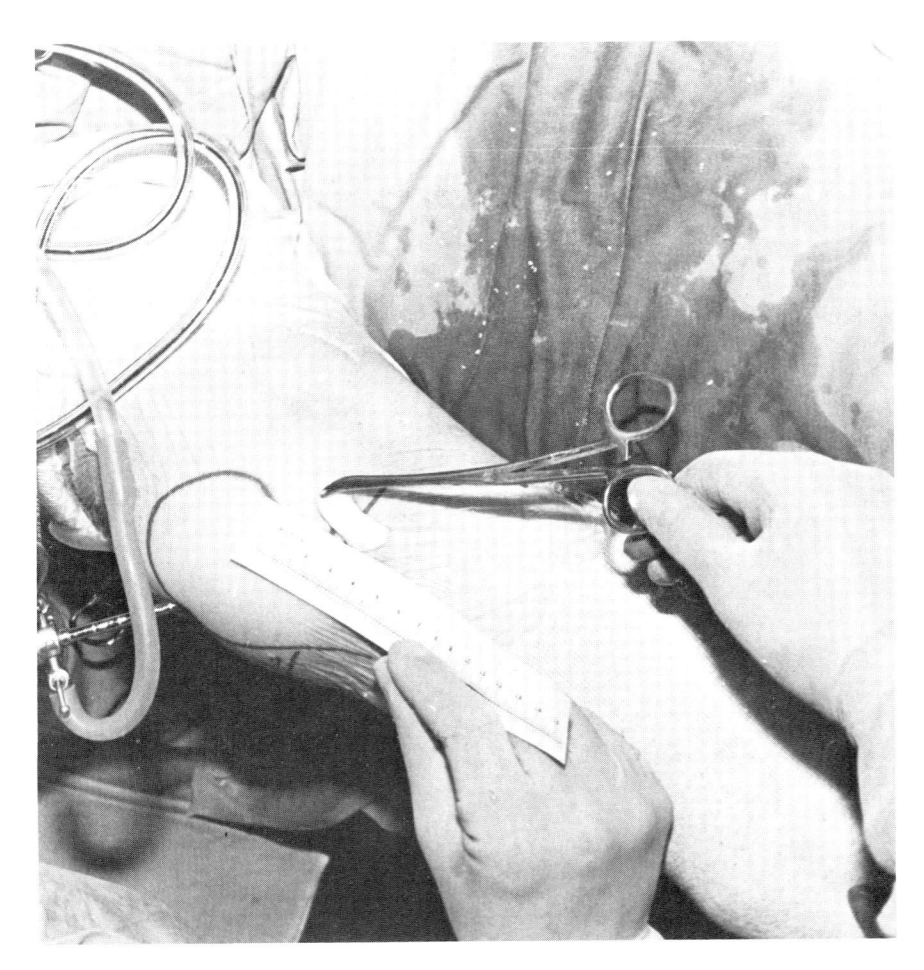

Dr. Patel measures the cartilage removed from the knee.

room. When the anesthesia wore off, Susan said she felt fine.

By late afternoon of the same day, Susan checked out of the hospital. Dr. Patel told her to walk with crutches to get extra support for her right knee.

The next day Susan was back at school. She began doing the knee exercises that Mr. Sakayan had shown her. Only ten days more and she was ready to play tennis again. Tests showed that over 90 percent of the original motion had been restored to her knee.

Arthroscopy was a fast, easy way for Dr. Patel to remove Susan's torn cartilage. This method, however, cannot be used for all knee surgery. Many knee operations require a longer incision and more destruction of tissue. Perhaps, in time, it will be possible to use arthroscopy more widely.

Discuss the Selection

1. What is sports medicine? Where did it get its start?
2. How are doctors using sports medicine to treat their patients?
3. How did you feel during the description of Susan's knee operation? Did you feel that you knew how it would turn out?
4. How successful was Susan's operation? Give reasons for your answer.
5. Find the part of the selection that mentions the kinds of doctors who specialize in various branches of sports medicine. Choose one branch of sports medicine and tell about the work done in it.

Apply the Skills

Authors use many details to describe certain aspects of a selection. In this selection, the author's step-by-step account of Susan's knee surgery is a good example of the use of details. Describe Susan's knee surgery. Cite as many specific details as possible from the selection.

Think and Write

Prewrite

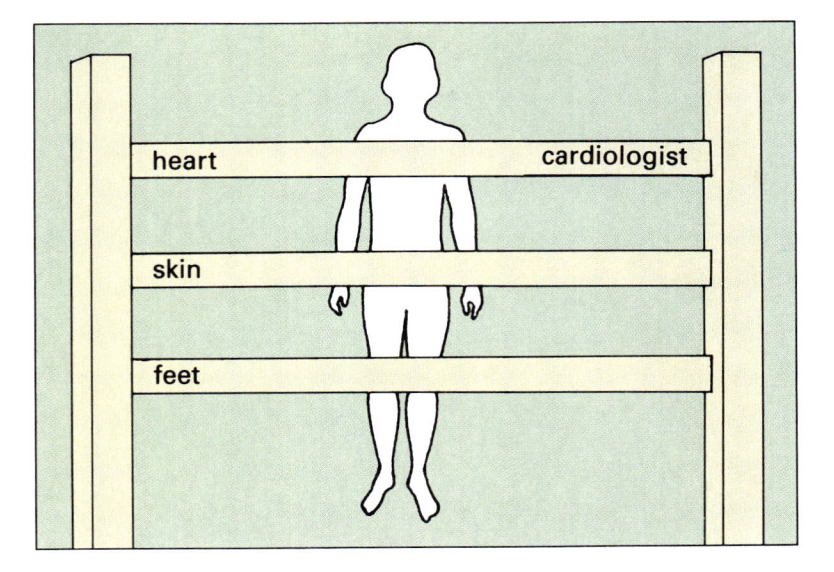

[Laddergram showing a human figure with three rungs labeled: "heart" — "cardiologist", "skin", and "feet".]

The left side of the laddergram shown above lists human body parts. The right side lists types of doctors who treat particular body parts. Copy the laddergram, and complete it by matching the specialist to the proper body part.

Compose

Write a paragraph describing a sports injury that might require a particular medical specialist. Refer to the laddergram and selection as needed. Your first sentence might be *Sometimes a runner's feet become too sore in the race, and the runner needs to see a podiatrist.*

Revise

Read your paragraph. Did you correctly match each body part with the doctor who specializes in treating it? Could someone who hasn't read the selection understand from your paragraph what that doctor does? If not, revise your work.

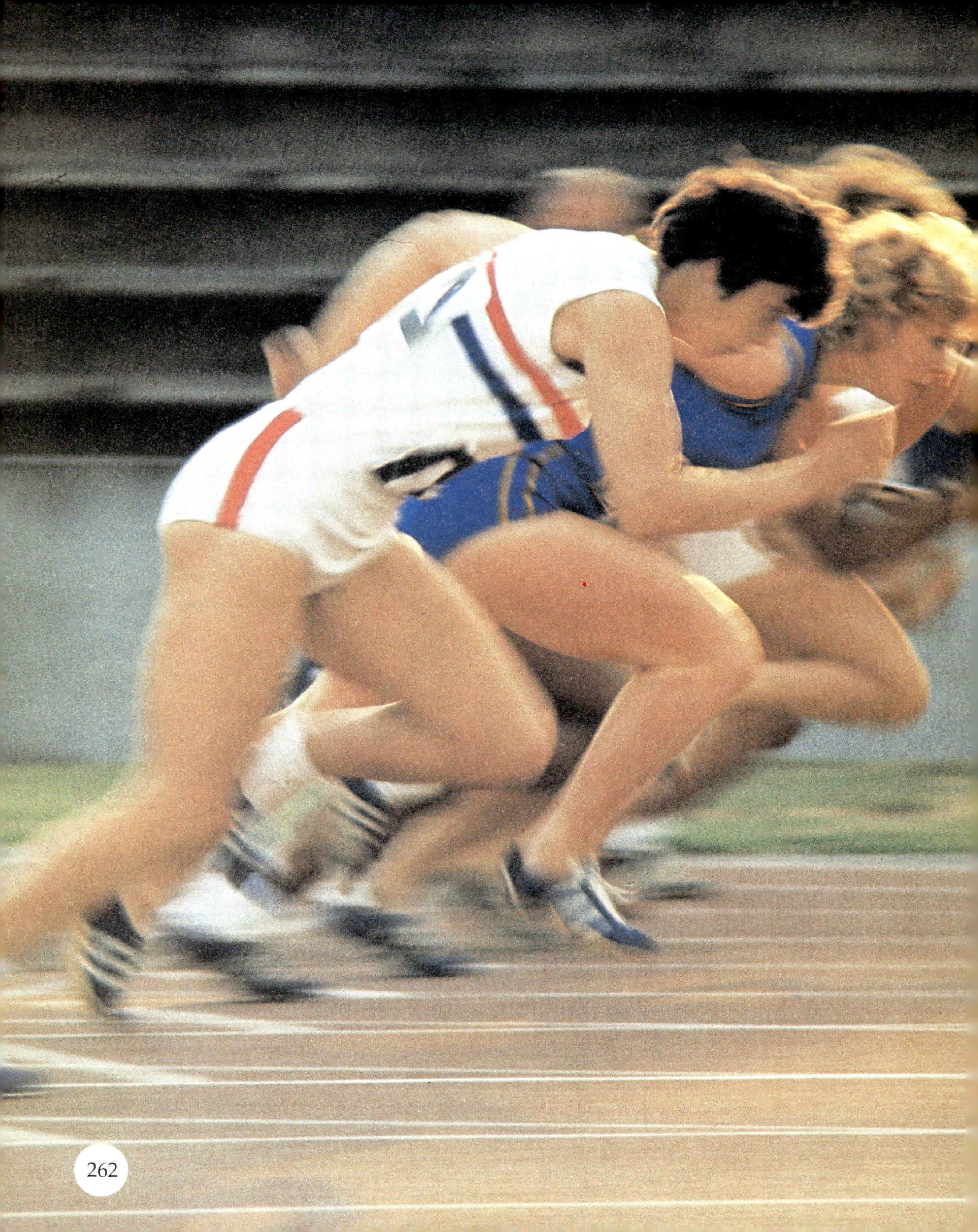

The Sprinters
by Lillian Morrison

The gun explodes them.
Pummeling, pistoning they fly
In time's face.
A go at the limit
A terrible try
To smash the ticking glass,
Outpace the beat
That runs, that streaks away
Tireless, and faster than they.

Beside ourselves
(It is for us they run!)
We shout and pound the stands
For one to win
Loving him, whose hard
Grace-driven stride
Most mocks the clock
And almost breaks the bands
Which lock us in.

Literature Study

Characterization

An author tells readers about a character in a number of ways:

1. through a physical description of the character
2. through the character's words and actions
3. through the character's thoughts and feelings
4. through the comments and reactions of other characters
5. through direct statements (writer's opinion of the character)

Direct and Indirect Characterization

The first four methods together are called indirect characterization. The fifth method is called direct characterization. **Indirect characterization** dramatizes character. **Direct characterization** tells rather than dramatizes. An author may use any or all of these methods to describe a character.

The easiest way to tell about a character is through direct characterization. Sometimes an author tells readers about a character at the beginning of a story. Here is an example:

> Ms. Cartwright came into the room. She was a tall woman with large brown eyes. Her face was framed by dark, curly hair. She wore a tailored outfit and walked rapidly. Her drawn face hinted at the sadness and pain of the past few days.

Indirect characterization, on the other hand, is presented more subtly. It is given bit by bit, often as part of the dialogue or action. As a result, there is no obvious description of the character.

Complex Characterization

Perhaps you know people who seemed unfriendly when you first met them. After you got to know them, however, you realized that they were warm and friendly. You changed your mind about them. Likewise, in reading a story, you sometimes change your mind about a certain character. At first, he or she seems to be one kind of person. As you continue to read the story, however, your thoughts and ideas about the character change. The author has guided your thoughts about the character by giving certain information early in the story and other information later.

The terms *flat* and *round* are sometimes used to describe characters. A **flat** character is one who has only one noticeable trait. That single trait becomes the label by which the character is identified. Every person in the real world, however, has a great many traits. A story character who is shown as having many sides, both good and bad, is a **round** character.

Static and Dynamic Characterization

Static characters do not change from the way the author first presents them. **Dynamic** characters, on the other hand, change because of what happens in the story.

Protagonist and Antagonist

A **protagonist** is a character in a story with whom the reader sympathizes. An **antagonist** is a character in the story who is in conflict with the protagonist. In the best stories, both the protagonist and the antagonist are round characters. Each one has many character traits.

Characterization by Stereotype

"All good" or "all bad" characterization is flat, static, and uninteresting. It also leads to **stereotypes**. A villain always looks mean. A hero is always smiling. When authors describe a character as being all one way, or all another way, they are **stereotyping**.

Stereotyping is often used to attack or insult groups or classes of people by making fun of some of their characteristics. Good writers try not to stereotype unless they have a good reason for doing so.

Think about the methods of characterization as you read stories. This will help you understand the characters and will also add to your enjoyment of the stories. While some writers may tell you that a character is honest or dishonest, courageous or fearful, or ambitious or lazy, most writers let you draw your own conclusions about a character's personal qualities.

Author Profile

Rosemary Sutcliff

When Rosemary Sutcliff was two years old, she suffered a serious illness that kept her bedridden for the next few years. She could not go to school, so her mother became her teacher. Luckily for Rosemary, her mother never tired of reading stories to her. The little girl loved the stories of Rudyard Kipling. She especially loved those set in her native England during the times when Romans ruled the British Isles.

As Sutcliff grew up, she displayed a talent for painting and at first set out to become an artist. Because of the physical disabilities that resulted from her childhood illness, she found that she could not paint on large canvasses. Instead, she turned to painting miniatures and became accomplished at this delicate art. After a while, she found herself drawn to writing, where she could use her imagination to create a world as vast and complicated as she wished.

Her writing career began when she was twenty-five years old. Her first book for young people was published five years later. Since that time, she has been a full-time author of historical fiction for young readers.

Some of Sutcliff's best known books have been set in Roman Britain from the first to the fifth centuries A.D. During this four-hundred-year period, Rome ruled what is now England, Ireland, and Wales. "A Crown of Wild Olive," the story you will read next, is set in ancient Greece during the fifth century B.C.

Sutcliff's stories recreate the life of ancient times so well that readers feel as if they are actually there. Sutcliff paints a detailed, realistic picture of the people and activities of each time and place she writes about.

Sutcliff says: "Writing historical fiction is one of those things that happened, I suppose, because I had so much time to read when I was small. . . . To me half the fun of writing a book is the research [involved in it]. I love trying to piece together historical background and to catch the right smell of the period. Every period has very much its own subtle difference in smell, and the whole atmosphere changes a little bit every few years through history. It's a fascinating exercise to try and catch this difference.

"Usually I prepare myself by getting a great many books together from the county library. This acts like a snowball. Every book has a bibliography and I get a great many more books from each bibliography. I just go on until I am completely embedded in the period and place that I'm writing about. Generally, the plot comes from the historical background, not the other way around. The two things gradually move together in my mind as I get the research further, so that the plot grows with it. They just grow fairly naturally, side by side.

"I keep a little red exercise book with notes and get a new one each time I'm writing a book. In this I write down all that I'm going to write about the characters, real and imaginary. I gradually think these people out, what their personal appearance is going to be, any kind of habits and likes and dislikes that they've got, their backgrounds, anything I can think of that makes them into real people. By the time I've got all this locked together, they've become kind of acquaintances. As I write about them, I get to know them better. By the time I've finished a book, our acquaintance has ripened and I know them as one knows a person whom you've known through the years and got to know very well. If I make them do something out of character, I know instantly."

Reading fictional stories about other historical periods is an enjoyable way to make history come alive. When asked why history is important for today's young people, Sutcliff said: "I think it's important to children today because it's how we got to be where we are now. You can't properly understand where you are now if you don't know how you grew to be there — what your roots are, where you came from, because we're still part of history. It's not complete unless you see what's behind you."

Two boys, Amyntas and Leon, worlds apart in their backgrounds, compete in a sporting event. Amyntas makes a discovery about himself and about friendship. Read to find out what he discovers.

As you read, notice the methods used to develop the characters of Amyntas and Leon.

A Crown of Wild Olive

by Rosemary Sutcliff

It was still early in the day, but already it was growing hot; the white dry heat of the Greek summer. The faint offshore wind that made it bearable had begun to feather the water, breaking and blurring the reflections of the galleys lying at anchor in Pireaus Harbor.

Half of Athens, it seemed, had crowded down to the port to watch the *Paralos*, the State Galley, sail for the Isthmus, taking its finest athletes on the first stage of their journey to Olympia.

Every fourth summer it happened; every fourth summer for more than three hundred years. Nothing was allowed to stand in the way, earthquake or pestilence or even war — even the long and weary war which, after a while of uneasy peace, had broken out again last year between Athens and Sparta.

Back in the spring the Herald had come, proclaiming the Truce of the Games; safe conduct through all lands and across all seas, both for the athletes and for those who went to watch them compete. And now, from every Greek state and from colonies and settlements all round the Mediterranean, the athletes would be gathering.

Aboard the *Paralos* was all the ordered bustle of departure. Ropes were being cast off; rowers were in their places at the oars. The Athenian athletes and their trainers with them had gathered on the afterdeck. Amyntas, son of Ariston, had drawn a little apart from the rest. He was the youngest there, still several months from his eighteenth birthday and somewhat conscious that he had not yet sacrificed his boy's long hair to Apollo. The rest, even of those entered for the boys' events — you counted as a boy at Olympia until you were twenty — were already short-haired and doing their military service. A few of them even had scars gained in border clashes with the Spartans, to prove that their real place, whatever it might be on the race track or in the wrestling pit, was with the men. Amyntas envied them. He was proud that he had been picked so young to run for Athens in the Boys' Double Stade, the Four Hundred Yards. But he was lonely. He was bound in with all the others by their shared training. They were bound together by something else, by another kind of life, other loyalties and shared experiences and private jokes, from which he was still shut out.

The last ropes holding ship to shore were being cast off now. Fathers and brothers and friends on the jetty were calling last-moment advice and good-luck wishes. Nobody called to Amyntas, but he turned and looked back to where his father stood among the crowd. Ariston had been a runner too in his day, before a Spartan spear wound had stiffened his left knee and spoiled his own hopes of an Olympic Olive Crown. Everyone said that he and Amyntas were very alike. Looking back now at the slight dark man who still held himself like a runner, Amyntas hoped, with a warm rush of pride, that they were right. He wished he had said so, before he came aboard. There were so many things he would have liked to have said, but he was even more tongue-tied with his father than he was with the rest of the world, when it came to saying the things that mattered. Now, as the last ropes fell away, he flung up his hand in salute, and tried to put them all into one wordless message. "I'll run the best race that's in me, Father — and if I win it, I'll remember that I'm winning for us both."

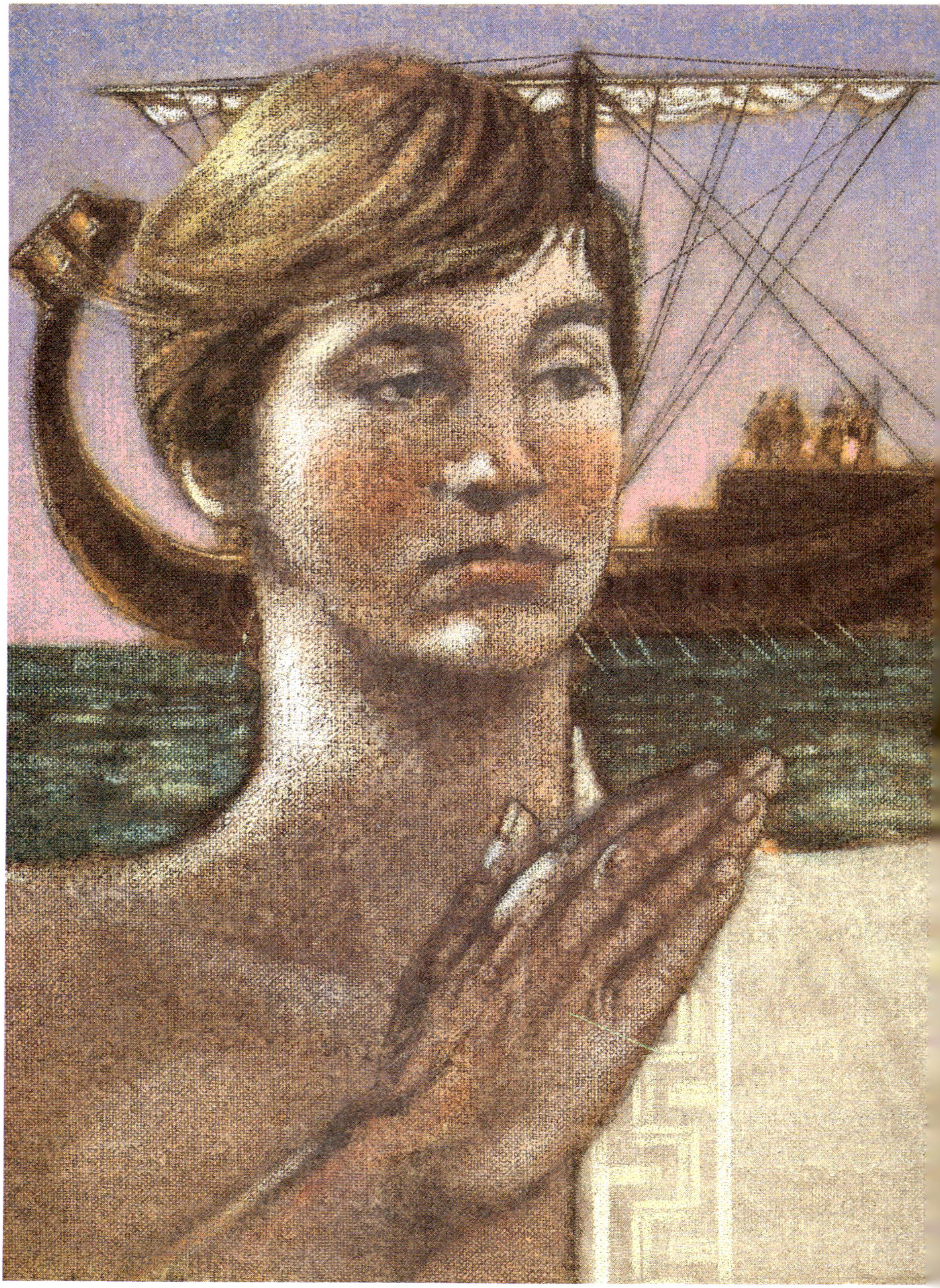

Among the waving crowd, his father flung up an answering hand, as though he had somehow received the message. The water was widening between ship and shore. The bos'n struck up the rowing time on his flute, and the rowers bent to their oars, sending the *Paralos* through the water towards the harbor mouth. Soon the crowd on shore was only a shingle of dark and light along the waterfront. But far off beyond the roofs of the warehouses and the covered docks, a flake of light showed where high over Athens the sunlight flashed back from the upraised spear-blade of the great Athene of the Citadel, four miles away.

They were out round the breakwater now. The one sail broke out from the mast, and they headed for the open gulf.

That night they beached the *Paralos* and made camp on the easternmost point of the long island of Salamis. Not long past noon next day they went ashore at the Isthmus and took horse for Corinth on the far side, where a second galley was waiting to take them down the coast. At evening on the fifth day they rode down into the shallow valley where Olympian Zeus, the Father of gods, had his sanctuary, and where the Sacred Games were celebrated in his honor.

What with the long journey and the strangeness of everything, Amyntas took in very little of the first evening. They were met and greeted by the Council of the Games, whose president made them a speech of welcome. Then the Chief Herald read them the rules. Afterwards they ate the evening meal in the athletes' mess; food that seemed to have no more taste nor substance than the food one eats in a dream. Then the dream blended away into a dark nothingness of sleep that took Amyntas almost before he had lain down on the narrow stretcher bed in the athletes' lodging, which would be his for the next month.

He woke to the first dappled fingers of sunlight shafting in through the doorway of his cell. They wavered and danced a little, as though broken by the shadows of tree branches. Somewhere farther down the valley a cuckoo was calling, and the world was real again, and his, and new as though it had been born that morning. He rolled over, and lay for a few moments, his hands behind his head, looking up at the bare rafters. Then he shot off the bed and through the doorway in one swallow-dive of movement, to wash his head and shoulders in the icy water trickling from the mouth of a stone bull into a basin just outside. He came up for air, spluttering and shaking the water out of his eyes. For a moment he saw the colonnaded court and the plane tree arching over the basin through a splintered brightness. There stood a boy of about his own age, who must have come out of the lodging close behind him. A boy with a lean, angular body, and dark, bony face under a shock of hair like the crest of an ill-groomed pony. For a long moment they stood looking at each other. Then Amyntas moved aside to let the other come to the water pipe.

As the stranger ducked his head and shoulders under the falling water, Amyntas saw his back. From shoulder to flank it was crisscrossed with scars, past the purple stage but not yet faded to the silvery white that they would be in a few years' time; pinkish scars that looked as though the skin was still drawn uncomfortably tight over them.

He must have made some betraying sound or movement, because the other boy ducked out from under the water, thrusting the wet reddish-brown hair back out of his eyes, and demanded curtly, "Have you never seen a Spartan back before?" So that was it. Amyntas, like everyone else, had heard dark stories of Spartan boys flogged, sometimes to death, in a ritual test of courage, before the shrine of Artemis Orthia, Lady of the Beasts.

"No," he said, "I am Athenian." And did not add that he hoped to see plenty of Spartan backs when once he had started his military service. It was odd, the cheap jibe came neatly into his head, and yet he did not even want to speak it. It was as though here at Olympia, the Truce of the Games was not just a rule of conduct, but something in one's heart. Instead, he added, "And my name is Amyntas."

They seemed to stand confronting each other for a long time. The Spartan boy had the look of a dog sniffing at a stranger's fist and taking his own time to make sure whether it was friendly. Then he smiled; a slow, rather grave smile, but unexpectedly warm. "And mine is Leon."

"And you're a runner." Amyntas was taking in his build and the way he stood.

"I am entered for the Double Stade."

"Then we race against each other."

Leon said in the same curt tone, "May we both run a good race."

"And meanwhile — when did you arrive, Leon?"

"Last night, the same as you."

Amyntas, who usually found it nearly as difficult to talk to strangers as he did to his own father, was surprised to hear himself saying. "Then you'll have seen no more of Olympia than I have. Shall we go and get some clothes on and have a look round?"

But by that time more men and boys were coming out into the early sunshine, yawning and stretching the sleep out of their muscles. And Amyntas felt a hand clamp down on his shoulder, and heard the voice of Hippias, his trainer. "Oh no you don't, my lad! Five days' break in training is long enough. I've work for you before you do any sightseeing!"

After that, they were kept hard at it, on the practice track and in the wrestling school that had the names of past Olympic victors carved on the colonnade walls. For the last month's training for the Games had to be done at Olympia itself. The last month's training was hard, in the old style that did not allow for rest days in the modern fashion that most of the Athenian trainers favored. Everything at Olympia had to be done the old way, even to clearing the stadium of its four years' growth of grass and weeds and spreading it with fresh sand. At other Crown Games, the work was done by paid laborers; but here, the contending athletes must do it themselves, to the glory of the gods, as they had done it in the far-off days when the Games were new. Some of them grumbled a good deal and thought it was time that the Priests of Zeus and the Council of the Games brought their ideas up to date. To Amyntas there seemed to be a sort of rightness about the thing as it was.

His training time was passed among boys from Corinth and Epidauros, Rhodes and Samos and Macedon. At first they were just figures in outline, like people seen too far off to have faces. He watched them with interest at track work, at javelin or discus-throwing or in the wrestling pit, trying to judge their form as he knew they were trying to judge his and one another's. But gradually as the early days went by, they changed into people with faces, with personal habits and likes and dislikes, suffering from all the strains and stresses of the last weeks before the Games. But even before those first few days were over, he and the Spartan boy had drifted into a companionable pattern of doing things together. They would wash each other down in the stone hip-baths in the washing room after practice and scrape the mess of rubbing oil and sand off each other's backs. It took Amyntas a little while to learn to scrape the bronze blade of the strigil straight over the scars on Leon's back as though they were not there. When they took their turn at scraping up the four years' growth of grass from the stadium, they generally worked together, sharing one of the big rush carrying-baskets between them. In the evenings, after the day's training was over, or in the hot noonday break when most people stretched themselves out in the shade of the plane trees for sleep or quiet talk, they seemed, more often than not, to drift into each other's company.

Once or twice they went to have a look at the town of tents and booths that was beginning to spring up all round the Sacred Enclosure and the Gymnasium buildings. A Games Festival drew many people besides those who came to compete or to watch — merchants, poets determined to get poems heard, horse dealers from Corinth and Cyrene, goldsmiths and leather workers, philosophers gathering for the pleasure of arguing with each other, sword and fire swallowers, and acrobats who could dance on their hands to the soft notes of Phrygian pipes. But Leon did not much like the crowded noisy tent-ground. Most often they wandered down to the river that flung its loop about the south side of Olympia. It had shrunk now in the summer heat, to little more than a chain of pools in the middle of its pale dried-out pebbly bed; but there was shade under the oleander trees, and generally a whisper of moving air. And lying on the bank in the shade was free. It had dawned on Amyntas quite early that the reason Leon did not like the fairground was that he had no money. The Spartans did not use money, or at least, having decided that it was a bad thing, they had no coinage but iron bars so big and heavy that nobody could carry them about, or even keep a store at home that was worth enough to be any use. They were very proud of their freedom from wealth, but it made life difficult at a gathering such as this, when they had to mix with people from other states. Leon covered up by being extremely scornful of the bright and foolish things for sale in the merchants' booths, and the acrobats who passed the bowl round for contributions after their performance; but he was just that shade too scornful to be convincing. And anyway, Amyntas had none too much money himself, to get him through the month.

So they went to the river. They were down there one hot noontide something over a week after they had first arrived at Olympia. Amyntas was lying on his back, his hands behind his head, squinting up into the dark shadow-shapes of the oleander branches against the sky. Leon was sitting beside him with his arms round his updrawn knees, staring out into the dazzle of sunlight over the open riverbed. They had been talking runners' talk, and suddenly Amyntas said, "I was watching the Corinthian making his practice run this morning. I don't *think* we have either of us much to fear from him."

"The Rhodian runs well," said Leon, not bringing back his gaze from the white dance of sunlight beyond the oleanders.

"But he uses himself up too quickly. He's the kind that makes the front running at first, and has nothing left for the home stretch. Myself, I'd say that the redheaded runner from Macedon had the better chance."

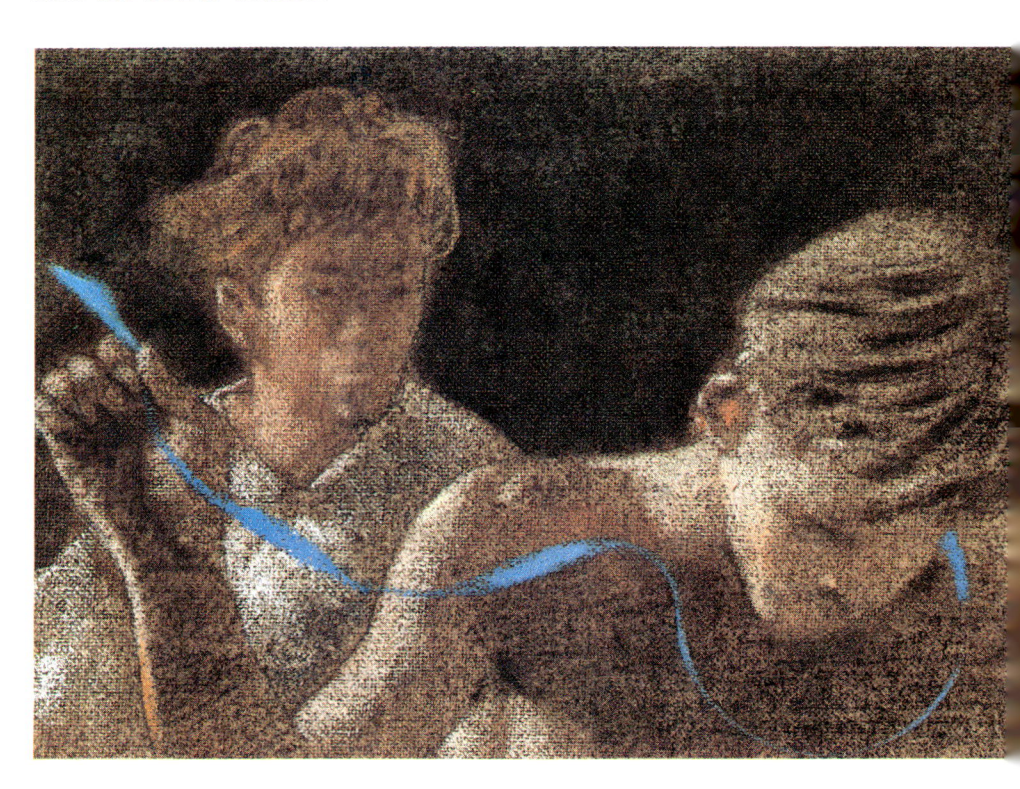

"He's well enough for speed. He knows how and when to use it. What do you give for Nikomedes's chances?"

"Nikomedes? — The boy from Megara? It's hard to say. Not much, from the form he's shown so far; but we've only seen him at practice. He's the sort that sometimes catches fire when it comes to the real thing."

There was a long silence between them, and they heard the churring of the grasshoppers, like the heat-shimmer turned to sound. And then Amyntas said, "I think you are the one I have most to fear."

Leon turned his head slowly and looked down at him. He said, "Have you only just woken to that? I knew the same thing of *you*, three days ago."

They were both silent again, and suddenly a little shocked. You might think that kind of thing, but it was best not to put it into words.

Leon made a quick sign with his fingers to avert ill luck; and Amyntas scrambled to his feet. "Come on, it's time we were getting back." They were both laughing, but a little breathlessly. Leon dived to his feet also, and shot ahead as they went up through the riverside scrub. But next instant, between one flying leap and the next, he stumbled slightly, and checked. Then he turned back, stooping to search for something among the dusty root-tangle of dry grass and camomile. Amyntas, swerving just in time to avoid him, checked also.

"What is it?"

"Something sharp. . . ." Leon pulled out, from where it had lain half-buried, the broken end of a sickle blade that looked as though it might have lain there since the last Games. "Seems it's not only the Stadium that needs clearing up." He began to walk on, carrying the jagged fragment in his hand. But Amyntas saw the blood on the dry ground where he had been standing.

"You have cut your foot."

"I know," Leon said, and went on walking.

"Yes, I *know* you know. Let me look at it."

"It's only a scratch."

"All the same — show me."

Leon stood on one leg, steadying himself with a hand on Amyntas's shoulder, and turned up the sole of his foot. "Look then. You can hardly see it."

There was a cut on the hard brown sole, not long, but deep, with the blood welling slowly. Amyntas said in sudden exasperation, "Haven't you any sense? Oh we all know about the Spartan boy with the fox under his cloak. Nobody but you Spartans thinks it's a particularly clever or praiseworthy story. But if you get dirt into that cut, you'll like enough have to scratch from the race!"

Leon suddenly grinned. "Nobody but we Spartans understand that story. But about the dirt, you could be right."

"I could. And that bit of iron is dirty enough for a start. Best get the wound cleaned up, in the river before we go back to the Gymnasium. Then your trainer can take over."

So with Leon sitting on a boulder at the edge of the shrunken river, Amyntas set to work with ruthless thoroughness to clean the cut. He pulled it open, the cool water running over his hands, and a thin thread of crimson fronded away downstream. It would help clean the wound to let it bleed a little; but after a few moments the bleeding almost stopped. No harm in making sure. He ducked his head to the place, sucked hard and spat crimson into the water. Then he tore a strip from the skirt of his tunic. He would have commandeered Leon's own — after all, it was Leon's foot — but he knew that the Spartan boys were only allowed to own one tunic at a time. If he did that, Leon would be left without a respectable tunic to wear at the Sacrifices. He lashed the thin brown foot tightly. "Now — put your arm over my shoulder and try to keep your weight off the cut as much as you can."

"Cluck, cluck, cluck!" said Leon, but he did as Amyntas said.

As they skirted the great open space of the Hippodrome, where the chariot races would be held on the second day of the Games, they came up to some members of the Athenian team, strolling under the plane trees. Eudorus the wrestler looked round and his face quickened with concern. "Run into trouble?"

"Ran into the remains of a sickle blade someone left in the long grass," Amyntas said, touching the rusty bit of metal he had taken from Leon and struck in his own belt. "It's near the tendon, but it's all right, so long as there's no dirt left in it."

"Near the tendon, eh? Then we'd best be taking no chances." Eudorus looked at Leon. "You are Spartan, I think? Amyntas, go and find the Spartan trainer. I'll take over here." And then to Leon again, "Will you allow me to carry you up to lodging? It seems the simplest way."

Amyntas caught one parting glimpse of Leon's rigid face as Eudorus lifted him, lightly as a ten-year-old, and set off towards the gymnasium buildings. Laughter caught at his stomach, but mixed with the laughter was sympathy. He knew he would have been just as furious in Leon's place. All this fuss and to-do over a cut that would have been nothing itself — if the Games had not been only three weeks off.

He set off in search of the trainer.

In the middle of that night, Amyntas woke up with a thought already shaped and complete in his mind. It was an ugly thought, and it sat on his chest and mouthed at him slyly. "Leon is the one you have most to fear. If Leon is out of the race. . . ."

He looked at it in the darkness, feeling a little sick. Then he pushed it away, and rolled over onto his face with his head in his arms. After a while he managed to go back to sleep again.

Next day, as soon as he could slip away between training sessions, he went out into the growing town of tents and booths and found a seller of images and votive offerings. He bought a little bronze bull with silvered horns. It cost nearly all the money that he had to spare, so that he would not now be able to buy the hunting knife with silver inlay on the hilt that had caught his fancy a day or two before. With the little figure in his hand, he went to the Sacred Enclosure. There, among altars shaded by plane trees, and statues of gods and Olympic heroes, the great Temple of Zeus faced the older and darker house of Hera his wife.

Before the Temple of Zeus, the ancient wild olive trees from which the victors' crowns were made cast dapple-shade across the lower steps of the vast portico. He spoke to the attendant priest in the deep threshold shadows beyond.

"I ask leave to enter and make an offering."

"Enter then, and make the offering," the man said.

And he went through into the vastness of the Temple itself, where the sunlight sifting through under the acanthus roof tiles made a honeycomb glow that hung high in the upper spaces and flowed down the gigantic columns. He scarcely touched the pavement underfoot, so that he seemed to wade in cool shadows. At the far end, sheathed in gold and ivory, his feet half lost in shadows, his head gloried with the dim radiance of the upper air, stern and serene above the affairs of mortal men, stood the mighty statue of the god himself. Olympian Zeus, in whose honor the Sacred Games had been held for more than three hundred years. Three hundred years, such a little while. Looking up at the heart-stilling face above him, Amyntas wondered if the god had even noticed yet that they were begun. Everything in the god's House was so huge. For a moment his head swam. He had no means of judging the size of anything, even himself, here where all the known landmarks of the world of men were left behind. Only one thing, when he looked down at it, remained constant in size; the tiny bronze bull with the silvered horns that he held in his hand.

He went forward to the first of the Offering Tables before the feet of the gigantic statue, and set it down. Now, the tables were empty and waiting. By the end of the festival, they would be piled with offerings; small humble ones like his own, and silver cups and tripods of gilded bronze to be taken away and housed in the Temple treasury. On the eve of the Games they would begin to fill up, with votive offerings made for the most part by the athletes themselves, for their own victory, or the victory of a friend taking part in a different event. Amyntas was not making the offering for his own victory, nor for Leon's. He was not quite sure why he was making it, but it was for something much more complicated than victory in the Double Stade. With one finger still resting on the back of the little bronze bull, he sent up the best prayer he could sort out from the tangle of thoughts and feelings within himself. "Father of all things, lord of these Sacred Games, let me keep a clean heart in this. Let me run the best race that is in me, and think of nothing more."

Outside again, beyond the dapple-shade of the olive trees, the white sunlight fell dazzling across his eyes. The world of humans, in which things had returned to their normal size, received him back. He knew that Hippias was going to be loudly angry with him for having missed a training session. But unaccountably, everything, including Hippias's anger, seemed surprisingly small.

Leon had to break training for three days, at least so far as track work was concerned. It was several more days before he could get back into full training; so for a while it was doubtful whether he would be able to take his place in the race. But with still more than a week to go, both his trainer and the Doctor-Priest of Asklepius declared him fit. His name remained on the list of entrants for the Double Stade.

And then it was the first day of the Festival; the day of solemn dedication, when each competitor must go before the Council to be looked over and identified, and take the Oath of the Games before the great bronze statue of Zeus of the Thunderbolts.

The day passed. And next morning before it was light, Amyntas woke to hear the unmistakable, unforgettable voice of the crowds gathering in the Stadium. A shapeless surf of sound, pierced by the cries of the jugglers and acrobats, and the sellers of water and honeycakes, myrtle and victors' ribbons calling their wares.

This was the day of the Sacred Procession; the Priests and Officials, the beasts garlanded for sacrifice, the athletes marching into the waiting Stadium, while the Herald proclaimed the name and state of each one as he passed the rostrum. Amyntas, marching in with the Athenians, heard his own name called, and Leon's, among names from Samos and Cyrene, Crete and Corinth and Argos and Megara. And he smelled the incense on the morning air, and felt for the first time, under his swelling pride in being Athenian, the thread of his own Greekness interwoven with the Greekness of all those others. This must have been, a little, the thing their great grandfathers had felt when they stood together, shield to shield, to hurl back the whole strength of invading Persia, so that they might remain free. That had been in a Games year, too.

The rest of that day was given over to the chariot and horse races. That night Amyntas went to his sleeping cell with the thunder of hooves and wheels still sounding somewhere behind his ears. He seemed to hear it in his dreams all night, but when he woke in the morning, it had turned into the sound that he had woken to yesterday, the surf-sound of the gathering crowd. But this morning it had a new note for him, for this was the Day. The crowd that was gathering out there round the Stadium was his crowd, and his belly tightened and the skin prickled at the back of his neck as he heard it.

He lay for a few moments, listening, then got up and went out to the stone fountain. Leon came out after him as he had done that first morning, and they washed down as best they could. The water barely dribbled from the mouth of the stone bull now. With the vast gathering of people, and the usual end-of-summer drought, the water shortage was getting desperate, as it always did by the time the Festival days arrived.

"How is the foot?" Amyntas asked.

"I can't remember where the cut was, unless I look for it."

They stood looking at each other, the friendship that they had never put into words trying to find some way to reach across from one to the other. "We cannot even wish each other luck," Amyntas said at last, helplessly.

And Leon said, almost exactly as he had said it at their first meeting, "May both of us run a good race."

They reached out and touched hands quickly and went their separate ways.

The next time they saw each other, they were waiting and ready for the track, with the rest of the Double Stade boys just outside the arched way into the Stadium. The Dolichus, the long distance race, and the Stade had been run, each with its boys' race immediately after. Now the trumpet was sounding to start the Double Stade. Amyntas's eyes went to meet Leon's, and found the Spartan boy's slightly frowning gaze waiting for him. He heard the sudden roar of the crowd, and his belly lifted and tightened. A little stir ran through the waiting boys. The next time the starting trumpet sounded, the next time the crowd gave that roar, it would be for them. Hippias was murmuring last-minute advice into Amyntas's ear, but he did not hear a word of it. He was going out there before all those thousands upon thousands of staring eyes and yelling mouths, and he was going to fail. Not just fail to win the race, but *fail*. His belly was churning now. His heart banged away right up in his throat so that it almost choked him. His mouth was dry and the palms of his hands were wet. The beginnings of panic were whimpering up in him. He looked again at Leon, and saw him run the tip of his tongue over his lips as though they were suddenly dry. It was the first time he had ever known the Spartan boy to betray anything of what was going on inside him. The sight gave him a sense of companionship that somehow steadied him. He began to take deep quiet breaths, as he had been taught, and the rising panic quieted and sank away.

The voice of the crowd was rising, rising to a great roar; the Men's Double Stade was over. He heard the Herald crying the name of the winner, and another roar from the crowd. Then the runners were coming out through the arched entrance. The boys pressed back to let them past, filthy with sweat and sand and oil. Amyntas looked at the face of the man with the victor's ribbons knotted round his head and arms, and saw that it was gray and spent and oddly peaceful.

"Now it's us!" someone said; and the boys were sprinting down the covered way, out into the open sun-drenched space of the Stadium.

The turf banks on either side of the broad track, and the lower slopes of the Kronon Hill that looked down upon it, were packed with a vast multitude of onlookers. Halfway down on the right-hand side, raised above the tawny grass on which everybody else sat, were the benches for the Council, looking across to the white marble seat opposite. There the Priestess of Demeter sat as still as though she herself were carved from marble, among all the jostling, swaying, noisy throng. Men were raking over the silver sand on the track. The trumpeter stood ready.

They had taken their places now behind the long white limestone curbs of the starting line. The Umpire was calling: "Runners! Feet to the lines!"

Amyntas felt the scorching heat of the limestone as he braced the ball of his right foot into the shaped groove. All the panic of a while back had left him. He felt light, and clearheaded, and master of himself. He had drawn the sixth place, with Leon on his left and the boy from Megara on his right. Before him the track stretched white in the sunlight, an infinity of emptiness and distance.

The starting trumpet yelped. The line of runners sprang forward like a wave of hunting dogs slipped from the leash.

Amyntas was running smoothly and without hurry. Let the green front-runners push on ahead. In this heat they would have burned themselves out before they reached the turning post. He and Leon were running neck and neck with the redheaded Macedonian. The Rhodian had gone ahead now after the front-runners; the rest were still bunched. Then the Corinthian made a sprint and passed the boy from Rhodes, but fell back almost at once. The white track was reeling back underfoot, the turning post racing towards them. The bunch had thinned out. The front-runners had begun to drop back already. As they came up towards the turning post, first the boy from Macedon, and then

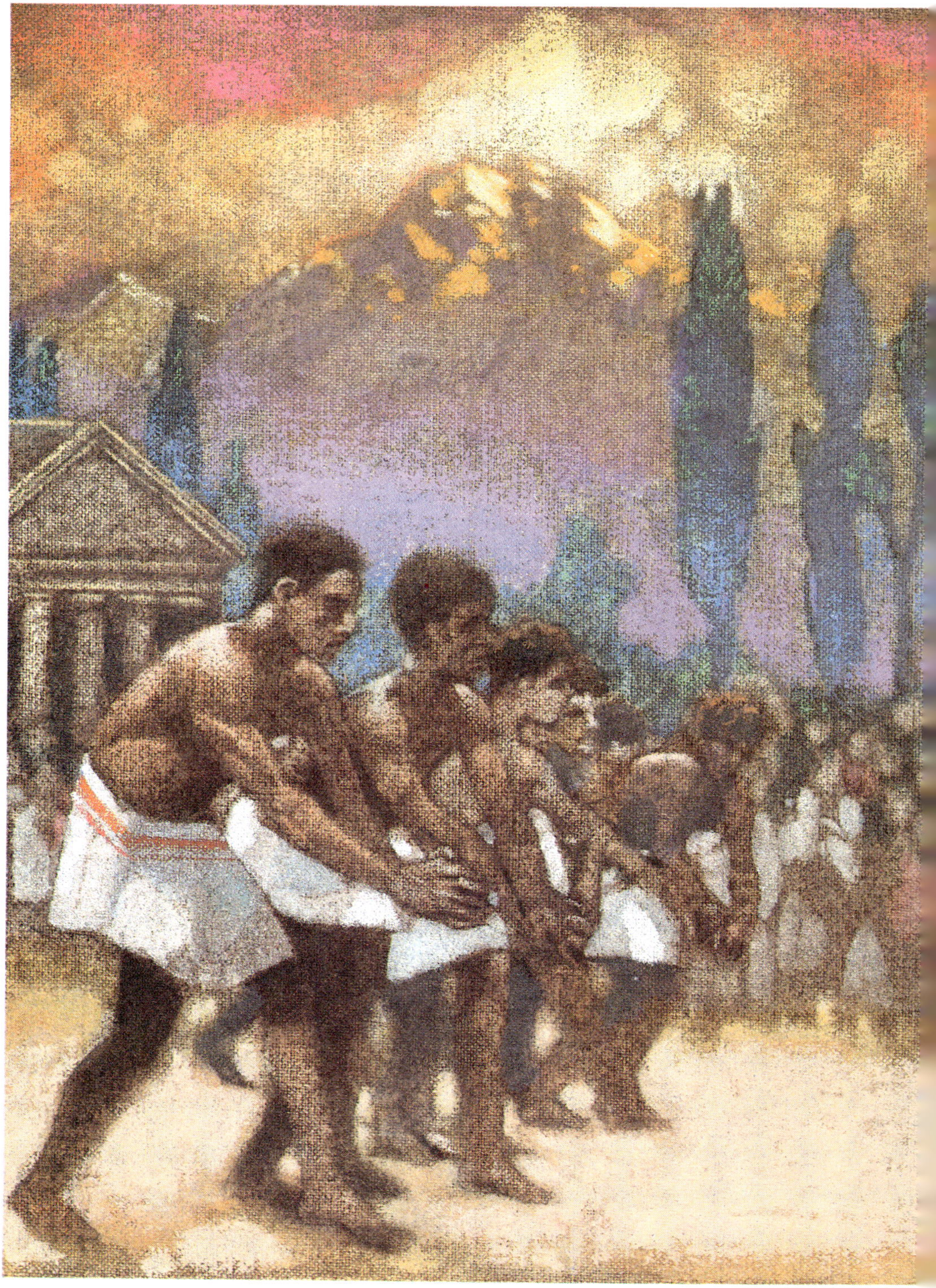

Nikomedes catching fire at last, slid into the lead, with Amyntas and Leon close behind them. Rounding the post, Amyntas skidded on the loose sand and Leon went ahead. It was then, seeing the lean scarred back ahead of him, that Amyntas lengthened his stride, knowing that the time had come to run. They were a quarter of the way down the home lap when they passed Nikomedes; the Megaran boy had taken fire too late. They were beginning to overtake the redhead. Amyntas knew in his bursting heart that unless something unexpected happened, the race must be between himself and Leon. Spartan and Macedonian were going neck and neck now. The position held for a few paces, and then the redhead gradually fell behind. Amyntas was going all out. There was pain in his breast and belly and in the backs of his legs, and he did not know where his next breath was coming from; but still the thin scarred back was just ahead. The crowd was beginning to shout, seeing the two come through to the front, a solid roar of sound that would go on rising now until they passed the finishing post. And then suddenly Amyntas knew that something was wrong. Leon was laboring a little, beginning to lose the first keen edge of his speed. Snatching a glance downward, he saw a fleck of crimson in the sand. The cut had reopened.

His body went on running, but for a sort of splinter of time his head seemed quite apart from the rest of him, and filled with an unmanageable swirl of thoughts and feelings. Leon might have passed the top of his speed anyway, it might be nothing to do with his foot — but the cut had reopened. To lose the race because of a cut foot. . . . It would be so easy not to make that final desperate effort that his whole body was crying out against. Then Leon would keep his lead. And at the same time another part of himself was remembering his father standing on the quayside at Piraeus as the *Paralos* drew away — crying out that he was not running only for himself but for Athens, his City and his people. A crown of wild olive would be the greatest thing that anyone could give to his friend. It would be to insult Leon to let him win . . . you could not do that to your friend. . . . And then, like a clean cold sword of light cutting through the swirling tangle of his thoughts, came the knowledge that greater than any of these things were the gods. These were the Sacred Games, not some mere struggle between boys in the gymnasium. For one fleeting instant of time he remembered himself standing in the Temple before the great statue of Zeus, holding the tiny bronze bull with the silvered horns. "Let me run the best race that is in me, and think of nothing more."

He drove himself forward in one last agonizing burst of speed. He was breathing against knives, and the roar of the blood in his ears drowned the roar of the crowd. He was level with Leon — and then there was nothing ahead of him but the winning post.

The onlookers had crowded right down towards it. Even above the howl of the blood in his head he heard them now, roar on solid roar of sound, shouting him in to victory. And then Hippias had caught him as he plunged past the post. Now he was bending over the trainer's arm, bending over the pain in his belly, snatching at his breath and trying not to be sick.

People were throwing sprigs of myrtle. He felt them falling on his head and shoulders. The sickness eased a little and his head was clearing. He began to hear friendly voices congratulating him; and Eudorus came shouldering through the crowd with a colored ribbon to tie round his head. But when he looked round for Leon, the Spartan boy had been swept away by his trainer. And a strange desolation rose in Amyntas and robbed his moment of its glory.

Afterwards in the changing room, some of the other boys came up to congratulate him. Leon did not come; but when they had cleaned off the sand and oil and sweat, and washed down with the little water that was allowed them, Amyntas hung about, sitting on the well curb outside while the trainer finished seeing to his friend's foot. And when Leon came out at last, he came straight across to the well, as though they had arranged to meet there. His face was as unreadable as usual.

"You will have cooled off enough by now. Do you want to drink?" Amyntas said, mainly because somebody had to say something. He dipped the bronze cup that always stood on the well curb in the pail that he had drawn.

Leon took the cup from him and drank, and sat down on the well curb beside him. As Amyntas dipped the cup again and bent his head to drink in his turn, the ends of the victor's ribbon fell forward against his cheek, and he pulled it off impatiently, and dropped it beside the well.

"Why did you do that?" Leon said.

"I shall never be sure whether I won that race."

"The judges are not often mistaken, and I never heard yet of folk tying victors' ribbons on the wrong man."

Amyntas flicked a thumb at Leon's bandaged foot. "You know well enough what I mean. I'll never be sure whether I'd have come first past the post, if that hadn't opened up again."

Leon looked at him a moment in silence, then flung up his head and laughed. "Do you really think that could make any difference? It would take more than a cut foot to slow me up, Athenian! You ran the better race, that's all."

It was said on such a harsh, bragging note that in the first moment Amyntas felt as though he had been struck in the face. Then he wondered if it was the overwhelming Spartan pride, or simply Leon, hurt and angry and speaking the truth. Either way, he was too tired to be angry back again. And whichever it was, it seemed that Leon had shaken it off already. The noon break was over, and the trumpets were sounding for the Pentathlon.

"Up!" Leon said, when Amyntas did not move at once. "Are you going to let it be said that your own event is the only one that interests you?"

They went, quickly and together, while the trainer's eye was off them, for Leon was under orders to keep off his foot. And the people cheered them both when they appeared in the Stadium. They seldom cared much for a good loser, but Leon had come in a close second, and they had seen the blood in the sand.

The next day the heavyweight events were held; and then it was the last day of all, the Crowning Day. Ever after, Amyntas remembered that day as a quietness after great stress and turmoil. It was not, in truth, much less noisy than the days that had gone before. The roaring of the Stadium crowds was gone; but in the town of tents the crowds milled to and fro. The jugglers with knives and the eaters of fire shouted for an audience and the merchants cried their wares. Within the Sacred Enclosure where the winners received their crowns and made their sacrifices before the Temples of Zeus and Hera, there were the flutes and the songs in praise of the victors, and the deep-voiced invocations to the gods.

But in Amyntas himself, there was the quiet. He remembered the Herald crying his name, and the light springy coolness of the wild olive crown as it was pressed down on his head, and later, the spitting light of pine torches under the plane trees, where the officials and athletes were feasting. And he remembered most, looking up out of the torchlight, and seeing, high and remote above it all, the winged tripods on the roof of the great Temple, outlined against the light of a moon two days past the full.

The boys left before the feasting was over. In his sleeping cell Amyntas heard the poets singing in praise of some chariot team, and the applause, while he gathered his few belongings together, ready for tomorrow's early start, and stowed his olive crown among them. Already the leaves were beginning to wilt after the heat of the day. The room that had seemed so strange the first night was familiar now; part of himself; and after tonight it would not know him anymore.

Next morning in all the hustle of departure, he and Leon contrived to meet and slip off for a little on their own.

The whole valley of Olympia was a chaos of tents and booths being taken down, merchants as well as athletes and onlookers making ready for the road. But the Sacred Enclosure itself was quiet, and the gates stood open. They went through, into the shade of the olive trees before the Temple of Zeus. A priest making the morning offering at a side altar looked at them; but they seemed to be doing no harm, and to want nothing, so he let them alone. There was a smell of frankincense in the air, and the early morning smell of last night's heavy dew on parched ground. They stood among the twisted trunks and low-hanging branches, and looked at each other and did not know what to say. Already they were remembering that there was war between Athens and Sparta, that the Truce of the Games would last them back to their own states, but no further. The longer the silence lasted, the more they remembered.

From beyond the quiet of the Enclosure came all the sounds of the great concourse breaking up; voices calling, the stamping of impatient horses. "By this time tomorrow everyone will be gone," Amyntas said at last. "It will be just as it was before we came, for another four years."

"The Corinthians are off already."

"Catching the cool of the morning for those fine chariot horses," Amyntas said, and thought, There's so little time, why do we have to waste it like this?

"One of the charioteers had that hunting knife with the silver inlay. The one you liked. Why didn't you buy it after all?"

"I spent the money on something else." For a moment Amyntas was afraid that Leon would ask what. But the other boy only nodded and let it go.

He wished suddenly that he could give Leon something, but there was nothing among his few belongings that would make sense in the Spartan's world. It was a world so far off from his own. Too far to reach out, too far to call. Already they seemed to be drifting away from each other, drifting back to a month ago, before they had even met. He put out a hand quickly, as though to hold the other boy back for one more moment, and Leon's hand came to meet it.

"It has been good. All this month it has been good," Leon said.

"It has been good," Amyntas agreed. He wanted to say, "Until the next Games, then." But military service was only a few months away for both of them. If they did meet at another Games, there would be the faces of dead comrades, Spartan or Athenian, between them; and like enough, for one of them or both, there might be no other Games. Far more likely, if they ever saw each other again, it would be over the tops of their shields.

He had noticed before how, despite their different worlds, he and Leon sometimes thought the same thing at the same time, and answered each other as though the thought had been spoken. Leon said in his abrupt, dead-level voice, "The gods be with you, Amyntas, and grant that we never meet again."

They put their arms round each other's necks and strained fiercely close for a moment, hard cheekbone against hard cheekbone.

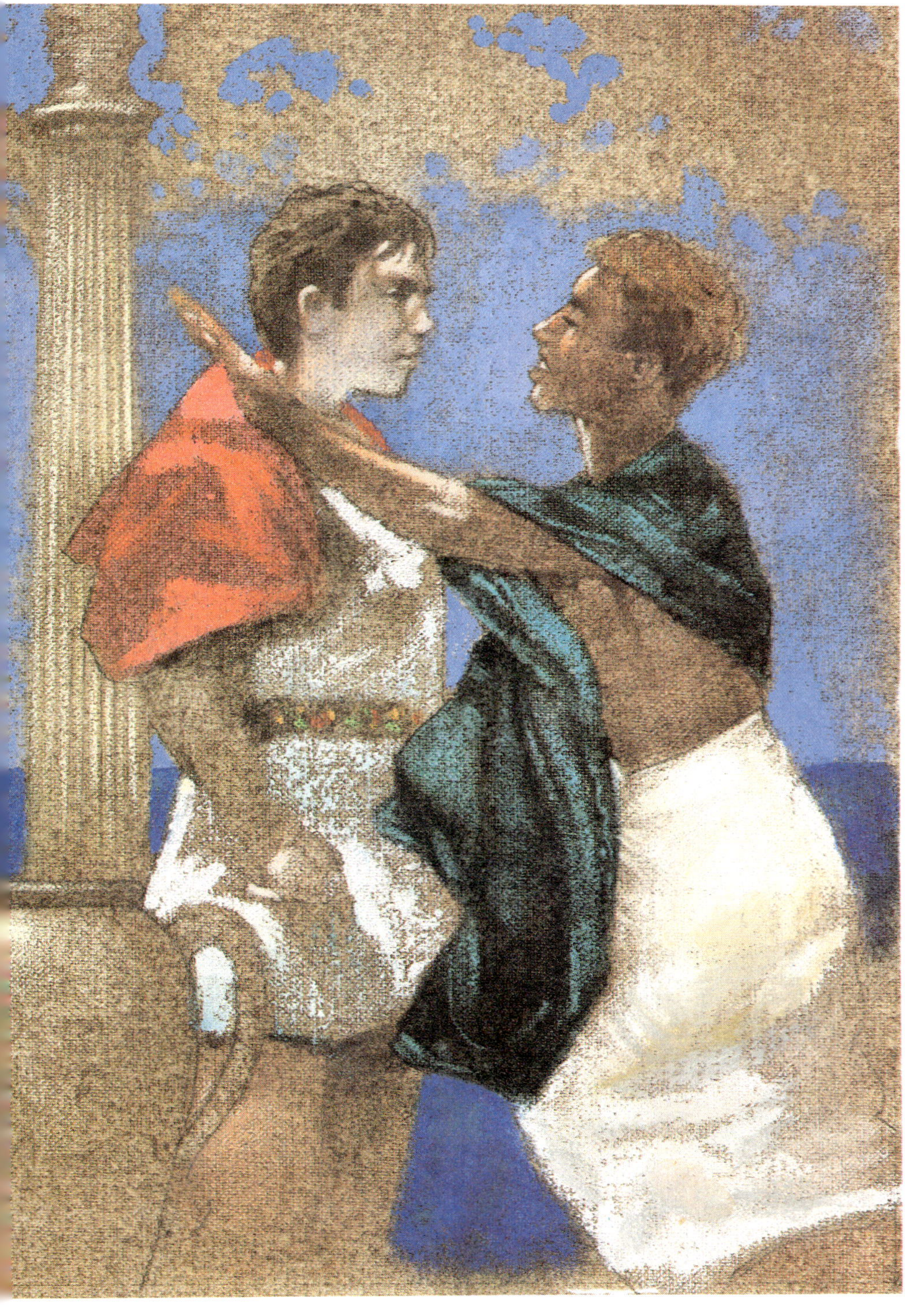

"The gods be with you, Leon."

And then Eudorus was calling, "Amyntas! Amyntas! We're all waiting!"

And Amyntas turned and ran — out through the gateway of the Sacred Enclosure, towards where the Athenian party were ready to start, and Eudorus was already coming back to look for him.

As they rode up from the Valley of Olympia and took the track towards the coast, Amyntas did not look back. The horses' legs brushed the dry dust-gray scrub beside the track, and loosed the hot aromatic scents of wild lavender and camomile and lentisk upon the air. A yellow butterfly hovered past. Watching it out of sight, it came to him suddenly that he and Leon had exchanged gifts of a sort, after all. It was hard to give them a name, but they were real enough. And the outward and visible sign of his gift to Leon was in the little bronze bull with the silvered horns that he had left on the Offering Table before the feet of Olympian Zeus. And Leon's gift to him. . . . That had been made with the Spartan's boast that it would take more than a cut foot to slow him up. He had thought at the time that it was either the harsh Spartan pride, or the truth spoken in anger. But he understood now, quite suddenly, that it had been Leon giving up his own private and inward claim to the olive crown, so that he, Amyntas, might believe that he had rightfully won it. Amyntas knew that he would never be sure of that, never in all his life. But it made no difference to the gift.

The track had begun to run downhill, and the pale dust cloud was rising behind them. He knew that if he looked back now, there would be nothing to see.

You may want to read the other two stories in the book **Heather, Oak, and Olive** *by Rosemary Sutcliff.*

Discuss the Selection

1. What did Amyntas discover about friendship?
2. What event created tension between Amyntas and Leon?
3. What were the two gifts that Amyntas realized his friend and he had exchanged?
4. Do you think that Amyntas won the race fairly? Give reasons for your answer.
5. Find the passage in which Leon says, "The gods be with you, Amyntas, and grant that we never meet again." What do you think he meant by this statement?

Apply the Skills

Authors develop characters through physical descriptions, actions, dialogue, inner thoughts and feelings, comments and reactions of others, and direct comments.

1. What methods did the author use to develop Amyntas's character? Give examples from the story.
2. What methods did the author use to develop Leon's character? Give examples from the story.

Thinking About "Galaxies"

In this unit, you have read about young people who made important discoveries about themselves. Sylvia, in "A White Heron," discovered that protecting a living creature was more important to her than winning a friend's approval. Miranda discovered the difficulty of growing up. Amyntas, in "A Crown of Wild Olive," discovered his deepest beliefs and values through his experiences at the Olympic Games. Both he and Leon learned that people from different backgrounds can become true friends.

In the excerpt from *A Deaf Child Listened*, you met Thomas Gallaudet at a turning point in his life. A chance encounter with a deaf child led Thomas to a way to teach her the meaning of words and to a rewarding career as a teacher of the deaf.

Another character, Sherlock Holmes, discovered his talent for observing details. He used his talent to solve mysteries and bring criminals to justice. In "The Adventure of the Musgrave Ritual," you were able to discover the method used by this famous fictional detective.

Folktales often help us discover important truths about life. The folktale you read taught an important lesson. Ologbon-Ori discovered that it is important to use common sense rather than simply to accept the opinions of others.

The discoveries and inventions of modern medicine make fascinating reading. As you read about Susan's knee operation, you discovered how new technology is used in the operating room.

Any of the selections you read in this unit might lead you to new horizons of thinking. Perhaps you enjoyed the Sherlock Holmes mystery. There are many more to discover. Perhaps you'd like to know more about the language of American Sign. A book can get you started. Or perhaps you want to learn more about sports medicine. The information can be found in books. The path to discovery begins at the nearest library.

1. Several stories in "Galaxies" are about friendship. Choose two characters who became friends. Tell how their friendship started and what each one learned from the friendship.

2. Some of the stories in "Galaxies" contained realistic elements. Choose a character from two different stories and tell how each character acted in a true-to-life way in solving his or her problem.

3. Think about the stories in "Galaxies." Choose a story character who seemed very real to you. In the story find examples that show how the author lets you know what the character is thinking or feeling.

4. The folktale in "Galaxies" taught a lesson about life. Think of other folktales that you have read or heard that taught lessons. Choose one folktale, describe the story briefly, and tell the lesson you learned from it.

5. Tell about a recent scientific discovery that you think is important. In your opinion, how will this discovery benefit humankind?

6. "A Crown of Wild Olive" involved the Olympic Games of ancient Greece. Compare and contrast these games with the modern Olympic Games. In what ways are they alike? How are they different?

7. Have you read a book about a hobby or interest of yours recently? Tell briefly what you learned from the book. How did it add to your enjoyment of the hobby or interest?

Read on Your Own

Sports Medicine by Melvin Berger. Crowell. The latest advances in preventing and treating sports injuries, as well as advice on staying physically fit and performing well in sports, are discussed in this book.

The Great Auto Race by Ruth Carlsen and G. Robert Carlsen. Scholastic. In this collection of factual and fictional stories, persons who faced challenges today and long ago are portrayed.

Dolphin Island by Arthur C. Clarke. Holt, Rinehart and Winston. In this novel a runaway boy in the twenty-first century finds himself a castaway on Dolphin Island. He has exciting adventures and gets a chance to carry out scientific experiments about dolphin communication.

Olode the Hunter and Other Tales from Nigeria by Harold Courlander. Harcourt Brace Jovanovich. In this collection of folktales from Nigeria, a country in western Africa, a noted folklorist retells tales from native storytellers.

Johnny Tremain by Esther Forbes. Houghton Mifflin. In this novel Johnny Tremain, a silversmith's apprentice with a maimed hand, becomes a dispatch rider actively involved in the events leading to the Boston Tea Party and the Battle of Lexington.

Challenging the Deep by Hans Hass. Morrow. In this autobiography, with the author's own photography, Hass tells about the dangers and rewards of his career as a marine biologist.

They Accepted the Challenge by Charles Kuntzleman. St. Martin's. In these eighteen stories of physically handicapped teenagers, each one overcomes a handicap to succeed in a challenging situation.

A Deaf Child Listened by Anne Neimark. Morrow. This is the biography of Thomas Gallaudet, who founded the first school for the deaf in the United States.

Sir Arthur Conan Doyle's The Adventures of Sherlock Holmes Adapted by Catherine E. Sadler. Avon Books. Books 1-4. The best of these famous mysteries appear in these four paperback volumes.

The Red Pony by John Steinbeck. Viking. In this novel, when Jody Tiflin receives a red pony from his father, he learns not only about horse raising, but also about himself, and joy and sorrow.

Heather, Oak and Olive by Rosemary Sutcliff. Dutton. Three stories of historical fiction from this book tell about the lives of young people in ancient Britain, Ireland, and Greece.

Dear Greta Garbo by Toby Talbot. Putnam. Thirteen-year-old Miranda and her grandmother discover that they share similar problems.

The Prince and the Pauper by Mark Twain. Bantam Books. In this classic, a poor boy and an English prince trade lives.

The Other Side of the Mountain by F. G. Valens. Warner Books. In this biography, champion skier Jill Kinmont, now a paraplegic after a skiing accident, faces her greatest challenge — returning to a normal life.

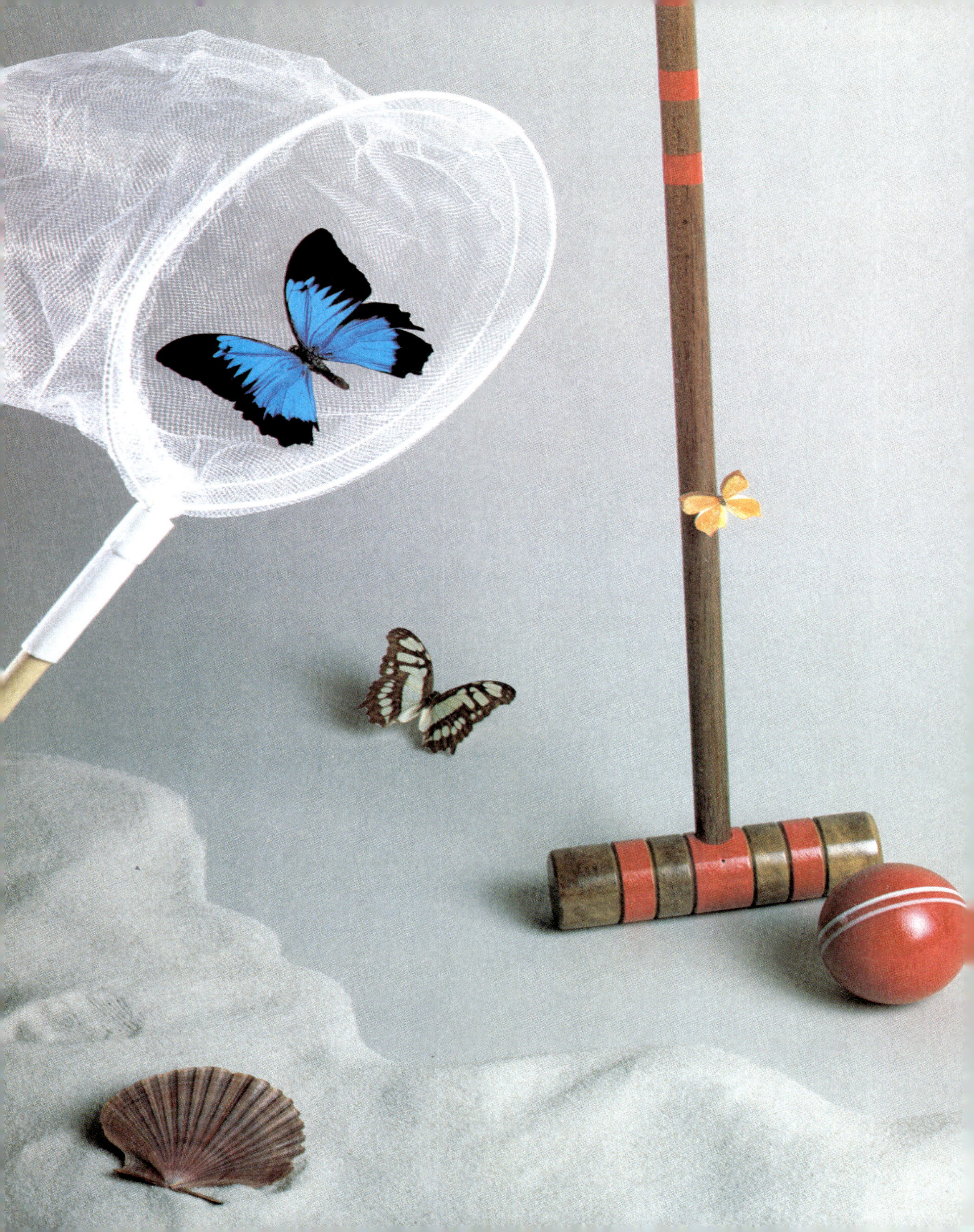

Unit 3
Wit and Wisdom

Often times we are confronted with problems that we are unable to solve by ourselves. We ask others for opinions, advice, and answers, hoping that we will be guided to a decision. We seek the wisdom of others — those who might have experienced a similar problem.

Writers sometimes disguise the problems of everyday life through humor. Our real world is not all problems, and we do laugh. Sometimes our problems are not such a burden to us if we can see the lighter side of a situation.

In this unit, you will discover how writers develop the wit and wisdom of their characters through actions and dialogue. You will be able to evaluate and judge the decisions some of the characters make. Some of the things the characters say and do may make you snicker. Some are meant to make you laugh out loud. You might even see yourself in some of the characters.

As you read, notice the techniques each writer uses to create witty situations and wise characters. Remember, too, that humor has its serious side. A story told from a humorous point of view can be meant to teach a serious lesson. Look for the wisdom as well as the wit as you enjoy the selections in this unit.

Literature Study

Essays and Anecdotes

The line between fiction and nonfiction is sometimes difficult to define. We can say, however, that **fiction** deals with imaginary characters and events. **Nonfiction** deals with real people's lives. Many kinds of writing are classified as nonfiction. In this unit, you will study one kind of nonfiction — the essay.

An **essay** is a short piece of nonfiction with a particular point of view. The subject is discussed only briefly. *Essay* comes from the French word *essai*, which means "try." It's as though the writer is saying, "Try out these ideas. See what you think of them." This was the thinking of Michel de Montaigne, a famous French essayist. Montaigne's thoughts still hold true today for both formal and informal essays.

Formal Essays

The **formal essay** is serious in tone, tightly organized, and objective. It has an introduction, a body, and a conclusion. Formal writing also lends itself to figures of speech. For example, Dr. Lewis Thomas uses *personification,* the representing of a thing as a person, in his essay "To Err Is Human," when he states: "We are at our human finest, *dancing with our minds,* when there are more choices than two."

Dr. Thomas also uses *alliteration*, two or more words having the same beginning sound. For example, Thomas uses phrases such as *complex computers* and *machine-made miscomputation*.

Another formal essayist was an English writer, Sir Francis Bacon. Much of his work shows that even the formal essay needs wit to make the writing interesting. In one of his essays, Bacon tells us how to read books: "Some books are to be tasted, others to be swallowed, and some few to be chewed and digested."

Informal Essays

In an **informal essay**, the reader may be as interested in the writer's personality and point of view as in what is said.

The mood of an informal essay can range from sad to very funny. The message can be understated or bold in tone. Informal essays can even mock the formal essay by pretending to be serious. Read the following example:

> There is a grave crisis which all citizens must be called upon to face. This is the lack of any new jokes about the hot spell currently attacking our metropolis.

The American writer James Thurber was good at writing informal essays. One of his methods was to focus on a subject's experience. He then added experiences unrelated to the original subject. Through this method, Thurber shared much about himself.

Anecdotes

An **anecdote**, like an informal essay, is conversational in tone, short, and often humorous. Instead of giving an opinion, an anecdote tells what happened. Informal essays often use anecdotes to make certain points. The element of surprise sometimes appears in formal and informal essays and in anecdotes. Surprise is a device to keep the reader interested. Suppose an essay were describing the worries of a boy on his first day at a new school. This surprise might follow: "I'm a little embarrassed to admit that the terrified boy described above was, in fact, me."

Read the following passages. Decide which kind of writing each represents: the formal essay, the informal essay, or the anecdote.

1. I watched the woman at the checkout counter in the store. She had a can of peas in one hand. Suddenly another person came forward. "Let me pay for those," he said.
2. Many people forget that our own country began in conflict. They are the very ones who seem to fear any disagreement.
3. There is nothing as hard as taking a test for which one has not studied. After years of faking and bluffing, I stand as a prime specimen of test disease. Here is how I got by—until today.

Knowing whether an essay is formal or informal, or whether it contains anecdotes, will help you understand its message.

The author of this informal essay has definite ideas about why some animals become lost. Read to find out what his ideas are.

As you read, notice how Thurber uses anecdotes to communicate his ideas about his problems with his own dog.

Look Homeward, Jeannie

by James Thurber

The moot and momentous question as to whether some lost dogs have the mysterious power of being able to get back home from distant places over strange terrain has been argued for years by dog-owners, dog-haters, and other persons who know nothing whatever about dogs. Mr. Bergen Evans in his book *The Natural History of Nonsense*, sides with the cynics who believe that the lost dog doesn't have any more idea where he is than a babe in the wood. (Author's note, 1955: I have come, somewhat reluctantly, to agree with Mr. Evans in almost all, but not quite all, cases.) "Like pigeons," Mr. Evans wrote, "dogs are thought to have a supernatural ability to find their way home across hundreds, even thousands, of miles of strange terrain. The newspapers are full of stories of dogs who have miraculously turned up at the doorsteps of baffled masters who had abandoned them afar. Against these stories, however, can be set the lost-and-found columns of the same papers, which in almost every issue carry offers of rewards for the recovery of dogs that, apparently, couldn't find their way back from the next block."

Now I don't actually have any empirical knowledge of the dogs that are supposed to have returned from strange, distant places as surely as an Indian scout or a locomotive engineer, but I am not quite fully prepared to write all of them off as figures of pure legend. Skepticism is a useful tool of the inquisitive mind, but it is scarcely a method of investigation. I would like to see a trained reporter or private investigator set out on the trail of the homing dog and see what he would find.

I happen to have a few haphazard clippings on the fascinating subject, but they are unsupported, as always, by convincing proof of any kind, one way or the other. The most interesting case is that of Bosco, a small dog who is reported to have returned to his house in Knoxville, Tennessee, in the winter of 1944 from Glendale, California, thus setting what is probably the world's distance record for the legendary event, twenty-three hundred miles in seven months. His story is recorded in a book called *Just a Mutt* by Eldon Roark, a columnist of the Memphis *Press-Scimitar*. Mr. Roark relates that he got his tip on the story from Bert Vincent on the Knoxville *News-Sentinel*, but in a letter to me Mr. Vincent wrote that he had some doubts of the truth of the long trek through towns and cities and over rivers and deserts.

Bosco belonged to a family named Flanigan, and Mr. Vincent does not question the sincerity of their belief that the dog that turned up on their porch one day was, in fact, Bosco come home. The dog bore no collar or license, however, and identification had to be made on the tricky basis of markings and behavior. The long-distance record of Bosco must be finally set down as a case that would stand up only, if I may be permitted the expression, in a court of lore.

Far-traveling dogs have become so common that jaded editors are inclined to turn their activities over to the society editors, and we may expect before long to encounter such items as this: "Rover, a bull terrier, owned by Mr. and Mrs. Charles L. Thompson of this city, returned to his home at 2334 Maybury Avenue yesterday, after a four-months' trip from Florida where he was lost last February. Mr. and Mrs. Thompson's daughter Alice Louise is expected home tomorrow from Shipley, to spend the summer vacation."

Incidentally, and just for the sake of a fair record, my two most recent clippings on the Long Trek deal with cats: Kit-Kat,

Lake Tahoe to Long Beach, California, 525 miles; Mr. Black, Stamford, Connecticut, to Atlanta, Georgia, 1,000 miles.

The homing dog reached apotheosis some years ago when the movie *Lassie Come Home* portrayed a collie returning to its young master over miles of wild and unfamiliar country in darkness and in storm. This million-dollar testament of faith, a kind of unconscious memorial to the late Albert Payson Terhune, may possibly be what inspired Bergen Evans's essay.

In the case of the "lost" dog in the next block, however, I suspect that he is on somewhat insecure ground. He assumes that the dog does not come back from the next block because it can't find its way. If this reasoning were applied to the thousands of men who disappear from their homes every year, it would exonerate them of every flaw except disorientation, and this is too facile an explanation for man or beast. Prince, the dog, may have just as many reasons for getting and staying . . . out as George, the husband: an attractive female, merry companions, change of routine, words of praise, small attentions, new horizons, an easing of discipline. The dog that does not come home is too large a field of research for one investigator, and so I will confine myself to the case history of Jeannie.

Jeannie had no show points to speak of. Her jaw was skimpy, her haunches frail, her forelegs slightly bowed. She thought dimly, and her coordination was only fair. Even in repose she had the strained, uncomfortable appearance of a woman on a bicycle.

Jeannie adjusted slowly and reluctantly to everything, including weather. Rain was a hand raised against her personally, snow a portent of evil, thunder the end of the world. She sniffed even the balmiest breeze with an air of apprehension, as if it warned of the approach of a monster at least as large as a bus.

Jeannie did everything the hard way, digging with one paw at a time, shoving out of screen doors sideways. When she was six months old, she tried to bury a bone in the second section of *The New York Times*, pushing confidently and futilely at the newsprint with her muzzle. She developed a persistent, troubled frown, which gave her the expression of someone who is trying to repair a watch with his gloves on.

   Jeannie spent the first two years of her life in the city, where her outdoor experiences were confined to trips around the block. When she was taken to the country to live, she clung to the hearth for several weeks, poking her nose out now and then for a dismaying sniff of what she conceived to be God's great Scotty trap. The scent of lawn moles and the scurry of squirrels brought her out in the yard finally for tentative explorations, but it was a long time before she followed the woodchuck's trail up to the edge of the woods.

   Within a few months Jeannie took to leaving the house when the sun came up and returning when it began to get dark. Her outings seemed to be good for her. She began to look sleek, fat, smug, and at the same time pleasantly puzzled, like a woman who finds more money in her handbag than she thought was there. I decided to follow her discreetly one day, and she led me a difficult two-mile chase to where a large group of summer people occupied a row of cottages near a lake. Jeannie, it came out, was the camp mascot. She had muzzled in, and for some time had been spending her days shaking down the cottagers for hamburgers, fried potatoes, cake, and marshmallows. They wondered where the cute little dog came from in the morning and where she went at night.

Jeannie had won them over with her only trick. She could sit up, not easily, but with amusing effort, placing her right forefoot on a log or a stone, and pushing. Her sitting-up stance was teetery and precarious, but if she fell over on her back or side, she was rewarded just the same, if not, indeed, even more bountifully. She couldn't lose. The camp was a pushover.

Little old One Trick had a slow mind, but she gradually figured out that the long trip home after her outing was a waste of time, an unnecessary loop in her new economy. Oh, she knew the way back all right — by what improbable system of landmarks I could never guess — but when she got home there was no payoff except a plain wholesome meal once a day. That was all right for young dogs and very old dogs and spaniels, but not for a terrier who had struck it rich over the hills. She took to staying away for days at a time. I would have to go and get her in the car and bring her back.

One day, the summer people, out for a hike, brought her home themselves, and Jeannie realized the game was up, for the campers obviously believed in what was, to her, the outworn principle of legal ownership. To her dismay they showed themselves to be believers in one-man loyalty, a virtue which Jeannie had outgrown. The next time I drove to the camp to get her she wasn't there. I found out finally from the man who delivered the mail where she had gone. "Your little dog is on the other side of the lake," he said. "She's stayin' with a schoolteacher in a cottage the other side of the lake." I found her easily enough.

The schoolteacher had opened her door one morning to discover a small Scotty sitting up in the front yard, begging. The cute little visitor had proceeded to take her new hostess for three meals a day, topped off now and then with chocolates. But I had located her hiding place, and the next time she disappeared from home she moved on to fresh fields. "Your little dog's stayin' with some folks over near Danbury," the mailman told me a week later. He explained how to get to the house. . . . a few hours later I got in the car and went after her. . . .

She was lying on the front porch of her current home in a posture of truculent possession. When I stopped the car at the curb she charged vociferously down the steps, not to greet the master, but to challenge a trespasser. When she got close enough to recognize me, her belligerence sagged. "Better luck next time," I said, coldly. I opened the door, and she climbed slowly into the car and up onto the seat beside me. We both stared straight ahead all the way home.

Jeannie was a lost dog, lost in another way than Bergen Evans realizes. There wasn't anything to do about it. After all, I had my own life to live. Before long I would have had to follow her as far as Stamford or Darien or wherever the gravy happened to be thickest and the clover sweetest. "Your little dog—" the mailman began a few days later.

"I know," I said. "Thanks," and went back into the house. She came home of her own accord about three weeks later, and I think she actually made an effort to adjust herself. It was too late, though, and a couple of changes had recently taken place in the house that had once been hers exclusively. A poodle had joined the family (this was Medve) earlier and had just produced a litter of four males and seven females. This had divided Jeannie's power and popularity by twelve, and it had disheartened her. There can be no doubt but that the advent of the newcomers caused her to begin the wanderings that had taken her farther and farther away for longer and longer sojourns. Then came the final and most crushing blow, the birth of a girl baby to her owners.

Jeannie's last and futile attempt at adjustment, however sincere it may have been, and I doubt that her heart was really in it, lasted only until the baby was able to toddle around. This was, after all, a long, long time by a dog's calendar, and the fact that she was no longer the favorite in the household caused her to snap at the baby one day and bite her under the eye. This happens often, much too often, when an infant takes precedence over an old-established pet. It is a safe and highly recommended rule to follow Thurber's Law in such a situation: Never bring the baby to the dog, always bring the dog to the baby.

Getting rid of a dog is not easy for any owner, but it becomes absolutely necessary if the dog turns on a child, for its hostility can never be dependably overcome. We gave Jeannie to a man and his wife who had no children and who loved dogs. They were generous with food and candy, and the new home was a paradise for a free-loader. In 1935, at the age of nine, Jeannie died, full of years and, I have no doubt, chocolates. We got a very nice letter from the people with whom she had spent her declining days. I doubt that she would have recognized us if we had called on her, or, if she had, that she would have spoken civilly to us. In a way, I suppose, you can't blame her, and I don't.

Discuss the Selection

1. What does James Thurber think about animals that cannot find their way home?
2. Explain how Jeannie's life changed once she began to go on outings.
3. How did Jeannie's master resolve the problem of her strange behavior?
4. What do you think of the author's decision to give Jeannie away?
5. At what point in the selection did you realize that Jeannie had made a successful adjustment to country living?

Apply the Skills

James Thurber was a master of the informal essay. One of the ways that he entertained his readers was by using anecdotes to introduce ideas and experiences intentionally unrelated to—or in opposition to—the original subject. In "Look Homeward, Jeannie," Thurber begins by discussing the mysterious power of some dogs to find their way home from distant places. Give two examples from the essay of Jeannie's very different, and thus comical, behavior.

Think and Write

Prewrite

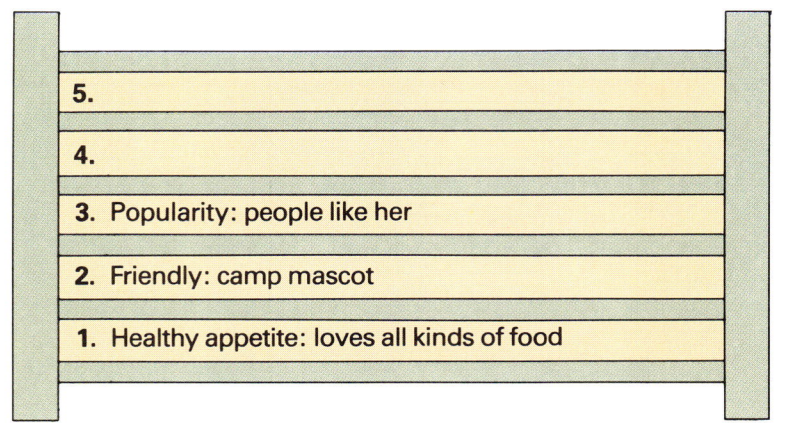

5.

4.

3. Popularity: people like her

2. Friendly: camp mascot

1. Healthy appetite: loves all kinds of food

An important reason for writing is to persuade other people to agree with you. When you write to persuade, first give your opinion and then give reasons to support that viewpoint. In "Look Homeward, Jeannie," the author finds that he must get rid of his dog. Study the laddergram shown above. The first three steps give reasons why someone would want to adopt Jeannie. Copy the laddergram and add two more reasons for adopting Jeannie.

Compose

Using the information in the laddergram, write a paragraph persuading the couple in the story to adopt Jeannie. Put yourself in the place of the owner of the dog. Give three or four reasons telling why Jeannie should be adopted. You might begin this way: *You'd like being the proud owner of a dog like Jeannie.*

Revise

Read your paragraph. Did you state your opinion in a way that would persuade someone to adopt Jeannie? If not, revise your paragraph to make it as convincing as possible. Be sure it includes all the reasons listed on the laddergram.

The Hairy Dog
by Herbert Asquith

My dog's so furry I've not seen
His face for years and years:
His eyes are buried out of sight,
I only guess his ears.

When people ask me for his breed
I do not know or care:
He has the beauty of them all
Hidden beneath his hair.

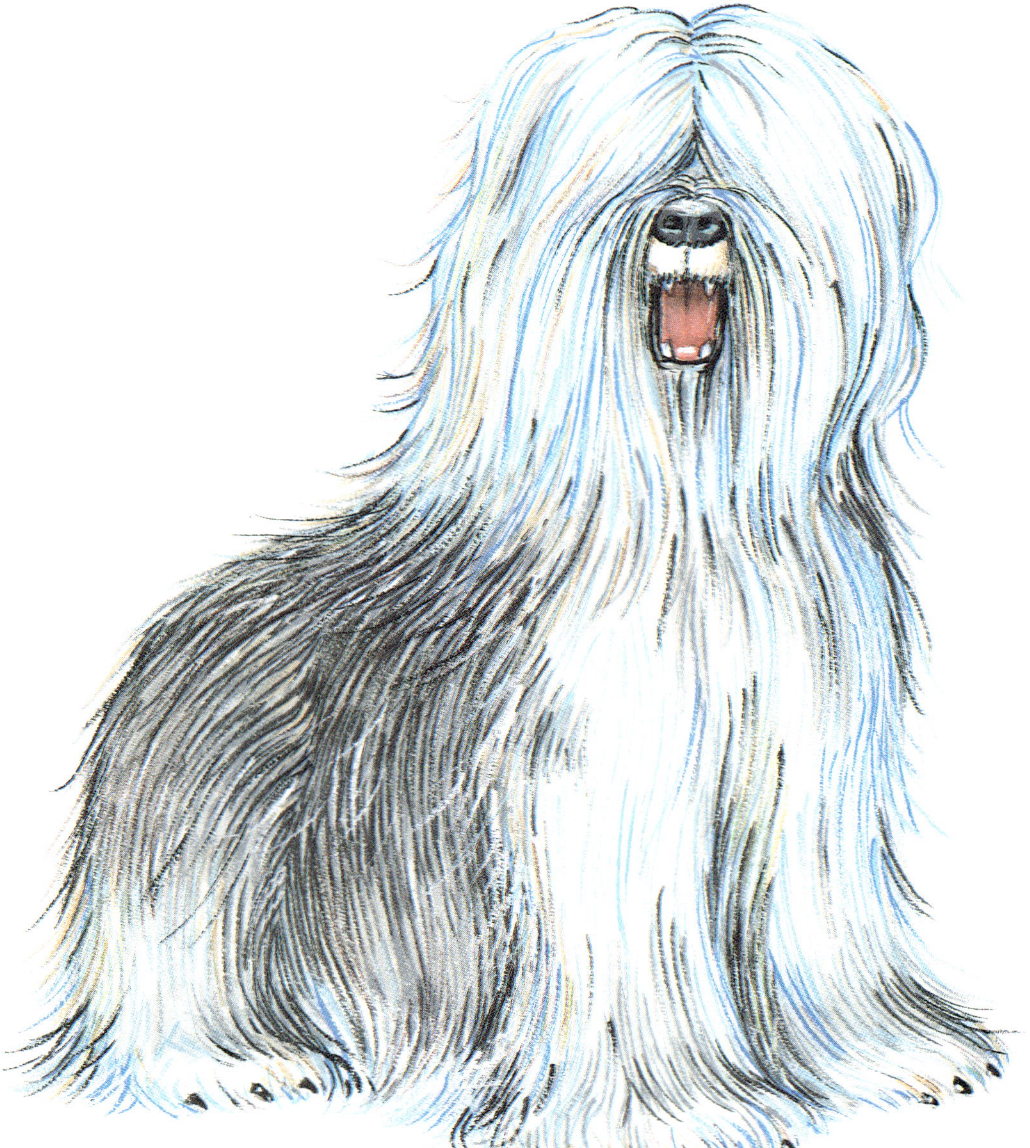

Comprehension Study

Main Idea

A well-written story or book contains paragraphs that have been carefully organized. The **topic**, or what the paragraph is about, can usually be stated in a word or a phrase. As you read the following paragraph, look for the topic. What word or phrase would you use to tell the topic?

> In spite of their genius, some of the greatest composers in history had surprisingly strange work habits. Ludwig van Beethoven, for example, insisted on pouring ice water over his head before composing music. He thought that the ice water would make him think better. Gioacchino Antonio Rossini would write operas only while hiding under a blanket to shut out distractions. Christoph Willibald Gluck refused to compose a note until he was seated in the middle of a field. Franz Joseph Haydn could write music only on pure white paper, and he wouldn't compose at all without wearing a good-luck ring given to him by Frederick the Great.

The topic of the paragraph that you just read might be *habits* or *composers' work habits*. Each sentence in the paragraph supports the topic by describing a habit that the composers had before starting to write music.

You know that the **main idea** of the paragraph is the most important thing that the author is saying. In the paragraph that you just read, the main idea is stated in the first sentence: *In spite of their genius, some of the greatest composers in history had surprisingly strange work habits.*

Notice that all the facts presented by the author in support of this idea give examples of great composers who refused to work until they did something that most people might find silly.

- Beethoven poured ice water over his head.
- Rossini ducked under a blanket.

- Gluck set off to find a field.
- Haydn hunted for pure white paper and a ring.

The Main Idea Stated in Two Sentences

An author will sometimes use two sentences to state the main idea of a paragraph. In such cases, it is necessary to combine the information from each sentence in order to find the main idea.

Read the following paragraph. What is the topic? What two sentences tell the main idea?

> Is anyone or anything wise enough to tell when someone is telling a lie? Some people claim that lie detectors are able to identify a liar every time. These machines can sense when a person has some of the symptoms that go along with lying. These symptoms include a faster pulse rate, heavy perspiration, blushing, rapid breathing, and frequent swallowing. Sensors are attached to the people being tested to record their responses to various questions. The detector is supposed to record strong physical responses every time the subject tells a lie. Yet a lie detector can be fooled by responses from people who are unaware that they are lying. Their responses don't change as they answer falsely.

The topic of the paragraph is a clue to the main idea. Which of the following expresses the topic of the paragraph that you have just read?

A. lie detectors   B. nervousness   C. machines

Choice A is the topic of the paragraph. To find the main idea of the paragraph, ask yourself, "What is the most important thing that the author wants to say to the reader?" In this case, it is: *Some people claim that lie detectors are able to identify a liar every time. Yet a lie detector can be fooled by responses from people who are unaware that they are lying.* To express the main idea of this paragraph, you had to combine information from two sentences at opposite ends of the paragraph.

Unstated Main Ideas

Sometimes the main idea of a paragraph cannot be found stated in a sentence or sentences. Instead, all the details imply a main idea. In such cases, the main idea is **unstated**.

As you read the following paragraph, look first for its topic. Notice the details in the paragraph that support that topic. Those details can lead to the unstated main idea.

> One of the best-known poets of the ancient world was Vergil, who once held a funeral for a dead fly. The funeral was the same as any funeral. The ceremony included speeches about the fly's life and pallbearers who carried the miniature coffin on a tray. After the funeral, the little fly was laid to rest in Vergil's garden, under a marble tombstone engraved with its date of death. While all this makes Vergil sound pretty strange, the funeral was, in fact, inspired by the tax laws of Rome, where cemetery land was exempt from taxes. Vergil turned the land around his house into tax-free burial ground.

Which choice best summarizes the topic of the paragraph?

A. funeral customs of Rome
B. the death of a fly
C. Vergil's burial of a fly

Although the author mentions a few funeral customs of ancient Rome, the emphasis of the paragraph is not funeral customs. Therefore, choice A is not the topic of the paragraph. Choice B, the death of a fly, is not the topic of the paragraph either, because the author didn't really discuss the fly. The topic of the paragraph is C, *Vergil's burial of a fly*. Notice that all the details in the paragraph describe this topic. What is the most important thing the author says about the topic? *Vergil buried a fly to avoid paying property taxes.* Another way to state the main idea is: *People in Rome did strange things to avoid paying taxes.*

Paragraphs Without a Main Idea

Not all paragraphs have a main idea. **Transitional paragraphs**, which connect the ideas stated in two other paragraphs, may not have a main idea of their own. Likewise, **summary paragraphs** often do not have a main idea. They simply review the main ideas of the rest of the article or selection. Finally, there are **descriptive paragraphs**, which list some interesting facts about a topic. If those facts don't have a main idea, the descriptive paragraph probably doesn't have one either. For example, read the following paragraph:

Since its establishment in 1917, the Pulitzer prize has been one of the most coveted awards for achievement in journalism, literature, music, and drama. The prize is awarded in the United States. It was named after Joseph Pulitzer, a newspaper publisher who left two million dollars to found a school of journalism at Columbia University in New York. The school was to give the awards on an annual basis. Prizes for journalism are awarded for material appearing in a U.S. newspaper. Books that have been awarded the prize for literature include *The Grapes of Wrath, Gone With the Wind,* and *The Good Earth.*

In the paragraph that you just read, the author doesn't want to make a specific point about the Pulitzer prize. Rather, the author's purpose is to present general information about the prize. The author also mentions a few prizewinners as part of what could be called "Facts about the Pulitzer Prize." Still, the paragraph does not, in fact, have a main idea.

Now read the next paragraph and answer the questions that follow.

In ancient China, patients were well protected against poor medical treatment. Doctors were paid only as long as their patients stayed well. If one got sick, the doctor had to pay the patient. Therefore, doctors took great care to avoid unnecessary or improper medical procedures. If a patient died, a special lantern was hung outside the doctor's house. Any doctor with too many lanterns didn't continue practicing medicine very long.

Which of the following choices states the topic of the paragraph that you just read?

A. Chinese lanterns   B. medical practice in ancient China   C. treating rare diseases

Choice B is the topic of the paragraph. Which sentence states the main idea, or most important thing about the topic? Although the paragraph gives interesting facts about the topic, it doesn't really have a main idea.

319

Textbook Application: Main Idea in Health

Health textbooks discuss the complicated subject of the human body and what it needs to stay in good health. Your knowledge of topics and main ideas will help you understand the information in health textbooks.

Read the following information from a health textbook. Use the sidenotes to help you locate topics and main ideas.

Why Do Some People Start to Smoke?

Most people know that smoking cigarettes can damage their health. Yet every day more people begin smoking. Although they cannot buy tobacco products legally, many teenagers are among these new smokers.

> What is the topic of this paragraph?
> Which sentence states the main idea?

Researchers believe that most young people begin smoking to satisfy some of their personal needs. They might want to be like someone they admire who is a smoker, or someone whose picture they saw in a cigarette advertisement. Others believe that smoking will make them seem more adult. Some people first start smoking because their friends are smoking. These people are unable to resist the pressure to go along with the group. Finally, there are those who smoke their first cigarette out of curiosity, to see what it is like.

> What is the unstated main idea of this paragraph?

People who smoke heavily for a long time find it difficult to stop. Many people who try to stop, start again after a few days, or even a few hours. Some people find that they cannot stop at all. Other people are able to stop smoking all at once and never smoke again. In time, they find that their desire to smoke goes away.

    Studies show that people who stop smoking can reverse most of the damage to their bodies. After people stop smoking, the parts of the respiratory system that were damaged begin to return to normal. Symptoms of chronic bronchitis seem to disappear. To some extent, damaged lung tissues repair themselves. Mucus buildup clears, smoker's cough vanishes, and breathing becomes easier. ← *What is the main idea of this paragraph? How do you know?*

    The best way to avoid the health problems caused by smoking is not to smoke. By not starting, you can avoid the physical and psychological dependence that may come with regular smoking, and you can prevent serious damage to your body. ← *What kind of paragraph is this?*

—*HBJ Health,*
Harcourt Brace Jovanovich

    Being able to recognize main ideas is an important part of reading. As you read, look for details that support main ideas.

In this story set in the 1800's, a reformed bank robber shows wisdom while making a lifesaving decision. Read to find out what Jimmy Valentine risks losing by his actions.

The topic of this story is that we must often make decisions in life that affect more than just ourselves. As you read, watch for such examples in the supporting details.

Jimmy Valentine

by O. Henry

A guard came to the prison shoe shop, where Jimmy Valentine was hard at work stitching uppers, and escorted him to the front office. There the warden handed Jimmy his pardon, which had been signed that morning by the governor. Jimmy took it in a tired kind of way. He had served nearly ten months of a four-year sentence. He had expected to stay only about three months, at the longest. When a man with as many friends on the outside as Jimmy Valentine had is received in the "stir" it is hardly worthwhile to cut his hair.

"Now, Valentine," said the warden, "you'll go out in the morning. Brace up, and make an honest man of yourself. You're not a bad fellow at heart. Stop cracking safes, and live straight."

"Me?" said Jimmy, in surprise. "Why, I never cracked a safe in my life."

"Oh, no," laughed the warden. "Of course not. Let's see, now. How was it you happened to get sent up on that Springfield job? Was it because you wouldn't prove an alibi for fear of compromising somebody in extremely high-toned society? Or was it simply a case of a mean old jury that had it in for you? It's always one or the other with you innocent victims."

"Me?" said Jimmy, still blankly virtuous. "Why, warden, I never was in Springfield in my life!"

"Take him back, Cronin," smiled the warden, "and fix him up with outgoing clothes. Unlock him at seven in the morning, and let him come to the bullpen. Better think over my advice, Valentine."

At a quarter past seven on the next morning, Jimmy stood in the warden's outer office. He had on a suit of the villainously fitting, ready-made clothes and a pair of the stiff, squeaky shoes that the state furnishes to its discharged compulsory guests.

The clerk handed him a railroad ticket and the five-dollar bill with which the law expected him to rehabilitate himself into good citizenship and prosperity. The warden and Jimmy shook hands. Valentine, 9762, was chronicled on the books "Pardoned by Governor," and Mr. James Valentine walked out into the sunshine.

Disregarding the song of the birds, the waving green trees, and the smell of the flowers, Jimmy headed straight for a restaurant. There he tasted the first sweet joys of liberty in the shape of a broiled chicken dinner. From there he proceeded leisurely to the depot. He tossed a quarter into the hat of a blind man sitting by the door, and boarded his train. Three hours set him down in a little town near the state line. He went to the cafe of one Mike Dolan and shook hands with Mike, who was alone behind the bar.

"Sorry we couldn't make it sooner, Jimmy, me boy," said Mike. "But we had that protest from Springfield to buck against, and the governor nearly balked. Feeling all right?"

"Fine," said Jimmy. "Got my key?"

He got his key and went upstairs, unlocking the door of a room at the rear. Everything was just as he had left it. There on the floor was still Ben Price's collar button that had been torn from the eminent detective's shirt band when they had overpowered Jimmy to arrest him.

Pulling out from the wall a folding bed, Jimmy slid back a panel in the wall and dragged out a dust-covered suitcase. He opened this and gazed fondly at the finest set of burglar's tools in the East. It was a complete set, made of specially tempered steel, the latest designs in drills, punches, braces and bits, jimmies, clamps, and augers, with two or three novelties invented by Jimmy himself, in which he took pride. Over nine hundred dollars they had cost him to have made at — a place where they make such things for the profession.

In half an hour Jimmy went downstairs and through the cafe. He was now dressed in tasteful and well-fitting clothes, and carried his dusted and cleaned suitcase in his hand.

"Got anything on?" asked Mike Dolan, genially.

"Me?" said Jimmy, in a puzzled tone. "I don't understand. I'm representing the New York Amalgamated Short Snap Biscuit Cracker and Frazzled Wheat Company."

This statement delighted Mike to such an extent that Jimmy had to take a seltzer-and-milk on the spot. He never touched "hard" drinks.

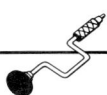

A week after the release of Valentine, 9762, there was a neat job of safe-burglary done in Richmond, Indiana, with no clue to the author. A scant eight hundred dollars was all that was secured. Two weeks after that a patented, improved burglar-proof safe in Logansport was opened like a cheese to the tune of fifteen hundred dollars, currency; securities and silver untouched. That began to interest the rogue-catchers. Then an old-fashioned bank safe in Jefferson City became active and threw out of its crater an eruption of bank notes amounting to five thousand dollars. The losses were now high enough to bring the matter up into Ben Price's class of work. By comparing notes, a remarkable similarity in the methods of the burglaries was noticed. Ben Price investigated the scenes of the robberies, and was heard to remark:

"That's Dandy Jim Valentine's autograph. He's resumed business. Look at that combination knob — jerked out as easy as pulling up a radish in wet weather. He's got the only clamps that can do it. And look how clean those tumblers were punched out! Jimmy never has to drill but one hole. Yes, I guess I want Mr. Valentine. He'll do his bit next time without any short-time or clemency foolishness."

Ben Price knew Jimmy's habits. He had learned them while working up the Springfield case. Long jumps, quick getaways, no confederates, and a taste for good society — these ways had helped Mr. Valentine to become noted as a successful dodger of retribution. It was given out that Ben Price had taken up the elusive safecracker, and other people with burglar-proof safes felt more at ease.

One afternoon Jimmy Valentine and his suitcase climbed out of the mail hack in Elmore, a little town five miles off the railroad down in the blackjack country of Arkansas. Jimmy, looking like an athletic young senior just home from college, went down the board sidewalk toward the hotel.

A young lady crossed the street, passed him at the corner, and entered a door over which was the sign "The Elmore Bank." Jimmy Valentine looked into her eyes, forgot what he was, and became another man. She lowered her eyes and colored slightly. Young men of Jimmy's style and looks were scarce in Elmore.

Jimmy collared a boy that was loafing on the steps of the bank as if he were one of the stockholders, and began to ask him questions about the town, feeding him dimes at intervals. By and by the young lady came out, looking royally unconscious of the young man with the suitcase, and went her way.

"Isn't that young lady Miss Polly Simpson?" asked Jimmy, with specious guile.

"Naw," said the boy. "She's Annabel Adams. Her pa owns this bank. What'd you come to Elmore for? Is that a gold watch chain? I'm going to get a bulldog. Got any more dimes?"

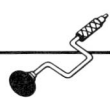

Jimmy went to the Planters' Hotel, registered as Ralph D. Spencer, and engaged a room. He leaned on the desk and declared his platform to the clerk. He said he had come to Elmore to look for a location to go into business. How was the shoe business, now, in the town? He had thought of the shoe business. Was there an opening?

The clerk was impressed by the clothes and manner of Jimmy. He, himself, was something of a pattern of fashion to the youth of Elmore, but he now perceived his shortcomings. While trying to figure out Jimmy's manner of tying his necktie, he cordially gave information.

Yes, there ought to be a good opening in the shoe line. There wasn't an exclusive shoe store in the place. The dry goods and general stores handled them. Business in all lines was fairly good. Hoped Mr. Spencer would decide to locate in Elmore. He would find it a pleasant town to live in, and the people very sociable.

Mr. Spencer thought he would stop over in the town a few days and look over the situation. No, the clerk needn't call the boy. He would carry up his suitcase, himself; it was rather heavy.

Mr. Ralph Spencer, the phoenix that arose from Jimmy Valentine's ashes — ashes left by the flame of a sudden and alternative attack of love — remained in Elmore, and prospered. He opened a shoe store and secured a good run of trade.

Socially he was also a success, and made many friends. And he accomplished the wish of his heart. He met Miss Annabel Adams, and became more and more captivated by her charms.

At the end of a year the situation of Mr. Ralph Spencer was this: He had won the respect of the community, his shoe store was flourishing and he and Annabel were engaged to be married in two weeks. Mr. Adams, the typical, plodding, country banker, approved of Spencer. Annabel's pride in him almost equaled his affection. He was as much at home in the family of Mr. Adams and that of Annabel's married sister as if he were already a member.

One day Jimmy sat down in his room and wrote this letter, which he mailed to the safe address of one of his old friends in St. Louis:

Dear Old Pal:

I want you to be at Sullivan's place, in Little Rock, next Wednesday night at nine o'clock. I want you to wind up some little matters for me. And, also, I want to make you a present of my kit of tools. I know you'll be glad to get them — you couldn't duplicate the lot for a thousand dollars. Say, Billy, I've quit the old business — a year ago. I've got a nice store. I'm making an honest living, and I'm going to marry the finest girl on earth two weeks from now. It's the only life, Billy — the straight one. I wouldn't touch a dollar of another man's money now for a million. After I get married I'm going to sell out and go West, where there won't be so much danger of having old scores brought up against me. I tell you, Billy, she's an angel. She believes in me; and I wouldn't do another crooked thing for the whole world. Be sure to be at Sully's, for I must see you. I'll bring along the tools with me.

Your old friend, Jimmy.

On the Monday night after Jimmy wrote this letter, Ben Price jogged unobtrusively into Elmore in a livery buggy. He lounged about town in his quiet way until he found out what he wanted to know. From the drugstore across the street from Spencer's shoe store he got a good look at Ralph D. Spencer.

"Going to marry the banker's daughter, are you, Jimmy?" said Ben to himself, softly. "Well, I don't know!"

The next morning Jimmy took breakfast at the Adamses'. He was going to Little Rock that day to order his wedding suit and buy something nice for Annabel. That would be the first time he had left town since he came to Elmore. It had been more than a year now since those last professional "jobs," and he thought he could safely venture out.

After breakfast quite a family party went downtown together — Mr. Adams, Annabel, Jimmy, and Annabel's married sister with her two little girls, aged five and nine. They came by the hotel where Jimmy boarded, and he ran up to his room and brought along his suitcase. Then they went on to the bank. There stood Jimmy's horse and buggy and Dolph Gibson, who was going to drive him to the railroad station.

All went inside the high, carved oak railings into the banking room — Jimmy included, for Mr. Adams's future son-in-law was welcome anywhere. The clerks were pleased to be greeted by the good-looking, agreeable young man who was going to marry Miss Annabel. Jimmy set his suitcase down. Annabel, whose heart was bubbling with happiness and lively youth, put on Jimmy's hat and picked up the suitcase. "Wouldn't I make a nice salesman?" said Annabel. "My! Ralph, how heavy it is. Feels like it was full of gold bricks."

"Lot of nickel-plated shoe horns in there," said Jimmy, coolly, "that I'm going to return. Thought I'd save express charges by taking them up. I'm getting awfully economical."

The Elmore Bank had just put in a new safe and vault. Mr. Adams was very proud of it, and insisted on an inspection by everyone. The vault was a small one, but it had a new patented door. It fastened with three solid steel bolts thrown simultaneously with a single handle, and had a time lock. Mr. Adams beamingly explained its workings to Mr. Spencer, who showed a courteous but not too intelligent interest. The two children, May and Agatha, were delighted by the shining metal and funny clock and knobs.

While they were thus engaged Ben Price sauntered in and leaned on his elbow, looking casually inside between the railings. He told the teller that he didn't want anything; he was just waiting for a man he knew.

Suddenly there was a scream or two from the women, and a commotion. Unperceived by the elders, May, the nine-year-old girl, in a spirit of play, had shut Agatha in the vault. She had then shot the bolts and turned the knob of the combination as she had seen Mr. Adams do.

The old banker sprang to the handle and tugged at it for a moment. "The door can't be opened," he groaned. "The clock hasn't been wound nor the combination set."

Agatha's mother screamed again, hysterically.

"Hush!" said Mr. Adams, raising his trembling hand. "All be quiet for a moment. Agatha!" he called as loudly as he could. "Listen to me." During the following silence they could just hear the faint sound of the child wildly shrieking in the dark vault in a panic of terror.

"My precious darling!" wailed the mother. "She will die of fright! Open the door! Oh, break it open! Can't you do something?"

"There isn't anyone nearer than Little Rock who can open that door," said Mr. Adams, in a shaky voice. "Spencer, what shall we do? That child — she can't stand it long in there. There isn't enough air, and, besides, she'll go into convulsions from fright."

Agatha's mother, frantic now, beat the door of the vault with her hands. Somebody wildly suggested dynamite. Annabel turned to Jimmy, her large eyes full of anguish, but not yet despairing.

"Can't you do something, Ralph — try, won't you?"

He looked at her with a strange soft smile on his lips and in his keen eyes.

"Annabel," he said, "give me that rose you are wearing, will you?"

Hardly believing that she heard him right, she unpinned the bud from the front of her dress, and placed it in his hand. Jimmy stuffed it into his vest pocket, threw off his coat and pulled up his shirtsleeves. With that act Ralph D. Spencer passed away and Jimmy Valentine took his place.

"Get away from the door, all of you," he commanded, shortly.

He set his suitcase on the table, and opened it out flat. From that time on he seemed to be unconscious of the presence of anyone else. He laid out the shining, strange implements swiftly and orderly, whistling softly to himself as he always did when at work. In a deep silence and immovable, the others watched him as if under a spell.

In a minute Jimmy's pet drill was biting smoothly into the steel door. In ten minutes — breaking his own burglarious record — he threw back the bolts and opened the door.

Agatha, almost collapsed, but safe, was gathered into her mother's arms.

Jimmy Valentine put on his coat, and walked outside the railings toward the front door. As he went he thought he heard a faraway voice that he once knew call "Ralph!" But he never hesitated.

At the door a big man stood somewhat in his way.

"Hello, Ben!" said Jimmy, still with his strange smile. "Got around at last, have you? Well, let's go. I don't know that it makes much difference, now."

And then Ben Price acted rather strangely. "Guess you're mistaken, Mr. Spencer," he said. "Don't believe I recognize you. Your buggy's waiting for you, isn't it?"

And Ben Price turned and strolled down the street.

Discuss the Selection

1. What did Jimmy risk losing when he decided to open the safe?
2. How did Jimmy resolve his problems in life?
3. What do you think finally caused Jimmy to reform his life?
4. Do you think that Ben was right or wrong to let Jimmy go without punishment? Support your opinion.
5. What words did the author use to let you know that Jimmy thought Ben would arrest him? Find them in the story.

Apply the Skills

The topic of O. Henry's "Jimmy Valentine" is that we must often make decisions that affect more than just ourselves. Several characters make choices that affect the lives of other characters in the story. Give an example of a decision made by each of the characters listed below.

1. Jimmy Valentine
2. Ben Price

Think and Write

Prewrite

Decision-maker	Decision	Supporting Reasons	Opposing Reasons
Jimmy	Whether to open safe	1. To save child	
Ben	Whether to arrest Jimmy	2. To prove he is a good detective	

In "Jimmy Valentine" both Jimmy Valentine and Ben Price are faced with difficult decisions. Copy the chart shown above, including the reasons in support of: (1) Jimmy's opening the safe, and (2) Ben's arresting Jimmy. Now add the *opposing* reasons; that is, at least one reason why Jimmy should *not* open the safe and one reason why Ben should *not* arrest him.

Compose

Using the information from the story and in the chart, write a paragraph telling why Jimmy should, or should not, open the safe. Then write a second paragraph telling why Ben should, or should not, arrest Jimmy. State your position in the topic sentence of each paragraph. Then give reasons to convince the reader that you made the right choice. In other words, try to persuade the reader to think the way you do. End each paragraph with an especially convincing statement.

Revise

Carefully read the paragraphs that you wrote. Did you express your opinions in a persuasive manner? Did you end each paragraph with a strong appeal to the reader? If not, revise your first draft, adding any details needed to convince the reader to share your opinions.

In her witty autobiography, Hildegarde Dolson describes the people and events that made growing up in her family a memorable experience. As you read, see if you can tell why she used the title she did.

The author uses numerous anecdotes held together by a main idea. What is the main idea of the selection?

We Shook the Family Tree
by Hildegarde Dolson

The Dolsons lived in a small town in Pennsylvania in the years after the Armistice—the end of World War I. The family consisted of father and mother and their four children: Hildegarde, the oldest; Bobby; Sally; and the youngest, Jimmy. Life in this energetic family was often full of surprises, fun, and even scary moments that seemed humorous when the family looked back on them.

Many families have a set of favorite stories or anecdotes about the humorous things that have happened to them. Hildegarde Dolson's family seems to have many such anecdotes. Perhaps her family had an unusual capacity for hilarity. Or is it just that Miss Dolson knows how to tell a story to bring out the humor in their family life? Decide for yourself when you read this excerpt from *We Shook the Family Tree*, a book about her family.

It was two years after the Armistice when Mother saw The House. My Grandmother Brown, a lively, beautiful old lady, was visiting us at the time, and she and Mother discovered it one afternoon when they were out walking. At dinner that night, they tackled my father.

The House was not only for sale, they said, but would cost even less than the one we now owned. It would actually be a saving to move. They described how it sat on the hill at the top of Buffalo Street, and Mother kept stressing the view, and how important it was to have room to breathe. Whenever my father asked what the house itself was like, both my mother and grandmother would say, "Oh, Cliff, it's so original."

My father found this description rather ominous, but he consented amiably enough to go and see the house that Saturday afternoon. My mother and grandmother had been truthful in saying it was original. It was indeed. I can still hear my father's roar of pained surprise when he discovered there wasn't even a washstand in the whole house and that the bathroom was downstairs next to the kitchen. The house itself was about the size of the one we owned, but much older, solider, and sweeter somehow. It sat there built into the hill with a beautiful view of the town below. There was certainly room to breathe, too, especially in the vast, desolate expanse of backyard, consisting entirely of rocks and overgrown grass clumps, all spreading uphill at a breakneck angle to the woods just behind. In fact, the yard rose so steeply from front to rear that the back bedroom upstairs had a door opening onto a wooden bridge that leaped over space straight out into the hilly backyard. To us children, it was the most fascinating, wonderful place we'd ever seen. To my father, it was a house without a furnace. Bobby, Sally, and I hung on to him squealing, "Oh, please." My mother and Grandma Brown began talking very fast and brightly about "adding a sun porch here with some ponds there" — and told my father he must be blind not to see the marvelous possibilities. Father spoke with the natural caution of a man who has learned when not to argue. His actual words were, "We'll see."

The next evening, just after dinner, my mother sat reading the paper. Suddenly she squealed, "Oh, Cliff!" Then she jumped up and kissed my father, who was looking very pleased with himself. What Mother had read was an item saying "C. B. Dolson has bought the Evans property at the top of Buffalo Street Hill." Bobby and I read the item over at least a dozen times. We went to school the following day with the swaggering walk of new landowners.

We moved into the house soon afterward. Then we lived for weeks in a lovely bedlam of carpenters knocking out partitions, electricians trying to bore through solid hundred-year-old oak beams, and plumbers carrying the bathtub upstairs. Bobby and I spent most of our time exploring the woods behind. We dammed up streams, cuddled pollywogs, ate any kind of berry growing on a bush, and hammered hundreds of the carpenters' best nails into odds and ends of wood, to build what we thought of as a lean-to.

It was nature, and not our neighbors, that presented the really tough problem. Mother said she didn't want a backyard that looked like everybody else's. There was small danger of this, since few of our neighbors went in exclusively for boulders and tall grass in landscaping. In order to arouse my father's enthusiasm for working around the grounds, she encouraged him to dig for fishing worms all over the place. In this way, he not only acquired a lot of juicy night crawlers for bait, but spaded up quite a tidy stretch of the backyard, painlessly.

Bobby and I, being disinterested in gardening, put up a croquet set. We leaped from rock to hillock, whamming our balls up hill and down dale in a game that combined the liveliest features of professional polo and an Easter Sunday egg hunt. Frequently a croquet ball would roll right on down the Buffalo Street hill, and we'd chase it for blocks. If we were tired after this jaunt, before going back home we'd drop in at my father's new insurance office. Then we'd trudge back up the hill, the croquet ball heavy in one hand, and go right on with the game.

Another hazard of our mountainside croquet was the two goats. Mother had acquired them soon after we moved in. She kept them tied to a post in the backyard. Give them enough rope and they'd clear quite a good piece of property, she figured. It's true that because of their huge appetites they eliminated the worst grass clumps, which is more than my brother and I did. On the other hand, none of us children ate the clothesline, so this makes us all about even. The goats were named Belle and Beauty, perhaps to fool the neighbors about the way they smelled. They

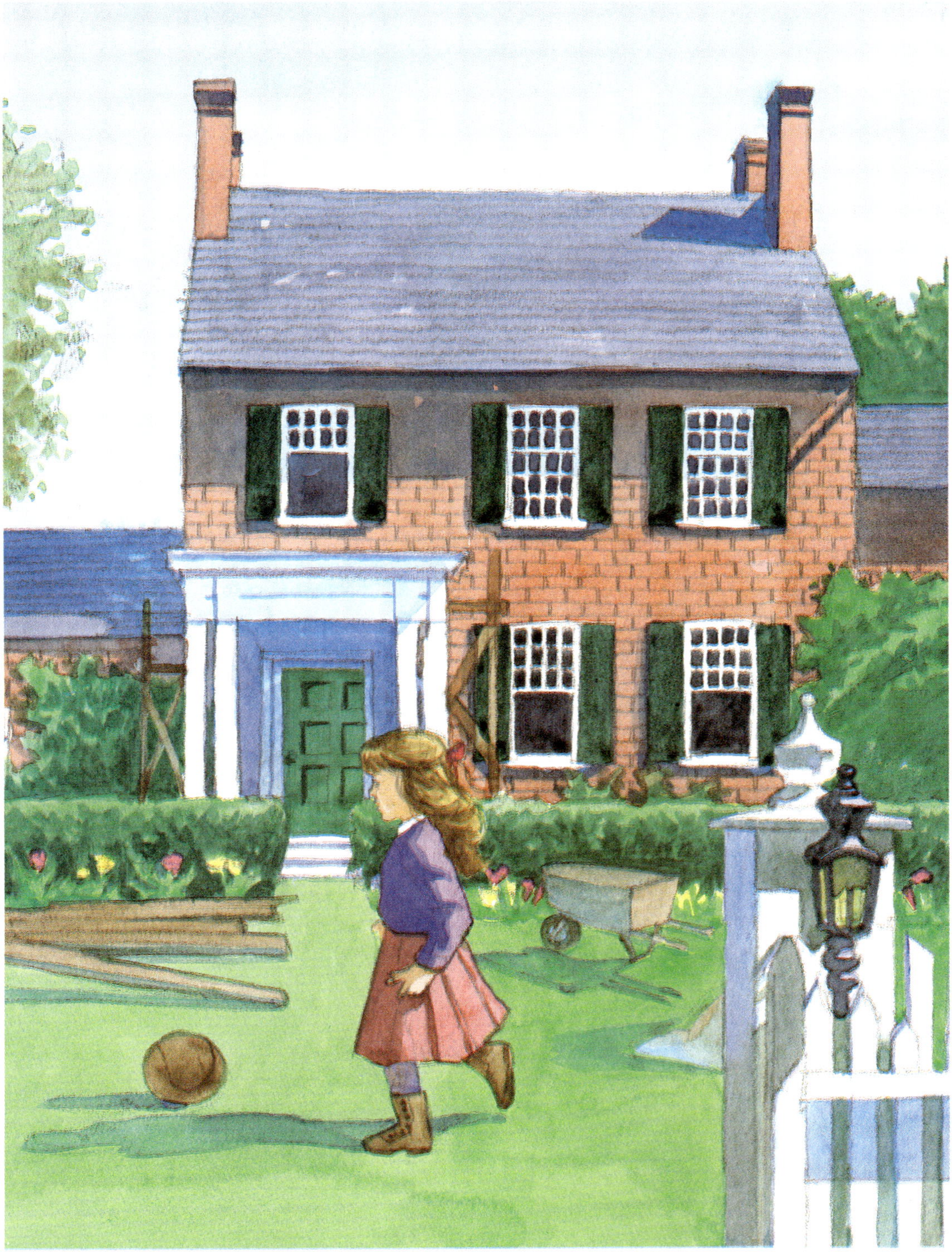

had been given to us, along with a little red goat cart, by a family leaving town who had managed to contain their joy as they bid the goats good riddance.

Theoretically, one of the goats' chief duties, besides mowing the grass, was to pull Bobby, Sally, and me, one at a time, in the goat cart. However, for some curious reason, Belle and Beauty were always confused about this. They thought it was we children who were supposed to pull *them*. After we'd ridden a few hundred feet, both goats would sit down and wait to be hauled home. It was an awfully unsatisfactory arrangement. Nobody cried when Belle and Beauty were given to a farmer who came to sell us eggs each week and admired the red goat cart. After he'd had the goats a week, he stopped bringing us eggs, probably to get even.

Anyway, it was my mother, and not the goats, who gradually succeeded in making the backyard into one of the prettiest in town. She put in rock gardens, pools, little fir trees, and a leveled-off terrace for eating outdoors. When I say that she was working uphill, I speak literally. And when I think of the original boulders that dotted our backyard, it seems to me that Mother's accomplishments were a fine example of what happens when an irresistible force meets an immovable object. I remember one time when she wanted a bird bath in a hurry. Thinking quickly, she sawed off our stationary clothes pole until it was just about four feet tall. Then she grabbed the lid off the garbage can, stuck it on the pole upside down, and covered the whole business with cement. It made a dandy bird bath — and still does.

The total transformation of the yard must have taken years, with the aid of my father and a few friends. As children, we didn't really appreciate all that work. Just after my father and mother had coddled along grass seed to get a velvety front lawn, we took to playing Blind Man's Bluff on that very spot. Some woman who had come to call told Mother she mustn't let us trample over the new lawn. Mother said serenely, "But I'm more interested in raising children than grass."

Bobby and I used to feel rather hurt when we went to a friend's house and were only allowed to enter the back door, after carefully wiping our feet on a door mat. At our own house, there were five doors leading to the outside. We could bang in and out of any of them, with no fuss about muddy feet. Sometimes when we were playing quietly in a friend's home, one of the children

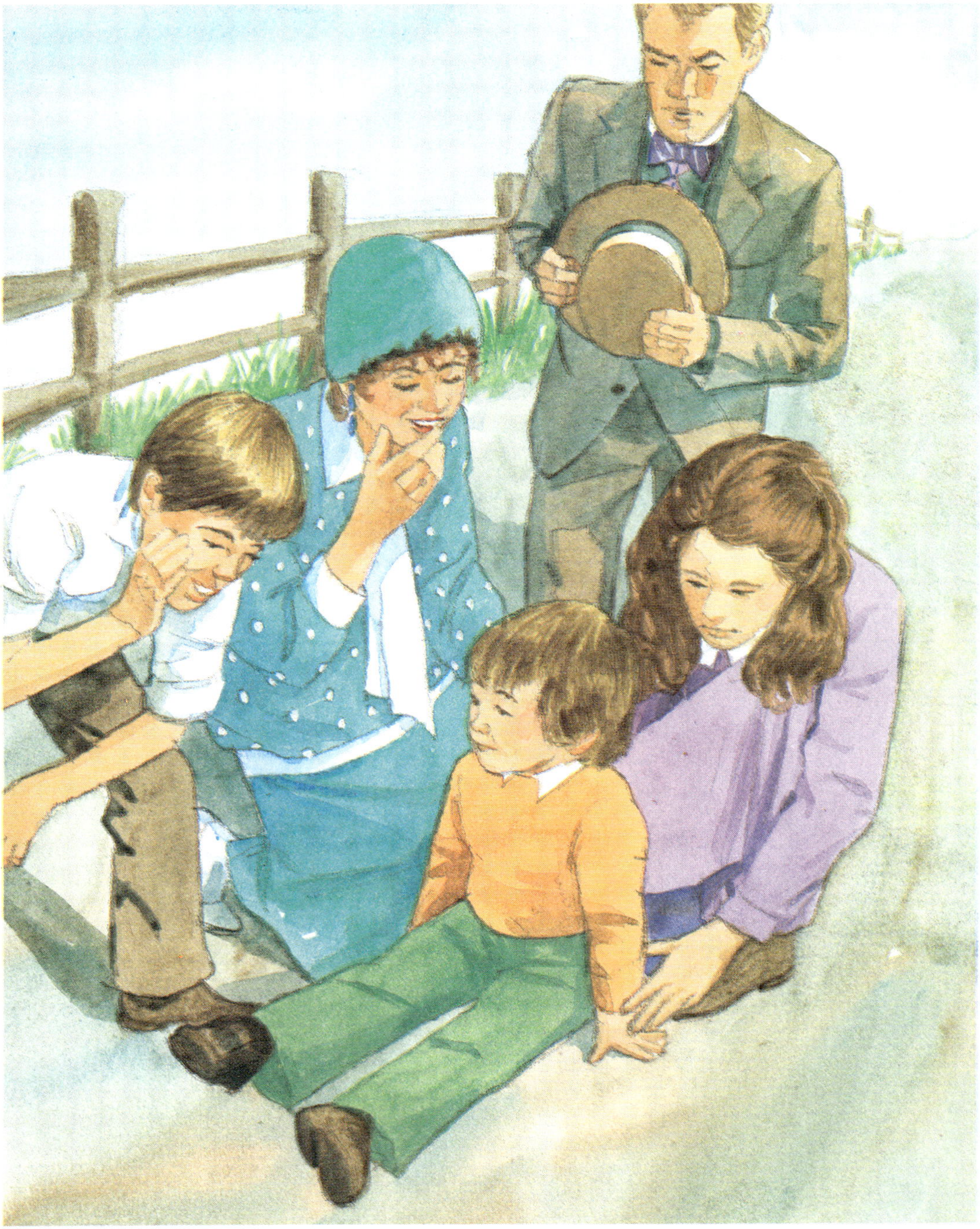

would say, "Aw, let's go up to the Dolsons', where we can bounce on the beds." This was a game we liked very much. Each child would take a turn standing on the bed, after first taking off his or her shoes to be polite. Then he'd jump up and down with high, bouncy leaps and end up sprawled flat on the mattress — winded and happy.

Another of the charms of our new home was sled-riding to school. The Buffalo Street hill was so steep that we could run out at three minutes of nine in the morning, slam ourselves on our sleds, and be at the school four blocks down the street as the nine o'clock bell rang. Every self-respecting child rode his or her sled in a fashion known as "belly gutter." Mother didn't think it was nice to say "belly." So, we Dolson kids rode "billy gutter." It was exactly the same thing but sounded more refined. Soon after moving up on the hill we'd been given an Airedale named Trouble. The dog loved to dash down between our sleds barking with uproarious gaiety and pretending to nip at our legs. He also had a lovable trick of following me into school if he were coaxed hard enough, and we never missed coaxing him.

Soon after Bobby began taking violin lessons, he discovered that by scraping his bow a certain way when practicing, he could produce discords that made Trouble howl like a werewolf in pain. Bobby's violin bow would eeeek and aaawk in hideous disharmony. Trouble would howl in mournful accompaniment. The total effect was excruciatingly wonderful — for us, if not for our parents.

Besides Trouble, the other addition to our household was a new baby brother, Jimmy, born in 1921. When my teacher at school asked me what our new baby looked like, I said briefly, "He's bright red," and let the matter rest there.

One of Jimmy's accomplishments was his ability to stand on his head for a remarkably long period of time. Once Mother complained to our friend and family doctor, Dr. Mac Brown, that she didn't think it was good for a little child to stand upside down so much. Dr. Brown said nonsense, no child could stand on its head long enough to matter. The next time he came to see us, Mother called my little brother in from the yard and said, "Jimmy, stand on your head."

Jimmy was rather surprised at this command, because Mother had been trying to discourage his favorite stance. However, he obeyed happily, and not only stood on his head, but was well on his way to breaking all previous endurance records. As his face turned purple and his eyeballs bulged, Dr. Brown got so nervous he urged my brother to stop. "You see," Mother said. Dr. Brown saw, all right. He had a nice little talk with Jimmy. He told him he must save his strength to grow up and be a good big football player. After that, Jimmy only stood on his head on very special occasions, or when somebody offered him a nickel.

Like my father, my brothers were ardent fishermen from the time they were old enough to recognize a night crawler from a crab. Even before they could actually accompany my father on his Saturday afternoon fishing sprees, they were allowed the exquisite pleasure of digging for worms, and filling a can full of bait. One day Jimmy forgot to take the tin can up to the far corner of the backyard, where he was helping Bobby dig for bait. When he came back down to the house, looking adorable in his little cowboy suit and cowboy hat, my mother was entertaining several women friends on the sun porch. "Dear, take off your hat and say how-do-you-do to the ladies," she told him. Jimmy said he didn't want to take off his hat. My mother persisted, although she was soon to regret it. When my brother finally took off his hat, a live mass of fishing worms sat on his head, wriggling. Lacking a bait can, Jimmy had been keeping them safe and warm. Mother helped Jimmy pick up all the worms and get them into a can before she served her friends tea. She said there was no sense in wasting good bait.

Besides being a good fisherman, Bobby was very smart at setting traps in the woods and catching various animals. The State Game Commission had offered a one-dollar bounty for each weasel caught. Bobby and his fellow-trapper, Tim Ely, naturally preferred weasels, but they weren't too fussy. On the day that my mother was to give a fancy dinner party, they came rushing down from the woods with their newest catch. "Mommy," Bobby shouted. "Look!" Mother didn't have to look. She had already sniffed. My brother deposited on our doorstep the most powerfully perfumed skunk in Pennsylvania.

For an hour Mother ran around opening windows and trying to air out the house. It didn't do much good, partly because the outdoors smelled as awful as we did indoors. It just wasn't the atmosphere Mother had intended for her nice dinner party, and her guests ignored the etiquette of "Never eat and run."

From the time he was a baby, my youngest brother Jimmy loved chasing butterflies. By the time he was four, his daily costume was a cowboy suit, plus a butterfly net with a bamboo handle six feet long, and an ether jar for chloroforming his catch. When friendly neighbors stopped Jimmy on the street and asked him playfully what the jar was for, his reply was short and to the point. "I kill butterflies."

Once Mother decided he belonged in kindergarten. After the first day Miss Wynne, the teacher in that haven for tots, sent him home with a note saying he was a child of nature, and shouldn't be cooped up indoors. This was a graceful way of putting it, all right. At least she didn't send my parents any bill for breakage.

Almost every Sunday, my father would suggest we take a little drive. There would follow a touching scene, in which Father tried to sell Jimmy on the idea of leaving Trouble, our Airedale, and the butterfly net at home. Nobody really expected anything to come of this. I'll say for Father he used persuasive arguments, so persuasive that they convinced everybody but Jimmy and the dog. Then off we'd go, with three of us wedged into the front seat of the Ford, three in the rear, and Trouble bounding from lap to lap like a happy cow, or licking Father's neck in gratitude for being included in the party. Meanwhile the butterfly net hanging from a car window called forth a frenzy of shouts from the drivers of passing cars.

Jimmy wasn't allowed to sit next to the door, because we had discovered that if he saw a butterfly, he'd go after it willy-nilly.

This had become alarmingly clear when he was two. One day he spotted a swallowtail as we drove down a country road. One minute our baby brother was with us, the next minute he wasn't. Upon realizing she was one child short, Mother screamed. Father pulled on the brakes and they ran back to find Jimmy lying in the road. As they bent over him, frantically looking for signs of life, Jimmy sat up and said in a pleasant conversational tone, "I watched the wheels go round." He was very philosophical in his pursuit of nature. Except for some cinder scratches, received when he fell out of the car on his face, he was in dandy shape. After that, however, Father had such trick safety catches put on the door handles to thwart Jimmy that we could hardly get out of the car ourselves without a crowbar. As a further precaution, Jimmy had to sit in the middle, and a rope loop attached to his cowboy belt was fastened to Mother's wrist.

On one of Father's fishing trips he had seen what he thought was an ideal picnic spot. For weeks afterward, whenever we went driving, he kept looking for this Shangri-la in which to eat our deviled eggs. "Now I think it's just over that next hill," he'd say. Each time, we four children peered out. "Is this it, Father?" we'd chorus. We said it so often that Father began to clench his teeth and stare straight ahead. When we finally found the picnic spot, on a Fourth of July, it was all Father had claimed. It had mossy places to sit, a stream for wading, and a lovely clump of trees. While Mother and I were laying out the picnic, Father took Sally and Bobby down to the stream. Jimmy roamed around us with his butterfly net. It must have been at least ten minutes before Mother realized he was missing. Her method of calling us home was to clap with the palms of her hands curved in a way that produced a startling amount of noise. (Even now, if I absentmindedly clap Mother's way in a New York movie house, people for rows around turn and gape.) After clapping for Jimmy and getting no answer, we called Father and he started out with Bobby and me on a casual searching party. Just on the other side of the clump of trees, we came to a fenced-in field. My youngest brother was inside it, at the end nearest us, stalking a butterfly. Then we saw the bull. It was a very big bull, and it was standing there gazing at Jimmy. Perhaps it had never before seen a miniature cowboy waving a butterfly net, and was trying to decide how to react. My father made a leap

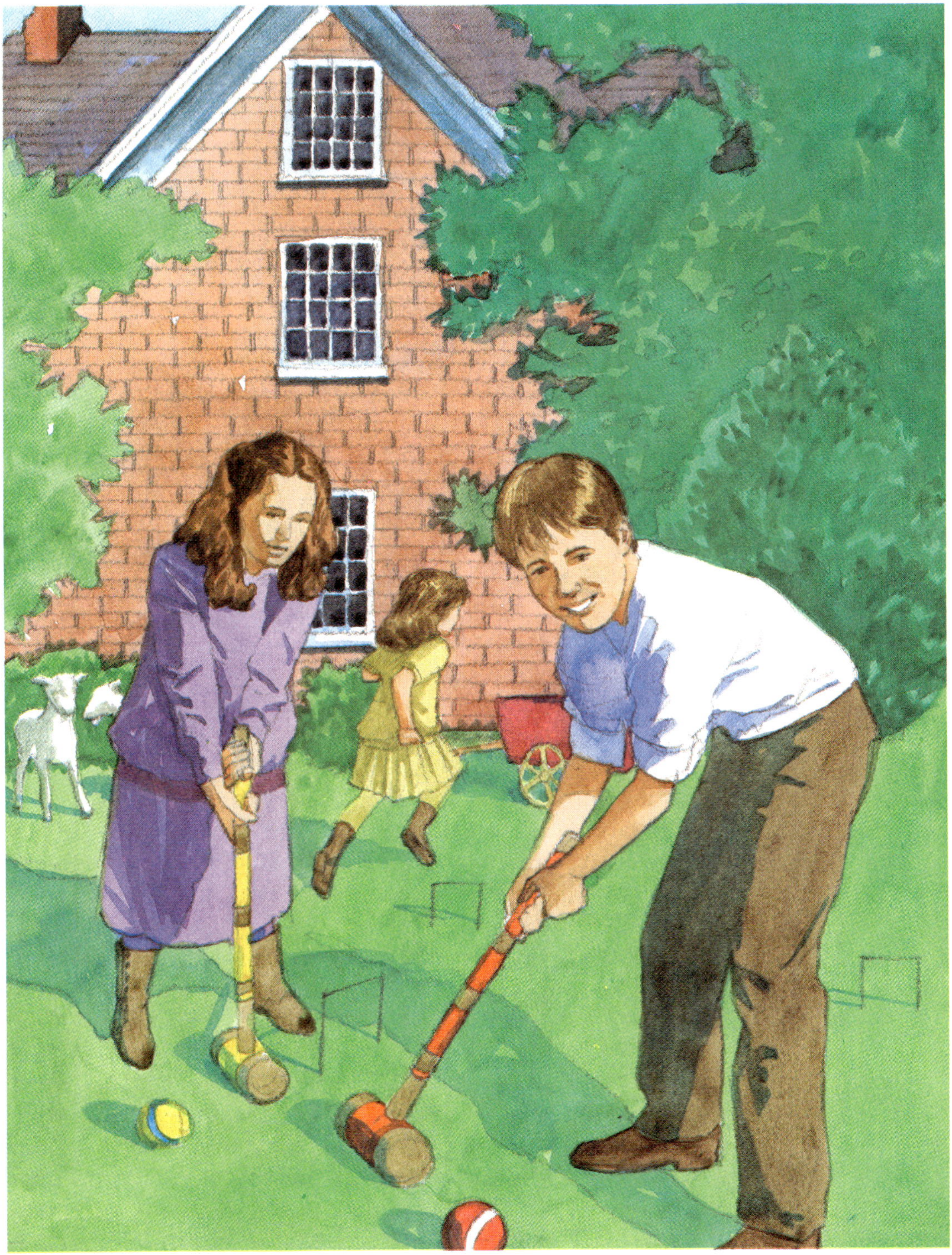

that would have done credit to a ballet dancer, and was inside the field grabbing Jimmy just as the bull decided to close in. Perhaps he just wanted to be friendly, but Father didn't have time to inquire into his intentions.

It's rather awkward to be chased by a bull when you're carrying a little boy, but Father got back to the fence near us, tossed Jimmy over, and scrambled over himself, at least three feet ahead of the horns. The bull looked more hurt than mad at this exit. All of us thought it was a highly successful rescue. That is, all of us but the rescued Jimmy. He was furious because his butterfly net had been left behind in the field and he wanted to go right back and get it. We had to promise that we'd fix him a new net and catch him a Luna moth, before he'd calm down enough to eat a deviled egg.

Butterfly chasing wasn't the only hobby in the family. My brother Bobby, in his early teens, found his hobby through his hero — Earl Liederman. Every picture Bobby had of Mr. Liederman was a stunning expanse of muscular flesh. He was one of the world's strongest men — physically, I mean — and he was Bobby's ideal. When Bobby first urged my parents to let him take the Earl Liederman correspondence course and become an iron-muscled man, Mother and Father thought it was funny. As the months wore on, and Bobby wore my parents down, in the slow, sure fashion of water dripping on rock, they stopped seeing the humor. We had Earl Liederman for breakfast, lunch, and dinner, and as warmed-over hash for Sunday night supper. Bobby argued from the standpoint of health: "You want me to be brawny, don't you?" He also argued from the standpoint of efficiency: "If I built up my muscles like Earl Liederman, I could mow the whole lawn in ten minutes." This campaign started in June. He got the course for Christmas. Measured in terms of light-years, it was only a jiffy, but it seemed like more.

I think the lessons came every other week, but the one piece of equipment arrived by express, at the very beginning of the course. Earl Liederman called it Tension Cables, and the word *tension* had a certain rightness throughout this phase of our lives. The contraption itself consisted of two wooden handles with coil springs. Between these was stretched a long black rubber cable about as big in diameter as a child's finger. With a handle held in each fist, the cable was stretched as far as possible, on the same principle as pulling taffy, only tougher. As the pupil grew stronger and stretchier, he could add more and more cables. Bobby claimed that Earl Liederman himself used ten. Also, Mr. Liederman had suggested, in one of the lessons, that the pupil put up an iron gymnasium bar "in some unused spot," to practice chinning himself. Bobby and Tim Ely rigged up a bar across the upstairs hall, a thoroughfare about as unused in our house as Broadway is in New York. It was enough higher than Bobby and Tim to give them a nice jumping range. But any tall and unwary visitor, traveling down the dusky narrow hall, ran the risk either of being decapitated by the bar, or of getting an awful conk on the head.

I'm still dazed and pleased to remember that Bobby's muscles actually did expand. At times, you could almost see them growing, like morning-glory seeds. An early lesson had included a diagram of all the important muscles, explaining which ones to concentrate on. Bobby's superior knowledge was hard on the rest of us. "You've neglected your deltoid, Father," he'd explain kindly. "That's why your shoulders are narrow." Or grabbing Sally, a small, exquisitely made child, by the scruff of the neck, he'd say, "Just feel her trapezius. It's terrible." Sally would insist stoutly she didn't care, but all of us felt a bit sullen. Bobby was especially critical of my scrawny frame. "If you'd chin yourself ten times a day, Hildegarde," he'd say, "you'd have a bigger latissimus dorsi in no time. You'd get so you could even lift a horse." At that state of my life, I wasn't much interested in lifting a horse. I'll admit now it could be quite an effective parlor trick.

We of the inferior latissimus dorsi and trapezius were still human, and we couldn't help feeling a solid satisfaction when the Liederman method finally boomeranged on Bobby. It was Lesson Number Nine that egged him on to new and interesting usage for the tension cables. Instead of just holding a handle in each fist and stretching, Mr. Liederman explained, it was also possible to put one handle on the floor, hold it there with the foot, and pull upward on the rubber cable with both hands. Bobby was pulling in this fashion, with all his new iron muscles, when his foot slipped. Immediately the released cable snapped up to hit him a good wallop on the nose. He went around for days in adhesive tape, but the only one of us who showed a decent amount of sympathy was little Jimmy.

Discuss the Selection

1. Why do you think Hildegarde Dolson called her autobiography "We Shook the Family Tree"?
2. How did Jimmy surprise his mother's friends at tea?
3. How did the family resolve the problem of Jimmy's interest in butterflies during their Sunday drives?
4. Which part of the selection did you think was the funniest? Why?
5. Do you think that Mr. Dolson shared the family's opinion of the house? Why or why not?

Apply the Skills

Most stories have a main idea connecting the author's thoughts. Sometimes the author states this idea directly. Other times, the main idea is unstated. In "We Shook the Family Tree," Hildegarde Dolson does not directly state the story's main idea.

1. In your own words, give the main idea of the selection.
2. Give three examples from the selection that tell the reader about the author's childhood.

Think and Write

Prewrite

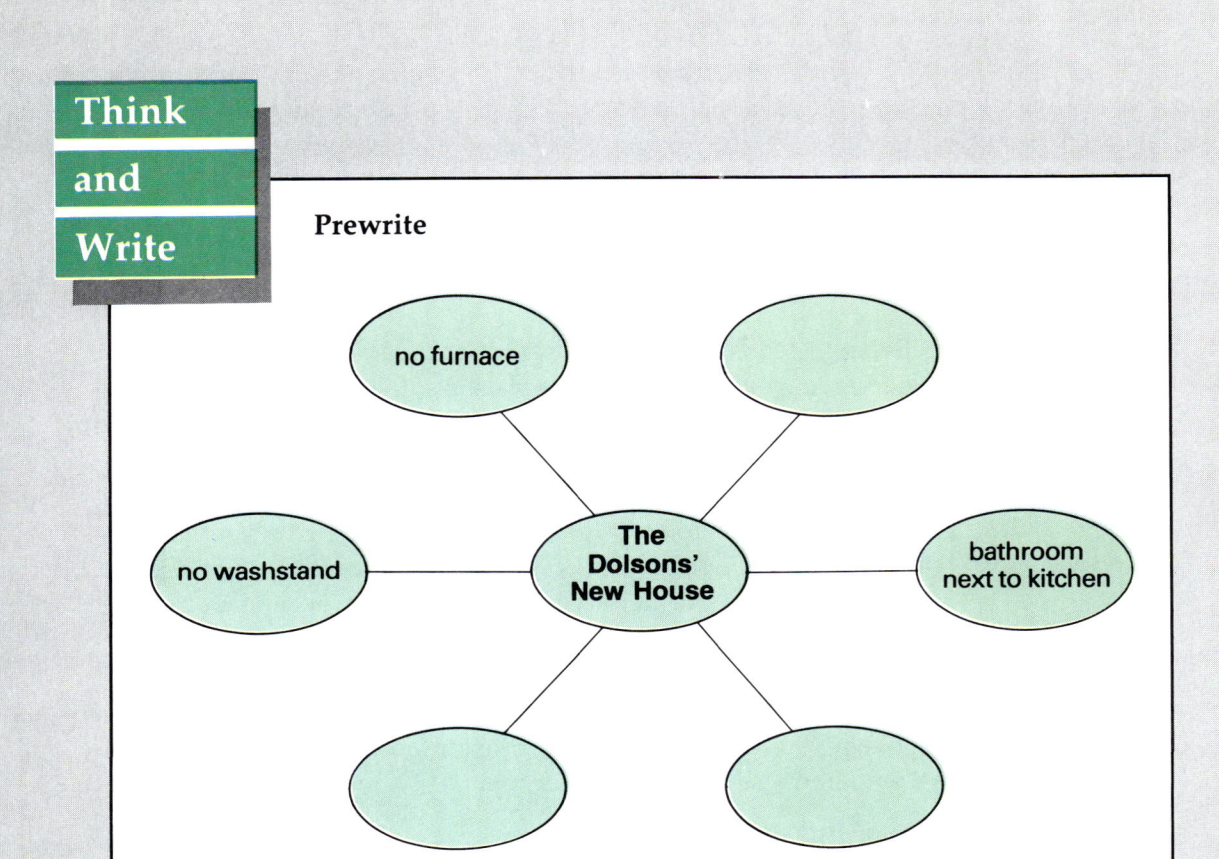

[Diagram: central oval "The Dolsons' New House" connected to six ovals — "no furnace", "no washstand", "bathroom next to kitchen", and three blank ovals]

A good descriptive paragraph gives the reader a vivid picture of a person, place, or thing. Copy the diagram shown above, including the author's descriptions of the Dolsons's new house. Then extend the diagram by fill-in the blank circles with other descriptions of the house. Refer to the story as needed.

Compose

Using the information in the diagram and the story, write a paragraph describing the Dolson house. Your first sentence might be *When Miss Dolson and her mother said the new house was original, they were not exaggerating.*

Revise

Read the paragraph you wrote. Does it contain all the details in the diagram? Does it give a clear picture of the Dolsons's house? If not, revise it to make sure the reader understands what made the house so original.

Study Skills

Tests

Being tested is a big part of school and of life. Just as you are tested in language arts, social studies, mathematics, science, and other subjects, adults are constantly being tested in their careers. In fact, every job is a kind of test. For example, the chef who prepares food that is tasty has passed, but the one who prepares and serves food that is too salty has failed. Likewise, a lawyer who files poorly organized, inaccurate court papers has failed by not doing the best job for his or her client. The client may even lose the case because the lawyer didn't follow a plan.

By going into each test situation — in or out of school — with a plan, you can improve your chances for success. Good planning will help you to achieve the two most important parts of test-taking — preparedness and self-confidence.

Preparing for the Test

Have you ever become nervous about taking a test? One reason that some people get "butterflies" in their stomachs before a test is that they do not start to study until the night before the test. You will feel more confident and better prepared if you make it a habit to follow a *daily* study plan.

Set aside time each afternoon or evening to review your notes about what was covered in class that day.

Complete any gaps in your notes by referring to the parts of the book on which your notes are based.

Make a note about anything that you didn't understand, in class or in the book, and ask your teacher about it the next morning, or as soon as possible.

Make an outline of your daily notes.

Use your outline to create a sample test. The real test is likely to be similar to the one that you make up as part of your study plan.

Always try to find a place to study that is quiet and comfortable. Your study place should, of course, have good lighting. Finally, try to find a study spot with no distractions.

Get plenty of sleep the night before the test so that you will be alert during the test. By planning ahead and following a daily study plan, you'll be able to go to bed at a reasonable hour instead of staying up all night to study.

Now answer these questions about the material that you have just read.

1. What two important parts of test-taking will a good study plan help you achieve?
2. Can you summarize the steps that will help you to be prepared and self-confident on the day of the test? In other words, what steps should you follow in your daily study plan, and what should you try to do the night before the test?

Test-taking Strategies

You have reviewed how to prepare for a test. If you follow that study plan, you should be well prepared and self-confident on the day of the test.

During the test itself, try to keep in mind the following test-taking strategies:

- Make sure that you understand all directions. If any directions are unclear, ask your teacher about them before the test begins.
- Read each question carefully before answering it.
- Do not spend too much time on any one question. If you are not sure of an answer, try to make an intelligent guess.
- Answer the easy questions first and the difficult ones last.
- Number each answer correctly if you are using a separate sheet of paper.
- Try to save enough time to check your answers, and, if necessary, to revise them.

Different Kinds of Tests

There are several kinds of tests; that is, formats for presenting questions. These formats include **multiple-choice, fill-in-the-blank,** and **essay** tests. With a special test-taking plan for each kind of test, you can improve your chances for good results.

Multiple-Choice Tests

Multiple-choice tests are those in which you are given several answers from which to choose the correct one. The test-taking strategies that you reviewed earlier are particularly useful in taking multiple-choice tests.

Read the directions carefully to be sure that you know exactly how to mark your answers. For example, notice whether the directions tell you to circle or to underline your answers. If you mark your answers in the wrong way, you could fail the test even if you know the right answers.

Look over the entire test, answering every question that you can. Temporarily skip over those that you can't answer.

Go back to the beginning of the test and make strategic guesses about the unanswered questions. A strategic guess on a multiple-choice test is best done systematically. First eliminate any choices that you know are wrong. From the remaining choices, make an intelligent guess. If you have a choice of four answers and you can eliminate two of them as wrong, you have a better chance of guessing right because you have narrowed the choices.

Fill-in-the-Blank Tests

Fill-in-the-blank tests are those that ask you to complete a sentence with a word or phrase. As with multiple-choice tests, read the directions carefully to be sure that you understand how to mark your answers. First, answer all the easy questions. Next, reread the difficult questions and try to answer them, even if you have to guess. If you don't give any answer at all, you'll miss that question anyway. Finally, try to save some time to check the accuracy of your answers. For example, a right answer that is spelled wrong may lower your test score.

Essay Tests

When you take an **essay test**, you have to do more than circle an answer or fill in a blank. You must express what you know in complete sentences or paragraphs. To succeed in taking an essay test, you will have to recall information. Then you will have to organize and summarize your knowledge of the subject on which you are being tested. To accomplish this task effectively, you will need to follow a plan especially designed for taking essay tests.

Read the directions carefully to make sure that you understand how long your answers are supposed to be and where you should write them.

Read each question carefully. Notice the important parts of each question. Who or what is the question about? The proper nouns will tell you. What aspect of that person or thing does the essay question ask you to discuss? The verbs, particularly the main verbs, will tell you.

Write notes on a piece of scrap paper about information related to the question. Jot down everything you think the answer should include.

Now begin writing your essay answers. First, write the introductory sentences by simply turning the essay instructions into statements. Study the following examples:

Essay Instruction
Compare the strategies for taking multiple-choice and fill-in-the-blank tests.

Introductory Statement
There are several similarities in the strategies for taking multiple-choice and fill-in-the-blank tests.

Finally, write at least two detail sentences to support your introductory statements. Refer to your notes as you write.

Start preparing for your next test now. Set up a daily study plan and follow it.

In this tall tale from Japan, a famous and mighty wrestler meets three wise and witty women. What does he learn about them? How are some surprising facts discovered?

A tall tale is a story in which the author uses exaggeration to create humor. As you read, notice which elements the author stretches beyond normal.

Three Strong Women

by Claus Stamm

Long ago, in Japan, there lived a famous wrestler, and he was on his way to the capital city to wrestle before the Emperor.

He strode down the road on legs thick as the trunks of small trees. He had been walking for seven hours and could, and probably would, walk for seven more without getting tired.

The season was autumn, the sky was a cold, watery blue, the air chilly. In the small bright sun, the trees along the roadside glowed red and orange.

The wrestler hummed to himself, "Zun-zun-zun," in time with the long swing of his legs. Wind blew through his thin brown robe, and he wore no sword at his side. He felt proud that he needed no sword, even in the darkest and loneliest places. The icy air on his body only reminded him that few tailors would have been able to make expensive warm clothes for a man so broad and tall. He felt much as a wrestler should —strong, healthy, and rather conceited.

A soft roar of fast-moving water beyond the trees told him that he was passing above a riverbank. He "zun-zunned" louder; he loved the sound of his voice and wanted it to sound clearly above the rushing water.

He thought: They call me Forever-Mountain because I am such a good strong wrestler—big, too. I'm a fine, brave man and far too modest ever to say so. . . .

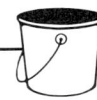

Just then he saw a girl who must have come up from the river, for she steadied a bucket on her head.

Her hands on the bucket were small, and there was a dimple on each thumb, just below the knuckle. She was a round girl with red cheeks and a nose like a friendly button.

Her eyes looked as though she were thinking of ten thousand funny stories at once. She clambered up onto the road and walked ahead of the wrestler, jolly and bounceful.

"If I don't tickle that fat girl, I shall regret it all my life," said the wrestler under his breath. "She's sure to go 'squeak' and I shall laugh and laugh. If she drops her bucket, that will be even funnier—and I can always run and fill it again and even carry it home for her."

He tiptoed up and poked her lightly in the ribs with one huge finger.

"Kochokochokocho!" he said, a ticklish sound in Japanese.

The girl gave a satisfying squeal, giggled, and brought one arm down so that the wrestler's hand was caught between it and her body.

"Ho-ho-ho! You've caught me! I can't move at all!" said the wrestler, laughing.

"I know," said the jolly girl.

He felt that it was very good-tempered of her to take a joke so well, and started to pull his hand free.

Somehow, he could not.

He tried again, using a little more strength.

"Now, now—let me go," he said. "I am a very powerful man. If I pull too hard I might hurt you."

"Pull," said the girl. "I admire powerful men."

She began to walk, and though the wrestler tugged and pulled until his feet dug great furrows in the ground, he had to follow. She couldn't have paid him less attention if he had been a puppy—a small one.

Ten minutes later, still tugging while trudging helplessly after her, he was glad that the road was lonely and no one was there to see.

"Please let me go," he pleaded. "I am the famous wrestler Forever-Mountain. I must go and show my strength before the Emperor"—he burst out weeping from shame and confusion—"and you're hurting my hand!"

The girl steadied the bucket on her head with her free hand and dimpled sympathetically over her shoulder. "You poor, sweet little Forever-Mountain," she said. "Are you tired? Shall I carry you? I can leave the water here and come back for it later."

"I do not want you to carry me. I want you to let me go, and then I want to forget I ever saw you. What do you want with me?" moaned the pitiful wrestler.

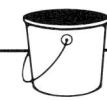

"I only want to help you," said the girl, now pulling him steadily upward on a narrow mountain path. "Oh, I am sure you'll have no more trouble than anyone else when you come up against the other wrestlers. You'll win, or else you'll lose, and you won't be too badly hurt either way. But aren't you afraid you might meet a really strong man someday?"

Forever-Mountain turned pale. He stumbled. He was imagining being laughed at throughout Japan as "Hardly-Ever-Mountain."

She glanced back.

"You see? Tired already," she said. "I'll walk more slowly. Why don't you come along to my mother's house and let us make a strong man of you? The wrestling in the capital isn't due to begin for three months. I know, because Grandmother thought she'd go. You'd be spending all that time in bad company and wasting what little power you have."

"All right. Three months. I'll come along," said the wrestler, feeling that he had nothing more to lose. Also, he feared that the girl might become angry if he refused, and place him in the top of a tree until he changed his mind.

"Fine," she said happily. "We are almost there."

She freed his hand, which had become red and a little swollen. "But if you break your promise and run off, I shall have to chase you and carry you back."

Soon they arrived in a small valley in the middle of which stood a simple farmhouse with a thatched roof.

"Grandmother is at home, but she is an old lady and she's probably sleeping." The girl shaded her eyes with one hand. "But Mother should be bringing our cow back from the field —oh, there's Mother now!"

She waved. The woman coming around the corner of the house put down the cow she was carrying and waved back.

She smiled and came across the grass, walking with a lively bounce like her daughter's. Well, maybe her bounce was a little more solid, thought the wrestler.

"Excuse me," she said, brushing some cow hair from her dress and dimpling, also like her daughter. "These mountain paths are full of stones. They hurt the cow's feet. And who is the nice young man you've brought, Maru-me?"

The girl explained. "And we have only three months!" she finished anxiously.

"Well, it's not long enough to do much, but it's not so short a time we can't do something," said her mother, looking thoughtful. "But he does look terribly feeble. He'll need a lot of good things to eat. Maybe when he gets stronger he can help Grandmother with some of the easy work about the house."

"That will be fine!" said the girl, and she called her grandmother—loudly, for the old lady was a little deaf.

"I'm coming!" came a creaky voice from inside the house, and a little old woman leaning on a stick and looking very sleepy tottered out of the door. As she came toward them she stumbled over the roots of a great oak tree.

"Heh! My eyes aren't what they used to be. That's the fourth time this month I've stumbled over that tree," she complained and, wrapping her skinny arms about its trunk, pulled it out of the ground.

"Oh, Grandmother! You should have let me pull it up for you," said Maru-me.

"Hm. I hope I didn't hurt my poor back," muttered the old lady. She called out, "Daughter! Throw that tree away like a good girl, so no one will fall over it. But make sure it doesn't hit anybody."

"You can help Mother with the tree," Maru-me said to Forever-Mountain. "On second thought, you'd better not help. Just watch."

Her mother went to the tree, picked it up in her two hands, and threw it. Up went the tree, sailing end over end, growing smaller and smaller as it flew. It landed with a faint crash far up the mountainside.

"Ah, how clumsy," she said. "I meant to throw it over the mountain. It's probably blocking the path now, and I'll have to get up early tomorrow to move it."

The wrestler was not listening. He had very quietly fainted.

"Oh! We must put him to bed," said Maru-me.

"Poor, feeble young man," said her mother.

"I hope we can do something for him. Here, let me carry him, he's light," said the grandmother. She slung him over her shoulder and carried him into the house, creaking along with her cane.

The next day they began the work of making Forever-Mountain over into what they thought a strong man should be. They gave him the simplest food to eat, and the toughest. Day by day they prepared his rice with less and less water, until no ordinary man could have chewed or digested it.

Every day he was made to do the work of five men, and every evening he wrestled with Grandmother. Maru-me and her mother agreed that Grandmother, being old and feeble, was the least likely to injure him accidentally. They hoped the exercise might be good for the old lady's rheumatism.

He grew stronger and stronger but was hardly aware of it. Grandmother could still throw him easily into the air — and catch him again — without ever changing her sweet old smile.

He quite forgot that outside this valley he was one of the greatest wrestlers in Japan and was called Forever-Mountain. His legs had been like logs; now they were like pillars. His big hands were hard as stones, and when he cracked his knuckles the sound was like trees splitting on a cold night.

Sometimes he did an exercise that wrestlers do in Japan — raising one foot high above the ground and bringing it down with a crash. Then people in nearby villages looked up at the winter sky and told one another that it was very late in the year for thunder.

Soon he could pull up a tree as well as the grandmother. He could even throw one — but only a small distance. One evening, near the end of his third month, he wrestled with Grandmother and held her down for half a minute.

"Heh-heh!" She chortled and got up, smiling with every wrinkle. "I would never have believed it!"

Maru-me squealed with joy and threw her arms around him — gently, for she was afraid of cracking his ribs.

"Very good, very good! What a strong man," said her mother, who had just come home from the fields, carrying, as usual, the cow. She put the cow down and patted the wrestler on the back.

They agreed that he was now ready to show some *real* strength before the Emperor.

"Take the cow along with you tomorrow when you go," said the mother. "Sell her and buy yourself a belt—a silken belt. Buy the fattest and heaviest one you can find and wear it when you appear before the Emperor, as a souvenir from us."

"I wouldn't think of taking your only cow. You've already done too much for me. And you'll need her to plow the fields, won't you?"

They burst out laughing. Maru-me squealed, her mother roared. The grandmother cackled so hard and long that she choked and had to be pounded on the back.

"Oh, dear," said the mother, still laughing. "You didn't think we used our cow for anything like *work*! Why, Grandmother here is stronger than five cows!"

"The cow is our pet." Maru-me giggled. "She has lovely brown eyes."

"But it gets tiresome having to carry her back and forth each day so that she has enough grass to eat," said her mother.

"Then you must let me give you all the prize money that I win," said Forever-Mountain.

"Oh, no! We wouldn't think of it!" said Maru-me. "Because we all like you too much to sell you anything. And it is not proper to accept gifts of money from strangers."

"True," said Forever-Mountain. "I will now ask your mother's and grandmother's permission to marry you. I want to be one of the family."

"Oh! I'll get a wedding dress ready!" said Maru-me.

The mother and grandmother pretended to consider very seriously, but they quickly agreed.

Next morning Forever-Mountain tied his hair up in the topknot that all Japanese wrestlers wear, and got ready to leave. He thanked Maru-me and her mother and bowed very low to the grandmother, since she was the oldest and had been a fine wrestling partner.

Then he picked up the cow in his arms and trudged up the mountain. When he reached the top, he slung the cow over one shoulder and waved good-by to Maru-me.

At the first town he came to, Forever-Mountain sold the cow. She brought a good price because she was unusually fat from never having worked in her life. With the money, he bought the heaviest silken belt he could find.

When he reached the palace grounds, many of the other wrestlers were already there, sitting about, eating enormous bowls of rice, comparing one another's weight and telling stories. They paid little attention to Forever-Mountain except to wonder why he had arrived so late this year. Some of them noticed that he had grown very quiet and took no part at all in their boasting.

All the ladies and gentlemen of the court were waiting in a special courtyard for the wrestling to begin. They wore many robes, one on top of another, heavy with embroidery and gold cloth, and sweat ran down their faces and froze in the winter afternoon. The gentlemen had long swords so weighted with gold and precious stones that they could never have used them, even if they had known how. The court ladies, with their long black hair hanging down behind, had their faces painted dead white, which made them look frightened. They had pulled out their real eyebrows and painted new ones high above the place where eyebrows are supposed to be, and this made them all look as though they were very surprised at something.

Behind a screen sat the Emperor — by himself, because he was too noble for ordinary people to look at. He was a lonely old man with a kind, tired face. He hoped the wrestling would end quickly so that he could go to his room and write poems.

The first two wrestlers chosen to fight were Forever-Mountain and a wrestler who was said to have the biggest stomach in the country. He and Forever-Mountain both threw some salt into the ring. It was understood that this drove away evil spirits.

Then the other wrestler, moving his stomach somewhat out of the way, raised his foot and brought it down with a fearful stamp. He glared fiercely at Forever-Mountain as if to say, "Now you stamp, you poor frightened man!"

Forever-Mountain raised his foot. He brought it down. There was a sound like thunder, the earth shook, and the other wrestler bounced into the air and out of the ring, as gracefully as any soap bubble.

He picked himself up and bowed to the Emperor's screen.

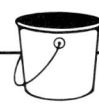

"The earth god is angry. Possibly there is something the matter with the salt," he said. "I do not think I shall wrestle this season." And he walked out, looking very suspiciously over one shoulder at Forever-Mountain.

Five other wrestlers then and there decided that they were not wrestling this season, either. They all looked annoyed with Forever-Mountain.

From then on, Forever-Mountain brought his foot down lightly. As each wrestler came into the ring, he picked up his opponent very gently, carried him out, and placed him before the Emperor's screen, bowing most courteously every time.

The court ladies' eyebrows went up even higher. The gentlemen looked disturbed and a little afraid. They loved to see fierce, strong men tugging and grunting at each other, but Forever-Mountain was a little too much for them. Only the Emperor was happy behind his screen, for now, with the wrestling over so quickly, he would have that much more time to write his poems. He ordered all the prize money handed over to Forever-Mountain.

"But," he said, "you had better not wrestle anymore." He stuck a finger through the screen and waggled it at the other wrestlers, who were sitting on the ground weeping with disappointment like great fat babies.

When Forever-Mountain promised not to wrestle anymore, everybody looked relieved. The wrestlers almost smiled.

"I think I shall become a farmer," Forever-Mountain said, and left at once to go back to Maru-me.

Maru-me was waiting for him. When she saw him coming, she ran down the mountain, picked him up, together with the heavy bags of prize money, and carried him halfway up the mountainside. Then she giggled and put him down. The rest of the way she let him carry her.

Forever-Mountain kept his promise to the Emperor and never fought in public again. His name was forgotten in the capital. But up in the mountains, sometimes, the earth shakes and rumbles, and they say that it is Forever-Mountain and Maru-me's grandmother practicing in the hidden valley.

Discuss the Selection

1. What surprising fact did Forever-Mountain learn about Maru-me, her mother, and her grandmother?
2. How did Forever-Mountain end up spending three months at Maru-me's home?
3. Why do you think Forever-Mountain asked Maru-me to marry him?
4. Why wasn't Forever-Mountain upset when the Emperor commanded him to give up wrestling?
5. At first, Forever-Mountain was conceited about his strength. When did you notice that he was becoming less conceited?

Apply the Skills

Tall tales combine realism with exaggeration to produce a comic effect. This combination allows the author to surprise and amuse the reader.

In "Three Strong Women," realistic characters are given superhuman traits and placed in absurd situations. As the story proceeds, it becomes more comical and extreme while maintaining an element of reality.

1. Give an example of a realistic description in the story.
2. Give an example of exaggeration in the story.

Think and Write

Prewrite

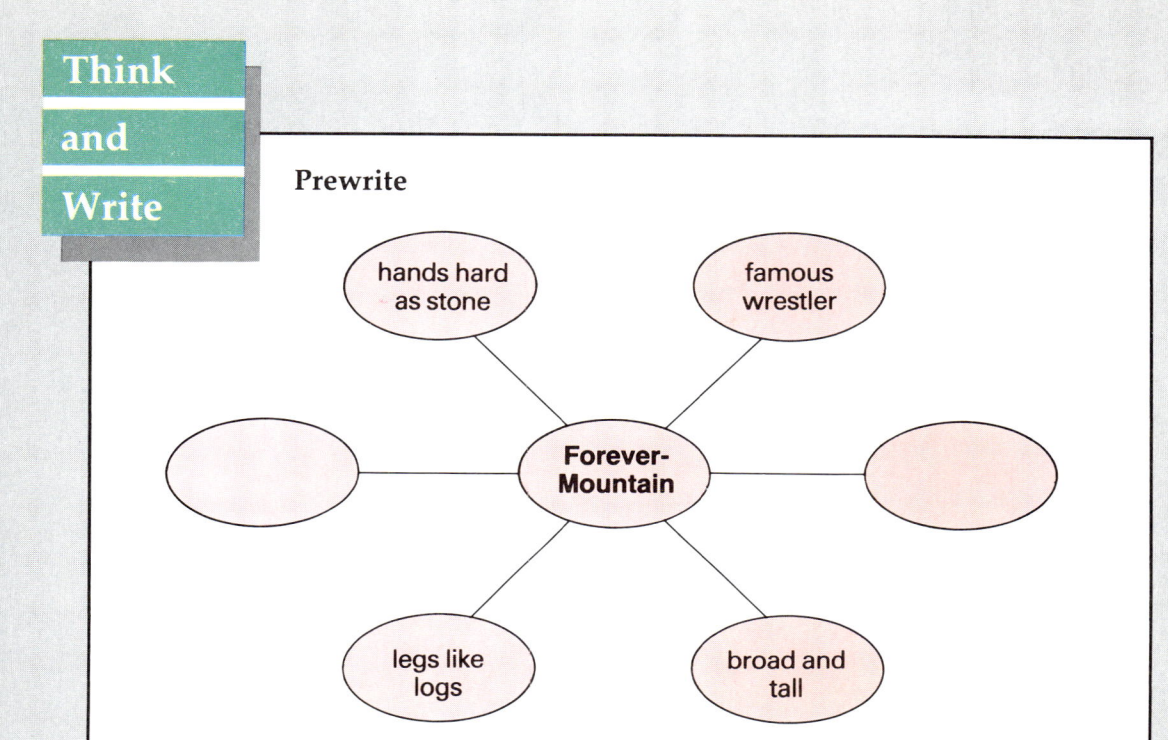

```
        hands hard          famous
         as stone           wrestler
              \              /
               \            /
                Forever-
    ( )────────Mountain────────( )
               /            \
              /              \
         legs like         broad and
           logs              tall
```

A descriptive paragraph is used to create a vivid image of a person, place, or thing. A well-written descriptive paragraph can be like a sharp photograph, only better. Copy the diagram shown above and add other words or phrases from the story that tell something about Forever-Mountain.

Compose

Using the information in the diagram and from the story, write a paragraph describing Forever-Mountain. You might start with this topic sentence: *Forever-Mountain, a famous Japanese wrestler, boasted of his incredible strength.*

Revise

Check to see if your paragraph stays on the topic—Forever-Mountain. It should include all the parts in the diagram. Then critically examine your writing for awkward sentences, inexact language, and other errors. Revise any words, phrases, or whole sentences that are unclear.

Comprehension Study

Predict Outcomes

When you give an opinion about what you think will happen, you are **predicting an outcome**. Predicting outcomes is a skill used both in reading and in everyday life. When you read a good story, you probably try to figure out what will happen next by thinking about what has already happened. Before a big sports event, you probably have an opinion about which team will win. Your opinion is probably based on both teams' scores in past games. Those scores are details of events that have already occurred.

When you predict outcomes in reading or in everyday life, try not to make wild guesses. It is better to base your predictions on the *details of the situation*. Also, consider *what you know from your own experience*.

A predicted outcome that is based on details of events that have already occurred and on your own experience is said to be **probable**. This means that it is *likely* that your prediction will come true, although it is *not certain*.

As you read the following paragraph, try to predict probable outcomes of the situation described. As you make your predictions, pay special attention to the details. Also, consider anything that you know from your own experience that might be similar to the situation in the paragraph.

> At the meeting of the city council, the subject of "No Parking" signs on streets leading to the beach was discussed. Some city residents said that the many "No Parking" signs made it difficult for them to use the beach because they had no place to park their cars. Residents who lived within walking distance of the beach said that the signs were meant only to discourage traffic, not to keep people from the city away. The city council president disagreed, insisting that something must be done. She pointed out that both city and beach-area

residents paid taxes for upkeep of the beaches. If people living in the city were excluded, she suggested, perhaps only beach-area residents should pay for upkeep of the beach. Both sides agreed to study the question and meet again next week.

Which of the following do you think are probable outcomes of the city council meeting?

A. Beach-area residents will agree to remove some "No Parking" signs.
B. The city council president will oppose further discussion of the problem.
C. The city council will vote to raise funds for a parking lot near the beach.
D. The city council will vote to close the beach.

Two of the choices listed are probable outcomes of the meeting. You can eliminate choice B because the paragraph states that the city council president is insisting that something be done to resolve the problem. You also can eliminate choice D because it is unlikely that the board will vote to close the beach.

Choice A is a probable outcome. In conflicts between people, partial solutions that don't cost much money often will be tried first. Choice C is also a probable outcome. If funding can be found, the new parking lot will solve the objections of drivers from the city without causing problems for beach-area residents.

Remember, the *probable* outcomes of the next meeting may not be the *actual* outcomes. When you predict an outcome, you are not stating what *will* happen. You are only stating what *could* happen, based on the facts and on what you know.

Speculation

Although predicting outcomes is not wild guessing, it might be described as educated guessing. Such educated guesswork is called **speculation**. Speculating is different from predicting because speculation doesn't depend entirely on details of events that have already occurred. Another difference is that when you predict an outcome, you are making a statement about what you think will happen at some point in the near or distant future. When you speculate, however, you might make a statement about the following:

- the past (for example, how the alphabet first came into use)
- the existence of something (for example, planets in other solar systems)
- the behavior or appearance of something (for example, how people made the first cave paintings)

Study these two sentences:

1. If Susan practices a lot, she might become a champion tennis player.
2. Susan will probably win the tennis tournament because she has won over half the matches, and she practices every day.

The first sentence is an example of speculation. It doesn't depend on any event that has already occurred. The second sentence is an example of a prediction. It relies on fact and personal knowledge. The fact is that Susan has won over half the games. The personal knowledge, or experience, relied on is that daily practicing can improve your game.

In the following paragraphs, the author is speculating about the spread of African honeybees in the United States.

A honeybee from Africa was accidentally released a few years ago in Brazil. This African honeybee has been spreading north through Latin America. African bees are more aggressive than ordinary honeybees. They become quickly disturbed and attack intruders.

There are several possibilities concerning the spread of the African bee. American bee handlers may be able to isolate the new strain of bee and destroy it before it becomes widespread in the United States. Or, the bee may find the cooler climate of North America uncomfortable. It is even possible that American bees will interbreed with African bees and become very fierce.

The author is making educated guesses about what will happen to the African bee in the United States. In other words, the author is making the following speculations:
- The African bee may spread rapidly through North America.
- Bee handlers may be able to isolate the new strain of bee.
- The cooler climate may stop the spread of this bee.
- The American bee may become fierce as it interbreeds with African bees.

Notice that the speculations are based on details from the paragraphs on African bees. Depending on conditions that may or may not exist, the author tells you what *might* occur.

Textbook Application: Predict Outcomes in Mathematics

Being able to predict outcomes is an important reading skill. Study the following mathematics-textbook excerpt. The sidenotes will help you solve the problems.

> How many red marbles are there?

> What are the chances of picking a green marble instead of a red one?

There are six marbles in a bag. Each is a different color. Lisa will pick one without looking. What is the chance that she will pick a red marble?

There are six marbles, and so there are six possible outcomes. All of the outcomes are equally likely. In other words, the chances of picking a red marble are 1 out of 6. The probability of picking a red marble is 1/6. If Lisa picks a red marble, you might say that this is a **favorable outcome**.

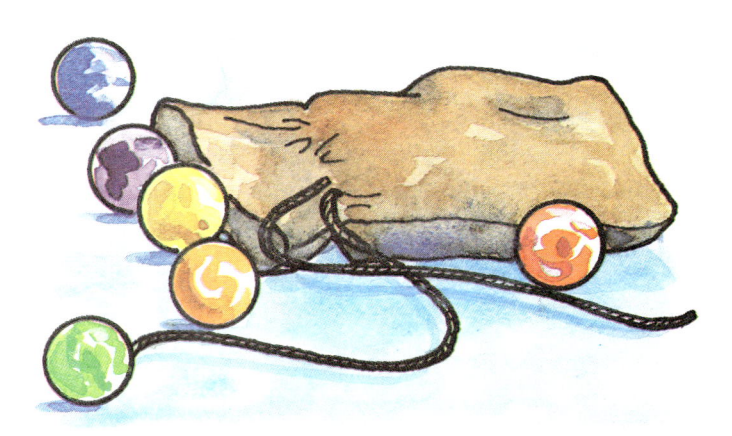

> How many total parts does the spinner contain?

Look at the spinner in the illustration that follows.
How many times would you expect the spinner to point to green if you spin 8 times? Since the probability that the pointer will point to green is 1/8, the expected outcome is 1/8 × 8, or 1 time.

Remember, if you know the probability that an event will occur, you can make a prediction about the **expected outcome** of many trials.

> How many green parts are there?

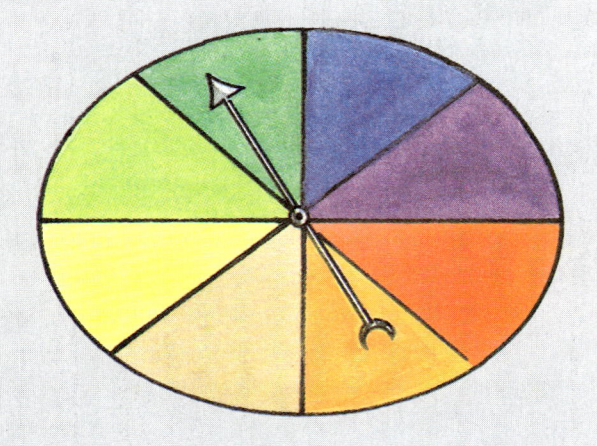

Sometimes you do not know the probability of an event, however. In such cases, you have to base your prediction on information that you already know. Look at the following example.

Lisa got 20 hits out of the last 25 times that she was at bat. The probability that she will get a hit on her next turn at bat is 80% because $^{20}/_{25} = 0.80 = 80\%$.

> What information do you know about Lisa's batting record?

— *Mathematics Today,*
Harcourt Brace Jovanovich

Pay special attention to the information provided. This information will form the basis for your predictions.

Basing your predictions on the information that is known, try to answer the following probability questions.

1. Cheryl received an A on 4 out of 8 math tests. What is the probability that she will get an A on her next test?
2. According to weather bureau records, it snowed 25 times on February 3 during the last 100 years. What is the probability of snow for next February 3?

Predicting outcomes is an important reading skill. Trying to figure what will come next in a story will add to your enjoyment and understanding.

373

Annie John is anxious about her first day at a new school. How does Annie use her wits to adjust to the new situation?

Annie copes with problems by recalling other difficult situations when things turned out fine. As you read, notice Annie's problems and see if you can predict the outcome of her concerns.

Annie John
by Jamaica Kincaid

Jamaica Kincaid is a young writer from the beautiful tropical island of Antigua in the Caribbean. In her novel *Annie John* she tells the story of a girl's experiences from the age of ten to seventeen.

In poetic language and through many anecdotes, both humorous and sad, the author explores the inner feelings of a girl as she moves from childhood to adulthood. The writer draws upon her own experiences growing up in the West Indies. Colorful details make the incidents vivid to the reader.

In this excerpt, Annie John is twelve and entering a new school. At her old school, Annie was an exceptionally bright pupil. Her ability at games and her mischievous personality won her many friends. But this is a new school and no one knows her. Her problem is the universal one of all newcomers—"How do I get accepted?"

On opening day, I walked to my new school alone. It was the first and last time that such a thing would happen. All around me were other people my age — twelve years — girls and boys, dressed in their school uniforms, marching off to school. They all seemed to know each other, and as they met they would burst into laughter, slapping each other on the shoulder and back, telling each other things that must have made for much happiness. I saw some girls wearing the same uniform as my own, and my heart just longed for them to say something to me, but the most they could do to include me was to smile and nod in my direction as they walked on arm in arm. I could hardly blame them for not paying more attention to me. Everything about me was so new: My uniform was new, my shoes were new, my hat was new, my shoulder ached from the weight of my new books in my new bag; even the road I walked on was new, and I must have put my feet down as if I weren't sure the ground was solid. At school, the yard was filled with more of these girls and their most sure-of-themselves gaits. When I looked at them, they made up a sea. They were walking in and out among the beds of flowers, all across the fields, all across the courtyard, in and out of the classrooms. Except for me, no one seemed a stranger to anything or anyone. Hearing the way they greeted each other, I couldn't be sure that they hadn't all come out of the same woman's belly, and at the same time, too. Looking at them, I was suddenly glad that because I had wanted to avoid an argument with my mother, I had eaten all my breakfast, for now I surely would have fainted if I had been in any more weakened a condition.

I knew where my classroom was, because my mother and I had kept an appointment at the school a week before. There I met some of my teachers and was shown the ins and outs of everything. When I saw the school then, it was nice and orderly and empty and smelled just scrubbed. Now it smelled of girls milling around, fresh ink in inkwells, new books, chalk and erasers. The girls in my classroom acted even more familiar with each other. I was sure I would never be able to tell them apart just from looking at them, and I was sure that I would never be able to tell them apart from the sound of their voices.

When the school bell rang at half past eight, we formed ourselves into the required pairs and filed into the auditorium. Our headmistress gave us a little talk, welcoming the new students and welcoming back the old students, saying that she hoped we had all left our bad ways behind us, that we would be good examples for each other and bring greater credit to our school than any of the other groups of girls who had been there before us. My palms were wet, and quite a few times the ground felt as if it were seesawing under my feet, but that didn't stop me from taking in a few things. For instance, the headmistress, Miss Moore. I knew right away that she had come to Antigua from England, for she looked like a prune left out of its jar a long time and she sounded as if she had borrowed her voice from an owl. The way she said, "Now, girls . . ." When she was just standing still there, listening to some of the other activities, her gray eyes going all around the room hoping to see something wrong, her throat would beat up and down as if a fish fresh out of water were caught inside. I wondered if she even smelled like a fish. Once when I didn't wash, my mother had given me a long scolding about it, and she ended by saying that it was the only thing she didn't like about English people: they didn't wash often enough, or wash properly when they finally did. My mother had said, "Have you noticed how they smell as if they had been bottled up in a fish?" On either side of Miss Moore stood our other teachers, women and men — mostly women. I recognized Miss George, our music teacher; Miss Nelson, our homeroom teacher; Miss Edward, our history and geography teacher; and Miss Newgate, our algebra and geometry teacher. I had met them the day my mother and I were at school. I did not know who the others were, and I did not worry about it. Since they were teachers, I was sure it wouldn't be long before, because of some misunderstanding, they would be thorns in my side.

We walked back to our classroom the same way we had come, quite orderly and, except for a few whispered exchanges,

quite silent. But no sooner were we back in our classroom than the girls were in each other's laps, arms wrapped around necks. After peeping over my shoulder left and right, I sat down in my seat and wondered what would become of me. There were twenty of us in my class, and we were seated at desks arranged five in a row, four rows deep. I was at a desk in the third row, and this made me even more miserable. I hated to be seated so far away from the teacher, because I was sure I would miss something she said. But, even worse, if I was out of my teacher's sight all the time, how could she see my industriousness and quickness at learning things? And, besides, only dunces were seated so far to the rear, and I could not bear to be thought a dunce. I was now staring at the back of a shrubby-haired girl seated in the front row — the seat I most coveted, since it was directly in front of the teacher's desk. At that moment, the girl twisted herself around, stared at me, and said, "You are Annie John? We hear you are very bright." It was a good thing Miss Nelson walked in right then, for how would it have appeared if I had replied, "Yes, that is completely true" — the very thing that was on the tip of my tongue.

As soon as Miss Nelson walked in, we came to order and stood up stiffly at our desks. She said to us, "Good morning, class," half in a way that someone must have told her was the proper way to speak to us and half in a jocular way, as if we secretly amused her. We replied, "Good morning, Miss," in unison and in a respectful way, at the same time making a barely visible curtsy, also in unison. When she had seated herself at her desk, she said to us, "You may sit now," and we did. She opened the roll book, and as she called out our names each of us answered, "Present, Miss." As she called out our names, she kept her head bent over the book, but when she called out my name and I answered with the customary response she looked up and smiled at me and said, "Welcome, Annie." Everyone, of course, then turned and looked at me. I was sure it was because they could hear the loud racket my heart was making in my chest.

It was the first day of a new term, Miss Nelson said, so we would not be attending to any of our usual subjects; instead, we were to spend the morning in contemplation and reflection and writing something she described as an "autobiographical essay." In the afternoon, we would read aloud to each other our autobiographical essays. (I knew quite well about "autobiography" and "essay," but reflection and contemplation! A day at school spent in such a way! Of course, in most books all the good people were always contemplating and reflecting before they did anything. Perhaps in her mind's eye she could see our futures and, against all prediction, we turned out to be good people.) On hearing this, a huge sigh went up from the girls. Half the sighs were in happiness at the thought of sitting and gazing off into clear space, the other half in unhappiness at the misdeeds that would have to go unaccomplished. I joined the happy half, because I knew it would please Miss Nelson, and, my own selfish interest aside, I liked so much the way she wore her ironed hair and her long-sleeved blouse and box-pleated skirt that I wanted to please her.

The morning was uneventful enough: A girl spilled ink from her inkwell all over her uniform; a girl broke her pen nib and then made a big to-do about replacing it; girls twisted and turned in their seats and pinched each other's bottoms; girls passed notes to each other. All this Miss Nelson must have seen and heard, but she didn't say anything — only kept reading her book: an elaborately illustrated edition of *The Tempest* that later, passing by her desk, I saw. Midway in the morning, we were told to go out and stretch our legs and breathe some fresh air for a few minutes; when we returned, we were given glasses of cold lemonade and a slice of bun to refresh us.

As soon as the sun stood in the middle of the sky, we were sent home for lunch. The earth may have grown an inch or two larger between the time I had walked to school that morning and the time I went home to lunch, for some girls made a small space for me in their little band. But I couldn't pay much attention to them; my mind was on my new surroundings, my new teacher, what I had written in my nice new notebook with its black-all-mixed-up-with-white cover and smooth lined pages (so glad was I to get rid of my old notebooks, which had on their covers a picture of a wrinkled-up woman wearing a crown on her head and a neckful and armfuls of diamonds and pearls — their pages so coarse, as if they were made of cornmeal). I flew home. I must have eaten my food. I flew back to school. By half past one, we were sitting under a flamboyant tree in a secluded part of our schoolyard, our autobiographical essays in hand. We were about to read aloud what we had written during our morning of contemplation and reflection.

In response to Miss Nelson, each girl stood up and read her composition. One girl told of a much revered and loved aunt who now lived in England and of how much she looked

forward to one day moving to England to live with her aunt; one girl told of her brother studying medicine in Canada and the life she imagined he lived there (it seemed quite odd to me); one girl told of the fright she had when she dreamed she was dead, and of the matching fright she had when she woke and found that she wasn't (everyone laughed at this, and Miss Nelson had to call us to order over and over); one girl told of how her oldest sister's best friend's cousin's best friend (it was a real rigmarole) had gone on a Girl Guide jamboree held in Trinidad and met someone who millions of years ago had taken tea with Lady Baden-Powell; one girl told of an excursion she and her father had made to Redonda, and how they had seen some booby birds tending their chicks. Things went on in that way, all so playful, all so imaginative. I began to wonder about what I had written, for it was the opposite of playful and it was the opposite of imaginative. What I had written was heartfelt, and, except for the very end, it was all too true. The afternoon was wearing itself thin. Would my turn ever come? What should I do, finding myself in a world of new girls, a world in which I was not even near the center?

It was a while before I realized that Miss Nelson was calling on me. My turn at last to read what I had written. I got up and started to read, my voice shaky at first, but since the sound of my own voice had always been a calming potion to me, it wasn't long before I was reading in such a way that except for the chirp of some birds, the hum of bees looking for flowers, the silvery rush-rush of the wind in the trees, the only sound to be heard was my voice as it rose and fell in sentence after sentence. At the end of my reading, I thought I was imagining the upturned faces on which were looks of adoration, but I was not; I thought I was imagining, too, some eyes brimming over with tears, but again I was not. Miss Nelson said that she would like to borrow what I had written to read for herself, and that it would be placed on the shelf with the books that made up our own class library, so that it would be available to any girl who wanted to read it. This is what I had written:

"When I was a small child, my mother and I used to go down to Rat Island on Sundays right after church, so that I could bathe in the sea. It was at a time when I was thought to have weak kidneys and a bath in the sea had been recommended as a strengthening remedy. Rat Island wasn't a place many people went to anyway, but by climbing down some rocks my mother had found a place that nobody seemed to have ever seen. Since this bathing in the sea was a medicine and not a picnic, we had to bathe without wearing swimming costumes. My mother was a superior swimmer. When she plunged into the seawater, it was as if she had always lived there. She would go far out if it was safe to do so, and she could tell just by looking at the way the waves beat if it was safe to do so. She could tell if a shark was nearby, and she had never been stung by a jellyfish. I, on the other hand, could not swim at all. In fact, if I was in water up to my knees I was sure that I was drowning. My mother had tried everything to get me swimming, from using a coaxing method to just throwing me without a word into the water. Nothing worked. The only

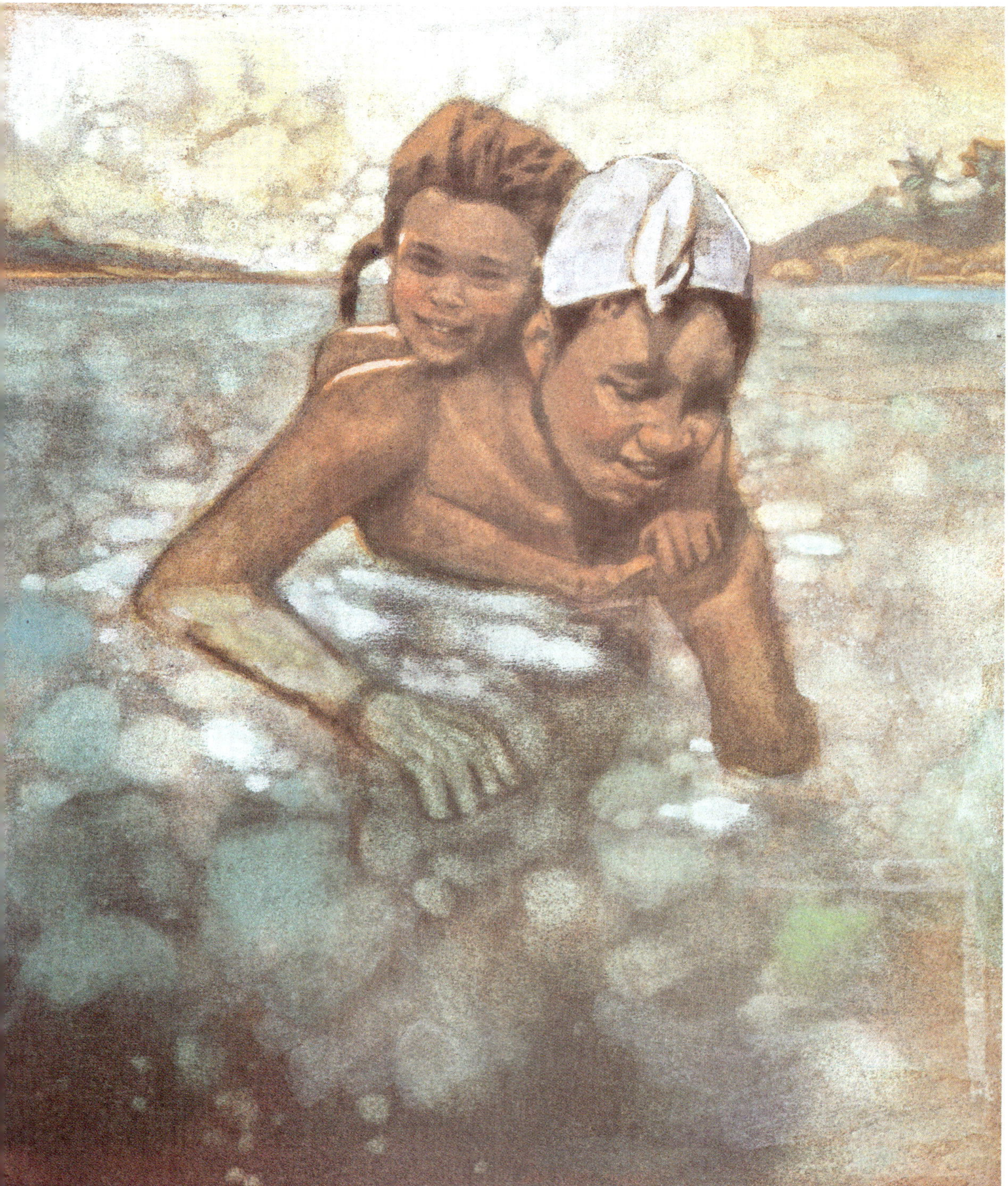

way I could go into the water was if I was on my mother's back, my arms clasped tight around her neck, and she would then swim around not too far from the shore. It was only then that I could forget how big the sea was, how far down the bottom could be, and how filled up it was with things that couldn't understand a nice hallo. When we swam around in this way, I would think how much we were like the pictures of sea mammals I had seen, my mother and I, naked in the water, my mother sometimes singing to me a song in a French patois I did not yet understand, or sometimes not saying anything at all. I would place my ear against her neck, and it was as if I were listening to a giant shell, for all the sounds around me — the sea, the wind, the birds screeching — would seem as if they came from inside her, the way the sounds of the sea are in a seashell. Afterward, my mother would take me back to the shore, and I would lie there just beyond the farthest reach of a big wave and watch my mother as she swam and dove.

"One day, in the midst of watching my mother swim and dive, I heard a commotion far out at sea. It was three ships going by, and they were filled with people. They must have been celebrating something, for the ships would blow their horns and the people would cheer in response. After they passed out of view, I turned back to look at my mother, but I could not see her. My eyes searched the small area of water where she should have been, but I couldn't find her. I stood up and started to call out her name, but no sound would come out of my throat. A huge black space then opened up in front of me and I fell inside it. I couldn't see what was in front of me and I couldn't hear anything around me. I couldn't think of anything except that my mother was no longer near me. Things went on in this way for I don't know how long. I don't know what, but something drew my eye in one direction. A little bit out of the area in which she usually swam was my mother, just sitting and tracing patterns on a large rock. She wasn't paying any attention to me, for she didn't know that I had missed her. I was glad to see her and started jumping up and down and waving to her. Still she didn't see me, and then I started to cry,

for it dawned on me that, with all that water between us and I being unable to swim, my mother could stay there forever and the only way I would be able to wrap my arms around her again was if it pleased her or if I took a boat. I cried until I wore myself out. My tears ran down into my mouth, and it was the first time that I realized tears had a bitter and salty taste. Finally, my mother came ashore. She was, of course, alarmed when she saw my face, for I had let the tears just dry there and they left a stain. When I told her what had happened, she hugged me so close that it was hard to breathe, and she told me that nothing could be farther from the truth — that she would never ever leave me. And though she said it over and over again, and though I felt better, I could not wipe out of my mind the feeling I had had when I couldn't find her.

"The summer just past, I kept having a dream about my mother sitting on the rock. Over and over I would have the dream—only in it my mother never came back, and sometimes my father would join her. When he joined her, they would both sit tracing patterns on the rock, and it must have been amusing, for they would always make each other laugh. At first, I didn't say anything, but when I began to have the dream again and again, I finally told my mother. My mother became instantly distressed; tears came to her eyes, and, taking me in her arms, she told me all the same things she had told me on the day at the sea, and this time the memory of the dark time when I felt I would never see her again did not come back to haunt me."

I didn't exactly tell a lie about the last part. That is just what would have happened in the old days. But actually the past year saw me launched into young-ladyness, and when I told my mother of my dream — my nightmare, really — I was greeted with a turned back and a warning against eating certain kinds of fruit in an unripe state just before going to bed. I placed the old days' version before my classmates because, I thought, I couldn't bear to show my mother in a bad light before people who hardly knew her. But the real truth was that I couldn't bear to have anyone see how deep in disfavor I was with my mother.

As we walked back to the classroom, I in the air, my classmates on the ground, jostling each other to say some words of appreciation and congratulation to me, my head felt funny, as if it had swelled up to the size of, and weighed no more than, a blown-up balloon. Often I had been told by my mother not to feel proud of anything I had done and in the next breath that I couldn't feel enough pride about something I had done. Now I tossed from one to the other; my head bowed down to the ground, my head held high up in the air. I looked at these girls surrounding me, my heart filled with just-sprung-up love, and I wished then and there to spend the rest of my life only with them.

Discuss the Selection

1. Annie was anxious about her new school and was afraid that no one would like her. How did she win over her new classmates?
2. How did Annie resolve her problem of feeling anxious in a new situation?
3. Why do you think Annie chose to write about going swimming with her mother?
4. What did you like best about Annie? Cite examples from the story.
5. At what point in the story did Annie finally feel accepted by her classmates? Find that part of the story.

Apply the Skills

An important reading skill is the ability to predict probable outcomes from a given set of events. This helps you to think critically about what you read.

As you were reading "Annie John," how did you predict Annie's situation would turn out?

Think and Write

Prewrite

Introduction	Body	Conclusion
On the first day of school, I felt terrible	Each girl stood up to read her composition	I couldn't believe the reaction to my composition
1. faced sea of strangers	1. about an aunt in England	1. adoring looks
2. longed to talk to someone	2. about brother studying medicine in Canada	2. upturned faces

A paragraph that tells a story is a **narrative paragraph**. A short narrative paragraph drawn from a personal experience is called a **personal anecdote**. Like most other kinds of paragraphs, a personal anecdote has a definite plan of organization. This plan includes a beginning, a body, and an end.

Copy the chart shown above and add two details that support each part—the introduction, the body, and the conclusion.

Compose

Using the information on the chart and details from the story, write an anecdote describing Annie John's first day at school. In the introduction, provide necessary background information and try to arouse the reader's interest. Make sure that your anecdote also includes a body and a conclusion. Remember, in a good paragraph, one action leads to another in a way that seems right and natural.

Revise

Carefully read the anecdote that you wrote. Does it contain an introduction, a body, and a conclusion? If not, revise your first draft until each part flows smoothly into the other.

This well-known author has learned much from the wisdom and way of life of the Eskimos and northern Canadian Indians. Read to find out how he uses this knowledge in his writing.

As you read, notice the sequence of events in James Houston's early life that helped to develop his interest in northern Canadian Indians and Eskimos.

James Houston: Tales of the Far North
by Bernice E. Cullinan

Storytelling is an ancient art that all peoples have used to pass on information and to keep the traditions of their society alive. Canadian-born James Houston is a modern-day master storyteller. He skillfully combines his own fascinating stories of adventure with tales of the northern Canadian Indians and Eskimos. These tales have never before been written down.

When James Houston was very young, his father visited the American Indians of the prairies and the Far West almost every year and brought back gifts of beaded moosehide moccasins. Both Houston and his sister watched and listened as their father drew pictures and told them of the wonderful things he had seen.

The family spent many summers on Lake Simcoe in Ontario. There Houston met an old man who introduced the boy to his Ojibwa people. Sometimes the Ojibwa Indians would invite James to fish with them or to gather wild rice in their canoes. They lived in complete harmony with nature. The Ojibwa were not only a strong link with the past but also a strong influence on Houston's future.

Houston remembers an incident from when he was twelve that shaped his future. He took art classes at the Toronto Art Gallery. There, he and his friends laughed and painted and happily hit each other over the head with rulers. One morning, Dr. Arthur Lismer, a great Canadian art teacher who had just returned from a trip to Africa, played African music and danced through the galleries, his face covered with a huge carved mask. The vision of that mask impressed young Houston deeply and hooked him forever on the art and lives of primitive people. From that time onward, he wanted to travel to the farthest corners of the earth.

After studying at the Ontario College of Art, he served with the Toronto Scottish Regiment during World War II. He traveled to the North Atlantic and the Pacific with that Canadian regiment. When World War II was over, Houston went to Paris to finish his training as a professional artist. Later, he returned to Canada, traveling slowly through Cree, Nascopi, and Chippewa Indian country, sketching what he saw. In Canada's Far North, he lived with the Inuit (Eskimo) people for

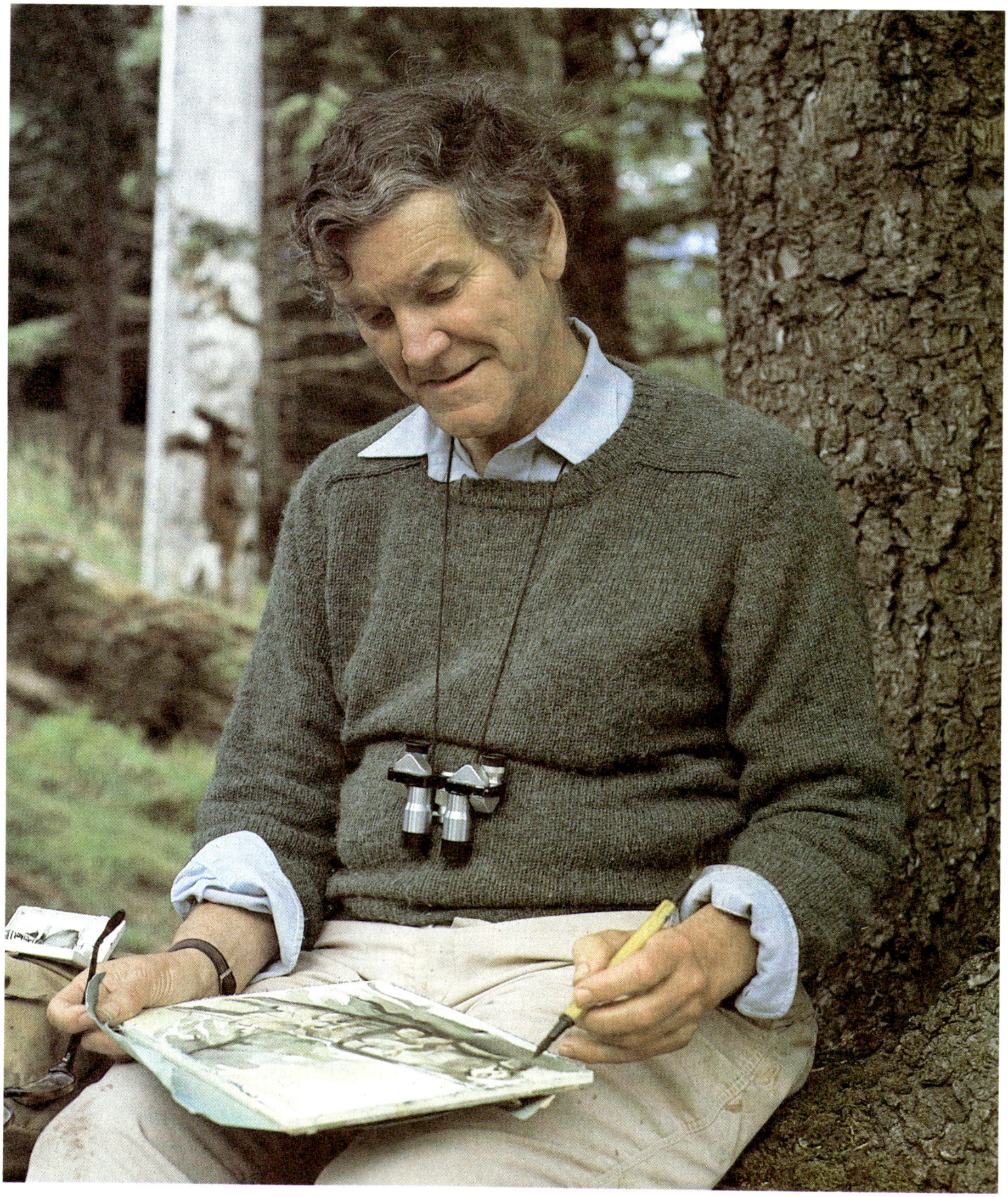

twelve years. Most of that time was spent on West Baffin Island with the Sikusalingmiut, an Eskimo tribe. Their way of thinking and their deep understanding of nature had a great effect on his art and his way of life.

Those far northern people did not use the written word to record their legends and their histories. Instead, they developed skillful ways of telling stories aloud. Special tribal storytellers passed these stories and storytelling techniques on from generation to generation. The storytellers were experts at creating suspense and excitement for their audience. They could imitate many sounds of animals and of nature. While they told the stories, there would often be dancing and drum playing. The sound of the howling Arctic winds outside was used to highlight the stories. Sometimes the storyteller's helper clicked a goose quill against his teeth to make sounds that helped build excitement and suspense. By listening to the master storytellers of the Inuit people tell about present-day adventures and past legends, Houston learned how to tell stories well himself.

Since then, James Houston has written and illustrated many stories for children and adults about the northern Canadian Indians and the Inuit. These stories include the tales and legends of these tribes. Houston retells them so that a reader today can understand them. To do this, he has to include many details that an Inuit storyteller would leave out. Since the Inuit live in a small, closely-knit group, every piece of information is shared and known by all the people. The storyteller has little need to explain many things that must be made clear to a modern reader.

To write an exciting and understandable story of the Far North for children of other lands, James Houston listens carefully to the ancient tales for some strange and fascinating core of truth that everyone can appreciate. Then he uses this truth as a theme. It becomes the center of dozens of important facts about the people, their lives, and further details about the special way they do things. He weaves these into the story in his own style. He believes that this is an excellent method to use when writing stories about other people and ways of life in far-off lands.

In *The White Archer*, a novel for young people, James Houston tells about an exciting Indian and Inuit conflict that ends in a surprising way. It was a story told to him by his dog-team traveling companion, Oshaweetok. To this story, Houston added a caribou hunt that he remembered from his own experience in the Far North. *Frozen Fire* was based on the true adventure of a contemporary boy who was lost on moving ice and of how he survived. The story was combined with a second plot about a boy from the south, a search for gold, and a helicopter.

Discuss the Selection

1. How does James Houston use his knowledge of Eskimo and northern Indian life in his writing?
2. What was the turning point in James Houston's life that helped shape his future?
3. What can you learn by reading the tales and legends of people from foreign lands or very different ways of life?
4. How does James Houston make a story of the Far North understandable to a modern reader?
5. What advice would you follow if you wished to write a story about people in a foreign land? Where in the selection would you find this advice?

Apply the Skills

Noting the correct sequence of events in a selection may help you remember the information it contains.

List the events, in the order in which they happened, that led to Houston's interest in northern Canadian Indians and Eskimos.

Think and Write

Prewrite

1. As a result of an incident that occurred at the Toronto Art Gallery when James Houston was twelve years old, he became keenly interested in the art and lives of tribal people.

2. Houston listened to master storytellers tell about the adventures of the Inuit people; thus he, too, learned to be a skillfull storyteller.

3.

Many ideas and events are connected in cause-and-effect relationships.

In "James Houston: Tales of the Far North," you learned of events that shaped his future as a master storyteller. Copy the chart shown above. Then complete it by adding another sentence that shows a cause-and-effect relationship.

Compose

Using the sentences from the chart and supporting details from the selection, write three paragraphs showing cause-and-effect relationships. Try to use connecting words or phrases such as *because, since, then, therefore,* and *as a result.* As shown in the chart, these words or phrases help signal cause-and-effect relationships.

Revise

Read the paragraphs you wrote. Does each paragraph contain at least one cause and one effect? Does your writing clearly show how events in Houston's life had an effect on his craft? If not, revise your work.

Vocabulary Study

Analogies

Recognizing the meaning of a word is only one part of building vocabulary. Another part is being able to understand the connection between words. This process, which is called using word analogies, examines not only your knowledge of word meanings, but also your ability to think clearly.

Many of the vocabulary tests that you will take will test your ability to understand word **analogies,** the relationships between words. For example, you may be asked to identify how the words *pink* and *color* are related. This relationship is obvious because you know that *pink* is a *color*.

Notice the relationship between the words in each of the following pairs. Which words are related in the same way that the word *pink* is related to the word *color*?

1. brush/paint   2. flower/daisy   3. snow/weather

Brush/paint is not related in the same way as *pink/color* because a brush is not a kind of paint. The second pair isn't a good choice, either, because it is not expressed in the *pink/color* order. A flower is not a kind of daisy; rather, a daisy is a kind of flower. The third pair is the logical choice because snow is a kind of weather, just as pink is a kind of color.

Think about this word pair: *cat/kitten*. Which words in the following pairs are related in the same way that *cat* is related to *kitten* in the word pair?

1. puppy/dog   2. deer/fawn   3. cow/calf

The only wrong choice is *puppy/dog* because it is out of order. In all the other pairs, the young animal is the second word in the pair, as in *cat/kitten*.

Analogies Between Parts and a Whole

Some word analogies express the relationship between a whole and one of its parts. A part of a book is a page. A part of a week is a day. Which of the following word pairs express first the whole and then one of its parts?

    1. bouquet/flower   2. sentence/word   3. lamp/sofa

The logical choices are numbers 1 and 2. Number 3 is illogical because a sofa is not part of a lamp.

Cause/Effect Analogies

Some word analogies express the relationship between something that happens and the effect that follows. For example, in the word pair *joke/laughter*, you can identify the relationship by saying that a joke usually *causes* laughter. You could also say that laughter is generally the *effect* of a joke.

Look at the following word pairs and identify the cause/effect relationships. Why is the other choice illogical?

    1. tragedy/tears   2. blood/wound   3. throw/catch

The logical choices are numbers 1 and 3. Tears are an effect of tragedy. Catch is an effect of something being thrown. The other pair is illogical because it gives the effect before the cause. In cause/effect relationships, the cause produces the effect.

Analogies Between Subjects and Characteristics

An analogy can express the relationship between a subject and one of its characteristics. For example, in the word pair *Nile/river*, you can identify the relationship by saying "The Nile is a river."

Examine the following word pairs. Identify the pair that shows the relationship between the subject and one of its characteristics.

    1. tennis/bowling   2. Texas/state   3. typewriter/paper

The logical choice is number 2 because the word *state* tells what *Texas* is. *Bowling* does not describe *tennis*; *paper* does not describe *typewriter*.

Analogies Express Many Different Kinds of Relationships

Analogies show many kinds of relationships between words. Understanding word analogies requires an ability to reason. Analogy questions are part of many standardized tests such as the Scholastic Aptitude Test (SAT), which you will take if you plan to enter college. As you read, think about word analogies.

In this witty fantasy, an English clergyman appears to communicate with strange creatures during an unbelievable journey. Are these surprising events real, or does he just imagine them?

As you read, think about relationships between words and the different kinds of analogies.

The Far Forests

by Joan Aiken

They were playing Twenty Questions in the study of the old house. The room was full of the gentle ticktock of clocks — one on the desk, and one on the mantelpiece, not to mention the grandfather clock in the hall adding his slow, thoughtful reminder that, even in this retreat, time moved on its measured way.

Outside, the night wind stirred the branches of ancient trees.

"Is it plankton?" said Miss Dallas, concealing a yawn. For years past, Twenty Questions had bored her to tears, but her brother, the old Canon, had a childish delight in the game, and so she indulged him.

"My dear Delia!" he said mildly. "Plankton would be animal, not vegetable. Have another question. That leaves you with three to go."

"Seaweed, then. If it's vegetable and not on any continent or island, it *must* be in the sea."

The parchment-like wrinkles around his eyes extended at this evidence of her illogicality.

"Think, Delia! There are other elements."

Miss Dallas looked around the room for inspiration. The ginger-brown velvet curtains were drawn, the fire slumbered in its black marble grate. A Persian cat, almost as elderly as the brother and sister, slept on the worn bearskin hearthrug. Innumerable books held dust and memories. A clutter of

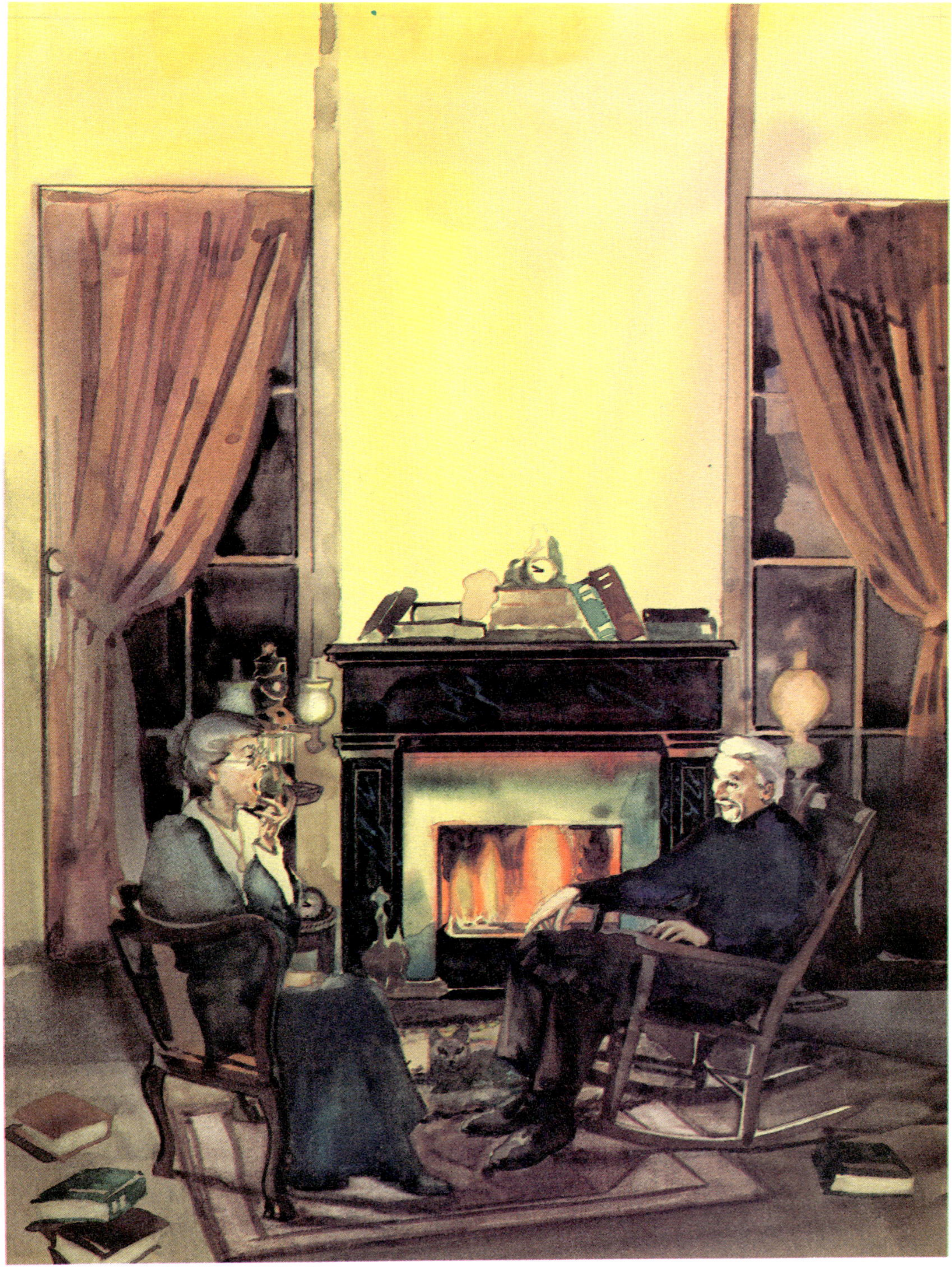

objects on the mantelpiece, never to be thrown away, included a paperweight from Italy, some curious lumps of rock, porcupine quills, and a silver statue of an angel with three pairs of wings.

"Well, I've never heard of vegetables floating in the air," Miss Dallas said impatiently. "Is it thistledown?"

"No. One more."

"I give up."

"Think!"

But she refused to think anymore, finding thought a troublesome exercise. She got up and began tidying the room with a sort of affectionate exasperation. The Canon eyed her mildly. He resembled the White Knight — his eyes were set deeply in great hollows, his large, noble, polished brow sloped back into a sparse halo of white hair like soft thistledown. He had a smile of great sweetness and a general air of being slightly mad.

"No," said Miss Dallas decisively. "I give up. What was it?"

"The forests of Mars."

"*Mars?*"

"Don't you remember that TV program the other night? The scientist who said the red patches might be forests?"

"It's not proved," Miss Dallas snapped. "You should have called it abstract, not vegetable. You can't count that as a point."

"Very well, my dear," he said patiently. "That makes me three thousand, three hundred, and ninety-four and you two thousand, nine hundred, and seventeen. You are catching up to me. Now I shall just go out for a stroll while you brew the cocoa."

"Don't be long," she said, turning out the oil lamp. "It's a very dark night."

The Canon was occasionally known to lose his memory and wander away. Sometimes he was found and returned by a neighbor. Sometimes he returned of his own accord after intervals of varying length, amounting once to five days. He never knew where he had been. His sister worried about it a little, but not unduly, relying, perhaps with reason, on his appearance of obvious saintliness to protect him from harm. But she did try to guard him from catching a chill.

"Henry! Your galoshes."

"Oh, yes. Yes, my dear. You do not happen to know, do you, where they are? I seem to have misplaced them."

Miss Dallas lit a candle and searched impatiently among the clutter of umbrellas, walking sticks, lawn-tennis racquets, polo clubs (what were *they* still doing here?) in the front hall. The galoshes were presently found in the laundry basket.

"I cannot think how they got there," said the Canon resignedly, and ambled out through the trellised porch into the garden.

It was indeed a dark night. Not a single star could be seen. The sky seemed as low as the roof. Not a sound came from the village, three-quarters of a mile distant. The Canon thought contentedly, as he strolled on the velvety lawn under his walnut trees (although the night was black, he knew to a hairsbreadth where each tree stood), that his house in its acre of garden might as well have been isolated in a thousand miles of woodland, even on a planet of its own. It was so dark, and the air smelled of leaves.

Delia called and he returned dutifully, sighing, to the kitchen door.

"Leave your galoshes by the stove, then you'll know where to look in the morning."

"So I shall, my dear, so I shall."

"And drink your cocoa while it's hot."

Notwithstanding this reminder the Canon went off several times into a dream as he sipped. "You know, my dear," he emerged once to say, "in spite of your doubt I like to think there are forests on Mars. In these sad days of deforestation, it gives me pleasure to think that at least on another planet there may be huge tracts of unspoiled forest, quite unspoiled by human greed. How many trees did the man say had to be cut each day to produce one issue of *The New York Times*?"

"I can't remember," said Miss Dallas shortly. "But has it occurred to you, Henry, that if there are forests on Mars there may also be inhabitants, cutting them down?"

"Oh, no," said the Canon, gently but firmly. "I am sure that if there are beings on Mars they are of a high enough order of intelligence and integrity to leave the forests unspoiled."

"Well—" said Miss Dallas, softening, "I hope you are right. Good night, Henry. Straight to bed now. No wandering about." She gave his cheek a brisk peck.

"No, indeed," said the Canon, turning absently towards the back door. She redirected him to bed. As she rinsed the cups and saucepan she heard him upstairs, singing his evening hymn:

"That, when black darkness closes day,
And shadows thicken round our way,
Faith may no darkness know, and night
From faith's clear beam may borrow light . . ."

Like all the old, the Canon slept lightly and woke early. Next morning he was up at half-past five. After paying a visit to his cherished butterfly collection in the spare room, he went in search of his galoshes, intending to take an early-morning stroll, as he often did before his sister came down.

The downstairs part of the house, with curtains drawn, was still veiled in twilight. It was a close, dark, quiet morning. The leaves, as so often on a gray morning in early summer, seemed to take all light from the sky. No birds were singing.

"I fear it will rain later," said the Canon, unlocking the back door, and forgetting his galoshes. He stepped out, and paused in mild surprise. For the green, hushed darkness was quite as intense outside the house as inside. In fact, the whole sky was hidden by a dull pall which lay close above the tops of the trees.

"What a remarkable phenomenon," said the Canon. "Can it mean a typhoon or hurricane? I can remember observing this curious opacity and greenness of sky in the tropics, before such storms. But the atmosphere is not electric, nor unusually warm. The light is certainly most strange. Shall I awaken Delia? But no, poor girl, she has such a busy life. I will let her sleep a little longer."

He strolled away from the house, enjoying the pleasant gloom.

"And what a powerful — what an unusually powerful smell of vegetation," he said. "I suppose it is the moisture in the air drawing out scents from the leaves. But really, even for this time of year, I do not recall ever having experienced anything quite like it. The odor is fragrant — like that of walnut leaves — but yet there is something stronger and quite distinctive . . ."

He paused, and his voice trailed away.

He was now standing at the edge of his garden, beyond a little orchard of apple and pear trees which ran from the far end of the lawn to a brook. The babbling of the water was very loud in the quietness. The dark green sky seemed even lower here. It seemed to be resting like a tent on the tips of the pear branches, some of which were still hung with blossoms. As he watched it, this tentlike sky appeared to bulge and sway.

"One would almost believe," the Canon murmured, "that some bird had alighted. But it must be the effect of the approaching storm. Dear me — and I have forgotten my galoshes."

But next moment he had forgotten them again, for the improbable happened. A rip appeared in the green covering of sky. A clear, three-cornered patch of brightness showed beyond it and rapidly extended, flooding daylight onto the blossoming branches and bluebell-starred grass below. The startled birds immediately began to sing.

"Can it be," said Canon Dallas, "that something is *nibbling* the sky?"

He continued to watch attentively and was confirmed in his opinion. Other rips appeared. The greenness curled back rapidly, like bits of burning paper. More and more daylight poured into the orchard. Soon the Canon was able to see the creatures that were demolishing this dark canopy.

There was not a doubt about it, they were moths. But of a size! Four of them, each rather larger than a tractor, were hovering twenty feet up, rapidly munching and consuming the green cover that lay over the house and its surrounding land. A shred of green the size of a tablecloth fluttered down beside the Canon, and a long proboscis followed it down and caught it as it fell.

The Canon stood rapt, gazing up. He was not in the least alarmed. True, not all moths were vegetarian, but these ones appeared to be so, for if they were moths, and they must be, what could they be eating but a single gigantic leaf that had fallen from heaven knew where, completely covering the area?

At first he was too absorbed in the beauty of the moths to think of anything else. Their hovering wings moved too fast for a clear view — all that he saw was a shimmering blue of iridescent purple and black and green. But their bodies, covered with thick, soft golden fur, could plainly be seen, as well as their long antennae and large, softly glowing eyes. They had almost finished the leaf now — only a few shreds remained.

One of the moths settled on the lawn for a moment or two and put itself to rights. Businesslike as a cat, it shook its fur into place, folding and unfolding its wings. The Canon gave an incredulous gasp at the sudden spread of color, patterned in unimagined shades of unimagined brilliance.

"Oh!" he cried. "Wait! Don't go — please don't go!"

But it was too late. The moths, communicating silently by means of their antennae, had risen and were fluttering together, seeking, it seemed, the right direction.

"Just a moment longer — oh, please!"

Did they turn their great shining eyes on him in pity? They hovered an instant. Then, as if carried by a thermal current, they soared together up and up, past the pale early-morning sun, until his dazzled eyes could follow them no farther.

He turned, stricken, to search the orchard for some reminder of their presence — a bit of golden fur, scrap of leaf, anything. But it almost seemed as if they had been bent on removing all evidence of themselves. There was nothing. Nothing at all.

"Their fur was golden," the Canon said, spooning down his porridge. "And their wings were — oh, every color, and close to ten feet wide. Their eyes were —" What color had their eyes been? A steely blue? Gold? Crystalline? He found it hard to remember. "I shall write to *The Times*," he said. "And ask in the village. Find out if anyone else saw them. Oh, Delia, I am sorry I had no time to wake you. They were gone so quickly."

He was silent again, numb with the anguish of their departure without him. Oh, to have gone with those travelers, to have shared their voyage and seen the forests that nurtured them!

His sister was looking at him with troubled eyes.

"You're sure you're all right. Henry? You haven't caught a chill, going out like that without your galoshes?"

"Of course not, Delia," he said somewhat impatiently. "If it matters to you so much, I will put my galoshes on now, before I write my letter to *The Times*."

Nobody in the village had seen the moths. *The Times* was too cautious to publish, without additional confirmation, such a letter from an eighty-five-year-old Canon who was well known to be somewhat dreamy and subject to fits of absent-mindedness. His letter was put aside to wait for others. People were kind to the Canon about his vision, for everybody was fond of him. But it did gradually become apparent to him that nobody really believed he had seen the moths — or not with his physical eyes at any rate. His feelings were hurt, and he stopped talking about the incident, even to Delia. But deep in his heart he cherished the faint, faint hope that some day the moths would come back.

Time passed, summer waned, autumn came. Miss Dallas went off one day on a Women's Club outing, and the Canon made haste to seize such a golden opportunity for cutting down the brambles at the end of the orchard, a job he greatly enjoyed.

The sight of her brother with pruning shears in his hand always filled Miss Dallas with terror. If she had known his intentions she would have stopped him by getting a man up from the village.

After working for half an hour he uncovered a large object which had been buried in nettles and brambles and half sunk in the grass. It seemed to be spherical, about as large as a piano, not hard, but sticky, and faintly iridescent.

He laid down the pruning shears and began clearing away the brambles with trembling hands, wonder and hope and incredulous joy growing in his heart. The hope was justified. Unmistakably, what lay among the cut vegetation was a crumpled corner of the great leaf, dry and brown now, but still slightly fragrant, wrapped about a gigantic cocoon.

His first thought was, "I shall see one of them again! I have another chance." His second thought was, "People will believe me now." His first worry was, "What shall I feed it on when it comes out?"

He fetched the wheelbarrow and transported the cocoon with immense care (it was not heavy) to the unused stables. He decided, for the moment at least, to say nothing of his discovery to anyone, not even to Delia. Delia would fuss, and take his temperature, and make him put on his galoshes. For the rest, there would be commotion and publicity and undesirable visitors. They might even take the cocoon away and put it in the Natural History Museum, or decide it belonged to the government. And he did want, he wanted so terribly badly, to see the unbelievable colors on those wings once more, in peace and solitude. Was it selfish of him? he wondered, or was it, perhaps, what the moths would have wished?

So he kept silent through the winter, remembered his galoshes, remembered to drink his cocoa when it was hot, chatted to his parishioners, and preached a sermon in the cathedral from time to time. And if he seemed more than usually vague and preoccupied—if the sermons were more than usually dreamy and full of unexplained ideas—well, as people said to one another, after all, the old Canon's getting on and he's really wonderful for his age.

Only to his sister did he sometimes still talk about the forests of Mars.

"The tragedy of it is," he said, "that we may have spoiled our chances of seeing them. They must know that we have wrecked our own forest. Naturally they won't, if they can help it, give us the opportunity of doing the same to theirs. If they can help it, they won't even let us know those forests exist."

"Who won't let us?"

"The inhabitants," he said, and his eyes became filled with inner visions of wonderful colors. "But perhaps they'd let just one or two go, people of proved integrity. But why should I be so foolish as to think that?" And he looked so humble and dejected that Miss Dallas, worried, insisted on his taking some medicine.

The Canon presently took steps unknown to his sister. He bought two enormous drums of honey and put them in the unused stable beside the cocoon. Winter slowly passed and May came around again.

"Do you think it's good for you to spend so much time in the old stables?" Miss Dallas said. "You are becoming quite thin and pale. I think I must get you away for a holiday."

"On no account — I mean, not just yet," her brother said hurriedly. "I feel extremely well, Delia."

Next week Miss Dallas was obliged to go to London for an annual conference of Women's Organizations. She left her brother anxiously. He had hardly seen her off before he hastened back to the stable where the cocoon was beginning to move and make faint noises. He fetched a chair and sat patiently, hour after hour, forgetting to eat or sleep in his intense excitement.

Only once did he leave the stables, and then it was to fetch a hammer and chisel to break open the drums of honey.

When Miss Dallas returned from her conference, the Canon was nowhere to be found. At first she was not seriously alarmed, for the weather was warm. But when a day had gone by, and then three days, and then three weeks, and still the police had found no trace of him, she became desperate.

Country-wide appeals were broadcast. Prayers were said in the parish church and in the cathedral, but still no one came forward to say that an elderly white-haired clergyman with a mild and benevolent expression had been found wandering.

And then one night when Miss Dallas, grimly blinking back her tears, was just about to heat the milk for a solitary cup of cocoa, the kitchen door opened and her brother walked in. Just like that! Mild, serene, unruffled, exactly as she had last seen him three weeks before.

"I am so sorry, my dear," he said. "I fear I forgot again and went out for a walk without my galoshes."

"Henry!" she cried, and embraced him. "Where have you been?"

"Been?" He looked vaguely surprised, a little troubled. "Why—to tell you the truth, I can't quite remember. But it will come back in time I hope—I devoutly hope." He looked wistfully around the familiar kitchen. "I see you were just about to make some cocoa, my dear. A cup of cocoa would be most welcome."

Miss Dallas wiped her eyes and set her trembling lips together. She had him back, and safe, that was the main thing. If she never discovered where he had been—why, it could not be helped.

"You are *sure* your feet are not wet, Henry? Why, what curious yellow stuff all over your shoes—it looks like down, or pollen."

"So it does," he said, staring at his shoes with a puzzled frown. "Where can it have come from? Ah, thank you, my dear. Cocoa—most acceptable and sustaining."

"Well, it's very nice to have you back, Henry," his sister said gruffly. "I was a little worried. However, it's over now. What would you say to a nice game of Twenty Questions?"

Discuss the Selection

1. Did the Canon imagine his experience with the moths or did it actually happen?
2. What part did the game of Twenty Questions play in the story?
3. Why do you think the Canon eagerly awaited the emergence of the moth from the cocoon?
4. Where do you think the Canon went during the days that he was missing?
5. There are some clues in the story that the Canon might have been telling the truth. Find those clues.

Apply the Skills

An analogy can be used to express a relationship between a whole and one of its parts, a cause and the resulting effect, or a subject and one of its characteristics. Decide what kind of relationship is expressed by each of the following pairs of words. Explain your answers.

1. insect/moth   2. forest/tree   3. shoes/galoshes

Think and Write

Prewrite

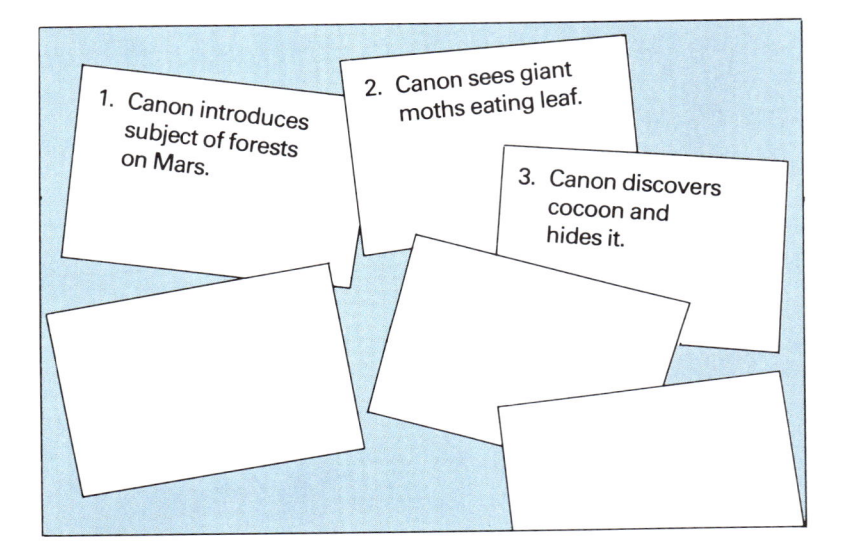

1. Canon introduces subject of forests on Mars.
2. Canon sees giant moths eating leaf.
3. Canon discovers cocoon and hides it.

When reading a story, it is important to understand the time order; that is, the order in which events occur. The note cards shown above list four important events in "The Far Forests." These events are numbered in the order in which they occur. Copy the note cards and add note cards that will complete the list of events that took place in the story.

Compose

Using the events on the note cards and in the story, write a paragraph summarizing "The Far Forests." In your paragraph, use time-order words such as *first*, *next*, and *later*. Your first sentence might be *The Canon's mind was on a recent TV program about possible forests on Mars.*

Revise

Read your paragraph. Did you present each event in the correct time order and link the events with time-order words? If not, revise your first draft to make the sequence of events as clear as possible.

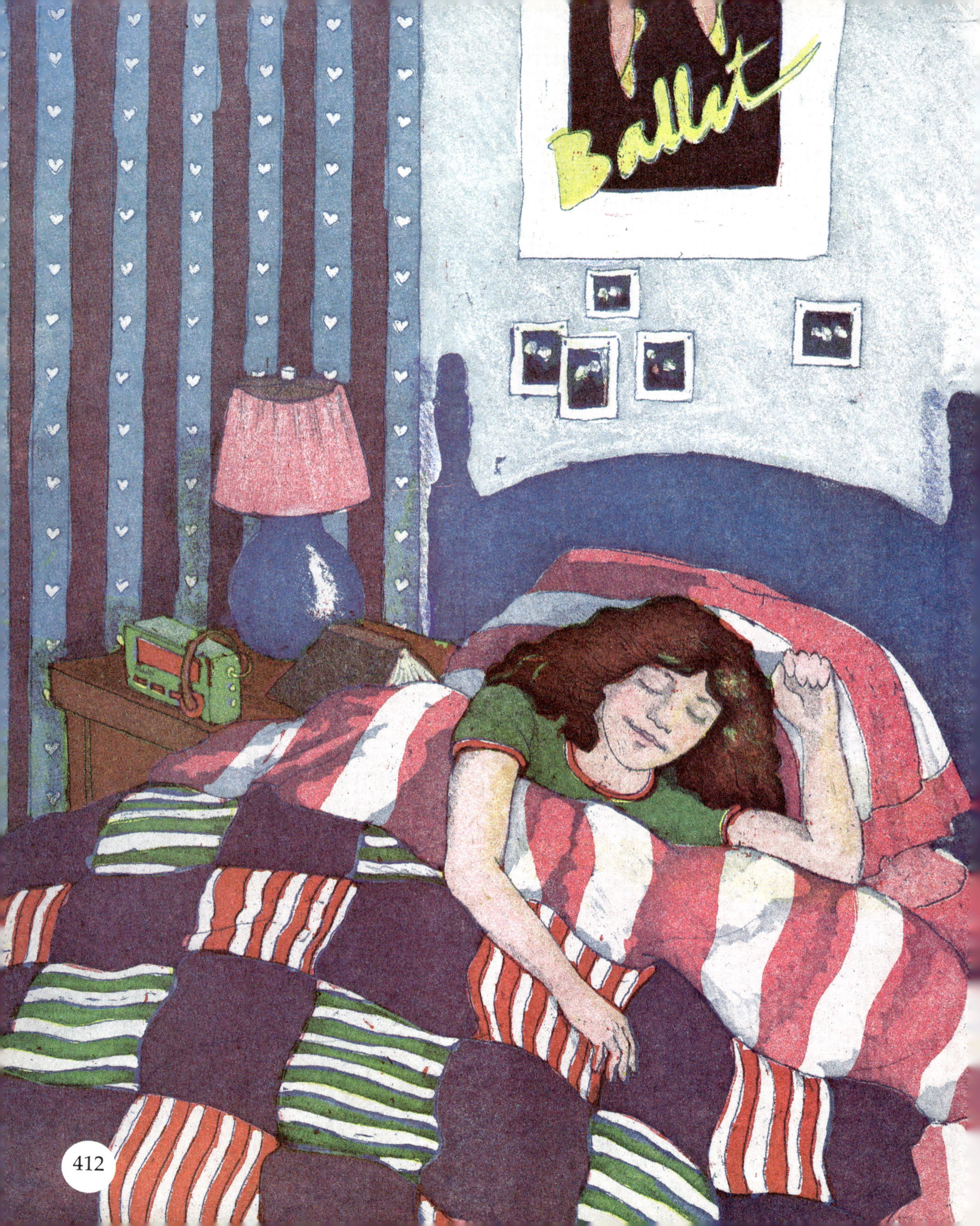
Ballet

What Did I Dream?

by Robert Graves

What did I dream? I do not know—
    The fragments fly like chaff.
Yet, strange, my mind was tickled so
    I cannot help but laugh.

Pull the curtains close again,
    Tuck me grandly in;
Must a world of humour wane
    Because birds begin

Complaining in a fretful tone,
    Rousing me from sleep—
The finest entertainment known,
    And given rag-cheap?

Literature Study

Point of View

Point of view is the angle or position from which a story is told. Just as a movie camera may remain at a distance to take in a large scene, or may move up close to focus on one face, so the point of view in a story determines the distance between reader and characters. A story can be told from the point of view of one character, or several characters, or of an outside observer.

First-Person Point of View: Participant and Observer

In first-person narration—the telling of a story from a first-person point of view—the narrator speaks from the *I*, first-person, vantage point. Although first-person point of view is a limited point of view, since the reader is told only what one character knows and observes, it gives a sense of immediacy to a story. Study the following passage written from the point of view of a **first-person participant**.

> I woke up early that morning, already filled with excitement about the camping trip. As I made my bed, I was thinking that tonight I'd be sleeping in a sleeping bag.

In another kind of first-person narration, the speaker is placed at some distance from the action. Here, the speaker is more of an observer than a direct participant. Study the following passage written from the point of view of a **first-person observer**.

> I observed the strange neighbors next door for about a year, but I never spoke with them. Then one day, I was a witness to an incredible drama at their house.

A first-person observer is like a reporter who witnesses an action. Although removed from the main characters, the observer often expresses personal judgments about what happens in the story.

Third-Person Point of View: Omniscient and Limited

In third-person point of view, the narrator uses third-person pronouns (*he* or *she*). The story is sometimes told from the point of view of an outsider, a third party. This outsider has full knowledge of the actions, words, physical characteristics and even the unspoken thoughts and feelings of the characters. Such an observer is *omniscient, all-knowing*. The story is told from the **omniscient point of view**. This point of view allows a reader to explore both the internal and external lives of characters. As an example, read this excerpt from O. Henry's "The Gift of the Magi":

> Now there were two possessions of the James Dillingham Youngs in which they both took mighty pride. One was Jim's gold watch that had been his father's and his grandfather's. The other was Della's hair.

An author might also tell a story in the third person from the point of view of only *one* character. This is called **limited third-person point of view**. In the following example from Doris Lessing's "A Mild Attack of Locusts," everything is told from Margaret's vantage point. The reader knows only what Margaret sees and feels. Thoughts and feelings of the others are not included.

> Margaret began to cry. It was all so hopeless — if it wasn't a bad season, it was locusts; if it wasn't locusts, it was army worms or veldt fires. Always something.

A skilled author uses the advantages of both first-person and third-person points of view. From which point of view is each of the following passages written?

1. Jackson was debating whether to rush for the bus. Athalia looked away. She had already decided to walk home.
2. As the courtroom drama unfolded, I was relieved that no one would be able to guess who I was, or why I was there.
3. As the courtroom drama unfolded, he was relieved that no one recognized him. He could watch the trial in safety.
4. I knew that my adventures in the deserted house would be remembered for a long time, but I wanted to keep my eyes and ears open, and get out as fast as I could.

Understanding the viewpoint from which stories are written will help you understand them better and enjoy them more.

Author Profile

Kathryn Forbes

Kathryn Forbes's writing career began in 1938, when she was twenty-nine. At that time, she sold some short stories to small magazines and newspapers. Like most unknown beginning writers, she realized that she would probably have to wait a long time for success. That is, if she were lucky enough to ever achieve it.

Forbes's career, however, was not destined to follow a roundabout route to success. Instead, she had the magic combination for a successful writer — talent and luck!

Only a few years after she sold her first story, Forbes wrote one about an immigrant family living in San Francisco at the turn of the century. It was based on her own family life.

Although it was fiction, the characters and the situations were very realistic. In fact, she modeled each of the characters on a member of her own family, and one, Katrin, on herself. The main character of the story was Katrin's mother, simply called Mama.

Forbes sold the story to a Canadian newspaper, *The Toronto Weekly Star*. An editor at *The Reader's Digest* magazine saw the story and liked it so much that the magazine bought it. When the story ran in the following issue, the magazine's readers went wild. Thousands of letters streamed in, asking for more stories about Mama and her family.

When the readers responded just as strongly to Forbes's second story, she decided to write an entire book about Mama. In 1943, only five years after she had sold her first piece of writing, Forbes had completed her first book, *Mama's Bank Account*. It was an immediate success.

The New York Times summed up what attracted people to *Mama's Bank Account*. Their reviewer said that Mama was one of the most likable mothers to be encountered on the printed page, that she was cheerful and funny as well as wise and understanding. It was Mama, calm and certain in her judgment, determined to succeed in her new homeland of America, that appealed to the readers. At a time when almost everyone in the world was fighting — for this was during World War II — Mama was a true heroine. She was a rare being who could solve everybody's problems peacefully and wisely.

Less than a year later, a stage play was based on *Mama's Bank Account*. It was called *I Remember Mama* and was written by John van Druten. The play opened on Broadway in 1944. It was an immediate success.

The success of Forbes and her stories about Mama does not end there, however. In 1948, RKO Pictures made a movie, also called *I Remember Mama*, that was based on the book. The movie, too, was a big success. One year later, there was a TV series simply called "Mama," about Forbes's fictional family. The program, which was one of the first family dramas on TV, ran for eight years. When the network tried to cancel the show in 1956, a flood of letters from viewers forced them to bring it back for another season.

Kathryn Forbes wrote only a few other books in her lifetime, and no others about Mama. She, her husband, and her two sons were great fans of outdoor sports, and the family enjoyed camping in their home state of California. Forbes died in 1966.

John van Druten's play tells about a Norwegian family living in America at the turn of the century. Observe how both wit and wisdom make the family's adjustment easier.

As you read, notice how the play is told from one character's point of view: Katrin's memories of life on Steiner Street.

Scenes from
I Remember Mama
by John van Druten

Scene 1

The period of the play is around 1910.
　Scene:　On either side of the stage are two small turntables on which the shorter scenes are played against very simplified backgrounds. As each scene finishes, the lights dim and the table revolves out, leaving an unobstructed view of the main stage. The main stage is raised by two steps, above which traveler curtains open and close.

　When the curtain rises, Katrin, in a spotlight, is seated at a desk on the right turntable, facing the audience. She is writing. Katrin is somewhere in her early twenties. She should be played by an actress who is small in stature, and capable of looking sufficiently like a child not to break the illusion in subsequent scenes. She is a blonde. Her hair, when we see her first, is in a modern "up" style, capable of being easily loosened to fall to shoulder length for the childhood scenes. She wears a very short dress, the skirt of which is concealed for the prologue by the desk behind which she is seated.

　Katrin writes in silence for a few moments, then puts down her pen, takes up her manuscript, and begins to read aloud what she has written.

Katrin (*reading*): "For as long as I could remember, the house on Steiner Street had been home. Papa and Mama had both been born in Norway, but they came to San Francisco because Mama's sisters were here. All of us were born here. Nels, the oldest and the only boy — my sister Christine — and the littlest sister, Dagmar." (*She puts down her manuscript and looks out front.*) It's funny, but when I look back, I always see Nels and Christine and myself looking almost as we do today. I guess that's because the people you see all the time stay the same age in your head. Dagmar's different. She was always the baby — so I see her as a baby. Even Mama — it's funny, but I always see Mama as around forty. She couldn't always have been forty. (*She picks up her manuscript and starts to read again.*) "Besides us, there was our boarder, Mr. Hyde. Mr. Hyde was an Englishman who had once been an actor, and Mama was very impressed by his flowery talk and courtly manners. He used to read aloud to us in the evenings. But first and foremost, I remember Mama." (*The light dims down, leaving Katrin only faintly*

visible. Lights come up on the main stage, revealing the house on Steiner Street — a kitchen room. It has a black flat, with a dresser, holding china. On either side of the dresser is a door, one leading to the pantry, the other to the rest of the house. The wall on the left is a short one. It is the wall of the house, and contains a door leading into the street, being presumably the back door of the house, but the one most commonly used as the entry door. Beyond it the street is visible, with a single lamppost at left, just outside the house. Behind the room rises the house itself with upper windows lighted, and behind

it a painted backdrop of the San Francisco hills, houses, and telegraph posts. The furniture of the kitchen is simple. A center table, with two chairs above it, armchairs at either end, and a low bench below it. Against the right wall, a large stove, below it another armchair. The window is below the door in the left wall and has a low Norwegian chest under it. Katrin's voice continuing in the half-dark, as the scene is revealed.) "I remember that every Saturday night Mama would sit down by the kitchen table and count out the money Papa had brought home in the little envelope."

(*By now the tableau is revealed in full, and the light on Katrin dwindles further. The picture is as she described. Mama — looking around forty — is in the armchair at right of the table, emptying the envelope of its silver dollars and smaller coins. Papa — looking a little older than Mama — stands above her. His English throughout is better than hers, with less accent.*)

Mama: You call the children, Lars. Is good they should know about money.

(*Papa goes to the door at the back and calls.*)

Papa: Children! Nels — Christine — Katrin!
Children's Voices (*off, answering*): Coming, Papa!
Mama: You call loud for Katrin. She is in her study, maybe.
Papa: She is where?
Mama: Katrin make the old attic under the roof into a study.
Papa (*amused*): So? (*shouting*) Katrin! Katrin!
Katrin (*still at her desk*): Yes, Papa. I heard.
Papa (*returning to the room*): A study now, huh? What does Katrin study?
Mama: I think Katrin wants to be author.
Papa: Author?
Mama: Stories she will write. For the magazines. And books, too, maybe, one day.
Papa (*taking out his pipe*): Is good pay to be author?
Mama: I don't know. For magazines, I think maybe yes. For books, I think no.
Papa: Then she become writer for magazines.
Mama: Maybe. But I like she writes books. Like the ones Mr. Hyde reads us. (*Dagmar enters from the pantry. She is a plump child of about eight and carries an alley cat in her arms.*) Dagmar, you bring that cat in again?
Dagmar: Sure, she's my Elizabeth — my beautiful Elizabeth!

(*She crosses to the chest under the window, and sits, nursing the cat.*)

Papa: Poor Elizabeth looks as if she had been in fight again.
Dagmar: Not poor Elizabeth. *Brave* Elizabeth. Elizabeth's a Viking cat. She fights for her honor!

Papa (*exchanging an amused glance with Mama*):   And just what is a cat's honor, little one?

Dagmar: The honor of being the bravest cat in San Francisco. (*Christine comes in. She, like Katrin, should be played by a small young actress, but not a child. Her hair is to her shoulders, her dress short, her age indeterminate. Actually, she is about thirteen at this time. She is the cool, aloof, matter-of-fact one of the family. She carries a box of crayons, scissors, and picture book.*) Aren't you, Elizabeth?

Christine (*sitting above the table and starting to color the picture book with the crayons*): That disgusting cat!

Dagmar: She's not disgusting. She's beautiful. Beautiful as the dawn!

Christine: And when have you ever seen the dawn?

Dagmar: I haven't seen it, but Mr. Hyde read to us about it. (*Mr. Hyde comes in from back door. He is a slightly seedy, long-haired man in his fifties. Rather of the old-fashioned English "laddie" actor type. He wears a very shabby long overcoat, with a deplorable fur collar, and carries his hat. His accent is English.*) Didn't you, Mr. Hyde? Didn't you read to us about the dawn?

Mr. Hyde: I did, my child of joy. The dawn, the rosy-finger-tipped Aurora.

Dagmar: When can I get to *see* the dawn, Mama?

Mama: Any morning you get up early.

Dagmar: Is there a dawn every morning?

Mama: Sure.

Dagmar (*incredulous*): It's all that beautiful, and it happens every morning? Why didn't anyone *tell* me?

Mr. Hyde: My child, that is what the poets are for. To tell you of all the beautiful things that are happening every day, and that no one sees until they tell them. (*He starts for the door.*)

Mama: You go out, Mr. Hyde?

Mr. Hyde: For a few moments only, dear Madam. I shall be back in time for our nightly reading. (*He goes out.*)

Mama (*who has gone to the back door, calls with a good deal of sharpness and firmness*): Nels! Katrin! You do not hear Papa call you?

Nels (*from upstairs*): Coming, Mama!

Katrin (*at her desk*): Yes, Mama. I'm coming. (*She rises. In her few moments in the dark, she has loosened her hair to her shoulders and we see that her skirt is short as she walks from her desk, and up the steps into the set. As soon as she has left it, the turntable revolves out. Immediately after her, Nels comes in from the back. He is a tall, strapping young fellow — old enough to look eighteen or nineteen, or fifteen or sixteen, according to his dress, or demeanor. Now, he is about fifteen.*)

Katrin (*to Christine*): Move over. (*She shares Christine's chair at the table with her.*)

Papa: So now all are here.

Mama: Come, then. (*Christine, Nels, and Katrin gather around the table. Dagmar remains crooning to Elizabeth, but rises and stands behind Papa. Sorting coins.*) First, for the landlord. (*She makes a pile of silver dollars. It gets pushed down the table from one member of the family to the next, each speaking as he or she passes it. Papa comes last.*)

Nels (*passing it on*): For the landlord!

Katrin (*doing likewise*): For the landlord!

Christine (*passing it to Papa*): The landlord.

Papa: For the landlord. (*He dumps the pile at his end of the table, writing on a piece of paper, which he wraps around the pile.*)

Mama (*who has been sorting*): For the grocer. (*The business is repeated. During this repeat, Dagmar's crooning to the cat becomes audible, contrapuntally to the repetitions of "For the Grocer."*)

Dagmar (*in a crescendo*): In all the United States no cat was as brave as Elizabeth. (*Fortissimo.*) In all the *world* no cat was as brave as Elizabeth!

Mama (*gently*): Hush, Dagmar. Quietly. You put Elizabeth back into the pantry.

Dagmar (*in a loud stage whisper, as she crosses to pantry*): No cat is as brave as Elizabeth! (*She goes out with the cat.*)

Mama: For Katrin's shoes to be half-soled. (*She passes a half dollar.*)

Nels: Katrin's shoes.

Katrin (*proudly*): My shoes!

Christine (*contemptuously*): Katrin's old shoes.

Papa: Katrin's shoes.

Christine (*rising and coming to Mama*): Mama, Teacher says this week I'll need a new notebook.

Mama: How much it will be?

Christine: A dime.

Mama (*giving her a dime*): For the notebook. You don't lose it.

Christine: I won't lose it. (*She wraps it in her handkerchief.*)

Mama: You take care when you blow your nose.

Christine: I'll take care. (*She returns to her seat.*)

Papa: Is all, Mama?

Mama: Is all for this week. Is good. We do not have to go to the Bank. (*She starts to gather up the few remaining coins. Katrin leaves the group, comes and sits on steps.*)

Nels (*rising*): Mama . . . (*She looks up, catching an urgency in his tone.*) Mama, I'll be graduating from grammar school next month. Could I . . . could I go on to High, do you think?

Mama (*pleased*): You want to go to high school?

Nels: I'd like to . . . if you think I could. (*Papa nods approvingly.*)

Nels (*awkwardly*): It . . . it'll cost a little money. I've got it all written down. (*Producing a piece of paper from his pocket.*) Carfare, clothes, notebooks — things I'll really need. I figured it out with Cy Nichols. He went to High last year.

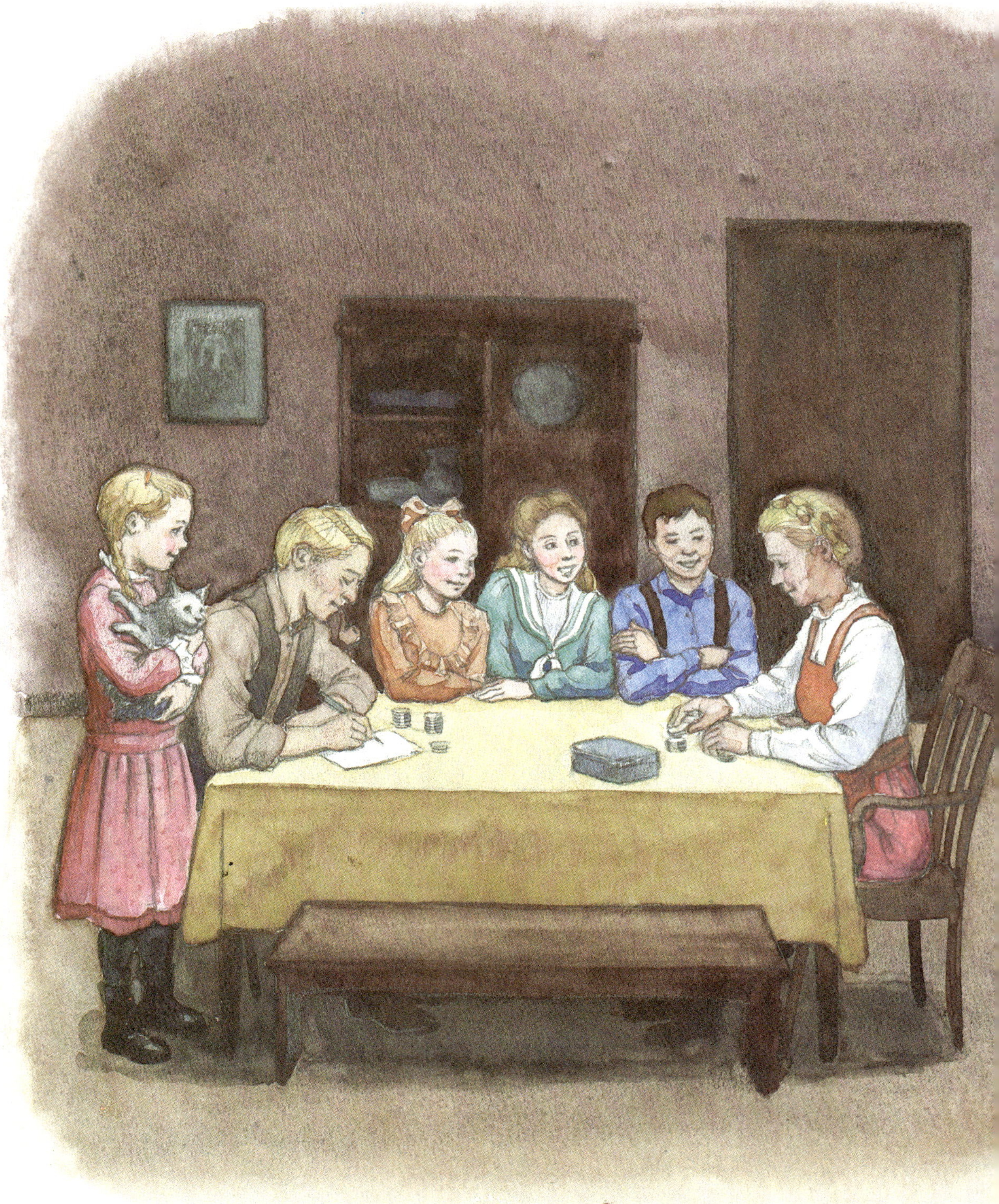

(*Papa rises and comes behind Mama to look at the paper Nels puts before them.*)

Mama: Get the Little Bank, Christine. (*Christine gets a small box from the dresser.*)

Katrin (*from the steps — herself again, in the present — looking out front*): The Little Bank! That was the most important thing in the whole house. It was a box we used to keep for emergencies — like the time when Dagmar had croup and Papa had to go and get medicine to put in the steam kettle. I can smell the medicine now! The things that came out of the Little Bank! Mama was always going to buy herself a warm coat out of it, when there was enough, only there never was.

(*Meanwhile, Mama has been counting the contents.*)

Nels (*anxiously*): Is there enough, Mama?

Mama (*shaking her head*): Is not much in the Little Bank right now. We give to the dentist, you remember? And for your roller skates?

Nels (*his face falling*): I know. And there's your warm coat you've been saving for.

Mama: The coat I can get another time. But even so . . . (*She shakes her head.*)

Christine: You mean Nels can't go to High?

Mama: Is not enough here. We do not want to have to go to the Bank, do we?

Nels: No, Mama, no. I'll work in Dillon's grocery after school.

(*Mama writes a figure on the paper and starts to count on her fingers. Papa looks over and does the sum in his head.*)

Papa: Is not enough.

Mama (*finishing on her fingers against her collarbone*): No, is not enough.

Papa (*taking his pipe out of his mouth and looking at it a long time*): I give up tobacco. (*Mama looks up at him, almost speaks, then just touches his sleeve, writes another figure and starts on her fingers again.*)

Christine: I'll mind the Maxwell children Friday nights. Katrin can help me.

(*Mama writes another figure. Papa looks over — calculates again, nods with satisfaction.*)

Mama (*triumphantly*): Is good! Is enough!

Nels: Gee! (*He moves beside Papa and plays with a wire puzzle.*)
Mama: We do not have to go to the Bank.

(*Dagmar returns, without the cat.*)

Dagmar (*hearing the last line*): Where is the Bank?
Christine (*leaving the table, cutting out the picture which she colored*): Downtown.
Dagmar: What's it look like?
Christine: Just a building.
Dagmar (*sitting on the bench, below the table*): Like a prison?
Christine (*sharply*): No, nothing like a prison.
Dagmar: Well, then why does Mama always say, "We don't want to go to the Bank?"
Christine: Because . . . well, because no one ever wants to go to the Bank.
Dagmar: Why not?

Christine: Because if we went to the Bank all the time, there'd be no money left there. And then if we couldn't pay our rent, they'd turn us out like Mrs. Jensen down the street.
Dagmar: You mean, it's like saving some of your candy for tomorrow?
Mama (*busy with coffee and cups at the stove and the dresser*): Yes, my Dagmar. Is exactly like saving your candy.
Dagmar: But if . . . if all the other people go to the Bank, then there won't be any money left for us, either.
Nels (*kindly*): It isn't like that, Dagmar. Everyone can only get so much.
Dagmar: How much?
Nels: However much you've got there . . . put away. You see, it's our money that we put there, to keep safe.
Dagmar: When did we put it there?
Nels: I . . . I don't know when. A long time back, I guess. Wasn't it, Mama?
Mama: Is enough about the Bank.
Dagmar: How much money have we got in the Bank?
Nels: I don't know. How much, Mama?
Mama: Enough.

(*The lights fade and curtains close on the main stage.*)

Scene 2

(*The time is several years later. The lights fade and the turntable revolves out. Curtains part on kitchen, slightly changed, smartened and refurnished now. Mama and Papa seated as usual. Mama is darning. Dagmar, looking a little older, is seated on the chest, reading a solid-looking book. Nels enters from the back door, carrying a newspaper. He wears long trousers now, and looks about nineteen.*)

Nels (*hitting Papa playfully on the head with the paper*): Hello! Here's your evening paper, Papa.

(*Papa puts down the morning paper he is reading and takes the evening one from Nels.*)

Papa (*at table*): Is there any news?
Nels: No. Oh, I forgot. There's a letter for Katrin. I picked it up on the mat as I came in. (*Going to back door and calling*): Katrin! Katrin! There's a letter for you.
Katrin (*answering from off stage*): Coming!
Mama (*at table*): Nels, you know who the letter is from?
Nels: Why, no, Mama. (*Hands it to her.*) It looks like her own handwriting.
Mama (*gravely inspecting it*): Is bad.
Papa: Why is it bad?
Mama: She get too many like that. I think they are stories she send to the magazines.
Dagmar (*closing her book loudly, rising*): Well, I'll go and see if I have any puppies yet. (*Crosses below the table and then turns.*) Mama, I've just decided something.
Mama: What have you decided?
Dagmar: If Nels is going to be a doctor, when I grow up, I'm going to be a — (*looking at the book title, and stumbling over the word*) — vet-vet-veterinarian.
Mama: And what is that?
Dagmar: A doctor for animals.
Mama: Is good. Is good.
Dagmar: There are far more animals in the world than there are human beings, and far more human doctors than animal

ones. It isn't fair. (*She goes to the pantry door.*) I suppose we couldn't have a horse, could we? (*This only produces a concerted laugh from the family. She turns, sadly.*) No . . . I was afraid we couldn't. (*She goes into the pantry.*)

(*Katrin comes in. She wears a slightly more adult dress than before. Her hair is up; she is about eighteen.*)

Katrin: Where's the letter?
Mama (*handing it to her*): Here.

(*Katrin takes it, nervously. She looks at the envelope, and her face falls. She opens it, pulls out a manuscript and a rejection slip, looks at it a moment, and then replaces both in the envelope. The others watch her covertly. Then she looks up, with determination.*)

Katrin (*above table*): Mama . . . Papa . . . I want to say something.
Papa: What is it?
Katrin: I'm not going to go to college.
Papa: Why not?
Katrin: Because it would be a waste of time and money. The only point in my going to college was to be a writer. Well, I'm not going to be one, so . . .
Mama: Katrin, is it your letter that makes you say this? It is a story come back again?
Katrin: Again is right. This is the tenth time. I made this one a test. It's the best I've ever written, or ever shall write. I know that. Well, it's no good.
Nels: What kind of story is it?
Katrin: Oh . . . it's a story about a painter, who's a genius, and he goes blind.
Nels: Sounds like *The Light That Failed*.
Katrin: Well, what's wrong with that?
Nels (*quickly*): Nothing. Nothing!
Katrin (*moving down*): Besides, it's not like that. My painter gets better. He has an operation and recovers his sight, and paints better than ever before.
Mama: Is good.
Katrin (*bitterly unhappy*): No, it isn't. It's rotten.

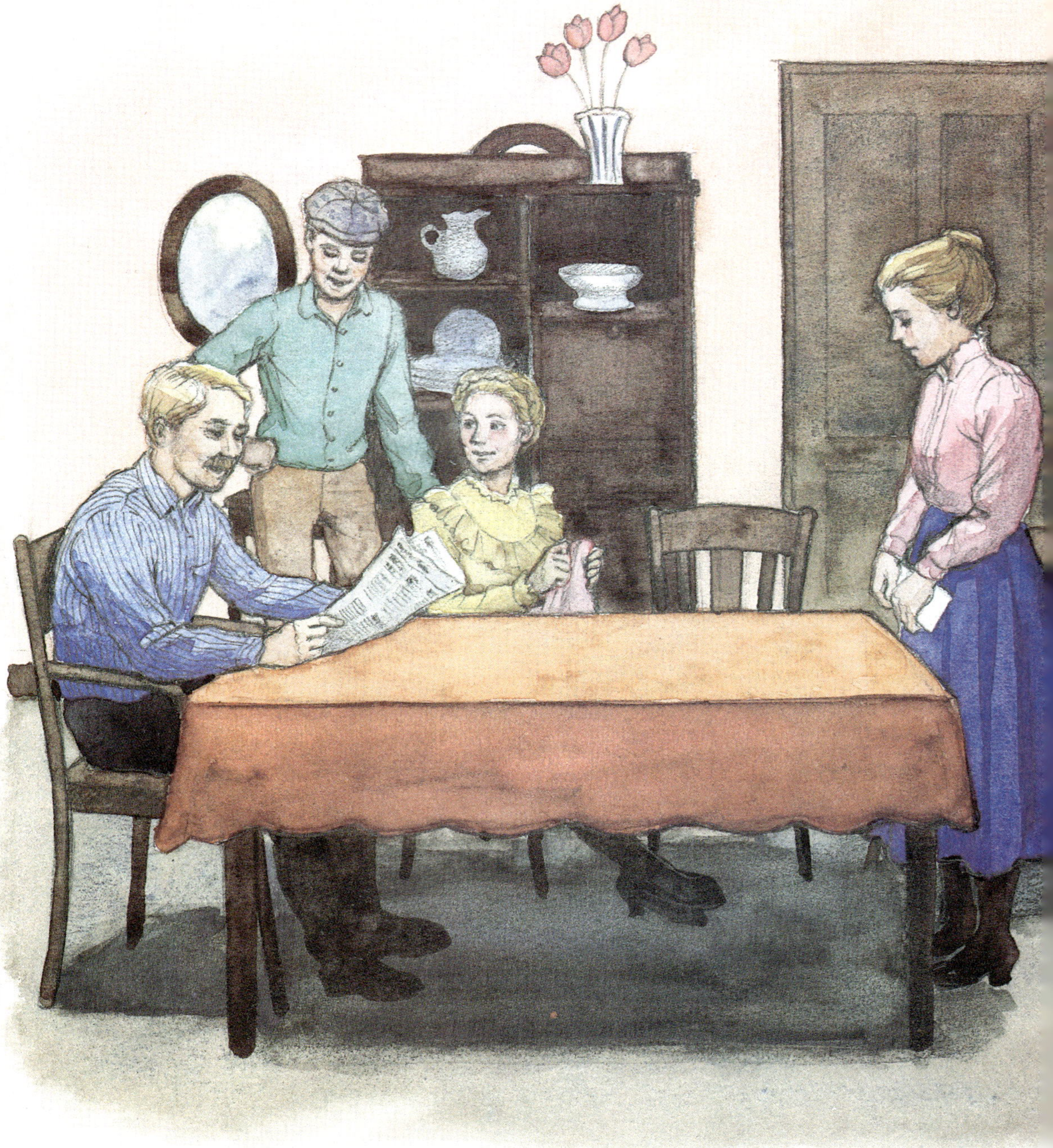

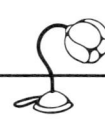

Mama: You have asked your teachers about this?

Katrin: Teachers don't know anything about writing. They just know about literature.

Mama: If there was someone in the world we could ask . . . for advice . . . to tell us . . . tell us if your stories are good.

Katrin: Yes. Well, there isn't. And they're not.

Papa (*looking at the evening paper*): There is something here in the paper about a lady writer. I just noticed the headline. Wait. (*He reads.*) "Woman writer tells key to literary success."

Katrin: Who?

Papa: A lady called Florence Dana Moorhead. It gives her picture. A fat lady. You have heard of her?

Katrin: Yes, of course. Everyone has. She's terribly successful. She's here on a lecture tour.

Mama: What does she say is the secret?

Papa: You read it, Katrin. (*He hands her the paper.*)

Katrin (*grabbing the first part*): "Florence Dana Moorhead, celebrated novelist and short story writer . . . blah-blah-blah . . . interviewed today in her suite at the Fairmont . . . blah-blah-blah . . . pronounced sincerity the essential quality for success as a writer." (*Throwing aside the paper.*) A lot of help that is.

Mama: Katrin, this lady . . . maybe if you sent her your stories, she could tell you what is wrong with them?

Katrin (*wearily*): Oh, Mama, don't be silly.

Mama: Why is silly?

Katrin (*behind table*): Well, in the first place because she's a very important person . . . a celebrity . . . and she'd never read them. And in the second, because . . . you seem to think writing's like . . . well, like cooking, or something. That all you have to have is the recipe. It takes a lot more than that. You have to have a gift for it.

Mama: You have to have a gift for cooking, too. But there are things you can learn, if you have the gift.

Katrin: Well, that's the whole point. I haven't. I know . . . now. So, if you've finished with the morning paper, Papa, I'll take the want ad section, and see if I can find myself a job. (*She takes the morning paper and goes out.*)

Mama: Is bad. Nels, what you think?

Nels: I don't know, Mama. Her stories seem all right to me, but I don't know.

Mama: It would be good to know. Nels, this lady in the paper . . . what else does she say?

Nels (*taking up the paper*): Not much. The rest seems to be about her and her home. Let's see . . . (*He reads — walking down.*) "Apart from literature, her main interest in life is gastronomy."

Mama: The stars?

Nels: No — eating. "A brilliant cook herself, she says that she would as soon turn out a good soufflé as a short story, or find a new recipe as she would a first edition."

Mama (*reaching for the paper*): I see her picture? (*She looks at it.*) Is kind face. (*Pause while she reads a moment. Then she looks up and asks.*) What is first edition?

(*Blackout. Lights up on turntable, representing the lobby of the Fairmont Hotel. A couch against a column with a palm behind it. An orchestra plays softly in the background. Mama is discovered seated on the couch, waiting patiently. She wears a hat and a suit, and clutches a newspaper and a bundle of manuscripts. A couple of guests come through the curtains and cross, disappearing into the wings. Mama watches them. Then Florence Dana Moorhead enters through the curtains. She is a stout, dressy, good-natured middle-aged woman. A Bellboy comes from the right, paging her.*)

Bellboy: Miss Moorhead?

F.D. Moorhead: Yes?

Bellboy: Telegram.

F.D. Moorhead: Oh, . . . Thank you. (*She tips him, and he goes. Mama rises and moves towards her.*)

Mama: Please. . . Please. . . Miss Moorhead . . . Miss Moorhead.

F.D. Moorhead (*looking up from her telegram, on the steps*): Were you calling me?

Mama: Yes. You are . . . Miss Florence Dana Moorhead?

F.D. Moorhead: Yes.

Mama: Please . . . might I speak to you for a moment?

F.D. Moorhead: Yes — what's it about?

Mama: I read in the paper what you say about writing.

F.D. Moorhead (*with a vague social smile*): Oh, yes?

Mama: My daughter, Katrin, wants to be a writer.

F.D. Moorhead (*who has heard that one before*): Oh, really? (*She glances at her watch.*)

Mama: I bring her stories.

F.D. Moorhead: Look, I'm afraid I'm rather in a hurry. I'm leaving San Francisco this evening . . .

Mama: I wait two hours here for you to come in. Please, if I may talk to you for one, two minutes. That is all.

F.D. Moorhead (*kindly*): Of course, but I think I'd better tell you that if you want me to read your daughter's stories, it's no use. I'm very sorry, but I've had to make a rule never to read anyone's unpublished material.

Mama (*nods — then after a pause*): It said in the paper you like to collect recipes . . . for eating.

F.D. Moorhead: Yes, I do. I've written several books on cooking.

Mama: I, too, am interested in gastronomy. I am good cook. Norwegian. I make good Norwegian dishes. Lutefisk. And Kjötboller. That is meat balls with cream sauce.

F.D. Moorhead: Yes, I know. I've eaten them in Christiania.

Mama: I have special recipe for Kjötboller . . . my mother give me. She was best cook I ever knew. Never have I told this recipe, not even to my own sisters, because they are not good cooks.

F.D. Moorhead (*amused*): Oh?

Mama: But . . . if you let me talk to you . . . I give it to you. I promise it is a good recipe.

F.D. Moorhead (*vastly tickled now*): Well, that seems fair enough. Let's sit down. (*They move to the couch and sit.*) Now, your daughter wants to write, you say? How old is she?

Mama: She is just eighteen. Just . . .

F.D. Moorhead: *Does* she write, or does she just . . . *want* to write?

Mama: Oh, she write all the time. Maybe she should not be author, but it is hard to give up what has meant so much.

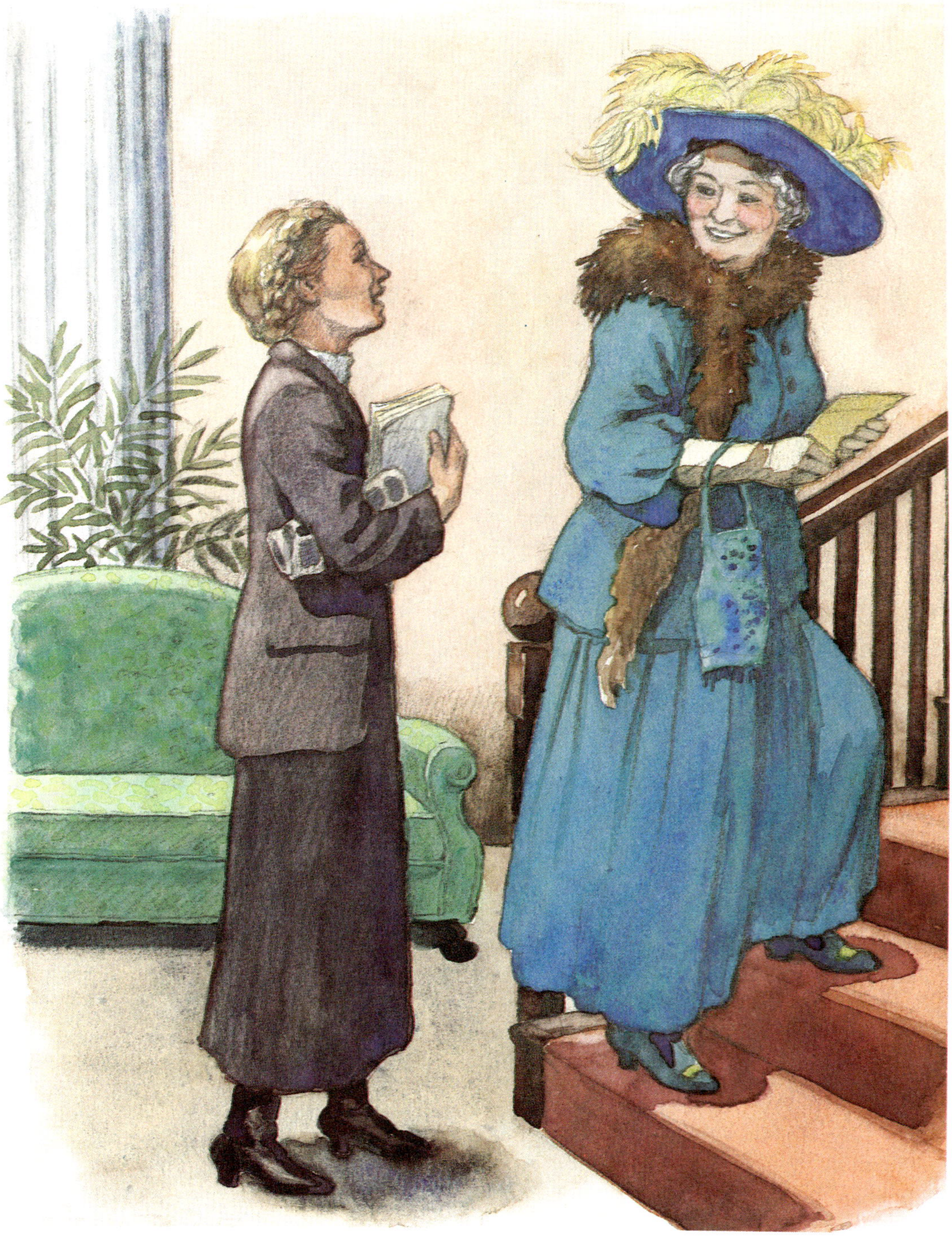

F.D. Moorhead: I agree, but . . .
Mama: I bring her stories. I bring twelve.
F.D. Moorhead (*aghast*): Twelve!
Mama: But if you could read maybe just one . . . To know if someone is good cook, you do not need to eat a whole dinner.
F.D. Moorhead: You're very persuasive. How is it your daughter did not come herself?
Mama: She was too unhappy. And too scared . . . of you. Because you are celebrity. But I see your picture in the paper.
F.D. Moorhead: That frightful picture!
Mama: Is the picture of woman who like to eat good . . .
F.D. Moorhead (*with a rueful smile*):   It certainly is. Now, tell me about the Kjötboller.
Mama: When you make the meat balls you drop them in boiling stock. Not water. That is one of the secrets.
F.D. Moorhead: Ah!
Mama: And the cream sauce. That is another secret. It is half sour cream, added at the last.
F.D. Moorhead: That sounds marvelous.
Mama: You must grind the meat six times. I could write it out for you. And . . . (*tentatively*) while I write, you could read?
F.D. Moorhead (*with a laugh*):   All right. You win. Come upstairs to my apartment. (*She rises.*)
Mama: Is kind of you. (*They start out.*) Maybe if you would read two stories, I could write the recipe for Lutefisk as well. You know Lutefisk . . . ?

(*They have disappeared into the wings, and the turntable revolves out. Katrin is at her desk.*)

Katrin: When Mama came back, I was sitting with my diary, which I called my Journal now, writing a Tragic Farewell to my Art. It was very seldom that Mama came to the attic, thinking that a writer needed privacy, and I was surprised to see her standing in the doorway. (*She looks up. Mama is standing on the steps.*) Mama!
Mama: You are busy, Katrin?
Katrin (*jumping up*):   No, of course not. Come in.

Mama (*coming down*):   I like to talk to you.
Katrin: Yes, of course.
Mama (*seating herself at the desk*):   You are writing?
Katrin (*on the steps*): No. I told you, that's all over.
Mama: That is what I want to talk to you about.
Katrin: It's all right, Mama. I was planning to tear up all my stories this afternoon, only I couldn't find half of them.
Mama: They are here.
Katrin: Did you take them? What for?
Mama: Katrin, I have been to see Miss Moorhead.
Katrin: Who's Miss . . . ? You don't mean Florence Dana Moorhead? (*Mama nods.*) You don't mean . . . (*She comes down to her.*) Mama, you don't mean you took her my stories?
Mama: She read five of them. I was two hours with her.
Katrin: What . . . did she say about them?
Mama (*quietly*):   She say they are not good.
Katrin (*turning away*): Well, I knew that. It was hardly worth your going to all that trouble just to be told that.
Mama: She say more. Will you listen, Katrin?
Katrin (*trying to be gracious*):   Sure. Sure. I'll listen.
Mama: I will try and remember. She say you write now only because of what you have read in other books, and that no one can write good until they have felt what they write about. That for years she write bad stories about people in the olden times, until one day she remember something that happen in her own town . . . something that only she could know and understand . . . and she feels she must tell it . . . and that is how she write her first good story. She say you must write more of things you know . . .
Katrin: That's what my teacher always told me at school.
Mama: Maybe your teacher was right. I do not know if I explain good what Miss Moorhead means, but I think I do. Your story about the painter who is blind . . . that is because . . . forgive me if I speak plain, but it is important to you . . . because you are the dramatic one, as Papa has said . . . and you think it would feel good to be a painter and be blind and not complain. But never have you imagined how it would be. Is true?

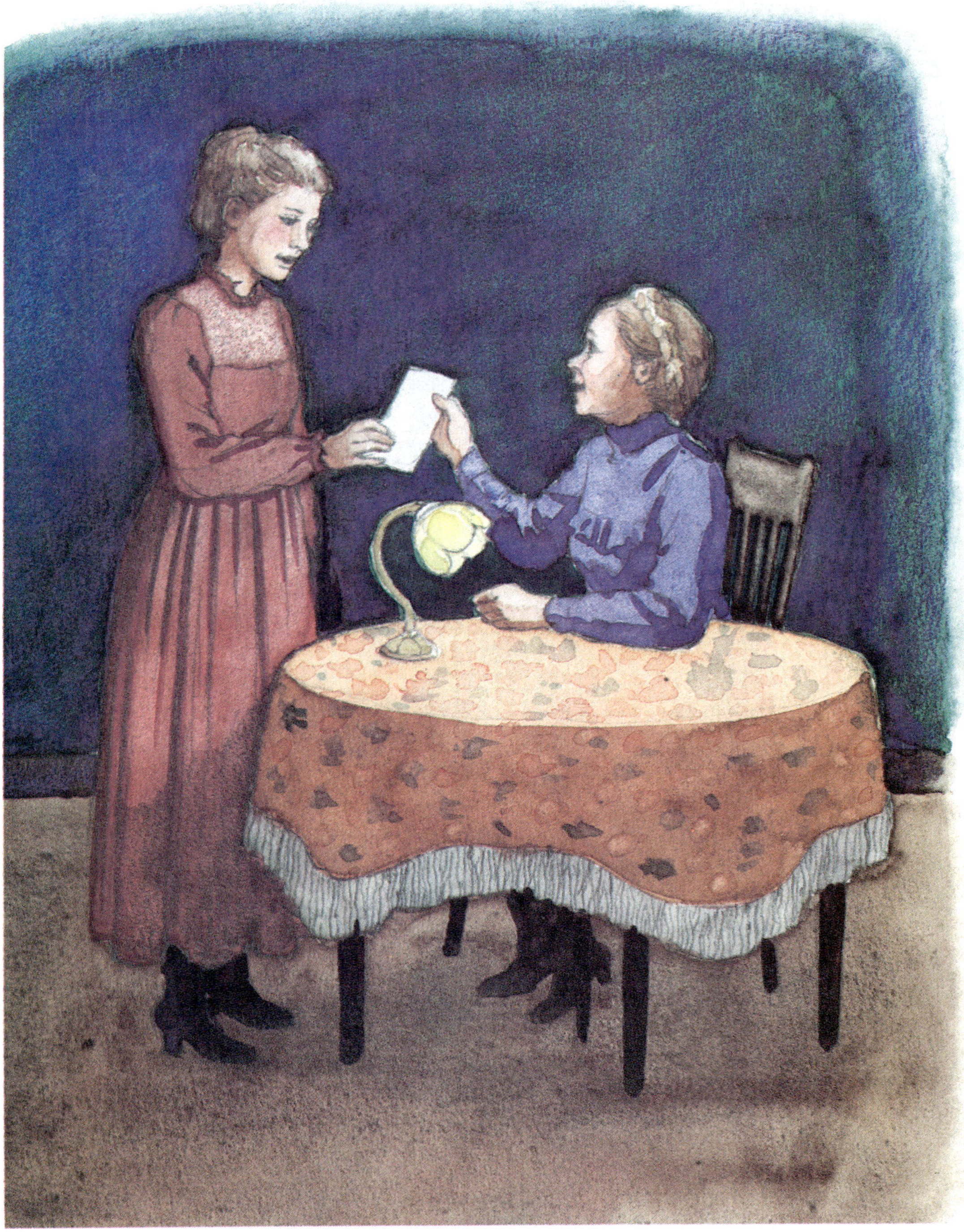

Katrin (*subdued*): Yes, I . . . guess it's true.

Mama: But she say you are to go on writing. That you have the gift. (*Katrin turns back to her, suddenly aglow.*) And that when you have written story that is real and true . . . then you send it to someone whose name she give me. (*She fumbles for a piece of paper.*) It is her . . . agent . . . and say she recommend you. Here. No, that is recipe she give me for goulash as her grandmother make it . . . here . . . (*She hands over the paper.*) It helps, Katrin, what I have told you?

Katrin (*subdued*): Yes, I guess it helps. Some. But what have I got to write about? I haven't seen anything, or been anywhere.

Mama: Could you write about San Francisco, maybe? Is fine city. Miss Moorhead write about her home town.

Katrin: Yes, I know. But you've got to have a central character or something. She writes about her grandfather . . . he was a wonderful old man.

Mama: Could you maybe write about Papa?

Katrin: Papa?

Mama: Papa is fine man. Is wonderful man.

Katrin: Yes, I know, but . . .

Mama (*rising*): I must go fix supper. Is late. Papa will be home. (*She goes up the steps to the curtains, and then turns back.*) I like you should write about Papa. (*She goes inside.*)

Katrin (*going back to her seat behind the desk*): Papa. Yes, but what's he ever done? What's ever happened to him? What's ever happened to *any* of us? Except always being poor and having illness, like the time when Dagmar went to hospital and Mama . . . (*The idea hits her like a flash.*) Oh . . . Oh . . . (*Pause—then she becomes the Katrin of today.*) And that was how it was born . . . suddenly in a flash . . . the story of "Mama and the Hospital" . . . the first of all the stories. I wrote it . . . oh, quite soon after that. I didn't tell Mama or any of them. But I sent it to Miss Moorhead's agent. It was a long time before I heard anything . . . and then one evening the letter came. (*She takes an envelope from the desk in front of her.*) For a moment I couldn't believe it. Then I went rushing into the kitchen, shouting . . . (*She rises from the desk, taking some papers with her, and rushes upstage, crying.*) Mama. Mama. (*The curtains have parted on the* *kitchen—and the family tableau—Mama, Papa, Christine, and Nels. Dagmar is not present. Katrin comes rushing in, up the steps. The turntable revolves out as soon as she has left it.*) Mama . . . Mama . . . I've sold a story!

Mama (*at table*): A story?

Katrin: Yes, I got a letter from the agent . . . with a check for . . . (*gasping*) five hundred dollars!

Mama: Katrin . . . is true?

Katrin: Here it is. Here's the letter. Maybe I haven't read it right. (*She hands the letter. Papa and Mama huddle and gloat over it.*)

Christine (*behind Mama's chair*): What will you do with five hundred dollars?

Katrin: I don't know. I'll buy Mama her warm coat, I know that.

Christine: Coats don't cost five hundred dollars.

Katrin: I know. We'll put the rest in the Bank.

Nels (*kidding*): Quick. Before they change their mind.

Katrin: Will you, Mama? Will you take it to the Bank downtown tomorrow? (*Mama looks vague.*) What is it?

Mama: I do not know how.

Nels: Just give it to the man and tell him to put it in your account, like you always do.

(*Mama looks up at Papa.*)

Papa: You tell them . . . now.

Christine: Tell us what?

Mama (*desperately*): Is no bank account! (*She rises, feeling hemmed in; sits on bench.*) Never in my life have I been inside a bank.

Christine: But you always told us . . .

Katrin: Mama, you've always said . . .

Mama: I know. But was not true. I tell a lie.

Katrin: But why, Mama? Why did you pretend?

Mama: Is not good for little ones to be afraid . . . to not feel secure. (*rising again*) But now . . . with five hundred dollar . . . I think I can tell.

Katrin (*going to her, emotionally*): Mama!

Mama (*stopping her*): You read us the story. You have it there?
Katrin: Yes.
Mama: Then read.
Katrin: Now?
Mama: Yes. No — wait. Dagmar must hear. (*She opens pantry door and calls.*) Dagmar.
Dagmar (*off*): Yes, Mama?
Mama (*calling*): Come here, I want you.
Dagmar (*off*): What is it?
Mama: I want you. What is it called . . . the story?
Katrin: It's called "Mama and the Hospital."
Papa (*delighted*): You write about Mama?
Katrin: Yes.

(*Dagmar comes in.*)

Dagmar: What is it? What do you want?
Mama: Katrin write story and get five hundred dollars. She read it to us. I want you should listen. (*Dagmar sits on the floor at Mama's feet.*) You are ready, Katrin?
Katrin: Sure.
Mama: Then read.
Katrin (*reading*): "For as long as I could remember, the house on Steiner Street had been home. All of us were born there. Nels, the oldest and the only boy . . ." (*Nels looks up, astonished to be in a story.* "my sister, Christine . . ." (*Christine does likewise.*) "and the littlest sister, Dagmar . . ."
Dagmar: Am I in the story?
Mama: Hush, Dagmar. We are all in the story.
Katrin: "But first and foremost, I remember Mama." (*The lights begin to dim and the curtain slowly to fall. As it descends, we hear her voice continuing.*) "I remember that every Saturday night Mama would sit down by the kitchen table and count out the money Papa had brought home in the little envelope . . ."

(*By now, the curtain is down.*)

You may want to read **Mama's Bank Account** *by Kathryn Forbes to learn more about Mama and her family.*

Discuss the Selection

1. How do wit and wisdom — especially that of Mama — help the family adjust to life in America?
2. When Katrin's manuscript is rejected, she thinks about quitting school and giving up writing. At this point, Mama steps in and tries to help. Summarize what Mama did in this example of motherly love.
3. Katrin resolved her writing problem by acting on Mama's advice from the famous writer. Specifically, what did Katrin do?
4. Miss Moorhead told Mama that Katrin should write about what she knows herself. What do you think of this advice?
5. Katrin received a letter from her literary agent and a $500 check for her story. What was revealed when Katrin said that she wanted to put the money in Mama's account at the bank? How did you feel about that revelation?

Apply the Skills

Point of view is the vantage point from which a story is told. In the first-person point of view, the story is told by one of the characters in his or her own words, from the "I" vantage point, as in "I Remember Mama."

In this play, Katrin's memories seem to come alive on the stage. Why do you suppose the storyteller chose to use Katrin's point of view?

Thinking About "Wit and Wisdom"

Wit can mean several things. It can mean a sense of humor. It can mean an ability to use words cleverly to make a point. And it can mean intelligence in dealing with life. All three kinds of wit are valuable assets for a person. Each of the stories in this unit shows characters who have wit in one or more of its varieties. Their wit helps them to acquire wisdom, the knowledge of what is right and true, and to apply this wisdom to life.

Hildegarde Dolson learned the value of a sense of humor as she grew up in a large and lively family. The Dolsons had the wit to cope cleverly with many family problems. So did Mama, in her family. She used her wit, and her wisdom, to help Katrin with her problems as an aspiring writer.

James Thurber had the wit to laugh at situations that others might find exasperating. He maintained his sense of humor as he dealt with his wandering dog, Jeannie. Similarly, the Canon's sister, Delia, dealt wisely with her brother's absent-minded wanderings. And the Canon certainly had the wit to make the most of his adventure.

A sense of humor gives us the ability to laugh at ourselves. Forever-Mountain was conceited about his wrestling ability until he was defeated by three strong women. Through this humbling experience, he learned not to take himself so seriously.

A person who has the wit to express thoughts well can do so in a serious as well as a humorous way. Annie John, who had a mischievous sense of humor, could also write a serious essay.

Another character with wit and wisdom is Jimmy Valentine. He had always dealt shrewdly with life. But when he abandoned his cleverness and made an unselfish decision, he acted with the greatest wisdom of all.

As you read other fiction and nonfiction stories, look for the three kinds of wit — sense of humor, cleverness with words, and intelligence in dealing with life. And observe how often wit and wisdom go hand in hand.

1. State the theme (main idea) of "Jimmy Valentine" and of "Annie John." One theme is presented in a humorous way and the other in a serious way. Which story did you like better? How did the humorous or serious tone of the story help communicate the theme?

2. Find an example of humorous dialogue in two of the selections. Tell why you find these examples funny.

3. Tell a humorous anecdote about an imaginary family.

4. Write a brief essay in which you express your point of view on a subject of interest to you. The essay can be humorous or serious. Make sure your essay has an introduction, a body, and a conclusion.

5. "We Shook the Family Tree" contains many humorous anecdotes. Retell one of these anecdotes from a serious point of view.

6. The authors of "We Shook the Family Tree" and "Scenes from I Remember Mama" wrote about their own life experiences. Why does their writing strike a sympathetic chord in their readers?

7. Retell a story in the unit from the point of view of a first-person participant. To make it more interesting, pick someone who is not a main character. For example, tell the story of "Jimmy Valentine" from the point of view of his fiancée, Annabel. Or, tell the story of "The Far Forests" from the point of view of a giant moth. Keep your story brief.

Read on Your Own

The Far Forests by Joan Aiken. Viking. Included are fifteen tales of fantasy, mystery, and wit by a master storyteller.

Suds by Judie Angell. Bradbury Press. You should recognize your favorites in this entertaining spoof of soap operas. It features a teenage girl, her parents, and her friends.

My Tang's Tungled and Other Ridiculous Situations collected by Sara and John Brewton. Crowell. A collection of humorous poems, limericks, tongue-twisters, and other nonsense by such poets as Lewis Carroll, Ogden Nash, and David McCord.

The Brainstormers: Humorous Tales of Ingenious American Boys edited by Dale B. Carlson. Doubleday. Twenty stories of humorous escapades, madcap schemes, pranks, and "brilliant" inventions by such well-known fictional characters as Tom Sawyer, Henry Huggins, and Homer Price.

Bagthorpes vs. the World by Helen Cresswell. Macmillan. One of five books of the Bagthorpe Saga, which chronicles the wacky adventures of a very unusual British family and their dog, Zero, who is the star of TV dog food commercials.

We Shook the Family Tree by Hildegarde Dolson. Random House. The hilarious adventures of the Dolson family and of Hildegarde, who goes to New York City to seek fame and fortune as a writer.

Mama's Bank Account by Kathryn Forbes.
Harcourt Brace Jovanovich. Included are the seventeen short stories that inspired the productions of *I Remember Mama*.

Growing Up Laughing compiled by Charles Keller. Prentice-Hall. In these short selections, notable humorists from Mark Twain to Bill Cosby tell about the funny side of growing up.

Annie John by Jamaica Kincaid. Farrar, Straus & Giroux. This talented young writer has the power to draw the reader into Annie John's thoughts and feelings as she experiences growing up on an island in the West Indies.

Three Comedies of American Family Life: I Remember Mama by John van Druten; **Life with Father** by Howard Lindsay and Russell Crouse; **You Can't Take It with You** by Moss Hart and George Kaufman. Edited by Joseph Mersand. Washington Square Press. Three very funny plays that were long-running Broadway hits and later were popular movies. The plays present three very different families, their adventures, and their misadventures.

Tatterhood and Other Tales edited by Ethel Johnson Phelps. Feminist Press. A collection of folktales from all over the world about daring, wise, and clever girls and their exploits.

Whoppers: Tall Tales and Other Lies Collected from American Folklore by Alvin Schwartz. Lippincott. This collection of outlandish ''lies'' told by early American settlers is as funny today as it was in frontier days.

Thurber's Dogs by James Thurber. Simon & Schuster. This is a collection of Thurber's best stories, fables, essays and cartoons, all dealing with one of his favorite subjects — dogs.

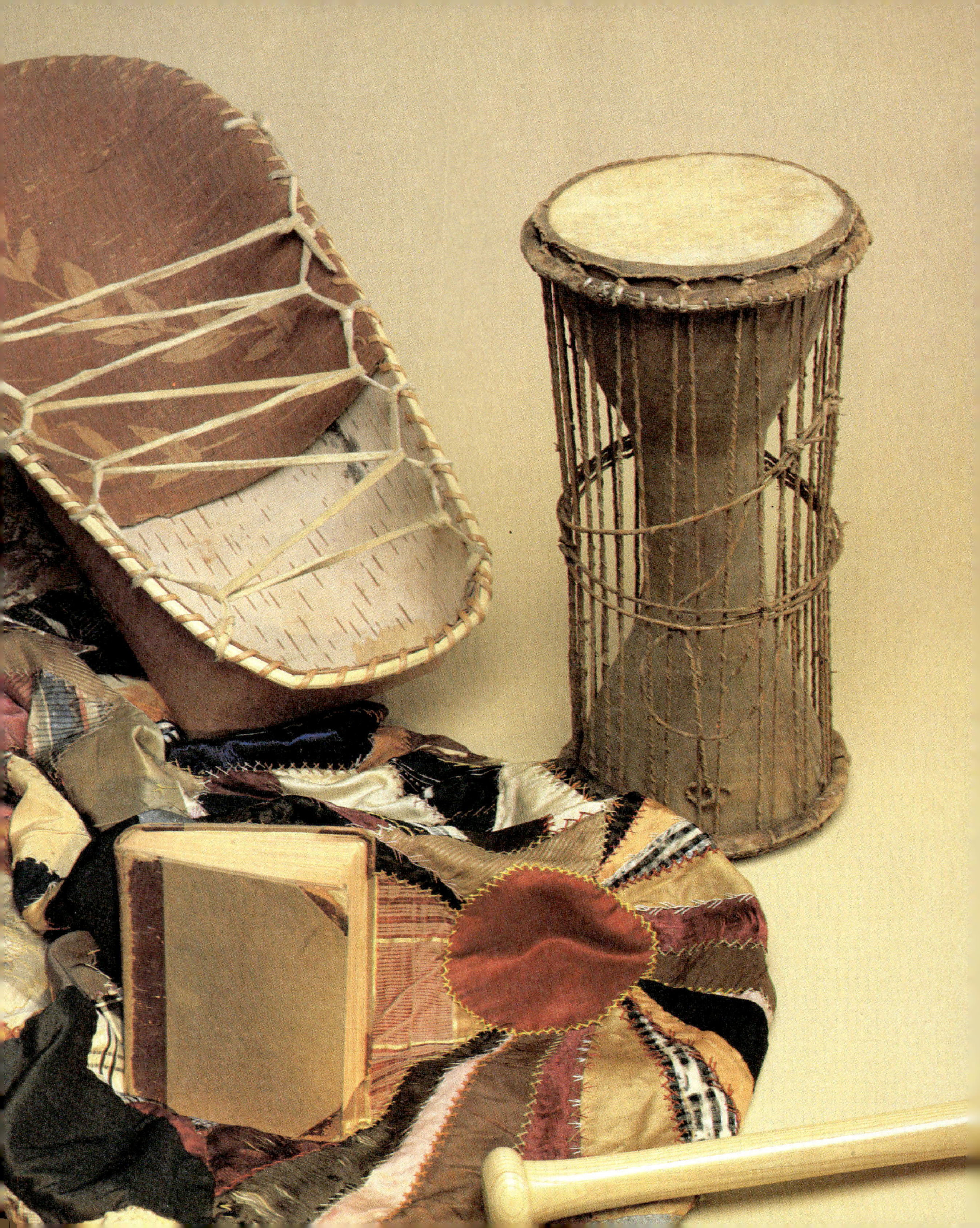

Unit 4
Legacies

Each of us is more than just an individual. We are all part of the great chain of history. Each of us receives a valuable inheritance—a legacy—from those who lived before us. Our knowledge comes from discoveries of the past. Almost everything we value comes from those who have lived before us.

Our heritage comes first from our family and later from our national identity. We are all Americans, but each of us has another tradition—that of our ancestors from Europe, Africa, Asia, South America, and the Caribbean, or from the native Americans: the American Indians and the Eskimos.

This legacy—of being Americans and also part of another tradition—gives us many things of value. We learn languages and customs. We have special celebrations and holidays, music and dances, foods we love and games we play. Within our families, there are traditions that are part of our heritage. Some traditions consist of ways of working and playing, family ideals and beliefs, family jokes and stories. Some parts of family heritage are things we can touch—photo albums, paintings, diaries and letters, a quilt, an old piece of furniture, or a special piece of jewelry.

The selections you will read in this unit are all about legacies and how they affected the lives of different people. As you read, notice what part of their heritage became important to them and how this heritage influenced their actions.

Literature Study

Nonfiction

Nonfiction describes real people, events, and ideas. Instead of whisking you off to an imaginary place like Oz, nonfiction presents the world as it is now or as it once was. Any person, event, or idea can be the topic of a nonfiction work. These works are wide and varied. They include biographies and autobiographies, interviews, essays, news stories, and journals. Nonfiction also includes hundreds of textbooks on different subjects.

Biographies, Autobiographies, Interviews

Many works are written about people, especially famous people. A work that describes a person's life can be in the form of an autobiography, a biography, or an interview. In **autobiographies** people describe the events of their lives. The story of one person's life written by another person is called a **biography**. Biographies and autobiographies are very popular because they allow readers to share parts of famous people's lives.

An **interview** is a conversation between an interviewer and another person. An interviewer might ask a famous person, such as a movie star, "Why did you decide to become an actor? What was it like to grow up in Texas?" Since the reader is interested in what the famous person has to say, good interviewers try to keep their own opinions to themselves.

Essays

An **essay** is a short piece of writing that presents a point of view. An essay may be humorous or serious. The informal essay is conversational and often tells much about the writer's personality, while the formal essay is more serious.

News Stories, Features, Editorials

Straight news stories make up most of the first page of a newspaper. These news stories present up-to-date events of wide public interest. **Feature stories** cover information that was not covered in the straight news stories of the day. Feature stories often have a distinctive viewpoint. Unlike straight news, **editorials** focus on writers' opinions on topics of interest to the public.

Diaries, Journals

Diaries are day-by-day accounts of events in a person's life. Diaries are also known as **journals**. By keeping a diary, you can express your experiences, thoughts, and wishes. A diary also serves as a record of events that might be difficult to recall at a later time.

Nonfiction can entertain, inform, explain, or persuade. In nonfiction, as in fiction, you will find these four styles of writing: description, narration, persuasion, and exposition.

Description is writing that presents details about a person, place, event, or almost anything else. Descriptive writing appeals to the senses of sight, sound, touch, smell, and taste. Some description is direct and factual; but more often, description helps establish a mood or stir an emotion.

Narration is writing that tells a story. In good narration, the order of events is clear. One event leads smoothly to the next. The writer tries to catch your interest at the very beginning. This makes you more alert and able to draw your own conclusions about the writing. A narrative may be book length, or a single paragraph such as an anecdote.

Persuasion is writing commonly found in newspaper editorials, political speeches, and print and broadcast advertisements. Persuasion is used to make you agree with the author's point of view on a topic, or perform an action, or do both.

Exposition is writing that presents information on a given topic. For example, the information in an article about sports medicine is exposition. Good expository writing focuses on ideas, logical presentation, and well-detailed facts. Although exposition is used in fiction as well as nonfiction, the most popular form it takes is in essays. Exposition is also that part of a play in which important background information is revealed to the audience.

Nonfiction has many categories of writing, including information on science, music, art, history, and other subjects. Many authors write nonfiction. Like fiction writers, nonfiction writers use description, narration, persuasion, and exposition in their craft.

Katherine Dunham was a pioneer in presenting the legacy of African and West Indian dance. How did she trace the roots of black American dance?

As you read this biography, think about the unusual steps Dunham took to accomplish her goal.

The African Roots of American Dance
from KATHERINE DUNHAM

by James Haskins

Katherine Dunham is known throughout the world as a dancer and choreographer, a creator of dances. She was the first to bring the rich heritage of West Indian and African dances to the stage so that people all over the world could enjoy them. Her dances were a reminder to other American blacks of the legacy of dance and music that their ancestors brought from Africa.

Katherine Dunham's lifelong interest in dance and theater began when she was a child in Chicago. She began to study ballet and modern dance as a teenager. By the time she was in college, she had decided to become a professional dancer. To help pay her college expenses, Dunham opened her own dance school. While teaching ballet to black youngsters, she realized that they and their parents did not value their own black dance heritage highly enough.

Katherine Dunham found out that it was tough making a go of a dancing school. But just when she was despairing most and thinking about giving up and becoming a schoolteacher, she had an exciting experience.

One day she heard that Dr. Robert Redfield, a professor in the University of Chicago's Department of Anthropology, was going to give a lecture on the bits and pieces of African culture that had survived in the New World after slavery. She went to hear this lecture, and she came away filled with excitement. Dr. Redfield had talked about African survivals in many areas of black American culture, but what had interested Dunham was what he had said about dance. Popular dances in America, like the lindy hop and the cakewalk, could be traced back to Africa!

Dunham had long felt that black dancing had a particular style about it. Now she knew why. These dances had roots in African dances. She wished she could go to Africa and find out just how the dances of the two cultures did connect. But since there didn't seem to be any way to do that, she decided that she could at least put what she had learned into her own dancing. And she decided that she could teach other young black dancers that they had a long tradition to be proud of.

Most black people were not proud of their African heritage in those days. The majority of books published in the United States talked about Africans as villagers who lived in grass huts and didn't wear enough clothes and had always been ruled by Europeans. In those days, if you really wanted to know about Africa, you had to go to a big library and find some musty old book that hardly anyone had taken out for years to find out the truth. Only in such a book could you find out that there had been great societies in Africa, with rich and powerful kings, more civilized than those in Europe at the same time. Katherine Dunham had started reading those musty old books. She didn't need them to convince her that modern popular dances started by blacks had their roots in Africa. She had felt it all along. She was excited by the idea.

At about this time she had something else to think about that gave her hope. Her friend Ruth Page had composed a ballet that was just what Katherine had been dreaming could be done. Based on a folktale from Martinique, an island in the

Lesser Antilles off Venezuela, it told of a devil woman who lured men to their death. Ruth asked Katherine to dance the major role, and Katherine's husband, Jordish McCoo, got to be part of the chorus of dancing men. The ballet was staged at the Chicago Opera House.

The ballet, which was called *La Guiablesse*, got very good reviews in the newspapers, and so did the dancing of its star, Katherine Dunham. As a result of her performance, she was chosen to hire and train one hundred fifty young black dancers for a program to be presented at the 1934 Chicago World's Fair. It also brought her to the attention of Mrs. Alfred Rosenwald Stern and the Rosenwald Fund.

The Julius Rosenwald Fund had established the Museum of Science and Industry in Chicago in 1929. It had also given large contributions to the University of Chicago. But its main reason for being was to help black people, especially in education. Altogether, the Fund helped to build five thousand schools for blacks in fifteen southern states. It also gave fellowships to individual black students so they could continue their education.

By the time Katherine Dunham came into contact with the Rosenwald Fund, she wanted very much to continue her education. She wanted to study anthropology and find out more about the peoples of the world and their cultures. She especially wanted to study the dances of black people and to trace those dances back to their roots in Africa. Ever since she had heard Dr. Redfield lecture on the subject at the university, she had been excited to learn all she could about black dancing. She had taken as many courses in anthropology as she could and was completely absorbed by the field. But she had noticed that these courses paid very little attention to dance, and by now she was convinced that dance wasn't just entertainment, it was an important social act.

People danced to communicate. They danced in a shared tradition. The dances of a culture were as important as their other customs. But few anthropologists had really studied the dances of various cultures and those that had did not study them closely enough.

Katherine Dunham recalls:

> I would wonder why reports on American Indian dancing, for example, were so disappointing. And of course the answer was that these anthropologists were not dancers. They could not participate, and so they could not really understand. They did their best work studying things they could participate in. . . . But dancing is different. It's very hard to describe, and it is almost impossible to understand unless you are a dancer.

Dunham realized that she would have to find out about the dances of various cultures herself. So when she learned that the Rosenwald people were interested in her, she decided to ask the Scholarship Fund to give her a grant so she could find out what she wanted to know.

The members of the Scholarship Committee of the Rosenwald Fund listened to many pleas for support each year. They were used to seeing hopeful young black students talk earnestly about their plans for study, and present books and manuscripts and college papers as evidence that they were serious about their work. But Katherine Dunham arrived for her interview without this kind of evidence. When the chairman of the committee asked her to explain why she wanted its financial support, Dunham said it was hard to explain in words. It would be much easier if she could show the committee what she wanted to do. The chairman told her to go ahead.

Katherine stood up, and before the eyes of the astonished committee she took off the jacket and skirt of her suit and removed her shoes. Dressed now in her black dancing leotard and tights, she began an exhibition of basic ballet steps. Then suddenly, she launched into a wild display that was her own idea of an African tribal dance. While the committee recovered from its shock, she put her suit and shoes back on and began to explain what it was she wanted to do.

She wanted to go where people still danced such ancient tribal dances. She wanted to find out why they danced this way. She wanted to learn how these dances had survived in the dancing of American blacks. Most of all, she explained, she wanted to understand dance as it began originally. American dancing was stilted and inhibited, and most Americans seemed to dance mostly because it was the thing to do. She believed that the original purpose of dancing, or at least the original effect of it, was to make people feel a part of the community. She emerged from the meeting with the feeling that she had impressed the committee. In fact, one member had suggested that the West Indies would be an excellent place for her to go to study. And she had agreed that it would. But all she could do was wait for their decision.

In January 1935 she received word that she had been granted a fellowship to go to the West Indies. At the age of twenty-five she had at last found her direction and people who believed in her enough to support her in pursuing her chosen path.

Once she had won the Rosenwald Fund grant, Dunham did not just pack up and take off for the West Indies, although that is what she wanted to do. The older and wiser people of the Rosenwald Scholarship Committee knew that if she was going to make the most of her chance to travel, she would have

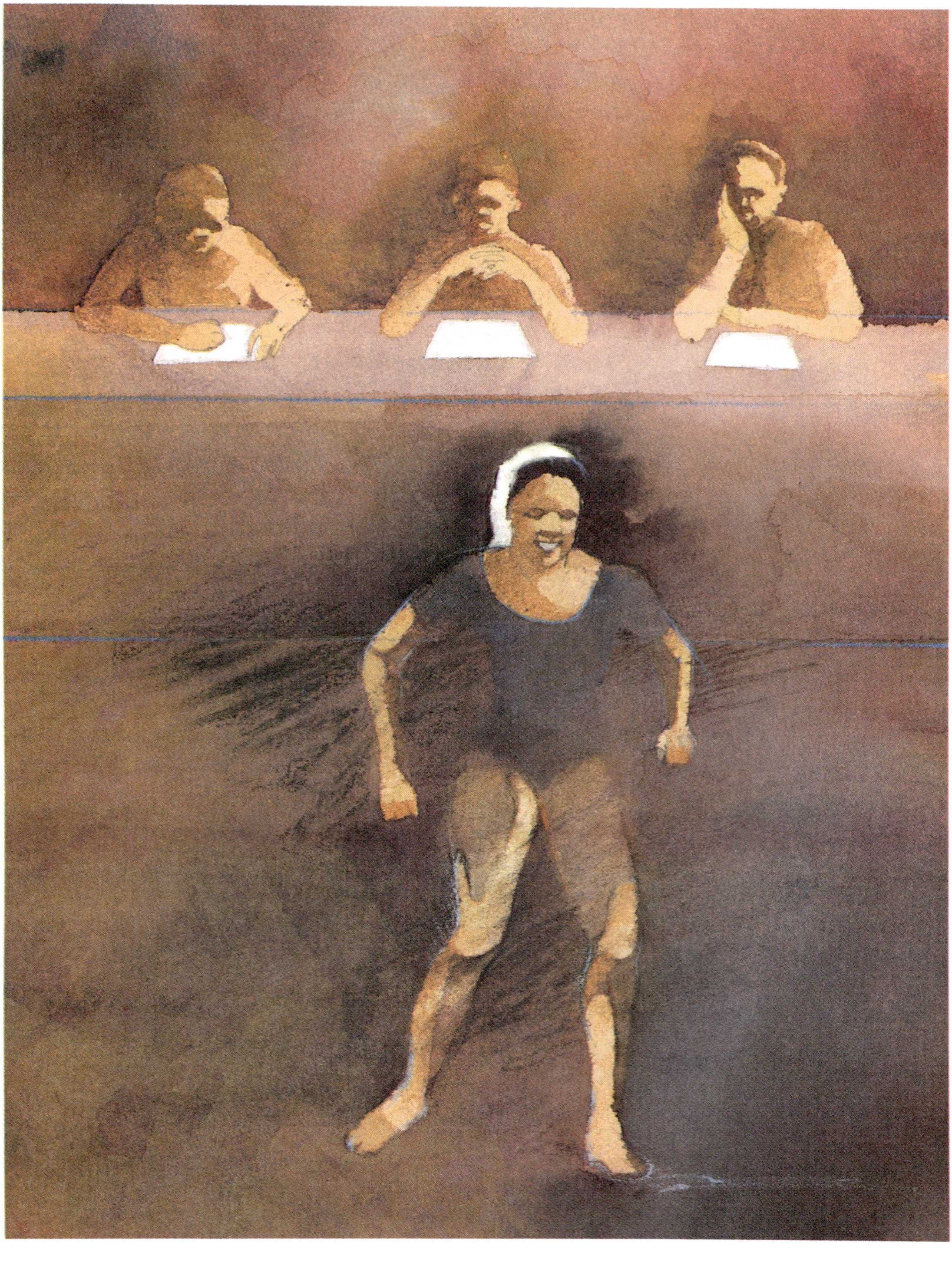

to be fully prepared. Of the $2,400 grant she received, $500 was for tuition and living expenses from March to June 1935 while she studied under Dr. Melville Herskovits, chairman of the Department of African Studies at Northwestern University in Chicago.

Dr. Herskovits is dead now, but he is still considered one of the greatest African scholars who ever lived. Nowadays, many colleges and universities have African Studies departments and fine scholars, but back in 1935 there were hardly any such departments. And there were hardly any professors like this man whose books and other writings remain required reading for anyone who wants to trace the African heritage of the black peoples of the world.

At first, Dunham was impatient with the work she had to do under Dr. Herskovits. She wanted to get out into "the field." But she soon learned that the professor had many important things to teach her. He taught her that she couldn't expect to learn much if she studied dance and nothing else. To really learn about the dances, she had to learn about the whole culture — what the people wore and what they ate and how they moved and spoke. He also taught her that if she wanted scholars to respect her work, she would have to learn how to make proper reports. She could not rely on just her memory or her notes. She would have to make records of her findings — photographs and tape recordings. To do this, she had to learn how to operate and take care of cameras and tape recorders.

She had to learn also how to enter and be accepted in a new culture. She could not just barge in and tell people she was going to study them. She had to understand that the people would be suspicious of her and that she would have to show them that she could be trusted. If she failed to do that, they would not accept her; her trip would be wasted because she would learn no more than an ordinary tourist. And finally, she had to learn to take care of herself because she was going into an entirely different world. Years before, she may have thought that going from Joliet to Chicago was going from one world to another, but at least both those worlds had the same food and the same conveniences like feather beds and toilets and hospitals. In the West Indies there were foods she had never eaten, a climate she had never lived in, diseases she had never

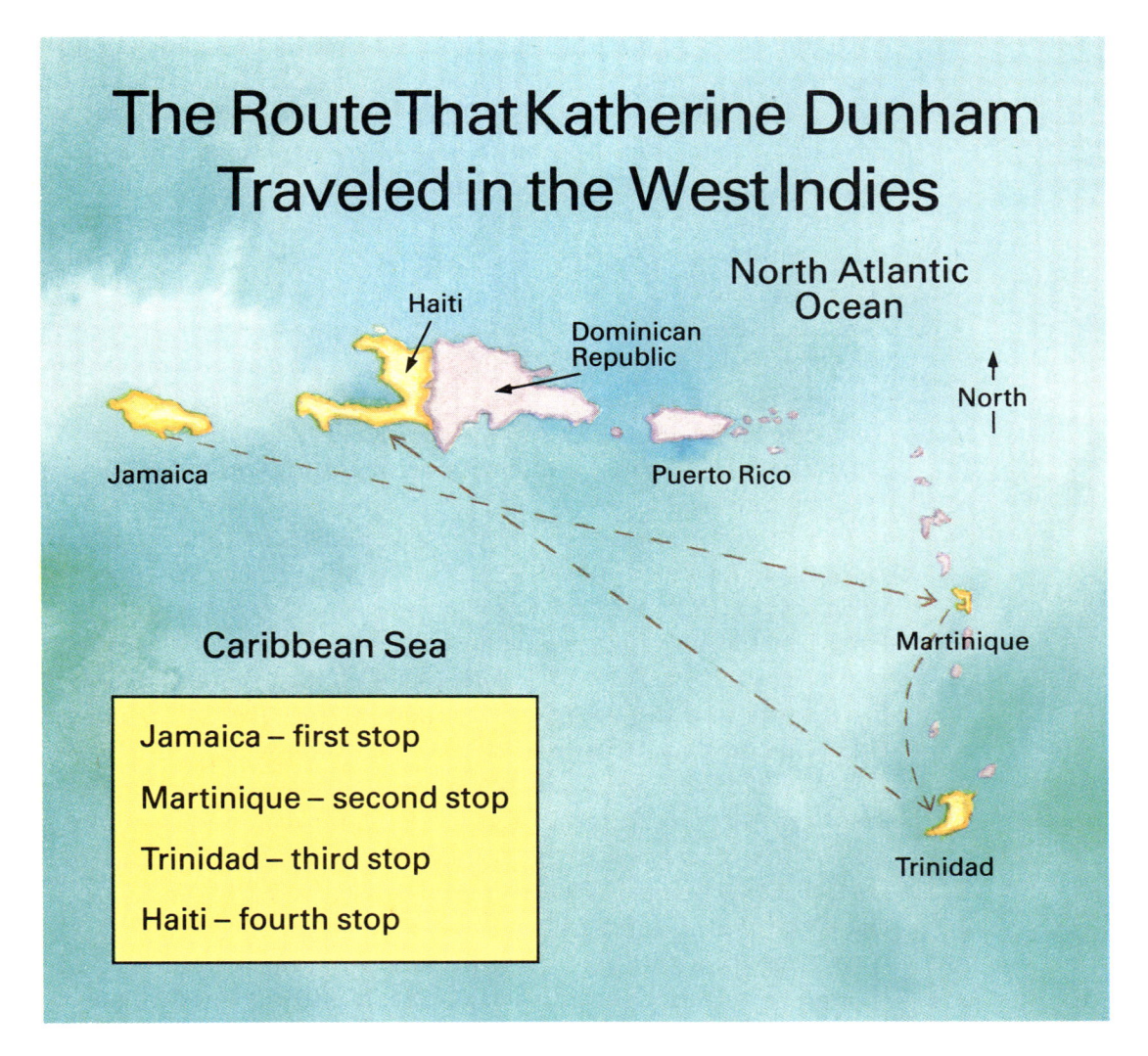

The Route That Katherine Dunham Traveled in the West Indies

Jamaica – first stop

Martinique – second stop

Trinidad – third stop

Haiti – fourth stop

heard of, and very few feather beds, porcelain toilets, or hospitals. She had to learn about medicines and what ailments they were for, what kinds of clothes were best for a tropical climate, how to keep her note paper and film and tapes from being destroyed by the abundant moisture. It was not long before Katherine Dunham forgot her impatience to get on with her trip. In fact, as June arrived, she wished she could spend many more months studying under Dr. Herskovits. She wondered if this three-month crash course in anthropology field work had prepared her enough for this exciting adventure that now seemed to be a little bit frightening, too.

In nervous moments, Dunham wondered how she could possibly gain acceptance among the people she wanted to study. She had learned from Dr. Herskovits that it was not enough to have some romantic idea of these people. She might want to study them, but they might not want to be studied. If she was not careful she could wind up as a tolerated outsider, and all she had learned about the techniques of field work would be useless.

In July 1935 the young woman whose former idea of a big trip had been to go to St. Louis, Missouri, took off for the West Indies. Her destination was the small village of northeast Jamaica called Accompong where Dr. Herskovits had recommended that she study the culture of the descendants of the famous Maroons.

The Maroons were slaves who escaped from their Spanish masters in Jamaica in 1655. Originally, these people had been brought to the Caribbean islands from Africa because the Spanish colonists in this part of the New World needed workers in their sugar cane fields. Britain also had colonies in the Caribbean, and in the 1650's the British began to take over the Spanish colonies. When the British attacked Jamaica in 1655, the slaves of the Spaniards saw their chance to escape. They went up into the mountains, and from their mountain strongholds they managed to beat back both the Spanish and the British. They began to be called Maroons because in old Spanish the word *maroon* means "mountaintop."

After a time, the new British rulers of the island gave up trying to defeat the Maroons. Instead, they signed a peace treaty with them. The Maroons got legal right to the lands they already controlled, and the British got relief from an embarrassing situation. Even now, people who know anything about the history of slavery, especially in the West Indies, have great respect for the Maroons. These people managed not only to escape from slavery but to stay free, even though armies were sent to recapture them. When Katherine Dunham went among them, they were still a proud, free people living in the mountains and very suspicious of outsiders. Dr. Herskovits and a few others had visited them for brief periods, but no outsider had ever lived among them for any length of time before Dunham arrived.

By the time Dunham went to Maroon country, she was twenty-six years old. By the standards of the hard life the Maroons lived she was already middle-aged. Maroon women her age had given birth to many children already, and their bodies were tired and worn, not lithe and supple as hers was. She was worlds away from them in experience, too. Most of the people she was about to study had never even been down from the mountains. Also, she might think of herself as somehow related to them because she was a black and so were they, but they could not see any relationship between themselves and her. The Maroons had intermarried in the nearly three hundred years since their escape. As a result, they were dark-skinned. By contrast, there stood Katherine Dunham, whose ancestry was not just African but Madagascan, French-Canadian, and even American Indian. She might have been of medium skin color in the United States, but here she was considered white.

Dunham had barely gotten used to these ideas when she came smack up against the practical differences of culture that Dr. Herskovits had warned her about. She slept on a mattress of river rushes that was laid on the floor. The Maroon food was so highly seasoned that she got stomachaches. She soon found out that the kerosene lamp she made notes by at night was such a luxury that she started feeling guilty about using it. And for a while she found herself in the defensive position of having to explain so much about who she was, what she was doing, and how her equipment worked that she began to wonder who was doing the field research — the Maroons or her.

After Katherine Dunham had been with the Maroons for a few days, she was overjoyed to be asked to attend a dance. She was so excited she could hardly wait. The invitation meant that she had behaved properly and was going to be let in on the tribe's ancient secrets, or so she thought. But when she arrived at the dance she was astonished and disappointed at what she saw. The women wore dresses and the men wore trousers. The one musician played a fiddle, and the dance was not much different from a plain old square dance. "For heaven's sake," she thought, "I could have stayed in Chicago and seen this!"

But she did not give up. Dr. Herskovits had warned her that she would not be accepted right away. She had an idea that the Maroons didn't just do square dances all the time. She watched and listened every day, and at night by her kerosene lamp she made notes about how the people dressed and behaved. She made friends among the Maroons, and gradually she learned that they had many ancient dances and rites. But these were discouraged by their chief, who thought that the ancient customs got in the way of the progress of his people. She learned, too, that most of the young people disapproved of the old dances. In feeling this way, they were no different from the young people of any culture, who think their parents' way of doing things is old-fashioned.

Although Dunham eventually got to see some of the old tribal dances, including a war dance that had come directly from Africa, she was disappointed in her visit to the Maroons. These people had been exposed to the outside world enough so that their culture was no longer the "pure" culture she wanted to find. She hoped she would have better luck in other parts of the West Indies.

In Martinique she was able to watch the war dance called *Ag'Ya* and other dances that had been done on the island as far back as anyone could remember. In Trinidad, she saw part of a Shango ceremony. Shango was the god of thunder and lightning worshiped by the Yoruba tribe in West Africa and brought to the New World by Yoruba slaves.

At last, in Haiti, she found what she had been looking for. Out in the "bush country," far away from the cities and towns, she found people whose belief in voodoo was as strong as it had been hundreds of years earlier.

The country now known as Haiti was discovered by Christopher Columbus in 1492 and was a Spanish possession until 1697, when Spain gave it up to France. Both the Spanish and the French imported African slaves to work the island's large sugar and coffee plantations, and because the plantations were so large and isolated from each other, the slaves were able to continue many of their African customs, including their religion. The majority of the slaves were of the Fon tribe from the Dahomey region of West Africa. Their religion, called *vodun* after the Fon word for god, came to be commonly known in the United States as voodoo. It was this strong religious tradition that helped the slaves to unite and overthrow their French masters in 1804. The new nation, which the revolutionaries called Haiti, was governed for a long time after that by men who were actually *vodun* priests.

By the time Katherine Dunham arrived on the island, Haiti was much like other Caribbean countries, at least on the surface. Dunham won immediate acceptance among the Haitian upper classes, but she was not interested in them. She traveled out to the country villages, where the people lived in grass huts and slept on rush floor mats. She made friends with these country people who lived and thought very much like their ancestors had a hundred or more years earlier. As they came to know and trust her, they told her more and more about their customs and their religious rites. She was invited to witness a ceremony in which an important priest who had died returned from the dead to name his successor. And finally she was allowed to take part in a ceremony of initiation into the ancient *vodun* cult. She eagerly accepted because, as she explains, "You can't know dances in Haiti without knowing the cult worship, because dance grows out of the demands of the gods. You hear a certain rhythm and without seeing what is being danced you know by the rhythm what the dance is and to what god it is being danced."

Katherine Dunham loved Haiti. It was the most beautiful place she had ever seen. She had made many friends of all classes there, and she did not want to leave them. But in June 1936 the period of her Rosenwald study grant was up, and she had to return to the United States. She had accomplished what she had set out to do. She had gathered material on the customs and ceremonies of people of African heritage. She had learned dances that seemed to her to link the dances of black Americans with the dances of Africans. On the personal level, she had discovered her own proud heritage and gained an understanding of her African roots. And she had learned that in order to dance the dances, or even interpret the dances, of the cultures she had visited, she would have to use every bit of her anthropological knowledge, and more.

Katherine Dunham

At age 40, she was world-renowned as a dancer and choreographer.

Katherine at age 6 or 7, about 1915.

She brought the dance and music of the West Indies to America.

Her costumes were authentic.

Many dances were set in Haiti.

467

Katherine Dunham's first career was as a dance teacher. She is shown here teaching ballet to black youngsters in 1938.

Since 1967, Katherine Dunham has been teaching dance, drama, and music to ghetto youth in East St. Louis, Illinois. Through her efforts Americans, both black and white, have gained a deeper appreciation of black dance in America and of its roots in Africa and the Caribbean.

She influenced a new generation of black dancers.

The dance "Rites of Passage" was based on her research in the West Indies. It was first performed in 1951.

Discuss the Selection

1. How did Katherine Dunham trace the roots of black American dance?
2. Describe the steps Dunham had to take to prepare for her journey to the West Indies.
3. Did Dunham personally feel she had achieved the purpose of her journey? Explain.
4. How did you feel when Dunham appeared before the Rosenwald Committee and danced for them instead of showing them a written application?
5. In what kind of ancient dance was Dunham finally allowed to participate? Why did she take part? Find that passage of the story and read it again.

Apply the Skills

The story of one person's life written by another person is called a biography. The subject is usually a famous person; for instance, an actor, an artist, or a sports figure.

In "The African Roots of American Dance," the author related Katherine Dunham's determination to find out more about the legacy of African and West Indian dance. What unusual steps did Dunham take to accomplish her goal? Cite two examples from this biography about her.

Think and Write

Prewrite

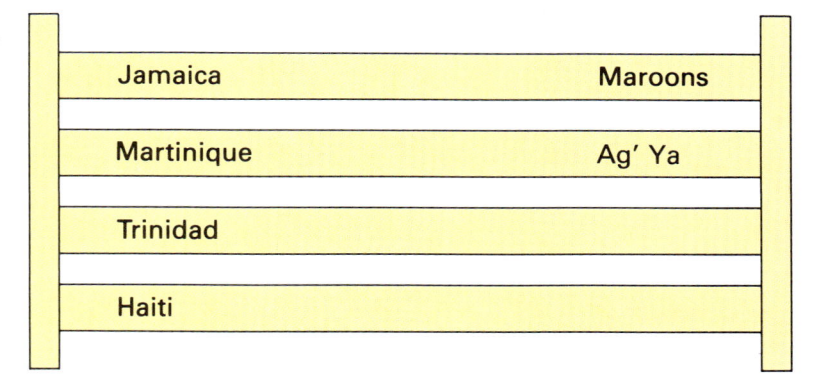

Jamaica	Maroons
Martinique	Ag' Ya
Trinidad	
Haiti	

Katherine Dunham visited four countries to learn about their customs and native dances. On the laddergram shown above, the four countries are shown on the left side. On the right side, native words from two of the countries are named. Copy the laddergram, adding the native words for the ceremonies Dunham saw in Trinidad and Haiti.

Compose

An explanatory paragraph tells how something is made or done.

Using the information in the laddergram and the selection, write an explanatory paragraph about the dances and ceremonies Dunham saw during her travels. Organize your explanation in logical order. Try to put yourself in the place of readers who may know nothing about your subject. You might start with this sentence: *In Jamaica, Katherine Dunham was invited to the dances of the Maroons.*

Revise

Read the paragraph you wrote. Check to make sure you haven't left something out. Is your explanation written in a clear, logical way? If not, revise your paragraph so that it is as clear and interesting as possible.

Comprehension Study

Fact and Opinion

Most of us have opinions about the people and events in our lives. We even have opinions about ourselves. An **opinion** is what a person thinks about someone or something. It is a belief, a view, or an attitude. While an opinion summarizes what we *believe* to be true, that viewpoint is not necessarily true.

Unlike an opinion, a **fact** is something that is known to be true or that can be proved to be true. Read the advertisement that follows. As you read, try to notice which sentences state facts and which sentences state opinions.

ANNOUNCEMENT:
HOT RIFFS TO PLAY SPECIAL CONCERT

The Hot Riffs are giving a special performance Friday, January 3, 1986, at 8:00 P.M. in the school cafeteria. Once you hear them, you'll agree that they are sensational. Attending this concert is the perfect way to start your weekend. They keyboard player uses a brand new synthesizer — the Omega. Once you hear this music, you won't want to listen to anything else!

As a skeptical reader of advertisements, what facts did you learn about the Hot Riffs after reading this announcement? Since it can be proved when and where the Hot Riffs are performing, the first sentence states a fact. The second sentence, however, is the advertiser's opinion. It cannot really be proved that this group is sensational. Some people may not find the Hot Riffs sensational. The third sentence is also an opinion. Attending the concert might be a perfect start to the weekend in the advertiser's opinion, but probably not in everyone's view. The advertiser's claim is not one that can be proved. The fourth sentence states a fact. The kind of synthesizer used by the keyboard player can be proved. The player either uses the Omega or does not. It also can be proved whether the Omega is a new synthesizer. The last sentence is sheer opinion. It is unlikely that after hearing the music, you won't want to hear any other music. The statement is slanted and cannot be proved.

Opinions Based on Facts

When scientists work with proven facts, they try to find ways to explain those facts. A **hypothesis** is an idea assumed to be true for the sake of argument or further study. It is an attempt to explain scientific facts. As you read the following paragraph, look for what could be called hypothesis and what could be called fact.

> A French scientific team has suggested that changes in the earth's climate may be caused by changes in the earth's core. The core radius of the earth is 2,180 miles, but only its outer layer is thought to affect climate. This molten layer is sixty miles thick and may circulate unevenly. The result would be changes in the earth's spin rate. The movement of oceans and the air would also be affected, causing major climate changes. Such changes have happened in recent years. The North Pole, for example, moved seventy miles in 1973. Skeptics argue that these changes are merely local. Others say sunspots also cause such changes. All agree that more observation is needed to find out what is happening in the earth's core.

The first sentence presents a hypothesis offered by a group of French scientists. The second and third sentences present information about the earth's core radius and molten layer. The fourth and fifth sentences try to support the hypothesis by describing changes in the earth's spin rate and air and ocean movement. Information about these changes and the movement of the North Pole follows in the sixth and seventh sentences. In the eighth and ninth sentences the author reveals the opinions of those who disagree with the French team's hypothesis. Finally, in the last sentence, the author tells you that more facts are needed before the hypothesis, the scientific opinion in the first sentence, can be proved true or false.

Opinions Based on Demonstrated Facts

Authors do not always choose to support their opinions with stated facts. In such cases, they probably think that the facts are obvious to the reader. For example, consider the following opinion: *I think that the Mojave Desert is an awful place to live.* Why do you suppose that an author might not find it necessary to support that opinion with stated facts? What facts might the author expect most readers to know about the Mojave Desert?

> Temperatures are extremely hot.
> The supply of water is limited.
> Food and other necessities are scarce.
> Population is sparse.

Since the author could expect most readers to know something about desert life, it would not be necessary to state all the facts.

Sources of Opinions

A good writer can help you decide how reliable an opinion is. Some opinions are more reliable than others. The value of a particular opinion depends on its source. For example, suppose you wanted an opinion about which microphone to use in taping the school chorus. Of the following sources, which would be most likely to give you valuable opinions?

- **a.** an advertisement for stereo components
- **b.** an article in an audio magazine
- **c.** an article in an independent consumers' magazine

In the advertisement for stereo components, the opinion would probably be that of the component maker or of the store selling the component. Both the maker and the seller want to sell their microphones. Therefore, the advertisement is unlikely to contain all the facts. It would give only the facts that said good things about the microphone.

How valuable are the opinions expressed in an audio magazine? Chances are the author examined different kinds of microphones before writing the article. You can also assume that the author knows something about components. If the author has nothing to gain or lose by expressing opinions about microphones, those opinions are likely to be valuable. Unlike the advertiser, the writer of a magazine article does not work for the company selling the product.

   An independent consumer's magazine is another source of valuable opinions. These magazines make detailed studies of the products they are reporting about. They generally present all the facts and then give opinions based on those facts.

Textbook Application: Fact and Opinion in Science

As a critical reader, it is important for you to be able to distinguish between fact and opinion. Read the following excerpt from a science textbook. Use the sidenotes to help you identify the facts and opinions.

Quasars and the Big Bang

Are the details about quasars in this paragraph presented as opinions or facts?

Quasars are by far the most distant objects in our universe, as well as the speediest and the most energetic. Some are billions of light-years away. They shine with the light of fifty to one hundred ordinary galaxies like the Milky Way. The speed at which quasars are moving away ranges from about 155,000 kilometers per second to 248,000 kilometers per second.

The Big Bang theory cannot be proved. It is a hypothesis.

The discovery of quasars furnishes evidence that may help scientists decide on a theory of the origin of the universe. The most generally accepted theory is that the universe began billions of years ago with a vast explosion. Hence this theory is known as the Big Bang theory. Since the universe is now expanding, the theory goes, there must have been a time when all the matter was close together. An explosion started to form the galaxies and gave them enough energy to move away from each other.

Where do quasars fit into the Big Bang theory? Some scientists think that a galaxy comes into being with a giant explosion, and that a quasar is just such an explosion — the birth of the galaxy. The quasar later becomes an ordinary galaxy.

Does this paragraph give a fact or an opinion about quasars and galaxies?

Astronomers have seen a quasar 9 billion light-years away. Think what this means. Astronomers looking at a quasar may be looking back at the birth of the universe itself! However, more information must be gathered. Perhaps some very different theory will come out of the work astronomers are now doing.

This much we do know. Quasars, galaxies, our own Milky Way, the stars, our sun, and the earth, in orbit around the sun, are all in motion. Stars, bright or dim, cool or hot, blue, yellow, or red, are changing — changing size, changing color, and changing luminosity. Galaxies are changing, too. The universe of which we are a part is always changing.

Why are the stars near the edge of the universe moving faster than those near the center? Even though the universe is billions of years old, most of its mass, according to the Big Bang theory, is located near its center. Therefore, gravitation would be strongest near the center of the universe. The stars closest to the center, then, are those most affected by the gravitational pull. The stars farther away from the center, where the gravitation is weaker, can move faster. Will these stars ever slow down?

Albert Einstein provided one possible answer. The stars could not continue to move faster and faster, he said, since no object can ever move faster than the speed of light. He proposed that when stars reached this maximum speed, they would reverse direction, moving back toward the center again. Thus, the universe would be continually expanding and contracting. Each contraction would result in a new big bang that would start the cycle all over again!

> Which facts in the paragraph that you just read support Einstein's theory — that is, his opinion — in this paragraph?

—*Matter: An Earth Science*,
Harcourt Brace Jovanovich

Answer these questions about the textbook excerpt.

1. Have astronomers settled the questions about the universe?
2. What statement about the universe is probably true?

American Indians have left us a rich legacy that has become part of our American heritage. In this piece of historical fiction, you will read how a Sioux woman won a new name for herself.

Although this story is fiction, it seems real because it is based on fact. As you read, notice the author's use of vivid factual details to describe Whirlwind's tribe.

How Whirlwind Saved Her Cub

by Dorothy M. Johnson

The Sioux Indians called themselves Lakotas, meaning "allies." The woman named Whirlwind in this story was born into the Oglala tribe of Lakotas in 1820. At that time these Plains Indians were prosperous hunters who owned huge herds of ponies. At thirteen, Whirlwind became a Buffalo Maiden in a religious ceremony that marked the beginning of her womanhood.

The story of Whirlwind's life is told in the novel *Buffalo Woman*. As the years go by, Whirlwind sees her tribe lose much of their hunting and grazing territory to the white settlers. By the 1870's the life of the Lakotas has become difficult. However, the Indians' pride in their heritage and way of life are still strong. In this episode, it is the spring of 1876. Whirlwind, now a grandmother, lives up to the high standard of courage that is her legacy as a Lakota woman.

Living in the Lodge:

Morning Rider, 36, head of the family
Young Bird, 32, wife of Morning Rider
Reaches Far Girl, 8, daughter of Young Bird and Morning Rider
Angry, 12, son of Young Bird, stepson of Morning Rider
Round Cloud Woman, 21, sister of Young Bird
Jumps, infant son of Round Cloud
Shoots, 13, motherless son of Morning Rider
Strikes Two, 24, son of Pemmican Woman, nephew of Whirlwind
Grandmother Whirlwind, 56, the old-woman-who-sits-by-the-door

---

There was plenty of work to be done in the lodge of Morning Rider, but there were plenty of women there to do it, so Whirlwind left on a project of her own.

"I'm going to dig roots," she explained to Round Cloud Woman. "Shall I take the baby for company?"

"He has just been fed, so take him if you like," her daughter-in-law agreed. His ears had not yet been pierced, so he did not have a boy name yet; his baby name was Jumps.

Whirlwind slung her baby grandson's cradleboard onto her back with the ease of long practice and went walking at a brisk pace, answering the baby when he made small sounds. She had two things hidden under her dress: her digging stick and a soft leather bag for carrying roots. She thought she knew where biscuit root would be growing—desert parsley. The roots were good to eat raw, or she might dry and grind them to make big flat cakes. The biscuit root made good mush with a wild onion cooked in it.

As a rule she liked company when she worked, but there was no point in inviting some other busy woman to come along to dig something that might not be there.

She did tell her destination to one person, her grandson Shoots, thirteen years old. She met him when he was returning on foot from his turn at guarding part of the vast pony herd.

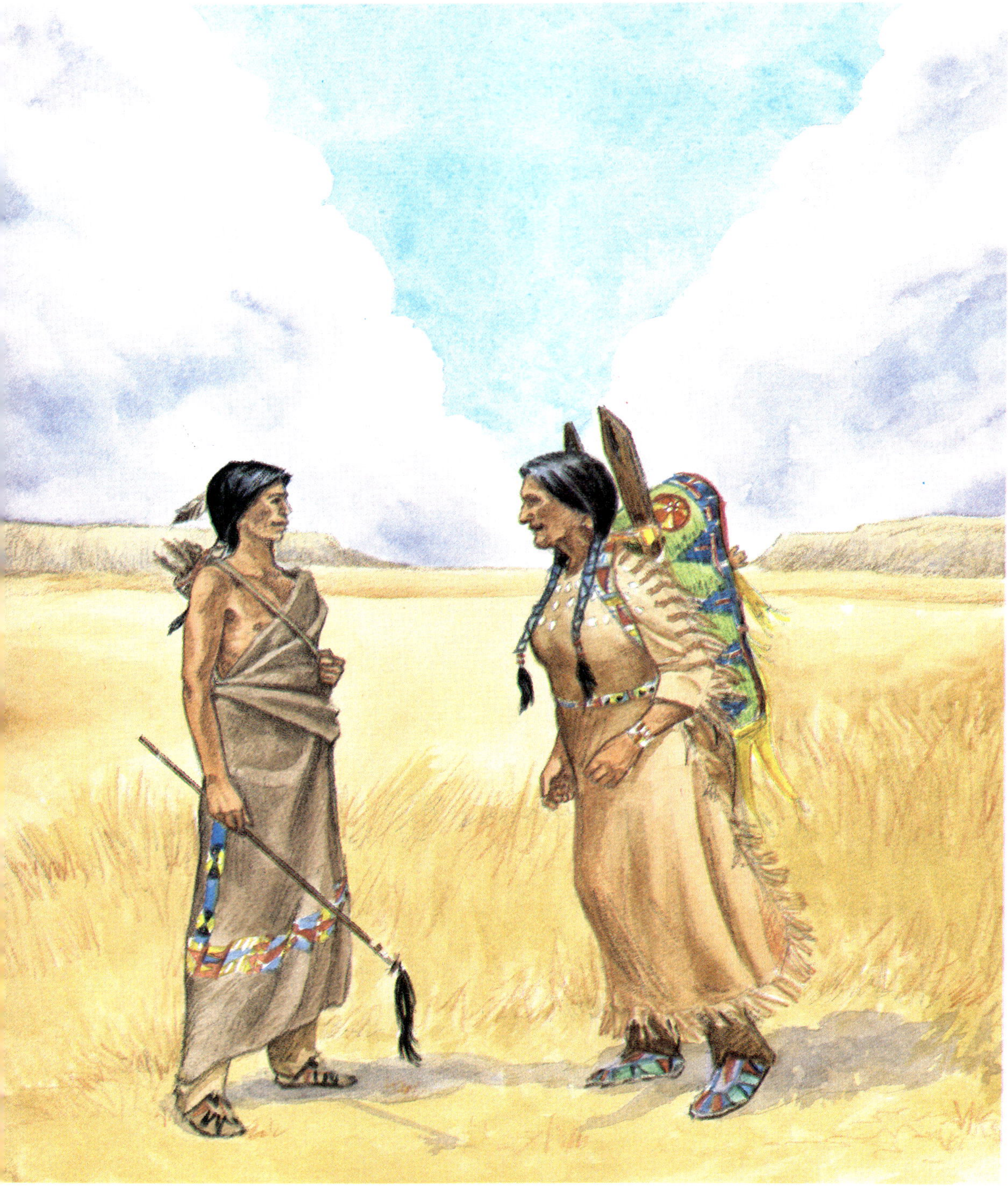

"Your little kinsman is going to help me dig biscuit root over there," she said. "Don't tell anybody where we are. Let the other women be sharp-eyed and find their own roots."

Shoots smiled and promised. He patted his baby kinsman's cheek and said, "Ho, warrior, old man chief. Take care of Grandmother." The baby jumped in his buckskin wrappings and cooed.

The biscuit root was plentiful on flat ground under a cutbank, just out of sight of the lodges. Whirlwind carefully propped the baby's cradleboard against a rock so the sun wouldn't shine in the child's face. Then, talking to him quietly, she began to dig skillfully, filling her buckskin bag, stooping and kneeling and rising again like a young woman. She was not young, she had lived through fifty-six winters, but she was strong and happy and healthy.

Her back was toward the baby when she heard him shriek with glee. She turned instantly—and saw a dreadful thing. Between her and the baby was another kind of baby, an awkward little bear cub, the cub of the frightfully dangerous grizzly bear. The cub itself was harmless, but the old-woman bear, its mother, must be near, and she would protect it.

Whirlwind did not even think of danger to herself. She ran to save *her* cub. She snatched up the baby on his cradleboard and threw him, with all her strength, above her head toward the level top of the cutbank.

At that moment the old-woman bear appeared. She snarled and came running, a shambling, awkward-looking run but very fast.

Whirlwind saw with horror the cradleboard with its precious burden sliding back down the cutbank. She had been too close when she threw the baby upward. The baby was screaming. Grandmother Whirlwind ran, picked up the cradleboard, ran back a few steps, and then threw hard again. This time the bundle stayed up there.

Whirlwind ran again toward the cutbank and climbed as fast as she could, digging into the dirt frantically with clutching fingers and digging toes.

The upper part of her body was on the flat ground and she was gripping a small tree as she tried to pull up her legs. Just then the old-woman grizzly reached up and tore at the legs with long, curved claws.

Whirlwind thought, I am dead — but my cub is safe if the sow bear does not come up here. No, I am not dead yet. I have something more to do. She screamed as hard as she could.

And her scream was heard.

Shoots was an untried boy. He had never even asked to go along with a war party to do errands for men of proved courage, to watch how a man should act. He had only thought of going on the hill to starve and thirst and lament to the Powers, praying for a powerful spirit helper. He had not yet done this thing. He believed his heart was strong. That day he found out.

  He was only playing when he heard the she-bear snarl. He was practicing a stealthy approach, intending to startle Grandmother Whirlwind. He was creeping quietly through thin brush, pretending that she was an enemy. He did not really expect to surprise her; she was usually very alert. She would scold when she discovered what he was up to, and then she would laugh at him because she had caught him.

He saw a bundle fly through the air and slide down the cutbank. It happened too fast for him to see that it was the cradleboard with his little kinsman. He heard fast movement in the weeds as Whirlwind ran back and threw the cradleboard again. He stood up, mouth open, just as she scrambled up the bank. With horror he saw the old-woman bear's claws rake her struggling legs.

With his heart in his mouth he did the best thing he could think of. He dropped his bow and grabbed the cub with both hands, so that it squalled with fear and pain. Then he threw it hard — past its mother.

Hearing her child cry, the woman bear whirled away from the cutbank to protect her cub. Shoots snatched up his bow; it was a good one, as strong as he could pull, and in a quiver on his shoulder he had six hunting arrows tipped with sharpened iron. At his waist he had a good steel knife.

But his enemy was better armed, with twenty immensely long, curved, sharp, death-dealing claws and a mouthful of long, sharp teeth, and she weighed more than five times as much as he did. She was protected by thick fur. Shoots was lightly clad.

He stood his ground and fired his arrows at her, fast but very carefully. Few grizzlies had ever been killed by one man alone; there were true tales of some bears killing men even after they should have been dead themselves. The woman bear yelled in pain and fury. She batted at the arrows deep in her flesh. She bit at them. But she kept coming.

Then Shoots did the last thing he could do, because it was too late to run. While the grizzly fought at the arrows, especially one that had gone into her left eye, he leaped on her back. With all his strength he sank his good steel knife into her throat, through the heavy fur and hide.

Then, as Grandmother Whirlwind had done, he clambered up the cutbank while the bear groped and swiped at him. He wondered why he could not see very well. He wondered who was screaming. He wondered if this was the day he was going to die.

Whirlwind, lying helpless, screamed louder when she saw him with blood running down his face, but he did not even know blood was there.

She cried, "Take the baby and run!" in so commanding a voice that he never thought of doing otherwise. With the cradled baby under one arm, he ran toward camp, howling for help, but stumbling.

His yells were heard. Two men on horseback lashed their ponies and met him. One seized the squalling baby. The other pulled Shoots up behind him on the pony. They rode fast toward where Whirlwind lay.

They leaped off — the one with the baby hung the cradleboard on a tree branch — and Shoots tumbled off. He had just realized that there was something he ought to do to prove his valor. He did something that his people talked about for many years afterward. While the men knelt by Whirlwind, he slid down the cutbank, picked up his bow, and struck the bear with it. She was coughing and dying. He shouted, as warriors do, "I, Shoots, have killed her! I count the first coup!"

Whirlwind and the men above heard him say it. They shouted in wonder and admiration. For a man to kill a grizzly without help was a very great thing indeed, and he had actually gone back into danger to count coup and claim the credit that was due him. He had counted coup against an armed enemy, after he was wounded, although he had never gone to war before that day. Now he was entitled to wear an eagle feather upright in his hair for first coup, a feather tipped with red paint because he had been wounded in battle.

He was the one who rode toward camp for more help while the two men stayed with Whirlwind and did what they could to make her comfortable. A crowd of people came hurrying after he delivered his message. There were women on horseback with poles and hides to make a pony drag for Whirlwind, because a great chunk of the muscles in the calf of one leg had been torn out by the she-bear's claws. There were men riding and boys riding, leading horses. More women brought supplies to help the wounded, and a medicine woman came with them, carrying her bundle of magic things. Round Cloud Woman came riding, crying, and Morning Rider came at a hard gallop to see about his mother and the infant.

Whirlwind fought them off, so keyed up and triumphant that she did not yet feel much pain. "Let me carry my grandchild!" she ordered when Round Cloud tried to take him away.

"I saved your cub," Whirlwind kept boasting, laughing and proud. "And Shoots saved us both. He is not a cub any more. He is a warrior!" She tried to make a victory trill in his honor, but as they lifted her gently onto the pony drag she fainted.

Morning Rider himself attended to the wound of his son Shoots, who did not even remember when the old-woman bear had slashed his forehead. The boy was able to laugh as he said, "She tried to scalp me!"

Morning Rider covered the wound with clotted blood from the bear and tied the flap of skin down with a strip of buckskin around the boy's head. He remarked fondly, "You will have a big scar there. The girls will keep asking you to tell how you got it. I am very proud of you."

Now maybe Grandmother Whirlwind would stop treating him like a little boy, to be ordered around.

He heard her shouting, laughing: "Behold Shoots—he is a warrior. He fought a grizzly bear and killed her."

Shoots shouted back, "Behold Whirlwind! She is a warrior. She was wounded in battle."

He began to sing a praise song for her, although he was feeling weak all of a sudden.

She laughed. "I am a warrior who was wounded while running away! Take the hide of the enemy—it belongs to Shoots."

Women were skinning out the dead bear and fighting with a horse that reared, not wanting to carry the hide on its back. The medicine woman filled a big dish with bear blood. She washed the great wound of Whirlwind's leg with water, chanting prayers. She covered the wound with the bear's thickening blood and then cut a big piece of the bear's hide, covering the wound and the blood with the raw side of the fresh hide.

She said with pity, "My friend, I think you will have trouble walking—always, as long as you live. But nobody will ever forget how you saved the boy cub today."

They cut off the immense claws of the woman bear; these were for Shoots. Not long afterward, when he went out to lament for a vision, his dream was a powerful one and when he made up his protective medicine bag, one of the claws was in it. The others he wore for a necklace when he dressed up.

That night the people had a victorious kill dance over the bloody hides of the great bear and the little one. Morning Rider rode around the camp circle leading a fine horse to give away, with Shoots riding beside him. Morning Rider sang:

> "A bear killed a mother long ago.
>   Now the woman's son has avenged her.
>   The warrior son has avenged his mother!"

Morning Rider gave the fine horse to a very brave old warrior, who gave Shoots a new name. The warrior shouted,

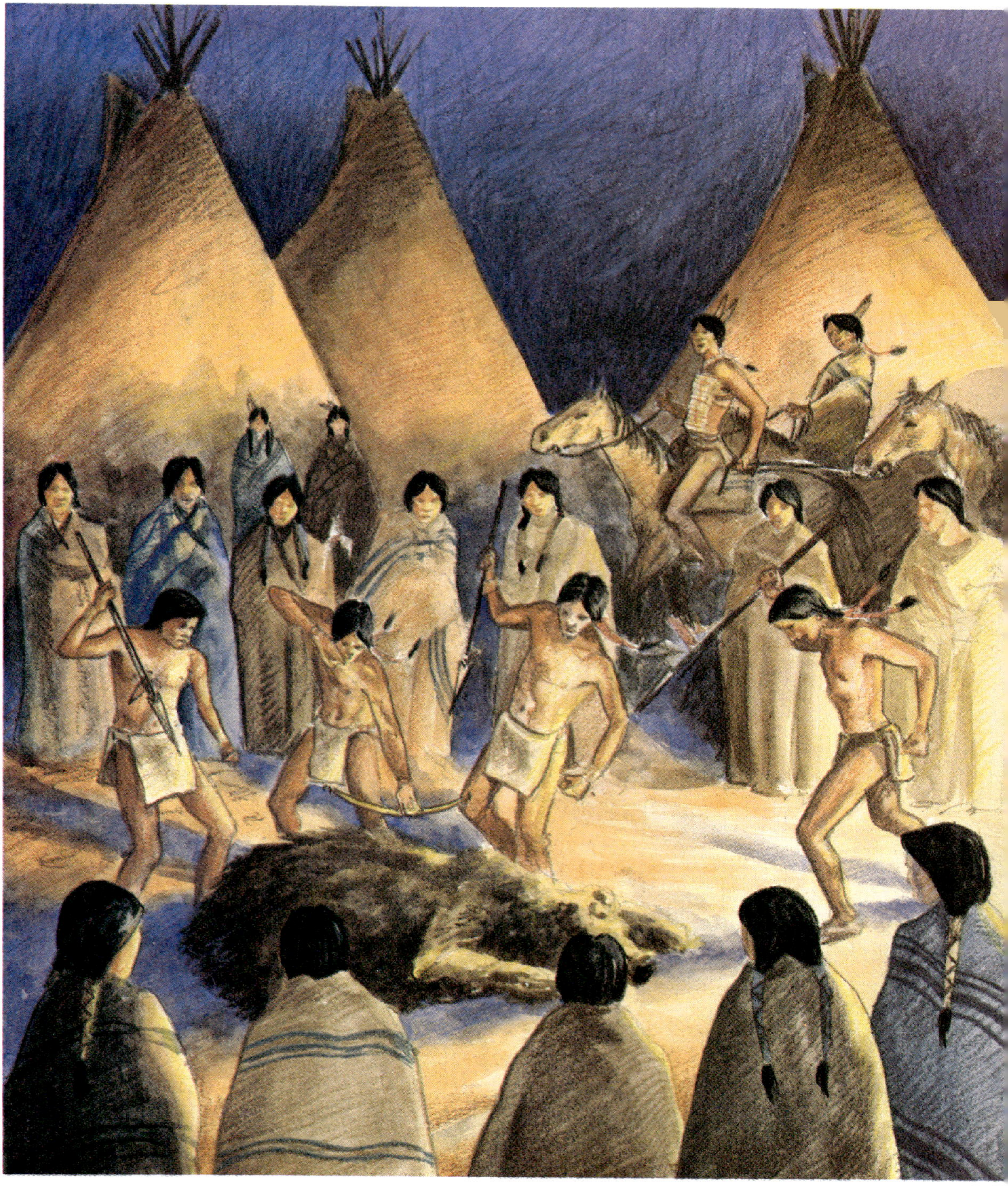

"The boy Shoots counted first coup on a grizzly bear and killed her to save two people. So I give him an honorable name. Kills Grizzly is his name!"

Grandmother Whirlwind lay on her bed, smiling as she listened to the singing and the triumphant drumming of the kill dance in honor of Shoots — no, now she must remember to call him Kills Grizzly. The medicine woman used all her spells and prayers and medicines to try to ease the pain. No matter how Whirlwind lay, with her foot propped up, the pain was very great, but her pride was greater.

"It does not hurt," she said. "It is nothing." She pretended to sleep.

Brings Horses stayed, and the sleepy women came back with the sleepy children. They spoke softly but were full of talk that Whirlwind wanted to hear: about how everyone was honoring Shoots for his courage and talking about how brave Whirlwind herself was.

"Everybody wants to see you," one of them remarked, smiling, "but we refused them all — all except one, who will come soon."

They were hurrying around, Whirlwind noticed, to tidy up the lodge — her work, but she could not do it now. It must be an important visitor or the women would not be so careful to have everything neat and nice this late at night with the baby and the little girl, Reaches Far, asleep.

Men's voices came nearer, two men. One was Morning Rider; his mother did not recognize the other one. Morning Rider entered and ushered in his companion. He said, "This is Whirlwind Woman, my mother. She saved her baby grandson."

The other man stood looking down at her. He smiled a little and said, "I am Crazy Horse."

Whirlwind gasped. For once in her life, she had nothing to say. This was the great chief, the quiet one, whose very presence made the hearts of his people big.

Morning Rider told her, "I have asked Crazy Horse to name the baby, and he agrees. When the boy is old enough, we will have the ear-piercing ceremony. But today Crazy Horse will give the child a name."

Round Cloud Woman brought the sleeping infant. She was shaking with excitement.

Crazy Horse looked long at the sleeping little face. Then he touched the child's forehead and said, "I give you a name that you can make great in honor of your grandmother, who saved you, and your kinsman, who counted first coup on the bear. I name the child She Throws Him."

A murmur of delight went up among Morning Rider's family: "Thank you, friend, thank you!"

Round Cloud Woman said to her child, "Wake up, She Throws Him, so that sometime you can say you looked on the face of Crazy Horse the day he gave you your name." The baby opened his eyes, yawned, and went to sleep again.

Now Whirlwind thought of something to say: "My son has forgotten his manners. I did not raise him right. He has not asked our visitor to sit down in the place of honor beside him."

The two men chuckled, and Morning Rider explained, "I asked him before we came, but he thought he would not stay long enough. Will the visitor sit down and smoke?"

Crazy Horse would. Morning Rider filled and lighted the sacred pipe and smoked it to the Powers of the six directions. Then he passed it to Crazy Horse, who did the same and gave back the sacred pipe.

"I wish also to speak to the warrior woman," he said. "Grandmother, how is it with you in your pain?" He used the term "grandmother" in the sense of great respect.

"Not so bad," she replied stoutly, as a warrior should. Crazy Horse stood up, then knelt beside her and looked into her face. "I give you a name, too, Grandmother. Your name is Saved Her Cub."

Then he nodded and left the lodge, leaving Whirlwind speechless for the second time that day.

When she got her wits back, she complained happily, "But I am too old to remember another name for myself!"

Morning Rider replied, "Others will remember."

Discuss the Selection

1. How did Whirlwind win a new name for herself?
2. Describe in detail the fight with the grizzly bear.
3. What did you think would happen after the grizzly bear slashed Whirlwind's leg?
4. In what way did the tribe honor Whirlwind for her courage in the fight with the bear?
5. The wounds of Shoots and Whirlwind were treated in different ways, but one detail of the treatment is the same. Find the part of the story that explains how their wounds were treated.

Apply the Skills

An opinion expresses a personal belief or attitude. A fact, however, is information that can be proved true or false. "How Whirlwind Saved Her Cub" has examples of both facts and opinions. Read the following sentences from the story. Decide which are statements of opinion and which are statements of fact.

1. The biscuit root made good mush with a wild onion cooked in it.
2. The biscuit root was plentiful on flat ground under a cutbank, just out of sight of the lodges.
3. Then Shoots did the last thing he could do, because it was too late to run.
4. "Nobody will ever forget how you saved the boy cub today."

Think and Write

Prewrite

Old Name	New Name
Shoots	
Jumps	
Whirlwind	

The left side of the chart shown above lists the names of three characters in "How Whirlwind Saved Her Cub." Copy the chart and complete it by adding the new name given to each of the characters at the end of the story.

Compose

Choose one pair of the names from the chart as your subject. Then write a paragraph describing what happened in the story that caused the change of name. Refer to the chart or selection as needed. Your first sentence might be *As a result of his fight with the bear, Shoots is renamed "Kills Grizzly."*

Revise

Read the paragraph you wrote. Could someone who hasn't read the selection understand from your writing what the character did to earn a new name? If not, revise your work.

Ute Indian Poem
by Nancy Wood

All is a circle within me.
I am ten thousand winters old.
I am as young as a newborn flower.
I am a buffalo in its grave.
I am a tree in bloom.

All is a circle within me.
I have seen the world through an eagle's eyes
I have seen it from a gopher's hole.
I have seen the world on fire
And the sky without a moon.

All is a circle within me.
I have gone into the earth and out again.
I have gone to the edge of the sky.
Now all is at peace within me.
Now all has a place to come home.

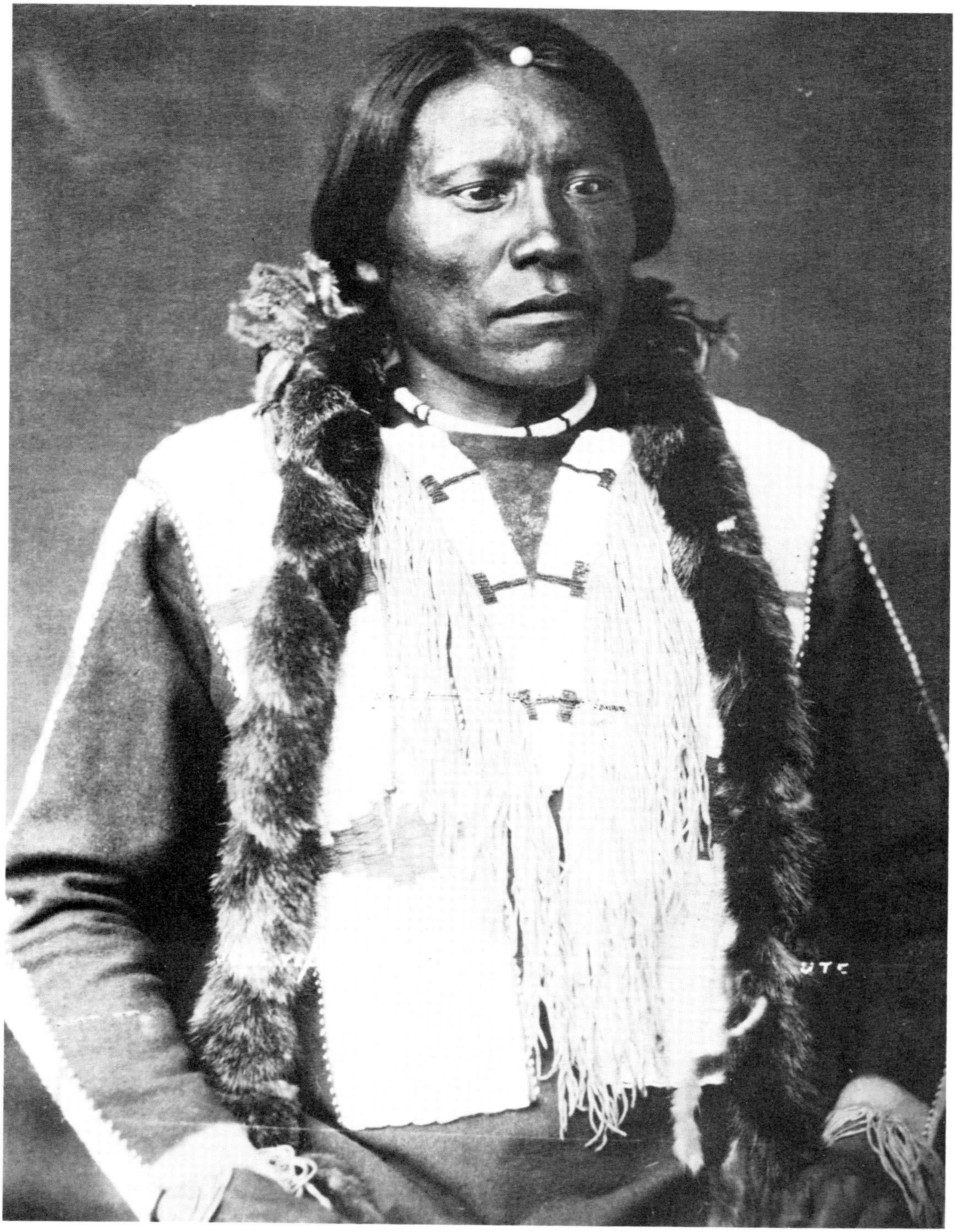
UTE

Many ordinary people have contributed to our American heritage by leaving us their journals. Read to find out how the author uses the journal of Catherine Cabot Hall, a New England schoolgirl, to address a major issue in American history.

As you read, notice how Catherine uses her journal to comment on events in her life.

A Gathering of Days

by Joan W. Blos

Imagine that you are browsing through an attic in a farmhouse in New England. At the bottom of a trunk you find a diary kept by someone your age, but written over one hundred fifty years ago. What better way to learn about the past than to see these long-ago events through an eyewitness.

Not everyone is lucky enough to discover a long-forgotten diary in an attic trunk. The next best thing, however, is a fictional diary, such as *A Gathering of Days*, created by author Joan Blos. This diary presents a picture of life in a small town in New England in 1830, as seen by thirteen-year-old Catherine. As you read her diary, you will find out about Catherine's family life, her school days, and the fun she had with her friends.

When Catherine began her diary, she had no idea that 1830 would be a year of changes and memorable events. One such event, which affected Catherine deeply, is the subject of this selection.

Sunday, October 17, 1830

I, Catherine Cabot Hall, aged 13 years, 7 months, 8 days, of Meredith in the State of New Hampshire, do begin this book.

It was given to me yesterday, my father returning from Boston, Massachusetts, where he had gone to obtain provisions for the months ahead.

My father's name is Charles: Charles Hall. I am daughter also of Hannah Cabot Hall, dead of a fever these four long years; and older sister of Mary Martha (called Matty) whose dark, curling hair resembles our mother's, but I have our mother's blue eyes.

My dearest friend is Cassie. The Shipmans' farm lies South of ours, and is rather larger. Cassie is older than I by a year, but the same in height. We tell each other everything; and each of us in the other's dear heart finds secret dreams reflected. Cassie's brothers are: David Horatio, older by a full two years; Asa Hale, my age exactly; and William Mason, the youngest. He is but a baby and called by every one "Willie."

This day being the Sabbath we attended services both morning and afternoon.

Thursday, November 4, 1830

Returning home from school this day I had a dreadful fright! Clearly I saw presented to me the dark silhouette of a lanky man, his coat all tattered against the sky, his bony hand above his eye as if to give it shade.

Although I quickly pointed him out, so swiftly did he vanish away that nothing remained when Cassie and Asa obeyed my pointing finger. Then, stumble-tongue'd, I must explain what I had wished them to see.

Asa determined that nothing would do unless we followed after. Cassie, ever more prudent, demurred; therefore must I, as the third of the party, cast the deciding ballot. As it was coming on to dark, and I still had our supper to set, I announced with Cassie. Asa, at this, scowled ruefully. But soon thereafter we all joined hands, in most perfect companionship resumed the homeward journey.

Wednesday, November 10, 1830

I saw my phantom again today—this time it stayed a longer while, peering and peering into the dusk, and in the same location, over by Piper's Woods.

I am resolved to examine the spot, and prove myself to A. and Cassie, both inclined to tease me still, about my apparition. "Now, Cath," they'll say, "what being will you find today?" Or: "Have you stray'd hogs, Catherine Hall, to take you in to the woods?"

Sophy told us today in school her father says when she turns fifteen she's to be sent to Lowell, Massachusetts, there to work in the mills. The Perkinses are badly off, and as she's strong she could make good money, being also healthy and well used to hard work.

But Sophy to go to Lowell? I should be quite terrified to be thus torn from all I love — people, place, and ways.

Sophy says the recruiter said the houses there have parlors for the girls, and are very well kept. Some of them even have pianos! Sophy is musical — like all of the Perkinses — and oft will sing so prettily when her father fiddles. I dare say she will learn to play and soon delight them all.

Monday, November 29, 1830

I have searched just everywhere! Today I carried my writing book home — Father had said he wished to see it, and Teacher Holt had granted permission exactly on that account. Now neither I nor M. can find it, looking with care throughout the house and in unlikely places.

I do recall that I set it down next to my cap and muffler and mittens as we started home. We only paused but once on the way, and that to pick some pods and grasses close by the side of the road.

I have not yet told Father of this: And how will I tell Teacher Holt how I've misused his trust? I pray the book be safe where it is and that I find it tomorrow!

Wednesday, December 1, 1830

I can not think what has *transpired*; still is my lesson book missing. Fortunately none seemed to notice that I wrote my lessons on foolscap pages. I feared discovery all the day.

Did another scholar mistake it? Surely he would have brought it to school — unless kept home on some account, & will bring it tomorrow?

The pond ice being thick and black, as will happen when cold persists with no snow between, we disported there after school. When we girls grew weary of skating, the boys cut branches of evergreens, and quickly pronounced them royal sleighs upon which we might ride. How festively we laughed and called, pretending we were ermine'd queens, and leaning back against the boughs while, before us, the boys' long strokes carried us over the ice.

Thursday, December 2, 1830
Lo! my lesson book is returned, and in the strangest way!

There is a nubbly boundary stone that separates the school house lot from the woods that belong to Wally Piper where both lots front the road. My book was there at the close of school, just as plain as anything, as if it had been set down. At first I dared not trust my eyes, certain it could not have fallen there, and who, I asked, would place it thus, and in such risk of harm?

However, I dwelt not on such thoughts, but taking it gladly in to my hands turned the familiar pages, each of them a friend. Then on the cover's inner side, just below my name and the place, a stranger and intruder amidst that company:

Pleez Miss
Take Pitty
I Am Cold

The letters seem drawn with charcoal and are raggedly formed. I know not what to make of it, nor can wait to tell Cassie and Asa.

Saturday, December 4, 1830
When I stepped out to the yard this morning a bit of paper held beneath a stone promptly attracted my eye. Altho' my fingers were clumsy with cold I hastened to smooth it open.

"Wait at the rock," it said. Altho' it lacked a signature, I knew the writer was Asa.

What rock, however, and *when* ought I wait? No other meaning seeming to fit, at last I concluded that A. knew *something* about my lesson book. Could he be the one to have taken it? No, it seemed not likely. Mayhap, its reappearance? I knew I could not puzzle it out; therefore with what *eagerness* did I await our meeting! How hard it was to not begrudge Father and Matty the time they took with their preparations and the morning meal. 'Twas a little of this and a little of that and "Catherine do stop fidgeting, it makes a man uneasy!" I thought he never had tarried so long over common

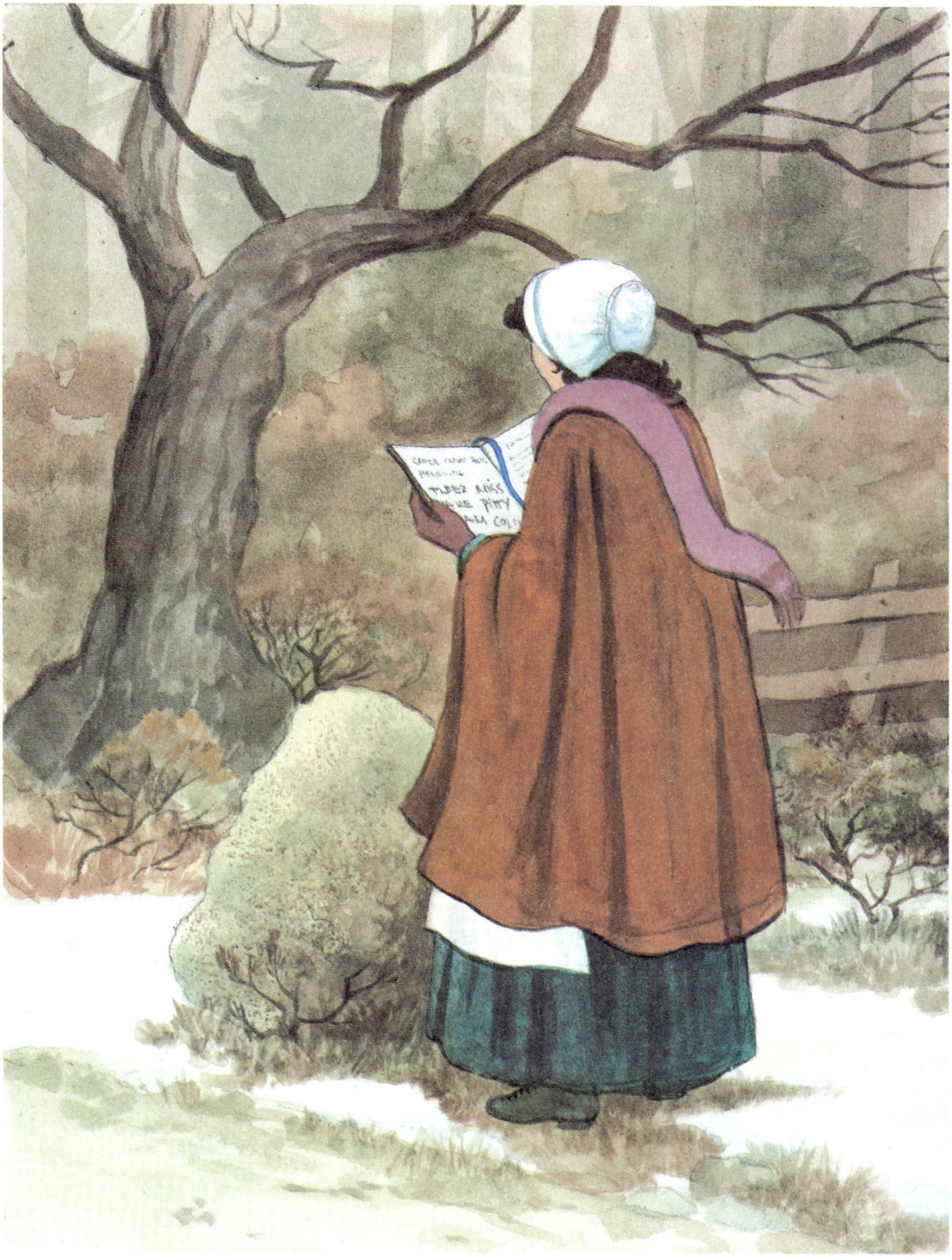

meat and cakes — and asked for bacon too! At last with all in tidiness I set out for school.

The sky had brightened, giving light, when I came to the rock. The wind, tho' light, seemed to glaze my cheek, and brought tears to my eyes. I stood there clapping my feet together — they taking turns to be clapper and clapped — and marking how thin are the soles of my boots, never intended for frozen ground or standing about of a morning. Had he been there before me or would he not come? Had I misread Asa's message? At last I heard the school bell ring and knew I could wait no longer. Public mortification now compounded my woes. On account of my late arrival I must pass before all the scholars, and so to my place. My face turned red as a smithy's in summer! Teacher Holt did not rebuke me. He must have seen the extent of my shame, considered it sufficient.

During the recess interchange, when girls going out meet boys coming in, Asa contrived to approach me. "After school! In the same place." Then he must pass on. There is so much more to tell. But I can write no longer now; shall resume tomorrow.

The next day I followed A. in to the woods, he having appeared as he said he would, and soon showed me the boot prints he'd found near where I'd seen my phantom. They were sharp, and deeply imprinted, as if they'd been made when the ground was soft, then caught fast by a freeze. Clearly a man's boots they were as to size; the prints themselves being widely spaced to suggest a long-legged stride.

"Whose?" I asked.

"O, Cath! You know! Your phantom and no other!"

"But this would be a *real* man, Asa; no mere vision'd phantom. What manner of man do you suppose—"

"A black man you said, at least dark complected. I'd supposed a run-away slave come to here for hiding."

"A black man, Asa? We've had none before, neither slave nor free. So I couldn't know what it might mean to call him dark complected." Tho' I tried to give lively argument I knew him to be right. "Any man will leave prints where he walks, and these say naught of his color. Perhaps it was just a run-away lad not liking his indenture."

What Asa liked not was my timid suggestion. "No," he asserted, "it need not be a poor slave! It might be a thief, or a man convicted. Maybe he was meant to hang, and escaped to our woods? Is that what you would have him be, rather than a slave? Besides, what difference would it make—"

Behind Asa's figure I saw tall trees, and hidden by them what manner of man; where in these woods might he be? Then Asa looked at me levelly and I, staring back, to return his gaze, noticed as I never had that one of his eyes is lighter in color than is its companion!

"It doesn't really matter," he said. "Suppose that he was wrongly convicted and this his hope of freedom, a good life later on."

I was in such a whirl! Asa was saying, "Whoever he is, he's cold and needs us to help him, Cath. Who are we to judge?" Thus was it revealed to me that Asa had found my book on the rock and read the inscription there.

"Asa," I said, "we must go home. I have to think on it."

(I have not spoken to Cassie yet; intend to do so tomorrow.)

Sabbath-day, December 12, 1830

I could not speak with C. today, her mother keeping close by her side at morning service, and after.

I am so mindful of the stranger — everything reminds me of him — the cold we felt on going out, the grateful warmth of home. Yet sadly I am in no way nearer to knowing what is right, in this instance, and what I ought to do.

"Please, miss . . . I am cold." Sinned against or dangerous sinner? I do so long to speak of it, yet who can give me counsel? "I am cold . . . Take pity." I wish he had never come to our place, disturbing the quiet of our woods, enforcing his words in my book.

Monday, December 13, 1830

Some of the Shipmans' pies are stolen, that had been put in the buttery after Thanksgiving meal. They were meant to freeze and keep, and would have been good till March.

Asa, whose sweet tooth is well known, was thrashed for the offense. As I am quite certain 'tis the phantom's work, again are wrong and right confused, and by what plausible signs.

Asa's brother David noted that the footprints in the snow matched not Asa's boots. But there was Asa, accepting guilt — this to protect the phantom I'm sure — and Asa's father brushing him off, saying that yesterday's snowfall was fine and, what with the wind and drifting over, no print would hold its shape.

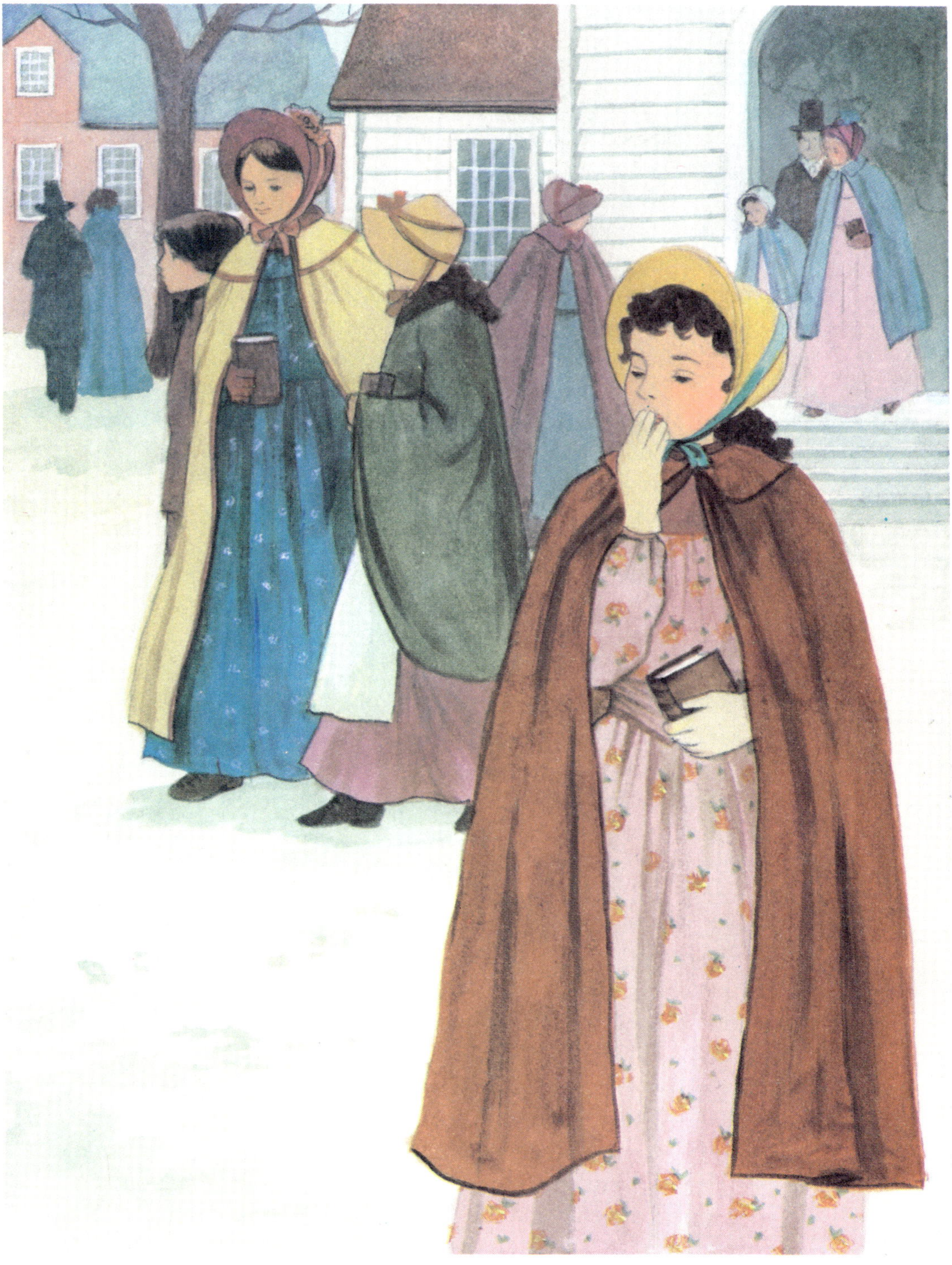

Friday, December 17, 1830

Cassie and I this afternoon selected one of my mother's quilts — one with plenty of warmth in it yet tho' some parts worn and faded. This would be our answer to the fugitive's appeal. Could he have known when he wrote in my book that I, tho' a child, had been installed in my deceased mother's place? If so, were he a local man? Did Providence guide his hand? Folding the quilt as small as we might, and wrapping some sausage and apples within, we crossed behind the Shipmans' house, reached the road, and thence proceeded to the phantom's stone. Asa dubbed it thus one day, and the name has taken.

As part of our plan I carried along the fateful lesson book. Should we be seen, or questioned, by neighbors, I was well rehearsed to say that I was in search of a certain tree which I intended sketching. Cassie had come to companion me; and see, she carried a worn-out quilt should we become too cold. A pat excuse, we all believed, to fit the situation. A second purpose might be served by taking the book in hand: Should we meet the stranger himself he'd know our purpose instantly; thus would not, likely, harm us.

The woods, as ever, were still and cold; the only sound the clacking of branches as, frozen, they touched one another. Sketchbook or no we did not tarry and tho' we saw no human sign, sped about our errand.

I turned but once as we left the spot where A. had discovered the Fugitive's prints and which he'd occasioned to show to me along with a fire's remains. Of this I shall remember forever the look of that cold and wintry clearing, the quilt tucked in the foot of a tree and folded carefully to display a patch of brightest scarlet. I meant it also as a greeting — a flash of color, a bit of warmth; the only thing man made, or brought, to that desolation.

Asa was at the gate. "Did you do it," he asked, low-voiced. "Yes," we said; and all of a sudden hot tears over-flowed. Again I saw that patch of scarlet and remembered my mother's voice, as she told her stories about that quilt that she had made with her own hands. "That gray," she'd said, "was a waistcoat once, the drab's my father's trousers. 'Tis said the pieces of scarlet are old, cut from the back of a Hessian soldier's coat left behind in battle during the Revolution. . . ."

"There, there, Cath," said Asa at last. Then he shifted from foot to foot, reached out for the edge of my cloak, and with it, wiped my cheek.

Monday, December 20, 1830

No more can I take my mind from the phantom than dare to re-enter the woods. Yesterday when a tree burst open, the cold and frost being very severe, the explosive sound set my heart to pounding — so certain was I the report was a rifle's, and my phantom discovered.

Saturday, December 25, 1830

We attended services, this being Christmas Day. Can there, I wonder, be a chill more fierce than that which gathers in a building all week, then hurls itself, as if too long caged, at those who venture in. Although we wore our heaviest clothing it availed us not. The wooden pews gave forth great chill and the flooring, tightly laid, creaked when we walked across it. 'Tis much like a Winter Sabbath misplaced, and Sabbath it is tomorrow!

Later, our father read from the Bible as he often does. When it came time to prepare our meal Matty helped me to set things out: a loaf of bread baked yesterday, mugs of cider, and our own good soup which I made in November, and we've had frozen in the buttery for these winter days. So we dined most plentifully; grateful for the warmth of home, all mindful of the newborn babe born in Bethlehem long ago and the sweet young mother.

Monday, December 27, 1830

I was startled to think, this morning, I saw my phantom again! This time it proved a phantom phantom — an upright stump seen through flung snow revealed as being naught but that when the wind subsided.

Asa promises, the first he can, that he will venture in to the woods to see if the quilt be taken. There have been, these two weeks past, reports of modest thefts. A chicken here, some dried roots there, the largest of the Shipman pies. We presume this the work of our phantom, and do not speak of it.

Once I asked Asa about his thrashing and had it been very painful? "Skin soon cools," he said with a shrug, "and I had rather accept a beating than, by my denial, risk another's life."

Wednesday, December 29, 1830
   The quilt we left for the phantom is gone; likewise the trail of footprints, and every other sign. So said Asa yesterday, after he went to the woods. He thinks the prints to have been erased — mayhap with a log or stone — but certain it is that care was taken, and that the stranger is gone.

   With Asa's words I felt released, even as if my feet would fly which have been heavily freighted during these past weeks.
   Then I thought of he who must travel, slowly over frozen ground, and in unknown land.
   "May he enjoy safe transport," I pray'd, "a safe end to his journey."

   In the months that followed, Catherine continued writing about her family life, her school days, and the times she had with her friends. She didn't think about the phantom after that until late September 1831, when she received a small package in the mail. In an instant, Catherine sensed the signer and the source. Opened, the package disclosed two matched pieces of crocheted lace and a brief message.

>   Sisters Bless you.
>   Free Now.
>   Curtis.
>   IN CANADA

   The man Catherine had helped had indeed been a slave; and was now free!

Discuss the Selection

1. How did the author tie the events in this story to a major issue in American history?
2. In what ways did Catherine and Curtis make contact with each other?
3. How did you feel when Asa took a thrashing for the stolen pies rather than endanger the runaway?
4. What did Curtis's final message mean to Catherine?
5. When Catherine left the quilt for the runaway, why did she let a piece of scarlet show? Find that part of the story and read it again.

Apply the Skills

A journal is a daily record or account of the writer's thoughts. This piece of fiction is told in the form of a schoolgirl's journal. Read the following passages from the story. Why do you think Catherine included them in her journal?

1. I am so mindful of the stranger—everything reminds me of him—the cold we felt on going out, the grateful warmth of home. Yet sadly I am in no way nearer to knowing what is right, in this instance, and what I ought to do.
2. Of this I shall remember forever the look of that cold and wintry clearing, the quilt tucked in the foot of a tree and folded carefully to display a patch of brightest scarlet.

Think and Write

Prewrite

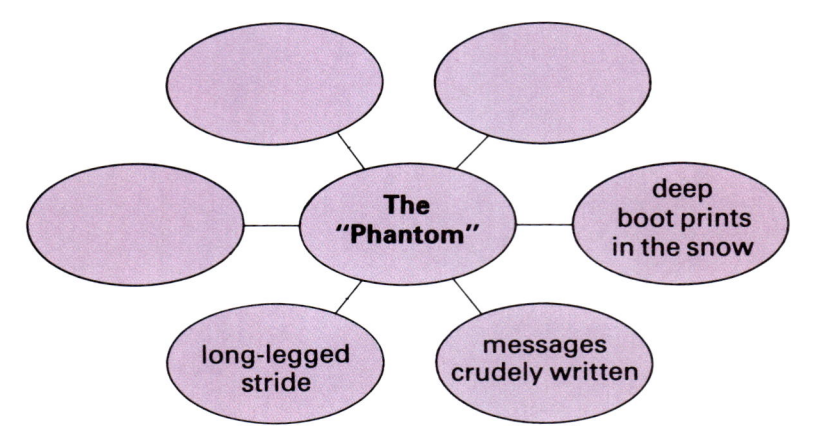

[Diagram: central oval "The 'Phantom'" connected to surrounding ovals — "deep boot prints in the snow", "messages crudely written", "long-legged stride", and three blank ovals]

A descriptive paragraph is used to create a vivid image of a person, place, or thing. In Catherine's journal, she describes Curtis, one of the central characters in this selection. A vivid picture of him emerges from her description.

Copy the diagram shown above, including the descriptive information given. Add three more descriptions of the "phantom" from the selection.

Compose

Referring to the diagram and the selection, write a paragraph describing Curtis. Make sure that you show his unique qualities. Arrange your details in an order that is easy to follow. Use language vivid enough to create a clear and colorful picture of Curtis.

Revise

Read the paragraph you wrote. Did you include the most important details from the story? Can a clear picture of Curtis be seen through your paragraph even by someone who hasn't read the story? If not, revise your work.

Study Skills

Job Applications

Adults are not the only people who look for jobs. Many teenagers look for jobs, too, so it's not too early to learn how to go after the one you want. The job-hunting skills you learn now will be useful to you during your entire work life. There are three important job-seeking skills:

1. finding job openings   2. writing résumés   3. interviewing

Job Openings

Like a detective looking for clues, you have to find out where the jobs are before you can get one. Just as detectives check out each lead, so should you. Newspapers, magazines, friends, relatives, and teachers can all offer you leads.

The newspaper is the source most job hunters turn to first. Although the daily newspaper has a listing of jobs, the largest listing is in the Sunday paper. An example of an advertisement you might find in a newspaper is shown on the next page.

Notice the skills that you would need for this job, and where and when to call for an appointment.

In addition to newspapers, other publications carry job listings. Most professions and industries publish special-interest magazines. For example, if someone wants to work in a law office for the summer, that person might look in a publication for that profession.

Besides looking for advertised jobs, you can also advertise your own skills. You can advertise in a local or neighborhood newspaper. Or, you can prepare a flyer, a sheet of paper advertising your skills. Then, post flyers on bulletin boards at school and other places in your neighborhood.

Another step that no job hunter should overlook is **networking**. Networking means letting your friends and relatives know that you are looking for a job. Be sure to let your network of helpers know the kind of job you hope to find. Often they can tell you about a job that is available. Sometimes they can tell you the name of an employer whom you can approach in person, call, or write. For example, if you are looking for a job as a baby-sitter, tell your neighbors. Your network can probably help you locate families with young children who might need your services. A network works like a net; it helps you "capture" the job you want.

PHOTOGRAPHY

Photo Studio seeks P/T trainee.

Must have basic photographic

skills and knowledge.

Call betw. 9-11 A.M. for appt.

676-2386

B. MICHAELS STUDIO

Résumé

Once you hear about a job opening that interests you, the next step is to send a **résumé**. A résumé is a written summary of your education and skills and of any jobs or volunteer positions that you have held. The purpose of a résumé is to interest an employer in calling you for an interview, a personal meeting about the job. If your résumé is clearly written and matched to the employer's needs, there is a good chance it will lead to an interview. If not, your résumé is likely to be tossed aside.

MARGARET PALMER
7700 Burr Oak Lane
University City, Missouri 63130
(314) 725-2940

OBJECTIVE: Summer job as a library aide.

SPECIAL SKILLS

Writing and Editing:
- Edited junior-high school magazine.
- Wrote a letter to the editor that was published in local newspaper.
- Won award for report on interview with local author.

Clerical:
- Assisted school librarian with filing.
- Typing speed: 40 words per minute.

Proofreading:
- Knowledge of proofreading symbols.

EDUCATION   1985-Present, Hanley High School, University City, Missouri.

WORK HISTORY   Summer 1984, Assistant clerk, Washington University, St. Louis, Missouri.
Summer 1983, Volunteer storyteller, Bates Public Library, St. Louis, Missouri.

References available on request.

You have to work hard to prepare your résumé. Remember, you are trying to sell your skills. It is often necessary to write several drafts before your résumé sounds convincing. Here are the main parts of a résumé:

- name, address, and telephone number
- job objective (kind of job you want)
- skills (examples: well-organized, good writer)
- work experience (examples: baby-sitting; junior lifeguard)
- volunteer work (example: hospital volunteer)
- education (schools attended; special honors)
- references (people who know you well or who know the quality of your work)

There are several ways to organize a résumé, but all résumés should be alike in certain ways. They should be brief (one page is usually best). Information should be clearly stated. The appearance should be neat. Study the sample résumé on page 514.

Job Interview

A person who is thinking about hiring you will want you to come in for an **interview**. Interviews allow the employer to get to know you. Interviews also give you a chance to get to know the employer. Careful preparation will make you feel more confident at an interview. Here are some ways you can prepare:

- Learn all you can about the company before the interview. This will help show the interviewer that you are interested in working for that company.
- Make sure that your clothing is clean and well pressed. Avoid jeans, sneakers, and very casual or flashy clothing.
- Try to anticipate some of the questions that you will be asked, and practice answering them before the interview.
- Think about any questions that you might want to ask about how the business is run, but ask them in a respectful way.

Besides a good résumé and good skills, there are two things that every employer looks for in a worker. One is the desire to work. The other is reliability. At the interview, show that you are interested in the job and are reliable. Even if you don't get the job, what you learn at an interview can help you the next time.

The work of an artist is an important part of his or her legacy. Read to find out how one artist, Margaret Sanfilippo, goes about creating story illustrations.

An interview contains both facts and opinions. As you read, notice the opinions of both Sanfilippo and her interviewer.

Margaret Sanfilippo: A Discriminating Artist

by Neil Ryder Hoos

Some adults have a hard time remembering the details of their childhoods. Margaret Sanfilippo, a successful book illustrator, has vivid impressions of her youth. She uses the memories of her own childhood to draw children with such realism that they seem almost lifelike. It is as if each painting suggests a real child who is part of a family that we all might know.

Margaret Sanfilippo's childhood was an ordinary one, with the exception of one surprise. When she was five years old, her family decided upon an adventure. They packed the family car, waved good-bye to California, and headed toward Central America. They were going to San Salvador, the capital of El Salvador. They went there to visit an uncle and congratulate him on his marriage. The Sanfilippo family loved the natural beauty of the countryside and the simple lifestyle of El Salvador. They moved there and stayed for five years. It was during these years that Margaret took her first art lessons.

Her family wished to fit quickly into this new way of life. Margaret went to local schools where she spoke only Spanish. She also went to an after-school program called "Bellas Artes." This program introduced young people to the "Beautiful Arts." There she first studied drawing, painting, sculpture, drama, and dance.

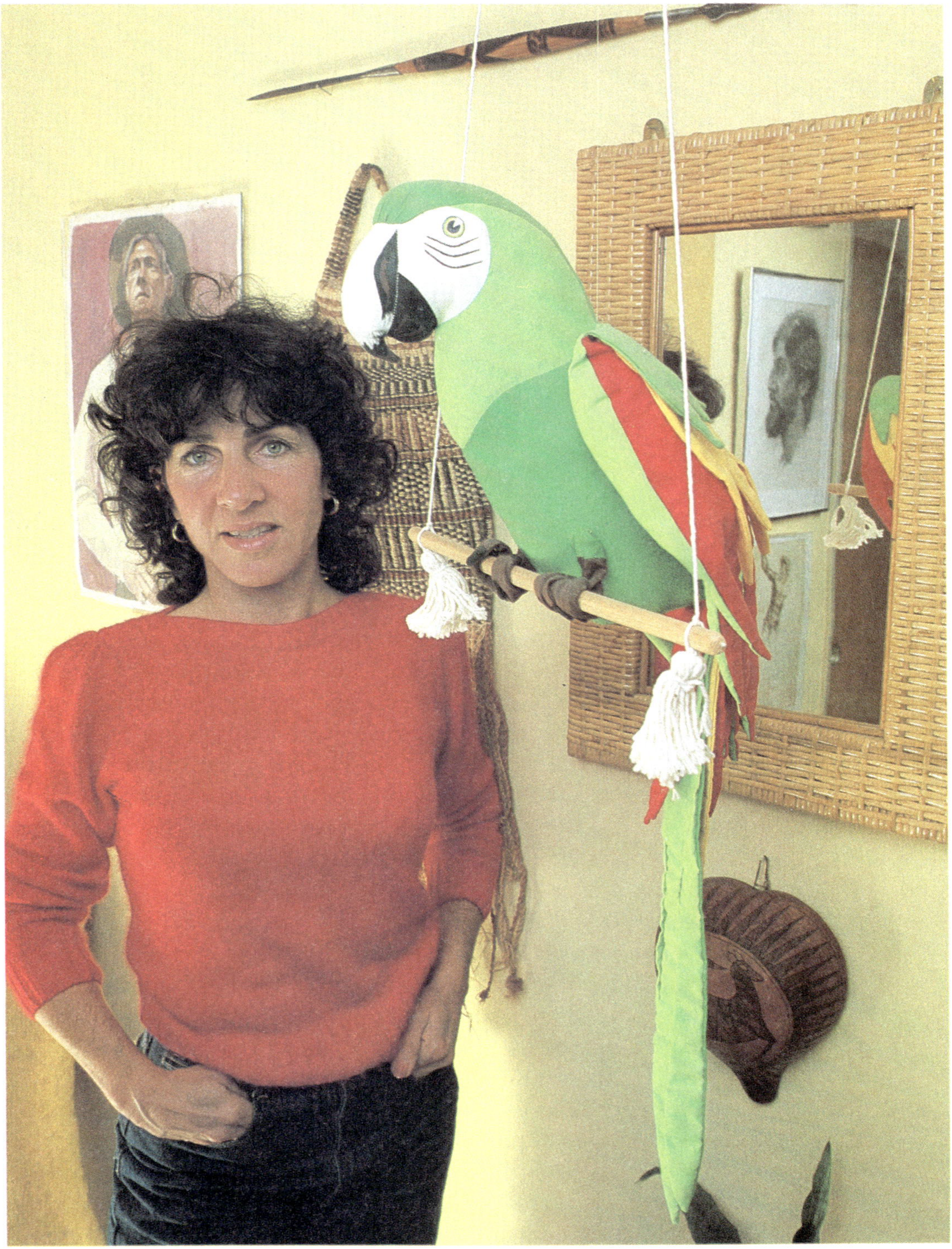

This special program was started as a means for children to express themselves artistically. They were taught to notice and appreciate the rich array of colors and sights that were all around them. The teachers believed that most children are really good artists. After the age of ten, most children go through a stage when they become too demanding of themselves and can become discouraged. This art program was designed to give all children the discipline and support they needed so they would not give up easily.

Sanfilippo still recalls being told, "You can, if you think you can." The school tried to inspire and motivate the children to develop their talents. Margaret Sanfilippo was encouraged to draw. Amid the lush tropical setting, the mountain lakes, beaches and farms, busy marketplaces full of colorful foods and ornaments, she began to draw the people of El Salvador.

Sanfilippo believes that people are the most challenging and the most interesting of all subjects to draw. She knows that there is more to drawing a portrait than most people think. Human beings are social creatures. In order to picture them realistically, they must be shown in social situations. To make someone appear lifelike, the artist must show the subject in an activity or reacting to a particular situation. For example, a picture of an American Indian boy shearing sheep would be more believable than just an isolated view of his face.

   A good illustrator must labor over the details of every drawing. Margaret Sanfilippo agrees with the saying "Inspiration is ninety percent perspiration." An accurate illustration is the result of careful observations. For example, some people in El Salvador would be at home in Paris or New York. They dress in the latest fashions. They are aware of the trends that they see on television, in movies, and in magazines. In contrast, other El Salvadoreans wear the traditional clothing of their ancestors. They express their rich cultural heritage by wearing brightly colored apparel. These people do not have television and are not easily influenced by the outside world. Sanfilippo understands that although these two groups of people come from the same country, they cannot be drawn in the same way. She must show subtle differences that reveal each person's background and heritage.

   Sanfilippo studied drawing throughout high school and college. She remembers one teacher who assigned many book reports

519

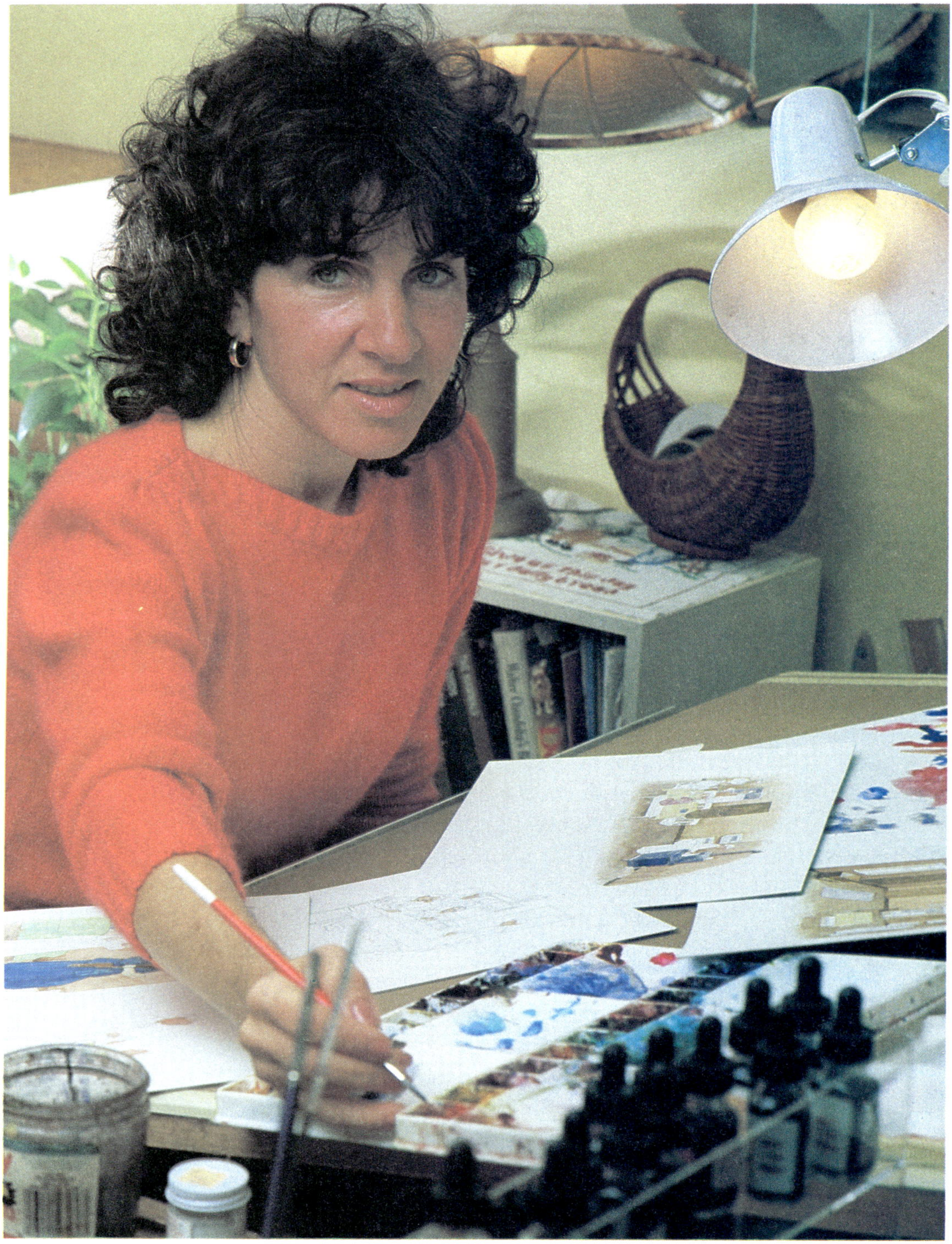

and asked that each book report be illustrated by the student. Sanfilippo enjoyed this approach to learning. She especially liked to draw the same book character in many different settings. It was at this time that Margaret Sanfilippo realized that book illustrating would be an ideal career for her. It would make it possible for her to combine two activities she loved, reading books and drawing pictures.

She still takes art classes as often as she can. Her goal is to make each illustration more "real" than the one before. Her profession has made it important that she understand people. She is often asked to draw different types of people who live within one community, yet look completely different from each other. Her keen eye catches both the differences and the similarities with the delicacy of a fine artist and humanitarian.

As an adult, Sanfilippo returned to El Salvador, the country that first encouraged her artistic talents. She also traveled to Mexico City. There she was introduced to the larger-than-life murals (wall paintings) by the famous Mexican artist Diego Rivera. The scenes that he painted on the walls of important buildings showed Mexican people in the activities of their daily life. She enjoyed these paintings very much. She was able to see how another artist interpreted the local colors and flavors of a community.

In Mexico City, Margaret Sanfilippo also studied the many ancient objects kept in the museums. These objects represent the traditions and history of Mexico. She uses this knowledge when she is called upon to draw Mexican people. On a trip to Peru she watched the colorful processions and festivals that display the traditions of the Indian and Hispanic past.

Knowing the heritage of people enables her to draw interesting and believable characters. This is one reason why her story illustrations are in great demand. She is currently busy illustrating children's textbooks, readers, and preschool stories. Her specialty is illustrating books with children of different racial and national backgrounds. To portray with sympathy the differences that make people unique is only part of the artistic challenge to an illustrator. Margaret Sanfilippo has been able to give the children she draws a unique sparkle in their eyes. This lifelike gleam animates each picture with real emotions. She recreates the wonders of her own childhood in each of the children she draws.

Discuss the Selection

1. How does Margaret Sanfilippo create story illustrations?
2. Summarize the events in Margaret Sanfilippo's life that helped her become an artist.
3. Look back at Margaret Sanfilippo's illustrations. Tell why you think they do or do not make the selection clearer to you.
4. Do you agree with the author's opinion that an artist must know the heritage of the people he or she draws? Find the reasons the author gives to support his opinion.
5. Sanfilippo thinks that drawing people is very challenging. Find that part of the selection that tells what is involved in drawing people.

Apply the Skills

An author's opinion can be very useful in helping you make an evaluation. Some opinions, however, are more valuable than others.

The author of "Margaret Sanfilippo: A Discriminating Artist" based his statements on an actual interview with Sanfilippo. You can, therefore, assume that he knows something about her life and work. His opinions are thus likely to be valuable.

1. Quote an opinion expressed by the author in the selection.
2. Now, give a detail from the selection that supports the opinion you cited.

Think and Write

Prewrite

[Notecards shown:]
- Margaret Sanfilippo: successful artist with vivid childhood memories.
- "You can, if you think you can."
- Exposure to art at "Bellas Artes" project.

Good note taking is writing down only what is important to you. Notes can serve as a valuable aid to writers in organizing information and ideas.

Study the notecards shown above. They give important information from the selection.

Copy the notecards. Then write three more notecards that give additional important information about the life and work of Margaret Sanfilippo.

Compose

Use the six notecards and supporting details from the selection on Sanfilippo to write a one-page composition in your own words. Try to make your writing as informative, accurate, and interesting as possible. Your first sentence might be *Margaret Sanfilippo is a successful artist who has vivid childhood memories.*

Revise

Read the composition you wrote. Did you include the information in the notecards and supporting details from the selection? Did you write in a clear and interesting way? If not, revise your work.

Comprehension Study

Paraphrase Information

Paraphrasing is the rewording of information. Paraphrasing what you have read is a good test of comprehension. If you can express someone else's ideas in your own words, you know that you have understood what you read or were told.

Read the following paragraph and then notice the way it is paraphrased. Look for the differences between the original paragraph and the paraphrase.

> You have probably seen glamorous movie stars in interviews on television. Some of the interviews take place in their homes, perhaps next to a large swimming pool or a dining table filled with elegant silver, china, and crystal. You know that many of these people lead exciting lives. What you don't see on television talk shows is the fact that famous people also work very hard. Entertainers spend many years learning their craft. Then, when they become successful, they often continue to study acting. They go to classes between rehearsals. This can be exhausting. Some performers begin working as early as 6 A.M., and they study and rehearse until after midnight.

Here is a paraphrase of the paragraph that you just read:

> Although the life of a movie star is glamorous in some ways, it is filled with many hours of hard work.

Notice that the paraphrase you just read is much shorter than the original paragraph. While the details have been combined, the original idea is not changed. It is only reworded.

Recognizing Paraphrasing

Authors often paraphrase the writing and statements of others. Read the following paragraph. Notice that some of the statements are the author's original ideas, some are paraphrases of other people's ideas, and some are direct quotes.

> Many people are asking whether the new Medicare rules hurt health care. According to Professor Karen Davis, hospital care for the elderly needs to be changed. She suggests that elderly people who live alone may need a better home health-care plan. Dr. Raymond Scalettar disagrees. He says, "I think we are in danger of throwing the baby out with the bath water."

The author's main idea is expressed in the first sentence. Notice that this sentence is not enclosed in quotation marks and is not identified as belonging to someone other than the author. On the other hand, the second sentence is a paraphrase of someone else's opinion. The phrase *according to Professor Karen Davis* tells you that the idea belongs to Professor Davis, not to the author. You know that the last sentence expresses Dr. Scalettar's idea because of the quotation marks. Before paraphrasing a selection, make sure you know who said what, so that you can credit the right person.

A **direct quotation** is identified by the use of quotation marks around the quoted words. When you see quotation marks, they alert you to the words of someone other than the author. The statement by Dr. Scalettar in the paragraph on Medicare has quotation marks around it. It is a direct quotation of the doctor's exact words.

An **indirect quotation**, however, gives a person's idea without quoting that person directly. Thus, quotation marks are not used. The second and third sentences in the paragraph on Medicare are indirect quotations.

Note Taking

Samuel Pepys was one of the world's best note takers. Much of the information about late seventeenth-century England is from the notes he made before he went to bed each night. His diary includes paraphrases of the long talks he had with King Charles II. Well-paraphrased notes can be important to you, too.

Since the purpose of note taking is to help you remember information, good notes are an important study tool. Before you begin taking notes, skim the selection to determine its point. In almost anything you read, the author will make one central point. This is true of an entire book, a single story, or just a short article.

You know that the subject of a paragraph is called the topic. You also know that the main idea in a paragraph is a specific statement about the topic. By using some of the methods by which you learned to find the topic and main idea of a paragraph, you can find the central point of a selection of any length. Once it is identified, jot down the topic and main idea or ideas on a card. Then write down the details that support the main idea. You might want to use numbered cards so that you can quickly find the information when needed. Remember to use quotation marks to indicate all words belonging to someone other than the author.

Suppose you want to paraphrase an article you read about the history of Flag Day. Read the article carefully, paying special attention to the central point and to noteworthy details.

Flag Day

Flag Day is a very special day for all Americans. It is celebrated on June 14 in memory of the day in 1777 when the Stars and Stripes became the official flag of the United States. Flag Day is not a national holiday. Some states, such as Pennsylvania, do celebrate it as a legal holiday.

On Flag Day, people all over the United States fly the flag on their homes and businesses. Public buildings also fly the flag.

Flag Day was first observed in 1877 to celebrate the one hundredth anniversary of the selection of the flag. In 1885, Bernard J. Cigrand, a schoolteacher from Wisconsin, began a lifetime fight to establish Flag Day as an annual celebration. President Woodrow Wilson established Flag Day as an annual national celebration in a proclamation issued on May 30, 1916.

Read the following notes about the article:

> **Flag Day**
>
> When, why, how celebrated:
>   Celebrated on June 14th
>   Memorializes selection of Stars
>   and Stripes as official flag
>   Not a nat'l holiday
>   Some states don't celebrate it
>   People fly flags on homes and
>   businesses
>
> History:
>   First observed in 1877
>   Officially proclaimed on May 30, 1916
>   by Woodrow Wilson
>
>   Encyclopedia, pg. 176

Notice how the notes are recorded.

First, the notes are short. Main ideas and important details are stated in phrases instead of full sentences. Abbreviations are used. For example, *nat'l* is used for *national*.

Second, notes are taken only on topics of interest to the reader.

Third, the information is written down by topic. Phrases are indented for clarity. Neat, well-written notecards are easier to understand and more helpful for future studying.

Finally, the source of the article on Flag Day is given.

Although a notecard doesn't tell you everything, it does give you enough information to enable you to rewrite the article in your own words.

Textbook Application: Paraphrasing in Social Studies

As you read the following excerpt from a social studies textbook, pay careful attention to the sidenotes. They will help you paraphrase the information.

A Giant Birthday Party

The year 1876 marked the one-hundredth anniversary of the Declaration of Independence. To celebrate the event, the United States gave itself a birthday party in Philadelphia, the birthplace of the nation. The party was a world's fair called the Centennial Exhibition. Those who planned the exhibition determined that it would be the biggest, fanciest, and most awe-inspiring show on earth, fit for a glorious and growing nation.

> Describe the giant engine that symbolized the new industrial age by paraphrasing details about its size and capability.

The Centennial Exhibition was just that. Main Hall, which stretched for a third of a mile, was the world's largest building. In Machinery Hall stood a symbol of the new industrial age — a giant steam engine, 40 feet tall, which supplied the power that ran eight hundred other machines in the hall. All in all, there were some two hundred buildings sprawled over several hundred acres. Fifty countries entered exhibits, making this one of the largest world's fairs.

> This paragraph identifies the most popular building at the fair and tells why it was popular.

The most popular building was Machinery Hall. There one could see all the latest machines and inventions from all over the world — everything from the typewriter and the telephone to the Westinghouse air brake and the railroad sleeping car. Americans noted with pride that machines from their own country compared well with those from the most advanced countries in the world.

The Centennial Exhibition opened May 10, 1876, and ran for six months. During that time, 10 million people — more than one in every five Americans — visited the exhibition. It was one of the most successful birthday parties of all time.

— *One Flag, One Land,*
Silver Burdett

Use your own words to restate the information in this paragraph.

Try paraphrasing information in selections. Paraphrasing is a good way to remember what you read.

529

Heroes are part of a nation's heritage. Roberto Clemente was a baseball hero to millions of fans. Read to find out how he became another kind of hero because he cared about those in need.

As you read sentences or paragraphs that you find hard to understand, try paraphrasing the ideas in your own words.

Roberto Clemente, Batting King

by Arnold Hano

New Year's Eve, 1972, the man named Roberto Clemente paced restlessly near an airplane at San Juan International Airport in Puerto Rico. His wife, Vera, who had come to see him off on a mission of mercy, said the plane looked old and overloaded. There had been too many delays. Why not wait until tomorrow?

Clemente told her not to worry. "But if there's one more delay," he said, "we'll leave this for tomorrow."

The thirty-eight-year-old Clemente had become a hero to his fellow Puerto Ricans. One of baseball's superstars, he had a lifetime batting average of .317 — the highest among active players. Though his team, the Pittsburgh Pirates, had narrowly missed winning the National League pennant in the 1972 season, Clemente had maintained his reputation of being one of the all-time greats in the game. On his last hit of the season he had become only the eleventh man in baseball history to get three thousand hits.

To Roberto Walker Clemente it was instinctive to share the good things of life. He had done so with his family, with his friends, and as much as possible with other citizens of Puerto Rico. Human suffering always challenged him like a pitcher's fast ball: He wanted to knock it out of sight.

Recently the city of Managua, capital of Nicaragua, had been shattered by an earthquake. Thousands were dead; many thousands more injured, homeless, hungry. Clemente had no close associations with Nicaragua, but he was well acquainted with suffering. As instinctive to him as sharing the good things in life was devoting himself wholeheartedly to everything he undertook. Thus, when he decided that Puerto Ricans should help their fellow Latin Americans in Nicaragua, he worked as hard as or harder than any member of the committee he helped to organize.

He and his committee worked all day Christmas Day and the day after in their headquarters at Hiram Bithorn Stadium in San Juan, where the star outfielder had often played in the Puerto Rico League. That week he went on radio and television frequently, exhorting people to give all they could to aid the Nicaraguan victims. When Clemente spoke, Puerto Ricans listened and followed, for no man on the island was more respected and admired. Within a few days they had contributed more than $150,000 and about twenty-six tons of food, clothing, and other materials.

All that December 31 Clemente and others had been toiling at loading a small cargo vessel with supplies for stricken Managua. An airplane — a four-engine propeller-driven DC-7 — had been hired from a Miami concern and already had made two mercy flights to Nicaragua. Now, on New Year's Eve, it was about to make a third. Was it necessary that he go with it?

Clemente, with his dedicated thoroughness, believed so. His friend Cristobal Colon, who had driven him and Mrs. Clemente to the airport, said, "He had received reports that some of the food and clothing he had sent earlier had fallen into the hands of profiteers." And so Clemente was determined to make the flight himself and see to it that the supplies went directly to the people who needed them.

At last, when Clemente had almost decided to postpone the flight until New Year's morning, the pilot arrived. Though Mrs. Clemente was uneasy about the airplane, Clemente was not; he knew that the piston-powered DC-7 is a sturdy model, a steady workhorse in many parts of the world today.

Having kissed his wife good-bye, he boarded the DC-7 with an associate, Rafael Lozano, and three crew members. The laden airplane was cleared for takeoff at 9:22 P.M.

The next anyone knew, the DC-7 was flying very low and trying to return to the airport. A man named Jose Antonio Paris, who lived on the beach, described what he saw:

"I was afraid [the airplane] would hit the palm trees. Before it got to the water's edge, there was an explosion. There were three more explosions after that, the fourth one just as the plane was plunging nose first into the ocean. It sank quickly. Not more than five minutes passed before it was completely underwater."

Roberto Clemente was dead, and his companions with him. But he would live long in the history of baseball.

Puerto Rico lies in the Caribbean Sea, warmed by the Gulf Stream and an unfrowning sun, yet cooled by ocean breezes. Frost and snow never visit the island, and a tropical garden of infinite variety and color flourishes lushly over the land. Royal poinciana trees blaze forth their bright red blossoms. Hibiscus blooms unfold until they are the size of dinner plates. Bougainvillea vines drape rooftops with their tiny crisp blood-red petals. The air is scented with jasmine. Mangoes, breadfruit, papayas, sapodillas — pulpy, sweet, and juicy — fall in clusters about the feet.

This was Roberto Clemente's home, an island slightly smaller than the state of Connecticut. Its name—*Puerto Rico*—means "Rich Port." Sugarcane and pineapple grow swiftly and full from the dark earth.

Yet do not be lulled by the abundance of fruit and trees. This land is one of the most crowded places in the world. Many of its approximately 3.5 million people live in incredibly tight quarters in the cities of the island, and though the slums are being torn down, the poor live poorly in Rich Port. And for all the soft ocean breezes and the scent of jasmine, each year tropical storms howl across the island and batter at thousands of flimsy homes; hurricanes make Puerto Rico a yearly stopover in July, August, September, October.

Yet the island continues to grow, and to grow strong. It has been part of the United States ever since the Spanish-American War of 1898, when America overthrew the Spanish Empire in the Caribbean, and Puerto Rico and Guam were ceded to the United States. Its ties with the United States are actually over four hundred years old, for it was Puerto Rico that Christopher Columbus set foot on, when he discovered America.

Today Puerto Rico is a commonwealth, a self-governing territory under the protection of the United States. Its citizens are citizens of the United States. When they sing their nation's anthem, they begin, "Oh, say can you see. . . ." The island has been for years a showcase of democracy in the Caribbean. Its constitution is a model for emerging nations.

The assimilation of Puerto Rico into the American nation is not complete, and many Puerto Ricans in this nation feel they are strangers, though the United States is their country just as much as it is the country of a Kansan or a Californian or a Connecticut Yankee. Not even military service under the Stars and Stripes has wiped out the feeling of difference. No fighting man acquitted himself more nobly or bled more profusely in defense of American freedom than Puerto Rico's brave 65th Infantry Regiment in the Korean War.

This sense of difference marks most Latin-American ballplayers. They speak freely of it. There are problems of race, of language, of adapting to the customs of a strange land. Habits are different, food is different, life—in all its aspects—is vastly different. So when a Latin ballplayer's career in the United States is noted, let it also be noted that whatever he accomplished has come about in a strange and difficult land.

Roberto Clemente, of course, knew none of this when he was born on August 18, 1934, in the town of Carolina, a suburb of San Juan. Life was more pleasant for young Roberto Walker Clemente than it was for many Puerto Rican children. His father was not a laborer in a sugar plantation, but the foreman of the plantation. Roberto's parents ran a grocery and a meat market for the plantation workers. Roberto's father also owned some trucks, which he used for small shipping jobs.

There were seven children, six boys and a girl. Roberto was the youngest. Latin-American families are very close, very protecting, very loving. The youngest is loved not only by his parents, but by his older brothers and sisters. Thus, Roberto was a very well-cared-for child.

Though Roberto was born in the Depression year of 1934, there was no Depression in his family. "My father always worked," Clemente recalled. "We lived in a big wooden house, with a large front porch. Five bedrooms, living room, dining room, kitchen. Indoor bathroom."

Indoor bathroom. So many Latin-American families had no indoor plumbing, no water on their land at all. When he was a child in the Dominican Republic, Felipe Alou, another Latin baseball star, used to walk a mile to the river and carry water on his head and shoulders for the family.

Roberto had less difficult chores. In the summer, when his father would hire out his trucks for jobs, Roberto often helped out, loading or unloading sand. Not difficult, he insisted later.

But more important than the amount of physical labor were the attitude and atmosphere within the Clemente house. "When I was a boy, I realized what lovely persons my mother and father were," Clemente said. "I was treated real good. I learned the right way to live. I never heard any hate in my house. Not for anybody. I never heard my mother say a bad word to my father, or my father to my mother. During the war, when food all over Puerto Rico was limited, we never went hungry. They always found a way to feed us. We kids were first, and they were second."

As a boy, Roberto played ball every day. Mainly, it was softball, in playgrounds at first, and later in a municipal league. He played shortstop or he pitched. When he was not playing ball, he squeezed a hard rubber handball hour after hour, to strengthen the muscles in his throwing arm. That arm became one of the strongest in baseball history.

When he did not play softball, he played sandlot baseball. And when he played neither, he often crouched over the family radio, listening to reports of ball games in the Puerto Rican winter league. His idol, when he was a youngster, was Monte Irvin, the slugging Giants' outfielder who played ball in Puerto Rico in the winter. Irvin did two things Clemente admired: he could hit, throw. For a spell, Roberto's nickname was Monte Irvin.

If you think this obsession with baseball occasionally jangled his folks' nerves, you're right. Even in a permissive home where the children came first, Roberto's mother sometimes became edgy over her son's total occupation with ball.

"I would forget to eat because of baseball," Clemente said, "and one

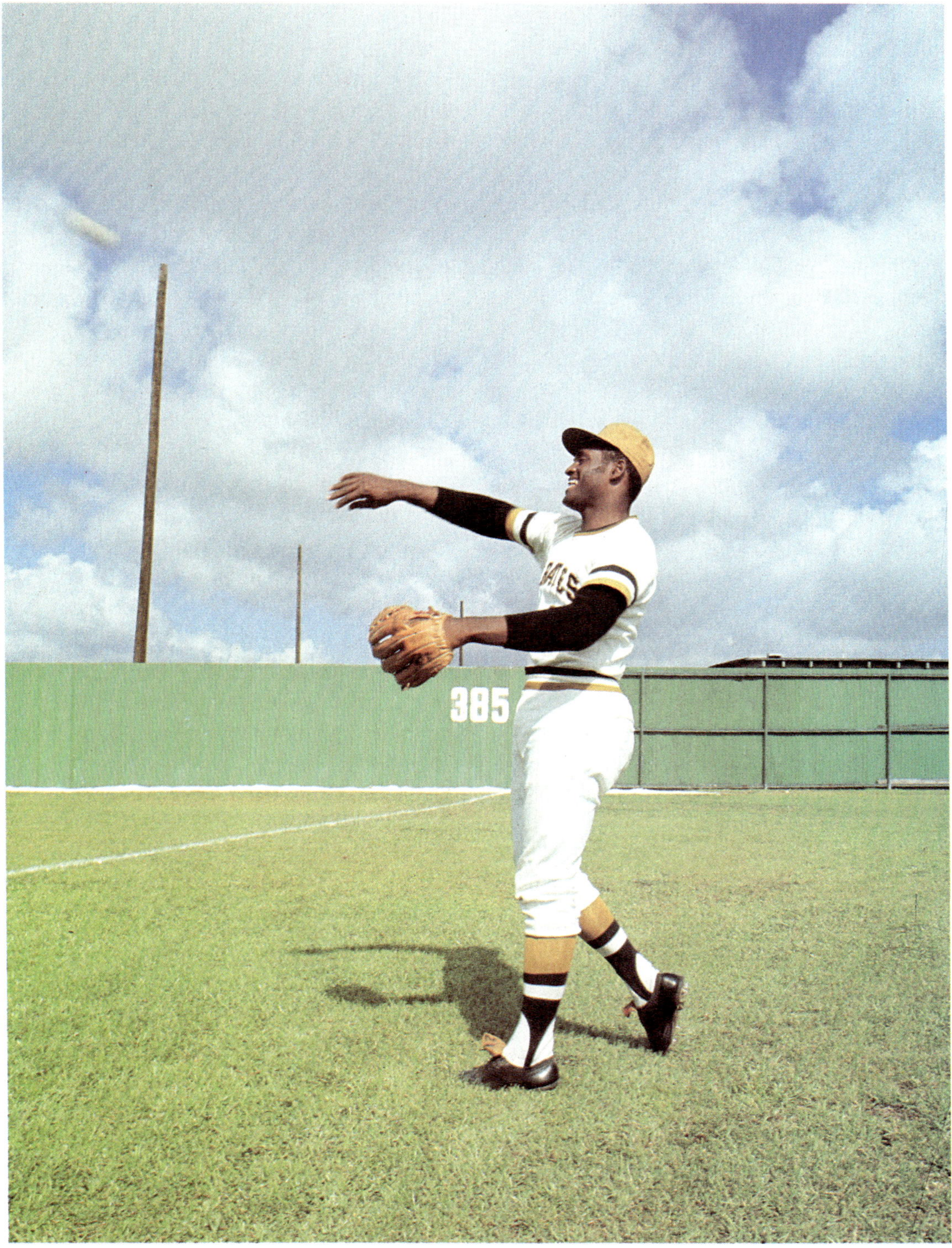
385

time my mother wanted to punish me. She started to burn my bat, but I got it out of the fire and saved it. Many times today she tells me how wrong she was and how right I was to want to play baseball."

But Clemente's mother did not always oppose her son's involvement. She couldn't. We read today of ballplayers who inherit their skills from their fathers. With Clemente, it was his mother who passed on the natural talent. Clemente says he got his arm from his mother. "She can still throw a ball from second base to home plate." Clemente told how his mother was invited to throw out the first ball of the amateur winter league in Puerto Rico, back in 1963. "She was seventy-three at the time," Clemente said. "She threw the ball from a box seat to home plate. She had something [a spin or a curve] on it, too."

Roberto intended to go to college and become an engineer. And though baseball was his life, at high school he managed to spread himself over other sports as well. He played baseball for his high school team, but he also made the track team, where he became an all-round sensation. Roberto threw the javelin; he high-jumped; he performed in what was then called the hop, skip, and jump, and which today is the triple jump. His best marks were outstanding. He tossed the javelin 195 feet; he high-jumped 6 feet; and he triple-jumped over 45 feet. Roberto Clemente was considered a sure member of Puerto Rico's Olympics squad for the 1956 event in Melbourne, Australia.

But professional baseball interfered with such a schedule. A high school history teacher, Roberto Marin, who also coached a softball team, became impressed with Clemente's skills. Marin passed the word to Pedro Zorilla, owner of the Santurce baseball team, in Puerto Rico, and one of the wisest judges of baseball talent in the Caribbean.

Zorilla shrugged off the unsolicited advice. Perhaps he had heard of too many high school stars from too many amateur scouts.

Later Zorilla took in a baseball game in the town of Manati, west of San Juan, where Zorilla lived. A seventeen-year-old center fielder caught his eye. Caught it? Filled it. The young man slammed a 390-foot triple and two doubles, and rifled a long throw to catch an opposing runner at third.

In the stands, Zorilla whistled. "Who is he?" he asked.

"His name is Roberto Clemente," a fan said.

"Hmm. Sounds familiar," Zorilla said.

Zorilla approached the player he once could have had for nothing. This time he offered a bonus of $300. Elated, Roberto went home, but to his astonishment his parents said, "Not enough." Until then he had no idea they were aware of bonuses and other by-products of play.

Zorilla eventually agreed to pay Clemente a $500 bonus, plus $60 a month (and one free baseball glove), and Clemente put on a Santurce uniform while still in high school. The notion of attending college to become an engineer faded once Clemente looked about at the other Santurce players. The team employed such men as Willie Mays, Orlando Cepeda, Ruben Gomez. Its manager was a former big league catcher, Herman Franks.

The idea that Latin Americans could not play big league ball also began to fade. Back in the states, Minnie Minoso had burst into stardom. In 1954, Bobby Avila would lead the American League in batting. More than any others, these two men — Minoso and Avila — brought sharply home to young Clemente that a player from the island might someday be a headlined performer on the mainland. "I thought stateside players were better than Latin players," he once said. "I thought you had to be Superman to make it. But when Minoso and Avila made it big, I realized others could do it, too."

Clemente played at Santurce in the winters of 1952-53, 1953-54, and 1954-55. In his third season, he batted .356.

Even before that .356, big league scouts tailed Clemente. Al Campanis, of the then Brooklyn Dodger office, organized a clinic in Puerto Rico. Clemente was one of a hundred prospects. As soon as Clemente began to hit and throw, to snare fly balls and run, Campanis — like Zorilla before him — had eyes for no one else. "Campanis asked me to do everything," said Clemente. "Run, hit, field, throw."

When the one-man show ended, Campanis suggested that Roberto join the Dodger farm system Clemente's father turned down the idea. He wanted Roberto to finish high school.

More big league scouts clustered about the wiry young player who rifled line drives to all fields, ran like the wind, and threw like — well, like nobody. During his senior year of high school in 1953, nine teams approached Clemente. They held fire until graduation. Then the Dodgers made a concrete offer: a $10,000 bonus for signing. It was one of the largest bonuses paid a Latin player. It becomes particularly large when measured against the $200 paid Felipe Alou, the $500 given Juan Marichal.

Yet it might have been much bigger.

Clemente verbally and jubilantly accepted the Dodger offer of $10,000.

Later that same day, the Milwaukee Braves came along with a bonus of over $30,000.

The confused young man brought the dilemma home to his folks.

His mother said sternly, "If you gave the word, you keep the word."

Some things are more important than money. Honor, for one.

Clemente signed with the Dodgers.

Which is not to say he played with the Dodgers. He finished the winter league season at Santurce, and in the spring of 1954 joined a Dodger farm club.

Roberto Clemente was nineteen years old, just a youth. The Dodgers owned six minor league teams, and had working agreements with ten other clubs.

Clemente could have been assigned to any of them. He might have begun at the very bottom, either at Class D Thomasville of the Georgia-Florida League, or Shawnee of the Sooner State League, or Hornell of the P.O.N.Y. League.

Clemente began instead at the top of the minor league pyramid. He joined former league pitching ace Joe Black and future big leaguers Ken Lehman, Ed Roebuck, Chico Fernandez, Norm Larker, Sandy Amoros, and Gino Cimoli. This was the meat of the roster on the Montreal ball club, in the Triple-A International League.

Roberto Clemente was one short step from the big leagues.

In 1954, Roberto Clemente, twenty-one years old, was drafted into the Pittsburgh Pirates. He soon became a top hitter, winning the award for best batter in both leagues four times. In 1966, he was voted Most Valuable Player in his league by the Baseball Writers of America. He beat out Sandy Koufax for the title, although Koufax had the best season of his career that year. Clemente was the first Puerto Rican to win the title and the second Latin (the first was a Cuban, Zoilo Versalles). From 1967 until his untimely death in 1972, Clemente enjoyed on the mainland the popularity and respect for his talents that had long been granted him in his native Puerto Rico.

In Puerto Rico, from his first year in the major leagues, Clemente had been idolized. Because of his success and that of other Latin players, Puerto Rican youngsters began to dream of major league baseball careers. Clemente loved children as much as he did baseball. After the 1971 World Series, he returned to San Juan to start building a "sports city," a dream that had absorbed him for a long time. The idea was to interest youngsters less fortunate than he in sports. The facility would have a variety of coaches, each a specialist in a particular sport, instead of the general physical education teachers found in most schools. Youngsters would use the facility weekdays, and on weekends it would be turned over to adults.

Clemente was always eager to get home to Puerto Rico. But when he went there, he had little time to relax. One of his troubles was that he could not say no to people or causes where he might be of help.

Clemente died on December 31, 1972.

Nowhere was he more deeply mourned than in the barrios of the Puerto Rico he loved. To the underprivileged, especially, he had assumed the stature of a folk hero. His strong brown face, his compassion, and his extraordinary success at a game that once had been the restricted sport of mainland whites—from these elements a hero was made. To thousands of Puerto Ricans even the house where he lived was not so much a dwelling place as a shrine to be visited.

Governor Luis A. Ferre of Puerto Rico declared three days of official mourning. Church bells tolled; there was an interfaith memorial service in Hiram Bithorn Stadium; radio stations canceled regular programs for somber music. The governor joined Pirate players Manny Sanguillen, Bob Johnson, and Rennie Stennett in a visit to Clemente's widow and three children.

From both North and Latin America there was an outpouring of eulogies.

"He was one of the greatest persons I knew," said John Galbreath, chairman of the board of the Pirates. "If you have to die, how better could your death be exemplified than by being on a mission of mercy?"

Baseball Commissioner Bowie Kuhn said: "Somehow Roberto transcended superstardom. His marvelous playing skills rank him among the truly elite. He had about him a touch of royalty."

"Image," as it is called, was important to Roberto Clemente. But, unlike the situation with many other ballplayers, Clemente's image and his *real* self were nearly identical. He was soft-spoken and gentle, decent and compassionate. He was also fiery, a man who demanded his due. Thus he sometimes seemed a man of contradictory characteristics. It is another way of saying that Roberto Clemente was *human*. And he did not pretend to be anything else.

Discuss the Selection

1. In what ways was Roberto Clemente a hero?
2. What special problems did Clemente and other Latin American players encounter when they entered major league baseball?
3. How did Roberto Clemente's personality enable him to deal successfully with the problems of being a Latin American in major league baseball?
4. How did you feel about Roberto Clemente's decision to accompany the supplies to Nicaragua? Tell why you agree or disagree with his reasons for going.
5. What words did the author use to tell you about Clemente's outstanding abilities in areas other than baseball? Find three sentences that describe Clemente's special abilities.

Apply the Skills

In paraphrasing a selection, or part of a selection, the original idea is not changed. It is only reworded. Sometimes synonyms are used in place of the original words. The paraphrase may be shorter than the original passage. Try paraphrasing the following paragraph from the selection, "Roberto Clemente, Batting King."

> As a boy, Roberto played ball every day. Mainly it was softball, in playgrounds at first, and later in a municipal league. He played shortstop or he pitched. When he was not playing ball, he squeezed a hard rubber handball hour after hour, to strengthen the muscles in his throwing arm. That arm became one of the strongest in baseball history.

Think and Write

Prewrite

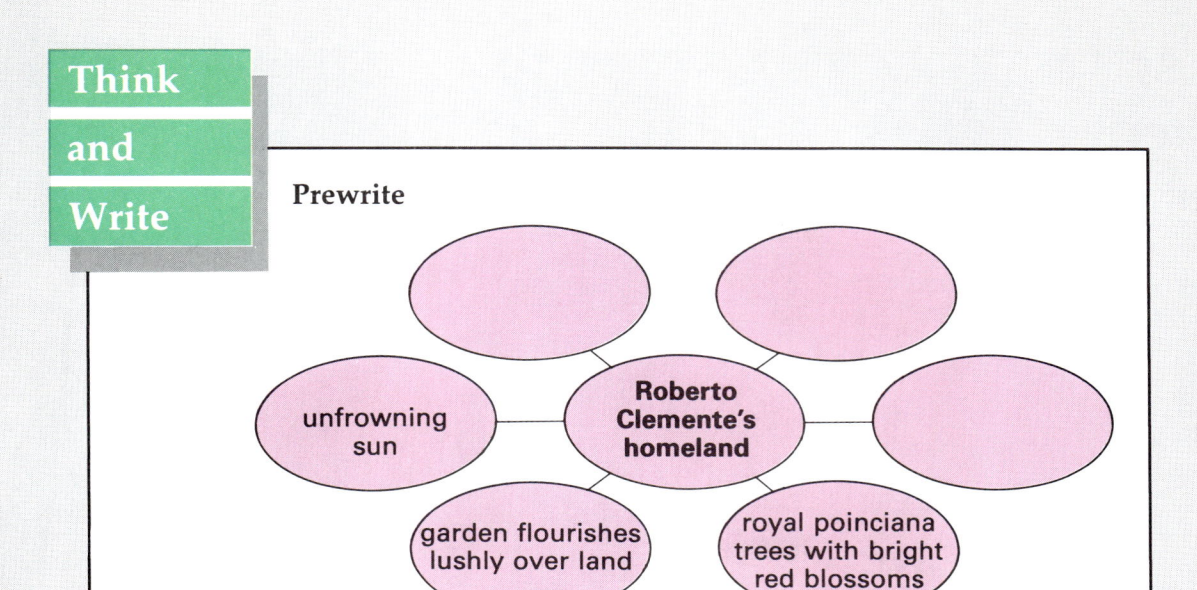

```
        (      )            (      )
                Roberto
 unfrowning     Clemente's    (      )
    sun         homeland
        garden flourishes   royal poinciana
        lushly over land    trees with bright
                            red blossoms
```

Language that appeals to any sense, or any combination of senses, creates **imagery**. Most imagery appeals to the sense of sight but can also suggest the way things sound, smell, taste, or feel.

Study the diagram shown above. Notice the words that describe Roberto Clemente's homeland, Puerto Rico. These words were included in the selection. Copy the diagram, adding other sensory words or phrases from the selection.

Compose

Using the information in the diagram and what you know about figurative language, compose your own paragraph describing the physical beauty of the island of Puerto Rico. Remember to choose words that convey the most vivid images. Your first sentence might be *Puerto Rico is a beautiful island paradise in the Caribbean Sea.*

Revise

Read the paragraph that you wrote. Does it give a vivid picture of the island of Puerto Rico? If you were the reader, would the description make you want to visit this picturesque place? If not, revise your paragraph as necessary to create a colorful picture of Puerto Rico.

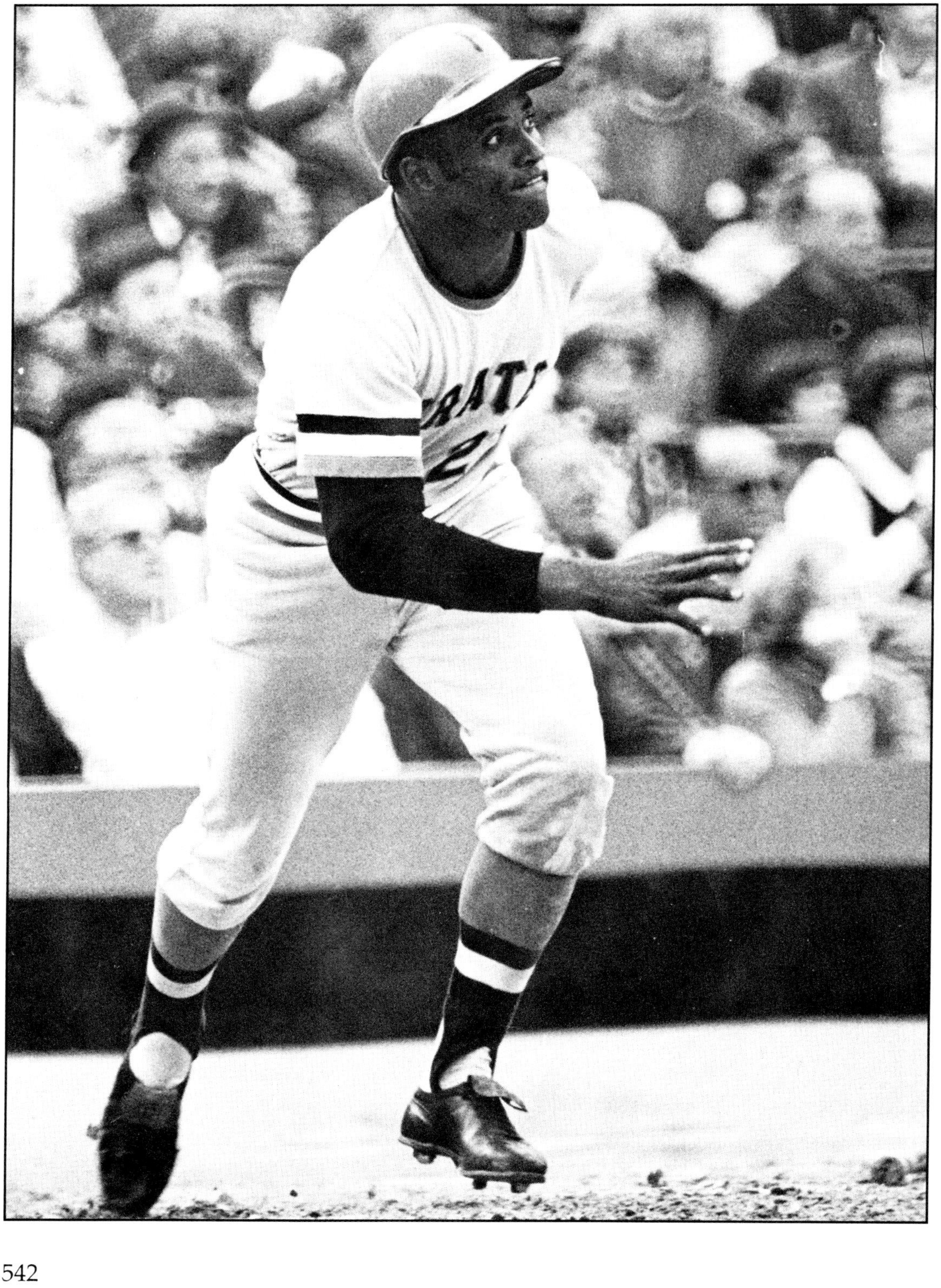

Clemente
(1934–72)
by Tom Clark

won't forget
his nervous
habit of
rearing his
head back
on his neck
like a
proud horse

Vocabulary Study

Context Clues

There are several methods to help you read unfamiliar words. One method is to look for clues in the words or sentences that surround the unfamiliar word. This method is called using **context clues**.

The context of a word is what comes before and after it to influence its meaning. To use the context as a clue to word meanings, you need to pay close attention to the whole sentence and possibly to several surrounding sentences. For example, suppose you don't know the meaning of the word *triumphant*. Read the following sentence:

> Nancy felt triumphant as she claimed her award for writing the winning eighth-grade essay.

Do you know the meaning of the word *triumphant*? From the context of the sentence you just read, it is fairly easy to see that the word *triumphant* means "happy over a victory."

The words surrounding an unfamiliar word may not always contain enough context clues to help you to figure out a word's meaning. Likewise, reading the entire sentence may not provide enough clues. In such cases, you can use a larger context to discover the meaning of the unfamiliar word. Using a larger context is simply reading more surrounding sentences, perhaps a full paragraph or two, to find the clues you need. From this larger context, you can often figure out what a word means.

The Synonym as a Context Clue

A **synonym** is a word that has the same, or almost the same, meaning as another word. For example, the word *friend* is a synonym for the word *companion*. In the following sentence, you can substitute the word *friend* for the word *companion* without changing the meaning:

Paul and his companion, Juan, usually spend Saturday afternoons together.

Suppose you didn't know the meaning of the word *barbarous* in this sentence:

He was a rough, barbarous ruler of an uncivilized land.

The word *barbarous* in this context is grouped with *rough* and *uncivilized*. Both *rough* and *uncivilized* are synonyms for *barbarous*. All three words have about the same meaning.

The Antonym as a Context Clue

An **antonym** is the opposite, or nearly the opposite, of another word. The word *ebullient* is the opposite of the word *dull*. Read the sentence below:

Judy is ebullient and full of life, but her sister's personality is just the opposite: somber, serious, and rather dull.

You can easily figure out the meaning of *ebullient* from the context clue. You're told that *ebullient* means "full of life." When a difficult word is followed by an easy word, you can usually figure out the meaning of the difficult word. It was also stated that *ebullient* is the opposite of *dull*, so if you know the meaning of *dull*, you have another clue to the meaning of the unfamiliar word.

The Appositive

An **appositive** is a word or a phrase that is placed next to another word or phrase to tell more about it. An appositive is usually set off with commas. Commas are not used, however, if the appositive is so closely related to what it explains that it seems to be part of that word or phrase. Read the following sentences. See if you can figure out the meanings of *dermis* and *dental caries*.

The dermis, the lower layer of your skin, contains living skin cells.

Dental caries, also called tooth decay, break down the structure of the tooth.

The explanatory phrases, or appositives — set off by commas — should have helped you figure out the meanings of *dermis* and *dental caries*.

As you read, look for context clues to help you figure out the meanings of unfamiliar words.

Acts of courage are among the legacies that make up our American heritage. Read to find out how a teenage girl, Elizabeth Lloyd, shows great courage.

As you read this story, use context clues to help you understand the meaning of any words that might be unfamiliar to you.

The Sampler

by Cornelia Meigs

Because the Lloyds' household was a very regular one, Elizabeth sat down every afternoon at exactly the same hour to sew on her sampler. Sewing was no easy task for an active girl who liked to be doing other things. But nobody, of course, ever thought of excusing her from it or ever dreamed of her growing up without having covered at least one square of linen with neat letters and figures.

The sampler was supposed to give her practice in all the different stitches of embroidery. Below the alphabet and the figures up to ten, it showed a small, carefully outlined picture of a willow tree and a tombstone. It was to be finished with her name and a motto such as WASTE NOT, WANT NOT.

There was so much to do in that thick-walled stone house, looking from its low hill out upon the bay, that there was no real time during the day when any older person could say with reason, "Elizabeth, you should be at your sewing." But when candlelight came — when the baking and sweeping, the dressing of chickens, and the curing of hams could not go forward so quickly by the dimmer light, then it was that her mother always said, "Now, Elizabeth," and the girl knew the sampler could not be avoided. It never occurred to her to hate it; she only knew that she liked doing anything else a great deal better.

Elizabeth had sat down to her needlework this October evening, with a wild wind swinging about the house and making the waves crash upon the shore below the hill. Elizabeth was alone, or almost alone; for her father and mother had driven five miles to the nearest town for the weekly marketing and had left Elizabeth with only deaf old Nora, the cook, who as everyone knew would fall asleep in her rocking chair in the little room above the kitchen the moment the last of the work was finished.

Not even the wind that blew in around the deep-framed windows, setting the candles to flickering — not even the slamming of the shutters — could rouse her. But as Elizabeth paused to slip the end of a thread into the slim eye of her needle there came a sound that, it seemed, would wake any sleeper on earth. *Boom*!

The great crash sounded from out on the water, where just at twilight she had looked out to see the smooth surface of the bay with not even a fishing boat in sight. *Boom*! This time all the windows in the house rattled and the glasses clattered on the dresser. *Boom*! The sound came a third time.

Elizabeth jumped up and ran to the window. What could it be? This was a time of peace, the year of 1810. It had been thirty years since the guns of the Revolution had echoed along those shores, and it would be two more years before another war was to break out between England and America.

She wondered for a puzzled minute if it could be pirates. It was quite true that pirates had landed on this coast within the memory of people not very much older than herself. She pressed her face against the pane, trying to peer out. How dark it was outside!

Yet there beyond the point was the ghostly form of a ship, dark against the duller darkness of the water. It was a bigger ship than those that usually came up the bay. She saw a great flash of red flame as once again a cannon crashed, and against its light she could make out, near the shore and struggling on the top of a towering wave, the dark shape of a small boat with three men in it.

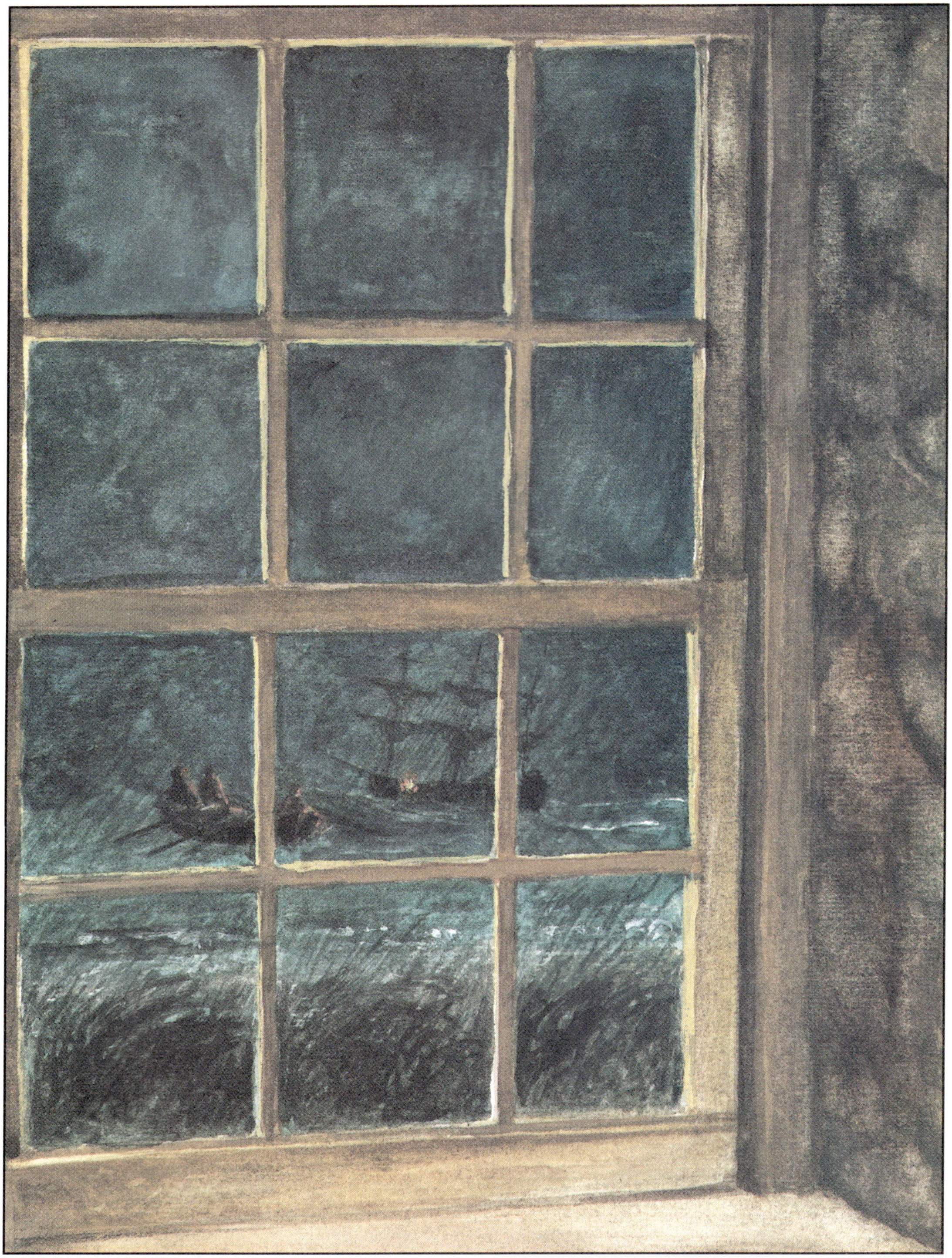

The blackness shut down again and there was nothing to be heard except the roaring of the wind. Then in a moment of brief calm there came a sound more surprising than any she had yet heard—a voice, little and distant, calling out, calling her own name.

"Elizabeth! Elizabeth Lloyd!"

She rushed to the door, lifted the latch, and immediately felt the wind snatch it from her hand and swing it wide, letting in a driving splatter of rain. Old Nora had actually been awakened by the cannon shots, which shook the house, and was thumping down the stairs. Elizabeth stood on the sill, holding back the door so that all the light that was possible would come shining out upon the darkness of the night.

The men in the boat needed a signal to guide them to the strip of beach just below the house. Her flash of light seemed to have shown them the direction; for she was almost certain that she heard, in another quiet moment, the sound of the bow on the gravel. She waited. How the wind roared!

Again there was a crash of the ship's cannon, its report followed a moment later by the splitting of wood. Voices and the tramp of feet were coming up the path. Somebody said, "They got our boat that time." And a deeper voice answered: "It's lucky we were no longer in it. Go easy there, mate; he's too tired to move another step." Three figures came out of the darkness, two of them supporting a third. The little group stumbled across the doorstep and stood blinking in the light of the warm kitchen.

Elizabeth closed the door against the rain and, as is always the duty of a hostess when guests come in out of the cold and wet, bent to put another log on the fire. One did that and then asked questions. But when she straightened up to look at the unexpected visitors, she had no need to ask. She cried out quickly, "Why, it's Cousin Nathaniel!"

"We thought this must be my uncle's house and that you at least would hear our hail."

Her cousin Nathaniel Holmes was only a year or two older than her own fourteen years; but he looked like a man indeed with his tall figure, his pale, tired face, and his rough seaman's coat.

The broad-shouldered man beside him said in a big, friendly voice, " 'Tis a shame to frighten you, young mistress, but men who are fleeing for their lives will take shelter anywhere."

"You did not frighten me," she answered bravely.

They were helping their comrade into the armchair in which she had been sitting. When once the tall man with graying hair had dropped back on the cushions, her cousin Nat stooped, picked something off the floor, and handed it to her.

"Your sampler, Elizabeth," he said with a broad smile. "I know how you love to sew, and I see how prettily you have made the willow. I fear you are to be badly interrupted in your favorite work this night. You wonder why we are here? Have you ever heard men speak of the custom of the British Navy — that of taking seamen by force?"

She had indeed, and her cheeks colored angrily as she thought of it. All America was excited over this same matter, which was to end by leading two friendly nations into war with each other. England had need of sailors and gunners for her warships, and since the life on board was hard, cruel, and dangerous, very few men would offer themselves for it. As a result the officers were ordered by their government to take men where they could, and take them they did.

They had fallen into the way of stopping American vessels at sea, searching them, and declaring that certain able seamen were really British and must be carried on board English ships to serve in His Majesty's Navy. It was of little use for the American captains to fight against them. The English battleships always had a row of cannon with which to back up their demands. Many a good man was rowed away and taken on board a proud, tall-sailed English vessel, each looking back to his own ship and to his comrades, whom perhaps he was never to see again. But here it seemed were three, at least, who had dared to refuse and had made this bold effort to escape.

"Yes," Nat said, looking up to answer the question in Elizabeth's eyes, "they took us all three, though Bo'sun

Leonard here is an old sailor, and though I am not yet a real seaman, for I sailed only six months ago. We swore to one another that we were not going to fight for the British king."

He held out his thin, cold hands to the blaze, saying no more, for he did not seem to think it was necessary to tell just what they had done. It was the broad-shouldered man, Dan Peters, who finished the account. He gave it in the most matter-of-fact way in the world. It was plain to see that all three were too weary to think of much of anything except that they were warm and safe here, at least for a few minutes.

Peters told of how they were carried away in a boat with four British sailors and a lieutenant, all armed with pistols and heavy swords. They made Peters pull an oar in the middle of the boat; but as they came near the towering side of the British vessel he saw, to his amazement, that Nat had leaped up to seize the officer around the middle, pinning his arms so that he could not draw his sword. The brief, hard struggle ended in the lieutenant's being flung overboard, while the two older Americans each fought with the sailor nearest him.

"We swung them over the side like sacks of gravel," Peters told them cheerfully. "They were so taken by surprise that they had no time to fight. The last one jumped to save us the trouble, and we caught up the oars and slipped away into the twilight, for it was just beginning to get dark. All those we dropped overboard got to the ship, and before she could get her cannon aimed at us we were hidden in among the islands. But we didn't dare land anywhere along these swampy shores."

The war vessel had followed, most of the shots from it going wide in the dark, but a few of them were good guesses that almost hit their mark. Higher and higher up the bay they had come, the men in the boat fighting so hard against wind and tide that Leonard, the old sailor, was fainting at the oars, and even the other two could scarcely lift and dip the heavy blades.

"Then we saw your light."

Old Nora, like Elizabeth, had without a word turned herself to caring for the comfort of the guests. She brought a great bowl of stew from the cupboard, poured it into a big iron kettle, and hung the kettle on the swinging hook. Nat helped her to lift it, and she nodded thanks and greeting to him, but she asked no questions. She had been deaf so long that she was used to the idea of not having things explained to her. She trotted back and forth, casting curious looks at the weary and dripping guests, but she stirred and seasoned the soup, cut bread from the long loaf, and said nothing. Elizabeth, however, kept no such silence.

"What will you do next?" she asked, looking from one to the other.

They were all three quiet, so that the beat of the rain outside and the harsh voice of the wind were the only sounds. The storm roared, then dropped an instant, and in the stillness there came to all of them the sound that no person who lives by the sea can ever fail to recognize—the creak of oars in their oarlocks. Even Bo'sun Leonard, sitting with closed eyes in the big chair, heard it and raised his drooping head.

"It's only a matter of minutes before they'll be here." It was the first time he had spoken, but his words were quick and very clear. "They can't fail to visit the only house that's in sight. You're to go on, you two. Do you hear me? That's orders. I can't move but you're to get away, and I will stay here."

It is the habit of every sailor to obey the commands of his superior. Nat and Peters hesitated a minute. Then Nat turned suddenly to the door of the bedroom opening from the kitchen. "Carry him in there," he said. "There's no time even to get him upstairs. And by some chance they may not search the house."

They lifted Leonard, bore him into the room, and laid him on the bed. He did not speak again or even open his eyes, but he made an impatient motion with his hand. He was anxious for them to go.

"If we could get across the hill to the Mallorys' house," Nat said, "we could get Ephraim Mallory and his three sons to stand by us, that I know. We could make a dash back and get Leonard away safe, even if the British had already laid hands on him. But if harm should come to you, Elizabeth—"

"No harm will come to us—two women who have done nothing," Elizabeth answered boldly, more boldly than she felt. "We will keep them back as long as we can." She put her mouth close to Nora's ear and shouted. "We are going to have still more guests. Pile up the fire and bring out the biggest ham."

Nat hesitated a moment in the doorway. Peters said, as he went through the door, "And if they do follow us, little mistress, would you try to flash a light at the window, maybe, if you could do it without danger? Then we would know where to make a stand." The door banged, and Elizabeth was left in the kitchen, listening.

The wind, roaring over the hill, drowned the noise of their retreating steps, but in the shelter of the house another sound began to be very plain, the heavy, orderly tramp of marching feet coming up from the landing—many of them, it seemed, oh, very many. Then there were voices, a thundering knock, and a command, "Open, in the king's name."

They all came in together—a tall officer wrapped in a dripping cape, a file of men behind him, their shoes, their hair, their rough blue coats streaming with the rain.

Elizabeth made her most polite curtsy, just as she had seen her mother do when important guests arrived. "My parents are away from home," she said calmly, "but we shall do our best to make you comfortable. You—you look as though you might be in need of refreshment."

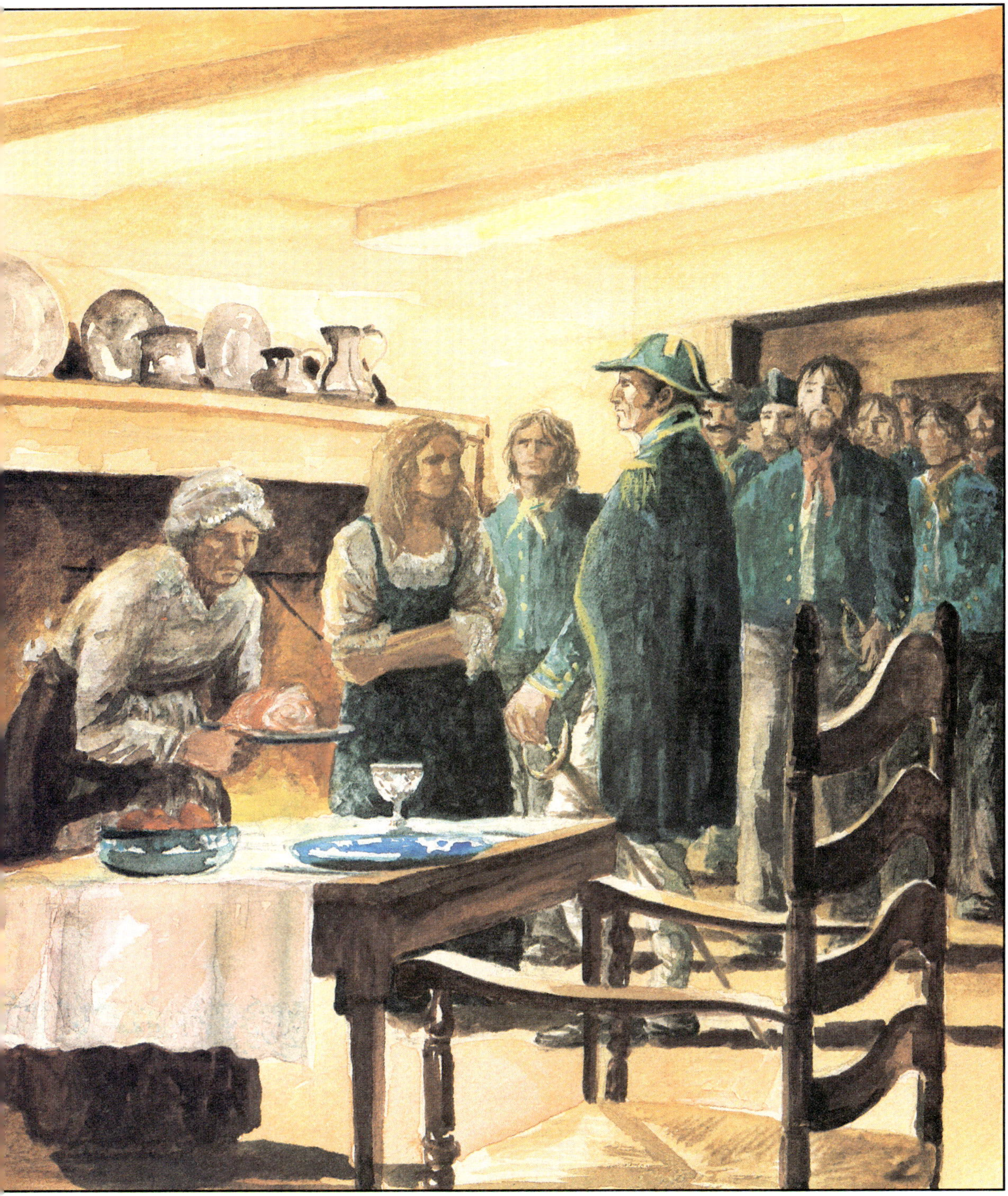

The officer—it might possibly have been the same lieutenant whom Nat had thrown out of the boat—swung his rapid glance about the room. The big, spotless kitchen was bright with the leaping fire and its reflection in the polished copper pots and pans. Elizabeth was laying a white cloth on the long table. Nora had unwrapped the ham and was already cutting delicate, rosy slices. The officer looked, hesitated, and then sat down in the big chair.

"The men will march better if they have some food," he said. "That was a long row we had, searching along the shore. Dobbs, go out and see that guards are placed around the house. If there is anyone hiding here it will be impossible to get away while they are watching. We may as well give ourselves the relief of a little warmth and food and look for those runaway rascals later on. Well, young woman, let me see what your house has to offer."

It was a splendid feast that the old farmhouse gave its guests that night. The whitest linen out of the great chest in the parlor, the glass dishes and the blue plates that had come from England with Elizabeth's great grandmother, the polished silver spoons were all brought forth. The choicest preserves, the last vegetables from the garden, the ham cured by a recipe a hundred years old made a supper fit for King George III himself instead of one of his officers. "Have you this?" the blue-uniformed man would ask now and again. "Do you not have that?"

"In a minute, sir; in just a minute," Elizabeth would answer. She lingered over the serving as long as she dared, she ducked curtsies when she received an order, she did everything to make the meal last a little longer.

Nora went back and forth, waiting on the men who sat humbly upon the benches by the fire while their commander dined alone at the long table. It was fortunate that farmhouses of that day had generous supplies in their storerooms. A large company it was, ten men, with even larger appetites.

The minutes went by, oh, so slowly. Nat and his comrade would be across the farm, Elizabeth was thinking; they would be climbing the hill; once over the top they would be within reach of the Mallorys' house. How long, how very long it took to reach shelter on this stormy night. But time was passing. Triumph colored her cheeks. They were growing safer every minute, safer. . . .

"And now," ordered the British officer, pushing his chair back suddenly, "I have even a mind to lay me down to take a little rest before I start out in the storm again. Light me a candle. I will go into the bedroom yonder and sleep a little."

No! Oh, no! Elizabeth had almost cried out the words in her terror, but she put her hand over her mouth and held them back. "We have better rooms above," she managed to say, her voice shaking, "if it would please you just to walk up the stairs."

"In an American farmhouse the best bed is always in the spare chamber below," he answered stubbornly. "I have been on shore often enough to learn that." He yawned widely and got up. "In our wandering life we must learn how to sleep comfortably when we can."

He walked across the kitchen. Elizabeth had lighted the candle and stood shaking, holding out her arm to bar the door. How, how could she stop him? She looked hopefully past him to old Nora beside the fire. Could not Nora think of something? But no, what did she understand?

The officer stopped, staring at her as she barred the way. His heavy brows drew together in a suspicious frown. "What is this? You have, after all, something hidden in that room? Out of my way!" He stepped forward.

Old Nora dropped a spoon with a great clatter. She took one limping step across the floor and flung the kitchen door wide open. "Don't waste time," she cried in her trembling old voice. "It was that way they went. Can't you see the marks of their feet beyond the doorstone? Go, if you have any hope of catching them."

There was a thump of heavy feet, a clash of swords drawn, a hail of orders as the men jumped up, seized their arms, and swung toward the door. The officer snatched up his cloak.

"Why did you not tell me this before?" he roared at Nora.

"Eh? I'm so deaf, how was I to know your errand? Nobody tells me anything." He was over the sill, but he swung around on the doorstep to give a final order.

"Dobbs, stand here and do not let either of these women pass. Keep three men to guard the windows so that they cannot make a signal. Do not follow us until we are well away." He was gone, and the door slammed behind him.

Elizabeth stood for a second trembling, wondering what she should do next. Then she seized a lantern from its hook on the wall, lighted it at the fire, and sped up the stairs. The door as well as the windows was guarded, but the men would not be watching that little round opening, hardly a real window, just above the roof of the kitchen.

She was beside it; she had wrapped her skirt about the lantern to hide its light; and she had climbed out through the space, which was little bigger than the porthole of a ship. The shingles on the roof below were wet and slippery, but she knew how to run across them, knew that she must keep running or she would fall. She ended, with a bump, against the great stone chimney. Steadying herself with one arm against the warm, rough stones, she made her way around the chimney and was on the peak of the kitchen roof, facing the distant hill.

Fearlessly she swung the lantern once, and again and again. A deep voice below shouted to her to stop. She took no notice, and suddenly a humming bullet went past her and hit against the chimney. The crash of the big pistol would give warning, even if the swinging light was not enough. Nat and his companion would know that the British were coming behind them. The lantern fell from her hand and broke on the stones below, but she had given her wild signal of danger and could do no more.

It had taken but a few seconds to run across the roof, but now it was slow minutes as she crawled back in the wind and the wet. Once inside and downstairs, she stood close to Nora by the fire. Her knees felt suddenly like water and her voice was trembling.

"Nora," she said close to the old woman's ear, "how could you tell them where Nat had gone?"

"It was better to give the old one a chance, even at the cost of a bit of danger to the young ones," answered Nora. "Yes, you told me nothing, but it did not take me long to guess what was going on. I saw the Revolution; I've been by before this when hunted men were hiding from their enemies." She drew a great breath and smoothed her apron. "Sakes, but we have a lot of dishes to wash up."

Elizabeth was not much help in setting the place to rights. Again and again she stood at the back door, straining to hear any sound that the wind might carry. Was that a distant shout and another? What was that? Voices that were far-off. They

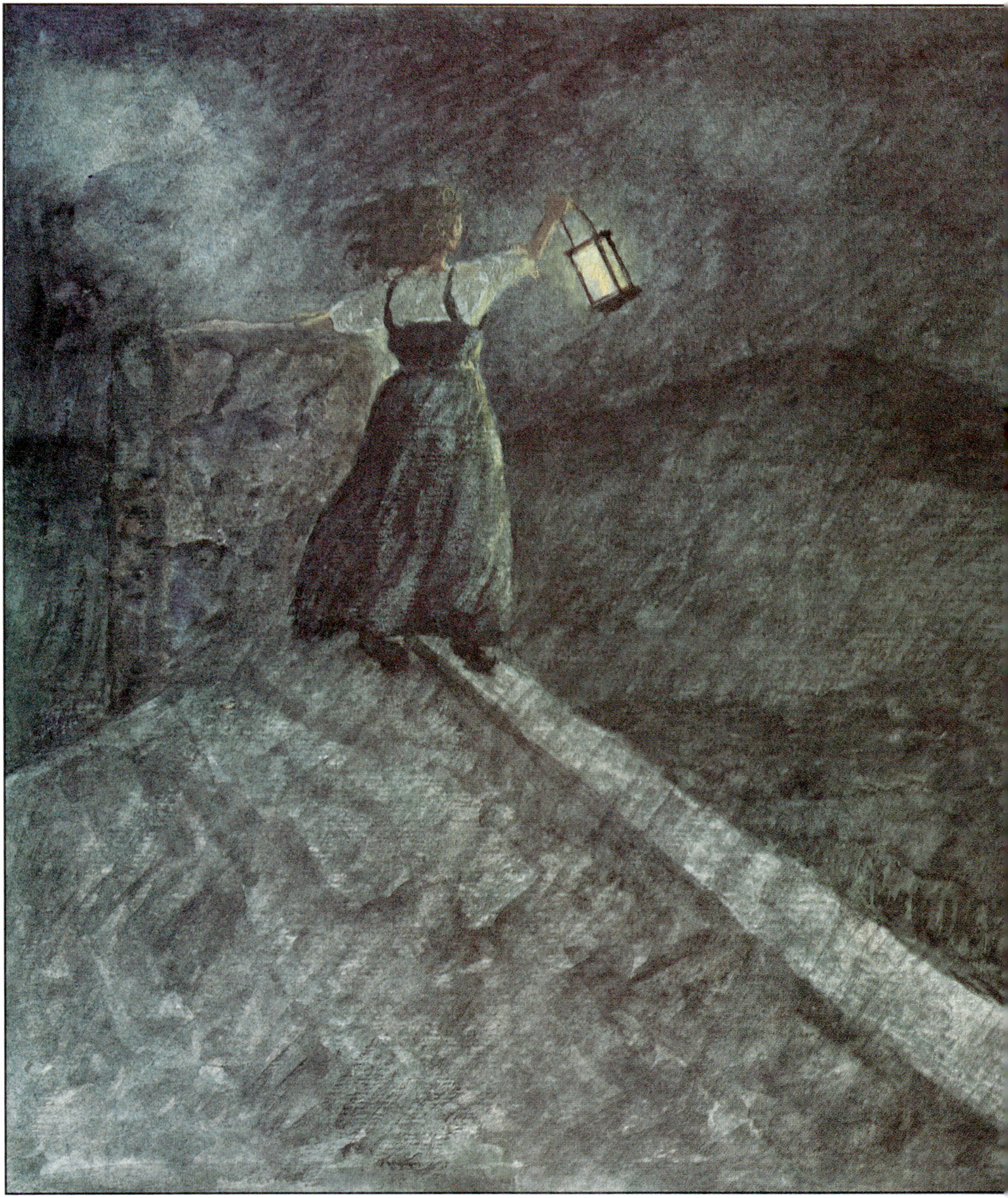

were nearer; they were coming this way. Had they taken her cousin? Would they in the end lay hands on poor Bo'sun Leonard, lying helpless within? Oh, Nat! Oh, Nat!

There was shouting and stumbling before the door. It swung back, and a dripping figure, sword in hand, was on the doorstep. Here was no blue coat or gold lace; here was no British seaman. This thin, long figure could be only one person — her cousin Nat!

Nathaniel threw his weapon down upon the table, where there were still standing the dishes and glasses that had been used for the lieutenant's dinner.

" 'Tis the wrong men who have feasted in this house tonight," he said. "Such a dinner! And we out there in the dark, hungry! May the Mallory boys come in?"

There was enough left; for the farmhouse could feed one company and still have plenty remaining for another. Nora, smiling broadly, brought them more and more food; the fire leaped on the hearth, and everyone together tried to give an account of what had happened. Nat and Peters were just coming over the hill with the Mallorys behind them when they saw Elizabeth's signal and found a favorable place to make a stand against the advancing British.

"They could not guess our numbers in the dark, and they decided, after the first attack, to retreat to their boat," Nat said. "They will have a pretty row out to their ship, for she has had to stand offshore in this wind. Here's a pleasant journey to them, and may they take profit by the lesson they have learned. It is not well to lay hands on American seamen."

"The whole British nation may learn an even better one in time," Dan Peters added; but most of his remark was lost in the hollow of the cup of cider he had raised to his lips.

It was easy to see by looking at Bo'sun Leonard that he must stay where he was for many days. Perhaps, indeed, he would never be able to go to sea again. But the other two stood up at last and said good night.

"We have to join our ship," Nathaniel said. "Our skipper will be in need of sailors, and he was to stop at Norfolk, where we can meet him." The night's adventures seemed to mean little to men whose days and hours were passed among the dangers of the sea. "No, we can spend no more time except to offer you our thanks, Elizabeth Lloyd."

Two hours later Elizabeth's father and mother came home. Their daughter was sitting by the table, quietly stitching away. She looked up as her parents came in.

"There is a guest in the spare chamber," she remarked calmly, "and there have been others here to supper. And see, Mother, I have finished my willow tree. Instead of the verse at the bottom I am going to embroider LIBERTY FOREVER. And then I am never going to sew another sampler. I think, now that I am fourteen, that I have other things to do besides stitching pictures of willow trees."

Discuss the Selection

1. How did Elizabeth show great courage?
2. What occurred between the first boom of the cannon and the return home of Elizabeth's parents?
3. Elizabeth's sampler was described twice in the story, once near the beginning, and once near the end. Find those parts of the story and read them again. How do the two descriptions differ?
4. What was your reaction when Elizabeth crawled on the roof with the lantern? When the British started shooting at her, did you think she would survive?
5. What changes took place in Elizabeth because of the events in the story? What happened at the end of the story to show what insight Elizabeth had gained?

Apply the Skills

By looking for clues in the words surrounding an unfamiliar word, you can often guess the meaning of the unfamiliar word. Use context clues to figure out the meaning of the italicized words in these passages.

1. Elizabeth was pleased about serving the Americans their victory feast. She was so pleased that she felt like doing a dance around the room, a little *gigue*.
2. She stirred the pot of soup warming in the fireplace. It hung on a *potlatch*, a big iron hook, fastened to the fireplace.
3. Leonard was a *bo'sun* on the ship. His job was to care for the deck crew and the rigging of the ship.

Think and Write

Prewrite

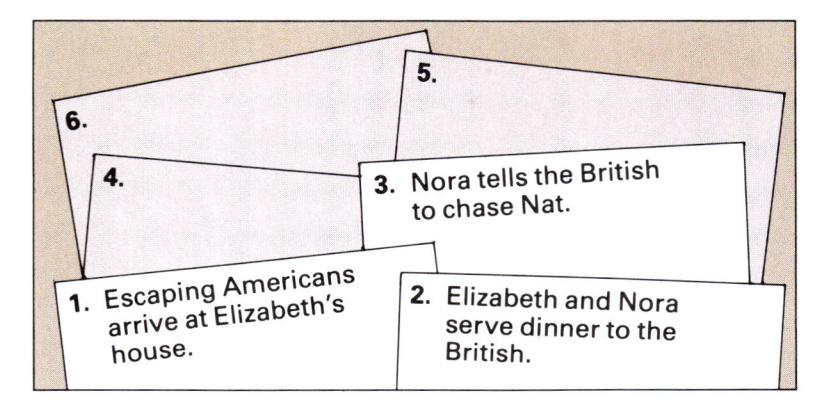

1. Escaping Americans arrive at Elizabeth's house.
2. Elizabeth and Nora serve dinner to the British.
3. Nora tells the British to chase Nat.
4.
5.
6.

A narrative paragraph tells a story or part of a story. It is usually written in chronological order. Each of the three notecards shown above describes an event from "The Sampler." The events are described in sequence, with the first card representing what happened first. Referring to the story, make three more notecards describing other events in the story. As you prepare your cards, pay attention to the chronological order of the events.

Compose

Using the information on the notecards, write a short narrative account of the main events from the story. Use chronological order, the order in which the events occur in the story. Try to use transition words, such as *while*, *next*, and *finally*, to help make the order of events clear. Your first sentence might be *While Elizabeth was embroidering, escaping sailors came to her house.*

Revise

Read the paragraph that you wrote. Have you included the events of the story in chronological order? Did you use transition words to make the sequence clear? If not, revise what you wrote by adding transition words and vivid details.

Freedom fighters of World War II left us a legacy of independence. Read to find out why a young woman of Jewish heritage, Hannah Senesh, chooses to risk her life on a dangerous mission.

Biographers often present social and historical details to help readers understand their subjects. As you read, notice the details that the author uses to explain Senesh's beliefs and heroic deeds.

Hannah Senesh

by Linda Atkinson

Hannah Senesh was born in Budapest, Hungary, in 1921. Her heritage from her Jewish family was one of culture and learning. She was popular in school and showed a talent for writing—especially poetry. As a teenager, Hannah began keeping a diary, and in it, she expressed her hopes and dreams for the future. In 1939, she emigrated to Palestine to live and work on one of the large farms called kibbutzim. At about this time, German armies were invading and conquering many European countries. Once under German rule, the Jews in these countries were in grave danger. In 1943, the Germans were about to occupy Hungary. Hannah's mother was still living in Budapest, although Hannah's brother George had escaped and was coming to join her in Palestine.

To save lives, Hannah volunteered to join a group of young Hungarian Jews on a dangerous mission.

March 1944

The roar of the airplane made it impossible for them to talk. They sat silently, stiffly, weighed down by their weapons, their parachutes, their bulky winter clothing. In forty minutes they would be over Yugoslavia, and the first part of their mission would begin.

There were four of them. Reuven, Yonah, Abba, and Hannah. Four young Jews on their way to Hitler's Europe. Each of them had been born there, in quieter times. Each had escaped and found safety in Palestine. But now, on the thirteenth of March, 1944, they were going back. Trained to fight by the British in the deserts of Palestine and Egypt, taught to use weapons, parachutes, radio transmitters, they were going back to gather information for the British about German defenses, to establish escape routes for captured Allied airmen, and to rescue as many Jews as they could.

The airplane buzzed and shook its way through the black night sky. Reuven studied the faces of the others: Abba and Yonah, deep in thought; Hannah, her blue eyes calm and clear. At twenty-two, Hannah was the youngest member of the crew, the only woman, and the only one who was positive that the mission would succeed. When she saw Reuven looking at her, she smiled and gave him the "thumbs up" sign, her favorite sign for victory.

Years later, Reuven described Hannah as a "poet-tomboy," a "girl who dreamed of being a heroine, and who was a heroine." On the night of the mission, "her excitement was contagious," he wrote. "We were all infected by it. Gradually tension relaxed, and the air seemed lighter."

According to the plan, Reuven and Hannah were going to jump first. Then the plane would circle and make a second pass over the target so Yonah and Abba could jump. Once on the ground, they would meet with the Yugoslavian partisans and make their way on foot to the border with Hungary. The German occupation was about to begin, and close to a million Jews were still living there. One of them was Catherine Senesh, Hannah's mother.

"Mother Darling," Hannah had written just before boarding the plane for Yugoslavia. "In a few days I'll be so close to you — and yet so far. Forgive me, and try to understand. With a million hugs. Your Annie."

Hannah hadn't seen her mother since 1939, when she had left her native Budapest for Palestine. She had begged her mother to go with her then. Anti-Jewish feeling in Hungary was already high and rising. The dangers faced by Jews all over Europe were the worst in recent memory. But no matter what arguments Hannah brought to bear, her mother would not leave Budapest. Like most of her friends and relatives, Catherine believed that the wave of bad feelings against Jews would soon recede and things would be once again the way they had been when she was a girl.

January 1943

As December turned to January 1943, Hannah had been in agony — afraid of

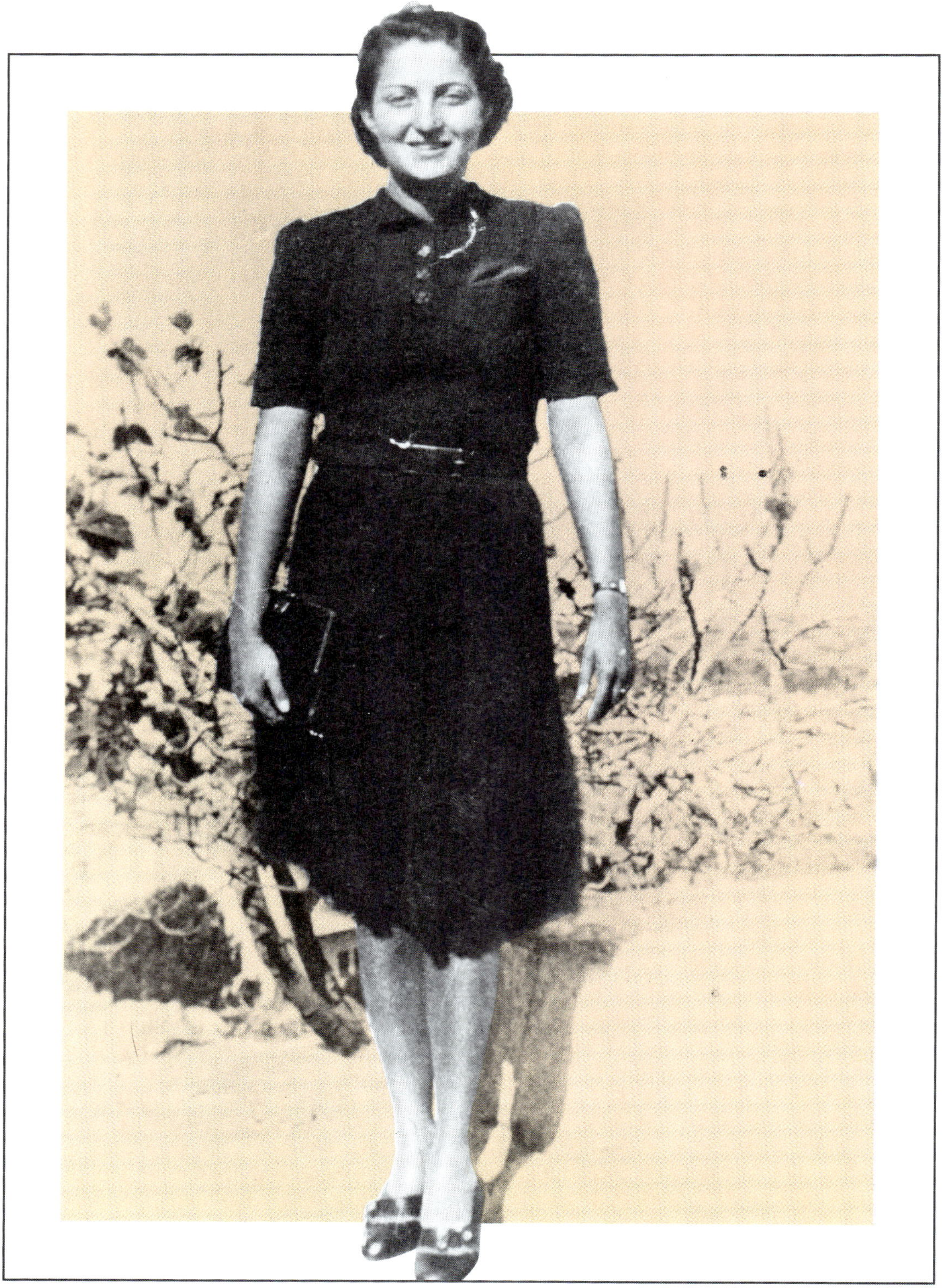

what might lie in store for Palestine, heartsick for her mother and brother in Europe. In spite of her best intentions, it seemed, she had failed to do what was needed. And now, like the young resistance fighters of Europe, she was faced with impossible choices. Should she stay in Palestine, in the Land she had come to love? What about the ones who could not come, the ones who were trapped in Europe and might be doomed to die there? What about her mother? How could Hannah not be among them at this time? If they could not escape, how could she not go to them and try to help?

On the eighth of January, 1943, Hannah's confusion suddenly ended. After a "shattering" week, she suddenly knew exactly what she must do: return to Hungary. She must help the people who were trapped there to escape. She must find her mother and bring her to Palestine. Although "I'm quite aware how absurd the idea is," she wrote, "it still seems both feasible and necessary to me, so I'll get to work on it and carry it through."

Almost a month and a half after Hannah's decision to return to Hungary, a young man named Yonah Rosen visited the settlement at Caesarea. Hannah had met him two years earlier when she was making the rounds of kibbutzim and had stopped briefly at his kibbutz, Ma'agan, on the Sea of Galilee. Most of the members there, like Rosen himself, were Hungarian. Now, in February 1943, she felt drawn to him, as to close kin. He too had left his family in Hungary when he came to Palestine. And he too was tormented by fears for them. Now he told Hannah that at Palmach Headquarters, which were being set up at his kibbutz, a rescue mission to Europe was being discussed. The idea was to drop parachutists behind the lines into the German-occupied countries. They would have to be natives of the countries to which they were sent so they could mix easily with the people and not arouse suspicion. Their job would be to help organize resistance to the Germans and to lead out the Jews who were trapped there. Rosen had already asked to be on the Hungarian mission — the Haganah. Hannah told him that was exactly what she wanted to do.

"I was truly astounded," Hannah wrote in her diary. "The *identical* idea! My answer, of course, was that I'm absolutely ready."

Rosen explained that the mission was not yet a sure thing. Haganah leaders had been trying for years to persuade the British to help organize a rescue mission to Eastern Europe. The British had never been interested. They didn't think such a mission would help the general war effort. But toward the end of January 1943, the Allied Air Command had sent bombers to destroy the Ploesti oil refineries of Rumania. Hundreds of Allied airmen — many more than had been anticipated — had been shot down and captured, making it clear that the Allies needed more and better information about German defenses in the area. Suddenly the idea of a parachute mission began to make sense to the British. Many Palestinian Jews were from the Balkan countries, including Rumania. They knew the languages of the area, the people, and the terrain. They would be able to act as spies, gather information, contact underground groups, and set up escape routes for the captured airmen. If they would do this first, and then go about the work of helping the Jews, the British said they would be willing to train them and supply the weapons, parachutes, and airplanes. Yonah promised to let Hannah know how things developed. He thought she was "admirably suited" for the mission.

"I see the hand of destiny in this," Hannah wrote in her diary, "just as I did at the time of my emigration to Palestine. I wasn't master of my fate then either. I was enthralled by one idea, and it gave me no rest. I knew I would emigrate, despite the many obstacles in my path. Now I again sense the excitement of something important and vital ahead, and the feeling of inevitability connected with a decisive and urgent step." She didn't know whether or not the people in charge would accept her. "But I think I have the capabilities necessary for just this assignment," she wrote, "and I'll fight for it with all my might."

Now her old enthusiasm returned. "I can't sleep at night," she wrote a few days after Yonah's visit, "because of the scenes I envisage: how I'll conduct myself in this or that situation . . . how I'll notify Mother of my arrival . . . how I'll organize the Jewish Youth."

On May 27, Yonah returned to Caesarea with the news Hannah had been waiting for. The rescue mission had been approved. Volunteers were going to be called and interviewed. Yonah had submitted Hannah's name. She could expect to be summoned soon. She wrote in her diary, "I pray for only one thing: that the period of waiting will not be too long, and that I can see action soon. As for the rest—I'm afraid of nothing. I'm totally self-confident, ready for anything."

In June, Hannah was called to Tel Aviv. She was interviewed by representatives of the British Army and representatives of the Haganah. The British were in charge of the interview. In response to a question about what Hannah thought the mission would entail, she calmly recited the priorities she knew the British insisted upon. The first, she said, was to contact local resistance fighters, and with their help, locate captured Allied airmen and help them to escape. The second priority, she said, was to help the Jews. In response to a question about what Hannah would do if she had to choose between saving her mother's life and the lives of twenty British soldiers, Hannah said she knew her mother would forgive her for the choice she would have to make.

Hannah was accepted for the mission. Now, her agony began in earnest. Working in the kitchen, in the garden, in the laundry, she waited for word that it was time to go. Meanwhile, she wrote poems and entries in her diary.

In December 1943, Hannah received orders to report to Kibbutz Ramat Hakovesh, not far from Tel Aviv, for the first part of her training. She did not write about this in her diary, but while in Tel Aviv, where she was to board the bus, she visited her friend Miryam and gave her a letter to be delivered to her brother George if he should arrive in Palestine while Hannah was gone. Miryam agreed not to ask any questions about the letter or about Hannah's mission, which was classified a military secret. Hannah had told members of Kibbutz Sdot-Yam just that she was reporting for basic training, which was partially true. Basic training was the first phase of Hannah's training. Parachute training was second. Later, in Egypt, she would be taught other important skills.

In all, two hundred forty youths had been accepted for the mission; thirty-two were being trained for the Balkans. In addition to Hannah, two others were women: Chaviva Reik and Sarah Braverman. Volunteers were trained in shifts. At Ramat Hakovesh, mission members were taught unarmed fighting, mostly based on judo, and armed fighting, using weapons. They also learned to disassemble and assemble the weapons, quickly, silently, and blindfolded.

From Ramat Hakovesh, Hannah returned briefly to her kibbutz, then she was back in Tel Aviv to board a bus to Ramat David, a kibbutz near Nahalal that housed the Middle East Training Center for Parachutists. While in Tel Aviv, Hannah tried to arrange immigration papers for her mother.

At Ramat David, she amazed everyone by her fearlessness in learning to parachute jump. "It's nothing," she said later to a new volunteer named Yoel Palgi. "You go up in a plane, you jump, and you're right back on the ground. I'll never forget how Nahalal looked from the air. It was a great experience. You'll love it."

"She spoke as naturally and plainly as if she were describing what she had had for breakfast that morning," Yoel wrote later.

Back at Caesarea to await orders for the third phase of her training, Hannah took walks on the beach, swam in the sea, worked, and waited. In mid-January 1944, she received orders to return to Tel Aviv. From there, members of the mission would depart together for Cairo and the final part of their training.

"We were all tense at the thought of leaving Palestine," Yoel Palgi wrote. "None dared admit to the other how difficult it was to leave; everyone wondered whether he would ever see the Land [Palestine] again. We were all parting from our dear ones, our settlements, our land. It was a silent parting, one that neither relieved tensions nor lightened spirits. We had to avoid arousing curiosity and questions. The mission itself was a silent one; no one must know we were going armed with a sling to do battle with the powerful enemy."

Hannah was worried about her mother in Budapest and about her brother, who was due to arrive in Palestine soon. The day Hannah's group was to leave for Egypt, Hannah got a message she could hardly believe: Her brother George was in Haifa. He had arrived on an immigrant ship called the *Nyassa* and had been interned in Atlit, a British-run camp for illegal immigrants. He had managed to persuade one of the British soldiers to search Hannah out and tell her of his arrival. Yoel Palgi was with Hannah when she got the news. "I hardly recognized in her the strong self-assured woman I had come to know so well," he wrote. "Tears flowed from her eyes. With difficulty I managed to obtain bus tickets for Haifa, and accompanied her there. . . ." Yoel also contacted their superiors and was able to have their departure for Egypt put off until the next day.

Hannah took back from Miryam the letter she had written in December and sent a telegram to her mother telling her George had arrived at last. At the Atlit camp, as an officer in the British Army, Hannah was able to make her way through the red tape and get permission for George to leave the compound for a few hours. Brother and sister walked out under the brooding late afternoon sky. Hannah could hardly believe that George had arrived at last. George could hardly believe that Hannah was going away. He told her part of the incredible story of his escape from Europe, how he had made his way from France to Spain, where he spent over a month in various prisons, passed himself off as a French-Canadian, and finally boarded an immigrant ship that got through the British patrols to Palestine.

Hannah could tell George almost nothing of what she was doing, where she was going, when she would be back. She told him only that she was a radio officer, and she gave him the letter she had retrieved from Miryam.

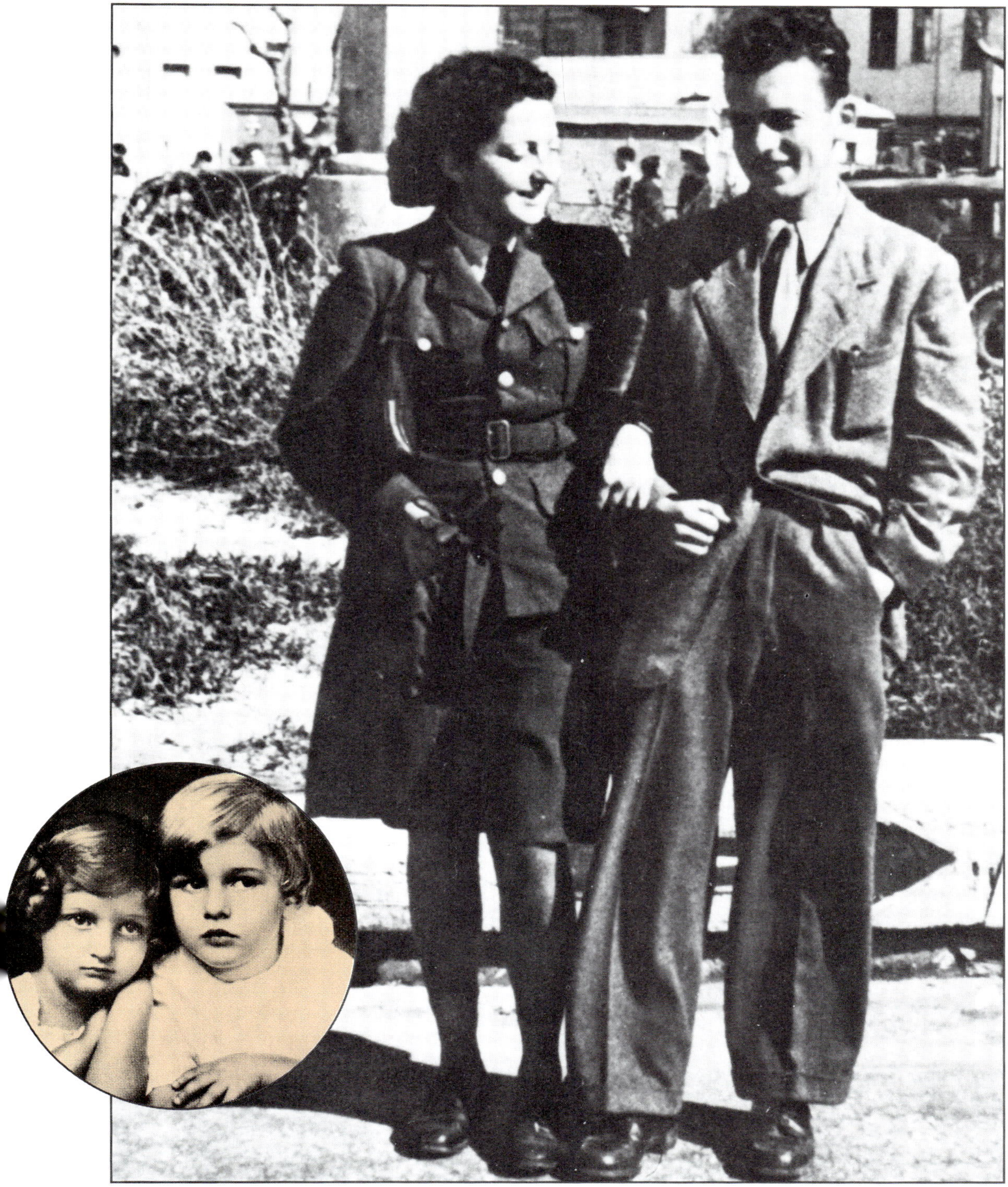

Darling George!

Sometimes one writes letters one does not intend sending. Letters one must write without asking oneself, "I wonder whether this will ever reach its destination."

Day after tomorrow I am starting something new. Perhaps it is madness. Perhaps it's fantastic. Perhaps it's dangerous. Perhaps one in a hundred — or one in a thousand — pays with his life. Perhaps with less than his life, perhaps with more. Don't ask questions. You'll eventually know what it's about.

George, I must explain something to you. I must exonerate myself. I must prepare myself for that moment when you arrive . . . waiting for that moment when, after six years, we will meet again, and you will ask, "Where is she?" and they'll abruptly answer, "She's not here."

I wonder, will you understand? I wonder, will you believe that it is more than a childish wish for adventure, more than youthful romanticism that attracted me? I wonder, will you feel that I could not do otherwise, that this was something I had to do?

There are events without which one's life becomes unimportant, a worthless toy; and there are times when one is commanded to do something, even at the price of one's life. . . .

We have need of one thing: people who are brave and without prejudices, who are not robots, who want to think for themselves and not accept outmoded ideas. It is easy to place laws in the hands of people, to tell them to live by them. It is more difficult to follow those laws. But most difficult of all is to impose laws upon oneself, while being constantly self-analytical and self-vigilant. I think this is the highest form of law enforcement, and at the same time the only just form. And this form of law can only build a new, contented life.

Don't think I see everything through rose-colored glasses. My faith is a subjective matter, and not the result of outer conditions. I see the difficulties clearly, both inside and out. But I see the good side, and above all, as I said before, I think this is the only way.

I did not write about something that constantly preoccupies my thoughts: Mother. I can't.

Enough of this letter. I hope you will never receive it. But if you do, only after we have met.

And if it should be otherwise, George dear, I embrace you with everlasting love.

Your sister

P.S. I wrote the letter at the beginning of the parachute training course.

Hannah took the letter back after George had read it. She told him she couldn't answer any questions about it and he did not ask. Then it was time for him to return to Atlit and for Hannah to return to Tel Aviv. The next day, she was gone.

The parachutists from Palestine were a small band, a whisper of defiance against the roaring forces of death in Europe. Like the fighters in the ghettos and the rebels in the death camps, their chances for success were very small. Perhaps there was no chance at all. But they were there. They came to help, the only group from outside Europe that did. Arriving on a death-drenched continent, they represented life. At a time when the bonds between people were betrayed in ways more cruel than can be comprehended, the bonds they felt held fast. "We go out to our brothers in exile," Hannah had written on her way back to Hungary. "Our hearts will bring tidings of springtime, our lips sing the song of light."

In all, two hundred forty parachutists were trained by the British for the rescue mission. Thirty-two were dropped into the Balkans of Eastern Europe. Seven were killed: Abba Berdichev, Peretz Goldstein, Zvi Ben Jacob, Chaviva Reik, Rafael Reis, Enzo Sereni, and Hannah, "wonderful, sparkling Hannah," twenty-three years old, executed on November 7, 1944, by an irregular firing squad in the yard of the Margit Boulevard Prison. In another age, she might have been a poet.

Discuss the Selection

1. Why did Hannah Senesh decide to leave Palestine and go on a dangerous rescue mission to Europe?
2. What training did Senesh receive in preparation for the mission?
3. In Senesh's interview with representatives of the British army, she was faced with some difficult questions. How did she resolve that challenge and get accepted for the mission?
4. How did you feel when Hannah Senesh met her brother before leaving on her mission?
5. In Hannah Senesh's letter to her brother, she identified the personal qualities she values. Locate that part of the selection and identify the qualities.

Apply the Skills

Biography is one of the most popular forms of nonfiction. Details of the social and historical circumstances in which the subject lived are often included. Locate three such details used by the biographer, Linda Atkinson, that explain young Hannah Senesh's heroic decision to go on a dangerous mission.

Think and Write

Prewrite

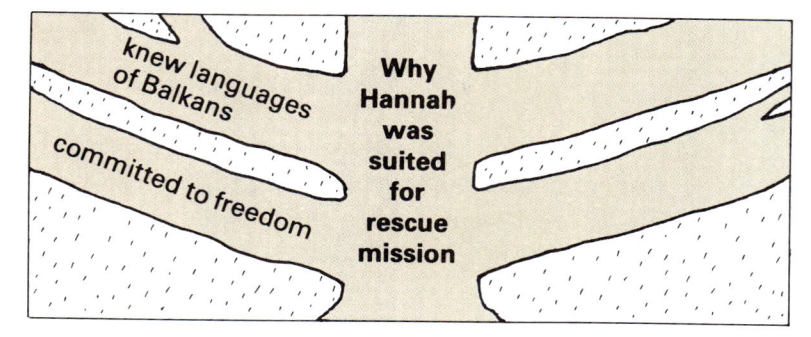

[Tree diagram showing "Why Hannah was suited for rescue mission" at center, with branches labeled "knew languages of Balkans" and "committed to freedom," and two empty branches.]

In the selection, "Hannah Senesh," Yonah thought Hannah was "admirably suited" for the rescue mission. In the tree diagram shown above, two reasons are given to support Yonah's belief in Hannah. Copy the diagram and complete it by filling in the empty branches with two more convincing reasons why Hannah was suited for the mission.

Compose

A persuasive paragraph states an opinion and supports it in a convincing way. The art of persuasion is an important life skill. Using the information in the tree diagram and the selection, write a persuasive paragraph to convince the British that Hannah has the capabilities to carry out the assignment. First, state your opinion. You might say: *Hannah Senesh is admirably suited for this mission.* Then, offer strong reasons as to why your opinion is worth their consideration. Finally, offer a convincing summary statement.

Revise

Read the paragraph you wrote. Did you begin with a statement of opinion? Does your paragraph give reasons to support that opinion? Did you conclude with a strong summary statement? If not, revise your paragraph until it is a clear and convincing presentation of Hannah's qualifications for the rescue mission.

Literature Study

Description

Description is any careful detailing of a person, place, or thing. Writers use description appealing to the senses of sight, sound, smell, touch, and taste to create more vivid mental pictures. A well-written description gives details to support the impression the author wants to make. The details are presented with carefully chosen descriptive words.

Read the following descriptions. As you read, pay special attention to the use of detail and descriptive words.

Description of a Person

> Karen Webster was a tall, thin woman with a vitality that sparkled through her sea-green eyes. The beige wool skirt and white cotton blouse she wore contrasted sharply with her colorful personality.

What does this description tell you about Karen Webster? What details support this idea?

Description of a Place

> The public market is an arena of sights, sounds, scents, and colors. Vendors call out their bargains from every corner. Bins of shiny red apples and pale green pears are sold at one stand, and huge watermelons at the next. Some yards away, the smell of freshly ground coffee lures tired shoppers.

What kind of impression is the author of this description trying to make? What details support this impression?

Description of an Object

> The little box was carefully handmade of the very best ebony and gold. The box stood on four button-like feet of real ivory.

As all the examples show, descriptive writing depends on colorful language and careful detailing. Read this sentence:

> The house was surrounded by grass and water.

Notice that the sentence does not give you a vivid description of the house. Here is a more descriptive sentence:

> The circular glass and steel house stretched out on a sea of grass leading to its own private lake of cool, crystal-clear water.

The best way to help a reader see the picture you want to create is to appeal to the reader's senses. Describe how things look, sound, smell, taste, and feel. You do not have to appeal to all five senses in every description. The more vivid the words you use, however, the better your description will be.

Mood

The mood of a story is the general feeling it gives the reader. Good descriptions help create mood. For example, spooky places, creaky stairs, and thunderstorms can create a mood of terror. Some writers create a feeling of mystery by presenting a situation that makes you crave an answer. Certain details in a story may create a mood of sadness. On the other hand, a humorous mood can result when an author tells you just the opposite of what you expect. Terror, mystery, sadness, and humor are moods created by authors of fiction and nonfiction.

Reading Description

In reading a description, try to grasp the main idea given by the details the author has chosen. Look closely at descriptions of persons, places, or things. Then ask yourself these questions:

1. Do you get a clear idea of what the author wants you to see or feel?
2. What details tell something special about the person, place, or thing that is being described?
3. Are the details arranged in a logical order?
4. Do all the words, phrases, and sentences give you a clear picture of what is being described?

Author Profile

Rudyard Kipling

Rudyard Joseph Kipling possessed a rare talent: He was able to entertain readers of all ages. His adult works earned many awards and honors, including the Nobel prize for literature. Kipling's books for young people were equally successful, whether they were written for the very young (the *Just So Stories*) or for older youth (*Captains Courageous, The Jungle Book*). No matter who his audience was, Rudyard Kipling was able to stir their imaginations with his exciting tales of adventure.

Rudyard Kipling was born in Bombay, India, in 1865. Both his parents were British; his father was a teacher at the Bombay School of Art. Although Rudyard spent only a small portion of his life in India, he never stopped writing about it. Almost all of his famous books are set in India.

When Kipling was seven years old, his parents sent him to England for his education. There he became an avid reader. With his teachers' help and encouragement, he also began composing poetry and short stories. By the time Kipling had finished his schooling, he knew that professional writing was the career for him.

Kipling left school at age seventeen to pursue his goal. He returned to India and was hired as a newspaper reporter in Bombay. Working on a newspaper improved Kipling's writing in several ways: First, it taught him to write quickly and clearly. Second, it forced him to write often, and he soon became confident of his skills. When the paper began printing some of Kipling's poems and short stories, his work was good enough to attract attention. Within a few years, Rudyard Kipling had his own following.

Kipling worked hard to satisfy his audience. When he was twenty-one he left the newspaper to work on a weekly magazine. In it he could write longer and more complicated stories than the ones he had previously written. During the next few years, he wrote many longer stories. One of them, "The Man Who Would Be King," was described by H.G. Wells, another famous writer of the time, as one of the finest short stories ever written.

These stories made Kipling famous in India, but he was not yet well known in England. In order to boost his career there he went to London in 1889. Again working with great speed, Kipling wrote many new pieces and published the stories he had written in India in book form. In almost no time he was a favorite of British readers. In fact, although he was very young, Kipling was already among the most successful English writers of his day. His popularity even began to spread to the United States, where Mark Twain was among his greatest fans.

Success did not slow Kipling down. On the contrary, the author continued writing at the same quick pace he had always maintained. He moved to America, married, and within a few years finished two classics, *Captains Courageous* and *The Jungle Book*. After four years in America, Kipling wished to return to England, which he now considered his true home. He and his family moved there and, this time, settled for good.

By now Kipling was a world-renowned author. He excelled in every literary form, writing poems, short stories, novels, and children's books with ease. With every book his reputation grew until, in 1907, he was awarded the Nobel prize for literature. At the age of forty-two, Kipling was an acknowledged master.

Kipling died in 1936. Today, Kipling's books are still read and enjoyed by millions. You may already be familiar with *The Jungle Book*, from which the next selection is taken, through the movie version made by Walt Disney.

In this story the boy Mowgli comes from a dual heritage. One is his human heritage and the other is the legacy of the jungle animals with whom he grew up. What does Mowgli learn as he grows up in the jungle?

As you read, notice how the author's carefully chosen details help you to get to know the animals who are part of Mowgli's life.

Mowgli's Brothers

by Rudyard Kipling

It was seven o'clock of a very warm evening in the Seeonee Hills when Father Wolf woke up from his day's rest, scratched himself, yawned, and spread out his paws one after the other to get rid of the sleepy feeling in their tips. Mother Wolf lay with her big gray nose dropped across her four tumbling, squealing cubs, and the moon shone into the mouth of the cave where they all lived. "*Augrh!*" said Father Wolf, "it is time to hunt again." And he was going to spring downhill when a little shadow with a bushy tail crossed the threshold and whined: "Good luck go with you, O Chief of the Wolves; and good luck and strong white teeth go with the noble children, that they may never forget the hungry in this world."

It was the jackal—Tabaqui the Dish-licker—and the wolves of India despise Tabaqui because he runs about making mischief, and telling tales, and eating rags and pieces of leather from the village rubbish-heaps. But they are afraid of him too, because Tabaqui, more than anyone else in the jungle, is apt to go mad, and then he forgets that he was ever afraid of anyone, and runs through the forest biting everything in his way. Even the tiger runs and hides when little Tabaqui goes mad, for madness is the most disgraceful thing that can overtake a wild creature. We call it hydrophobia, but they call it *dewanee* — the madness — and run.

"Enter, then, and look," said Father Wolf, stiffly, "but there is no food here."

"For a wolf, no," said Tabaqui, "but for so mean a person as myself a dry bone is a good feast. Who are we, the Gidur-log [the Jackal-People], to pick and choose?" He scuttled to the back of the cave, where he found the bone of a buck with some meat on it, and sat cracking the end merrily.

"All thanks for this good meal," he said, licking his lips. "How beautiful are the noble children! How large are their eyes! And so young too! Indeed, indeed, I might have remembered that the children of kings are men from the beginning."

Now, Tabaqui knew as well as anyone else that there is nothing so unlucky as to compliment children to their faces; and it pleased him to see Mother and Father Wolf look uncomfortable.

Tabaqui sat still, rejoicing in the mischief that he had made, and then he said spitefully:

"Shere Khan, the Big One, has shifted his hunting-grounds. He will hunt among these hills for the next moon, he has said."

Shere Khan was the tiger who lived near the Wainganga River, twenty miles away.

"He has no right!" Father Wolf began angrily. "By the Law of the Jungle he has no right to change his quarters without due warning. He will frighten every head of game within ten miles, and I — I have to kill for two, these days."

"His mother did not call him Lungri [the Lame One] for nothing," said Mother Wolf, quietly. "He has been lame in one foot from his birth. That is why he has only killed cattle. Now the villagers of the Wainganga are angry with him, and he has come here to make *our* villagers angry. They will scour the jungle for him when he is far away, and we and our children must run when the grass is set alight. Indeed, we are very grateful to Shere Khan!"

"Shall I tell him of your gratitude?" said Tabaqui.

"Out!" snapped Father Wolf.

"Out and hunt with thy master. Thou hast done harm enough for one night."

584

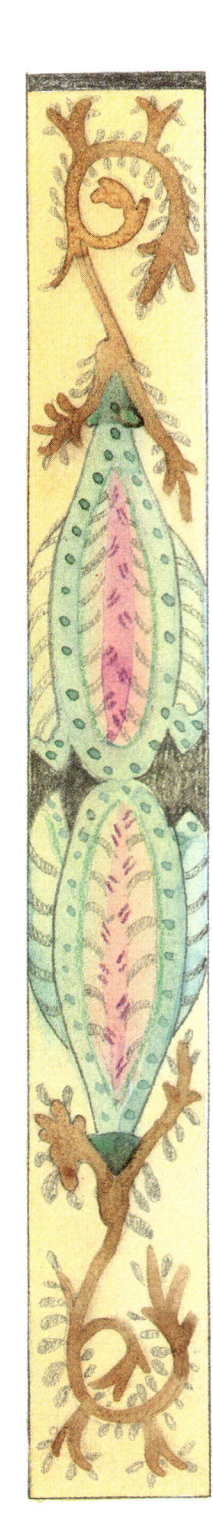

"I go," said Tabaqui, quietly. "Ye can hear Shere Khan below in the thickets. I might have saved myself the message."

Father Wolf listened, and below in the valley that ran down to a little river, he heard the dry, angry, snarly, sing-song whine of a tiger who has caught nothing and does not care if all the jungle knows it.

"The fool!" said Father Wolf. "To begin a night's work with that noise! Does he think that our bucks are like his fat bullocks?"

"Hsh. It is neither bullock nor buck he hunts tonight," said Mother Wolf. "It is a human." The whine had changed to a sort of humming purr that seemed to come from every quarter of the compass. It was the noise that bewilders people sleeping in the open, and makes them run sometimes into the very mouth of the tiger.

"Human!" said Father Wolf, showing all his white teeth. "*Faugh!* Are there not enough beetles and frogs in the tanks that he must eat a human, and on our ground too!"

The Law of the Jungle, which never orders anything without a reason, forbids every beast to eat humans except when he is killing to show his children how to kill, and then he must hunt outside the hunting grounds of his pack or tribe. The real reason for this is that human-killing means sooner or later, the arrival of men on elephants, with guns, and hundreds of men with gongs and rockets and torches. Then everybody in the jungle suffers. The reason the beasts give among themselves is that the human is the weakest and most defenseless of all living things, and it is unsportsmanlike to touch him. They say too—and it is true—that human-eaters become mangy, and lose their teeth.

The purr grew louder, and ended in the full-throated "*Aaarh!*" of the tiger's charge.

Then there was a howl—an untigerish howl—from Shere Khan. "He has missed," said Mother Wolf. "What is it?"

Father Wolf ran out a few paces and heard Shere Khan muttering and mumbling savagely, as he tumbled about in the scrub.

"The fool has had no more sense than to jump at a woodcutters' campfire, and has burned his feet," said Father Wolf, with a grunt. "Tabaqui is with him."

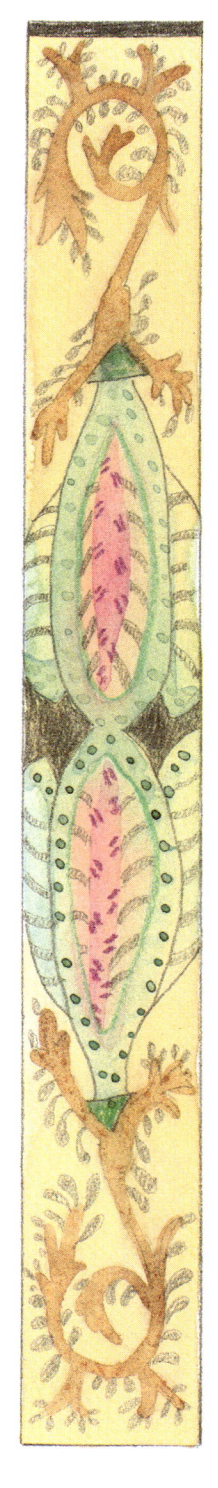

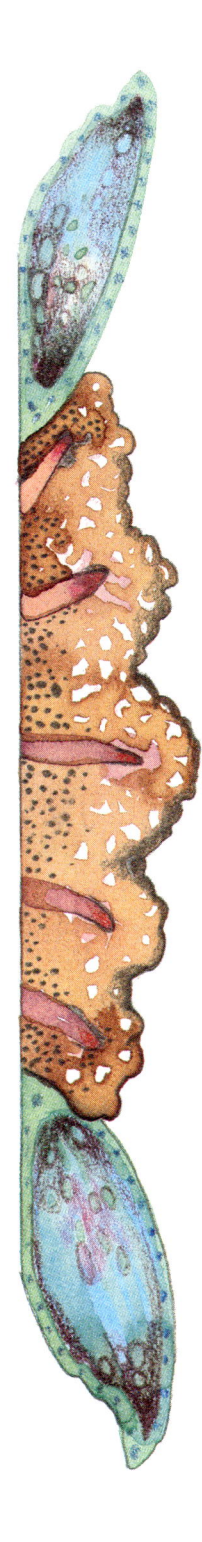

"Something is coming up hill," said Mother Wolf, twitching one ear. "Get ready."

The bushes rustled a little in the thicket, and Father Wolf dropped with his haunches under him, ready for his leap. Then, if you had been watching, you would have seen the most wonderful thing in the world — the wolf checked in mid-spring. He made his bound before he saw what it was he was jumping at, and then he tried to stop himself. He shot up straight into the air for four or five feet, landing almost where he left ground.

"Human!" he snapped. "A human's cub. Look!"

Directly in front of him, holding on by a low branch, stood a baby who could just walk — as soft and as dimpled a little atom as ever came to a wolf's cave at night. He looked up into Father Wolf's face, and laughed.

"Is that a human's cub?" said Mother Wolf. "I have never seen one. Bring it here."

A wolf accustomed to moving his own cubs can, if necessary, mouth an egg without breaking it, and though Father Wolf's jaws closed right on the child's back, not a tooth even scratched the skin, as he laid it down among the cubs.

"How little! How bold!" said Mother Wolf, softly. The baby was pushing his way between the cubs to get close to the warm hide. "*Ahai!* He is going among the others. And so this is a human's cub. Now, was there ever a wolf that could boast of a human's cub among her children?"

"I have heard now and again of such a thing, but never in our pack or in my time," said Father Wolf. "He is altogether without hair, and I could kill him with a touch of my foot. But see, he looks up and is not afraid."

The moonlight was blocked out of the mouth of the cave, for Shere Khan's great square head and shoulders were thrust into the entrance. Tabaqui, behind him, was squeaking: "My lord, my lord, it went in here!"

"Shere Khan does us great honor," said Father Wolf, but his eyes were very angry. "What does Shere Khan need?"

"My quarry. A human's cub went this way," said Shere Khan. "Its parents have run off. Give it to me."

587

Shere Khan had jumped at a woodcutters' campfire, as Father wolf had said, and was furious from the pain of his burned feet. But Father Wolf knew that the mouth of the cave was too narrow for a tiger to come in by. Even where he was, Shere Khan's shoulders and forepaws were cramped for want of room, as a human's would be if he tried to fight in a barrel.

"The wolves are a free people," said Father Wolf. "They take orders from the head of the pack, and not from any striped cattle-killer. The human's cub is ours — to kill if we choose."

"Ye choose and ye do not choose! What talk is this of choosing? By the bull that I killed, am I to stand nosing into your dog's den for my fair dues? It is I, Shere Khan, who speak!"

The tiger's roar filled the cave with thunder. Mother Wolf shook herself clear of the cubs and sprang forward, her eyes, like two green moons in the darkness, facing the blazing eyes of Shere Khan.

"And it is I, Raksha [the Demon], who answer. The human's cub is mine, Lungri — mine to me! He shall not be killed. He shall live to run with the pack and to hunt with the pack; and in the end, look you, hunter of little cubs — frog-eater — fish-killer — he shall hunt *thee*! Now get hence, or by the sambur that I killed (*I* eat no starved cattle), back thou goest to thy mother, burned beast of the jungle, lamer than ever thou camest into the world! Go!"

Father Wolf looked on amazed. He had almost forgotten the days when he won Mother Wolf in fair fight from five other wolves, when she ran in the pack and was not called the Demon for compliment's sake. Shere Khan might have faced Father Wolf, but he could not stand up against Mother Wolf, for he knew that where he was she had all the advantage of the ground, and would fight to the death. So he backed out of the cave mouth growling, and when he was clear he shouted:

"Each dog barks in his own yard! We will see what the pack will say to this fostering of human-cubs. The cub is mine, and to my teeth he will come in the end, O bushtailed thieves!"

Mother Wolf threw herself down panting among the cubs, and Father Wolf said to her gravely:

"Shere Khan speaks this much truth. The cub must be shown to the pack. Wilt thou still keep him, Mother?"

"Keep him!" she gasped. "He came, by night, alone and very hungry; yet he was not afraid! Look, he has pushed one of my babes to one side already. And that lame butcher would have killed him and would have run off to the Wainganga while the villagers here hunted through all our lairs in revenge! Keep him? Assuredly I will keep him. Lie still, little frog. O thou Mowgli—for Mowgli the Frog I will call thee—the time will come when thou wilt hunt Shere Khan as he has hunted thee."

"But what will our pack say?" said Father Wolf.

The Law of the Jungle lays down very clearly that any wolf may, when he marries, withdraw from the pack he belongs to; but as soon as his cubs are old enough to stand on their feet he must bring them to the pack council, which is generally held once a month at full moon, in order that the other wolves may identify them. After that inspection the cubs are free to run where they please, and until they have killed their first buck no excuse is accepted if a grown wolf of the pack kills one of them. The punishment is death where the murderer can be found; and if you think for a minute you will see that this must be so.

Father Wolf waited till his cubs could run a little, and then on the night of the pack meeting took them and Mowgli and Mother Wolf to the Council Rock—a hilltop covered with stones and boulders where a hundred wolves could hide. Akela, the great gray Lone Wolf, who led all the pack by strength and cunning, lay out at full length on his rock, and below him sat forty or more wolves of every size and color, from badger-colored veterans who could handle a buck alone, to young black three-year-olds who thought they could. The Lone Wolf had led them for a year now. He had fallen twice into a wolf-trap in his youth, and once he had been beaten and left for dead; so he knew the manners and customs of humans. There was very little talking at the rock. The cubs tumbled over each other in the center of the circle where their mothers and fathers sat, and now and again a senior wolf would go quietly up to a cub, look at him carefully, and return to his place on noiseless feet. Sometimes a mother would push her cub far out into the moonlight, to be sure that he had not been overlooked. Akela from his rock would cry: "Ye know the Law — ye know the Law. Look well, O wolves!" And the anxious mothers would take up the call: "Look — look well, O wolves!"

At last — and Mother Wolf's neck-bristles lifted as the time came — Father Wolf pushed "Mowgli the Frog," as they called him, into the center, where he sat laughing and playing with some pebbles that glistened in the moonlight.

Akela never raised his head from his paws, but went on with the monotonous cry: "Look well!" A muffled roar came up from behind the rocks — the voice of Shere Khan crying: "The cub is mine. Give him to me. What have the Free People to do with a human's cub?" Akela never even twitched his ears. All he said was: "Look well, O wolves! What have the Free People to do with the orders of any save the Free People? Look well!"

There was a chorus of deep growls, and a young wolf in his fourth year flung back Shere Khan's question to Akela: "What have the Free People to do with a human's cub?" Now the Law of the Jungle lays down that if there is any dispute as to the right of a cub to be accepted by the pack, he must be spoken for by at least two members of the pack who are not his father and mother.

"Who speaks for this cub?" said Akela. "Among the Free People who speaks?" There was no answer, and Mother Wolf got ready for what she knew would be her last fight, if things came to fighting.

Then the only other creature who is allowed at the pack council — Baloo, the sleepy brown bear who teaches the wolf cubs the law of the Jungle: old Baloo, who can come and go where he **pleases because he eats only nuts and roots and honey — rose up on his hindquarters and grunted.**

"The human's cub — the human's cub?" he said. "I speak for the human's cub. There is no harm in a human's cub. I have no gift of words, but I speak the truth. Let him run with the pack, and be entered with the others. I myself will teach him."

"We need yet another," said Akela. "Baloo has spoken, and he is our teacher for the young cubs. Who speaks besides Baloo?"

A black shadow dropped down into the circle. It was Bagheera the Black Panther, inky black all over, but with the panther marking showing up in certain lights like the pattern of watered silk. Everybody knew Bagheera, and nobody cared to cross his path, for he was as cunning as Tabaqui, as bold as the wild buffalo, and as reckless as the wounded elephant. But he had a voice as soft as wild honey dripping from a tree, and a skin softer than down.

"O Akela, and ye the Free People," he purred, "I have no right in your assembly, but the Law of the Jungle says that if there is a doubt which is not a killing matter in regard to a new cub, the life of that cub may be bought at a price. And the Law does not say who may or may not pay that price. Am I right?"

"Good! Good!" said the young wolves, who are always hungry. "Listen to Bagheera. The cub can be bought for a price. It is the Law."

"Knowing that I have no right to speak here, I ask your leave."

"Speak then," cried twenty voices.

"To kill a cub is shame. Besides, he may make better sport for you when he is grown. Baloo has spoken in his behalf. Now to Baloo's word I will add one bull, and a fat one, newly killed, not half a mile from here, if ye will accept the human's cub according to the Law. Is it difficult?"

There was a clamor of scores of voices, saying: "What matter? He will die in the winter rains. He will scorch in the sun. What harm can a frog do us? Let him run with the pack. Where is the bull, Bagheera? Let him be accepted." And then came Akela's deep bay, crying: "Look well — look well, O wolves!"

Mowgli was still deeply interested in the pebbles, and he did not notice when the wolves came and looked at him one by one. At last they all went down the hill for the dead bull, and only Akela, Bagheera, Baloo, and Mowgli's own wolves were left. Shere Khan roared still in the night, for he was very angry that Mowgli had not been handed over to him.

"Aye, roar well," said Bagheera, under his whiskers, "for the time comes when this thing will make thee roar to another tune, or I know nothing of humans."

"It was well done," said Akela. "Humans and their cubs are very wise. He may be a help in time."

"Truly, a help in time of need, for none can hope to lead the pack forever," said Bagheera.

Akela said nothing. He was thinking of the time that comes to every leader of every pack when his strength goes from him and he gets feebler and feebler, till at last he is killed by the wolves and a new leader comes up — to be killed in his turn.

"Take him away," he said to Father Wolf, "and train him as befits one of the Free People."

And that is how Mowgli was entered into the Seeonee Wolf Pack for the price of a bull and on Baloo's good word.

Now you must be content to skip ten or eleven whole years, and only guess at all the wonderful life that Mowgli led among the wolves, because if it were written out it would fill ever so many books. He grew up with the cubs, though they, of course, were grown wolves almost before he was a child, and Father Wolf taught him his business, and the meaning of things in the jungle, till every rustle in the grass, every breath of the warm night air, every note of the owls above his head, every scratch of a bat's claws as it roosted for a while in a tree, and every splash of every little fish jumping in a pool, meant just as much to him as the work of the office means to a business. When he was not learning he sat out in the sun and slept, and ate and went to sleep again; when he felt dirty or hot he swam in the forest pools; and when he wanted honey (Baloo told him that honey and nuts were just as pleasant to eat as raw meat) he climbed up for it, and that Bagheera showed him how to do. Bagheera would lie out on a branch and call: "Come along, Little Brother," and at first Mowgli would cling like the sloth, but afterwards he would fling himself through the branches almost as boldly as the gray ape. He took his place at the Council Rock, too, when the pack met, and there he discovered that if he stared hard at any wolf, the wolf would be forced to drop his eyes, and so he used to stare for fun. At other times he would pick the long thorns out of the pads of his friends, for wolves suffer terribly from thorns and burrs in their coats. He would go down the hillside into the cultivated lands by night, and look very curiously at the villagers in their huts, but he had a mistrust of humans because Bagheera showed him a square box with a dropgate so cunningly hidden in the jungle that he nearly walked into it, and told him that it was a trap. He loved better than anything else to go with Bagheera into the dark warm heart of the forest, to sleep all through the drowsy day, and at night to see how Bagheera did his killing. Bagheera killed right and left as he felt hungry, and so did Mowgli—with one exception. As soon as he was old enough to understand things, Bagheera told him that he must never touch cattle because he had been bought into the pack at the price of a bull's life. "All the jungle is thine," said Bagheera, "and thou canst kill everything that thou art strong enough to kill; but for the sake of the bull that bought thee thou must never kill or eat any cattle young or old. That is the Law of the Jungle." Mowgli obeyed faithfully.

And he grew and grew strong as a boy must grow who does not know that he is learning any lessons, and who has nothing in the world to think of except things to eat.

Mother Wolf told him once or twice that Shere Khan was not a creature to be trusted, and that some day he must kill Shere Khan. But though a young wolf would have remembered that advice every hour, Mowgli forgot it because he was only a boy — though he would have called himself a wolf if he had been able to speak in any human tongue.

Shere Khan was always crossing his path in the jungle, for as Akela grew older and feebler the lame tiger had come to be great friends with the younger wolves of the pack, who followed him for scraps, a thing Akela would never have allowed if he had dared to push his authority to the proper bounds. Then Shere Khan would flatter them and wonder that such fine young hunters were content to be led by a dying wolf and a human's cub. "They tell me," Shere Khan would say, "that at council ye dare not look him between the eyes." And the young wolves would growl and bristle.

Bagheera, who had eyes and ears everywhere, knew something of this, and once or twice he told Mowgli in so many words that Shere Khan would kill him some day. And Mowgli would laugh and answer: "I have the pack and I have thee; and Baloo might strike a blow or two for my sake. Why should I be afraid?"

It was one very warm day that a new notion came to Bagheera — born of something that he had heard. Perhaps Sahi the Porcupine had told him; but he said to Mowgli when they were deep in the jungle, as the boy lay with his head on Bagheera's beautiful black skin: "Little Brother, how often have I told thee that Shere Khan is thy enemy?"

"As many times as there are nuts on that palm," said Mowgli, who, naturally, could not count. "What of it? I am sleepy, Bagheera, and Shere Khan is all long tail and loud talk — like Mor the Peacock."

"But this is no time for sleeping. Baloo knows it; I know it; the pack knows it; and even the foolish, foolish deer know. Tabaqui had told thee, too."

"Ho! Ho!" said Mowgli. "Tabaqui came to me not long ago with some rude talk that I was a human's cub and not fit to dig pignuts; but I caught Tabaqui by the tail and swung him twice against a palm tree to teach him better manners."

"That was foolishness, for though Tabaqui is a mischief-maker, he would have told thee of something that concerned thee closely. Open those eyes, Little Brother. Shere Khan dare not kill thee in the jungle; but remember, Akela is very old, and soon the day comes when he cannot kill his buck, and then he will be leader no more. Many of the wolves that looked thee over when thou wast brought to the council first are old too, and the young wolves believe, as Shere Khan has taught them, that a human-cub has no place with the pack. In a little time thou wilt be a man."

"And what is a man that he should not run with his brothers?" said Mowgli. "I was born in the jungle. I have obeyed the Law of the Jungle, and there is no wolf of ours from whose paws I have not pulled a thorn. Surely they are my brothers!"

Bagheera stretched himself at full length and half shut his eyes. "Little Brother," said he, "feel under my jaw."

Mowgli put up his strong hand, and just under Bagheera's silky chin, where the giant rolling muscles were all hid by the glossy hair, he came upon a little bald spot.

"There is no one in the jungle that knows that I, Bagheera, carry that mark — the mark of the collar. And yet, Little Brother, I was born among humans, and it was among humans that my mother died — in the cages of the king's palace at Oodeypore. It was because of this that I paid the price for thee at the council when thou wast a little cub. Yes, I too was born among men. I had never seen the jungle. They fed me behind bars from an iron pan till one night I felt that I was Bagheera — the Panther — and no human's plaything, and I broke the silly lock with one blow of my paw and came away. And because I had learned the ways of humans, I became more terrible in the jungle than Shere Khan. Is it not so?"

"Yes," said Mowgli, "all the jungle fears Bagheera — all except Mowgli."

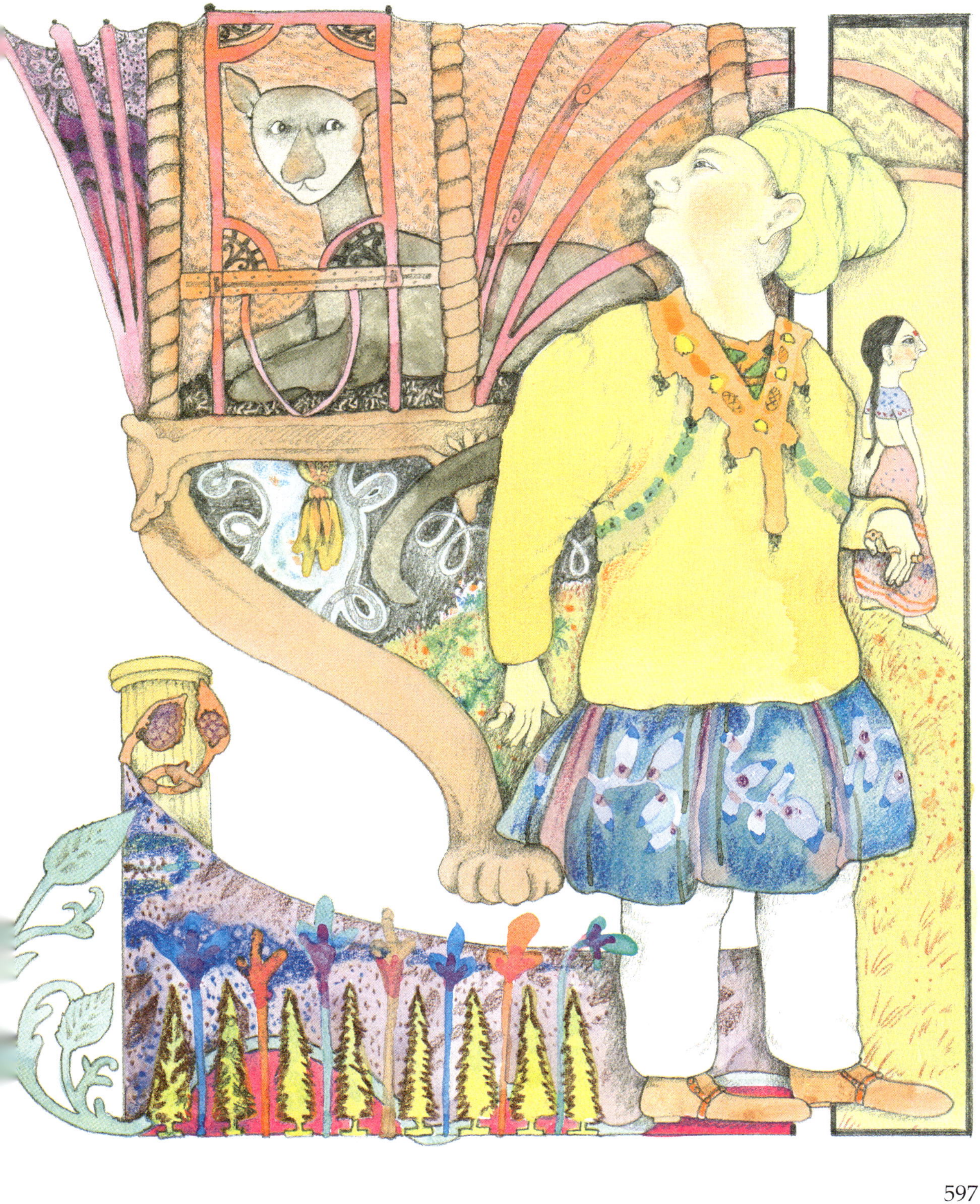

"Oh, thou art a human's cub," said the black panther, very tenderly, "and even as I returned to my jungle, so thou must go back to humans at last — to the humans who are thy brothers — if thou art not killed in the council."

"But why — but why should any wish to kill me?" said Mowgli.

"Look at me," said Bagheera, and Mowgli looked at him steadily between the eyes. The big panther turned his head away in half a minute.

"*That* is why," he said, shifting his paw on the leaves. "Not even I can look thee between the eyes, and I was born among humans, and I love thee, Little Brother. The others they hate thee because their eyes cannot meet thine; because thou art wise; because thou hast pulled out thorns from their feet — because thou art a human."

"I did not know these things," said Mowgli, sullenly, and he frowned under his heavy black eyebrows.

"What is the Law of the Jungle? Strike first and then give tongue. By thy very carelessness they know that thou art a human. But be wise. It is in my heart that when Akela misses his next kill — and at each hunt it costs him more to pin the buck — the pack will turn against him and against thee. They will hold a jungle council at the rock, and then — and then — I have it!" said Bagheera, leaping up. "Go thou down quickly to **the humans' huts in the valley, and take some of the Red Flower which they grow there,** so that when the time comes thou mayest have even a stronger friend than I or Baloo or those of the pack that love thee. Get the Red Flower."

By Red Flower Bagheera meant fire, only no creature in the jungle will call fire by its proper name. Every beast lives in deadly fear of it, and invents a hundred ways of describing it.

"The Red Flower?" said Mowgli. "That grows outside their huts in the twilight. I will get some."

"There speaks the human's cub," said Bagheera, proudly. "Remember that it grows in little pots. Get one swiftly, and keep it by thee for time of need."

"Good!" said Mowgli. "I go. But art thou sure, O my Bagheera"—he slipped his arm round the splendid neck, and looked deep into the big eyes—"art thou sure that all this is Shere Khan's doing?"

"By the broken lock that freed me, I am sure, Little Brother."

"Then, by the bull that bought me, I will pay Shere Khan full tale for this, and it may be a little over," said Mowgli, and he bounded away.

"That is a human. That is all a human," said Bagheera to himself, lying down again. "Oh, Shere Khan, never was a more evil hunting than that frog hunt of thine ten years ago!"

Mowgli was far and far through the forest, running hard, and his heart was hot in him. He came to the cave as the evening mist rose, and drew breath, and looked down the valley. The cubs were out, but Mother Wolf, at the back of the cave, knew by his breathing that something was troubling her frog.

"What is it, Son?" she said.

"Some bat's chatter of Shere Khan," he called back. "I hunt among the ploughed fields tonight." And he plunged downward through the bushes, to the stream at the bottom of the valley. There he checked, for he heard the yell of the pack hunting, heard the bellow of a hunted sambur, and the snort as the buck turned at bay. Then there were wicked, bitter howls from the young wolves: "Akela! Akela! Let the Lone Wolf show his strength. Room for the leader of the pack! Spring, Akela!"

The Lone Wolf must have sprung and missed his hold, for Mowgli heard the snap of his teeth and then a yelp as the sambur knocked him over with his forefoot.

He did not wait for anything more, but dashed on; and the yells grew fainter behind him as he ran into the croplands where the villagers lived.

"Bagheera spoke truth," he panted, as he nestled down in some cattle fodder by the window of a hut. "Tomorrow is one day both for Akela and for me."

601

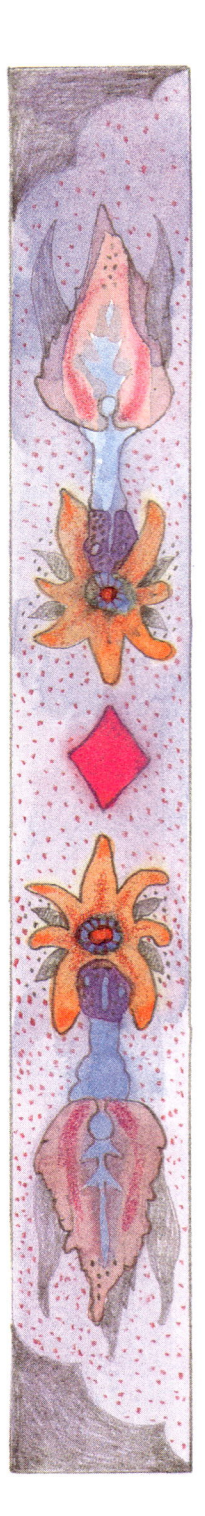

Then he pressed his face close to the window and watched the fire on the hearth. He saw the herder's wife get up and feed it in the night with black lumps; and when the morning came and the mists were all white and cold, he saw the human's child pick up a wicker pot plastered inside with earth, fill it with lumps of red-hot charcoal, put it under his blanket, and go out to tend the cows in the field.

"Is that all?" said Mowgli. "If a cub can do it, there is nothing to fear." So he strode round the corner and met the boy, took the pot from his hand, and disappeared into the mist while the boy howled with fear.

"They are very like me," said Mowgli, blowing into the pot, as he had seen the woman do. "This thing will die if I do not give it things to eat." And he dropped twigs and dried bark on the red stuff. Halfway up the hill he met Bagheera with the morning dew shining like moonstones on his coat.

"Akela has missed," said the panther. "They would have killed him last night, but they needed thee also. They were looking for thee on the hill."

"I was among the ploughed lands. I am ready. See!" Mowgli held up the fire pot.

"Good! Now, I have seen humans thrust a dry branch into that stuff and presently the Red Flower blossomed at the end of it. Art thou not afraid?"

"No. Why should I fear? I remember now — if it is not a dream — how, before I was a wolf, I lay beside the Red Flower, and it was warm and pleasant."

All that day Mowgli sat in the cave tending his fire pot and dipping dry branches into it to see how they looked. He found a branch that satisfied him, and in the evening when Tabaqui came to the cave and told him rudely enough that he was wanted at the Council Rock, he laughed till Tabaqui ran away. Then Mowgli went to the council, still laughing.

Akela the Lone Wolf lay by the side of his rock as a sign that the leadership of the pack was open, and Shere Khan with his following of scrap-fed wolves walked to and fro openly being flattered. Bagheera lay close to Mowgli, and the fire pot was between Mowgli's knees. When they were all gathered together, Shere Khan began to speak — a thing he would never have dared to do when Akela was in his prime.

"He has no right," whispered Bagheera. "Say so. He is a dog's son. He will be frightened."

Mowgli sprang to his feet. "Free People," he cried, "does Shere Khan lead the pack? What has a tiger to do with our leadership?"

"Seeing that the leadership is yet open, and being asked to speak —" Shere Khan began.

"By whom?" said Mowgli. "Are we all jackals, to fawn on this cattle-butcher? the leadership of the pack is with the pack alone."

There were yells of "Silence, thou human's cub!" "Let him speak. He has kept our Law." And at last the seniors of the pack thundered: "Let the Dead Wolf speak." When a leader of the pack has missed his kill, he is called the Dead Wolf as long as he lives, which is not long.

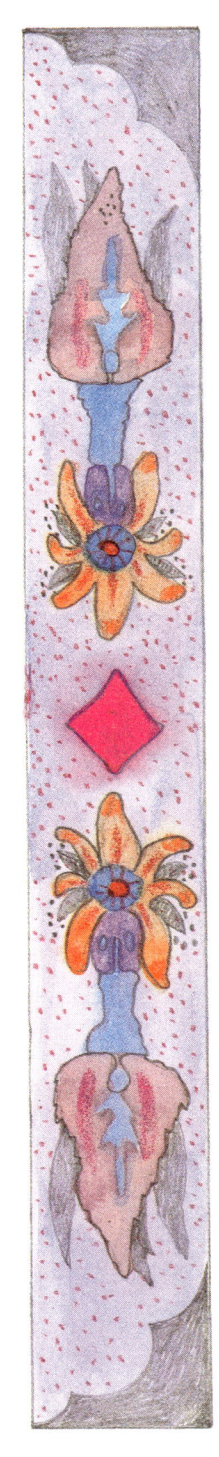

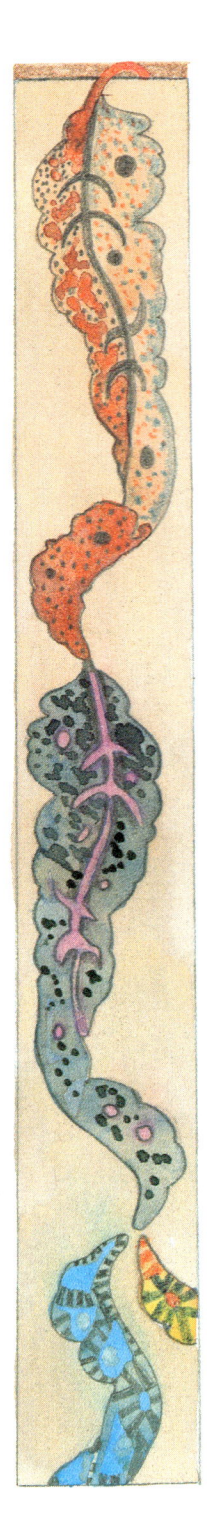

Akela raised his old head wearily:

"Free People, and ye too, jackals of Shere Khan, for twelve seasons I have led ye to and from the kill, and in all that time not one has been trapped or maimed. Now I have missed my kill. Ye know how that plot was made. Ye know how ye brought me up to an untried buck to make my weakness known. It was cleverly done. Your right is to kill me here on the Council Rock, now. Therefore, I ask, who comes to make an end of the Lone Wolf? For it is my right, by the Law of the Jungle, that ye come one by one."

There was a long hush, for no single wolf cared to fight Akela to the death. Then Shere Khan roared: "Bah! What have we to do with this toothless fool? He is doomed to die! It is the human-cub who has lived too long. Free People, he was my meat from the first. Give him to me. I am weary of this human-wolf folly. He has troubled the jungle for ten seasons. Give me the human-cub, or I will hunt here always, and not give you one bone. He is a human, a human's child, and from the marrow of my bones I hate him!"

Then more than half the pack yelled: "A human! A human! What has a human to do with us? Let him go to his own place."

"And turn all the people of the villages against us?" clamored Shere Khan. "No! Give him to me. He is a human, and none of us can look him between the eyes."

Akela lifted his head again, and said: "He has eaten our food. He has slept with us. He has driven game for us. He has broken no word of the Law of the Jungle."

"Also, I paid for him with a bull when he was accepted. The worth of a bull is little, but Bagheera's honor is something that he will perhaps fight for," said Bagheera, in his gentlest voice.

"A bull paid ten years ago!" the pack snarled. " What do we care for bones ten years old?"

"Or for a pledge?" said Bagheera, his white teeth bared under his lip. "Well are ye called the Free People!"

"No human's cub can run with the people of the jungle," howled Shere Khan. "Give him to me!"

"He is our brother in all but blood," Akela went on, "and ye would kill him here! In truth, I have lived too long. Some of ye are eaters of cattle, and of others I have heard that, under Shere Khan's teaching, ye go by dark night and snatch children from the villager's doorstep. Therefore I know ye to be cowards, and it is to cowards I speak. It is certain that I must die, and my life is of no worth, or I would offer that in the human-cub's place. But for the sake of the pack—a little matter that by being without a leader ye have forgotten—I promise that if ye let the human-cub go to his own place, I will not, when my time comes to die, bare one tooth against ye. I will die without fighting. That will at least save the pack three lives. More I cannot do; but if ye will, I can save ye the shame that comes of killing a brother against whom there is no fault—a brother spoken for and bought into the pack according to the Law of the Jungle."

"He is a human—a human—a human!" snarled the pack. And most of the wolves began to gather round Shere Khan, whose tail was beginning to switch.

"Now the business is in thy hands," said Bagheera to Mowgli. "*We* can do no more except fight."

Mowgli stood upright, the fire pot in his hands. Then he stretched out his arms, and yawned in the face of the council. But he was furious with rage and sorrow, for, wolflike, the wolves had never told him how they hated him. "Listen you!" he cried. "There is no need for this dog's jabber. Ye have told me so often tonight that I am a human (and indeed I would have been a wolf with you to my life's end), that I feel your words are true. So I do not call ye my brothers anymore, but say *dogs*, as a human should. What ye will do, and what ye will not do, is not yours to say. The matter is with *me*. And that we may see the matter more plainly, I, the human, have brought here a little of the Red Flower which ye, dogs, fear."

He flung the fire pot on the ground, and some of the red coals lit a tuft of dried moss that flared up, as all the council drew back in terror before the leaping flames.

Mowgli thrust his dead branch into the fire till the twigs lit and crackled, and whirled it above his head among the cowering wolves.

"Thou are the master," said Bagheera, in an undertone. "Save Akela from the death. He was ever thy friend." Akela, the grim old wolf who had never asked for mercy in his life, gave one piteous look at Mowgli as the boy stood, his long black hair tossing over his shoulders in the light of the blazing branch that made the shadows jump and quiver.

"Good!" said Mowgli, staring round slowly. "I see that ye are dogs. I go from you to my own people—if they be my own people. The jungle is shut to me, and I must forget your talk and your companionship; but I will be more merciful than ye are.

607

Because I was all but your brother in blood, I promise that when I am a human among humans I will not betray ye to humans as ye have betrayed me." He kicked the fire with his foot, and the sparks flew up. "There shall be no war between any of us in the pack. But here is a debt to pay before I go." He strode forward to where Shere Khan sat blinking stupidly at the flames, and caught him by the tuft on his chin. Bagheera followed in case of accidents. "Up dog!" Mowgli cried. "Up, when a human speaks, or I will set that coat ablaze!"

Shere Khan's ears lay flat back on his head, and he shut his eyes, for the blazing branch was very near.

"This cattle-killer said he would kill me in the council because he had not killed me when I was a cub. Thus and thus, then, do we beat dogs when we are humans. Stir a whisker, Lungri, and I ram the Red Flower down thy gullet!" He beat Shere Khan over the head with the branch, and the tiger whimpered and whined in an agony of fear.

"*Pah!* Singed jungle-cat — go now! But remember when next I come to the Council Rock, as a human should come, it will be with Shere Khan's hide on my head. For the rest, Akela goes free to live as he pleases. Ye will not kill him, because that is not my will. Nor do I think that ye will sit here any longer, lolling out your tongues as though ye were somebodies, instead of dogs whom I drive out — thus! Go!" The fire was burning furiously at the end of the branch, and Mowgli struck right and left round the circle, and the wolves ran howling with the sparks burning their fur. At last there were only Akela, Bagheera, and perhaps ten wolves that had taken Mowgli's part. Then something began to hurt Mowgli inside him, as he had never been hurt in his life before, and he caught his breath and sobbed, and the tears ran down his face.

"What is it? What is it?" he said. "I do not wish to leave the jungle, and I do not know what this is. Am I dying, Bagheera?"

"No, Little Brother. That is only tears such as humans use," said Bagheera. "Now I know thou art a human, and a human's cub no longer. The jungle is shut indeed to thee henceforward.

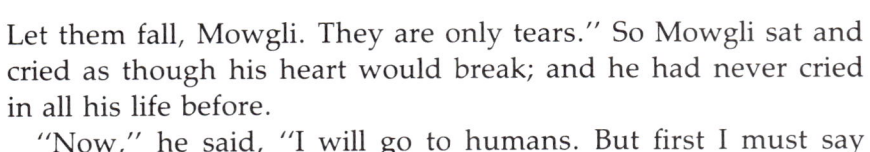

Let them fall, Mowgli. They are only tears." So Mowgli sat and cried as though his heart would break; and he had never cried in all his life before.

"Now," he said, "I will go to humans. But first I must say farewell to my mother." And he went to the cave where she lived with Father Wolf, and he cried on her coat, while the four cubs howled miserably.

"Ye will not forget me?" said Mowgli.

"Never while we can follow a trail," said the cubs. "Come to the foot of the hill when thou art a human, and we will talk to thee; and we will come into the croplands to play with thee by night."

"Come soon!" said Father Wolf. "Oh, wise little frog, come again soon, for we be old, thy mother and I."

"Come soon," said Mother Wolf, "little son of mine, for listen, child of human, I loved thee more than ever I loved my cubs."

"I will surely come," said Mowgli, "and when I come it will be to lay out Shere Khan's hide upon the Council Rock. Do not forget me! Tell them in the jungle never to forget me."

The dawn was beginning to break when Mowgli went down the hillside alone, to meet those mysterious things that are called humans.

Discuss the Selection

1. What lesson did Mowgli learn as he grew up in the jungle?
2. Describe the way that Bagheera helped Mowgli prepare for the final confrontation with Shere Khan.
3. How did you feel when Mowgli decided to return to the people of the villages?
4. Where did the end of the story leave the conflict between Mowgli and Shere Khan?
5. Why did Akela and Bagheera take Mowgli's side at the council meeting? Find that part of the story and read it again.

Apply the Skills

Good descriptive writing helps readers form a clear idea of how things look, sound, smell, taste, and feel. Description allows you to see characters, places, and objects.

In "Mowgli's Brothers," the author describes the animals in vivid detail. Find two examples of the author's use of description.

Thinking About "Legacies"

In the unit you just read, different people were influenced by their heritage to act in certain ways. Each person lived by values and ideals that were part of his or her heritage. Catherine Hall and Roberto Clemente shared the idea of helping those in need. Catherine Hall helped a runaway slave. Roberto Clemente collected food and medicine for earthquake victims in Nicaragua. Elizabeth Lloyd and Hannah Senesh fought against tyranny and injustice. Each of these young women braved danger to help others when her own freedom was threatened.

Whirlwind and her grandson Shoots lived by the Lakota Indians' code of bravery. This code inspired their courage in fighting a bear and in enduring the pain of the wounds they suffered. Mowgli was inspired by the code of behavior he learned from the wolf pack. He followed the laws of the jungle and lived by its values of cooperation, honor, and courage in facing one's enemies.

A person's heritage can influence the creation of works of art. Katherine Dunham used her legacy of African and Caribbean dancing and music to create the stage performances that made her famous. Margaret Sanfilippo found inspiration in the heritage of South American art and costumes when she created her book illustrations. American artists and crafts people today find inspiration in the beautiful quilts made in Catherine Hall's time.

Reading stories about the lives of real and fictional people teaches us about our heritage. We learn what values, ideals, and goals inspired others in the past. Members of each new generation can use this legacy to shape their own lives. They, in turn, can record their struggles and accomplishments to provide inspiration for future generations. And so the chain of heritage will gain new links to join it to the future.

1. Compare Elizabeth Lloyd and Hannah Senesh. What threat to her homeland did each fight against? How did each show courage in her fight against tyranny?

2. Choose two characters from "Legacies" whom you admire. Describe the personal qualities and actions that you found admirable.

3. What is the value of keeping a diary or journal? What can a person learn from reading diaries and journals written by people in other times and places?

4. Do you prefer to read biographies or autobiographies of famous people? What differences could there be between the story of a person's life told by an outsider and that story told in the person's own words?

5. Find at least one passage of effective description from each of two selections in "Legacies." Tell why the description made the character or scene come alive for you.

6. What parts of your heritage would you like to learn more about? Why? What are some things you could do to learn more about your heritage?

7. If you were going to write a biography of a living celebrity, what sources of information would you use? Which do you think would be most helpful?

Read on Your Own

In Kindling Flame by Linda Atkinson. Lothrop, Lee & Shepard. The biography of Hannah Senesh, heroine of World War II, is told in her diaries, letters, and poems.

Tall-Tale America by Walter Blair. Coward McCann. This collection of tall tales provides a legendary history of American folk heroes.

A Gathering of Days by Joan Blos. Scribner's. This fictional diary of a young girl in New England in 1830 tells of life in those days.

All the Dark Places by J. Allan Bosworth. Doubleday. A young cave explorer, Peter Torin, faces the ultimate challenge when he becomes lost in Preacher's End, a cave with a frightening legend.

Constance: A Story of Early Plymouth by Patricia Clapp. Lothrop, Lee & Shepard. The author is a descendant of the heroine of this fictionalized biography of a fifteen-year-old girl who came to the Plymouth colony on the Mayflower.

Women Astronauts: Aboard the Shuttle by Mary Virginia Fox. Julian Messner. These are brief biographies of women astronauts.

The Double Life of Pocohontas by Jean Fritz. Putnam. 1983. This fascinating biography is told from Pocohontas's point of view.

The Samurai's Tale by Erik Christian Haugaard. Houghton Mifflin. An orphan servant boy, Taro, grows from boyhood to become a samurai, a traditional warrior, in sixteenth-century Japan.

Roberto Clemente: Batting King by Arnold Hano. Putnam. This book is a biography of the baseball hero from Puerto Rico who was a humanitarian as well as a star athlete.

Katherine Dunham by James Haskins. Coward, McCann & Geoghegan. Now over seventy, Katherine Dunham has led a fascinating life as a dancer, choreographer, anthropologist, and champion of disadvantaged people in the United States and Haiti.

Buffalo Woman by Dorothy Johnson. Dodd, Mead. This novel portrays the way of life of Plains Indian hunters and warriors from 1820 to 1877 through episodes in the life of a woman of the Oglala tribe of the Lakota people.

The Jungle Book by Rudyard Kipling. Doubleday. This is the story of Mowgli the jungle boy, the jungle of India, and its animals.

Women Who Changed Things by Linda Peavy and Ursula Smith. Scribner's. Included are the stories of nine women who brought about significant changes in science and politics.

Words: A Book About the Origins of Everyday Words and Phrases by Jane Sarnoff and Reynold Ruffins. Scribner's. Learn about words used today that had strange or surprising meanings long ago.

Shadow of a Bull by Maia Wojciechowska. Atheneum. A famous bullfighter's son in a small town in Spain finds that his legacy can be a burden.

Glossary

The glossary is a special dictionary for this book. The glossary tells you how to spell a word, how to pronounce it, and what the word means.

The following abbreviations are used throughout the glossary: *n.*, noun; *v.*, verb; *adj.*, adjective; *adv.*, adverb; *interj.*, interjection; *prep.*, preposition; *conj.*, conjunction; *pl.*, plural; *sing.*, singular.

An accent mark (′) is used to show which syllable receives the most stress. For example, in the word *granite* [gran′ it], the first syllable receives more stress. Sometimes in words of three or more syllables, there is also a lighter mark to show that a syllable receives a lighter stress. For example, in the word *helicopter* [hel′ə·kop′tər], the first syllable has the most stress, and the third syllable has lighter stress.

The symbols used to show how each word is pronounced are explained in the "Pronunciation Key" on the next page.

Pronunciation Key*

a	add, map	m	move, seem	u	up, done
ā	ace, rate	n	nice, tin	û(r)	burn, term
â(r)	care, air	ng	ring, song	yōō	fuse, few
ä	palm, father	o	odd, hot	v	vain, eve
b	bat, rub	ō	open, so	w	win, away
ch	check, catch	ô	order, jaw	y	yet, yearn
d	dog, rod	oi	oil, boy	z	zest, muse
e	end, pet	ou	pout, now	zh	vision, pleasure
ē	equal, tree	o͝o	took, full	ə	the schwa, an unstressed vowel representing the sound spelled
f	fit, half	o͞o	pool, food		a in *above*
g	go, log	p	pit, stop		e in *sicken*
h	hope, hate	r	run, poor		i in *possible*
i	it, give	s	see, pass		o in *melon*
ī	ice, write	sh	sure, rush		u in *circus*
j	joy, ledge	t	talk, sit		
k	cool, take	th	thin, both		
l	look, rule	t̷h̷	this, bathe		

*The Pronunciation Key and the short form of the key that appears on the following right-hand pages are reprinted from the *HBJ School Dictionary,* copyright © 1985 by Harcourt Brace Jovanovich, Inc.

A a

ab·surd [ab·sûrd′ *or* ab·zûrd′] *adj.* Not reasonable; ridiculous: What an *absurd* idea! —**ab·surd′ly** *adv.*

ac·knowl·edge [ak·nol′ij] *v.* **ac·knowl·edged, ac·knowl·edg·ing** To admit, recognize, take responsibility for, answer for: to *acknowledge* an error.

ad·a·mant [ad′ə·mənt] *n.* An unbreakable stone or other substance.

ad·vance·ment [ad·vans′mənt] *n.* Forward movement; progress: Housing all the homeless will be a real *advancement*.

ad·ver·tise·ment [ad′vər·tīz′mənt *or* ad·vûr′tis·mənt] *n.* A sales notice promoting a product or service.

adze [adz] *n.* A cutting tool with a broad chisel-like blade.

aer·o·nau·tics [âr′ə·nô′tiks] *n.* A field of study involving the design, manufacture, and flight of airplanes.

ag·o·ny [ag′ə·nē] *n., pl.* **ag·on·ies** Extreme suffering of body or mind.

al·a·bas·ter [al′ə·bas·tər] *adj.* Smooth and white, like stone: an *alabaster* statue.

al·i·bi [al′ə·bī] *n.* The excuse of being somewhere else at the time of a crime.

al·ter·nate [ôl′tər·nit] *adj.* Different; substitute: an *alternate* life-style.

am·a·teur [am′ə·choor *or* am′ə·t(y)oor] **1** *n.* A person who practices any art, study, or sport for enjoyment rather than money. **2** *adj.* use: an *amateur* orchestra.

a·mi·a·ble [a′mē·ə·bəl] *adj.* Having a pleasant disposition; friendly.

am·u·let [am′yə·lit] *n.* A piece of jewelry worn to keep away evil or bad luck.

an·es·thet·ic [an′is·thet′ik] *n.* A drug or gas that cuts off sensation or causes unconsciousness, such as ether.

a·noint [ə·noint′] *v.* To place oil or ointment on, often in a religious ceremony.

an·thro·pol·o·gy [an′thrə·pol′ə·jē] *n.* The study of the physical, social, and cultural development of human beings.

an·tic·i·pate [an·tis′ə·pāt′] *v.* **an·tic·i·pat·ed, an·tic·i·pat·ing** To forsee and deal with beforehand: Try to *anticipate* grandfather's needs.

ap·pa·ra·tus [ap′ə·rā′təs *or* ap′ə·rat′əs] *n., pl.* **ap·pa·ra·tus** *or* **ap·pa·ra·tus·es** Equipment, such as a device or machine, for a particular use.

ap·pa·ri·tion [ap′ə·rish′ən] *n.* A ghostly appearance: An *apparition* took shape in the distance.

ap·pen·dix [ə·pen′diks] *n., pl.* **ap·pen·dix·es** *or* **ap·pen·di·ces** [ə·pen′də·sēz] Material added, as at end of book.

ap·pren·tice [ə·pren′tis] *n.* A learner in a trade.

ar·chae·ol·o·gist [är′kē·ol′ə·jist] *n.* An expert who studies past cultures, mainly by digging up and examining the remains of ancient cities and tombs.

Arch·mage [ärch′māj] *n.* A chief magician or wise person.

Arc·tic [är(k)′tik] The area around the North Pole.

arena — botany

a·re·na [ə·rē′nə] *n.* A space where spectacles are performed.

a·ris·to·crat·ic [ə·ris′tə·krat′ik] *adj.* On a high social level; of the nobility or upper classes.

ar·mi·stice [är′mə·stis] *n.* An arrangement to halt a battle or war: The *armistice* that ended World War I took place on November 11, 1918.

ar·ter·y [är′tər·ē] *n., pl.* **ar·ter·ies** A blood vessel that carries blood from the heart to the rest of the body.

Ar·tes, Be·llas [är′tās bā′yäs] *n.* Beautiful arts.

ar·thri·tis [är·thrī′tis] *n.* A disease in which joints become inflamed.

as·so·ci·ate [ə·sō′shi·āt] *v.* To connect in thought.

as·tron·o·my [ə·stron′ə·me] *n.* The study of the entire planetary system.

at·mos·phere [at′məs·fir] *n.* The quality of one's surroundings: an *atmosphere* of good cheer.

au·di·o·vis·u·al [ô′dē·ō·vizh′oo·əl] *adj.* Having both an auditory and a visual dimension: She runs the *audiovisual* equipment in our school.

a·vi·a·tion [ā·vē·ā′shən] *n.* A field of study related to aircraft.

a·ware [ə·wâr′] *adj.* Fully realizing; conscious. —**a·ware′·ness** *n.*

awe [ô] *n.* A feeling of wonder mingled with great respect: We had a feeling of *awe* at the sight of the Golden Gate Bridge. —**awe-in·spir·ing** [ô·in·spīr′ing] *adj.* Causing awe; awesome: The young astronomer thought that Halley's comet was truly an *awe-inspiring* sight.

B b

back mat·ter [bak′ mat′ər] *n.* Material at the back of a book, as the index, glossary, or appendix.

baf·fle [baf′əl] *v.* **baf·fled, baf·fling** To confuse, puzzle: The situation *baffled* me.

balk [bôk] *v.* To refuse to cooperate, thwart, hinder: We *balked* when it came to paying more dues.

bar·bar·ous [bär′bər·əs] *adj.* Not civilized; crude. —**bar·ba·rous·ly** *adv.*

bau·ble [bô′bəl] *n.* A showy trinket or jewel, usually of low value.

bed·lam [bed′ləm] *n.* A scene of noise and confusion.

bed·rid·den [bed′rid(ə)n] *adj.* Restricted to bed by sickness or injury.

blip [blip] *n.* A luminous signal shown on a radar screen.

bois·ter·ous [bois′tər·əs] *adj.* Loud and wild: a *boisterous* gang. —**bois·ter·ous·ly** *adv.*

bot·a·ny [bot′ə·nē] *n.* The scientific study of plant life. —**bot·an·ist** *n.*

a	add	i	it	oo	took	oi	oil
ā	ace	ī	ice	oo	pool	ou	pout
â	care	o	odd	u	up	ng	ring
ä	palm	ō	open	û	burn	th	thin
e	end	ô	order	yoo	fuse	th	this
ē	equal					zh	vision

ə = { **a** in *above* **e** in *sicken* **i** in *possible*
      o in *melon* **u** in *circus*

619

boundary   colleague

bound·a·ry [boun′də·rē *or* boun′drē] *n., pl.* **bound·a·ries** A line or mark that forms an outer limit, as of a political division or private property.

boun·ti·ful [boun′tə·fəl] *adj.* Abundant; plentiful: This year we had a *bountiful* harvest.

brace [brās] *n.* Something used as a support or to strengthen or hold in place: She had to wear a *brace* on her leg after the accident.

break·wa·ter [brāk′wô′tər] *n.* A barrier that protects a harbor or beach from destruction by waves.

bron·chi·tis [brong·kī′tis] *n.* Coughing caused by inflammation or infection of the bronchial tubes.

buc·ca·neer [buk′ə·nir′] *n.* A person who robs ships on the high seas, especially a leader or a member of a band of outlaw sailors; pirate.

buck·skin [buk′skin] *n.* A kind of soft yellow leather made from the skin of deer or sheep.

bush coun·try [boosh′ kun′trē] *n.* Unsettled, uncleared land covered with low, treelike shrubs.

byre [bir] *n. British* A cow stable.

C c

car·cass [kär′kəs] *n.* The body of a dead animal.

Car·ib·be·an Sea [kar′ə·bē′ən *or* kə·rib′ē·ən sē] *n.* The part of the Atlantic Ocean between the West Indies and Central and South America.

car·i·bou [kar′ə·boo′] *n., pl.* **car·i·bou** *or* **car·i·bous** A type of reindeer found in North America: We saw a *caribou* at the Museum of Natural History.

car·ies [kar′ēz] *n.* Decay in teeth.

cas·u·al [kazh′oo·əl] *adj.* Occasional; happening once in a while.

cat·a·log [kat′ə·log] *n.* A list of books and materials in a library.

cat·e·go·ry [kat′ə·gôr′ē] *n., pl.* **cat·e·go·ries** A division, as part of a system of classification: Botany is a *category* of science.

cease [sēs] *v.* **ceased, ceas·ing** To bring to a halt: *Cease* that racket.

cen·ten·ni·al [sen·ten′ē·əl] *adj.* Relating to a 100th anniversary: a *centennial* observance.

chafe [chāf] *v.* **chafed, chaf·ing** To rub against; cause friction.

cham·ber [chām′bər] *n.* A private room or office.

cho·re·o·graph [kor′ē·o·graf′] *v.* To create movements for a dance: to *choreograph* a ballet. —**cho·re·og·ra·pher** [kor′ē·og′rə·fər] *n.*

clam·or·ing [klam′ər·ing] *adj.* Making loud noises.

coal-scut·tle [kōl′skut′(ə)l] *n.* A pail used for carrying coal.

co·qui·na [kō·kē′nə] *n.* A small sea mollusk with a striped or banded shell.

col·ic [kol′ik] *n.* A pain in the abdomen caused by muscular spasms. —**col·ick·y** *adj.*

col·league [kol′ēg] *n.* A co-worker in a profession or organization: Bill was a *colleague* at the firm.

colonnade　　　　　　　　　　　　　　　　　　　　　　　　　　　　　　cutbank

col·on·nade [kol′ə·nād′] *n.* Columns set in a regularly spaced row.

com·mon·wealth [kom′ən·welth′] *n.* A democratic country; republic.

com·pas·sion [kəm·pash′ən] *n.* Pity for the sufferings of others, with a desire to help.

com·pli·cat·ed [kom′plə·kā′tid] *adj.* Complex, intricate: The rug had a *complicated* pattern.

com·rade [kom′rad *or* kom′rəd] *n.* A friend, companion. — **com·rade·ship** *n.*

con·cept [kon′səpt] *n.* A well-organized idea: the *concept* of self-help.

con·quis·ta·dor [kon·k(w)is′tə·dôr′] *n.* A 16th-century Spanish conqueror of Mexico and Peru.

con·so·la·tion [kon′sə·lā′shən] *n.* The act or condition of being comforted or cheered: We looked to our teammates for *consolation* when we lost the game.

con·ta·gious [kən·tā′jəs] *adj.* Easily spread to others: a *contagious* mood.

con·trail [kon′trāl] *n.* The streaks of condensed water vapor left in the air by an airplane.

con·tra·pun·tal [kän·trə·pənt′(ə)l] *adj.* In music, utilizing counterpoint, the technique of combining harmonizing melodic lines that keep their individual linear quality.

con·ver·sa·tion [kon′vər·sā′shen] *n.* An exchange of ideas; talk: a political *conversation* revolved around politics. — **con·ver·sa·tion·al** *adj.*

con·vul·sion [kən·vul′shən] *n.* (often *pl.*) An uncontrolled, violent muscular contraction.

cos·mic [koz′mik] *adj.* Universal.

coup [ko͞o] *n.* A victory by an Indian warrior over an enemy, human or animal.

cov·et [kuv′it] *v.* To desire possession of something belonging to someone else.

cra·dle·board [krād′(ə)l bôrd′] *n.* A stiff, wooden-backed device for carrying a baby, with a fabric or leather sack or pouch attached.

craft [kraft] *n.* Highly skilled handwork.

cre·scen·do [krə·shen′dō] *n.* A gradual rise in loudness or strength: The song ended with a *crescendo*.

crev·ice [krev′is] *n.* A narrow crack or split, as in a rock or wall.

croon [kro͞on] *v.* To sing softly or hum, as in a lullaby.

crouch [krouch] *v.* To stoop down, ready to spring forward.

crys·tal-clear [kris′təl·klir′] *adj.* Transparent, with no imperfections.

cul·ti·vate [kul′tə·vāt′] *v.* **cul·ti·vat·ed, cul·ti·vat·ing** To prepare soil for planting.

cun·ning [kun′ing] *adj.* Clever; sly.

cut·bank [kut′bangk] *n.* The side of a channel carved at an angle by water running through mostly level ground.

a	add	i	it	o͞o	took	oi	oil
ā	ace	ī	ice	o͞o	pool	ou	pout
â	care	o	odd	u	up	ng	ring
ä	palm	ō	open	û	burn	th	thin
e	end	ô	order	yo͞o	fuse	th	this
ē	equal					zh	vision

ə = { **a** in *above*　**e** in *sicken*　**i** in *possible*
　　　o in *melon*　**u** in *circus* }

621

D d

daz·zle·ment [daz′əl·mint] *n.* A glaring brightness.

de·cap·i·tate [di·kap′ə·tāt′] *v.* **de·cap·i·tat·ed, de·cap·i·tat·ing** To remove the head of; behead. —**de·cap·i·ta·tion** *n.*

de·for·est [dē·fôr′ist] *v.* To strip land of trees or woods. —**de·for·es·ta·tion** *n.*

de·form·i·ty [di·fôrm′ə·tē] *n.* Malformation of a body part.

del·i·ca·cy [del′ə·kə·sē] *n.* Refinement of feeling; sensitivity to others.

del·i·cate [del′ə·kit] *adj.* Fine, as in structure, design, or shape: a *delicate* snowflake.

de·mure [di·myoor′] *adj.* Modest, shy.

de·pen·dent [di·pen′dənt] *adj.* Needing someone or something for support: *dependent* children.

de·plor·a·ble [di·plôr′ə·bəl] *adj.* Disgraceful; regrettable.

de·pre·ci·ate [di·prē′shē·āt′] *v.* **de·pre·ci·at·ed, de·pe·ci·at·ing** To make or become lower in value: We refuse to *depreciate* our efforts.

der·mis [dur′mis] *n.* The layer of skin just below the outer skin.

di·a·logue [dī′·ə·lôg′ *or* dī′·ə·log′] *n.* Conversation between two or more speakers.

dis·ci·pline [dis′ə·plin] *n., pl.* **dis·ci·plines** Strict, formal training.

dis·cus [dis′kəs] *n.* A heavy wooden or metal disk used in athletic throwing contests.

dis·port [dis·pôrt′] *v.* To entertain or be entertained.

dis·sect [di·sekt′ *or* dī·sekt′] *v.* To cut apart in order to examine: to *dissect* a frog.

dis·tinc·tive [dis·tink′tiv] *adj.* Serving to distinguish or setting off as special: a *distinctive* style of dress.

dis·trac·tion [dis·trak′shən] *n.* Disruption of one's concentration: You need a place to study without *distractions*.

drawn [drôn] *adj.* Haggard in appearance.

du·bi·ous·ly [d(y)oo′·bē·əs·lē] *adv.* In an uncertain manner; doubtfully: Always react *dubiously* when a stranger asks you for something.

E e

eb·on·y [eb′ə·nē] *n.* A hard, heavy wood with a very dark color.

e·bul·lient [i·bool′yənt] *adj.* Filled with enthusiasm; high-spirited.

ec·o·nom·ics [ek′ə·nom′iks *or* ē′kə·nom′iks] *n.* The study of the production, distribution, and use of goods and services: In *economics*, money, taxes, and earnings are studied.

e·con·o·my [i·kon′ə·mē] *n., pl.* **e·con·o·mies** Making the most of what one has.

ef·fi·cient [i·fish′ənt] *adj.* Producing or handling something without waste.

el·e·gant [el′ə·gənt] *adj.* Tasteful, fine in quality, luxurious.

El Salvador — front matter

El Sal·va·dor [el sal'·və·dôr] The smallest country in Central America, on the Pacific Southeast of Guatemala.

e·lu·sive [i·lōō'siv] *adj.* Escaping or avoiding capture: The fox is an *elusive* creature.

em·i·nent [em'ə·nənt] *adj.* Distinguished because of high rank or great achievement.

en·ter·i·tis [en'tə·rī'təs] *n.* Inflammation of the intestines, the part of the body where food is digested.

en·tomb [in·tōōm'] *v.* To bury in or as if in a tomb.

en·try [en'trē] *n., pl.* **en·tries** A word, phrase, or number entered in a list or series.

en·vis·age [in·vis'ij] *v.* To make a mental picture in one's mind; to visualize.

e·pit·o·me [i·pit'ə·mē] *n.* A person or object that is the best example of some characteristic: The movie star was the *epitome* of glamour.

err [ur *or* er] *v.* **erred, err·ring** To make a mistake.

eth·ics [eth'iks] *n. pl.* The study and rules of morality in human behavior.

et·i·quette [et'ə·kət] *n.* The rules set for correct behavior.

ex·as·per·a·tion [ig·zas·pə·rā'shən] *n.* Angry feeling when patience is lost: She expressed *exasperation* by stamping her foot.

ex·cerpt [ek'sûrpt] *n.* A passage from a book or piece of writing: The teacher read us an *excerpt* from the novel.

ex·cur·sion [ik·skur'shən] *n.* A short recreational trip or outing.

ex·empt [ig·zempt'] *adj.* Freed or excused, as from a duty or obligation: Children are usually *exempt* from taxes.

ex·plo·ra·tion [eks·plə·rā'shən] *n.* Travel through a new region to find out about it: *exploration* of the ocean floor.

F f

fa·cil·i·ty [fə·sil'ə·tē] *n.* An establishment to accommodate the performance of something: a good sports *facility*.

fel·low·ship [fel'ō·ship'] *n.* Warm friendship in a group: The team had great *fellowship*.

flam·boy·ant [flam·boi'·ənt] *adj.* Brilliantly colored: a *flamboyant* Hawaiian shirt.

fly·er [flī'ər] *n.* A leaflet or handbill: The campaigner handed me a *flyer*.

fools·cap [fōōlz'kap'] *n.* A type of writing paper.

foot·sore [fōōt'sôr'] *adj.* Having sore or tired feet: I was *footsore* after the hike.

for·lorn [fôr·lôrn'] *adj.* Lonely and forgotten or neglected.

for·tis·si·mo [fôr·tis'·ə·mō] *adj., adv.* A musical direction for playing loudly.

front mat·ter [frunt' mat'ər] The pages that come before the main body of the book:

a	add	i	it	ōō	took	oi	oil
ā	ace	ī	ice	ōō	pool	ou	pout
â	care	o	odd	u	up	ng	ring
ä	palm	ō	open	û	burn	th	thin
e	end	ô	order	yōō	fuse	th	this
ē	equal					zh	vision

ə = { **a** in *above*, **e** in *sicken*, **i** in *possible*, **o** in *melon*, **u** in *circus* }

623

futilely

Front matter consists of title, copyright and acknowledgment pages, the table of contents, and a preface or introduction.

fu·tile·ly [fyōō′təl·ē] *adv.* Uselessly, in vain.

G g

ga·losh·es [gə·losh′əz] *n. pl.* Overshoes worn for protection from damp, rain, sleet, or snow.

gar·ret [gar′it] *n.* A small room or set of rooms in an attic, under a sloping roof.

gas·tron·o·my [gas·tron′ə·mē] *n.* The study and enjoyment of fine food and drink.

gen·er·a·tion [jen′ə·rā′shən] *n.* Any group born at about the same time, especially those who share similar beliefs and lifestyles: my parents' *generation.*

gen·ial [jēn′yəl] *adj.* Friendly and good-natured: a *genial* welcome.

ge·ol·o·gy [jē·ol′ə·jē] *n.* The study of the origin, history, and structure of the earth: Rocks are the main material of study in *geology.*

goad [gōd] *n.* A pointed stick for driving animals by prodding them.

graph·ic [graf′ik] *adj.* Pertaining to the art of writing; written representation.

grap·ple [grap′əl] *v.* **grap·pled, grap·pling,** *n.* To struggle, contend: to *grapple* with a puzzling matter.

hydrophobia

grav·el [grav′əl] *n.* Small pieces of stone or cement used on roads and paths.

grav·i·ta·tion [grav′ə·tā′shən] *n.* In physics, the force that pulls two bodies together.

griev·ous [grē′vəs] *adj.* Causing grief, sorrow, and pain: a *grievous* insult.

guile [gīl] *n.* The use of cunning.

gut·tur·al [gut′ər·əl] *adj.* Having a husky, grating sound; harsh: *guttural* speech.

H h

Hai·ti [hā′tē] A country in the West Indies, on the western part of Hispaniola.

haunch [hônch] *n.* A side of the body between the waist and thigh: They squatted on their *haunches* and held their hands out to the fire.

head·mis·tress [hed·mis′tris] *n.* A woman who is principal of a school, usually a private girls' school.

hearth [härth] *n.* The warm floor in front of a fireplace: People in colonial times often gathered around the *hearth.*

hi·lar·i·ty [hi·lâr′ə·tē] *n.* Gaiety and boisterous laughter.

hill·ock [hil′ək] *n.* A small hill or mound.

hum·ble [hum′bəl] *adj.* Not boastful or proud; meek.

hy·dro·pho·bi·a [hī′drə·fō′bē·ə] *n.* A disease of mammals said to cause madness: *Hydrophobia* is another name for rabies.

illusion — irresistible

I i

il·lu·sion [i·lōō′zhən] *n.* An appearance or impression contrary to reality: The snow bank gave an *illusion* of sand.

im·mense [i·mens′] *adj.* Tremendously large; huge: an *immense* rock.

im·mi·grant [im′ə·grənt] *n.* A person who comes to a new country or region to live.

im·mov·a·ble [i·mōō′və·bəl] *adj.* Permanently fixed in place.

im·pact [im·pakt] *n.* A strong effect; powerful blow: the *impact* of 100-foot waves.

im·preg·na·ble [im·preg′nə·bəl] *adj.* Not capable of being overcome: The fortress was *impregnable*.

in·an·i·mate [in·an′ə·mit] *adj.* Not alive: A table is an *inanimate* object.

in·ci·sion [in·sizh′ən] *n.* A cut or gash, as in surgery.

in·cred·i·ble [in·kred′ə·bəl] *adj.* Extraordinary, unbelievable: an *incredible* story.

in·doc·tri·nate [in·dok′trə·nāt′] *v.* To advocate, especially by teaching: to *indoctrinate* a belief.

in·ev·i·ta·ble [in·ev′ə·tə·bəl] *adj.* Certain to happen, unavoidable.

in·fer·no [in·fûr′nō] *n.* A place like hell, full of fire or great heat: The iron smelter was a roaring *inferno*.

in·fi·nite [in′fə·nit] *adj.* Extending without boundaries; limitless: The plains seemed *infinite*.

ink·well [ingk′wel′] *n.* A container to hold ink, sometimes set into a desk.

in·nu·mer·a·ble [i·n(y)ōō′mər·ə·bəl] *adj.* Numbering more than can be counted.

in·stinc·tive [in·stingk′tiv] *adj.* Having its origin in the instincts: Sneezing in the presence of dust is an *instinctive* response.

in·tact [in·takt′] *adj.* Whole, undamaged: The heirs kept the family land *intact*.

in·tel·lect [in′tə·lekt] *n.* The power of thought, understanding, and knowledge: Use your *intellect* to solve the problem.

in·ten·tion [in·ten′shən] *n.* Plan or purpose: I have no *intention* of quarreling with them.

in·te·ri·or [in·tir′ē·ər] *n.* The part that is inside: the *interior* of the building.

in·ter·sec·tion [in′tər·sek′shən] *n.* A street crossing.

in·trigue [in′trēg *or* in·trēg′] *n.* The making of plots and schemes: Spies engage in *intrigue*.

I·nu·it [in′ōō·it′ *or* in′yōō·it′] *n.* A people who live along the Arctic coasts of North America, also called Eskimo or Eskimos.

i·ron·ic [ī·ron′ik] *adj.* Odd because so unexpected: It was *ironic* that the minute we gave up the search, we found the missing clue. **i·ron·i·cal·ly** *adv.*

ir·re·sis·ti·ble [ir·i·zis′tə·bəl] *adj.* Not resistible: an *irresistible* grin. —**ir·re·sis·ti·bly** *adv.*

a	add	i	it	ōō	took	oi	oil
ā	ace	ī	ice	ōō	pool	ou	pout
â	care	o	odd	u	up	ng	ring
ä	palm	ō	open	û	burn	th	thin
e	end	ô	order	yōō	fuse	th	this
ē	equal					zh	vision

ə = { **a** in *above*, **e** in *sicken*, **i** in *possible*, **o** in *melon*, **u** in *circus* }

625

J j

jack·al [jak′əl] *n.* A doglike mammal of Asia and Africa.

Ja·mai·ca [jə·mā′kə] An island country in the West Indies, in the Caribbean Sea, to the south of Cuba.

jam·bo·ree [jam′bə·rē′] *n.* A large assembly of Scouts, often from many countries.

jaunt [jônt] *n.* A short trip, taken for pleasure.

jave·lin [jav′(ə·)lin] *n.* A light spear thrown for distance in athletic contests.

jeer [jir] *v.* to mock or ridicule with words.

joc·u·lar [jok′yə·lər] *adj.* Intended as or containing a joke: *jocular* remarks.

jos·tle [jos′(ə)l] *v.* To shove into; bump: She was *jostled* by the crowd in the street.

lig·a·ment [lig′ə·mənt] *n.* A strong band of tissue that connects bones or helps to support an organ of the body.

light-head·ed [līt′hed′id] *adj.* Slightly dizzy: He felt *light-headed* after the climb.

light-year [līt′yir′] *n.* The distance light travels in one year, about six trillion miles.

lin·ger [ling′gər] *v.* To stay longer than planned or expected: The guests *lingered* because the party had been so enjoyable.

lin·guis·tics [ling·gwis′tiks] *n.* The study of how language works and is learned.

liv·id [liv′id] *adj. informal* In a rage.

loft·y [lof′tē] *adj.* Highly placed; exalted: a *lofty* position.

loi·ter [loi′tər] *v.* To stand idly, linger: Don't *loiter* in the hallway.

lull [lul] *v.* To quiet by soothing sounds or motions.

lure [loor] *n.* Something offered to attract; bait: The bank offered free gifts as a *lure* to customers.

lux·u·ry [luk′shər·ē] *n., pl.* **lux·u·ries** An expensive but unnecessary item: A ruby pin is a *luxury*.

L l

lair [lâr] *n.* The cave or other place where wild animals live: the tiger's *lair*.

leg·en·dar·y [lej′ən·der′ē] *adj.* Famous in or as if in a legend: a *legendary* exploit.

lieu·ten·ant [loo·ten′ənt] *n.* An officer in the navy, ranking below a captain.

M m

mag·ni·fy [mag′nə·fī′] *v.* To enlarge in appearance: Microscopes *magnify* bacteria.

maim   nurture

maim [mām] *v.* To injure seriously a part of the body; cripple: The accident *maimed* the miner.

make·shift [māk'shift] *adj.* Put together, usually for temporary use: a *makeshift* costume for the party.

man·ne·quin [man'ə·kin] *n.* A life-sized model of the human figure used for displays.

man·u·fac·ture [man'yə·fak'chər] *v.* To make, as in a factory: They *manufacture* lamps in that building.

mar·ket·place [mär'kit·plās'] *n.* An open or indoor space with stalls and counters where goods are bought and sold.

Mar·ti·nique [mär'ti·nēk'] A French-ruled island in the eastern West Indies.

Med·i·care [med'i·kâr'] *n.* Health insurance for the aged, sponsored by the Federal government.

mer·cu·ry [mûr'kyə·rē] *n.* A heavy, poisonous silver-white metallic element that is liquid at ordinary temperatures: Pure *mercury* is used in thermometers and barometers.

me·trop·o·lis [mə·trop'ə·lis] *n.* A large urban area: This is a bustling *metropolis*.

mi·grate [mī'grāt] *v.* **mi·grat·ed, mi·grat·ing** To move from one region or climate to another: Geese *migrate* in autumn and spring. —**mi·gra·tion** *n.*

mil·li·ner·y [mil'ə·ner'ē] *n.* The design and creation of women's hats.

mis·com·pu·ta·tion [mis·kom'pyə·tā'shən] *n.* The wrong amount or number obtained by a mistake in computation.

Mo·ja·ve Desert [mō·hä'vē dez'ərt] A desert in southeastern California.

mon·i·tor [mon'ə·tər] *n.* An electronic device that allows continual observance of people or events.

mu·nic·i·pal [myoo·nis'ə·pəl] *adj.* Having to do with local government of a town or city: A *municipal* ordinance prohibits loud noises.

myth·o·log·i·cal [mith'ə·loj'i·kəl] *adj.* Coming from a myth; legendary: a *mythological* hero.

N n

naught [nôt] *n.* Nothing.

neu·tron [n(y)oo'tron'] *n.* A particle without electrical charge found in the nucleus of most atoms.

nur·ture [nûr'chər] *v.* **nur·tured, nur·tur·ing** To help grow, to nourish: We *nurtured* the plants until spring, when we could put them outdoors.

a	add	i	it	oo	took	oi	oil
ā	ace	ī	ice	oo	pool	ou	pout
â	care	o	odd	u	up	ng	ring
ä	palm	ō	open	û	burn	th	thin
e	end	ô	order	yoo	fuse	th	this
ē	equal					zh	vision

ə = { **a** in *above*   **e** in *sicken*   **i** in *possible*
      o in *melon*   **u** in *circus* }

O o

oc·cur·rence [ə·kûr′əns] *n.* Something that happens: The *occurrence* seemed like a miracle.

O·jib·wa [ō·jib′wā *or* ō·jib′wə] *n., pl.* **O·jib·wa** *or* **O·jib·was** A tribe of North American Indians once living on the shores of Lake Superior in the U.S. and Canada.

o·le·an·der [ō′lē·an′dər] *n.* A shrub with clusters of white, pink, or red flowers.

om·i·nous [om′ə·nəs] *adj.* Promising ill; threatening: an *ominous* forecast. — **om·i·nous·ly** *adv.*

o·pac·i·ty [ō·pas′ə·tē] *n.* The quality or condition of not allowing light to pass through: The *opacity* of the fog made driving dangerous.

or·i·gin [ôr′ə·jin] *n.* The primary cause or source: The *origin* of a word.

out·mod·ed [out·mōd′id] *adj.* Not in current use; old-fashioned: an *outmoded* typewriter.

P p

pall·bear·er [pôl′bâr′ər] *n.* A person who carries a coffin or walks beside it at a funeral.

pan·o·ram·a [pan′ə·ram′ə] *n.* A complete view of a subject or of passing events or sights: The exhibit showed a *panorama* of the development of the steam engine.

pan·to·mime [pan′tə·mīm′] *n.* Movements without speech: The drama was performed in *pantomime*.

pat·ent [pat′(ə)nt] *v.* To obtain a government document granting the exclusive right to make and sell an invention or to use a new process for a specified term: Edison *patented* many inventions.

pat·ois [pat′wä] *n.* A local dialect of a language: the French *patois* of Antigua.

peas·ant [pez′ənt] *n.* In Europe and Asia, a rural person of humble birth.

pem·mi·can [pem′ə·kən] *n.* Meat dried into a paste and pounded flat.

pen·dant [pen′dənt] *n.* An ornament that is hung on a chain.

pen·nant [pen′ənt] *n.* The prize awarded to a baseball team for winning a majority of league games.

per·ceive [per·sēv′] *v.* **per·ceived, per·ceiv·ing** To sense; become aware of: Animals *perceive* danger in many ways.

per·il·ous [per′əl·əs] *adj.* Risky; dangerous. —**per·il·ous·ly** *adv.* —**per·il·ous·ness** *n.*

per·pet·u·ate [pər·pech′o͞o·āt′] *v.* **per·pet·u·at·ed, per·pet·u·at·ing** To cause a continuation of: to *perpetuate* a story.

per·plex [per·pleks′] *v.* To cause confusion and doubt to: The math problem *perplexed* the whole class.

per·se·cute [pûr′sə·kyo͞ot′] *v.* **per·se·cut·ed, per·se·cut·ing** To keep up an attack on: Our society does not *persecute* witches.

per·son·al·i·ty [pûr′sən·al′ə·tē] *n., pl.* **per·son·al·i·ties** The unique qualities or characteristics of a person.

Pharaoh   pronunciation key

Phar·aoh [fâr′ō *or* fā′rō] *n.* A king of ancient Egypt.

phi·los·o·phy [fi·los′ə·fē] *n., pl.* **phi·los·o·phies** A system of thought dealing with truth and wisdom.

phys·ics [fiz′iks] *n.* The science that deals with matter, energy, and motion: *Physics* includes the study of mechanics, heat, sound, light, electricity, and magnetism.

pin·a·fore [pin′ə·fôr′] *n.* A sleeveless, apronlike garment, worn as a dress or protective smock.

pin·ion [pin′yən] *n.* The outer segment of a bird's wing.

pit·e·ous [pit′ē·əs] *adj.* Arousing or deserving pity: a *piteous* cry. —**pit·e·ous·ly** *adv.* —**pit·e·ous·ness** *n.*

plan·e·tar·i·um [plan′ə·târ′ē·əm] *n., pl.* **plan·e·tar·i·ums** or **plan·e·tar·i·a** A room or building with a domed ceiling for showing the stars and other celestial bodies as they appear or appeared at any point in time and from any location.

plau·si·ble [plô′zə·bəl] *adj.* Apparently reasonable: a *plausible* excuse. —**plau·si·bly** *adv.*

poise [poiz] *v.* **poised, poising** To be or hold in balance: The ballerina was *poised* on her toes.

por·tent [pôr′tənt] *n.* A warning sign of what is to come; omen: a *portent* of disaster.

pre·car·i·ous [pri·kâr′ē·əs] *adj.* Dangerous; hazardous: a *precarious* position to be in. —**pre·car·i·ous·ly** *adv.*

pre·cau·tion [pri·kô′shən] *n.* A step taken to avoid a possible danger or evil: As a *precaution* against fire, we put the tree in a pail of water.

pre·sum·a·ble [pri·zoo′mə·bəl] *adj.* Being assumed or taken for granted; likely: a *presumable* cause. —**pre·sum·a·bly** *adv.*

pre·tense [pri·tens′ *or* prē′tens] *n.* An appearance that is false; something pretended: Tyrants sometimes make a *pretense* of kindness.

pro·bos·cis [prə·bos′is] *n., pl.* **pro·bos·cis·es** A tubelike body part in some insects used for sucking.

pro·ceed [prə·sēd′] *v.* To start and carry forward an activity: The class *proceeded* to perform the play.

pro·ces·sion [prə·sesh′ən] *n.* A group arranged one behind the other and moving in a formal way.

pro·duce [prod′(y)oos] *n.* Products, as vegetables and fruits, grown on a farm for market.

pro·fes·sion [prə·fesh′ən] *n.* An occupation that requires a good education and in which the work is mental rather than physical: Medicine, law, and teaching are three *professions.*

prom·i·nent [prom′ə·nənt] *adj.* Well-known; eminent: *prominent* in the church— **prom·i·nent·ly** *adv.*

pro·nun·ci·a·tion key [prə·nun′sē·ā′shən kē] *n.* A table that explains the symbols

a	add	i	it	o͞o	took	oi	oil
ā	ace	ī	ice	o͞o	pool	ou	pout
â	care	o	odd	u	up	ng	ring
ä	palm	ō	open	û	burn	th	thin
e	end	ô	order	yo͞o	fuse	<u>th</u>	this
ē	equal					zh	vision

ə = { **a** in *above*   **e** in *sicken*   **i** in *possible*
     o in *melon*   **u** in *circus*

629

provision — respiratory

used to show how words are pronounced.

pro·vi·sion [prə·vizh′ən] *n.* **pro·vi·sions** Food or a supply of food: The ship was loaded with *provisions* for the long voyage.

pub·li·ca·tion [pub′lə·kā′shən] *n.* A book or magazine, or anything else that is published.

pur·pose·ly [pur′pəs·lē] *adv.* On purpose; deliberately: Did you fall *purposely*?

Q q

quaint [kwānt] *adj.* Charmingly odd or old-fashioned. —**quaint·ly** *adv.* —**quaint·ness** *n.*

qua·sar [kwā′zar] *n.* A very distant celestial object that emits radio waves and light. Its light spectrum shows that it is moving at a very high speed away from us. *Quasar* is an acronym formed from *quasi-stellar radio source*.

R r

ra·di·a·tion [rā′dē·ā′shən] *n.* The energy sent out from radioactive substances.

rav·ish·ing·ly [rav′ish·ing·lē] *adv.* Enchantingly; delightfully: *ravishingly* beautiful.

re·al·ism [rē′əl·iz′əm] *n.* A view of life as it really is, shown in literature and art: The *realism* of the painting was almost frightening.

re·cruit [ri·kroot′] *v.* To invite membership in a group or organization: We keep *recruiting* new members for our club when the old ones graduate. —**re·cruit·ment** *n.*

re·fresh·ment [ri·fresh′mənt] *n.* Something that refreshes, as food or drink.

reign [rān] *n.* The rule of a sovereign: The American Revolution took place during the *reign* of George III.

re·li·a·ble [ri·lī′ə·bəl] *adj.* Dependable; trustworthy: a *reliable* account. —**re·li·a·bil·i·ty** *n.* —**re·li·a·bly** *adv.*

re·luc·tant [ri·luk′tənt] *adj.* Unwilling; hesitant: *reluctant* to join in the dance. —**re·luc·tance** *n.* —**re·luc·tant·ly** *adv.*

Ren·ais·sance [ren′ə·säns′] *n.* The great production of art, literature, and learning that marked the 14th, 15th, and 16th centuries in Europe.

re·sent [ri·zent′] *v.* To feel or show anger based on real or imagined wrong: She *resented* her friend's insult.

Re·sis·tance [ri·zis′təns] *n.* Those who fought behind the lines in World War II: a member of the *Resistance*.

re·source [ri·sors′ or rē′sôrs] *n. (often pl.)* A valuable supply that can be used or drawn on: Natural *resources*, such as air and water, should not be polluted.

res·pi·ra·to·ry [res′pə·rə·tôr′ē or ri·spīr′ə·tôr′ē] *adj.* Of or having to do with the lungs and breathing: Joan wants to become a *respiratory* therapist.

630

resuscitate · spaniel

re·sus·ci·tate [ri·sus′ə·tāt′] *v.* **re·sus·ci·tat·ed, re·sus·ci·tat·ing** To revive; bring back from unconsciousness. —**re·sus·ci·ta·tion** *n.*

re·treat [ri·trēt′] *v.* To withdraw.

rig·ma·role [rig′·mə·rōl′] *or* **rig·a·ma·role** [rig′·ə·mə·rōl′] *n.* Senseless talk or writing; nonsense.

S s

sa·cred [sā′krid] *adj.* Viewed as holy in religion. —**sa·cred·ness** *n.*

sar·coph·a·gus [sär·kof′ə·gəs] *n., pl.* **sar·coph·a·gus·es** *or* **sar·coph·a·gi** [sär·kof′ə·jī] A stone coffin.

scep·ter [sep′tər] *n.* A staff carried as a sign of royal power.

schol·ar·ship [skol′ər·ship] *n.* A grant of money awarded to a student.

script [skript] *n.* **1** Handwriting. **2** A printing type designed to imitate handwriting. **3** A copy of a play or dramatic role, for the use of actors.

scorch [skôrch] *v.* To burn just a little on the surface; singe.

scrub [skrub] *n.* An area of small, stunted trees: We decided to picnic in the *scrub*.

se·cur·i·ties [si·kyŏŏr′ə·tēz] *n., pl.* Stocks and bonds.

sen·sor [sen′sər] *n.* A device that picks up a physical movement and records and transmits it through an electrical impulse: The *sensors* on the lie detector pick up the slightest movement.

sheaf [shēf] *n., pl.* **sheaves** [shēvz] A stalk of cut grain, as rye or wheat, bound together.

shear [shir] *v.* **sheared, sheared** *or* **shorn, shear·ing** To cut fleece from a sheep: Shepherds are busy at *shearing* time.

sheath [shēth] *n., pl.* **sheaths** [shēthz *or* shēths] Any narrow and close-fitting covering.

shrine [shrīn] *n.* A memorial place or object containing something sacred; a place to worship.

sim·i·lar·i·ty [sim′ə·lar′ə·tē] *n., pl.* **sim·i·lar·i·ties** The points on which things being compared are similar; likeness.

smite [smīt] *v.* **smote, smit·ten, smit·ing 1** To hit; strike hard. **2** To affect or impress suddenly and powerfully.

So·cial Se·cur·i·ty [sō′shəl si·kyŏŏr′ə·tē] A system of payments to the aged and the disabled.

som·ber [som′bər] *adj.* Dark and gloomy. —**som·ber·ly** *adv.* —**som·ber·ness** *n.*

span·iel [span′yəl] *n.* A small or medium-sized dog with large, floppy ears and often long, silky hair.

a	add	i	it	ŏŏ	took	oi	oil
ā	ace	ī	ice	ōō	pool	ou	pout
â	care	o	odd	u	up	ng	ring
ä	palm	ō	open	û	burn	th	thin
e	end	ô	order	yōō	fuse	th	this
ē	equal					zh	vision

ə = { a in *above*, e in *sicken*, i in *possible*, o in *melon*, u in *circus* }

sparse [spärs] *adj.* **spars·er, spars·est** Thinly scattered.

spawn [spôn] *v.* To produce in great numbers.

spe·cial·ist [spesh'əl·ist] *n.* A person who concentrates on one activity or subject.

spe·cious [spē'shəs] *adj.* Appearing correct or true but actually untrue: The idea that rotting meat produces maggots is *specious*.

spher·i·cal [sfir'i·kəl] *adj.* Shaped like a ball or globe.

sphinx [sfingks] *n., pl.* **sphinx·es** or **sphin·ges** [sfin'jēz] In Egyptian myths, a creature with a lion's body and the head of a man, ram, or hawk.

spin rate [spin rāt] *n.* The number of times that an object revolves in a set period: a *spin rate* of 60 times a second.

splen·did [splen'did] *adj.* Magnificent and glorious: a *splendid* sunset.

splut·ter [splut'ər] *v.* To make explosive sounds; hiss: Water *splutters* on a hot surface.

sprawl [sprôl] *v.* To sit or lie with the legs and arms stretched out in a relaxed way: to *sprawl* on a bed.

squig·gle [skwig'əl] *n.* An irregular, twisting line.

squire [skwīr] *n.* In England, a person who owns a great deal of land.

stam·ped·ing [stam·pēd'ing] *adj.* Rushing forward in panic, as a herd of animals.

ster·e·o·type [ster'ē·ə·tīp *or* stir'ē·ə·tīp'] *n.* A fixed mental image of a person, thing, or event that makes no allowances for individual differences. —**ster·e·o·typ·i·cal** [ster'ē·ə·tip'i·kəl] *adj.*

stra·te·gic [strə·tē'jik] *adj.* Having to do with the careful planning and direction of an effort: a *strategic* plan for winning the contest. —**stra·te·gi·cal·ly** *adv.*

stride [strīd] *v.* **strode, strid·den, strid·ing** *v.* To walk with long, proud steps.

strig·il [strij'əl] *n.* In ancient Greece and Rome, a long slender shaft of wood or ivory used by athletes to scrape off oil rubbed on the skin before exercising.

sub·sti·tute [sub'stə·t(y)o͞ot'] *v.* **sub·sti·tut·ed, sub·sti·tut·ing** To use in place of: to *substitute* oil for butter.

sum·ma·rize [sum'ə·rīz'] *v.* **sum·ma·rized, sum·ma·riz·ing** To make a short version of; sum up: to *summarize* a report.

su·pe·ri·or [sə·pir'·ē·ər] *adj.* Better than average: a *superior* performance.

su·per·nat·u·ral [so͞o·pər·nach'ər·əl] *adj.* Beyond the known laws or forces of nature; magical: *supernatural* strength.

swirl [swurl] *n.* A curved or twisting line; spiral.

symp·tom [sim(p)'təm] *n.* An indication of disorder or disease: Sneezing is a *symptom* of a cold.

syn·the·siz·er [sin'thə·sī'zər] *n.* An electronic device that produces and combines many kinds of sounds, used especially in music.

T t

tail·ored [tā'lərd] *adj.* Trim and well-made: a *tailored* look.

tar·mac [tar′mak] *n.* A paved surface, especially the area around an airplane hangar.

tech·nol·o·gy [tek·nol′ə·jē] *n., pl.* **tech·nol·o·gies** The application of scientific knowledge to practical uses: The computer is a product of *technology*.

tem·per·a·ment [tem′pər·ə·mənt] *n.* A sensitive, easily excitable emotional makeup.

tend [tend] *v.* To have an inclination: I *tend* to agree.

ten·ta·tive [ten′tə·tiv] *adj.* Hesitant; limited: a *tentative* effort. —**ten·ta·tive·ly** *adv.* —**ten·ta·tive·ness** *n.*

ter·rain [tə·rān] *n.* An area of land.

ter·ri·er [ter′ē·ər] *n.* A type of small dog.

the·o·ret·i·cal [thē′ə·ret′i·kəl] *adj.* Existing only as an idea; having to do with theory: a *theoretical* invention.

ther·mal [thûr′məl] *adj.* Hot or warm: a *thermal* current.

tod·dle [tod′(ə)l] *v.* **tod·dled, tod·dling** To walk unsteadily.

top·knot [top′not] *n.* A knot of hair worn on top of the head.

tor·ment [tor′mənt] *n.* Horrible bodily pain or mental agony. —**tor·men·tor** *or* **tor·men·ter** *n.*

tra·di·tion [trə·dish′ən] *n.* The transfer of customs, beliefs, and tales from one generation to another.

trait [trāt] *n.* A feature or quality of character or personality: Honesty is a good *trait*.

trel·lised [trel′ist] *adj.* Made of strips of wood or metal: We sat under the *trellised* arch in the garden.

tres·tle [tres′əl] *n.* A frame used to support part of a table top or platform.

tril·o·gy [tril′ə·jē] *n., pl.* **tril·o·gies** A group of three plays, novels, or musical compositions in a related series.

Trin·i·dad [trin′i·dad] An island off northeastern Venezuela, part of the country called Trinidad and Tobago.

tri·pod [trī′pod] *n.* Anything that stands on three legs, such as a table.

tri·umph [trī′əmf] *v.* To win a victory; be successful: The young man *triumphed* over his handicap.

tum·bler [tum′blər] *n.* A part of a lock that must be moved to a certain position, as by a key, before the lock will open.

U u

un·a·bridged [un′ə·brijd′] *adj.* Unshortened, complete: an *unabridged* dictionary.

un·ac·com·plished [un′ə·kom′plisht] *adj.* Not performed: The task went *unaccomplished* when they heard how hard it was.

a	add	i	it	o͞o	took	oi	oil
ā	ace	ī	ice	o͞o	pool	ou	pout
â	care	o	odd	u	up	ng	ring
ä	palm	ō	open	û	burn	th	thin
e	end	ô	order	yo͞o	fuse	th	this
ē	equal					zh	vision

ə = { **a** in *above*   **e** in *sicken*   **i** in *possible*
       o in *melon*   **u** in *circus* }

unanimous — yam

u·nan·i·mous [yōō·nan′ə·məs] *adj.* In full agreement: a *unanimous* vote.

un·bid·den [un·bid′(ə)n] *adj.* Not invited: Ants were *unbidden* guests at the picnic.

un·ob·struct·ed [un·əb·struk′təd] *adj.* Free of blockage or obstacle: an *unobstructed* view.

un·ob·tru·sive [un′əb·trōō′siv] *adj.* Not noticeable; inconspicuous: an *unobtrusive* sound.

ush·er [ush′ər] *v.* To help in, escort, or conduct, as to a seat. —**usher in:** To announce an arrival: to *usher in* the new era.

u·surp·er [yōō·sûrp′ər] *n.* Someone who seizes and holds without legal right.

V v

val·or [val′ər] *n.* Courage; bravery, especially in war.

van·tage point [van′tij point] A position from which evaluation is easily made: a *vantage point* on the problem.

veer [vir] *v.* To change direction sharply.

veld *or* **veldt** [velt *or* felt] *n.* An open grassy plain with no tall trees.

ven·dor [ven′dər] *n.* A person who sells goods, often out-of-doors.

ven·i·son [ven′ə·sən *or* ven′ə·zən] *n.* Deer meat.

Ve·nus [vē′nəs] *n.* In Roman myths, the goddess of love and beauty.

ver·sa·tile [vûr′sə·til] *adj.* Having many uses.

vi·brant [vī′brənt] *adj.* Energetic; vigorous: a *vibrant* feeling.

vir·tu·al [vur′chōō·əl] *adj.* Being something in effect, but not in fact: the *virtual* king of the country. —**vir·tu·al·ly** *adv.*

vi·tal [vī′t(ə)l] *adj.* Basic to life: *vital* nourishment.

vi·tal·i·ty [vī·tal′ə·tē] *n.* The characteristic of being energetic; vigor; liveliness: You need a lot of *vitality* for square dancing.

vo·tive [vō′tiv] *adj.* Having to do with an act of worship: a *votive* candle.

W w

waist·coat [wāst′kōt *or* wes′kət] *n. British* A vest worn by a man.

wea·ry [wir′ē] *adj.* **wea·ri·er, wea·ri·est** Tired; fatigued: The *weary* firefighters dragged the hoses back to the truck.

Y y

yam [yam] *n.* An edible plant root.

yoke [yōk] *v.* **yoked, yok·ing** To attach; join together: to *yoke* two horses.

yon·der [yon′dər] *adv.* Over there: Go *yonder* and fetch a brick.

Z z

zest [zest] *n.* Keen enjoyment; great pleasure: to dance with *zest*.

a	add	i	it	o͞o	took	oi	oil
ā	ace	ī	ice	o͞o	pool	ou	pout
â	care	o	odd	u	up	ng	ring
ä	palm	ō	open	û	burn	th	thin
e	end	ô	order	yo͞o	fuse	th	this
ē	equal					zh	vision

ə = { **a** in *above*, **e** in *sicken*, **i** in *possible*, **o** in *melon*, **u** in *circus* }

Pronunciation Guide to Names, Words, and Phrases

Abbe Sicard [ä·bā′ sē·kär′]
Accompong [ə·kom′pong]
Aea [ē′ə]
Aeetes [ē·e′tēz]
Aeson [ē′sən]
agheera [ə·gē′rə]
Ag'Ya [äg′yə]
ahai [ä·hī′]
Akela [ə·kē′lə]
Alliance Française [əl·lyons′ frä(n)·sez′]
Alou, Felipe [a·lōō′, fe·lē′pā]
Amyntas [ə·min′täs]
Ankhesenamun [ən·ke·se·nä′mən]
Antigua [an·tē′g(w)ə]
Antilles [an·til′ēz]
Arcas [är′kəs]
Archmage [ärch′māj]
Areas [a′rē·əs]
Ares [är′ēz]
Argonauts [är′gə·näts]
Argos [är′gos]
Ariston [a′rist·on]
Artemis Orthia [är′tə·mis ôr′thē·ə]
Asklepius [ask·lē′pē·əs]
Athene [ə·thē′nē]
Atlit [ät′lit]
Atuan [ə·tōō′ən]

Bagheera [bə·gē′rə]
barrios [bär′rē·ōs]
Beethoven, Ludwig van [bā′·tō·vən, lōōd′vig vän]
Bellas Artes [bā′əs är′täs]

bougainvillea [bōō·gən·vil′ē·ə]
Budapest [bōō′də·pest]
byre [bīr]

Caesarea [se·zə·rē′ə]
Calusa [kə·lōō′sə]
Carnarvon [kär·när′vən]
Carolina [ka·rō·lē′nə]
Cepeda, Orlando [sā·pā′də, ôr·land′ō]
Chalciope [kal·sē′ə·pē]
Clemente, Roberto [kle·ment′ā, rō′bâr′tō]
cochinas [ko·chē′·nəs]
Colchis [kol′kis]
Colchian [kol′kē·ən]
Colon, Cristobal [kôl·ôn′, krē·stə·bäl′]
conquistadores [kon·k(w)is·tə·dôr′es]
Cotugno, Domenico [kō·tōō′nyō, dō·men′i·kō]
Cyrene [sī·rē′nē]

Dahomey [də·hō′mē]
Demeter [di·mē′tər]
dewanee [də·wän′ē]
Dolichus [do′lik·əs]

Epidaurus [ep·i·dôr′əs]
essai [es·sā′]
Eudorus [yōō′dôr·əs]

Ferre, Luis [fə·rā′, lōō·ēs′]
fortissimo [fôr·tis′ə·mō]

Galilee [gal′ə·lē]
Gallaudet, Thomas [gal·ə·det′ tō·mäs′]
Ged [ged]
Gensher [gensh′ər]
Gidur-log [gid′ōōr log]
Gluck, Christoph Willibald [glōōk, kris′tof vil′ə·bôld]
Gothar [gō′thâr]

Haganah [hä·gä·nä′]
Haifa [hī′fə]
Haiti [hā′tē]
Haydn, Franz Joseph [hī′dən, fränz yō′səf]
Hecate [hek′ə·tē]
Hera [hir′ə]
Hippias [hip′ē·əs]
Hippocrates [hip·o′krə·tēz]
hippodrome [hip′ə·drōm]

Ioeth [yō′əth]
Iolcus [yôl′kəs]

kaluna [kə·lōō′nə]
kibbutz [ki·bōōts′]
kibbutzim [ki·bōōts′im]
kjotboller [kyot′bôl·ər]
Kronon [krô′nôn]

La Guiablesse [lə gē·ə·bles′]
Lakotas [lə·kō′təs]
lapis lazuli [lap′is laz′yōō·lī]
lastissimus dorsi [ləs·tis′i·məs dôr′sē]

637

Leon [lē'ōn]
Lozano, Rafael [lō·sä'nō, räf·ə·el']
Luxor [luk'sôr]
Linnl [lin'əl]
Lungri [lōōng'rē]
Lutefisk [lōōt'ə·fisk]

Ma'agan [mä·ä'gən]
Macedon [mas'ə·don]
Macedonian [mas·ə·dō'nē·ən]
machete [mə·shet'ē]
Madagascan [mad·ə·gas'kən]
magery [mā'jə·rē]
Magi [mā'jī]
Managua [mä·nä'gwä]
Manati [mä·nä·tē']
Marichal, Juan [mä·rē·chäl', hwän]
Marin, Roberto [mä·rēn', rō·bâr'tō]
Martinique [mär·ti·nēk']
Maru-me [mä'rōō mē]
Medea [mə·dē'ə]
Megara [meg'ə·rə]
Moisant, Matilde [mwə·sôn' mə·tēld']
Mojave [mō·hä'vē]
Montaigne, Michel de [mon·tān'yə, mē·chel' də]
Mowgli [mō'glē]

Nahalal [nä·hä·läl']
nakomik [nə·kō'mik]
Nigeria [nī·jir'ē·ə]
Nikomedes [nik'ō·mē'dēz]
Ninotchka [nə·noch'kə]
Nyassa [nē·äs'sə]

Ogion [ō'gē·on]
Oglala [og·la'la]
Ologbon-Ori [ol·og'bon ôr'ē]
Oodeypore [ōō·dā·pôr']

Osseo [os'ē·ō]
otak [ō'tak]

pa-hay-okee [pə hä ō'kē]
Palgi, Yoel [päl'gē, yō'əl]
Paralos [pär'ə·los]
Paris, Jose Antonio [pə·rēs', hō·sä' än·tō'nē·ō]
Patel, Dinesh [pa·tel', dē·nesh']
patois [pat'wä]
Pechvarry [pech·vä'rē]
Pelias [pē'lē·əs]
Pendor [pend'ôr]
Pepys [pēps]
petang [pə·tang']
Phrontis [fron'tis]
Phrygian [frij'ē·ən]
Piraeus [pī·rē'əs]
Ploesti [ploy·esht']
Pocahontas [pō·kə·hon'təs]
poinciana [poin·sē·än'ə]
Polydeuces [pol·ə·dyōō'sēz]
Puerto Rico [pwer'tō rē'kō]

Raksha [rak'shə]
Ramat Hakovesh [rə·mät' hə·kō'vəsh]
Rameses [ram'ə·sēz]
Reah [rē'ə]
Redonda [rə·don'də]
Reik, Chaviva [rīk, khä·vē' va]
Rhodes [rōdz]
Rhodian [rō'dē·ən]
Ricoletti [rē·kō·let'tē]
Rivera, Diego [rē·vir'rə, dē·ā'gō]
Rossini, Gioacchino Antonio [rō·sē'nē, jyo·ə·kē'nō än·tō'nē·ō]

Sahi [sä'hē]

Sakayan, Ara [sə·kī'ən, ä'rə]
sambur [sam'bōōr]
Samurai [sam'ōō·rī]
Santurce [san·tōōr'sā]
sapodillas [sap·ō·dē'äs]
saviksak [sə·vik'sək]
Sdot-Yam [zdôt yäm']
Seeonee [sē·ō·nē']
senet [sen'et]
Shango [shan'gō]
Shere Khan [shā'rä kän]
Sioux [sōō]
Squanto [skwän'tō]
strigil [stri'jəl]

Tabaqui [tä·bä·kwē']
tableau [tab·lō']
Telamon [tel·ə·mōn]
Tel Aviv [tel ə·vēv']
Theseus [thē'sē·əs]
Tirra [ti'rə]
Toogak [tōō'gək]
Ttil [til]
Tutankhamen [tōōt·ən·käm'ən]

ushabti [yōō·shäb'tē]
Ute [yōōt]
Utha [yōō'thə]

Vergil [vûr'jəl]
Versalles, Zoilo [vâr·sä'yes, zō·ē'lō]
vodun [vō·dōōn']

Wainganga [wä·in·gäng'ə]
werelight [wēr'līt]
Werr [wûr]

Yang Wei-t'e [yang wā'te]
Yevaud [ye·vōd]
Yoruba [yə·rōō'bə]

Zeus [zōōs]
Zorilla, Pedro [zō·rē'yə, pā'drō]
Zoron [zôr'on]

Index of Titles and Authors

Adventure of the Musgrave Ritual, The, 200
African Roots of American Dance, The, 452
Aiken, Joan, 396
Annie John, 374
Asquith, Herbert, 314
Atkinson, Linda, 566

Berger, Melvin, 250
Blos, Joan W., 496
Bradbury, Ray, 4

Clark, Tom, 543
Clemente (1934-72), 543
Colum, Padraic, 36
Courlander, Harold, 224
Cullinan, Bernice, 388

Dark They Were, and Golden-Eyed, 4
Deaf Child Listened, A, 180
Dear Greta Garbo, 230
Dolson, Hildegarde, 334
Doyle, Sir Arthur Conan, 200
Dragon of Pendor, The, 126

Far Forests, The, 396
Forbes, Kathryn, 416
Frozen Fire, 72

Gathering of Days, A, 496
George, Jean Craighead, 90
Going to the Dogs . . . and Cats, 110
Graves, Robert, 413

Haines, Gail Kay, 28
Hairy Dog, The, 314
Hano, Arnold, 530
Haskins, James, 452
Henry, O., 322
Herriot, James, 110
Hoban, Russell, 172
Hoos, Neil Ryder, 516
Houston, James, 72, 388
How Ologbon-Ori Sought Wisdom, 224
How Whirlwind Saved Her Cub, 478

Scenes from *I Remember Mama,* 418

Jason and the Golden Fleece, 36
Jewett, Sarah Orne, 156
Jigsaw Puzzle, 172
Jimmy Valentine, 322
Jocelyn Bell's Puzzle, 28
Johnson, Dorothy M., 478

Kincaid, Jamaica, 374
Kipling, Rudyard, 580, 582

Le Guin, Ursula K., 124, 126
Look Homeward, Jeannie, 304

Meigs, Cornelia, 546
Morrison, Lillian, 263
Mowgli's Brothers, 582

Neimark, Anne E., 180

Pace, Mildred Mastin, 54

Roberto Clemente: Batting King, The, 530

Sadler, Catherine Edward, 200
Sampler, The, 546
Sanfilippo, Margaret, 516
Sprinters, The, 263
Stamm, Claus, 354
Story-Teller, The, 20
Sutcliff, Rosemary, 266, 268

Talbot, Toby, 230
Talking Earth, The, 90

Three Strong Women, 354
Thurber, James, 304
Treasures of King Tutankhamen, The, 54

Ute Indian Poem, 494

van Doren, Mark, 20
van Druten, John, 418

We Shook the Family Tree, 334
What Did I Dream?, 413
What Is Sports Medicine?, 250
White Heron, A, 156
Wood, Nancy, 494